THE
Christian
Bed & Breakfast
DIRECTORY

1997-1998 Edition

THE
Christian
Bed & Breakfast
DIRECTORY

1997-1998 Edition

Edited by
Rebecca Germany

A Barbour Book

Front cover illustrations compliments of (clockwise from top left) The Main Stay Inn and Cottages of Kennebunkport, Maine; Eight Gables Inn of Gatlinburg, Tennessee; Run of the River Bed and Breakfast of Leavenworth, Washington, photography by Randy Wells; Eight Gables Inn of Gatlinburg, Tennessee; and Captain Tom Lawrence House of Falmouth, Massachusetts.

Published by Barbour and Company, Inc.
              P.O. Box 719
              Uhrichsville, Ohio 44683
              Email: books<barbour@tusco.net>
              Web site: http://www.barbourbooks.com

 Member of the
Evangelical Christian
Publishers Association

Printed in the United States of America

Table of Contents

How To Use This Book

Have you ever dreamed of spending a few days in a rustic cabin in Alaska? Would you like to stay in an urban town house while taking care of some business in the city? Would your family like to spend a weekend on a midwestern farm feeding the pigs and gathering eggs? Maybe a romantic Victorian mansion in San Francisco or an antebellum plantation in Mississippi is what you've been looking for. No matter what your needs may be, whether you are traveling for business or pleasure, you will find a variety of choices in the 1997-1998 edition of *The Christian Bed & Breakfast Directory*.

In the pages of this guide you will find over 1,400 bed and breakfasts, small inns, and homestays. All of the information has been updated from last year's edition, and many entries are listed for the first time. Although not every establishment is owned or operated by Christians, each host has expressed a desire to welcome Christian travelers.

The directory is designed for easy reference. At a glance, you can determine the number of rooms available at each establishment and how many rooms have private (PB) and shared (SB) baths. You will find the name of the host or hosts, the price range for two people sharing one room, the kind of breakfast that is served, and what credit cards are accepted. There is a "Notes" section to let you know important information that may not be included in the description. These notes correspond to the list at the bottom of each page. The descriptions have been written by the hosts. The publisher has not visited these bed and breakfasts and is not responsible for inaccuracies.

General maps are provided to help you with your travel plans. Included are the towns where our bed and breakfasts are located, some reference cities, major highways, and major recreational lakes. Please use your road map for additional assistance and details when planning your trip.

It is recommended that you make reservations in advance. Many bed and breakfasts have small staffs or are run single-handedly and cannot easily accommodate surprises. Also, ask about taxes, as city and state taxes vary. Remember to ask for directions, and if your special dietary needs can be met, and confirm check-in and check-out times.

Whether you're planning a honeymoon (first or second!), family vacation, or business trip, *The Christian Bed & Breakfast Directory* will make any outing out of the ordinary.

REBECCA GERMANY, EDITOR

ALABAMA

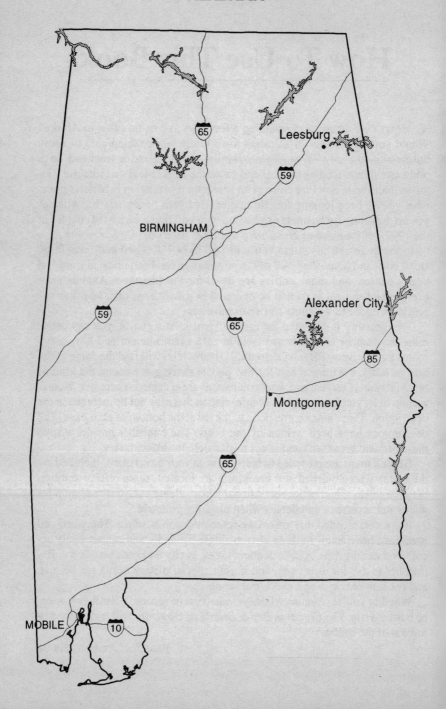

Alabama

ALSO SEE RESERVATION
SERVICES UNDER MISSIS-
SIPPI AND TENNESSEE

ALEXANDER CITY

Mistletoe Bough
Bed and Breakfast
497 Hillabee Street, 35010
(205) 329-3717; FAX (205) 234-0094

Mistletoe Bough is an elegant Queen
Anne house built in 1890 by Rueben
Herzfeld. The bed and breakfast offers
guests a retreat into years gone by with
all the comfort and convenience of modern days. Listed on the National Register of Historic Places, this lovely Victorian home offers elegance and charm
that you will sense the moment you enter the house.

Hosts: Carlice and Jean H. Payne
Rooms: 5 (3PB; 2SB) $65-95
Full Breakfast
Credit Cards: A, B
Notes: 2, 5, 7 (over 10), 9, 10, 12

Mistletoe Bough Bed and Breakfast

LEESBURG

The Secret
Bed and Breakfast Lodge
Route 1, Box 82, 35983-9732
(205) 523-3825; FAX (205) 523-6477
Web site: http://www.bbonline.com/~bbonline/
al/thesecret

A scenic view of seven cities and two
states, overlooking Weiss Lake from
Shinbone Ridge. Rooftop pool and

NOTES: Credit cards accepted: A Master Card; B Visa; C American Express; D Discover;
E Diners Club; F Other; 2 Personal checks accepted; 3 Lunch available; 4 Dinner available;
5 Open all year; 6 Pets welcome; 7 Children welcome; 8 Tennis nearby; 9 Swimming nearby;
10 Golf nearby; 11 Skiing nearby; 12 May be booked through travel agent.

vaulted ceiling in lodge area. Fireplace. Two queen-sized beds, TV, and private baths in every room. AAA star rating. A special place—a secret—with a view as spectacular in the day as it is enchanting at night. Come. Discover. Enjoy!

Hosts: Diann and Carl Cruickshank
Rooms: 4 (PB) $75-105
Full Country Breakfast
Credit Cards: A, B
Notes: 2, 5, 8, 9, 10

The Secret

MONTGOMERY

Red Bluff Cottage
551 Clay Street, PO Box 1026, 36101
(334)264-0056; FAX (334) 262-1872

This raised cottage, furnished with family antiques, is high above the Alabama River in Montgomery's Cottage Hill district near the state capitol, Dextor Avenue, King Memorial Baptist Church, the first White House of the Confederacy, the Civil Rights Memorial, and Old Alabama Town. It is convenient to the Alabama Shakespeare Festival Theater, the Museum of Fine Arts, and the expanded zoo.

Hosts: Mark and Anne Waldo
Rooms: 4 (PB) $65
Full Breakfast
Credit Cards: A, B, C, D
Notes: 2, 5, 7, 10, 12

NOTES: Credit cards accepted: A Master Card; B Visa; C American Express; D Discover; E Diners Club; F Other; 2 Personal checks accepted; 3 Lunch available; 4 Dinner available;

Alaska

ANCHORAGE

Artic Loon
Bed and Breakfast

PO Box 110333, 99511
(907) 345-4935 (voice and FAX)

Elegant accommodations await guests in this 6,500 square-foot Scandinavian home in the hillside area of South Anchorage. Breathtaking, spectacular views of Mount McKinley, the Alaskan Range, and the Anchorage Bowl are presented from every room. An eight-person jacuzzi hot tub, sauna, rosewood grand piano, and pool table provide relaxation after a full, gourmet breakfast served on English bone china. Fully licensed, quiet mountain setting near golf course, Chugack State Park, hiking trails, and zoo.

Hosts: Jamie and Lee Johnson
Rooms: 3 (1PB; 2SB) $85-105
Full Breakfast
Credit Cards: A, B
Notes: 2, 5, 7, 8, 9, 10, 11, 12

Elderberry B&B

8340 Elderberry, 99502
(907) 243-6968

Elderberry B&B is located by the air-port and has three guest rooms with private baths. We cater to each one of our guests on an individual basis. Situated on the greenbelt in Anchorage where moose can often be spotted. We serve full, homemade breakfasts. Linda and Norm, the hosts, love to talk about Alaska and are very active in their church.

Hosts: Norm and Linda Seitz
Rooms: 3 (PB) $50-75
Full Breakfast
Credit Cards: A, B
Notes: 2, 5, 7, 11, 12

Hospitality Plus

7722 Anne Circle, 99504-4601
(907) 333-8504

A comfortable home, delightful and thematically decorated rooms, caring and knowledgeable hosts, sumptuous breakfast elegantly served, a mountain range within reach, a profusion of wild-flowers and moose in the yard. Add to that years of various Alaskan adventures, a Hungarian refugee's escape story, exceptional tour and guiding experience, an avid fisherman, story-telling experts and artistic achievements, and then sum it all up in one

---

5 Open all year; 6 Pets welcome; 7 Children welcome; 8 Tennis nearby; 9 Swimming nearby; 10 Golf nearby; 11 Skiing nearby; 12 May be booked through travel agent.

ALASKA

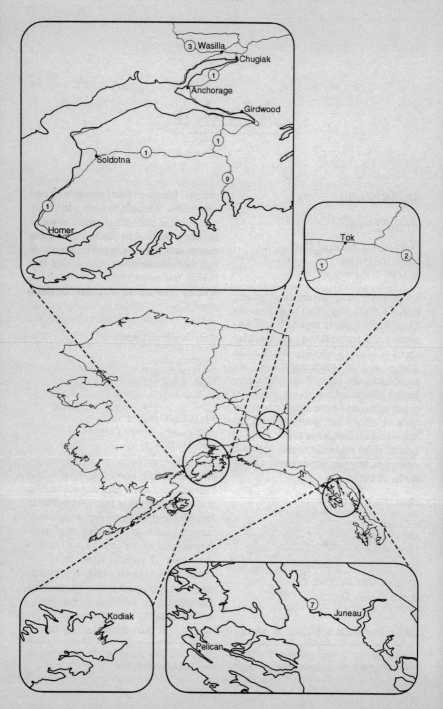

word: HOSPITALITY. It doesn't get better than this!

Hosts: Charlie and Joan Budai
Rooms: 3 (1PB; 2SB) $50-75
Full Breakfast
Credit Cards: none
Notes: 2, 5, 7, 8, 9, 10, 11, 12

CHUGIAK

Peter's Creek Bed and Breakfast

22626 Chambers Lane, 99567
(907) 688-3465; (800) 405-3465;
FAX (907) 688-3466

Located on 2.5 acres of wooded terrain on the north shore of Peter's Creek. Spacious, large custom home designed with physically challenged in mind and furnished with antiques. Theme decorated rooms have cable TV, VCR, and refrigerator. Full Alaskan breakfast. Smoke-free environment. Long-time Alaskans wish to make your stay a pleasure!

Hosts: Bob and Lucy Moody
Rooms: 3 (PB) $85
Full Breakfast
Credit Cards: A, B, C, D
Notes: 2, 5, 7, 9, 11, 12

"A" Cross Country Meadows B&B

GIRDWOOD

"A" Cross Country Meadows Bed and Breakfast

PO Box 123, 99587
(907) 783-3333; FAX (907) 783-3335

Come for a great winter/summer escape, stay for romance and relaxation! Enjoy deluxe accommodations, fabulous views, peaceful, and private. Girdwood offers famous restaurants for your dining pleasure . . . spice of romance always lingering in the atmosphere. Take home lasting memories of "A" Cross Country Meadows Bed and Breakfast stay. The only thing missing is you. "You've created a wonderful oasis here. Keep dedicating everything to God," says a guest from Eagle River, Alaska, July 27, 1996.

Hosts: Brent and Sylvia Stonebraker
Rooms: 2 (PB with king-sized beds) $95-100
"Country Style" Continental Breakfast
Credit Cards: A, B, C
Notes: 5, 11, 12

HOMER

Brass Ring Bed and Breakfast

PO Box 2090, 99603
(907) 235-5450

A two story log home located in the heart of Homer. Our five guest rooms are individually decorated. We serve a

---

NOTES: Credit cards accepted: A Master Card; B Visa; C American Express; D Discover; E Diners Club; F Other; 2 Personal checks accepted; 3 Lunch available; 4 Dinner available; 5 Open all year; 6 Pets welcome; 7 Children welcome; 8 Tennis nearby; 9 Swimming nearby; 10 Golf nearby; 11 Skiing nearby; 12 May be booked through travel agent.

full breakfast with fresh ground coffee. For your convenience, we have a coin laundry and limited freezer space.

Hosts: Dave and Vicki VanLiere
Rooms: 6 (1PB; 5SB) call for rates
Full Breakfast
Credit Cards: A, B
Notes: 2, 7 (over 5), 12

JUNEAU

Alaska Wolf House

PO Box 21321, 1900 Wickersham, 99802
(907) 586-2422; FAX (907) 586-9053

Alaska Wolf House is a 4,000 square foot western, red cedar log home located one mile from downtown Juneau. Built on the side of Mt. Juneau, it features a southern exposure enabling the viewing of sunrises and sunsets over busy Gastineau Channel and the moon rising over the statuesque mountains of Douglas Island. Hosts Philip and Clovis Dennis serve an excellent breakfast in The Glassroom overlooking the channel and mountains. Within a short walk is the Glacier hiking-jogging-biking trail and public transportation. Smoke-free rooms are available with private or shared bathrooms. Suites have kitchens. Plan to enjoy all the amenities of home while experiencing "Our Great Land of Foreverness."

Hosts: Philip and Clovis Dennis
Rooms: 5 (2PB; 3SB) $75-125
Full Breakfast
Credit Cards: A, B
Notes: 2, 5, 7, 8, 9, 10, 11, 12

Pearson's Pond Luxury Inn and Gardens

4541 Sawa Circle-CD, 99801-8723
(907) 789-3772; FAX (907) 789-6722

Private studio/suites on scenic pond. Hot tub under the stars, rowboat, bicycles, BBQ, guest kitchenette. Complimentary cappuccino, fresh breads, gourmet coffee, and popcorn. Near glacier, fishing, rafting, skiing, ferry, airport, and Glacier Bay departures. Smoke-free. Quiet, scenic, and lots of privacy in fully equipped studio with private entrance and deck. In-room dining and TV, VCR, and stereotapes provided. Hosts will make all travel, tours, excursion arrangements. Guests say it's a definite "10" . . . where great expectations are quietly met. Winner of AAA and ABBA excellence awards.

Hosts: Steve and Diane Pearson
Rooms: 3 (PB) $89-169
Continental Breakfast
Credit Cards: A, B, C, E
Notes: 2, 5, 8, 9, 10, 11, 12

KODIAK

Country Bed and Breakfast

1415 Zentner Avenue, 99615
(907) 486-5162; (voice and FAX)

Our bed and breakfast radiates a homey atmosphere with its homemade bread, granola, yeast rolls, abelskievers (a Danish donut), and "made-from-scratch" buttermilk pancakes and berry syrup. Thirteen skylights brighten the living room, kitchen, hall, bathroom and one of the bedrooms of our cedar-sided home located in a quiet neighborhood. All remodeling was done by my husband who retired five years ago from the Coast Guard base here in Kodiak after 38 years of federal employment, while I have majored in being a homemaker, wife, and mother which has prepared me well for a bed and breakfast hostess.

Hosts: Sally and Ken Van Dyke
Rooms: 4 (SB) $70-80 + tax
Full Breakfast
Credit Cards: none
Notes: 2, 5, 6, 7, 8, 9, 10, 11, 12

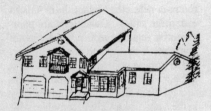

Country Bed and Breakfast

PELICAN

Beyond the Boardwalk Inn of Pelican

Summer: PO Box 12, Pelican, AK 99832
(907) 735-2463
Winter: PO Box 60, Indianola, WA 98342
(360) 297-3550

Our home resides in a small boardwalk fishing town nestled in a deep fjord, ninety miles west of Juneau, Alaska. My wife and I, being teachers, enjoy open-

Beyond the Boardwalk Inn of Pelican

ing our home in June, July, and August where you can appreciate the solitude beauty of waterfalls, hiking, fishing, wonderful food, and Christian fellowship. Our home, decorated uniquely Alaskan, features a log cabin with hot tub and three guest rooms. A truly Christian, rural Alaskan adventure.

Hosts: Ted and Anne Beth Whited
Rooms: 3 (1PB; 2 SB) $90
Full Breakfast
Credit Cards: A, B, C, D, E
Notes: 2, 4

SOLDOTNA

Denise Lake Lodge

PO Box 1050, 99669
(907) 262-1789; (800) 478-1789;
FAX (907) 262-7184

Denise Lodge is on a quiet lake setting two miles from Soldotna and the famous Kenai Rive king salmon fishing. Enjoy our log lodge and friendly atmosphere. Rooms and cabins have private baths and include full breakfast. Available are hot tub, sauna, exercise room, satellite TV, large covered deck and barbeque, laundry, fish cleaning room, and freezer

5 Open all year; 6 Pets welcome; 7 Children welcome; 8 Tennis nearby; 9 Swimming nearby;
10 Golf nearby; 11 Skiing nearby; 12 May be booked through travel agent.

space. No smoking in buildings.

Hostess: Elaine Hanson
Rooms: 12 (PB) $79-125
Full Breakfast
Credit Cards: A, B, C, D
Notes: 2, 5, 7, 9, 10, 11, 12

TOK

Cleft of the Rock
Bed and Breakfast

Sundog Trail, Box 122, 99780
(907) 883-4219; FAX (907) 883-5963
Email: cleftrck@polarnet.com

Cleft of the Rock Bed and Breakfast offers you sparkling, well-maintained accommodations and warm, friendly, Christian hospitality. Nestled in black spruce just three miles west of Tok. You can find an inviting, homelike atmosphere in one of our guest rooms, or cabins. A hot hearty Alaskan breakfast. Children 12 and under stay free. AAA approved.

Hosts: John and Jill Rusyniak
Rooms: 6 (4PB; 2SB) $65-105
Full Breakfast
Credit Cards: A, B
Notes: 2, 5, 6 (with approval), 7, 11, 12

Yukon Don's

WASILLA

Yukon Don's
Bed and Breakfast

1830 E. Parks Hwy., Suite 386, 99654
(907) 376-7472; (800) 478-7472;
FAX (907) 376-6515

When you're traveling in Alaska, or to and from Denali National Park, you don't want to miss staying at Yukon Don's Bed and Breakfast, "Alaska's most acclaimed B&B Inn." Each spacious, comfortable guest room is decorated with authentic Alaskana; stay in Iditarod, Fishing, Denali, Hunting rooms or select the Matanuska or Yukon executive suites. Our guests are pampered by relaxing in the Alaska room, complete with Alaskan historic library, video library, pool table, cable TV, and gift bar. The all-glass-view room on the second floor offers the grandest view in the Matanuska Valley, complete with fireplace, sitting chairs and observation deck. We also offer phones in each room, Yukon Don's own expanded continental breakfast bar, a sauna, exercise room, and, according to Commissioner Glenn Olds (world traveler) "the grandest view he has ever seen from a home." Judge William Hungate, St. Louis, MO said, "It's like seeing Alaska without leaving the house." Wasilla is home of the International Iditarod sled dog race.

Hosts: "Yukon" Don and Kristan Tanner
Rooms: 7 (3PB; 4SB) $85-125
Expanded Continental Breakfast
Credit Cards: A, B, C, D
Notes: 2, 5, 7, 8, 10, 11, 12

NOTES: Credit cards accepted: A Master Card; B Visa; C American Express; D Discover; E Diners Club; F Other; 2 Personal checks accepted; 3 Lunch available; 4 Dinner available;

Arizona

Advance Reservations Inn Arizona and Old Pueblo Homestays, RSO

PO Box 13603, **Tucson**, 85732
(520) 790-0030; (800) 333-9776;
FAX (520) 790-2399
Web site: http://www.tucson.com/inn

A statewide B&B reservation service featuring accommodations in individual homes, inns, and guest ranches in **Arizona**, ranging from the very modest to luxurious, including continental to gourmet breakfast. Some provide facilities for group meetings, weddings, reunions, etc. Near Arizona cities, suburbs, mountains, and country areas. Easy access to national parks, historic towns, universities, and Mexican border. Also representing places in **Hawaii, Mexico,** and **New Mexico**. MC and Visa accepted. William A. Janssen, coordinator.

Arizona Trails B&B Reservation Service

PO Box 18998, **Fountain Hills** 85269-8998
(602) 837-4284; (888) 799-4284;
FAX (602) 816-4224

The convenient and easy way to make your bed and breakfast reservations free of charge. **Statewide** accommodations from the Arizona Hhigh Country to the Land of the Old West. Specializing in traditional bed and breakfast homes and small inns. All properties are personally inspected and approved to ensure a comfortable, quality visit. Affiliated with Bed and Breakfast of Rhode Island and New England Hospitality Network. Stay out West with the folks who know it best. Major credit cards and personal checks accepted. Roxanne and Hank Boryczki, owners.

Mi Casa Su Casa Bed and Breakfast Reservation Service

PO Box 950, **Tempe**, AZ 85280-0950
(602) 990-0682; (800) 456-0682 (reservations);
FAX (602) 990-3390

Over 160 inspected and approved homestays, guest cottages, ranches, and inns in Arizona, Utah, New Mexico, and Nevada. In **Arizona**, listings include Ajo, Apache Junction, Bisbee, Cave Creek, Clarkdale, Dragoon, Flagstaff, Mesa, Page, Patagonia, Payson, Pinetop, Phoenix, Prescott, Scottsdale, Sedona, Sierra Vista, Tempe, Tucson, Tombstone, Yuma, and other cities. In

---

5 Open all year; 6 Pets welcome; 7 Children welcome; 8 Tennis nearby; 9 Swimming nearby; 10 Golf nearby; 11 Skiing nearby; 12 May be booked through travel agent.

ARIZONA

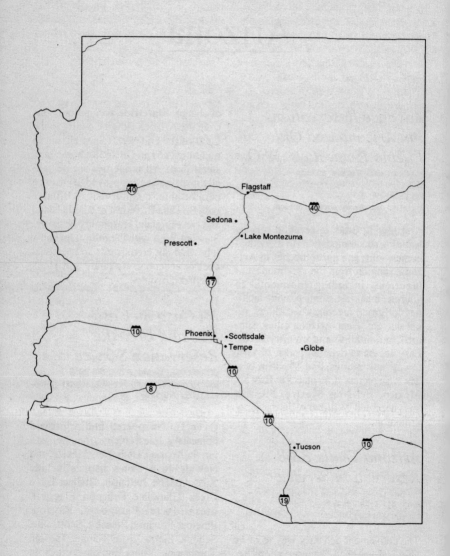

New Mexico, we have included Albuquerque, Algodones, Chimayo, Los Cruces, Silver City, Sante Fe, and Taos. In Utah, listings include Moab, Monroe, Salt Lake City, Springdale, St. George, and Tropic. In Nevada, we list Las Vegas. Rooms with private and shared baths range from $40-175. Credit cards welcomed. Full or continental breakfast. A book with individual descriptions, rates, and pictures is available for $9.50. Ruth Young, coordinator.

Comfi Cottages

FLAGSTAFF

Comfi Cottages

1612 N. Aztec Street, 86001
(520) 774-0731

Near the Grand Canyon, great for families. Five individual cottages with antiques and English country motif. Three cottages are two bedroom, one bath; one is a one-bedroom honeymoon cottage and another is a large three bedroom, two baths. All have gas fireplaces. Fully equipped with linens, towels, and blankets. Kitchens have dishes, pots, pans, coffeepot, etc. Ready-to-prepare breakfast foods in fridge. Color cable TV and telephone. Bicycles on premises, washer/dryer, picnic tables, and barbecue grills at each cottage. Arizona Republic's choice as "Best Weekend Getaway" for November 1995.

Hosts: Ed and Pat Wiebe
Rooms: 7 (PB) $65-195 (for entire cottage)
Guest Prepared Full Breakfast
Credit Cards: A, B, D
Notes: 2, 5, 7, 8, 9, 10, 11, 12

The Inn at 410 Bed and Breakfast

410 N. Leroux Street, 86001
(520) 774-0088; (800) 774-2008;
FAX (520) 774-6354

Explore the Grand Canyon, Indian Country, Sedona, and the San Francisco Peaks while relaxing at "the Place with the Personal Touch." The Inn at 410 offers four seasons of hospitality in a charming 1907 Craftsman home. Scrumptious gourmet breakfasts and afternoon cookies and tea. Uniquely decorated guest rooms, all with private baths, some with fireplace and oversized jacuzzi tubs; one room wheelchair accessible. Walk two blocks to shops, galleries, and restaurants in historic downtown Flagstaff.

Hosts: Howard and Sally Krueger
Rooms: 9 (PB) $100-165
Full Breakfast
Credit Cards: A, B
Notes: 2, 5, 7, 10, 11, 12

NOTES: Credit cards accepted: A Master Card; B Visa; C American Express; D Discover; E Diners Club; F Other; 2 Personal checks accepted; 3 Lunch available; 4 Dinner available; 5 Open all year; 6 Pets welcome; 7 Children welcome; 8 Tennis nearby; 9 Swimming nearby; 10 Golf nearby; 11 Skiing nearby; 12 May be booked through travel agent.

Jeanette's Bed and Breakfast

Jeanette's Bed and Breakfast

3380 E. Lockett Road, 86004-4043
(520) 527-1912; (800) 752-1912

Relax and enjoy while you step back in time. Architecture of the post Victorian era recalls Arizona's first statehood days. Experience Jeanette's four rooms filled with signs of the time. Private baths reflect the style of the era and a *"breakfast so divine"* is served with the flair and detail of a fine Sunday dinner. Flagstaff is the place to be for sights, sounds, and the smell of cool clean pine scented mountain air. So come, stay a day or stay a week at *"Jeanette's."*

Hosts: Jeanette and Ray West
Rooms: 4 (PB) $65 winter - $85 summer
Full Breakfast
Credit Cards: A, B
Notes: 2, 5, 7 (infants and children over 7), 8, 9, 10, 11, 12

Cedar Hill Bed and Breakfast

GLOBE

Cedar Hill B&B

175 East Cedar, 85501
(520) 425-7530

Cedar Hill B&B was built in 1903 by the Trojonavich family. Who were owners of Glober Lumber Company, which accounts for the wainscoting walls in the kitchen and rear porch. The property has many fruit trees and flower beds, including a grape arbor for the enjoyment of our guests. Guests may enjoy both a front porch with porch swings and our back patio with shade trees. The back yard is fenced for the protection of children and pets you may wish to bring! Cable TV and VCR are available in the living room. Within driving distance of both Tuscon and Phoenix. Discounts for senior citizens and for stays longer than overnight.

Hostess: Helen Gross
Rooms: 2 (SB) $40-50
Full Breakfast
Credit Cards: none
Notes: 2, 5, 6, 7, 9

LAKE MONTEZUMA

Sycamore Haven

3933 Meadow Lane, PO Box 5341, 86342
(520) 567-4414; (800) 209-8103 or 0597

Spend a few days in cool Lake Montezuma and you may never want to leave. We have two lovely suites, queen beds, private baths, and quiet, peaceful surroundings. Near by are churches, golf courses, the gurgling Beaver Creek, great restaurants, and the beautiful Grand Canyon. Historical

NOTES: Credit cards accepted: A Master Card; B Visa; C American Express; D Discover; E Diners Club; F Other; 2 Personal checks accepted; 3 Lunch available; 4 Dinner available;

sights galore and also train and river boat trips available. Must see to believe!

Hosts: Chuck and Millie Mabry
Rooms: 2 (PB) $95-125
Continental Breakfast
Credit Cards: none
Notes: 2, 5, 7, 8, 9, 10, 11

Whispering Waters Bed and Breakfast

PO Box 5633, 86342
(520) 567-4540 or 639-0459

Discover an unforgettable getaway. Whispering Waters sits on nearly one acre "on the banks of Beaver Creek." Nature is bountiful—see the many species of birds, including the Golden Eagle, and numerous water fowl. Enjoy afternoon tea on the ninety-foot covered deck or next to a cozy fire. Walk or bicycle around the picturesque community and visit the many area attractions. Non-smoking indoors.

Hosts: Mona Marszaiek, Dawn and Chris Mattson
Rooms: 3 (1PB; 2SB) $85-110
Full Country Breakfast
Credit Cards: A, B
Notes: 2, 5, 7, 8, 9, 10, 11, 12

PHOENIX

The Villa on Alvarado

2031 N. Alvarado Road, 85004
(602) 253-9352

Located in a quiet, historic neighborhood, the Villa features a spacious guest house with two bedrooms, two baths, and a kitchenette. The deck overlooks the manicured gardens and a sparkling pool. If royalty is your preference, our English tower will be perfect for you. It has a private entrance, sitting room, curved stairway that leads to a magnificent canopied king-sized bed, private bath, and balcony.

Hosts: Chris and Kay King
Rooms: 3 (PB) $70-125
Continental Breakfast
Credit Cards: none
Notes: 5, 8, 9, 10

PRESCOTT

Hassayampa Inn

122 E. Gurley St., 86301
(520) 778-9434 (voice and FAX)
(800) 322-1927

Times have changed, but the Inn, now listed on the National Register of Historic places, still retains the charm of yesteryear with the amenities of today. The classic overnight rooms, lace curtains, oak period furniture, and modern bathrooms, along with exceptional service provided by a caring staff, will enhance your visit. Discriminating travelers will find the Inn the ideal destination; just steps from the center of town, Courthouse square, antique shops, museums, and stately Victorian homes. For the finest in cuisine visit the acclaimed Peacock Room; for a light snack and beverage, relax in the quaint Bar and Grill, or just sit back and enjoy the beauty of the magnificent lobby at the Hassayampa Inn.

Hosts: William M. Teich and Georgia L. Teich
Rooms: 68 (PB) $89-175
Full Breakfast
Credit Cards: A, B, C, D, E
Notes: 2, 3, 4, 5, 7, 8, 9, 10, 12

5 Open all year; 6 Pets welcome; 7 Children welcome; 8 Tennis nearby; 9 Swimming nearby; 10 Golf nearby; 11 Skiing nearby; 12 May be booked through travel agent.

Mount Vernon Inn

Mount Vernon Inn

204 N. Mt. Vernon Avenue, 86301
(520) 778-0886; FAX (520) 778-7305

Built in 1900, the Inn is nestled amont the shade trees in the center of the Mount Vernon Historical District. The grand house with its candle snuffer turret, gables, pediments, and Greek revival porch, proudly recalls a time when imagination and frontier self-confidence expressed itself in an architecture best described as whimsical. Today, the Inn offers a glimpse of a past era that seems simpler, slower, and completely charming. Our three guest cottages, originally the carriage and tack houses and the studio house, are separate from the main house. Completely private, cottage guest can prepare breakfast in the convenient kitchen or stroll to any of the wonderful restaurants within easy walking distance.

Hosts: Michele and Jerry Neumann
Rooms: 4 (PB) $90
Full Breakfast ·
Credit Cards: A, B, D
Notes: 2, 5, 10, 12

SCOTTSDALE

Valley O' The Sun Bed and Breakfast

PO Box 2214, 85252
(602) 941-1281; (800) 689-1281

"*Cead Mile Faite*" are the words in Gaelic on the doormat of the Valley O' The Sun Bed and Breakfast. It means "100,000 welcomes." This B&B is more than just a place to stay. Kathleen wants to make your visit to the great Southwest a memorable one. Ideally located in the college area of Tempe, but still close enough to Scottsdale to enjoy the glamour of its shops, restaurants, and theaters. Two guestrooms can comfortably accommodate four people. One bedroom has a full-size bed and the other has twin beds. Each room has its own TV. Within minutes of golf, horseback riding, picnic area and swimming, bicycling, shopping, and tennis, and walking distance from Arizona State University.

Hostess: Kathleen Kennedy Curtis
Rooms: 2 (1SB,) $40
Continental Breakfast
Credit Cards: none
Notes: 2 (restricted), 5, 7 (over 10), 8, 9, 10, 11, 12

SEDONA

Briar Patch Inn

HC 30, Box 1002, 86336
(520) 282-2342; FAX (520) 282-2399

Eight acres of beautiful grounds along Oak Creek in spectacular Oak Creek

---

NOTES: Credit cards accepted: A Master Card; B Visa; C American Express; D Discover; E Diners Club; F Other; 2 Personal checks accepted; 3 Lunch available; 4 Dinner available;

Canyon. Rooms and cottages are all delightfully furnished with southwestern charm. A haven for those who appreciate nature amid the wonders of Sedona's mystical beauty. Suitable for small workshops.

Hosts: Joann and "Ike" Olson
Rooms: 16 (PB) (includes 12 cottages) $139-215
Full Breakfast
Credit Cards: A, B
Notes: 2, 5, 7, 8, 9, 10, 11, 12

The Graham Bed and Breakfast

The Graham Bed and Breakfast Inn

150 Canyon Circle Drive, 86351
(520) 284-1425; (800) 228-1425;
FAX (520) 284-0767

The Graham Inn is an impressive contemporary Southwest inn with huge windows allowing great views of Sedona's red rock formations. Each guest room has a private bath, balcony, and TV/VCR and some rooms have a jacuzzi and fireplace. All rooms have many individual features which make each unique and delightful. Pool and spa invite guests outdoors. Mobile Four Star

Award and AAA Four Diamond Award. Sedona's Finest.

Hosts: Carol and Roger Redenbaugh
Rooms: 6 (PB) $109-229
Full Breakfast
Credit Cards: A, B, D
Notes: 2, 5, 7, 8, 9, 10, 11, 12 (no fee)

Territorial House, An Old West B&B

65 Piki Drive, 86336
(520) 204-2737; (800) 801-2737;
FAX (520) 204-2230

Our large stone and cedar house has been tastefully decorated to depict Arizona's territorial era. Each room is decorated to recall different stages of Sedona's early history. Some rooms have private balcony, jacuzzi tub, or fireplace. An enormous stone fireplace graces the living room and a covered veranda welcomes guests at the end of a day of sightseeing around Sedona. Relax in our outdoor hot tub. A full hearty breakfast is served at the harvest table each morning. All of this is served with Western hospitality.

Hosts: John and Linda Steele
Rooms: 4 (PB) $95-155
Full Breakfast
Credit Cards: A, B
Notes: 2, 5, 7, 8, 9, 10, 11, 12

TUCSON

Casa Alegre B&B Inn

316 E. Speedway Boulevard, 85705
(520) 628-1800; (800) 628-5654;
FAX (520) 792-1880

Casa Alegre is a charming 1915 crafts-

---

5 Open all year; 6 Pets welcome; 7 Children welcome; 8 Tennis nearby; 9 Swimming nearby; 10 Golf nearby; 11 Skiing nearby; 12 May be booked through travel agent.

man-style bungalow, featuring mahogany, leaded glass, built-in cabinetry, and hardwood floors. the serene gardens, pool, and hot tub make an oasis of comfort in central Tucson, just minutes from the University of Arizona. Scrumptous full breakfast. Private baths. AAA and Mobile rated.

Hostess: Phyllis Florek
Rooms: 5 (PB) $80-95
Full Breakfast
Credit Cards: A, B, D
Notes: 2, 5, 8, 9, 10, 11, 12

El Presidio
Bed and Breakfast Inn

297 N. Main Avenue, 85701
(520) 623-6151; (800) 349-6151

Experience Southwestern charm in a desert oasis with the romance of a country inn. Garden courtyards with Old Mexico ambiance of lush, floral displays, fountains, and cobblestone surround richly appointed guest house and suites. Enjoy antique decors, robes, complimentary beverages, fruit, snacks, TVs, and telephones. The 1880s Victorian adobe mansion has been featured in many magazines and the book *The Desert Southwest*. Located in a historic district; walk to fine restaurants, museums, shops, and the Arts District. Close to downtown. Mobile and AAA three-star rated.

Hostess: Patti Toci
Rooms: 3 suites (PB) $85-110
Full Breakfast
Credit Cards: none
Notes: 2, 5, 8, 9, 10, 12

Jeremiah Inn

10921 E. Snyder Road, 85749
(520) 749-3072

For centuries travelers have paused at quiet inns to refresh themselves before continuing life's journey. The Jeremiah Inn is one such place (Jeremiah 9:2a). Santa Fe style with spacious contemporary comforts are offered in this 1995 constructed inn, a 3.3 acre desert retreat in the shadows of the Catalina Mountains. Birding, star-gazing, hiking, swimming, queen beds, afternoon cookies, and smoke-free premises are offered.

Hosts: Bob and Beth Miner
Rooms: 3 (PB) $55-100
Full Breakfast
Credit Cards: A, B
Notes: 2, 5, 7, 8, 9, 10, 11, 12

June's
Bed and Breakfast

3212 W. Holladay, 85746
(602) 578-0857

Mountainside home with pool. Majestic towering mountains. Hiking in the desert. Sparkling city lights. Beautiful rear yard and patio. Suitable for receptions.

Hostess: June Henderson
Rooms: 3 (1PB; 1SB) $45
Continental Breakfast
Credit Cards: none
Notes: 5, 9, 10, 12

NOTES: Credit cards accepted: A Master Card; B Visa; C American Express; D Discover; E Diners Club; F Other; 2 Personal checks accepted; 3 Lunch available; 4 Dinner available;

Arkansas

CALICO SPRINGS

Happy Lonesome Log Cabins

HC61, Box 72, 72519
(501) 297-8764

Perched on a 300 foot bluff overlooking the White River, these log cabins are surrounded by the Ozark National Forest. Decorated with the past in mind, they offer modern comforts. A sleeping loft sleeps two; downstairs has a hide-a-bed, woodstove in the living area, kitchenette, and bath. Relax on the porch swing and enjoy the river valley view and ever-present wildlife. The quiet and peacefulness makes this a quality "getaway" location.

Hosts: Christian and Carolyn Eck
Rooms: 4 (2PB; 2SB) $56
Expanded Continental Breakfast
Credit Cards: A, B, D
Notes: 2, 7, 12

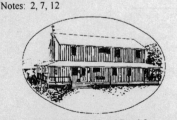

Beaver Lake Bed and Breakfast

EUREKA SPRINGS

Beaver Lake Bed and Breakfast

Route 2, Box 318, 72632
(501) 253-9210

Our comfortable country home has an awe inspiring view of Beaver Lake and the surrounding Ozark Mountains from every room! Experience peace and beauty away from the crowds and the stress of your daily life. Swim, fish, hike, or just relax on the wraparound porch and let gracious hosts pamper you—the perfect place to renew your spirit. Accommodations are for non-smoking adults only. Request our brochure or look for us on the Internet.

Hosts: David and Elaine Reppel
Rooms: 4 (PB) $55-85
Full Breakfast
Credit Cards: none
Notes: 2, 5, 9, 10, 12

Bonnybrooke Farm Atop Misty Mountain

Route 2, Box 335A, 72632
(501) 253-6903

If your heart's in the country . . . or longs to be . . . we invite you to share in the

5 Open all year; 6 Pets welcome; 7 Children welcome; 8 Tennis nearby; 9 Swimming nearby; 10 Golf nearby; 11 Skiing nearby; 12 May be booked through travel agent.

ARKANSAS

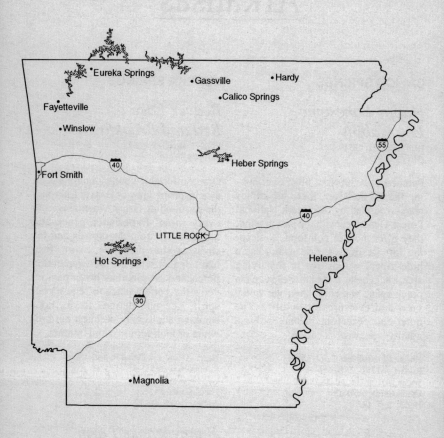

sweet quiet and serenity that awaits you in your place to come home to . . . . Five cottages, distinctly different in their pleasure to tempt you: fireplace and jacuzzi for two, full glass fronts and mountaintop views, shower under the stars in your glass shower, wicker porch swing in front of the fireplace and a wonderful jacuzzi . . . you're gonna love it! In order to preserve privacy our location is not made public and is given to registered guests only.

Hosts: Bonny and Josh Pierson
Rooms: 5 cottages (PB) $95-145
Basket Breakfast
Credit Cards: none
Notes: 2, 5, 9, 1

Bridgeford House

Bridgeford House

263 Spring Street, 72632
(501) 253-7853; FAX (501) 253-5497

Nestled in the heart of Eureka Springs' historic district, Bridgeford House is an 1884 Victorian delight. Outside are shady porches and beautiful gardens. A short walk to town on the trolley and horsedrawn carriage route. Each room

or suite has private entrances and baths. Desserts in-room as well as coffee. Large gourmet breakfasts served daily. Smoking outside.

Hosts: Denise and Michael McDonald
Rooms: 4 (PB) $85-105
Full Breakfast
Credit Cards: A, B
Notes: 2, 5, 7, 8, 9, 10, 12

The Brownstone Inn

75 Hillside Avenue, 72632
(501) 253-7505; (800) 973-7505

A present part of Eureka's past in this historical limestone building, located on trolley route to historic downtown and an easy short drive to the Great Passion Play. Victorian accommodations, private outside entrances, private baths, and gourmet breakfasts with coffee, tea, or juice at your doorstep before breakfast. Featured in *Best Places to Stay in the South.*

Hosts: Marvin and Donna Shepard
Rooms: 4 (PB) $90-105
Full Breakfast
Closed January and February
Credit Cards: A, B
Notes: 2, 5, 10, 12

Crescent Cottage Inn

211 Spring Street, 72632
(501) 253-6022; (800) 223-3246 (res.only)
FAX (501) 253-6234

Crescent Cottage Inn is a landmark Victorian home built in 1881 and is on the National Register. There are four guest areas all having private baths, queen beds, cable TV, and telephones—two

---

NOTES: Credit cards accepted: A Master Card; B Visa; C American Express; D Discover; E Diners Club; F Other; 2 Personal checks accepted; 3 Lunch available; 4 Dinner available; 5 Open all year; 6 Pets welcome; 7 Children welcome; 8 Tennis nearby; 9 Swimming nearby; 10 Golf nearby; 11 Skiing nearby; 12 May be booked through travel agent.

have private, double jacuzzi spas and refrigerators, also fireplaces. All rooms and two (of three) porches overlook forested mountains. A great full breakfast. Antiques throughout and recently redecorated. Walk to town, trolley stop, and 1886 church next door. AAA 3-diamond rating.

Hosts: Ralph and Phyllis Becker
Rooms: 3 + 1 two-room suite (PB) $75-125
Full Hearty Breakfast
Credit Cards: A, B, D
Notes: 2, 5, 8, 9, 10, 12

Dairy Hollow House: Country Inn

515 Spring Street, 72632
(501) 253-7444; (800) 562-8650;
FAX (501) 253-7223

A friendly innkeeper to welcome you . . . the smell of hot apple cider with cinnamon on a cool day . . . a stack of wood by an antique fireplace, a jug of tulips: everywhere delight. Choose between our 1800s Ozark Farmhause and the late 40s bungalow-style Main House in a peaceful, wooded green valley just a mile from our Victorian downtown. A full breakfast-in-a-basket is delivered right to your door each morning. Home of *The Dairy Hollow House Cookbook* and *Dairy Hollow House Soup and Bread: A Country Inn Cookbook* (James Beard, Julia Child award nominee). AAA 3-diamond.

Hosts: Ned Shank and Crescent Dragonwagon
Rooms: 6 (PB) $145-205
Full Breakfast delivered in a basket
Credit Cards: A, B, C, D, E
Notes: 2, 5 (closed January), 7, 9, 10, 12

Dairy Hollow House: Country Inn

Gardeners Cottage

11 Singleton, 72632
(501) 253-9111; (800) 833-3394

Tucked away in a private, wooded, historic district location, this delightful cottage is decorated in charming country decor with romantic touches, cathedral ceilings, skylight, full kitchen, and a jacuzzi for two. The spacious porch with its swing and hammock is for leisurely lounging. Great for honeymooners or a long peaceful stay.

Hostess: Barbara Gavron
Rooms: 1 cottage (PB) $95-115
No Breakfasts
Credit Cards: A, B, C, D
Notes: 2, 9, 10, 12

The Heartstone Inn and Cottages

35 Kings Highway, 72632
(501) 253-8916; (800) 494-4921;
FAX (501) 253-6821

An award-winning inn with all private baths, private entrances, and cable TV.

NOTES: Credit cards accepted: A Master Card; B Visa; C American Express; D Discover; E Diners Club; F Other; 2 Personal checks accepted; 3 Lunch available; 4 Dinner available;

King and queen beds. Antiques galore. Renowned gourmet breakfasts. In-house massage therapy studio. Golf privileges. Large decks and gazebo under the trees; great for bird-watching. Recommended by. *New York Times, Country Home Magazine, America's Wonderful Little Hotels and Inns, Recommended Inns of the South*, and many more.

Hosts: Bill and Iris Simantel
Rooms: 10 + a 1-bedroom cottage and a 2-bedroom cottage (PB) $65-120
Full Gourmet Breakfast
Closed Christmas through January
Credit Cards: A, B, C, D
Notes: 2, 9, 10, 12

Piedmont House Bed and Breakfast

165 Spring Street, 72632
(501) 253-9258; (800) 253-9258

Built as travelers' lodging in 1880, Piedmont House is located in the heart of the Victorian, historic district. Each room has private baths, air-conditioning, ceiling fans, and private entrance from the wraparound porches. Best mountain views and just a short walk to historic downtown shopping and great restaurants. A home away from home with the warmest hospitality you could ever find.

Hosts: Sheri and Ron Morrill
Rooms: 8 (PB) $69-129
Full Breakfast
Credit Cards: A, B, C, D, E
Notes: 2, 7 (over 12), 9, 10

Ridgeway House B&B

28 Ridgeway, 72632
(501) 253-6618; (800) 477-6618

Prepare to be pampered! Sumptuous breakfasts, luxurious rooms, antiques, desserts, quiet street within walking distance of eight churches, five-minute walk to historic downtown, trolley one block. Porches, decks, private jacuzzi suites for anniversaries/honeymoons. All our guests are VIPs!! Open all year.

Hosts: Becky and "Sony" Taylor
Rooms: 5 (3PB; 2SB) $79-139
Full Breakfast
Credit Cards: A, B, D
Notes: 2, 5, 7, 12

Ridgeway House B&B

Singleton House B&B

11 Singleton, 72632
(501) 253-9111; (800) 833-3394

This old-fashioned Victorian house with a touch of magic is whimsically decorated and has an eclectic collection of treasures and antiques. Breakfast is served on the balcony overlooking a wildflower garden and fish pond. Walk one block to the historic district, shops, and cafés. Passion Play and Holy Land

5 Open all year; 6 Pets welcome; 7 Children welcome; 8 Tennis nearby; 9 Swimming nearby; 10 Golf nearby; 11 Skiing nearby; 12 May be booked through travel agent.

tour reservations can be arranged. A guest cottage with jacuzzi is also available at a separate location. Hands-on apprenticeship program available! Featured in over 15 Bed and Breakfast Guidebooks. Celebrating our 13th year!

Hostess: Barbara Gavron
Rooms: 5 (PB) $60-95
Full Breakfast
Credit Cards: A, B, C, D
Notes: 2, 5, 7, 9, 10, 12
Cottage: 1 (PB) $95 (no breakfast)

Singleton House B&B

The Tweedy House

16 Washington Street, 73632
(501) 253-5435; (800) 346-1735

Built in 1883, Tweedy House is an elegant Victorian home located on the Historic Loop. Inside Tweedy House you will find three stories of antiques, family heirlooms, and quality furnishings. The third floor features a romantic honeymoon hideaway. The second floor features two large guest rooms with private baths, and one two-room suite. Amenities include: jacuzzi, TV/VCRs, guest sunroom, decks/porches, hot tub, refreshments, full breakfast,

evening dessert, and friendly service!

Hosts: Ed and Kathy Greiner
Rooms: 4 (2 are suites) (PB) $79-129
Full Breakfast plus evening dessert
Credit Cards: A, B, D
Notes: 2, 5, 8, 9, 10, 11 (water), 12

Wisteria Lane Lodging

RR 7, Box 575, 72632
(501) 253-7544; toll free (888) WISTERIA or 947-8374

Country style and grace are combined with Victorian glamour in our spacious, modern log cabins. Almost hidden in the lush woods, each private cabin features king, brass bed, whirlpool for two, fireplace, TV/VCR and stereo with CD, full kitchen, champagne, covered porch with swing, and barbeque grill. Come experience a little bit of magic in the country as you open the door to casual elegance . . . a wonderland of relaxing luxury in our incurably romantic log cabins.

Hosts: Bob and Peggy Mistark
Rooms: 2 cabins (PB) $100-120
Continental Breakfast
Credit Cards: A, B, D
Notes: 2, 5, 8, 9, 10, 12

FAYETTEVILLE

Hill Avenue Bed and Breakfast

131 S. Hill Avenue, 72701
(501) 444-0865

This century-old home is located in a residential neighborhood near the University of Arkansas, downtown square, Walton Art Center, and Bud Walton

---

NOTES: Credit cards accepted: A Master Card; B Visa; C American Express; D Discover; E Diners Club; F Other; 2 Personal checks accepted; 3 Lunch available; 4 Dinner available;

Arena. Accommodations are smoke free with king-size beds and private baths.

Hosts: Cecelia and Dave Thompson
Rooms: 3 (PB) $60
Continental Breakfast
Credit Cards: none
Notes: 5

FORT SMITH

Thomas Quinn Guest House

815 North "B" Street, 72901
(501) 782-0499

The house is located on the edge of Fort Smith's historic district convenient to the sights and restaurants. The original home, the first floor, was built in 1863. All suites have a furnished kitchen with bar, living room, bath, and one or two bedrooms with private dressing vanities. Live plants, local art, and antiques are scattered throughout. Secure accommodations are perfect for the business traveler or vacationer.

Hosts: Mike and Melody Conley
Rooms: 9 suites (PB) $59-79
Breakfast not included.
Credit Cards: A, B, C, D, E
Notes: 2, 5, 6 (some), 7, 8, 9, 10, 12

Lithia Springs Lodge

GASSVILLE

Lithia Springs Lodge

Route 1, Box 77A, Highway 126 N., 72635
(501) 435-6100

A lovingly restored, early Ozark health lodge, six miles southwest of Mountain Home in north central Arkansas. Fishing, boating, and canoeing in famous lakes and rivers. Scenic hills, valleys, and caverns. Silver Dollar City, Branson, and Eureka Springs are within driving distance. Enjoy walking in the meadow and woods and browse through the adjoining Country Treasures Gift Shop.

Hosts: Paul and Reita Johnson
Rooms: 5 (3PB; 2SB) $50-70
Full Breakfast
Credit Cards: A, B
Notes: 2, 5, 8, 9, 10, 12

HARDY

Hideaway Inn B&B

Route 1 Box 199, County Road #82, 72542
(501) 966-4770

Modern B&B on 376 acres. Three guest rooms, queen beds and central air. Gourmet breakfast and evening snack served. TV/VCR in common area. Beautiful setting, picnic sites, and outdoor pool. Children welcome. Log cabin with two bedrooms, two baths, living/dining/kitchenette combo. Located ten miles from Hardy and Spring River.

Hostess: Julia Baldridge
Rooms: 5 (3PB; 2SB) $55-95
Full Breakfast
Credit Cards: A, B, C, D
Notes: 2, 5, 7, 9, 10, 12

5 Open all year; 6 Pets welcome; 7 Children welcome; 8 Tennis nearby; 9 Swimming nearby; 10 Golf nearby; 11 Skiing nearby; 12 May be booked through travel agent.

Olde Stonehouse Bed and Breakfast Inn

511 Main Street, 72542
(501) 856-2983; (800) 514-2983;
FAX (501) 856-4036

Native stone house in historic district one block the from Spring River and Old Hardy Town's quaint antique and craft shops. Antiques, queen beds, private baths, central heat/air, ceiling fans, unusual stone fireplace with "Arkansas Diamonds", player piano. Full breakfast served family style. Separate 1904 cottage with opulant Victorian inspired suites. Nearby: Country Music-Comedy Theater with outdoor musicals, Antique Car and Verterans Museums, golfing, canoeing, trail rides, Mammoth Springs and Grand Gulf State Parks.

Hostess: Peggy Johnson
Rooms: 7 + 2 suites (PB) $55-95
Full Breakfast
Credit Cards: A, B, C, D
Notes: 2, 3, 4, 5, 8, 9, 10, 12

HEBER SPRINGS

The Anderson House Inn

201 E. Main Street, 72543-3116
(501) 326-5266; (800) 264-5279;
FAX (501) 362-2326
E-mail: hildebr@cswnet.com

A country inn in the bed and breakfast tradition. Enjoy a wonderful lodging alternative in a beautiful Ozark foothills setting. The Anderson House Inn is convenient to Greens Ferry Lake and Little Red River fishing and water sports. Trophy trout fishing is available. We feature handmade quilts, antiques, and a southern flavor. Our Great room has a large screen TV for guests to enjoy.

Visit our web site at http://www.bbonline.com/ar/anderson

Hosts: Jim and Susan Hildebrand
Rooms: 16 (PB) $68-98
Full Breakfast
Credit Cards: A, B, C, D
Notes: 2, 5, 8, 9, 10, 12

HELENA

Foxglove

229 Beech, 72342
(501) 338-9391 (voice and FAX); (800) 863-1926

On a ridge overlooking historic Helena and the Mississippi River, stunning antiques abound in this nationally registered inn. Parqueted floors, quartersawn oak woodwork, stained glass, and six original fireplaces are complimented by private marble baths, whirlpool tubs, phones, cable, FAX, air-conditioning, and other modern conveniences. Points of interest include Delta Cultural Center, Confederate cemetary, antique shops, and a casino, all within 5 minutes. Complimentary evening beverage and snack included.

Host: John Butkiewicz
Rooms: 8 (6PB; 2SB in suites) $69-109
Full Breakfast
Credit Cards: A, B
Notes: 2, 5, 12

HOT SPRINGS

Vintage Comfort Bed and Breakfast

303 Quapaw, 71908
(501) 623-3258 (voice and FAX); (800) 608-4682

Situated on a tree-lined street, a short walk from Hot Springs' historic Bath

---

NOTES: Credit cards accepted: A Master Card; B Visa; C American Express; D Discover; E Diners Club; F Other; 2 Personal checks accepted; 3 Lunch available; 4 Dinner available;

House Row, art galleries, restaurants, and shopping. Guests enjoy a comfortably restored Queen Anne house built in 1907. Four spacious rooms are available upstairs, each with private bath, ceiling fan, and period furnishings. A delicious full breakfast is served each morning in the inn's dining room. Vintage Comfort B&B is known for its comfort and gracious Southern hospitality.

Hostess: Helen Bartlett
Rooms: 4 (PB) $65-90
Full Breakfast
Credit Cards: A, B, C
Notes: 2, 5, 7 (over 6 years), 8, 9, 10, 12

Magnolia Place

MAGNOLIA

Magnolia Place

510 E. Main, 71753
(501) 234-6122; (800) 237-6122;
FAX (501) 234-1254

Your secure comfort and enjoyment is our main priority in five beautiful guest rooms, each decorated with spectacular antiques and each having a private bath, telephone, and TV. Imagine a re-freshing breeze as you relax on the large wraparound porch and enjoy the rockers and swing, just like the old days. Stroll along the flagstone path through the flower garden. Savor a full gourmet breakfast served in the elegant formal dining room, featuring an 1820 dining table once used by President Harding. Come and experience the charm and hospitality of the Old South in exquisite surroundings.

Hosts: Carolyne Hawley, innkeeper, and Ray Sullivent
Rooms: 5 (PB) $89-99
Full Breakfast
Credit Cards: A, B, C, D, E
Notes: 5, 9, 12

WINSLOW

Sky-Vue Lodge

22822 N. Highway 71, 72959
(501) 634-2003; (800) 782-2003

Located on Scenic 71 near Fayetteville, Sky-Vue Lodge offers a 25 mile view of the Ozarks. Enjoy the spectacular view from the porch of your charming cabin, which has heating and air-conditioning for year-round comfort. Hike our 83 acres, or enjoy activities at two nearby state parks. We are family oriented and alcohol free. Facilities are ideal for retreats, conferences, reunions, and weddings. Full breakfast included, other meals available.

Hosts: Glenn and Janice Jorgenson
Rooms: 7 cottages (PB) $45-55
Full Breakfast
Credit Cards: A, B, D
Notes: 2, 4, 5, 7, 8, 9

5 Open all year; 6 Pets welcome; 7 Children welcome; 8 Tennis nearby; 9 Swimming nearby; 10 Golf nearby; 11 Skiing nearby; 12 May be booked through travel agent.

CALIFORNIA (NORTHERN)

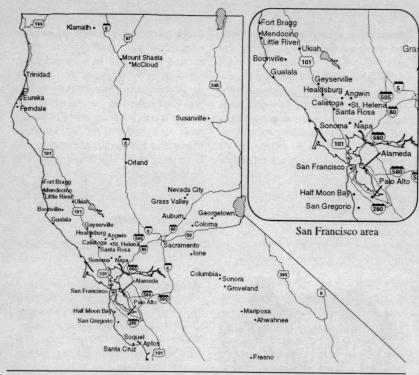

San Francisco area

CALIFORNIA (SOUTHERN)

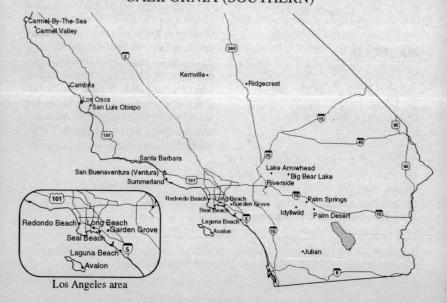

Los Angeles area

California

AHWAHNEE

Silver Spur
Bed and Breakfast
44625 Silver Spur Trail, 93601
(209) 683-2896

Silver Spur Bed and Breakfast is nestled in the Sierra Nevadas of California, just off historic Highway 49, key to the California Gold Country, near the South and West gates of famed Yosemite National Park, and minutes from many outdoor sports. We feature beautiful clean rooms with private baths and entrances, tastefully decorated in American Southwest. Outdoor rest and dining areas boast outstanding Sierra views. A continental breakfast is served daily. Come enjoy Yosemite and be treated to old-fashioned hospitality and great value!

Hosts: Patty and Bryan Hays
Rooms: 2 (PB) $45-60
Expanded Continental Breakfast
Credit Cards: A, B, D
Notes: 2, 5, 6 (sometimes), 7, 9, 10, 11, 12

ALAMEDA

Garratt Mansion
900 Union, 94501
(510) 521-4779; FAX (510) 521-6796

This 1893 Victorian halts time on the tranquil island of Alameda. Only twenty miles to Berkeley or downtown San Francisco. We'll help maximize your vacation plans or leave you alone to regroup. Our rooms are large and comfortable, and our breakfasts are nutritious and filling.

Hosts: Royce and Betty Gladden
Rooms: 7 (5PB; 2SB) $85-135
Full Breakfast
Credit Cards: A, B, C, E
Notes: 2, 5, 7, 8, 9, 10, 12

Garratt Mansion

NOTES: Credit cards accepted: A Master Card; B Visa; C American Express; D Discover; E Diners Club; F Other; 2 Personal checks accepted; 3 Lunch available; 4 Dinner available; 5 Open all year; 6 Pets welcome; 7 Children welcome; 8 Tennis nearby; 9 Swimming nearby; 10 Golf nearby; 11 Skiing nearby; 12 May be booked through travel agent.

ANGWIN (NAPA VALLEY WINE COUNTRY)

Forest Manor

415 Cold Springs Road 94508
(707) 965-3538; (800) 788-0364;
FAX (707) 965-3303

Tucked amongst world renowned vineyards in the Napa wine country and a forested wild life preserve is this secluded 20-acre English Tudor estate, described as "one of the most romantic country inns . . . a small exclusive resort." Enjoy the scenic countryside with wineries, ballooning, spas, shops, lake, water sports, and hiking and biking on forest trails or in the valley. Amenities include a 53 foot pool and spa, spacious luxurious suites (some with inroom whirlpools, fireplaces, verandahs), refrigerators, coffee makers, as well as afternoon cookies and tea.

Hosts: Dr. Harold and Corlene Lambeth
Rooms: 4 (PB) $119-239 off-season;
$149-249 in-season
Full Breakfast
Credit Cards: A, B
Notes: 2, 5, 8, 9, 12

Forest Manor

APTOS

Bayview Hotel, A Country Inn

8041 Soquel Drive, 95003
(408) 688-8654; (800) 4-BAYVIEW;
FAX (408) 688-5128

The Bayview Hotel is proud to be the oldest operating inn on the Monterey Bay. This elegant Victorian-Italianate structure was built in 1878 by Joseph Arano who imported fine furniture for his "grand hotel." All rooms have private baths, some have fireplaces and extra-large soaking tubs. Some of the original furniture is still at the Inn. One of the Bayview's contemporary amenities is the Bayview Grill and Bar which serves breakfast to inn guests as well as lunch and dinner. Visit us on the Internet at: http://BlueSpruce.com.

Hostess: Gwen Burkard
Rooms: 11(PB) $90-150
Full Breakfast
Credit Cards: A, B, C, D
Notes: 2, 3, 4, 5, 7, 8, 9, 10, 12

AUBURN

Power's Mansion Inn

164 Cleveland Avenue, 95603
(916) 885-1166; (916) 885-1386

Power's Mansion Inn, a Victorian mansion built in 1898, has been restored to its original splendor. The beautiful old house has bay windows with lace curtains, an oak staircase, and period furnishings. It is well known for the numerous happy occasions, including weddings and parties, that have been

---

NOTES: Credit cards accepted: A Master Card; B Visa; C American Express; D Discover; E Diners Club; F Other; 2 Personal checks accepted; 3 Lunch available; 4 Dinner available;

enjoyed here. For the comfort and pleasure of our guests, all of our rooms have queen-size beds, private baths, TV, direct dial telephones, and individual temperature control. There are two extra large suites and also a family room.

Hosts: Arno and Jean Lejniers
Rooms: 11 (PB) $79-149
Full Breakfast
Credit Cards: A, B, C
Notes: 2, 5, 7, 9, 10, 11, 12

Power's Mansion Inn

AVALON

Zane Grey Pueblo Hotel

PO Box 216, 90704
(310) 510-0966; (800) 3-PUEBLO;
FAX (310) 510-0639

Southwest Hopi Indian style pueblo built by Zane Grey in 1926. The pueblo is located on a hillside overlooking Avalon Bay and the Pacific Ocean. We offer a complimentary taxi pick-up upon arriving and a shuttle to and from town six times daily. We do have a swimming pool and a patio and deck that overlook the Avalon Bay.

Host: Kevin Anderson
Rooms: 18 (PB) $59-90 off-season;
$85-125 in-season
Continental Breakfast
Credit Cards: A, B, C
Notes: 5, 8, 9, 10, 12

BIG BEAR LAKE/FAWNSKIN

The Inn at Fawnskin Bed and Breakfast

880 Canyon Road, PO Box 378, Fawnskin 92333
(909) 866-3200

The Inn at Fawnskin is one of the few non-camping accommodations on the north shore of Big Bear Lake. A Beautiful custom log home nestled in its own pine forest, minutes from lake and forest trails. Living room with big rock fireplace and library; deck with lake and forest views. Dine by rock fireplace with a delicious homemade breakfast. Game room with wide screen TV, video library, pool table, game table, stereo, and wet bar. Breathtaking master suite; handmade quilts, terry robes. Exceptional hospitality provided by owner/operators.

Hosts: Susan and G.B. Sneed
Rooms: 4 (2PB; 2SB) $85 to 175
Full, Three Course Breakfast
Credit Cards: A, B, C
Notes: 5, 8, 9, 10, 11, 12

BOONVILLE

Anderson Creek Inn

12050 Anderson Valley Way (PO Box 217), 95415
(707) 895-3091; (800) 552-6202;
FAX (707) 895-2546

Delightfully blending elegance with rustic, this lovely inn is spacious and quiet, surrounded by spectacular valley views and rolling pastures full of friendly farm animals. There are five gracious guest rooms with king beds

5 Open all year; 6 Pets welcome; 7 Children welcome; 8 Tennis nearby; 9 Swimming nearby; 10 Golf nearby; 11 Skiing nearby; 12 May be booked through travel agent.

and private baths. Prices include wine, hors d'oeuvres, and a full gourmet breakfast. Some rooms have fireplaces; all have wonderful views and plenty of privacy.

Hosts: Rod and Nancy Graham
Rooms: 5 (PB) $95-165
Full "Scrumptious" Breakfast
Credit Cards: A, B
Notes: 2, 5, 6 (with prior approval), 7, 8, 9 (pool), 10

CALISTOGA

Calistoga Wayside Inn

1523 Foothill Boulevard, 94515
(707) 942-0645; (800) 845-3632;
FAX (707) 942-4169

A warm, inviting Mediterranean-style home, built in the 1920's and situated in a secluded garden setting. Rooms have king or queen beds and private baths. Enjoy the garden and patio, or curl up by the fireplace. Savor a Calistoga country breakfast, afternoon refreshments, and herb tea in the evening. Restaurants, shops, wineries, and spas nearby. Gift certificates.

Hosts: Cora Freitas, owner, and Jan Balcer
Rooms: 3 (PB) $100-145
Full Breakfast
Credit Cards: A, B, C, D
Notes: 2, 5, 7, 8, 9, 10, 12

Calistoga Wayside Inn

Foothill House

3037 Foothill Boulevard, 94515
(707) 942-6933; (800) 942-6933;
FAX (707) 942-5695

"The romantic inn of the Napa Valley," according to the *Chicago Tribune* travel editor. In a country setting, located in the western foothills just north of Calistoga, the Foothill House offers spacious suites individually decorated with antiques. All suites have private baths and entrances, fireplaces, small refrigerators, and air-conditioning. Some have jacuzzis. A luxurious cottage is also available. A gourmet breakfast is served each morning and appetizers and refreshments each evening.

Hosts: Gus and Doris Beckert
Rooms: 3 (PB) $135-250
Full Breakfast
Credit Cards: A, B, C, D
Notes: 2, 5, 8, 9, 10, 12

Hillcrest Bed and Breakfast

3225 Lake County Highway, 94515
(707) 942-6334

"My home is your home." Hillcrest is a rambling, secluded, country home with panoramic views of lush Napa Valley. Swimming, hiking, and fishing on 40 acres. The home is filled with family heirlooms from the family mansion which burned to the ground in 1964. Antique furniture, silver, crystal, Oriental rugs, photos, and artwork decorate the home. Fireplace and grand piano in the guest parlor with a breathtaking view. Large outdoor pool and spa.

Hostess: Debbie O'Gorman
Rooms: 6 (4PB; 2SB) $45-90
Continental Breakfast
Credit Cards: none
Notes: 2, 5, 6, 8, 9, 10, 11 (water), 12

Scarlett's Country Inn

Scarlett's Country Inn

3918 Silverado Trail, 94515
(707) 942-6669 (voice and FAX)

Three exquisitely appointed suites set in the quiet mood of green lawn and tall pines overlooking the famed Napa Valley Vineyards. Seclusion, romance, queen beds, private baths, antiques, fireplace, air-conditionin, secluded woodland swimming pool. Phone and television available in rooms on request. Home-baked breakfast and afternoon refreshments served in rooms or under the apple trees by the pool. Close to wineries and spas. Children welcome at no charge.

Hostess: Scarlett Dwyer
Rooms: 3 (PB) $ 110-175
Full Breakfast
Credit Cards: none
Notes: 2, 5, 7, 8, 9, 10, 12

CAMBRIA

The Pickford House Bed and Breakfast

2555 MacLeod Way, 93428
(805) 927-8619

Eight large rooms done in antiques. All private baths with clawfoot tubs and showers. The front three rooms have fireplaces and a view of the mountains and valley. All rooms have a TV and king- or queen-size bed. Wine and fruitbreads served at 5 PM. Located near beaches and wineries and only seven miles from the Hearst Castle. Third person only $20. Full breakfast served from 8-9 AM in our antique dining room with cozy fireplace. Gift certificates available. Abundance of parking space. Check in after 3 PM, check out at 11 AM.

Hostess: Anna Larsen
Rooms: 8 (PB) $89-130
Full Breakfast
Credit Cards: A, B
Notes: 2, 5, 7

CARMEL

Sunset House Bed and Breakfast

PO Box 1925, 93921
(408) 624-4884 (voice and FAX)

Sunset House, a romantic Inn, located on a quiet residential street, capturing the essence of Carmel. Experience the sound of the surf, being close to the beach and yet only two blocks from

---

5 Open all year; 6 Pets welcome; 7 Children welcome; 8 Tennis nearby; 9 Swimming nearby; 10 Golf nearby; 11 Skiing nearby; 12 May be booked through travel agent.

quaint shops, restaurants, and galleries that make Carmel famous. A special breakfast tray is brought to the room allowing guests to relax and enjoy the glow of the fire and the beauty of the view. Each room is uniquely decorated with considerable thought and care to insure guests an enjoyable stay.

Hosts: Camille and Dennis Fike
Rooms: 5 (PB) $130-190
Expanded Continental Breakfast
Credit Cards: A, B, C, D
Notes: 2, 5, 6, 7, 8, 9, 10, 12

CARMEL VALLEY

The Valley Lodge
Carmel Valley Rd. at Ford Road, PO Box 93, 93924
(408) 659-2261; (800) 641-4646;
FAX (408) 659-4558

A warm Carmel Valley welcome awaits the two of you, a few of you, or a small conference. Relax in a garden patio room or a cozy one or two bedroom cottage with fireplace and kitchen. Enjoy a sumptuous continental breakfast, our heated pool, sauna, hot spa, and fitness center. Tennis and golf are nearby. Walk to fine restaurants and quaint shops of Carmel Valley village, or just listen to your beard grow.

Hosts: Peter and Sherry Coakley
Rooms: 31 (PB) $99-149
Cottages: $159-249
Expanded Continental Breakfast
Credit Cards: A, B, C
Notes: 2, 5, 6 ($10 fee), 7, 8, 9 (on-site), 10, 12

COLOMA

Coloma Country Inn
345 High Street, PO Box 502, 95613
(916) 622-6919

Built in 1852, this country Victorian farmhouse is surrounded by five acres of private gardens in the middle of a 300-acre state park. Main house has five guest rooms and the carriage house has two suites. All rooms feature country decor, including quilts, stenciling, American antiques, and fresh flowers. Hot-air balloon with your host from the backyard meadow or white-water raft from the South Fork American River one block from the inn.

Hosts: Alan and Cindi Ehrgott
Rooms: 7 (5PB; 2SB) $84-170
Full Breakfast
Credit Cards: none
Notes: 2, 5, 7, 9, 10, 12

COLUMBIA

Fallon Hotel
11175 Washington Street, 95310
(209) 532-1479; (800) 532-1479;
FAX (209) 532-7027

Since 1857 the Fallon Hotel in the historic Colombia State Park has provided hospitality and comfort to travelers from all over the world. It has been authentically restored to its Victorian grandeur, and many of the antiques and furnishings are original to the hotel. We welcome you to come visit our Fallon Hotel, Fallon Theater, and old-fash-

NOTES: Credit cards accepted: A Master Card; B Visa; C American Express; D Discover; E Diners Club; F Other; 2 Personal checks accepted; 3 Lunch available; 4 Dinner available;

ioned ice cream parlor for a taste of the Old West.

Host: Tom Bender
Rooms: 14 (13PB; 1SB) $50-95
Continental Breakfast
Credit Cards: A, B, C, D
Notes: 2, 4, 5 (weekends only Jan-March), 7, 8, 9, 10, 11, 12

ESTABLISHED 1857
COLUMBIA STATE HISTORIC PARK

Fallon Hotel

EUREKA

"An Elegant Victorian Mansion" B&B Experience

1406 "C" Street, 95501
(707) 444-3144; FAX (707) 442-5594

An award-winning 1888 NATIONAL HISTORIC LANDMARK of opulence, grace, and grandeur, featuring spectacular gingerbread exteriors, opulent Victorian interiors, antique furnishings, and an acclaimed French-Gourmet breakfasts. Exclusively for the non-smoking traveler, the inn is a "Living history House-Museum" for the descriminating connoisseur of authentic Victorian decor, who also has a pas-

sion for quality, service, and the extraordinary. Breath-takingly authentic, with all the nostalgic trimmings of a century ago, this meticulously restored Victorian masterpiece offers both history and hospitality, combined with romance and pampering. Enjoy the regal splendor of this spectacular STATE HISTORIC SITE, and indulge in 4-star luxury. With complimentary horseless-carriage rides, bicycles, sauna, and laundry service, the Inn is recommended by AAA, Mobil, Fodor's, and more. Arthur Frommer calls it *"The very best that California has to offer— not to be missed."*

Hosts: Doug and Lily Vieyra
Rooms: 4 (2PB; 2SB) $65-165
Full French Gourmet Breakfast
Credit Cards: A, B
Notes: 2, 3, 5, 8, 9, 10, 11, 12

Carter House Victorians

301 "L" Street, 95501
(707) 444-8062; (800) 404-1390;
FAX (707) 444-8067

Carter Victorians encompassed three lovely Victorians: the Carter House Inn, an exact replica of a circa 1884 San Francisco house that was destroyed in the 1906 earthquake; the classic 25-room Hotel Carter, and the newest addition, the three-room, single-level Bell Cottage. Each offers a distinctly clean and artful blend of classic Victorian architecture with stylish, contemporary interior settings, all in a warm, hospitable environment. A great variety of luxurious rooms, each appointed with original local art, fine antiques, and gen-

5 Open all year; 6 Pets welcome; 7 Children welcome; 8 Tennis nearby; 9 Swimming nearby; 10 Golf nearby; 11 Skiing nearby; 12 May be booked through travel agent.

erous amenities such as fireplaces, whirlpools, bay views, skylights, double-head showers, soaking tubs with marina views, king-size beds, telephones, VCRs and a video tape library, honor bars, and minifridges. "The best of the best," according to *California Living Magazine*.

Hosts: Mark and Christi Carter
Rooms: 32 (PB) $115-225
Full Breakfast
Credit Cards: A, B, C, D, E, F
Notes: 2, 4, 5, 7, 8, 10, 12

The Daly Inn

The Daly Inn

1125 "H" Street, 91311
(707) 465-3638; (800) 321-9656;
FAX (707) 444-3636

This exquisite Colonial Revival mansion, built in 1905, has four fireplaces, lovely Victorian gardens, a third floor "Christmas Ballroon" and is completely furnished with turn of the century antiques. We are known for our wonderful breakfasts and making our guests feel at home in a quiet, romantic atmosphere. Eureka's Old Town, with its wonderful shops and restaurants, is within walking distance. The majestic

Redwoods and the Pacific Ocean are only minutes away. AAA approved, three diamond rating.

Hosts: Sue and Gene Clinesmith
Rooms: 5 (3PB; 2SB) $80-140
Full Breakfast and wine and cheese each evening
Credit Cards: A, B, C, D
Notes: 2, 5, 8, 10, 12

FERNDALE

The Gingerbread Mansion Inn

400 Berding Street, PO Box 40, 95536
(707) 786-4000; (800) 952-4136;
FAX (707) 786-4381

Nestled between the giant redwoods and the rugged Pacific Coast, is one of California's best-kept secrets: the Victorian village of Ferndale. A State Historic landmark and listed on the National Historic Register, Ferndale is a community frozen in time with Victorian homes and shops relatively unchanged since their construction in the mid-to-late 1800s. One of Ferndale's most well-known homes is the Gingerbread Mansion Inn. Decorated with antiques, the eleven, romantic guest rooms offer private baths, some with old-fashioned clawfoot tubs, and fireplaces. Also included is a full breakfast, high tea, four parlors, and formal English gardens. Rated four-diamonds by AAA.

Host: Ken Torbert
Rooms: 10 (PB) $140-350
Full Breakfast
Credit Cards: A, B, C
Notes: 2, 5, 10, 12

NOTES: Credit cards accepted: A Master Card; B Visa; C American Express; D Discover; E Diners Club; F Other; 2 Personal checks accepted; 3 Lunch available; 4 Dinner available;

FORT BRAGG

Grey Whale Inn

615 N. Main Street, 95437
(707) 964-0640; (800) 382-7244;
FAX (707) 964-4408
E-mail: gwhale@mcn.org

Handsome four-story Mendocino Coast Landmark since 1915. Cozy rooms to expansive suites, all have private baths. Ocean, garden, hill, or town views. Some rooms have fireplaces or TV, one has a jacuzzi tub, and all have phones. Recreation area: pool table/library, fireside lounge, and TV theater. Sixteen-person conference room. Full buffet breakfast features blue-ribbon breads. Friendly, helpful staff. Relaxed seaside charm, situated six blocks to beach. Celebrate your special occasion on the fabled Mendocino Coast!

Hosts: John and Colette Bailey
Rooms: 14 (PB) $85-180
Full Breakfast
Credit Cards: A, B, C, D
Notes: 2, 5, 7, 8, 9, 10, 12

Pudding Creek Inn

700 N. Main Street, 95437
(707) 964-9529; (800) 227-9529;
FAX (707) 961-0282

Two lovely 1884 Victorian homes, adjoined by a lush garden court, offer comfortable and romantic rooms. Your stay includes a complete, full breakfast buffet in the morning and a social hour in the evening with hot and cold beverages and a cheese platter. Common rooms open for guest use include forma

Victorian parlor and dining room with fireplace, TV/recreation room filled with books, games, and puzzles and lastly the beautiful enclosed garden court.

Hosts: Garry and Carole Anloff
Rooms: 10 (PB) $70-130
Full Breakfast Buffet
Credit Cards: A, B, C, D
Notes: 2, 5, 7, 8, 9, 10, 12

FRESNO

Mary Lou's B&B

5502 W. Escalon Avenue, 93722
(209) 277-2650

Mary Lou's B&B in Fresno, CA is just three miles east of Hwy. 99 off the Herndon ramp. Stop on your way to Yosemite or Sequoia National Parks. Twin beds, private bath, guest sitting room, and air-conditioning await your arrival.

Hosts: Mary Lou and Merle Robinson
Rooms: 1 (PB) $50-60
Full Breakfast
Credit Cards: none
Notes: 2, 5, 7, 10

GARDEN GROVE
(L.A./ORANGE COUNTY AREA)

Hidden Village B&B

9582 Hale Kulani Drive, 92641
(714) 636-8312

Charming Colonial home with antiques, rare Victorian lighting fixtures, hand-woven coverlets on brass beds. Four

5 Open all year; 6 Pets welcome; 7 Children welcome; 8 Tennis nearby; 9 Swimming nearby; 10 Golf nearby; 11 Skiing nearby; 12 May be booked through travel agent.

guest rooms, two with private bath. Full breakfast served in the dining room includes specialty egg dishes, muffins, and homegrown fruites. Air-conditioning and TV in rooms. One room have a fireplace and sun deck. Close to Disneyland and the convention center.

Hosts: Dick and Linda O'Berg
Rooms: 4 (2PB; 2SB) $65-75
Full Breakfast
Credit Cards: none
Notes: 2, 3, 5, 7, 9, 10, 12

GEORGETOWN—GOLD COUNTRY

Historic American River Inn

PO Box 43, Main at Orleans Street, 95634
(916) 333-4499; (800) 245-6566;
FAX (916) 333-9253

Innkeepers Will and Maria Collin carry on the century old tradition of graciousness in a setting far removed from the fast pace of modern living. You are invited to cool off in a beautiful mountain pool or relax in the spa. Some may choose a day of bicycling amid the colorful breathtaking daffodils, iris and the brilliant yellow-gold scotch broom. The bicycles are provided. Their historic Queen Anne Inn can provide the ideal setting for your corporate off-site meeting or retreat. All meeting necessities and food catering services are available. The inn can accommodate up to 17/60 participants. Please call for detailed information for your group.

Hosts: Will and Maria Collin
Rooms: 18 (12PB; 6SB) $85-115
Full Gourmet Breakfast
Credit Cards: A, B, C, D, E, F
Notes: 2, 3, 5, 7, 8, 9, 10, 11, 12

GEYSERVILLE

Campbell Ranch Inn

1475 Canyon Road, 95441
(707) 857-3476; (800) 959-3878;
FAX (707) 857-3239

A 35-acre country setting in the heart of the Sonoma County wine country

Campbell Ranch Inn

NOTES: Credit cards accepted: A Master Card; B Visa; C American Express; D Discover; E Diners Club; F Other; 2 Personal checks accepted; 3 Lunch available; 4 Dinner available;

between the Alexander Valley and Dry Creek Valley wine regions. Spectacular view, beautiful gardens, tennis court, swimming pool, hot tub, and bicycles. The Inn has four spacious rooms and a private cottage, private baths, king beds, and balconies. Quiet and peaceful. Full breakfast is served on the terrace, and an evening dessert of homemade pie or cake is offered. Visit wineries and Lake Sonoma for water sports, fishing, and hiking. The wine country destination resort. Color brochure available.

Host: Mary Jane and Jerry Campbell
Rooms: 5 (PB) $100-165
Full Breakfast, Evening Dessert
Credit Cards: A, B, C
Notes: 2, 5, 10, 12

GRASS VALLEY

Elam Biggs
Bed and Breakfast

220 Colfax Avenue, 95945
(916) 477-0906

This 1892 beautiful Queen Anne Victorian is set admist a large yard surrounded by grand old shade trees and a rose-covered picket fence. All this is just a short stroll to historic downtown Grass Valley. In the morning, enjoy brewed coffee and a hearty breakfast served in the lovely dining room or outside on the private porch.

Hosts: Barbara and Peter Franchino
Rooms: 5 (PB); $75-110
Full Breakfast
Credit Cards: A, B
Notes: 2, 5, 7, 8, 9, 10, 11, 12

Elam Biggs B&B

GUALALA

North Coast Country Inn

34591 S. Highway 1, 95445
(707) 884-4537; (800) 959-4537

Picturesque redwood buildings on a forested hillside overlooking the Pacific Ocean. The large guestrooms feature fireplaces, private baths, queen beds, decks, and mini-kitchens and are furnished with authentic antiques. There is a beautiful hilltop gazebo garden and romantic hot tub under the pines.

Hosts: Loren and Nancy Flanagan
Rooms: 4 (PB) $135
Full Breakfast
Credit Cards: A, B, C
Notes: 2, 5, 8, 10, 12

HALF MOON BAY

Old Thyme Inn

779 Main Street, 94019
(415) 726-1616; FAX (415) 712-0805

The Inn has seven guest rooms, all with

---

5 Open all year; 6 Pets welcome; 7 Children welcome; 8 Tennis nearby; 9 Swimming nearby; 10 Golf nearby; 11 Skiing nearby; 12 May be booked through travel agent.

private baths. The Inn is a restored 1889 Queen Anne Victorian, located on historic Main Street in the downtown area. Some rooms have fireplaces and double size whirlpool tubs. The theme is our English-style herb garden; all rooms are named after herbs. Atmosphere is friendly and informal. We serve beverages in the evening and a hearty breakfast each morning. Nearby activities include golf, whale-watching, tidepools, and shopping. Many fine restaurants are closeby, many within walking distance.

Hosts: George and Marcia Dempsey
Rooms: 7 (PB) $75-210
Full Breakfast
Credit Cards: A, B, C
Notes: 2, 5, 8, 9, 10, 11, 12

HEALDSBURG

The Honor Mansion
14891 Grove Street, 95448
(707) 433-4277; (800) 554-4667;
FAX (707) 431-7173

A beautifully restored 1883 "Italiante" Victorian in the heart of the Sonoma County Wine Country. Enjoy the comfort of immaculate guest rooms, a dip in the pool, or a peaceful rest beside the Koi pond waterfall. Wonderful food; warm hospitality. Your best vacation ever!

Hostess: Cathi Fowler
Rooms: 6 (PB) $120-195
Full Breakfast
Credit Cards: A, B, D
Notes: 5, 10, 12

IDYLLIWILD

Wilkum Inn Bed and Breakfast
PO Box 1115, 92549
(909) 659-4087; (800) 659-4086

Come home to warm hospitality and personal service in a friendly mountain ambiance. The two-story, shingle-sided inn is nestled among pines, oaks, and cedars. Warm knotty pine interiors and a cozy river rock fireplace are enhanced by the innkeepers' antiques and collectibles. Expanded continental breakfast of fruits and breads, such as crepes, Belgian Waffles or abelskivers, fortify guests for a day of hiking or visiting unique shops and art galleries.

Hostesses: Annamae Chambers and Barbara Jones
Rooms: 5 (3PB; 2SB) $65-95
Expanded Continental Breakfast
Credit Cards: none
Notes: 2, 5, 12

IONE

The Heirloom
214 Shakeley Lane, PO Box 322, 95640
(209) 274-4468

Travel down a country lane to a spacious, romantic English garden and a petite Colonial mansion built circa 1863. The house features balconies, fireplaces, and heirloom antiques, along with gourmet breakfast and gracious hospitality. Located in the historic gold country, close to all major northern California cities. The area abounds with antiques, wineries, and historic sites.

NOTES: Credit cards accepted: A Master Card; B Visa; C American Express; D Discover; E Diners Club; F Other; 2 Personal checks accepted; 3 Lunch available; 4 Dinner available;

Within walking distance to a golf course.

Hostesses: Melisande Hubbs and Patricia Cross
Rooms: 6 (4 PB; 2 SB); $60-92
Full Breakfast
Credit Cards: A, B, C
Closed Thanksgiving and Christmas
Notes: 2, 5, 8, 9, 10

The Heirloom

JULIAN

Butterfield Bed and Breakfast

2284 Sunset Drive, PO Box 1115, 92036
(619) 765-2179; (800) 379-4262;
FAX (619) 765-1229

Butterfield Bed and Breakfast captures the gold mining and apple growing heritage of the historic mountain hamlet of Julian. The inn's five guest rooms, each with private bath, offer guests day's end luxury in the French Bedroom Suite, Country Rose, Feathernest Room, Apple "Sweet," or the Rosebud Cottage. Each morning guests are treated to a gourmet breakfast. Butterfield offers holidays specials, carriage rides, and candlelight dinner or just a quiet place to relax. From the lilac and apple blossoms of spring, the wild flowers of summer, and the glorious hues of fall to the white frosting of winter, Butterfield Bed and Breakfast delivers a mother lode of hospitality all year long.

Hosts: Ray and Mary Trimmins
Rooms: 5 (PB) $105-135
Full Breakfast
Credit Cards: A, B, C, D
Notes: 2, 4, 5, 7, 8, 10, 12

Julian Gold Rush Hotel

PO Box 1856, 2032 Main Street, 92036
(619) 765-0201

Built in 1897 by a freed slave, Albert Robinson, and his wife, Margaret, the Hotel fit beautifully into the emerging Victorian society of the 1890's. The Hotel was often called the "Queen of the Back Country" and was a frequent stopping place of Lady Bronston, Admiral Nimitz, the Scripps, and the Whitneys. The hotel register even boasts the presence of many a senator and congressman. Popular also with the townfolk, the Hotel served as a Julian social center after the monthly townhall dances when Margaret Robinson hosted and prepared much anticipated midnight feasts.

Hosts: Steve and Gig Ballinger
Rooms: 14 (PB) $72-160
Full Breakfast
Credit Cards: A, B, C
Notes: 2, 5, 7, 8, 9, 10, 12

---

5 Open all year; 6 Pets welcome; 7 Children welcome; 8 Tennis nearby; 9 Swimming nearby; 10 Golf nearby; 11 Skiing nearby; 12 May be booked through travel agent.

KERNVILLE

Kern River Inn Bed and Breakfast

PO Box 1725, 119 Kern River Drive, 93238-1725
(619) 376-6750; (800) 986-4382;
FAX (619) 376-6643

A charming, classic country riverfront B&B located on the wild and scenic Kern River in the quaint little town of Kernville within the Sequoia National Forest in the southern Sierra Mountains. We specialize in romantic getaways. All bedrooms have private baths and feature river views; some with whirlpool tubs and fireplaces. Full breakfast. Walk to restaurants, shops, parks, and museum. A short drive to giant redwood trees. An all-year vacation area with fishing, skiing, hiking, biking, white-water rafting, and Lake Isabella.

Hosts: Jack and Carita Prestwich
Rooms: 6 (PB) $79-99
Full Breakfast
Credit Cards: A, B, C
Notes: 2, 5, 7, 9, 10, 11, 12

KLAMATH

Requa Inn

451 Requa Road, 95548
(707) 482-8205; FAX (707) 482-0844

Historic 1914 inn located at the mouth of majestic Klamath River, in the heart of Redwood National Park. Nearby activities include hiking, beaches, birding, whale watching, fishing, and boating. Four rooms with views of the river. Panoramic views from the lobby and dining room. Available for weddings, meetings, and parties. Special rates for large groups or extended stays.

Hosts: Sue Reese and Leo and Melissa Chavez
Rooms: 10 (PB) $70-95
Full Breakfast
Credit Cards: A, B, C, D
Notes: 3, 4, 5, 7, 12

LAGUNA BEACH

Eiler's Inn B&B

741 South Coast Highway, 92651
(714) 494-3004; FAX (714) 497-2215

Twelve rooms with private baths and a courtyard with gurgling fountain and colorful blooming plants are within walking distance of town and most restaurants; half block from the beach.

Host: Nico Wirtz
Rooms: 12 (PB) $100-145
Full Breakfast
Credit Cards: A, B, C, D
Notes: 2, 5, 8, 9, 10, 12

LAKE ARROWHEAD

Arrowhead Windermere Manor

263 S. State Hwy. 173, PO Box 2177, 92352
(909) 336-3292; (800) 429-BLUE;
FAX (909) 336-4748

The cozy elegance of European decor in an alpine setting welcomes you to the Arrowhead Windermere Manor (formerly the Bluebell House). Guests appreciate immaculate housekeeping, exquisite breakfasts, warm hospitality, and relaxing by the fire or out on the deck. Walk to charming lakeside vil-

---

NOTES: Credit cards accepted: A Master Card; B Visa; C American Express; D Discover; E Diners Club; F Other; 2 Personal checks accepted; 3 Lunch available; 4 Dinner available;

lage, boating, swimming, and restaurants. Private beach club and ice skating are nearby; winter sports 30 minutes away. Ask about discounts!

Hosts: Paul and Tudee Evers
Rooms: 5 (PB) $105-150
Full Gourmet Breakfast
Credit Cards: A, B, D
Notes: 2, 5, 9, 11

Eagles Landing B&B

27406 Cedarwood, 92652
Mail to: PO Box 1510, Blue Jay, CA 92317
(909) 336-2642 (voice and FAX); (800) 835-5085

The interesting architecture, forest and lake views, artistic decor, gourmet breakfasts, and social hour make Eagles Landing a landmark, but the fun, warmth, and hospitality of the hosts are why guests return. The three beautiful rooms are decorated with art, antiques, and crafts collected from around the world. The suite is cabin-like and done in Early California.

Hosts: Dorothy and Jack Stone
Rooms: 4 (PB) $95-185
Full Breakfast
Credit Cards: A, B, C, D
Notes: 2, 5, 8, 9, 11, 12

Eagles Landing B&B

LITTLE RIVER

The Victorian Farmhouse Inn

7001 N Highway 1, 95456
(707) 937-0697; (800) 264-4723

Built in 1877 as a private residence, the Inn has been completely renovated and furnished in period antiques to enhance its beauty and Victorian charm. All rooms have private baths, and most have fireplaces. Breakfast is served in your room. The Inn has a country setting with redwoods and fir trees, and the ocean is just across the street. Located two miles south of Mendocino.

Hostess: Carole Molnar
Rooms: 10 (PB) $85-155
Full Breakfast
Credit Cards: A, B, C
Notes: 2, 5, 6 (some), 7, 8, 9, 10, 12

LONG BEACH

Lord Mayor's B&B Inn

435 Cedar Avenue, 90802
(310) 436-0324 (voice and FAX)

An award-winning historical landmark, the 1904 home of the first mayor of Long Beach invites you to enjoy the ambiance of years gone by. Rooms have 10-foot ceilings and are decorated with period antiques. Each unique bedroom has its private bath and access to a large sundeck. Full breakfast is served in the dining room or on the deck overlooking the garden. Located near beaches, close to major attractions, within walking distance of convention and civic center and special events held down-

---

5 Open all year; 6 Pets welcome; 7 Children welcome; 8 Tennis nearby; 9 Swimming nearby;
10 Golf nearby; 11 Skiing nearby; 12 May be booked through travel agent.

town. The right touch for the business and vacation traveler.

Hosts: Laura and Reuben Brasser
Rooms: 5 (PB) $85-125
Full Breakfast
Credit Cards: A, B, C, D
Notes: 2, 5, 7, 9, 10, 12

LOS OSOS

Gerarda's Bed and Breakfast

1056 Bay Oaks Drive, 93402
(805) 534-0834

Gerarda's three bedroom ranch-style home is comfortably furnished and offers wonderful ocean and mountain views from the elaborate flower gardens in front and back. Gerarda, the hostess, speaks five languages and will welcome you warmly. She cooks a wonderful family-style breakfast. A few miles from state parks, Morro Bay, Hearst Castle, San Luis Obispo, universities, and shopping center.

Hostess: Gerarda Ondang
Rooms: 3 (1PB; 2SB) $30-45
Full Breakfast
Credit Cards: none
Notes: 2, 5, 7, 8, 9, 10

MARIPOSA (GOLD COUNTRY AND YOSEMITE NATIONAL PARK)

Finch Haven

4605 Triangle Road, 95338
(209) 966-4738 (voice and FAX)

A quiet country home on nine acres with panoramic mountain views. Birds, deer, and other abundant wildlife. Two rooms with private bath and private deck. Queen and twin beds. Nutritious breakfast. In the heart of the California Gold Rush Country near historic attractions. Convenient access to spectacular Yosemite Valley and Yosemite National Park. A restful place to practice Mark 6:31 and to enjoy Christian hospitality.

Hosts: Bruce and Carol Fincham
Rooms: 2 (PB) $75
Full Breakfast
Credit Cards: none
Notes: 2, 5, 7, 8, 9, 11, 12

Meadow Creek Ranch Bed and Breakfast Inn

2669 Triangle Rd./Hwy. 49 S., 95338
(209) 966-3843

Historical 1850's stage coach stop. Two story ranch house near Yosemite National Park. Lined by De Long Creek, meadows, pines, oaks, and black walnut trees. Relax on the porch, enjoy the country, yet be minutes from town. Wake up to fresh coffee and a full, sit-down, country breakfast by candlelight with guests from the world over. Appointed with European and American antiques, art, and nature's surroundings.

Hosts: Bob and Carol Shockley, owners
Rooms: 3 (1PB in cottage; 2SB in main house) $75-95 + tax
Full, Great, Country Breakfast
Credit Cards: A, B, C, D
Notes: 2, 8, 9, 10, 11, 12

NOTES: Credit cards accepted: A Master Card; B Visa; C American Express; D Discover; E Diners Club; F Other; 2 Personal checks accepted; 3 Lunch available; 4 Dinner available;

Shiloh B&B (guest house)

Shiloh Bed and Breakfast

3265 Triangle Park Road, 95338
(209) 742-7200

Shiloh is an old peaceful farmhouse with a private guest house nestled among Ponderosa pines in the foothills of Yosemite National Park. Two quaint knotty pine bedrooms in the main house share a private bath. The pleasantly decorated guest house sleeps five or six and has a full kitchen, living room, and private deck. Playground for the children, plus a swimming pool and horse shoe pits. Historic gold rush country and Yosemite to explore. Christian hospitality.

Hosts: Ron and Joan Smith
Rooms: 3 (1PB; 2SB) $55-85
Extended Continental Breakfast
Credit Cards: A, B, C, D
Notes: 2, 5, 7, 9, 10

Winsor Farms Bed and Breakfast

5636 Whitlock Road, 95338
(209) 966-5592

A country home seven miles north of Mariposa, just off Highway 140 to Yosemite National Park. This peaceful hilltop retreat among majestic pines and rugged oaks offers two rooms decorated for your comfort and convenience. An extended continental breakfast is served. The town of Mariposa is the Gateway to the Mother Lode Gold Country, with famous court house, museums, and history center. Yosemite National Park, a scenic wonder of the world with waterfalls, granite cliffs, Sequoia Big Trees, birds, and animals.

Hosts: Donald and Janice Haag
Rooms: 2 (SB) $40-50
Extended Continental Breakfast
Credit Cards: none
Notes: 2, 5, 7 (restricted)

MCCLOUD

McCloud River Inn

PO Box 1560, 325 Lawndale, 96057
(800) 2617831; FAX (916) 964-2730 (call first)

Beautifully restored 1900 Victorian style building on five acres at the base of Mount Shasta. All five rooms are furnished with romance in mind. Full breakfast is served in dining room. Downstairs enjoy our espresso bar, old-fashioned candy store, and art gallery. Near fishing, golf, hiking, swimming, skiing, and snowmobiling. Snowmobiles and mountain bike rentals available.

Hostess: Marina Mort
Rooms: 5 (2PB; 3SB) $55-76
Full, Home-cooked Breakfast
Credit Cards: A, B, C, D
Notes: 2, 3, 5, 7, 9, 10, 11, 12

---

5 Open all year; 6 Pets welcome; 7 Children welcome; 8 Tennis nearby; 9 Swimming nearby; 10 Golf nearby; 11 Skiing nearby; 12 May be booked through travel agent.

MENDOCINO

Antioch Ranch
39451 Comptche Road, 95460
(707) 937-5570; FAX (707) 937-1757

Antioch Ranch, providing a Christian atmosphere of peace, is a place for refreshment and renewal. Located just 5½ miles inland from the picturesque town of Mendocino, the Ranch features four guest cottages on 20 acres of rolling hills, redwoods, and apple orchards. Each cottage has its own style and ambiance. Rustic, yet comfortable, they feature woodstoves, complete kitchens with a microwave, two bedrooms, a bath, and open living/dining room.

Hosts: Jerry and Pat Westfall
Rooms: 4 two bedroom cottages (PB) $55-75
Breakfast on request basis.
Credit Cards: none
Notes: 2, 5, 7, 8, 9 (beach), 10

Blair House

Blair House
45110 Little Lake Street, 95460
(707) 937-1800; (800) 699-9296;
FAX (707) 937-2444

Blair House is perhaps the most well-known home in Mendocino. The popular television series "Murder She Wrote" features the exterior of this Victorian mansion as Jessica Fletcher's fictional home. The exterior of the house is almost as it was when it was built in 1888. The charm of Blair House begins when you walk through the gate of our picket fence into our garden. Ring the old-fashioned doorbell and step into simple elegance. You'll love the plush queen-size beds in all our rooms, complete with hand-crafted quilts and lovely ocean and village views to brighten each room. Blair House can be your home away from home.

Hosts: Geoffrey and Ming Hart
Rooms: 5 (2 PB; 3 SB) $80-155
Continental Breakfast
Credit Cards: A, B
Notes: 2, 5, 6, 7, 12

Mendocino Village Inn
44860 Main St., PO Box 626, 95460
(707) 937-0246; (800) 882-7029;
Email: mendoinn@aol.com

An 1882 Queen Anne Victorian with gardens, frog pond, and sun deck. Many rooms with fireplaces and ocean views. Style is eclectic with emphasis on clean, comfortable, and welcoming. We are close to the beach and walking distance to all shops and restaurants. "Please come and play our pump organ." Visit our web site at: http://www.mcn.org/cbc/bussect/villageinn/mendoinn.html.

Hosts: Kathleen and Bill Erwin
Rooms: 12 + 1 suite (11PB; 2SB) $75-175
Full Breakfast (two courses)
Credit Cards: none
Notes: 2, 5, 8, 9, 10

NOTES: Credit cards accepted: A Master Card; B Visa; C American Express; D Discover; E Diners Club; F Other; 2 Personal checks accepted; 3 Lunch available; 4 Dinner available;

Mendocino Village Inn

MT. SHASTA

Mt. Shasta Ranch Bed and Breakfast

1008 W. A. Barr Road, 96067
(916) 926-3870; FAX (916) 926-6882

The inn is situated in a rural setting with a majestic view of Mt. Shasta and features a main lodge, carriage house, and cottage. Group accommodations are available.Our breakfast room is ideally suited for seminars and retreats with large seating capacity. The game room includes piano, ping-pong, pool table, and board games. Guests also enjoy an outdoor jacuzzi. Nearby recreational facilities include alpine and Nordic skiing, fishing, hiking, mountain bike rentals, surrey rides, and museums. Call for pastor's discount.

Hosts: Bill and Mary Larsen
Rooms: 9 + 1 cabin (5PB; 5SB) $55-95
Full Breakfast
Credit Cards: A, B, C, D
Notes: 2, 5, 7, 8, 9, 10, 11, 12

NAPA

Blue Violet Mansion

443 Brown Street, 94559
(707) 253-2583; (800) 959-2583;
FAX (707) 257-8205

Cross the threshold of this graceful Queen Anne Victorian mansion and return to the elegance of the 1880s. Situated on a quiet street with an acre of private gardens in historic Old Town Napa and walking distance from downtown shops and restaurants. This lovingly restored inn is an intimate and romantic home offering large, cheerful faux and mural painted rooms with fireplaces, balconies, private baths or spas, and more. Guests are encouraged to feel at home in the grand front rooms and enjoy the new courtyard garden with fountains and stained glass skylight and swimming pool. Enjoy an evening of romantic elegance with a private candlelight champagne dinner, picnic lunches, bicycles, and much more. Hot air ballooning and golf packages available. Near Wine Train. Described by Bill Gleason in his book *50 Most Romantic Places in Northern California* as the cabernet of Napa Valley's inns.

Hosts: Bob and Kathy Morris
Rooms: 14 (PB) $145-240 (amenity extra)
Full Breakfast
Credit Cards: A, B, C, E, F
Notes: 2, 3, 4, 5, 7, 8, 9, 10, 12

Hennessey House

1727 Main Street, 94559
(707) 226-3774; FAX (707) 226-2975

Hennessey House, a beautiful Eastlake-style Queen Anne Victorian located in downtown Napa, is listed in the National Register of Historic Places. It features antique furnishings, fireplaces, whirlpools, patios, and a sauna. The dining room, where a sumptuous breakfast is served, features one of the finest examples of a hand-painted, stamped tin ceilings in California. Just a short walk to the Wine Train! *"My husband and I had the privilege of staying at your inn . . . and had a wonderful visit. We especially enjoyed meeting the other people and the great breakfast you served,"* Jennifer and Jeff Andions.

Hostesses: Andrea Lamar and Lauriann Delay
Rooms: 10 (PB) $80-155
Full Breakfast
Credit Cards: A, B, C, D
Notes: 2, 5, 7, 8, 10, 12

La Belle Epoque

1386 Calistoga Avenue, 94559
(707) 257-2161; (800) 238-8070;
FAX (707) 226-6314

Elaborate Queen Anne architecture and extensive use of stained glass are complimented by elegant period furnishings. This century-old Victorian boasts six tastefully decorated guest rooms, each with private bath and two with fireplaces. A generous, gourmet breakfast is offered each morning either by fireside in the formal dining room or in the more relaxed atmosphere of the inn's plant-filled sunroom. Complimentary evening wine and appetizers on the premises. Wine tasting room/cellar. Walk to Old Town, Wine Train, and

Opera House. On-grounds parking and air-conditioned throughout.

Hostess: Georgia Jump, owner
Rooms: 6 (PB) $125-185
Full Gourmet Breakfast
Credit Cards: A, B, C, D
Notes: 2, 5, 8, 9, 10, 12

NAPA VALLEY

Bartels Ranch and B&B Country Inn

1200 Conn Valley Road, St. Helena, 94574-9606
(707) 963-4001; FAX (707) 963-5100

"Heaven in the Hills." Situated in the heart of the world-famous Napa Valley wine country is this secluded, romantic, elegant country estate overlooking a "100-acre valley with a 10,000-acre view." Honeymoon "Heart of the Valley" suite has sunken jacuzzi, sauna, shower, stone fireplace, and private deck with vineyard view. Romantic, award-winning accommodations, expansive entertainment room, poolside lounging, personalized itineraries, afternoon refreshments, pool table, fireplace, library, and terraces overlooking the vineyard. Bicycle to nearby wineries, lake, golf, tennis, fishing, boating, mineral spas, and bird watching. Come dream awhile!

Hostess: Jami Bartels
Rooms: 4 (PB) $135-355
Full Breakfast
Credit Cards: A, B, C, D, E, F (JOB)
Notes: 2, 3, 4 (catered), 5, 7, 8, 9, 10, 12

NOTES: Credit cards accepted: A Master Card; B Visa; C American Express; D Discover; E Diners Club; F Other; 2 Personal checks accepted; 3 Lunch available; 4 Dinner available;

NEVADA CITY

The Parsonage
Bed and Breakfast Inn

427 Broad Street, 95959
(916) 265-9478; (916) 265-8147

History comes alive in this 125-year-old-home in Nevada City's historic district. Cozy guest rooms, parlor, and dining and family rooms are all lovingly furnished with the innkeeper's pioneer family's antiques. Breakfast is served on the veranda or in the formal dining room. Enjoy lunch or dinner at one of the 26 restaurants in the four block area.

Hostess: Deborah Dane, owner
Rooms: 6 (PB) $65-120
Expanded Continental Breakfast; Full Breakfast
on holidays and weekends.
Credit Cards: A, B
Notes: 2, 5, 7, 9, 10, 11, 12

ORLAND

Inn at Shallow Creek Farm

4712 Road DD, 95963
(916) 865-4093; (800) 865-4093

The Inn offers bed and breakfast at a working farm and orange orchard. Our two-story farmhouse offers spacious rooms furnished with antiques, creating a blend of nostalgia and comfortable country living. Our breakfasts feature home-baked breads and an assortment of fruit and juice from our own trees. Delicious homemade jams and jellies complement our farm breakfasts. Nearby Black Butte Lake and Sacramento National Wildlife Refuge offer outdoor recreation activities. French,

German, and Spanish are spoken.

Hosts: Mary and Kurt Glaeseman
Rooms: 4 (2PB; 2SB) $55-75
Full Breakfast
Credit Cards: A, B
Notes: 2, 5, 9, 10, 12

PALM DESERT

Tres Palmas B&B

73135 Tumbleweed Lane, 92260
(619) 773-9858; (800) 770-9858;
FAX (619) 776-9159

Tres Palmas is located just one block south of El Paseo, the "Rodeo Drive of the Desert," where you will find boutiques, art galleries, and many restaurants. Or stay "home" to enjoy the desert sun in and around the pool and spa. The guest rooms feature queen or king beds, climate controls, ceiling fans, and color televisions and are uniquely decorated in southwestern style. Lemonade and iced tea are always available. Snacks served in the late afternoons. AAA three diamond rated; AB&BA rated A+.

Hosts: Karen and Terry Bennett
Rooms: 4 (PB) $100-160 Oct. 1 to June 30
Expanded Continental Breakfast
Credit Cards: A, B
Notes: 2, 5, 8, 9, 10, 12

Tres Palmas Bed and Breakfast

---

5 Open all year; 6 Pets welcome; 7 Children welcome; 8 Tennis nearby; 9 Swimming nearby; 10 Golf nearby; 11 Skiing nearby; 12 May be booked through travel agent.

PALM SPRINGS

Casa Cody Bed and Breakfast Country Inn

175 S. Cahuilla Road, 92262
(619) 320-9346; (800) 231-CODY (2639);
FAX (619) 325-8610

A romantic, historic hideaway is nestled against the spectacular San Jacinto Mountains in the heart of Palm Springs Village. Completely redecorated in Santa Fe decor, it has 23 ground-level units consisting of hotel rooms, studio suites, and one- and two-bedroom suites with private patios, fireplaces, and fully equipped kitchens. Cable TV and private phones; two pools; secluded, tree-shaded whirlpool spa.

Hosts: Therese Hayes, Frank Tysen, and
    Elissa Yoforth
Manager: Elissa Goforth
Rooms: 17 (PB) $35 summer midweek to
    $185 (suite) winter weekend
Continental Breakfast
Credit Cards: A, B, C
Notes: 2, 5, 6 and 7 (limited), 8, 9, 10, 11

PALO ALTO

Adella Villa

PO Box 4528, 94309-4528
(415) 321-5195; FAX (415) 325-5121

Luxurious '20s Italian villa on one acre of lovely manicured gardens with pool, fountains, antiques, and a music room featuring Steinway grand piano. Four-thousand square-foot inn with all the amenities! Pamper yourself in one of our jacuzzi tubs. Enjoy a full breakfast. Refreshments available throughout the day. Thirty minutes from San Francisco.

Hostess: Tricia Young
Rooms: 5 (PB) $99-129
Full Breakfast
Credit Cards: A, B, C, E
Notes: 2, 5, 8, 10, 12

Hotel California

2431 Ash Street, 94306
(415) 322-7666; fax (415) 321-7358
Email: calhotel@aol.com

A unique bed and breakfast inn ideal for visiting professionals, out-of-town guest, and many international academic visitors (walk to Stanford University). One of the most reasonably-priced places to stay. Twenty comfortable rooms, each with private bathroom and attractively furnished with antique pieces. Close shops. A great and convenient place to stay if visiting Stanford or Palo Alto. Reservations or inquiries by email happily accepted. Visit our wed site at www.hotelcalifornia.com.

Hosts: Mark and Mary Ann Hite
Rooms: 20 (PB) $57-65
Continental Breakfast
Credit Cards: A, B, C, D, E
Notes: 5, 12

REDONDO BEACH

Breeze Inn

122 S. Juanita Avenue, 90277-3435
(310) 316-5123

Located in a quiet, modest neighborhood. Large suite with private entrance, private bath with spa, antiques, Oriental carpet, California king bed, and breakfast area with microwave and

---

NOTES: Credit cards accepted: A Master Card; B Visa; C American Express; D Discover; E Diners Club; F Other; 2 Personal checks accepted; 3 Lunch available; 4 Dinner available;

toaster oven, and stocked refrigerator for continental breakfast. Good ventilation with skylight and ceiling fan. Outside patio. One room also available with twin beds and private bath. A brochure is available with map. Near Los Angeles, Disneyland, Universal City, and approximately five blocks to pier and beach.

Hosts: Norris and Betty Binding
Rooms: 2 (PB) $45-65 (2 night minimum)
Continental Breakfast (extra charge for Full)
Credit Cards: none
Notes: 2, 5, 7 (over 5), 8, 9, 10

RIDGECREST

BevLen Haus Bed and Breakfast

809 N. Sanders Street, 93555
(619) 375-1988; (800) 375-1989;
FAX (619) 446-3220

"Once a guest, always a friend." Gracious, quiet, safe, and comfortable; your "secret high desert hideaway." Nearly 2,000 square feet, furnished with antiques, handmade quilts, and comforters in winter! Paved parking. Cooling air in summer. Old-fashioned kitchen has antique cast-iron cookstove, hand-hammered copper sink. In full-service community. Close to Sierra Nevada, Death Valley, Naval Air Warfare Center, China Lake, ghost towns, movie sites, and ancient Indian cultural sites. Wildflowers in spring. No smoking.

Hosts: Bev and Len de Geus
Rooms: 3 (PB) $45-65
Full Breakfast
Credit Cards: A, B, C, D
Notes: 2, 5, 8, 9, 10, 12

RIVERSIDE

Truffles Bed and Breakfast

PO Box 130649, (43591 Bow Canyon Rd.),
92315
(909) 585-2772

Gracious hospitality in peaceful surroundings describe this elegant, country, manor inn nestled on ¾ acre at a 7,000 foot high mountain resort. Skiing, golf, hiking, and lake close by. Five guest rooms are individually appointed with private baths and feathertop beds. Full breakfasts, afternoon appetizers, and evening desserts topped off with truffles on bedtime pillows make for a memorable stay. This spacious establishment includes comfortable traditional and antique furnishings with lots of attention to detail. No smoking.

Hostesses: Marilyn Kane and Carol Bracey
Rooms: 5 (PB) $110-135
Full Breakfast
Credit Cards: A, B, C, D
Notes: 2, 5, 7 (over 12), 10, 11

SACRAMENTO

Sterling Hotel

1300 "H" Street, 95814
(916) 448-1300 (voice and FAX);
(800) 365-7660

Circa 1894. The gables and bays, turrets and verandas of this 15,000 square-foot Queen Anne Victorian home testify to the affluence of its former owners, the Carter-Hawley Hale family, of Weinstocks department store fame. The foyer and drawing room boast black

5 Open all year; 6 Pets welcome; 7 Children welcome; 8 Tennis nearby; 9 Swimming nearby; 10 Golf nearby; 11 Skiing nearby; 12 May be booked through travel agent.

marble fireplaces and marble floors, while guest rooms feature writing desks, designer furnishings, private spas, and marble baths. A large, 3,200 square-foot, elegant ballroom is available for social events, weddings, and receptions. The inn's four star restaurant is Chanterelle.

Host: Rick Francis
Rooms: 15 (PB) $125-225
Continental Breakfast
Credit Cards: A, B, C, D, E
Notes: 2, 3, 4, 5, 7, 10, 12

Vizcaya Mansion

Vizcaya Mansion

2019 21st Street, 95826
(916) 455-5243; (800) 456-2019;
FAX (916) 455-6102

Built in 1899, this Colonial revival mansion is one of Sacramento's most significant Victorian residences. Oriental carpets, a working fireplace, and antique fixtures add to the feelings of relaxed elegance. The dining room, with its dark peach walls, lace curtains, and high ceilings, is also a comfortable space for small get-togethers. A large, elegant ballroom is available for social events, weddings, and receptions. For outdoor events, the inn has a large garden patio shaded by an enormous picture-perfect oak tree. Located in a residential neighborhood, the Vizcaya provides guests with quiet and privacy.

Host: Rick Francis
Rooms: 9 (PB) $95-225
Full Breakfast
Credit Cards: A, B, C, E
Notes: 2, 5, 7, 10, 12

ST. HELENA

Hilltop House Bed and Breakfast

9550 St. Helena Road, PO Box 726, 94574
(707) 944-0880; FAX (707) 571-0263

Poised at the very top of the ridge that separates the famous wine regions of Napa and Sonoma, Hilltop House is a country retreat with all the comforts of home and a view that you must see to believe. Annette and Bill Gevarter built their contemporary home with this mountain panorama in mind, the vast deck allows you to enjoy it at your leisure with a glass of wine in the afternoon, with breakfast in the morning, or with a long soak in the hot tub. From this vantage point, sunrises and sunsets are simply amazing. You'll cherish the natural setting, the caring hospitality, and the prize location.

Hostess: Annette Gevarter
Rooms: 4 (PB) $105-175
Full Breakfast
Credit Cards: A, B, C
Notes: 2, 5, 7, 8, 9, 10, 12

NOTES: Credit cards accepted: A Master Card; B Visa; C American Express; D Discover; E Diners Club; F Other; 2 Personal checks accepted; 3 Lunch available; 4 Dinner available;

SAN FRANCISCO

Dolores Park Inn

3641 17th Street, 94115
(415) 621-0482

This charming, two-story Italianate Victorian mansion was built in 1874. It sits in a subtropical garden behind a wrought iron fence in the sunny part of San Francisco. The guest rooms are appointed with antiques, queen-sized beds, and color TVs. A full breakfast is served in the formal dining room, and an evening beverage is served either on the patio or by the fireplace. Within walking distance to international restaurants, antique street cars, and easy transportation to the heart of San Francisco.

Host: Bernie Vielwerth
Rooms: 5 (1PB; 4SB) $95-165
Full Breakfast
Credit Cards: A, B
Notes: 5, 8, 12

The Grove Inn

890 Grove Street, 94117
(415) 929-0780; (800) 829-0780;
FAX (415) 929-1037

The Grove Inn is a part of a historic Victorian setting, the Alamo Square. Centrally located, the Grove Inn is within reach of the Golden Gate Park, symphony, operas, and the Museum for Modern Arts. It is reasonably priced and managed by experienced innkeepers. This is the fourteenth season for the Grove Inn.

Hostess: Rosetta Zimmerman
Rooms: 20 (14PB; 6SB) $65-85
Continental Breakfast
Credit Cards: A, B, C
Notes: 5, 8, 9, 12

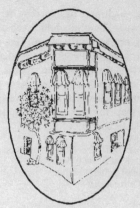

The Monte Cristo

The Monte Cristo

600 Prisido Avenue, 94115
(415) 931-1875; FAX (415) 931-6005

The Monte Cristo has been part of San Francisco since 1875, located two blocks from the elegantly restored Victorian shops, restaurants, and antique stores on Sacramento Street. There is convenient transportation to downtown San Francisco and to the financial district. Each room is elegantly furnished with authentic period pieces.

Host: George Yuan
Rooms: 14 (11PB; 3SB) $63-108
Full Buffet Breakfast
Credit Cards: A, B, C, D, E
Notes: 5, 7, 9, 10

The Red Victorian

1665 Haight Street, 94117
(415) 864-1978; FAX (415) 863-3293

Built in 1904, The Red Victorian Inn is a standing monument of history in the heart of San Francisco. The inn has 18

---

5 Open all year; 6 Pets welcome; 7 Children welcome; 8 Tennis nearby; 9 Swimming nearby; 10 Golf nearby; 11 Skiing nearby; 12 May be booked through travel agent.

rooms which were designed by the current owner Sami Sunchild. Each of the rooms are tastefully furnished with unique decor and come in a variety of styles with private or shared baths. The Red Victorian is the perfect place for a three-day mini-vacation or just an overnight stay for a wonderful bed and breakfast experience.

Hostesses: Sami Sunchild and Rosie Nguyen
Rooms: 18 (4PB; 14SB) $95-200
Continental Buffet Breakfast
Credit Cards: A, B, C
Notes: 2, 5, 12

Rancho San Gregorio

SAN GREGORIO

Rancho San Gregorio

5086 La Honda Road (Hwy. 84), 94074
(415) 747-0810; FAX (415) 747-0184

Five miles inland from the Pacific Ocean is an idyllic rural valley where Rancho San Gregorio welcomes travelers to share relaxed hospitality. Picnic, hike, or bike in wooded parks or on ocean beaches. Our country breakfast features local specialties. Located 45 minutes from San Francisco, Santa

Cruz, and the Bay area. Smoking outdoors only.

Hosts: Bud and Lee Raynor
Rooms: 4 (PB) $75-145 (extra person $15)
Full Breakfast
Credit Cards: A, B, C, D
Notes: 2, 5, 7, 9, 10, 12 (10%)

SAN LUIS OBISPO

Apple Farm Inn

2015 Monterey Street; 93401
(805) 544-2040; (800) 255-2040;
FAX (805) 546-9495

You'll enjoy the unique setting of the four-diamond rated Apple Farm Inn. All rooms feature a cozy fireplace and are uniquely appointed to create an atmosphere ranging from country Victorian charm to traditional elegance. Dine in our fine restaurant for breakfast, lunch, or dinner. Our extensive gift shop offers an abundance of gifts to please everyone. Stroll in the flower-filled garden and visit our creekside working millhouse and 14-foot waterwheel as an added highlight to your stay.

Hosts: Katy and Bob Davis
Rooms: 69 (PB) $95-190
Breakfast extra fee
Credit Cards: A, B, C, D
Notes: 2, 3, 4, 5, 7, 8, 9, 10, 12

SANTA BARBARA

Long's Seaview B&B

317 Piedmont, 93105
(805) 687-2947

Overlooking the ocean and Channel Islands. Quiet neighborhood of lovely homes. Breakfast usually served on

Apple Farm Inn

huge patio. Large bedroom with king-size bed. Private entrance, private bath. Convenient to all attractions and Solvang. Local information and maps. Fantastic views from patio.

Hostess: LaVerne Long
Rooms: 1 (PB) $75-79
Full Breakfast
Credit Cards: none
Notes: 12

Montecito B&B

167 Olive Mill Road, 93103
(805) 969-7992

Enjoy a spacious room with private bath, private entrance, TV, phone, desk, and eating area. Patio jacuzzi is available for your use. Includes homemade continental breakfast and coffee. Room has garden atmosphere and looks out on a vista of trees and mountains. Located close to Westmont College and just above coastal village shopping and restaurants. Approximately one-half mile to the beach.

Hostess: Linda Ryan
Rooms: 1 (PB) $50-60
Continental Breakfast
Credit Cards: none
Notes: 2, 5, 7, 8, 9, 10, 12

The Old Yacht Club Inn

431 Corona Del Mar Dr., 93103
(805) 962-1277; (800) 676-1676 (reservations);
FAX (805) 962-3989

The Inn at the beach! These 1912 California Craftsman and 1925 early California-style homes house nine individually decorated guest rooms furnished with antiques. Bicycles, beach chairs, and towels are included, and an evening social hour is provided. Gourmet dinner is available on Saturdays.

Hostesses: Nancy Donaldson and Sandy Hunt
Rooms: 9 (PB) $90-160
Full Breakfast
Credit Cards: A, B, C, D, E
Notes: 2, 4 (Saturdays), 5, 7, 8, 9, 10, 12

Simpson House Inn

121 E. Arrellaga Street, 93101
(805) 963-7067; (800) 676-1280;
FAX (805) 564-4811

The Inn is secluded behind sandstone walls and tall hedges in an acre of English Gardens, yet only a five minute walk along the tree-lined street to restaurants, theaters, museums, and shops. The Victorian estate is considered one to the most distinguished homes of its

5 Open all year; 6 Pets welcome; 7 Children welcome; 8 Tennis nearby; 9 Swimming nearby;
10 Golf nearby; 11 Skiing nearby; 12 May be booked through travel agent.

era in Southern California. It features the elegant 1874 home, restored 1878 barn, and three garden cottages. The Inn is elegantly appointed with antiques, English lace, Oriental rugs, and fine art.

Hostess: Dixie Adair Budke, general manager
Rooms: 14 (PB) $140-300
Full Gourmet Breakfast
Credit Cards: A, B, C, D
Notes: 2, 5, 8, 9, 10, 12

SANTA CRUZ

Babbling Brook Inn

1025 Laurel Street, 95060
(408) 427-2437; (800) 866-1131;
FAX (408) 427-2457

The foundations of the Inn date back to the 1790s when padres from the local mission built a grist mill to take advantage of the stream to grind corn. In the 19th century, a water wheel generated power for a tannery. Then a few years later, a rustic log cabin was built which remains as the heart of the inn. Most of the rooms are chalets in the garden, surrounded by pines and redwoods, cascading waterfalls, and gardens.

Hostess: Helen King
Rooms: 12 (PB) $85-165
Full Breakfast
Credit Cards: A, B, C, D, E, F
Notes: 2, 5, 8, 9, 10, 12

Chateau Victorian

118 First Street, 95060
(408) 458-9458

Chateau Victorian was turned into an elegant B&B with a warm, friendly atmosphere in 1983. Built around 1885,

the Inn is only one block from the beach. All seven rooms have a queen-size bed; a private, tiled bathroom, one of which has a clawfoot tub with shower; and a fireplace, with fire logs provided. Each room has its own heating system, controlled by the guest. Wine and cheeses are available for the guest in late afternoon. Chateau Victorian is within walking distance to downtown, the Municipal Wharf, the Boardwalk Amusement Park, and fine, as well as casual, dining.

Hostess: Alice June
Rooms: 7 (PB) $110-140 + tax
Expanded Continental Breakfast
Credit Cards: A, B, C
Notes: 2, 5, 8, 9, 10, 12 (no commissions)

Pleasure Point Inn and Boat Charters

2-3665 E. Cliff Drive, 95062
(408) 475-4657; (800) 872-3029;
FAX (408) 464-3045

On the water overlooking the beautiful Monterey Bay. Fantastic views from three of our rooms. Fireplaces and whirlpool tubs. Boat charters are underway daily for fishing or cruising. Your host is an accomplished captain of the "Margaret Mary" and your hostess is more than willing to arrange dinner reservations at a fine, local restaurant or point you to historic landmarks in the area. Within walking distance to the beaches and shopping villages.

Hosts: Sal and Margaret Margo
Rooms: 4 (PB) $125-145
Continentall Breakfast
Credit Cards: A, B
Notes: 5, 7, 8, 9, 10, 12

NOTES: Credit cards accepted: A Master Card; B Visa; C American Express; D Discover; E Diners Club; F Other; 2 Personal checks accepted; 3 Lunch available; 4 Dinner available;

SANTA ROSA (WINE COUNTRY)

The Gables Inn

4257 Petaluma Hill Road, 95404
(707) 584-5634 (voice and FAX);
(800) GABLESN

The Gables Inn is a beautifully restored Victorian mansion sitting grandly on 3½ acres in the center of Sonoma Wine Country. Elegant guest rooms feature fluffy goose down comforters, antiques, and all private bathrooms. A separate, cozy, creekside cottage features a whirlpool tub for two. Guests are treated to a sumptuous, four-course, gourmet breakfast. The Gables provides easy access to 140 premium wineries, the giant redwoods, the Russian River Resort, as well as, the craggy North coastline and is just one hour north of San Francisco.

Hosts: Mike and Judy Ogne
Rooms: 8 (PB) $110-190
Full Breakfast
Credit Cards: A, B, C, D
Notes: 2, 5, 8, 9, 10, 12

Pygmalion House Inn, Bed and Breakfast

Pygmalion House Inn, Bed and Breakfast

331 Orange Street, 95401
(707) 526-3407 (voice and FAX)

Pygmalion House is a lovely Victorian (1880s) furnished with many of Gypsy Rose Lee's antiques and memorabilia. The guest rooms all have private baths with tubs and showers. And, our prices are the most reasonable—"Mostest for the Leastest." Guests return again and again.

Hostess: Caroline
Rooms: 5 + 1 suite (PB) $65-75
Full Country Breakfast
Credit Cards: A, B
Notes: 2, 5, 10

SEAL BEACH

The Seal Beach Inn and Gardens

212 Fifth Street, 92740
(562) 493-2416; (800) HIDEAWAY;
FAX (562) 799-0483
Note: Old area code (310) good until Feb. 1997

Elegant, historic Southern California Inn, one block from ocean beach in a charming, prestigious, seaside town next to Long Beach. Lush gardens, lovely estate appearance. Exquisite rooms and suites. Pool, library, and kitchens available. Free full breakfast/ social hour. Modern amenities. Short walk to restaurants, shops, and beach pier. Three freeways close by. Easy drive to Disneyland and other major Los Angeles attractions and business centers. Meeting rooms available (24 maximum). Convenient to LAX, Long

5 Open all year; 6 Pets welcome; 7 Children welcome; 8 Tennis nearby; 9 Swimming nearby;
10 Golf nearby; 11 Skiing nearby; 12 May be booked through travel agent.

Beach, and Orange County Airports.

Hosts: Marjorie and Harty Schmaehl
Rooms: 23 (PB) $118-185
Full Gourmet Breakfast
Credit Cards: A, B, C, D, F
Notes: 3, 4, 5, 8, 9, 10, 12

The Seal Beach Inn and Gardens

SONOMA

Sparrow's Nest Inn

424 Denmark Street, 95476
(707) 996-3750; FAX (707) 938-5023

Sonoma's historic town square is one mile from this delightful cottage. Just right for rest or romance. Pretty English country decor, fresh flowers, chocolates, cozy beds, scrumptious breakfast, privacy, garden and courtyard for sunning and reading. The "Nest" is complete with bedroom, bath, small kitchen fully equipped, living room (including sofa bed) phone, cable TV/VCR, air-conditioning. Within three miles are five notable wineries, San Francisco Solano Mission, little shops, and wonderful restaurants.

Hosts: Thomas and Kathleen Anderson
Rooms: 1 single cottage (PB) $85-105
Both Full and Continental Breakfast available
Credit Cards: A, B, C, D
Notes: 2, 5, 6 (special arrangements), 7, 8, 9, 10

SONORA

Lavender Hill Bed and Breakfast Inn

683 S. Barretta, 95370
(209) 532-9024; (800) 446-1333 ext. 290

Come home . . . to a 1900s Victorian home overlooking the historic gold rush town of Sonora. At sunset you can watch the world from a wraparound porch, enjoy a country walk through year round flower gardens, and a covered patio, ideal for a small wedding. In the morning, you wake to a home-cooked breakfast and have the opportunity to listen and share experiences with others, perhaps planning your day to include hiking in Yosemite, fishing, biking, river rafting, or even a scenic steam train ride. Afternoons and evenings could include a stroll to downtown antique shops and boutiques, fine dining, and topped off with your enjoyment for one of the professional repertory theaters. We will be glad to plan a dinner theater package for your stay. Gift certificates also available. One visit will have you longing to return "home".

Hosts: Jean and Charlie Marinelli
Rooms: 4 (PB) $75-95
Full Breakfast
Credit Cards: A, B, C
Notes: 2, 5, 7, 8, 9, 10, 11, 12

SOQUEL

Blue Spruce Inn

2815 Main Street, 95073
(408) 464-1137; (800) 559-1137;
FAX (408) 475-0608

Spa tubs, fireplaces, quiet gardens, and

NOTES: Credit cards accepted: A Master Card; B Visa; C American Express; D Discover; E Diners Club; F Other; 2 Personal checks accepted; 3 Lunch available; 4 Dinner available;

original local art foster relaxation for our guests. The Blue Spruce is four miles south of Santa Cruz and one mile inland from Capitoal Beach—an ideal location that blends the flavor of yesteryear with the comfort of today. Hike or bike through the redwoods or country fields. Walk to fine dining then relax in the outdoor hot tub. Our Internet address is <http://BlueSpruce.com>. Visit us soon!

Hosts: Pat and Tom O'Brien
Rooms: 6 (PB) $90-150 Fri. & Sat.; $85-135 Sun. to Thurs.
Full Breakfast
Credit Cards: A, B, C
Notes: 2, 5, 8, 9, 10, 12

Blue Spruce Inn

SUMMERLAND

Inn on Summer Hill

2520 Lillie Avenue, 93067
(805) 969-9998; (800) 845-5566;
FAX (805) 565-9946

One of America's Top Rated B&Bs awaits you with visually captivating English country decor and world class amenities. Set in the seaside village of Summerland, just five minutes south of Santa Barbara, this California Craftsman-styled award-winning inn, built in 1989, offers sixteen mini-suites with ocean views, fireplaces, jacuzzi tubs, canopy beds, video cassette players and original art and accessories. Sumptuous full gourmet breakfasts, hor d'oeuvres and desserts add to the uncompromising comfort and charm. Guests rooms provide a directory of local activities along with concierge service and special packages for the discerning traveler in the mood for something out of the ordinary. The Automobile Club and *Country Inns Magazine* have also rated the Inn one of the "Best in the Country."

Hostess: Verlinda Richardson
Rooms: 16 (PB) $165-295
Full Breakfast
Credit Cards: A, B, C, D
Notes: 3 (picnic only), 5, 8, 9, 10, 12

SUSANVILLE

The Roseberry House

609 North Street, 96130
(916) 257-5675

The Roseberry House lives up to its name with roses in profusion in the carpets, wallpapers, and vases. It features an unusual collection of antiques, with each guest room distinctly different. Enjoy a tastefully prepared full breakfast in the formal dining room. This is our home and we want you to be comfortable here. Located just two blocks from Main Street in historic uptown Susanville and near a variety of Northern California recreational activities.

Hosts: Bill and Maxine Ashmore
Rooms: 4 (PB) $55-85
Full Breakfast
Credit Cards: A, B, C
Notes: 2, 5, 8, 9, 10, 11

TRINIDAD

The Lost Whale Inn

3452 Patrick's Point Drive, 95570
(800) 677-7859; FAX (707) 677-0284
Email: lmiller@northcoast.com
Web site: www.lost_whale_inn.com

Visit Humboldt's most romantic Inn, listen to sea lions, and relax on numerous decks overlooking the spectacular ocean view. Gardens and private beach accessed through the beautiful forest on our wonderful beach trail. Experience gourmet breakfasts and afternoon teas with complimentary drinks. Guests' children will enjoy the full playground, including a playhouse with loft. Minutes from parks, lagoons, and miles of unspoiled beaches. The Lost Whale Inn . . . serene and secluded on the rugged California coast.

Hosts: Susanne Lakin and Lee Miller
Rooms: 8 (PB) $100-150
Full Gourmet Breakfast
Credit Cards: A, B, C, D
Notes: 2, 5, 7, 8, 9, 10, 12

The Lost Whale Inn

Trinidad Bay Bed and Breakfast

560 Edwards Street, PO Box 849, 95570
(707) 677-0840

Our Cape Cod style home overlooks beautiful Trinidad Bay and offers spectacular views of the rugged coastline and fishing harbor below. Two suites, one with fireplace, and two upstairs bedrooms are available. We are surrounded by dozens of beaches, trails, and Redwood National Parks; within walking distance of restaurants and shops. Breakfast delivered to guests staying in suites, while a family style breakfast is served to guests in rooms.

Hosts: Paul and Carol Kirk
Rooms: 4 (PB) $125-155
Expanded Continental Breakfast
Credit Cards: A, B
Closed December and January
Notes: 2, 8, 10

UKIAH

Vichy Hot Springs

2605 Vichy Springs Road, 95482
(707) 462-9515; FAX (707) 462-9516

Vichy Springs is a delightful two-hour drive north of San Francisco. Historic cottages and rooms await with delightful vistas from all locations. Vichy Springs features naturally sparkling 90-degree mineral baths, a communal 104-degree pool, and olympic-size pool, along with 700 private acres with trails and roads for hiking, jogging, picnicing, and mountain bicycling. Vichy's idyllic setting is a quiet, healing environment. California state landmark #980.

Hosts: Gilbert and Marjorie Ashoff
Rooms: 17 (PB) $130-170
Full Breakfast
Credit Cards: A, B, C, D, E, F
Notes: 2, 3, 4, 5, 7, 8, 9, 10, 12

VENTURA

Bella Maggiore Inn

67 S. California Street, 93001
(805) 652-0277; (800) 523-8479

An intimate European-style B&B, one
hour north of Los Angeles. Garden
courtyard with fountain; lobby with fireplace and piano. Comfortable rooms
with suites, some have fireplaces and
spa tubs. Full breakfast served in our
courtyard restaurant, Nona's. Special
rates for business travelers and groups.
We are three blocks from the beach and
walking distance to several fine restaurants.

Hosts: Tom and Cyndi Wood
Rooms: 28 (PB) $75-150
Full Breakfast
Credit Cards: A, B, C, D, E
Notes: 3, 4, 5, 7, 8, 9, 10, 12

La Mer Gastehaus

411 Poli Street, 93001
(805) 643-3600; FAX (805) 653-7329

Built in 1890, this is a romantic European getaway in a Victorian Cape Cod
home. A historic landmark nestled on a
green hillside overlooking the spectacular California coastline. The distinctive
guest rooms, all with private entrances
and baths, are each a European adventure, furnished in European antiques to
capture the feeling of a specific country. Bavarian buffet-style breakfast and
complimentary refreshments; midweek
packages; antique horse carriage rides.
AAA and Mobil approved.

Hosts: Gisela and Michael Baida
Rooms: 5 (PB) $85-155
Full Breakfast
Credit Cards: A, B, C
Notes: 2, 5, 8, 9, 10, 12

YOSEMITE NATIONAL PARK (GROVELAND)

Lee's Middle Fork Resort

11399 Cherry Lake Road, Groveland 95321
(209) 962-7408; (800) 626-7408;
FAX (209) 962-7400

Conveniently located eleven miles from
Big Oak Flat entrance to Yosemite National Park, Lee's Middle Fork Resort
is the perfect place to stay for beautiful
scenic landscapes while you vacation
or simply pass through the charming
Yosemite area. Relax and enjoy the restful atmosphere as you discover why
Yosemite is so acclaimed for its beauty.
While there, you can take the opportunity to gaze upon some of the most
amazing rock formations and the most
stunning waterfalls, or enjoy an afternoon of activities which include hiking,
well-stocked river fishing, swimming,
or white-water rafting. For winter guests
there is downhill and cross-country skiing. Come and visit Lee's Middle Fork
Resort and discover for yourself the real
meaning of paradise.

Hosts: Lee and Nita L. Hilarides
Rooms: 20 (PB) $49-89
Continental Breakfast (May to Sept.)
Credit Cards: A, B, C, D, E
Notes: 3, 5, 7, 9, 10, 11, 12

5 Open all year; 6 Pets welcome; 7 Children welcome; 8 Tennis nearby; 9 Swimming nearby;
10 Golf nearby; 11 Skiing nearby; 12 May be booked through travel agent.

COLORADO

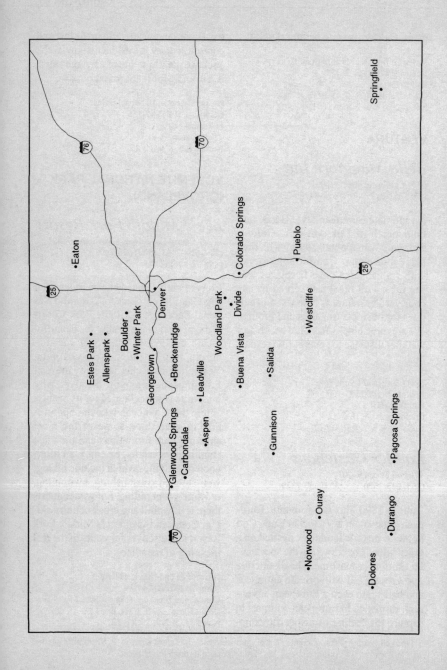

Colorado

ALLENSPARK

Allenspark Lodge

PO Box 247, 184 Main, 80510
(303) 747-2552 (voice and FAX, call first)

A classic high mountain bed and breakfast, nestled in a flower-starred village. Comfortable rooms, warm hospitality and magnificent surroundings make our historic, cozy, beautifully remodeled lodge the ideal place for that vacation weekend, reception, reunion, or retreat. Let the magic begin! Hot tub, hospitality, and game room; near Rocky Mountain National Park. Three small cabins are also available.

Hosts: Mike and Becky Osmun
Rooms: 12 (5PB; 9SB) $45-90
Continental Breakfast
Credit Cards: A, B
Notes: 2, 5, 11

ASPEN

Christmas Inn

232 W. Main Street, 81611
(970) 925-3822; (800) 625-5581;
FAX (970) 925-3328

Aspen, the affordable way! The Inn features clean, attractive rooms, all with private baths, telephones, and remote control cable TVs. Enjoy our sundeck with panoramic views of Aspen. Unwind in our whirlpool and sauna (winter only) and enjoy a hearty, full breakfast each morning. Walk to most shops and restaurants. On the route for the free skier shuttle and the shuttle to the music tent.

Hostess: Lynn Derfee
Rooms: 24 (PB) $56-120
Full Breakfast
Credit Cards: A, B, C
Notes: 5, 7, 10, 11, 12

Christmas Inn

NOTES: Credit cards accepted: A Master Card; B Visa; C American Express; D Discover; E Diners Club; F Other; 2 Personal checks accepted; 3 Lunch available; 4 Dinner available; 5 Open all year; 6 Pets welcome; 7 Children welcome; 8 Tennis nearby; 9 Swimming nearby; 10 Golf nearby; 11 Skiing nearby; 12 May be booked through travel agent.

Little Red Ski Haus

118 E. Cooper Avenue, 81611
(970) 925-3333; FAX (970) 927-9578

We are a quaint historic lodge that has had only one owner for 36 years. The 110-year-old Victorian house has additional rooms for a total of 21 bedrooms. Christian hosts look forward to welcoming you to their lodge. Located in the center of Aspen and surrounded by impressive 14,000 ft. peaks of the Rocky Mountains. Non-smoking lodge. We will accept Christian retreats.

Hosts: Marjorie Babcock, owner, and Derek
    Brown, manager
Rooms: 21 (4PB; 17SB) $52-118
Breakfast—Full (winter); Continental (summer)
Credit Cards: A, B
Notes: 7, 9, 10, 11

Brair Rose Bed and Breakfast

BOULDER

Brair Rose Bed and Breakfast

2151 Arapahoe Avenue, 80302
(303) 442-3007; FAX (303) 786-8440

English country cottage close to the University of Colorado and downtown Boulder. Nine unique rooms offer featherbed comforters, telephones, period antiques, fresh flowers, and good books. Friendly, attentive service includes afternoon and evening tea with our own shortbread cookies. Hearty, home-baked breakfast served in the dining room or on the sun porch. Schedule a 10-15 person retreat for the winter months.

Hosts: Margaret and Bob Weisenbach
Rooms: 9 (PB) $89-140
Continental Plus Breakfast
Credit Cards: A, B, C
Notes: 2, 5, 12

BRECKENRIDGE

Allaire Timbers Inn

9511 Highway 9, S. Main Street, 80424
(970) 453-7530; (800) 624-4904;
FAX (970) 453-8699

Award-winning log bed and breakfast, combining contemporary and rustic log furnishings in an intimate setting. Guest rooms have private bath and deck with mountain views. Suites offer private fireplace and hot tub. Great room, with fireplace, sunroom, loft, and outdoor hot tub, has spectacular views of the Colorado Rockies. Hearty breakfast and afternoon refreshments. Wheelchair accessible. In Breckenridge, offering an abundance of year-round activities. Featured on the Travel Channel's "Romantic Inn in America."

Hosts: Jack and Kathy Gumph
Rooms: 10 (PB) $120-245
Full Breakfast
Credit Cards: A, B, C, D
Notes: 2, 5, 10, 11, 12

NOTES: Credit cards accepted: A Master Card; B Visa; C American Express; D Discover; E Diners Club; F Other; 2 Personal checks accepted; 3 Lunch available; 4 Dinner available;

BUENA VISTA

Meister House Bed and Breakfast

PO Box 1133, 414 E. Main Street, 81211
(719) 395-9220; (800) 882-1821;
FAX (719) 395-9128

This historic landmark hotel was built over 100 years ago as a small, first-class hotel. Today it has been renovated to its current state as an intimate seven room bed and breakfast. It is nestled near the head waters of the world famous whitewater Arkansas River and at the base of the Collegiate Peaks Mountain Range, part of the rugged Rocky Mountains. After your fresh, gourmet breakfast in our courtyard, there are many recreational activities all within walking distance!

Hosts: Barbara and Frank Hofmeister
Rooms: 7 (3PB; 4SB) $55-105
Full Breakfast
Credit Cards: A, B, C, D
Notes: 2, 5, 7, 8, 9, 10, 11, 12

CARBONDALE

Mt. Sopris Inn

Box 126 (0165 Mt. Sopris Ranch Rd.), 81623
(970) 963-2209; (800) 437-8675 (reservations only); FAX (970) 963-8975
Email: MTSOPRISIN@compuserve.com

At Mt. Sopris Inn, country elegance surrounds the visitor who appreciates our extraordinary property. Central to Aspen, Redstone, and Glenwood Springs, the Inn offers 15 private rooms and baths professionally decorated. All rooms have king or queen beds, TV, telephone, and include full breakfast, some have fireplaces, jacuzzis, and steam baths. Guest use of swimming pool, whirlpool, pool table, library, great rooms, and seven-foot grand piano. Open to all.

Hostess: Barbara Fasching
Rooms: 15 (PB) $ 85-250
Full Breakfast
Credit Cards: A, B
Notes: 2, 5, 8, 9, 10, 11, 12

Van Horn House at Lions Ridge

0318 Lions Ridge Road, 81623
(970) 963-3605; FAX (970) 963-1681

Our country home is filled with antiques and Colorado hospitality. All four rooms feature a queen-sized bed with snuggly comforters in winter and bathrobes for your use. Two rooms with private baths also provide private balconies; two rooms with a shared bath have cozy alcoves. Each affords a spectacular view of the Roaring Fork Valley and majestic Mt. Sopris. A full breakfast is served daily; relax at night in the hot tub under the stars!

Hosts: Susan and John Laatsch
Rooms: 4 (2PB; 2SB) $60-70
Full Breakfast
Credit Cards: A, B
Notes: 2, 5, 7 (over 8), 8, 9, 10, 11, 12

COLORADO SPRINGS

Holden House—1902 Bed and Breakfast Inn

1102 W. Pikes Peak Avenue, 80904
(719) 471-3980; FAX available on request

Historic 1902 storybook Victorians and

---

5 Open all year; 6 Pets welcome; 7 Children welcome; 8 Tennis nearby; 9 Swimming nearby;
10 Golf nearby; 11 Skiing nearby; 12 May be booked through travel agent.

carriage house filled with antiques and family treasures. Guest rooms boast feather pillows, individual decor, period furnishings, and queen beds. One disabled access room available. Suites include fireplaces, "tubs for two," and more! Centrally located in residential area near historic Old Colorado City, shopping, restaurants, and attractions. "The Romance of the Past with the Comforts of Today." Two friendly resident cats. AAA/Mobil approved.

Hosts: Sallie and Welling Clark
Rooms: 6 (PB) $80-115
Full Gourmet Breakfast
Credit Cards: A, B, C, D, E
Notes: 2, 5, 8, 9, 10, 12

Pikes Peak Paradise

Pikes Peak Paradise

236 Pinecrest Road, **Woodland Park** 80863
(719) 687-6656; (800) 728-8282;
FAX (719) 687-9008

Enjoy a gorgeous view of Pikes Peak from your room. Hot tubs and fireplaces in rooms. Gourmet breakfast included. A great place to be quiet, stand in awe, and meditate peacefully! Without a doubt, you will find a most pleasant

experience as a guest at Pikes Peak Paradise Bed and Breakfast!

Hostess: Priscilla Arthur
Rooms: 6 (PB) $95-195
Full Gourmet Breakfast
Credit Cards: A, B, C, D
Notes: 2, 5, 6, 10, 12

Room at the Inn B&B

618 N. Nevada Avenue, 80903
(719) 442-1896; (800) 579-4621;
FAX (719) 442-6802

Experience a peek at the past in this elegant Victorian B&B. Enjoy . . . the charm of a classic three story turreted Queen Anne with pocket doors, oak staircase, and wood floors and furnished with period antiques . . . the romance of fireplaces, plush robes, whirlpool tubs for two and cut flowers . . . and gracious hospitality featuring full breakfasts, afternoon tea, and turn down service. Conveniently located near downtown and Colorado College. Wheelchair accessible, air-conditioning, and outdoor hot tub. Mobil three star rated.

Hostesses: Jan and Chick McCormick
Rooms: 7 (PB) $80-120
Full Breakfast
Credit Cards: A, B, C, D
Notes: 2, 5, 7 (over 12), 8, 10, 12

DENVER

Capitol Hill Mansion

1207 Pennsylvania Street, 80203
(303) 839-5221; (800) 839-9329;
FAX (303) 839-9046

Award-winning 1891 Victorian mansion with eight individually decorated

---

NOTES: Credit cards accepted: A Master Card; B Visa; C American Express; D Discover; E Diners Club; F Other; 2 Personal checks accepted; 3 Lunch available; 4 Dinner available;

guest rooms featuring antiques mixed with modern amenities such as cable TV, refrigerators, complimentary beverages, hair dryers, telephones, desks, private baths, off-street parking, and breakfast. Whirlpool tubs, fireplaces, and balconies are available. A short walk to downtown, government offices, museums, galleries, shopping, and restaurants and a short drive to all major sports venues and the Rocky Mountains. Perfect for business or romance.

Hostess: Kathy Robbins
Rooms: 8 (PB) $89-149
Full Breakfast
Credit Cards: A, B, C, D
Notes: 2 (with ID), 5, 7, 8, 9, 10, 11, 12

Capitol Hill Mansion

Castle Marne
A Luxury Urban Inn

1572 Race Street, 80206
(303) 331-0621; (800) 92 MARNE (reservations); FAX (303) 331-0623

Chosen by *Country Inns Magazine* as one of the "Top 12 Inns in North America." Come fall under the spell of one of Denver's grandest historic mansions. Your stay at the Castle Marne

combines Old World elegance with modern day convenience and comfort. Each guest room is a unique experience in pampered luxury. All rooms have private baths. Two suites with jacuzzi tubs for two. Three rooms with private balconies and hot tubs. Afternoon tea and a full gourmet breakfast are served in the cherry-paneled dining room. Castle Marne is a certified Denver Landmark and on the National Register of Historic Structures.

Hosts: The Peikers Family
Rooms: 9 (PB) $85-200
Full Breakfast
Credit Cards: A, B, C, D, E, F
Notes: 2, 3, 4, 5, 7 (over 10), 8, 9, 10, 11, 12

Queen Anne
Bed and Breakfast Inn

2147 Tremont Place, 80205
(303) 296-6666; (800) 432-INNS (4667);
FAX (303) 296-2151

Facing quiet Benedict Fountain Park in downtown Denver are two side-by-side National Register Victorian homes with fourteen guest rooms including four gallery suites. Fresh flowers, chamber music, period antiques, phone, and private baths are in all rooms. Six rooms have special tubs; one has a fireplace. There is air-conditioning and free parking. The Inn is only walking distance to the Capitol, 16th St. Pedestrian Mall, Convention Center, Larimer Square, restaurants, shops, and museums. Among its many awards: Best 12 B&Bs nationally, Ten Most Romantic, Best of Denver, and Best 105 in Great American Cities. Now in its tenth year, it is

---

5 Open all year; 6 Pets welcome; 7 Children welcome; 8 Tennis nearby; 9 Swimming nearby; 10 Golf nearby; 11 Skiing nearby; 12 May be booked through travel agent.

inspected/approved by AAA, Mobil, ABBA, and Distinctive Inns of Colorado.

Hosts: Tom and Chris King
Rooms: 14 (PB) $75-165
Full Breakfast
Credit Cards: A, B, C, D, E
Notes: 2, 5, 8, 9, 10, 11, 12

DIVIDE

Silver Wood Bed and Breakfast

463 County Road 512, 80814
(719) 687-6784; (800) 753-5592
Email: silver1007@aol.com

Silver Wood is a newly constructed, contemporary home located in rural Colorado near Divide. Your drive to Silver Wood winds through strands of aspen, open meadows, pine trees, and fantastic views of mountains. Only 22 miles from Cripple Creek, 30 miles from Colorado Springs, and 7 miles from Mueller State Park. Silver Wood offers a multitude of sight seeing opportunities in the Pikes Peak area with country quiet. Non-smoking residence.

Hosts: Larry and Bess Oliver and 2 resident cats
Rooms: 2 (PB) $65
Full Country/Gourmet Breakfast
Credit Cards: A, B, D
Notes: 2, 5, 7, 12

Silver Wood Bed and Breakfast

DOLORES

Mountain View Bed and Breakfast

28050 County Road P, 81323
(970) 882-7861; (800) 4592

Situated in the beautiful Southwest and surrounded by world famous archeological sites, this B&B has 22 acres of hiking trails, creek, and pond. The ranch style inn has porches, decks, and hot tub with marvelous mountain and sunset vews. Eight guest rooms/suites and cabin, all with private baths, full breakfast, laundry, and evening refreshments. Numerous specials can be viewed on the Internet, free gift with every stay. We welcome singles, families, and small groups of up to 36.

Hosts: Cecil and Brenda Dunn
Rooms: 8 (PB) $54-79
Full Breakfast
Credit Cards: A, B
Notes: 2, 5, 7, 8, 9, 10, 11, 12

DURANGO

Logwood Bed and Breakfast

35060 US Hwy. 550 N., 81301
(970) 259-4396; (800) 369-4082;
FAX (970) 259-7812

Built in 1988, this 4,800 square-foot red, cedar log home sits on 15 acres amid the beautiful San Juan Mountains and beside the Animas River. Guest rooms are decorated with a southwestern flair.

NOTES: Credit cards accepted: A Master Card; B Visa; C American Express; D Discover; E Diners Club; F Other; 2 Personal checks accepted; 3 Lunch available; 4 Dinner available;

Homemade country quilts adorn the country made queen-sized beds. Private baths in all guest rooms. A large, river rock fireplace warms the elegant living and dining areas in the winter season. Award-winning desserts are served in the evening. Pamper yourselves. Come home to LOGWOOD.

Hosts: Debby and Greg Verheyden and son Alan
Rooms: 6 (PB) $70-125
Full Breakfast
Credit Cards: A, B
Notes: 2, 5, 7 (over eight), 9, 10, 11, 12

Logwood Bed and Breakfast

Scrubby Oaks Bed and Breakfast

PO Box 1047, 81302
(970) 247-2176

Located on ten acres overlooking the Animas River Valley, this sprawling ranch syle inn has a quiet country feel with the convenience of being three miles from downtown Durango. Scrubby Oaks is beautifully furnished with family antiques, artworks, and fine books. Lovely gardens and patios frame the outside where guests can relax after a day of sightseeing around the Four Corners area. Snacks are offered afternoons and a full country breakfast is served each morning.

Hostess: Mary Ann Craig
Rooms: 7 (3PB; 4SB) $65-75
Full Breakfast
Credit Cards: none
Open end of April to end of October
Notes: 2, 7, 8, 9, 10, 12

Strater Hotel

699 Main Ave., 81301
(970) 247-4431; (800) 277-4431;
FAX (970) 259-2208

Strater Hotel has been around since 1887. Authentic Victorian walnut antiques and architecture. Romance and charm. Cable TV, phones, private baths, jacuzzi, restaurant, and Old West saloon. Located in the heart of the historic downtown shopping and entertainment district. Two blocks from D&SNG RR depot. Free parking. Near historic sites and outdoor activities. Melodrama on site.

Host: Rod Barker
Rooms: 93 (PB) $78-170 ($115-170 summer)
European Plan
Credit Cards: A, B, C, D
Notes: 2, 4, 6, 7, 8, 9, 10, 11, 12

EATON

The Country Rose Inn

725 Fourth St., 80615
(970) 454-3915

Country, Victorian decorated inn. The master suite is decorated with white wicker, antiques, lace, and rose stencils. Amenities include private bath, cable TV, second bedroom, shared bath, queen bed, and self-serve tea with

5 Open all year; 6 Pets welcome; 7 Children welcome; 8 Tennis nearby; 9 Swimming nearby; 10 Golf nearby; 11 Skiing nearby; 12 May be booked through travel agent.

home-baked cookies. The full breakfast is served on the patio or in the dining room.

Hosts: Don and Donna Anderson
Rooms: 2 (1PB; 1SB) $45-60
Full Breakfast
Credit Cards: none
Notes: 2 (+ travelers'), 10, 11

The Victorian Veranda Bed and Breakfast

515 Cheyenne Avenue, 80615
(970) 454-3890

We want to share with you our beautiful two-story Queen Anne home with a wraparound porch. It also has a view of the Rocky Mountains which are 45 minutes away. Our guests enjoy the spacious and comfortable rooms, balcony, fireplaces, bicycles-built-for-two, baby grand, player piano, and one room that has a private whirlpool bath. We are just 50 minutes from North Denver. A memorable and elegant stay for a moderate price.

Hostess: Nadine and Dick White
Rooms: 3 (1PB; 2SB) $45-60
Full Breakfast
Credit Cards: none
Notes: 2, 5, 7, 9, 10, 12

ESTES PARK

The Quilt House Bed and Breakfast

PO Box 399, 80517
(970) 586-0427

A beautiful view can be enjoyed from every window of this sturdy mountain home. Iit is just a 15-minute walk to downtown Estes Park and only four miles from the entrance of Rocky Mountain National Park. There are three bedrooms upstairs for guests plus a lounge where guests can read, look at the mountains, and have a cup of coffee or tea. A guest house beside the main house has a kitchenette. The hosts gladly help with information concerning hiking trails, car drives, wildlife viewing, shopping, etc. No smoking.

Hosts: Hans and Miriam Graetzer
Rooms: 4 (2PB; 2SB) $52-62
Full Breakfast
Credit Cards: none
Notes: 2, 5, 8, 9, 10

Hardy House Bed and Breakfast

GEORGETOWN

Hardy House Bed and Breakfast

605 Brownell, PO Box 156, 80444
(303) 569-3388; (800) 490-4802

The Hardy House with its late 19th century charm invites you to relax in the parlor by the potbellied stove, sleep under feather comforters, and enjoy a candlelight breakfast. Georgetown is only 55 minutes from Denver and the

NOTES: Credit cards accepted: A Master Card; B Visa; C American Express; D Discover; E Diners Club; F Other; 2 Personal checks accepted; 3 Lunch available; 4 Dinner available;

airport. Surrounded by mountains, it boasts unique shopping, wonderful restaurants, and close proximity to seven ski areas.

Hosts: Carla and Mike Wagner
Rooms: 4 (PB) $73-82
Full Breakfast
Credit Cards: A, B
Notes: 2, 5, 7 (over 13), 11, 12

GLENWOOD SPRINGS

Back In Time

927 Cooper, 81601
(970) 945-6183

A spacious Victorian home built in 1903 and filled with antiques, family quilts, and clocks. A full breakfast is served in the dining room: a hot dish accompanied by fresh hot muffins, fruit, and a specialty of June's mouth watering cinnamon rolls.

Hosts: June and Ron Robinson
Rooms: 5 (5PB) $70-85
Full Breakfast
Credit Cards: A, B, C
Notes: 2, 5, 8, 9, 10, 11, 12

GUNNISON

Waunita Hot Springs Ranch

8007 County Road 887, 81230
(970) 641-1266

A family-owned and operated American Plan dude ranch in the summer, Waunita Hot Springs offers B&B accomodations December through March. Guests may enjoy a comfortable lodge setting with pool and spa fed by

hot springs. Groups welcome. Winter sports available at nearby Monarch Ski Area. 8,946 foot altitude, with year-round access. Color brochure available.

Hosts: The Pringle Family
Rooms: 26 (22PB; 4SB) $68
Full Breakfast
Credit Cards: B
Notes: 2, 4, 7, 9, 11

LEADVILLE

The Ice Palace Inn

813 Spruce Street, 80461
(719) 486-8272

This gracious Victorian inn was built at the turn-of-the-century, using the lumber from the famous Leadville Ice Palace. Romantic guest rooms, elegantly decorated with antiques and quilts, each with an exquisite private bath, are named after the original rooms of the Ice Palace. Begin your day with a delicious gourmet breakfast served in this historic inn. Innkeepers are owners, Giles and Kami Kolakowski, welcome you!

Hosts: Giles and Kami Kolakowski
Rooms: 3 (PB) $79-119
Full Gourmet Breakfast
Credit Cards: F
Notes: 2, 5, 7, 8, 9, 10, 11, 12

Wood Haven Manor Bed and Breakfast

PO Box 1291, 809 Spruce, 80461
(719) 486-0109; (800) 748-2570;
FAX (719) 486-0210

Enjoy the taste and style of Victorian Leadville by stepping back 100 years

---

5 Open all year; 6 Pets welcome; 7 Children welcome; 8 Tennis nearby; 9 Swimming nearby;
10 Golf nearby; 11 Skiing nearby; 12 May be booked through travel agent.

in this beautiful home located in this prestigious "Banker's Row." Each room is distinctively decorated in Victorian style with private bath. One suite with whirlpool tub. Spacious dining room; comfortable living room with fireplace. Historic city with a backdrop of Colorado's highest mountains. Enjoy snow-mobiling, biking, hiking, and more.

Hosts: Bobby and Jolene Wood
Rooms: 7 (PB) $59-99
Full Breakfast
Credit Cards: A, B, C, D
Notes: 2, 5, 7, 8, 9, 10, 11, 12

Wood Haven Manor Bed and Breakfast

NORWOOD

Lone Cone Elk Ranch Bed and Breakfast

PO Box 220, 81423
(970) 327-4300

Located in the small agricultural town of Norwood where cattle ranches and farms dot the landscape. The complete downstairs of the two-story home is yours during your stay. It includes two bedrooms, a bath, a spacious living area with a fireplace, TV, and a private entrance. Choose the B&B plan which includes accommodations and breakfast, but no rance activities, or the guest ranch plan which includes accommodations, home-cooked meals, horseback riding, tack, equipment, and wranglers. Enjoy watching our elk. Other activies center on fishing, hiking, wildlife watching, hunting, and relaxing in some of the beautiful san Juan Mountains.

Hosts: Bob and Sharon Hardman
Rooms: 4 (SB) $40 (+$10 each child)
Full Breakfast
Credit Cards: none
Notes: 2, 3, 4, 5, 7, 10, 11

OURAY

The Damn Yankee Country Inn

100 6th Avenue, PO Box 709, 81427
(970) 325-4219; (800) 845-7512;
FAX (970) 325-0502

Relax your body. Ten uniquely appointed rooms await, each with a private bath and entrance, some with fireplaces. Cabins along the river will be available in 1996. Drift off to the soothing music of a mountain stream from your luxurious queen-size bed. Snuggle under a plush down comforter. Most rooms have fireplaces. Sit back and watch your favorite film on cable TV. Drink in the fresh mountain air. Relax in our hot tub. Or, gather around the parlor with friends and sing along to music from a baby grand piano. Feast your senses. Enjoy afternoon snacks in our towering observatory. And savor a hearty, gourmet

NOTES: Credit cards accepted: A Master Card; B Visa; C American Express; D Discover; E Diners Club; F Other; 2 Personal checks accepted; 3 Lunch available; 4 Dinner available;

breakfast, as you watch the sun glint over the mountaintops.

Hosts: Mike and Marj Manley
Rooms: 10 (PB) $68-165
Full Hearty Gourmet Breakfast
Credit Cards: A, D, C, D
Notes: 2, 3, 4 (winter), 5, 8, 9, 10, 11, 12

The Damn Yankee Country Inn

Ouray 1898 House

322 Main Street, PO Box 641, 81427
(970) 325-4871

This 100-year-old house has been carefully renovated and combines the old with the comfortable amenities of the today. Each room features antique furnishings, cable TV, and a private bath. From the deck off each guest room is a spectacular view of the San Juan Mountains, or enjoy this view from the unique Victorian gazebo and soothing spa. A full breakfast is served with a "variety for every appetite." Ouray is known as the "Jeep Capitol of the World" and is also known for its natural hot springs and marvelous hiking trails.

Hosts: Lee and Kathy Bates
Rooms: 4 (PB) $58-100
Full Breakfast
Credit Cards: A, B, C
Notes: 2, 7, 8, 9, 10

PAGOSA SPRINGS

Be Our Guest, A B&B/Guesthouse

19 Swiss Village Drive, 81147
(970) 264-6814

Nestled in the pines with easy access off Highway 160, Be Our Guest is a three level mountain home decorated in southwest style. It has three private rooms, an open sleeping loft area, and one entire level self-contained. A entire house can be reserved for groups of up to 30 people. Amenities include satellite TV, VCR, games, and wraparound deck. A short distance from many of Colorado's sights and year-round activities.

Hosts: Tom and Pam Schoemig
Rooms: 3 (1PB; 2SB) $38-58
Full Breakfast
Credit Cards: none
Notes: 2, 5, 6 (by prior arrangement), 9, 10, 11

Davidson's Country Inn

PO Box 87, 2763 Hwy. 160 E., 81147
(970) 264-5863; FAX (970) 264-9276

Davidson's Country Inn is a three-story log house located at the foot of the Rocky Mountains on 32 acres. The Inn provides a library, a playroom, a game room, and some outdoor activities. A two-bedroom cabin is also available. The Inn is tastefully decorated with family heirlooms and antiques, with a warm country touch to make you feel at home.

---

5 Open all year; 6 Pets welcome; 7 Children welcome; 8 Tennis nearby; 9 Swimming nearby; 10 Golf nearby; 11 Skiing nearby; 12 May be booked through travel agent.

Two miles east of Highway 160.

Hosts: The Gilbert Davidson Family
Rooms: 8 (3PB; 5SB) $46-95
Full Breakfast
Credit Cards: A, B, C, D
Notes: 2, 5, 6 (by prior arrangement), 7, 8, 9, 10, 11, 12

PUEBLO

Abriendo Inn

300 W. Abriendo Avenue, 81004
(719) 544-2703; FAX (719) 542-6544

Experience the elegance of an estate home as you delight in the pleasure of personal attention and hospitality. Antiques, crocheted bedspreads, and brass and four-poster beds take you to a getaway to yesterday with the conveniences you expect of today. Breakfast is always hearty, home-baked, and served in the oak wainscoted dining room or one of the picturesque porches. The inn is located within walking distance of restaurants, shops, and galleries . . . all in the heart of Pueblo. The Abriendo Inn is on the National Register of Historic Places.

Hostess: Kerrelyn Trent
Rooms: 10 (PB) $85-115
Full Breakfast
Credit Cards: A, B, C, F
Notes: 2, 5, 8, 9, 10, 12

The Tudor Rose

SALIDA

Gazebo Country Inn

507 E. 3rd., 81201
(719) 539-7806

A 1901, restored Victorian home with magnificent deck and porch views. Gourmet breakfasts and private baths. Located in the heart of the Rockies. Whitewater rafting on the Arkansas River and skiing at the Monarch Mountain Lodge are a few of the amenities. We are committed to your comfort and relaxation.

Hosts: Don and Bonnie Johannsen
Rooms: 3 (PB) $50-65 + tax
Full Breakfast
Credit Cards: A, B, C
Notes: 2, 5, 7 (over 8), 9, 10, 11, 12

The Tudor Rose

PO Box 89, 81201
(719)-539-2002; (800) 379-0889;
FAX (719) 530-0345

Stately country manor, high on a pinon hill, surrounded by 37 acres. Six distinctive rooms, including the Henry Tudor Suite with its raised jacuzzi, highlight the inn. A formal Queen Anne living room, formal dining room, relaxing "wolf's" den, deck with sunken spa, exercise room, and a full hot breakfast are all complimentary. Facilities include a barn, fenced paddocks, access to thousands of federal acres, and outdoor dog accommodations.

Hosts: John and Terre' Terrell
Rooms: 6 (4PB; 2SB) $50-105
Full Breakfast
Credit Cards: A, B, C, D
Notes: 2, 3, 5, 6, 7, 8, 9, 10, 11, 12

NOTES: Credit cards accepted: A Master Card; B Visa; C American Express; D Discover; E Diners Club; F Other; 2 Personal checks accepted; 3 Lunch available; 4 Dinner available;

SPRINGFIELD

Plum Bear Ranch

PO Box 241, 29461 County Road 21, 81073
(719) 523-4344; FAX (719) 523-4324

Plum Bear Ranch provides guests with an atmosphere of comfort and freedom; the opportunity for city dwellers to share in the bounty of the range. It's an ideal place to relax with panoramic views and peaceful, country setting with its gorgeous sunrises and spectacular sunsets.

Hosts: Wendy and Rory Lynch
Rooms: 7 (3PB; 4SB) $40-50
Full Breakfast
Credit Cards: A, B
Notes: 2, 5, 6, 7

WESTCLIFFE

Purnell's Rainbow Inn

104 Main Street, 81252
(719) 783-2313

Purnell's Rainbow Inn comfortable, hospitable, western-style inn situated between the magnificent Sangre de Cristos and Wet Mountains in historic West Cliffe. Four bedrooms, uniquely decorated, provide genuine comfort. A great room offers big screen TV, game table, books for reading pleasure, and a 7-8 person hot tub available. Full breakfast features freshly baked muffins, special entrees, and seasonal fruits. Mountain bike rentals, hiking supplies and maps, fly fishing pro shop

with instruction, and cross-country skiing opportunities are readily available for a memorable Wet Mountain experience.

Hosts: David and Karen Purnell
Rooms: 4 (2PB; 2SB) $50-60
Full Breakfast
Credit Cards: A, B
Notes: 2, 5, 7, 9, 10, 11, 12

WINTER PARK

Candlelight Mountain Inn

PO Box 600, 80482
(970) 887-2877; (800) KIM-4-TIM (546-4846)

Nestled on a mountainside among pine and aspen trees, the Candlelight Mountain Inn is located in Colorado's beautiful Fraser Valley. Married couples, retired folks, and families will enjoy the comfortable beds, full breakfasts, candlelit lane, game and toy room, hot tub under the stars, glider swings around the campfire, the beautiful view, and other surprises. Our inn is situated in the heart of a vacation paradise; it's just 15 minutes to the ski slopes, 30 minutes to the Rocky Mountain National Park, and only three minutes to the Pole Creek Golf Course and the YMCA of the Rockies . . . a fantastic family vacation spot.

Hosts: Kim and Tim Onnen
Rooms: 4 (2PB; 2SB) $40-80
Full Breakfast
Credit Cards: none
Notes: 2, 5, 7, 8, 9, 10, 11

5 Open all year; 6 Pets welcome; 7 Children welcome; 8 Tennis nearby; 9 Swimming nearby; 10 Golf nearby; 11 Skiing nearby; 12 May be booked through travel agent.

WOODLAND PARK

Woodland Inn Bed and Breakfast

159 Trull Road, 80863
(719) 687-8209; (800) 226-9565;
FAX (719) 687-3112

Guests enjoy the relaxing home-like atmosphere and fantastic views of Pikes Peak from this cozy country inn in the heart of the Rocky Mountains. Peacefully secluded on twelve private acres of woodlands, the Inn is convenient to a variety of attractions, some of which include limited stakes gambling in Cripple Creek, Pikes Peak, Cog Railway and highway; hiking; biking; golf; trail riding; and cross-country skiing. Hot air ballooning with host is also available! Expansions are planned that will add rooms, baths, comforts, and conveniences.

Hosts: Frank and Nancy O'Neil
Rooms: 6 (PB) $55-80
Full Breakfast
Credit Cards: A, B, C
Notes: 2, 5, 6, 7, 8, 10, 11, 12

Connecticut

Bed and Breakfast, Ltd.

PO Box 216, **New Haven** 06513
(203) 469-3260

Bed and Breakfast, Ltd. Offers over 125 accommodations throughout **Connecticut, Massachusetts, and Rhode Island**—from elegantly simple to simply elegant. We offer incredible variety, both in home styles and in price ranges. A quick call assures accurate descriptions and availability. (Host homes nationwide are invited to join our growing network.)

Director: Jack M. Argenio
Rooms: 125+ (60PB, 65SB) $50-125
Credit Cards: (at some) A, B, C
Notes: 2 (at some), 5, 7 (at some), 8, 9, 10, 11

CLINTON

Captain Dibbell House

21 Commerce Street, 06413
(860) 669-1646; FAX (860) 669-2300

Our 1886 Victorian, just two blocks from the shore, features a wisteria-covered century-old footbridge and gazebo on our half-acre of lawn and gardens. Spacious living rooms and bedrooms are comfort-

ably furnished with antiques and family heirlooms, fresh flowers, fruit baskets, and home-baked treats. There are bicycles, nearby beaches, and marinas to enjoy.

Hosts: Helen and Ellis Adams
Rooms: 4 (PB) $75-95
Full Breakfast
Credit Cards: A, B
Notes: 2, 8, 9, 10, 12

Butternut Farm

GLASTONBURY

Butternut Farm

1654 Main Street, 06033
(860) 633-7197 (voice and FAX)

This 18th century architectural jewel is furnished in period antiques. Prize-

---

5 Open all year; 6 Pets welcome; 7 Children welcome; 8 Tennis nearby; 9 Swimming nearby;
10 Golf nearby; 11 Skiing nearby; 12 May be booked through travel agent.

CONNECTICUT

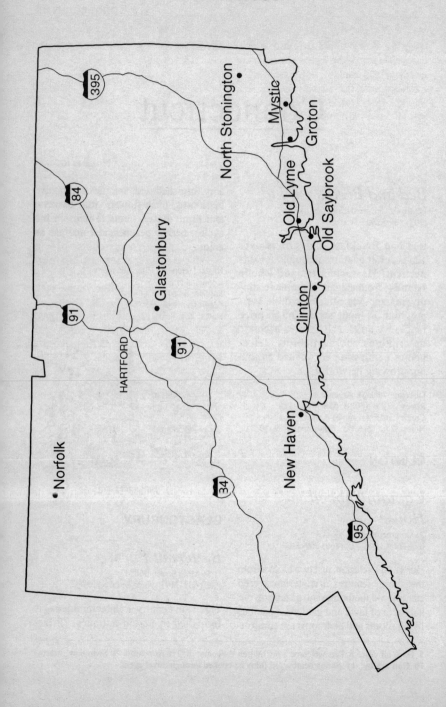

winning dairy goats, pigeons, and chickens roam in an estate setting with trees and herb gardens. Enjoy fresh eggs for breakfast. The farm is located ten minutes from Hartford by expressway; one and one-half hours to any place in Connecticut. Private baths. Sorry, no pets and no smoking.

Host: Don Reid
Rooms: 3 + suite and apartment (PB) $68-88
Full Breakfast
Credit Cards: C
Notes: 2, 5, 7, 8, 9, 10, 11

GROTON

Bluff Point Bed and Breakfast

26 Fort Hill Road, 06340
(860) 445-1314

A restored Colonial bed and breakfast (circa. 1850) located on U.S. Route #1 and adjacent to Bluff Point State Park Coastal Preserve. Conveniently located four miles from Mystic Seaport Museum. Large common area with shared TV is available for our guests. Our home is equipped with a central fire sprinkler system. No smoking or pets. We give warm and friendly service.

Hosts: Walter and Edna Parfitt
Rooms: 3 (1PB; 2SB) $85
Continental Breakfast
Credit Cards: none
Notes: 2, 5, 8, 9, 10

MYSTIC

Harbour Inne and Cottage

15 Edgemont Street, 06355
(860) 572-9253

The Harbour Inne and cottage is located on the Mystic River two block from historic downtown Mystic. Six rooms and a cottage. Three-room cottage with a fireplace and two double beds in the bedroom. Sleep sofa and color TV in living room with glider doors opening onto deck with hot tub spa. Shower/lavatory facilities, kitchen and dining area. Guest house has five rooms, each with double bed, color TV, shower or bath, and air-conditioning. Equipped galley and dining area for guests' use as well as social area with fireplace and antique piano.

Host: Charles Lecouras, Jr.
Rooms: 6 and cottage (PB) $75-250
Self-catered Breakfast
Credit Cards: none
Notes: 5, 6, 7, 8, 9, 10

Harbour Inne and Cottage

NOTES: Credit cards accepted: A Master Card; B Visa; C American Express; D Discover; E Diners Club; F Other; 2 Personal checks accepted; 3 Lunch available; 4 Dinner available; 5 Open all year; 6 Pets welcome; 7 Children welcome; 8 Tennis nearby; 9 Swimming nearby; 10 Golf nearby; 11 Skiing nearby; 12 May be booked through travel agent.

NORFOLK

Greenwoods Gate
Bed and Breakfast

105 Greenwoods Road E., 06058
(860) 542-5439

Warm hospitality greets you in this beautifully restored 1797 Colonial home. Small and elegant with four exquisitely appointed guest suites, each with private bath (one with jacuzzi). Fine antiques, fireplaces, and sumptuous breakfasts to indulge you. *Yankee Magazine*, calls this "New England's most romantic Bed and Breakfast." *Country Inns* Bed and Breakfast Magazine says: "A Connecticut Jewel." Home of Yale's summer music festival.

Hosts: George E. and Marian M. Schumaker
Rooms: 4 suites (PB) $165-225
Gourmet Breakfast (afternoon tea and refreshments before going out to dinner)
Credit Cards: none
Notes: 5, 7, 8, 9, 11, 12

Antiques and Accommodations

NORTH STONINGTON

Antiques
and Accommodations

32 Main Street, 06359
(860) 535-1736; (800) 554-7829

Stroll through our well-tended gardens filled with edible flowers and herbs. Relax on our porches and patios. Our country retreat is located 2.5 miles from I-95, minutes from Mystic Seaport, Aquarium, and superb beaches. Gracious hospitality awaits you at our lovingly restored homes: antiques, canopy beds, fireplaces, private baths, air-conditioned rooms, and cable TV. Greet the day with our acclaimed four-course candlelight breakfast. Always an abundance of flowers. We welcome children who appreciate antiques.

Hosts: Thomas and Ann Gray
Rooms: 3 + 2 cottages (PB) $95-195
Full Breakfast
Credit Cards: A, B
Notes: 2, 5, 7, 8, 9, 10, 12

OLD LYME

Old Lyme Inn

85 Lyme Street, 06371
(860) 434-2600; (800) 434-5352;
FAX (860) 434-5352

In the heart of a small Connecticut town, the Old Lyme Inn is a fine 19th century home restored to its full grandeur. A tree shaded-lawn leads up to the banistered front porch where each guest can relax and just watch the world go by. Built in

NOTES: Credit cards accepted: A Master Card; B Visa; C American Express; D Discover; E Diners Club; F Other; 2 Personal checks accepted; 3 Lunch available; 4 Dinner available;

the 1850s as a farmhouse, the Inn is now a lodging place with five guest rooms and eight suites. All rooms are handsomely furnished in Empire and Victorian with antiques and are equipped with air-conditioning, telephones, and TVs to make your stay even more enjoyable.

Hostess: Diana Field Atwood
Rooms: 13 (PB) $99-158
Country Continental Breakfast
Credit Cards: A, B, C, D, E
Notes: 2, 3, 4, 5 (except first 2 weeks of Jan.), 6, 7, 8, 10, 12

The Deacon Timothy Pratt Bed and Breakfast

OLD MYSTIC

Red Brook Inn

PO Box 237, 06372
(860) 572-0349 (voice and FAX)

Nestled on seven acres of old New England wooded countryside, bed and breakfast lodging is provided in two historic buildings. The Haley Tavern, circa 1770, is a Colonial built by sea captain Nathaniel Crary. Each room is appointed with period furnishings, including canopy beds, and there are many working fireplaces throughout the inn and guest rooms. A hearty breakfast is served family style in the ancient keeping room. Enjoy a quiet, Colonial atmosphere near Mystic Seaport Museum, antique shops, Foxwoods Casino, and Aquarium. Colonial dinner weekends are also available November and December. No smoking.

Hostess: Ruth Keyes
Rooms: 10 (PB) $95-189
Full Breakfast
Credit Cards: A, B, C, D
Notes: 2, 5, 7, 8, 9, 10

OLD SAYBROOK

The Deacon Timothy Pratt Bed and Breakfast

325 Main Street, 06475
(860) 395-1229

Step back in time and enjoy the splendor of yesteryear at the Deacon Timothy Pratt House. Guest rooms are romantically furnished in period style with working fireplaces. A full country breakfast is served in the elegant dining room. In Old Saybrook, Connecticut, where the Connecticut River meets Long Island Sound, the Pratt House is conveniently located in the historic and shopping district. Walk to shops, restaurants, theaters, town green, and Saybrook Point. Located near beaches, antique shops, museums, Mystic Seaport and Aquarium, Foxwoods Casino, Goodspeed Opera House, Ivoryton Playhouse, Essex Steam Train and Riverboat, and Gillette Castle State Park.

Hostess: Shelley Nobile
Rooms: 3 (2PB; 1SB) $100-125
Full Breakfast
Credit Cards: none
Notes: 2, 5, 7, 8, 9, 10, 11

---

5 Open all year; 6 Pets welcome; 7 Children welcome; 8 Tennis nearby; 9 Swimming nearby; 10 Golf nearby; 11 Skiing nearby; 12 May be booked through travel agent.

DELAWARE

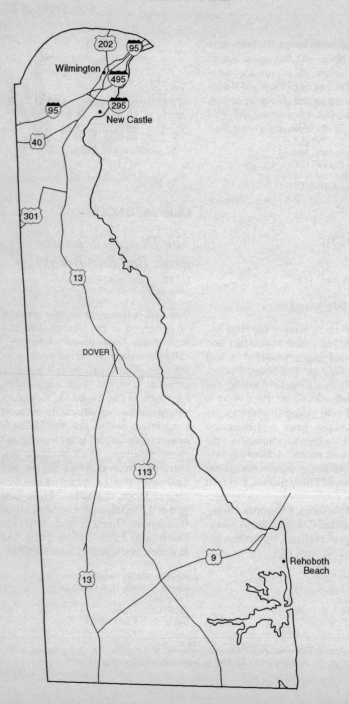

Delaware

NEW CASTLE

Armitage Inn

2 The Strand, 19720
(302) 328-6618; FAX (302) 324-1163

Built in 1732, the Armitage Inn is beautifully situated on the bank of the Delaware River in historic New Castle, Delaware. Elegantly furnished, air-conditioned guest rooms, all with private baths and most with whirlpool tubs, ·overlook the picturesque vistas of the grand Delaware River, the acres of parkland surrounding the Inn, and a peaceful walled garden. Gourmet buffet breakfast is served in the grand dining room or in the garden. The Inn is conveniently located in the heart of this historic town which was established in 1651 and functions today as a living museum, with buildings dating back to its founding years. New Castle is located in the heart of the Brandywine Valley with its numerous museums and attractions.

Hosts: Stephen and Rina Marks
Rooms: 5 (PB) $95-135
Breakfast Buffet
Credit Cards: A, B, C, D
Notes: 2, 5, 7 (over 12), 8, 12

William Penn Guest House

206 Delaware Street, 19720
(302) 328-7736

Visit historic New Castle and stay in a charmingly restored home, circa 1682, close to museums and major highways. Rates are $55 for shared baths and $75 for private baths.

Hosts: Richard and Irma Burwell
Rooms: 4 (1PB; 2SB) $55-75
Continental Breakfast
Credit Cards: none
Notes: 2, 8

REHOBOTH BEACH

The Royal Rose Inn Bed and Breakfast

41 Baltimore Avenue, 19971
(302) 226-2535

A charming and relaxing 1920's beach cottage, this bed and breakfast is tastefully furnished with antiques and a romantic rose theme. A scrumptious breakfast of homemade bread, muffins, egg dishes, and much more is served on a large screened-in porch. Air-con-

NOTES: Credit cards accepted: A Master Card; B Visa; C American Express; D Discover; E Diners Club; F Other; 2 Personal checks accepted; 3 Lunch available; 4 Dinner available; 5 Open all year; 6 Pets welcome; 7 Children welcome; 8 Tennis nearby; 9 Swimming nearby; 10 Golf nearby; 11 Skiing nearby; 12 May be booked through travel agent.

ditioned bedrooms, guest refrigerator, and off-street parking are real pluses for guests. Centrally located one and one half blocks from the ocean and boardwalk. Midweek specials, weekend packages, and gift certificates. Open April through November, other times by chance.

Hostess: Kenny and Cindy Vincent
Rooms: 7 (3PB; 4SB) $45-120
Continental Plus Breakfast
Credit Cards: none
Notes: 2, 7 (over 6), 8, 9, 10

Tembo
Bed and Breakfast
100 Laurel Street, 19971
(302) 227-3360

Tembo, named after Gerry's elephant collection, is a white frame beach cottage set among old shade trees in a quiet residential area just one block from the beach. Furnished with comfortable antique furniture, hand-braided rugs, paintings, and carvings by Delaware artists. A cozy ambiance pervades the casual, hospitable atmosphere.

Hosts: Don and Gerry Cooper
Rooms: 6 (1PB; 5SB)
Continental Breakfast
Credit Cards: none
Notes: 2, 7 (over 12), 8, 9, 10

SEAFORD

Nanticoke House
121 S. Conwell Street, 19973
(302) 628-1331

100 year old home located on the Nanicoke River in central Delmarva Peninsula. Convenient to ocean beaches, Delaware and Chesapeake Bays, Cape May-Lewis Ferry, and barrier islands of Assateague and Chincoteague. Many historical points of interest, antique shops, and outlet stores. River view, flower gardens, and a relaxing, congenial atmosphere. Plenty of good food, fun, and fellowship. A God-given home we enjoy sharing. Hebrews 13:2.

Hosts: Bob and Dianne Seiler
Rooms: 3 (1PB; 2SB) $50-60
Full Breakfast
Credit Cards: none
Notes: 2, 5, 7, 9, 10

WILMINGTON

The Boulevard
Bed and Breakfast
1909 Baynard Boulevard, 19802
(302) 656-9700; FAX (302) 656-9701

This beautifully restored city mansion was originally built in 1913. Impressive foyer and magnificent staircase leading to a landing complete with window seat and large leaded-glass windows flanked by 15-foot columns. Full breakfast served on screened porch or formal dining room. Bedrooms furnished with antiques and family heirlooms. Close to business district and area attractions.

Hosts: Charles and Judy Powell
Rooms: 6 (4PB; 2SB) $60-75
Full Breakfast
Credit Cards: A, B, C
Notes: 2, 5, 7, 8, 10

NOTES: Credit cards accepted: A Master Card; B Visa; C American Express; D Discover; E Diners Club; F Other; 2 Personal checks accepted; 3 Lunch available; 4 Dinner available;

District of Columbia

ALSO SEE LISTINGS UNDER MARYLAND AND VIRGINIA

Adams Inn

1744 Lanier Place NW, 20009
(202) 745-3600; (800) 578-6807;
FAX (202) 319-7958

This turn-of-the-century town house is in the Adams-Morgan neighborhood with over 40 ethnic restaurants. It has clean comfortable home-style furnishings. Adams Inn, located north of the White House and near the National Zoo, is convenient to transportation (Woodley Park Zoo Metro), convention sites, government buildings, and tourist attractions.

Hosts: Gene and Nancy Thompson with Anne
  Owens
Rooms: 25 (12PB; 13SB) $45-90
Expanded Continental Breakfast
Credit cards: A, B, C, D, E
Notes: 2, 5, 7, 12

Bed and Breakfast Accommodations, Ltd.

PO Box 12011, 20005
(202) 328-3510; FAX (202) 332-3885

A reservation service representing over 80 properties in Washington, DC, and nearby Maryland and Northern Virginia. Unique accommodations include private home bed and breakfast, guest houses, inns and hotels, and unhosted one and two bedroom apartments. Many restored and historic Victorians, some with jacuzzi tubs and fireplaces. Children welcome. Major credit cards accepted. Personal Checks accepted if presented two weeks prior to arrival. Wendy Serpan, coordinator.

The Dupont at the Circle

The Dupont at the Circle

1606 19th Street NW, 20009
(202) 332-5251, FAX (202) 408-8308

Restored Victorian townhouse com-

---

5 Open all year; 6 Pets welcome; 7 Children welcome; 8 Tennis nearby; 9 Swimming nearby; 10 Golf nearby; 11 Skiing nearby; 12 May be booked through travel agent.

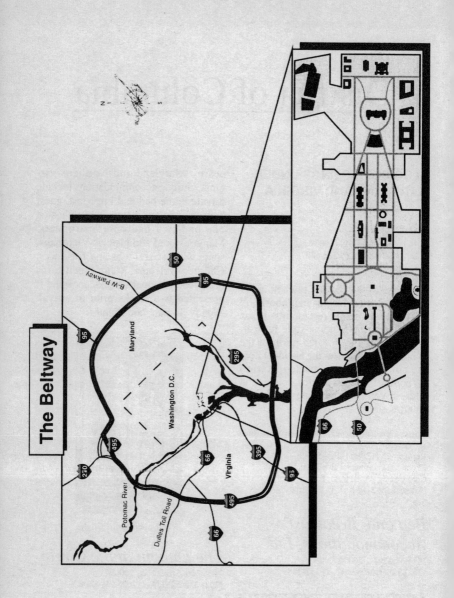

bines the charm of yesteryear with the conveniences of today. Its rooms all have private bathrooms, some with jacuzzis and TVs. The location is perfect—½ block to the metro with shops, wonderful restaurants and the White House and the museums are within walking distance. Continental breakfast included. All rooms are air-conditioned.

Hosts: Alan and Anexora Skvirsky
Rooms: 6 (PB); $95-175
Continental Breakfast
Credit Cards: A, B, C
Notes: 5, 8, 9, 12

Kalorama Guest House

Kalorama Guest House at Kalorama Park

1854 Mintwood Place NW, 20009
(202) 667-6369; FAX (202) 319-1262

Enjoy Washington, DC the right way! Try bed and breakfast in a charming Victorian townhouse. Lodge downtown, within an easy walk to the restaurants, clubs, and nightlife of Adams Morgan and Dupont Circle. Walk to the Metro (subway). Allow us to provide you with a complimentary continental breakfast when you awake, and an evening aperitif when you return to your "home-away-from-home." Most tourist attractions are only 10 minutes away.

Hosts: Tami, Carlotta, John, and Mark
Rooms: 31 (12PB; 19SB) $50-95
Continental Breakfast
Credit Cards: A, B, C, E
Notes: 2, 5, 7, 12

Kalorama Guest House at Woodley Park

2700 Cathedral Avenue NW, 20008
(202) 328-0860; FAX (202) 328-8730

This charming Victorian inn provides a cozy home-away-from-home. Located on a quiet street in a lovely downtown residential neighborhood, the House is a stroll from the Metro (subway), neighborhood restaurants, and shops. Guest rooms are tastefully decorated in period. Enjoy your breakfast in a sun-filled room and relax with an aperitif at day's end. Our hospitality and personal service is nationally known. Most tourist attractions are only ten minutes away.

Hosts: Michael and Mary Anne
Rooms: 19 (12PB; 7SB) $50-95
Continental Breakfast
Credit Cards: A, B, C, E
Notes: 2, 5, 7, 12

NOTES: Credit cards accepted: A Master Card; B Visa; C American Express; D Discover; E Diners Club; F Other; 2 Personal checks accepted; 3 Lunch available; 4 Dinner available; 5 Open all year; 6 Pets welcome; 7 Children welcome; 8 Tennis nearby; 9 Swimming nearby; 10 Golf nearby; 11 Skiing nearby; 12 May be booked through travel agent.

The Reeds

PO Box 12011, 20005
(202) 328-3510; FAX (202) 332-3885

Built in the late 1800s, this large Victorian home features original wood paneling, including a unique oak staircase, stained glass, chandeliers, Victorian-style lattice porch, and art nouveau and Victorian antiques and decorations. It is a double lot and it has a garden with fountains and an old-fashioned swing. The house has been featured in the *Washington Post* and the *Philadelphia Inquirer* and as part of "Christmas at the Smithsonian." It is located ten blocks from the White House at historic Logan Circle.

Hosts: Charles and Jackie Reed
Rooms: 6 (1PB; 5SB) $55-95
Continental Plus Breakfast
Credit Cards: A, B, C, E
Notes: 2 (2 weeks in advance), 5, 7, 8, 9

Swiss Inn

1204 Massachusetts Avenue NW, 20005
(202) 371-1816; (800) 955-7947

The Swiss Inn is a charming turn-of-the-century Victorian townhouse located in Washington, DC. Amenities include bay windows, high ceilings, and fully equipped kitchenettes. The small family-owned and operated inn is within walking distance of the White House, FBI, National Geographic, Chinatown, the Convention Center, the Smithsonian Museums, Ford's Theater, Women in the Arts Museum, the subway, and many other attractions. We are also just two blocks from the main business district. Grocery stores are within walking distance, as are many churches, including St. Matthew's Cathedral.

Host: Ralph Nussbaumer
Rooms: 7 (PB) $58-98
Breakfast is not served
Credit Cards: A, B, C, D, E
Notes: 2, 5, 6, 7

NOTES: Credit cards accepted: A Master Card; B Visa; C American Express; D Discover; E Diners Club; F Other; 2 Personal checks accepted; 3 Lunch available; 4 Dinner available;

Florida

Bailey House

AMELIA ISLAND/FERNANDINA BEACH

Bailey House

28 S. 7th Street, 32034
(904) 261-5390; (800) 251-5390;
FAX (904) 321-0103

Visit an elegant Queen Anne home furnished in Victorian period decor. The beautiful home, with magnificent stained glass windows, turrets, and a wraparound porch, was built in 1895 and is on the National Register of Historic Places. The recently renovated home offers the comfort of air conditioning and private baths. The location in Fernandina's historic district is within walking distance of excellent restaurants, antique shopping, and many historic churches. No smoking or pets please.

Hosts: Tom and Jenny Bishop
Rooms: 5 (PB) $85-115
Full Breakfast
Credit cards: A, B, C
Notes: 2, 5, 8, 9, 10, 12

AMELIA ISLAND

Elizabeth Pointe Lodge

98 S. Fletcher Avenue, 32034
(904) 261-1137; (800) 772-3359;
FAX (904) 277-6500

The main house of the lodge is constructed in an 1890s Nantucket shingle-style with a strong maritime theme, broad porches, rockers, sunshine, and lemonade. Located prominently by the Atlantic Ocean, the Lodge is only steps from often deserted beaches. Suites are available for families. A newspaper is delivered to your room in the morning and breakfast is served overlooking the ocean.

Hosts: David and Susan Caples
Rooms: 25 (PB) $100-175
Full Breakfast
Credit Cards: A, B, C
Notes: 2, 3, 4, 5, 7, 8, 9, 10, 12

---

5 Open all year; 6 Pets welcome; 7 Children welcome; 8 Tennis nearby; 9 Swimming nearby; 10 Golf nearby; 11 Skiing nearby; 12 May be booked through travel agent.

FLORIDA

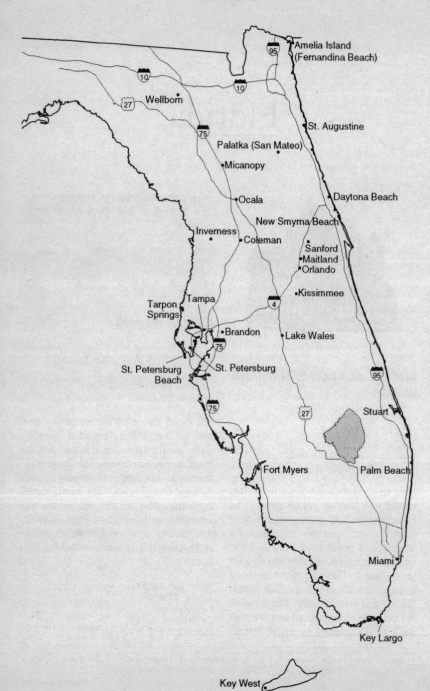

Florida House Inn

22 S. Third Street, PO Box 688, 32034
(904) 261-3300; (800) 258-3301 (reservations);
FAX (904) 277-3831

Located in the heart of our Victorian seaport village, Florida's oldest hotel dates from 1857. Recently restored, our award-winning inn is the perfect combination of historic charm and modern convenience. Each room is a comfortable blend of antiques and reproductions, vintage quilts, handmade rugs, and polished pine floors. Deluxe rooms offer fireplaces, jacuzzis, or original clawfoot tubs. A cozy English-style pub, original boardinghouse restaurants, and brick courtyard with gazebo are all a part of the Florida House experience.

Hosts: Bob and Karen Warner
Rooms: 11 (PB) $70-135
Full Breakfast each morning
Credit Cards: A, B, C, E
Notes: 2, 3, 4, 5, 7, 8, 9, 10, 12

COLEMAN

The Son's Shady Brook Bed and Breakfast

PO Box 551 (949 N. US 301), 33521
(352) PIT-STOP (748-7867)

A refreshing change for all who seek solitude and tranquility in a therapeutic, scenic setting. An escape from the humdrum of everyday life. Exclude the ordinary and enjoy the beautiful wooded area with a rapidly flowing creek. Atmosphere conductive to reading, writing, table games, or just relaxing. Comfortable beds with other interest-ing and enjoyable amenities. Delicious, satisfying breakfasts are served. Central Florida attractions are about 50 miles away. Brochures and gift certificates available.

Hostess: Ms. Jean Lake Martin
Rooms: 4 (PB) $50-60
Full Breakfast
Credit Cards: A, B, C
Notes: 2, 5, 8, 9, 10

The Son's Shady Brook Bed and Breakfast

DAYTONA BEACH

Live Oak Inn

444-448 South Beach Street, 32114
(904) 252-4667; (800) 881-4667;
FAX (904) 239-0068

Live Oak Inn stands where Mathias Day founded Daytona. Two carefully restored houses—both listed in the national register of historic places (1871 and 1881)—are among Florida's top ten historic inns and are the cornerstone of Daytona's historic district. Each of the Inn's rooms celebrates one of the people or events which helped shape Florida's history. All have private baths, king- or

---

NOTES: Credit cards accepted: A Master Card; B Visa; C American Express; D Discover; E Diners Club; F Other; 2 Personal checks accepted; 3 Lunch available; 4 Dinner available; 5 Open all year; 6 Pets welcome; 7 Children welcome; 8 Tennis nearby; 9 Swimming nearby; 10 Golf nearby; 11 Skiing nearby; 12 May be booked through travel agent.

queen-sized beds, and either jacuzzis or Victorian soaking tubs with showers. The Inn also has a restaurant and lounge, and is non-smoking. It offers the best of Daytona! Across the street from the downtown Halifax Harbor Marina and the restful atmosphere of the intra-coastal waterway, and the excitement of the "World's Most Famous Beach" is only one mile away. The Inn is one of those pleasant memory, return again places where hospitality is treated as an art.

Hosts: Jessie and Del Glock and Marcy Scott
Rooms: 12 (PB) $75-150
Continental Breakfast
Credit Cards: none
Notes: 2, 3, 4, 5, 8, 9, 10, 12

FORT MYERS

Island Rover Sailing Ship

Mailing: 11470 S. Cleveland Avenue, 33907
(914) 691-7777; FAX (941) 936-7391

The *Island Rover* is a 72-foot sailing ship which is Coast Guard approved for 49 passengers. We have five staterooms to accommodate ten passengers for overnight. Located under the Sky Bridge at Ft. Myers Beach on the beach side. We are a tall ship, designed like a 19th Century pirate ship. Relax and sail with us!

Rooms: 5 (2PB; 4SB) $89-169
Continental Breakfast
Credit Cards: A, B, C, D
Notes: 2, 5, 7, 8, 9, 10

Windsong Garden and Art Gallery

5570-4 Woodrose Court, 33907
(941) 936-6378

This town house-type home is designed to be your home away from home. The spacious accommodations include a bright and cheery suite with a large, private bath and dressing area. Located 15 minutes from the beaches, Sanibel and Captiva Islands, fine shopping, good restaurants, and the University of Florida. Resident Cat.

Hostess: Embe Burdick
Rooms: 1 (PB) $75
Continental Breakfast
Credit Cards: none
Notes: 2, 5, 8, 9, 10

INVERNESS

Crown Hotel

109 N. Seminole Avenue, 34450
352) 344-5555; FAX (352) 726-4040

Experience the elegance of authentic Victorian decor in one of our 34 individually styled rooms. Your choice of dining in Churchill's Grill or our British Fox and Hound Pub. Centrally located in the secluded hill of Inverness activities. Available activities within the area include canoeing, horseback riding, golfing, and bicycling trails. The perfect place for a quiet, relaxing getaway.

Hosts: Mr. and Mrs. Nigel Sumner
Rooms: 34 (PB) $55-75
Continental Breakfast
Credit Cards: A, B, C, E
Notes: 3, 4, 5, 7, 8, 9, 10, 12

NOTES: Credit cards accepted: A Master Card; B Visa; C American Express; D Discover; E Diners Club; F Other; 2 Personal checks accepted; 3 Lunch available; 4 Dinner available;

KEY LARGO

Jules' Undersea Lodge

Mailing: 51 Shoreland Drive, 33037
(305) 451-2353; FAX (305) 451-4789

Jules' Undersea Lodge is the world's first and only undersea hotel where guests actually scuba dive to enter their rooms. Luxury accommodations include air-conditioned rooms with VCR, stereo, phone, and well-stocked galley. Each room has a 42" round window which offers a unique underwater view. The hotel has two private bedrooms with shared common room and wet rooms areas. The hotel was originally built as an underwater research lab. It is still occasionally used by NASA to study the effects of extended space travel. Jules' Undersea Lodge has been featured on "Lifestyles of the Rich and Famous," in the Sports Illustrated Swimsuit Issue, and on every major television network in the world.

Host: Ian Koblick
Rooms: 2 (SB) $390-590
Full Breakfast
Credit Cards: A, B, C, D
Notes: 3, 4, 5, 9, 10, 12

KEY WEST

Center Court—Historic Inn and Cottages

916 Center Street, 33040
(305) 296-9292; (800) 797-8787;
FAX (305) 294-4104

Beautifully renovated Key West home from 1873, located one block from Duval and Truman Avenue. On quiet, historic lane, yet within walking distance of every Old Town attraction and beaches. This elegantly appointed and handicapped accessible inn has hair dryers, cable TV, telephones, air-conditioning, and fans in each room. One and two room cottages available. Common area has heated pools, jacuzzi, exercise pavilion, fish and lily pond, and lush, tropical gardens. Enjoy breakfast on the veranda overlooking the pool and gardens. AAA approved, three-diamonds. Winner of two Historic Preservation awards. Let us pamper you with Caribbean charm!

Hostess: Naomi Van Steelandt
Rooms: 7 (PB) $78-298
Expanded Continental Breakfast
Credit Cards: A, B, C, D
Notes: 5, 6, 7, 8, 9, 10, 12

Whispers Bed and Breakfast Inn

Whispers B&B Inn

409 William Street, 33040
(305) 294-5969; (800) 856-SHHH;
FAX (305) 294-3899

Located in the heart of Old Town, Whispers, a 150-year-old Victorian-style house, offers its guest the luxury of a

5 Open all year; 6 Pets welcome; 7 Children welcome; 8 Tennis nearby; 9 Swimming nearby;
10 Golf nearby; 11 Skiing nearby; 12 May be booked through travel agent.

private resort (free use of lap pool, private beach, and health spa) yet the quaintness of a B&B. Whispers also offers its guests a full and varied gourmet breakfast. So come down and enjoy Key West—and come home to Whispers.

Host: John W. Marburg
Rooms: 7 (5PB; 2SB) $69-150
Full Gourmet Breakfast
Credit cards: A, B, C, D
Notes: 2, 5, 8, 9, 10, 12

Unicorn Inn

KISSIMMEE

Unicorn Inn
English Bed and Breakfast

8 S. Orlando Avenue, 34741
(407) 846-1200; (800) 865-7212;
FAX (407) 846-1773

The Unicorn—the only bed and breakfast in Kissimmee—is located in Historic Downtown off the Broadway. A safe, peaceful, relaxing district 300 yards from Lake Tohopekalegia (fishing boats and other boats can be rented), the Unicorn is close to golf courses, horseback riding, and other attractions like Disney World, Sea World, and Wet and Wild. Orlando Airport is a 25 minute drive. Amtrak and Greyhound

stations are nearby. All rooms have TV and air-conditioning. Kitchen facilities with complimentary tea and coffee. Restored to its full grandeur, the Unicorn Inn has antique pottery, prints, and furniture. Many churches located nearby. British owned and run by Fran and Don Williamson of Yorkshire, England. Our rule is: "Make Yourself At Home." Airport pick-ups available. AAA three diamond rated.

Hostess: Don and Fran Williamson
Rooms: 8 (2 of which have space for children)
(PB) $55-65
Full or Light Breakfast
Credit Cards: A, B, C, D, E
Notes: 2, 5, 7, 8, 9, 10, 12

LAKE WALES

Chalet Suzanne Country Inn and Restaurant

3800 Chalet Suzanne Drive, 33853
(941) 676-6011; (800) 433-6011;
FAX (941) 676-1814

Nestled among orange groves halfway between Tampa and Orlando, Chalet Suzanne has been welcoming guests for over sixty years. The Restaurant has an international reputation for superb food and features waterfront dining, an award-winning wine list, and excellent service. Thirty romantic guest rooms, Lake Suzanne, airstrip, pool, manicured grounds, courtyards, and patios will make everyone in the family feel welcome.

Hosts: Carl and Vita Hinshaw
Rooms: 30 (PB) $135-195
Full Breakfast
Credit Cards: A, B, C, D, E
Notes: 2, 3, 4, 5, 6, 7, 8, 9 (on-site), 10, 12

NOTES: Credit cards accepted: A Master Card; B Visa; C American Express; D Discover; E Diners Club; F Other; 2 Personal checks accepted; 3 Lunch available; 4 Dinner available;

MIAMI

Banyan Treehouse B&B/ Agency of Bed and Breakfast Hosts

7436 SW 117 Avenue, PO Box 160, 33183
(305) 271-5422 (voice and FAX)

Private, five-acre, equestrian estate. Safe, clean, and beautiful. Three guest rooms, two apartments, all private whirlpool baths. Wraparound decks, lush tropical foliage, theraputic hot tubs, and a treehouse. Breakfast under giant orchid tree. Romantic. Five minutes to restaurants, great shopping, and movies. Fifteen minutes to zoo, Parrot Jungle, Monkey Jungle, and Orchid Jungle. Twenty-five minutes to Miami Beach and Art Deco Center. Thirty minutes to Florida Key for snorkeling, scuba diving, glass-bottom boats, and deep sea fishing. Twenty minutes to Everglades National Park, etc. Call for brochure.

Hostess: Ms. Beck
Rooms: 3 + 2 apartments (PB) $45-65
Continental Breakfast
Credit Cards: none
Notes: 2, 5, 8, 9, 10, 12 (20% com.)

Miami River Inn

118 SW South River Drive, 33130
(305) 325-0045; (800) HOTEL-89;
FAX (305) 325-9227
Email: miami100@ix.netcom.com

Built between 1906 and 1910, the Miami River Inn boasts four wooden cottages surrounding a pool and jacuzzi in a lush tropical garden. The Inn's 40 rooms are each individually decorated with antique furnishings, featuring cable television, touchtone phones, central air/heat, and private bathrooms. A quick walk to downtown offers shopping, dining, museums, and galleries. Office services available free to business travellers. Beaches, airport, and Port of Miami are within a 15-minute drive.

Hostess: Sallye Jude
Rooms: 40 (38PB; 2SB) $59-125
Extended Continental Breakfast
Credit Cards: A, B, C, D, E, F (Carte Blanche)
Notes: 5, 7, 8, 9 (on-site), 10, 12

Thurston House

MAITLAND

Thurston House

851 Lake Avenue, 32751
(407) 539-1911; (800) 843-2721;
FAX (407) 539-0365

Hidden amid five acres of beautiful wooded, lakefront land, Thurston House provides a perfect escape from the pressures of the day. The wraparound porch, garden areas, and walking paths provide places for peaceful reflection. Four guest rooms, all with queen-sized beds, private baths, and desk with phone await you in this circa 1885 Queen Anne Victorian home.

---

5 Open all year; 6 Pets welcome; 7 Children welcome; 8 Tennis nearby; 9 Swimming nearby; 10 Golf nearby; 11 Skiing nearby; 12 May be booked through travel agent.

Thurston House boasts beautifully restored woodwork, and is decorated using period antiques and fine reproductions.

Hosts: Carole and Joe Ballard
Rooms: 4 (PB) $90
Expanded Continental Breakfast
Credit Cards: A, B, C
Notes: 2, 5, 9, 10, 12

MICANOPY

Shady Oak
Bed and Breakfast

PO Box 236, 32667
(352) 466-3476

The Shady Oak stands majestically in the center of historic downtown Micanopy. A marvelous canopy of old, live oaks; quiet, shaded streets; and many antique stores offer visitors a memorable connection to Florida's past. This three-story, 19th century-style mansion features five beautiful, spacious suites, private baths, porches, jacuzzi, Florida room, and widow's walk. Three lovely, historic churches within walking distance. Local activities include antiquing, bicycling, canoeing, bird watching, and much more. "Playfully elegant accommodations, where stained glass, antiques, and innkeeping go together as kindly as warm hugs with old friends."

Hosts: Candy and Mark Lancaster
Rooms: 5 suites (PB) $75-125
Full Breakfast
Credit Cards: A, B
Notes: 2, 3, 4, 5, 6, 7, 9, 10, 12

NEW SMYRNA BEACH

Indian River Inn

1210 S. Riverside Drive, 32168
(904) 428-2491; (800) 541-4529 (reservations);
FAX (904) 426-2532

Built in 1916, this inn is the oldest extant hotel in Volusia County. It has been lovingly restored and remodeled to meet all current standards of security, comfort, and convenience without sacrificing its charm and character. A gracious atmosphere of warmth and friendliness, unsurpassed in today's often frantic lifestyle, can be found here. We are located on the Atlantic Intercoastal Waterway minutes from I-95 and I-4 between Daytona Beach and the Kennedy Space Center. Church groups and buses welcomed.

Hosts: Ed and Donna Ruby
Rooms: 27 + 15 suites (PB) $50-115
Continental Breakfast
Credit Cards: A, B, D
Notes: 2, 3 and 4 (available Thanksgiving—Easter), 5, 7, 8, 9 (on premises), 10, 12

Night Swan Intracoastal
Bed and Breakfast

512 S. Riverside Drive, 32168
(904) 423-4940; FAX (904) 427-2814

Come watch the pelicans, dolphins, sailboats, and yachts along the Atlantic Intracoastal Waterway from our beautiful front room, our wraparound porch, our 140-foot dock, or your room. Our spacious three-story home has kept its character and charm of 1906 in the Historic District of New Smyrna Beach,

---

NOTES: Credit cards accepted: A Master Card; B Visa; C American Express; D Discover; E Diners Club; F Other; 2 Personal checks accepted; 3 Lunch available; 4 Dinner available;

with its central fireplace and its intricate natural wood in every room. We are located between Daytona Beach and Kennedy Space Center, on the Indian River, just two miles from the beach. AAA approved.

Hosts: Martha and Chuck Nighswonger
Rooms: 8 (PB) $59-129
Full or Continental Breakfast
Credit Cards: A, B, C, D
Notes: 2, 5, 7, 8, 9, 10

Seven Sisters Inn

OCALA

ORLANDO

Seven Sisters Inn

820 SE Fort King Street, 34471
(352) 867-1170; (800) 250-3496;
FAX (352) 867-5266

Seven Sisters Inn, chosen "Inn of the Month" by *Country Inns Bed and Breakfast* Magazine, is located in the heart of Ocala's historic district. Built in 1888, this Queen Anne style Victorain house has been lovingly restored to its original statley elegance, with beautiful period furnishings. Each guest room has private bath, carefully chosen, elegant decor, sitting rooms, fireplaces, and much more. The owners, both airline pilots, have traveled all over the world, collecting suberb recipes. It's no wonder their gourmet dishes are received with such enthusiasm! Triple-Crown ABBA, AAA three diamond, and three star Mobil rated.

Hosts: Bonnie Morehardt and Ken Oden
Rooms: 8 (PB) $105-165
Full Breakfast
Credit Cards: A, B, C, D
Notes: 2, 5, 9, 10, 12

The Courtyard at Lake Lucerne

211 N. Lucerne Circle E., 32801
(407) 648-5188; (800) 444-5289;
FAX (407) 246-1368

A unique property made up of three historic buildings furnished with antiques and surrounding a tropically landscaped brick courtyard, this establishment is located in the historic district on the southern edge of downtown Orlando, convenient to everything central Florida has to offer. Rooms have phones and cable TV; two suites have double jacuzzis and steam showers. Selected by *Country Inns Magazine* as one of 1992's "Best Inn Buys" and by Herb Hillier for *The Miami Herald* as one of the ten best inns in Florida for 1992.

Hosts: Charles, Sam, and Eleanor Meiner with Paula Bowers
Rooms: 24 (PB) $69-165
Expanded Continental Breakfast
Credit Cards: A, B, C, E
Notes: 2, 5, 7, 10, 12

---

5 Open all year; 6 Pets welcome; 7 Children welcome; 8 Tennis nearby; 9 Swimming nearby; 10 Golf nearby; 11 Skiing nearby; 12 May be booked through travel agent.

Meadow Marsh B&B

940 Tildenville School Road, **Winter Garden**
34787
(407) 656-2064

Peace and tranquillity surround you as God's beauty unfolds in 12 acres of ol' Florida. Giant oaks, stately palms, and abundant wild life make your stay at meadow marsh one for relaxing and renewing of your spirit. The spacious lawn invites a romantic picnic or a hand-in-hand walk through the meadow to the adjacent rails-to-trails path. Old-fashioned swings, crochet, and badminton add to the feeling of yesteryears. You'll enjoy the 1877 Victorian farmhouse where cozy fireplaces, hardwood floors, and lace curtains add to the warmth and beauty of this country estate. Suites offer two-person jacuzzis while the smaller bedrooms have antique tubs which were saved during renovations. Pamper yourselves for a moment in an atmosphere of a sweeter time that existed not so very long ago.

Hosts: Cavelle and John Pawlack
Rooms: 2 + 2 suites (PB) $95-195
Full Breakfast
Credit Cards: A, B
Notes: 2, 5, 10, 12

PerriHouse B&B

10417 Centurion Ct., **Lake Buena Vista** 32836
(407) 876-4830; (800) 780-4830;
FAX (407) 876-0241

PerriHouse is a quiet, private country estate inn secluded on 20 acres of land adjacent to the Walt Disney World complex. (Disney Village, Pleasure Island, and EPCOT Center all only 3 to 5 minutes away.) It's the perfect vacation setting for families who desire a unique travel experience with a comfortable, convenient home away from home. An upscale continental breakfast awaits you each morning and a refreshing pool spal relaxes you after a full day of activities. Each guest room features its own private bath, entrance, TV, telephone, ceiling fan, and central air/heat. The PerriHouse grounds are being developed and landscaped to create a future bird sanctuary and wildlife preserve. Come bird watch on the peaceful, tranquil estate grounds and wake up to the bird songs outside your window. Your hosts instinctively offer their guests a unique blend of cordial hospitality, comfort, and friendship!

Hosts: Nick and Angi Perretti
Rooms: 6 (PB) $75-95
Continental Plus Breakfast
Credit cards: A, B, C, D
Notes: 2 (2 weeks ahead), 5, 7, 8, 9, 10, 12

Ferncourt Bed and Breakfast

PALATKA (SAN MATEO)

Ferncourt B&B

150 Central Ave, PO Box 758, **San Mateo** 32187
(904) 329-9755

Built in 1889, this centurian painted

lady, with its 17 plus rooms, has been lovingly restored by your host and hostess. They delight in sharing this small piece of Florida history with others. You will be served a complimentary gourmet breakfast in our dining room, breakfast room, or if you choose, our spacious wraparound veranda. Located in North Central Florida, historic San Mateo was a thriving little town just before the turn of the century. Now only a sleepy hamlet, it offers a quiet place to get away. Only minutes away from many of Florida's attractions.

Hosts: Jack and Dee Morgan
Rooms: 5 (PB) $55-75
Full Breakfast
Credit Cards: A, B, C, D
Notes: 2, 5, 10, 12

PALM BEACH

Palm Beach Historic Inn

365 S. County Road, 33480
(407) 832-4009; FAX (407) 832-6255

A historic landmark building, beautifully restored to preserve its original integrity and stately elegance, has every modern convenience. Four suites and nine guest rooms, tastefully and individually appointed, private baths and showers, air-conditioning, cable TV, and telephones. Guests will be served a complimentary deluxe continental breakfast in their rooms. Walk one block to the beach and two blocks to the world-famous Worth Avenue shopping. Perfect for weekend getaways, family vacations, relaxing retreats, business trips, and romantic

weekends. ABBA "A" rating for excellence.

Hostess: Brenda Lee Inniss
Rooms: 9 + 4 suites (PB) $75-250
Deluxe Continental Breakfast
Credit Cards: A, B, C, D, E
Notes: 5, 7, 8, 9, 10, 12

ST. AUGUSTINE

Carriage Way B&B

70 Cuna Street, 32084
(904) 829-2467; (800) 908-9832;
FAX (904) 826-1461

Built in 1833, a Victorian home located in the heart of the historic district amid unique and charming shops, museums, and historic sites. The atmosphere is leisurely and casual, in keeping with the general attitude and feeling of Old St. Augustine. All guest rooms have a private bath with a clawfoot tub or shower. Rooms are furnished with antiques and reproductions including brass, canopy, or four poster beds. A full home-baked breakfast is served.

Hosts: Bill and Diane Johnson
Rooms: 9 (PB) $69-125
Full Breakfast
Credit Cards: A, B, C, D
Notes: 2, 3 and 4 (picnic), 5, 7 (over 8), 8, 9, 10, 12

Carriage Way Bed and Breakfast

Castle Garden B&B

15 Shenandoah Street, 32084
(904) 829-3839

Stay at a Castle and be treated like royalty! Relax and enjoy the peace and quiet of "royal treatment" at our newly restored, 100-year-old castle of the Moorish Revival design. The only sounds you'll hear is the occasional roar of a cannon shot from the old fort 200 yards to the south or the creak of solid wood floors. Awaken to the aroma of freshly baked goodies as we prepare a full, mouth-watering, country breakfast just like "Mom used to make." The unusual coquina stone exterior remains virtually untouched while the interior of the former Castle Warden Carriage House boasts two beautiful bridal suites complete with soothing in-room jacuzzi, sunken bedrooms, and all of life's little pleasures! Amenities: complimentary wine, chocolates, bikes, and private parking. Packages and gift baskets available. We believe that every guest is a gift from God.

Hosts: Bruce Kloeckner and Kimmy VanKooten
Rooms: 6 (PB) $75-150
Full Breakfast
Credit Cards: A, B, C, D
Notes: 2, 5, 7, 8, 9, 10, 12

The Cedar House Inn

79 Cedar Street, 32084-4311
(904) 829-0079; (800) 233-2746;
FAX (904) 825-0916

Capture romantic moments at our 1893 Victorian home in the heart of the ancient city. Escape into your antique filled bedroom with private whirlpool bath or clawfooted tub, enjoy the comfortable parlor with its fireplace, player piano and antique Victrola, or sit on the shady veranda and watch time stroll by. Elegant full breakfast, evening snack, on premises parking, jacuzzi spa, and bicycles. Walk to historical sites or bicycle to beach. AAA approved, 3 diamond rated. Smoke free home.

Hosts: Russ and Nina Thomas
Rooms: 5 + 1 suite (PB) $59-150
Full Breakfast
Credit Cards: A, B, D
Notes: 2, 5, 7 (over 10), 8, 9, 10, 11, 12

Old Powder House Inn

38 Cordova Street, 32084
(904) 824-4149; (800) 447-4149;
FAX (904) 825-0143

Towering pecan and oak trees shade verandas with large rockers to watch the passing horse-drawn buggies. An introduction to a romantic escape in the charming turn-of-the-century Victorian inn. Amenities include high tea, hors d' oeuvres, jacuzzi, cable TV, parking, bicycles, family hospitality, picnics, special honeymoon packages, anniversaries, and birthdays.

Hosts: Al and Eunice Howes
Rooms: 9 (PB) $65-150
Full Gourmet Breakfast
Credit Cards: A, B, D
Notes: 2, 5, 7, 8, 9, 10, 12

St. Francis Inn

279 St. George Street, 32084
(904) 824-6068; (800) 824-6062;
FAX (904) 810-5525

Built in 1791, the Inn is a beautiful Spanish Colonial building. The court-

---

NOTES: Credit cards accepted: A Master Card; B Visa; C American Express; D Discover; E Diners Club; F Other; 2 Personal checks accepted; 3 Lunch available; 4 Dinner available;

yard garden provides a peaceful setting for traditional hospitality. Accommodations range from double rooms and suites to a five-room cottage—all private bath, cable TV, central air/heat, and many have fireplaces. The Inn is centrally located in the historic district within easy walking to restaurants, shops, and historical sites.

Host: Joe Finnegan
Rooms: 14 (PB) $52-125
Continental Plus Breakfast
Credit cards: A, B
Notes: 2, 5, 7 (limited), 8, 9, 10, 12

Southern Wind Inns East and West

Southern Wind East	Southern Wind West
Innkeeper: Jeanette	Innkeeper: Linda
18 Cordova Street,	34 Saragossa Street,
32084	32084
(904) 825-3623	(904) 808-7384

Stay with us at our two charming locations. Our East home is built of Coquina massonry with verandas overlooking the route of horse-drawn carriages. It houses eight rooms ranging from $75-139 per night.

Our West Inn, built in 1920, the cottage style craft era archetecture, is our family inn. It houses six rooms with private entrances. Prices range from $75-110 per night.

Both have off-street parking, air-conditioning, cable TV, and complimentary wine.

Hostesses: Jeanette Dean and Linda Nucci
Rooms: 14 total (PB) $75-139
Full Breakfast
Credit Cards: A, B, C, D, E
Notes: 2, 5, 7, 8, 9, 10, 12

Southern Wind West

ST. PETE BEACH

Island's End Resort

1 Pass-a-grille Way, 33706
(813) 360-5023; FAX (813) 367-7890

The compelling appeal of all that paradise can offer abounds at Island's End. Deep blue sky, turquoise waters, exotic sunrise, and sweets all work in concerts to relax and entertain you. Island's End features six unique, well-appointed guest homes including a fantastic three-bedroom house with atruim and private pool. Try your hand at fishing day or night from one of the best docks on Florida's west coast. Small private beach only a half block from our beautiful five mile beach.

Hosts: Jone and Millard Gamble
Rooms: 6 (PB) $61-160
Continental served Tues., Thurs., and Saturday
Credit cards: A, B
Notes: 2, 5, 7, 8, 9, 10

ST. PETERSBURG

Mansion House

105 Fifth Avenue NE, 33701
(813) 821-9391 (voice and FAX);
(800) 274-7520

Mansion House, built in 1904 and beau-

---

5 Open all year; 6 Pets welcome; 7 Children welcome; 8 Tennis nearby; 9 Swimming nearby; 10 Golf nearby; 11 Skiing nearby; 12 May be booked through travel agent.

tifully restored, has five rooms with private baths in the main house. A sixth room, the Carriage House, has a cathedral ceiling, four-poster bed, phone, and TV. Common areas include a library/TV room with VCR, sun porch, living room, and patio. Guests have access to kitchen and 24-hour snacks. Antiques from around the world are dispersed throughout the house. The Mansion House is convenient to cultural and sports attractions, water, restaurants, and shopping. Private boat cruises are available on the bay or gulf with your host as captain. Portuguese is spoken.

Hosts: Robert and Rose Marie Ray
Rooms: 6 (PB) $85-125
Full Breakfast
Credit Cards: A, B, C
Notes: 2 (deposit required), 5, 7, 8, 9, 12

SANFORD

The Higgins House Bed and Breakfast

420 Oak Avenue, 32771
(407) 324-9238; (800) 584-0014

Enjoy the romance of a by-gone era at this 102-year-old Queen Anne Victorian bed and breakfast. Three guest rooms and cottage all with private baths. Victorian gardens and hot tub. Located in historic Sanford near beautiful Lake Monre and the St. Johns River. Anitque shops nearby.

Hosts: Walter and Roberta Padgett
Rooms: 3 + cottage (PB) $85-115
Continental Plus Breakfast
Credit Cards: A, B, C, D
Notes: 2, 5, 8, 10, 12

The Homeplace B&B Inn

STUART

The Homeplace Bed and Breakfast Inn

501 Akron Avenue, 34994
(407) 220-9148; (800) 251-5473;
FAX (407) 221-3265

The Homeplace, Stuart's premier bed and breakfast inn, was built in 1913 and lovingly restored in 1989. The Inn is best known for its romantic ambiance, quality, and unequaled graciousness. Four guest rooms are air-conditioned and comfortably appointed with antiques. The "wickered" sun porch and turn-of-the-century parlor create a Victorian setting in which to recall pleasurable reminiscences of times gone by. The lush patio garden, pool, and heated spa beckon. Stroll or bike to Stuart's newly restored historic area for shopping and fine dining.

Hosts: Suzanne and Michael Pescitelli
Rooms: 4 (PB) $75-95 (subject to change)
Full Breakfast
Credit Cards: A, B
Notes: 2, 5, 8, 9 (on-site), 10, 12

NOTES: Credit cards accepted: A Master Card; B Visa; C American Express; D Discover; E Diners Club; F Other; 2 Personal checks accepted; 3 Lunch available; 4 Dinner available;

TAMPA

Behind the Fence Bed and Breakfast Inn

1400 Viola Dr. @ Countryside, **Brandon** 33511
(813) 685-8201; (800) 44-TAMPA

Retreat into the simplicity and tranquillity of life in a bygone era with all the conveniences of today's world. Come to Florida and choose your accommodations from a cottage by our pool to a private room in our antique-filled New England Salt-Box house. Nearby parks and river canoeing offer lots of opportunities for family activities. Homemade, Amish sweet rolls are featured and "relaxing" is the word most guests use to refer to their stay "behind the fence." Country furniture for sale and tours available upon request. AAA and 3-star approved.

Hosts: Larry and Carolyn Yoss
Rooms: 5 (3PB; 2SB) $65-75
Expanded Continental Breakfast
Credit Cards: none
Notes: 2, 5, 6 (some), 7, 8, 9, 10

TARPON SPRINGS

East Lake Bed and Breakfast

421 Old East Lake Road, 34689
(813) 937-5487

Private home on two and a half acres, situated on a quiet road along Lake Tarpon, close to the Gulf of Mexico. The hosts are retired business people who enjoy new friends and are well informed about the area. The room and adjoining bath are at the front of the house, away from the family quarters. The room has central air, color TV, and telephone. Breakfast includes fresh fruit, juice, entree, and homemade breads and jams. Close to many Florida attractions.

Hosts: Dick and Marie Fiorito
Rooms: 1 (PB) $40
Full Home-Cooked Breakfast
Credit Cards: none
Notes: 2, 5, 8, 9, 10

WELLBORN

1909 McLeran House B&B and Collectibles Shoppe

12408 CR 137, 32094
(904) 963-4603

The 1909 McLeran House offers guests a glimpse into the north Florida (Suwannee River Valley) of a century ago. Restoration of the home has been extensive and meticulous, including central air/heat. There is a huge wraparound front porch and six fireplaces, each with curly-pine mantle. Furnishings are a tasteful and appropriate blend of old and new. A cedar gazebo crowns the garden area which includes swing, fountain, arbor, walkways, goldfish pond, the original open well, and lush landscaping. Many local attractions nearby, including the Stephen Foster Folk Culture Center.

Hosts: Robert and Mary Ryals
Rooms: 2 (1PB; 1SB) $60
Deluxe Continental Breakfast
Credit Cards: none
Notes: 2, 5, 9, 10

---

5 Open all year; 6 Pets welcome; 7 Children welcome; 8 Tennis nearby; 9 Swimming nearby; 10 Golf nearby; 11 Skiing nearby; 12 May be booked through travel agent.

GEORGIA

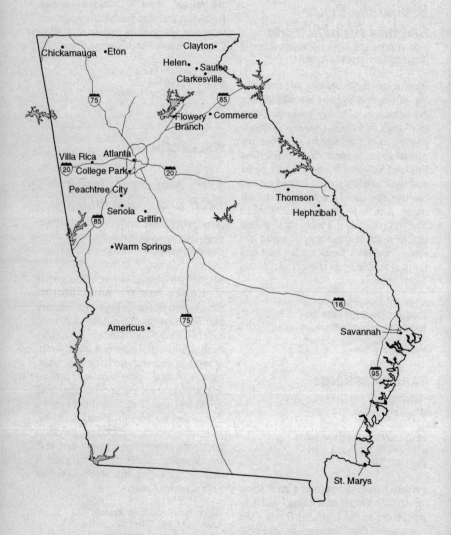

Georgia

RSVP GRITS, INC.

541 Londonberry Rd. NE, **Altlanta** 30327
(404) 843-3933; (800) 823-7787
FAX (404) 252-8886
Email: innfo@aol.com

RSVP GRITS, INC. (Great Reservations in the South) represents a select group of very special B&Bs and Inns in the **Atlanta** area, within 150 miles of Atlanta, in **North Georgia**, as far east as **Augusta** plus a sampling in **North and South Carolina** area. We provide personal service and are pleased to help plan get-away weekends, romantic retreats, or small business seminars or meetings. All properties are properly licensed and inspected. Free service. 40+ inns, all with private baths. Rates: $85-250. Credit cards and personal checks accepted. Marty Barnes, coordinator. Free brochure.

AMERICUS

1906—The Pathway Inn

501 S. Lee Street, 31709
(912) 928-2078 (voice and FAX);
(800) 889-1466

Parlors, porches, whirlpools, down comforters, fireplaces, friends, muffins, and more await you at a 1906 Greek Revival style inn with stained glass and a sumptuous candlelit breakfast. Between Plains (Home of President Carter) and historic Civil War Andersonville. 30 minutes west of I-75 / 2½ hours south of Atlanta. Home of Habitat for Humanity. We spoil our business travelers the same as tourists and honeymooners. Attend and hear President Carter teach Sunday School.

Hosts: David and Sheila Judah
Rooms: 5 (PB) $65-117
Full Breakfast
Credit Cards: A, B, C, D
Notes: 2, 5, 6 (with permission), 7, 10, 12 (10%)

1906—The Pathway Inn

NOTES: Credit cards accepted: A Master Card; B Visa; C American Express; D Discover; E Diners Club; F Other; 2 Personal checks accepted; 3 Lunch available; 4 Dinner available; 5 Open all year; 6 Pets welcome; 7 Children welcome; 8 Tennis nearby; 9 Swimming nearby; 10 Golf nearby; 11 Skiing nearby; 12 May be booked through travel agent.

ATLANTA

Beverly Hills Inn

65 Sheridan Drive, 30305
(404) 233-8520 (voice and FAX)
(800) 331-8520

A charming European-style hotel, with 18 suites uniquely decorated with period furnishings, offers fresh flowers, continental breakfast, and the little things that count. We're a morning star, not a constellation; a solitary path, not a highway. Only some will understand, but then, we don't have room for everybody.

Hosts: Bonnie and Lyle Klienhans
Rooms: 18 (PB) $80-450
Continental Breakfast
Credit Cards: A, B, C, E
Notes: 2, 5, 6, 7, 8, 9, 10, 12

Oakwood House
Bed and Breakfast

951 Edgewood Avenue NE, 30307
(404) 521-9320; FAX (404) 688-6034

Get away—in the city to our relaxing, small inn. Your hosts live next door. Located in Atlanta's oldest suburb, historic Inman park, just two miles east of downtown Atlanta, Oakwood House is perfect for business and pleasure travelers. Easy access via car and subway. There's lots to do in the city of Rhett and Scarlet, Coca Cola, Martin Luther King Jr., and Jimmy Carter. You'll enjoy our comfortable rooms which feel like a real home. New whirlpool suite. Free theater tickets (seasonal). Family room features trundle bed for two children. Board your pet nearby. No smoking.

Hosts: Robert and Judy Hotchkiss
Rooms: 5 (PB) $75-150
Enhanced Continental Breakfast
Credit Cards: A, B, C
Notes: 2, 5, 7, 8, 9, 10, 12

Shellmont
Bed and Breakfast

821 Piedmont Avenue NE, 30308
(404) 872-9290; FAX (404) 872-5379

Built in 1891, Shellmont is on the National Register of Historic Places and is a city of Atlanta Landmark Building. A true Victorian treasure of carved woodwork, stained and leaded glass, and unique architecture located in Midtown Atlanta's restaurant, theater, and cultural district, one mile from downtown. It is furnished entirely with antiques.

Hosts: Ed and Debbie McCord
Rooms: 5 (PB) $94-149
Full Breakfast
Credit Cards: A, B, C, D, F
Notes: 2, 5, 7 (limited), 8, 10, 12

Shellmont Bed and Breakfast

NOTES: Credit cards accepted: A Master Card; B Visa; C American Express; D Discover; E Diners Club; F Other; 2 Personal checks accepted; 3 Lunch available; 4 Dinner available;

The Woodruff B&B Inn

223 Ponce de Leon, 30308
(404) 875-9449; (800) 473-9449;
FAX (404) 870-0042

Prepare yourself for Southern charm, hospitality, and a full Southern breakfast. The Woodruff Bed and Breakfast Inn is conveniently located in Midtown Atlanta. It is a 1906 Victorian home built by a prominent Atlanta family and fully restored by the current owners. Each room has been meticulously decorated with antiques. The Woodruff has a very colorful past which lends to the charm and history of the building and the city. Close to everything. Ya'll come!

Hosts: Douglas and Joan Jones
Rooms 13 (PB) $69-295
Full Breakfast
Credit Cards: A, B, C, D
Notes: 2, 5, 7, 9, 12

CHICKAMAUGA

New Dawn Farm Bed and Breakfast

363 South Cedar Lane, 30707
(703) 799-1695 or (706) 539-2177;
FAX (703) 799-1695
Email: 103210,3666 Compuserve

Serene, rural setting within one hour to major recreation lakes, ski slope, historic Chickamauga Military Park, and state parks. Only 30 minutes to Chattanooga, TN. Modest, newly renovated, four-bedroom home with living room, dining room, and kitchen. Continental plus breakfast. Comfortable, affordable, and offering the most beautiful scenery

anywhere. Reservations requested.

Hostess: Chris Everett
Owner: Jennie Chandler
Rooms: 4 (1PB; 3SB) $30-60
Continental Plus Breakfast
Credit Cards: none
Notes: 2, 5, 6, 7, 10, 11

CLAYTON

English Manor Inns

PO Box 1605; US Hwy. 76 E., 30525
(706) 782-5789 (voice and FAX);
(800) 782-5780

English Manor is a cluster inn concept of seven individual inns scattered over seven acres of naturally landscaped property abutting the Chattahoochee National Forest. Ideal for honeymooners, anniversaries, family refreshers, corporate groups, whitewater rafters, and retreats. Full breakfast plus wine, juice, and appetizers served daily. Pool, year-round hot tub, and cable TV; some rooms and suites with fireplaces and/or jacuzzis.

Hosts: Susan and English Thornwell
Rooms: 42 (PB) $89-199
Full Breakfast
Credit Cards: none
Notes: 2, 5, 6, 7, 8, 9, 10, 11, 12

COLLEGE PARK

The Moore House

4385 Jailette Road, 30349
(404) 768-6092

Classic 1940 bungalow, nestled on 1½ acres of loveliness, is completely furnished in beautiful decor. Located ten minutes from Hartsfield Airport. The

---

5 Open all year; 6 Pets welcome; 7 Children welcome; 8 Tennis nearby; 9 Swimming nearby; 10 Golf nearby; 11 Skiing nearby; 12 May be booked through travel agent.

house is yours to enjoy. Twin beds for kids and king-sized bed for Mom and Dad. Ceiling fans, colored cable TV, VCR, central air, telephone, sitting room, bath, kitchen, and laundry room. Walking distance from park and tennis court. Ten minutes from mall and restaurants. Please, no smoking.

Hosts: Eddie and Beverly Moore
Rooms: 2 (SB) $85-100
Breakfast prepared by guests with food provided.
Credit Cards: none
Notes: 2 (2 weeks prior to stay), 5, 7, 8, 9, 10

The Pittman House

COMMERCE

The Pittman House B&B
81 Homer Road, 30529
(706) 335-3823

The Pittman House is located in the beautiful rolling hill of Northeast Georgia in the bustling town of historic Commerce. We invite you to come rock with us on the huge wraparound porch of our restored 1890s four-square Colonial house, which is furnished throughout with antiques that take you back to a quieter time and enhance the hominess of The Pittman House. Conveniently located within minutes of the University of Georgia, boating, historic Hurri-

cane Shoals, shopping, vineyards, restaurants, and more. Also, only an hour from Atlanta and its attractions. Three diamond AAA rating.

Hosts: Tome and Dot Tomberlin
Rooms: 4 (2PB; 2SB) $55-65
Full Breakfast
Credit Cards: A, B
Notes: 2, 5, 8, 9, 10, 11, 12

ETON

Ivy Inn
245 Fifth Avenue E., PO Box 406, 30724
(706) 517-0526; (800) 201-5477

Historic 1908 country home was one of the first homes built in Eton. Rocking-chair porches offer a break from a busy day shopping for antiques, clothes, or carpet; Eton is part of the carpet capital of the world. Hiking in Cohutta Wilderness or bicycling on the Inn's bikes refreshes the weary soul. In-room telephone and TV. Day trips to Atlanta, Chattanooga, and Ocoee River. Horses/stabling next door to the Inn. Restricted smoking.

Hosts: Gene and Juanita Twiggs
Rooms: 3 (PB) $87
Full Southern Breakfast
Credit Cards: A, B, C
Notes: 2, 5, 9, 10, 11 (water), 12

Ivy Inn

NOTES: Credit cards accepted: A Master Card; B Visa; C American Express; D Discover; E Diners Club; F Other; 2 Personal checks accepted; 3 Lunch available; 4 Dinner available;

FLOWERY BRANCH

Whitworth Inn

6593 McEver Road, 30542
(770) 967-2386; FAX (770) 967-2649

Contemporary country inn on five
wooded acres offers a relaxing atmosphere. Ten uniquely decorated guest
rooms with their own baths. Two guest
living rooms. Full, country breakfast
served in a large, sunlit dining room.
Meeting/party space available. Thirty
minutes northeast of Atlanta at Lake
Lanier. Nearby attractions and activities include boating, golf, beaches, and
water parks. Close to Road Atlanta and
Chateau Elen Winery/Golf Course. Easily accessible from major interstates.
Three diamond AAA rating.

Hosts: Ken and Christine Jonick
Rooms: 10 (PB) $55-70
Full Breakfast
Credit Cards: A, B, C
Notes: 2, 5, 7, 8, 9, 10, 12

GRIFFIN

Double Cabins Bed and Breakfast

3335 Jackson Road, 30223
(770) 227-6611

This National Register home was built
in 1842 in the Greek Revival Style char-
acteristic of Southern country homes.
The five bedroom home features an
original walnut staircase and gold leaf
cornice boards in the living room as well
as numerous additional accents of the
period. The doors throughout have their
original knobs and locks with brass
keys. The property was part of the Great
1823-1825 land purchase from the
Creek Indians and lies on the McIntosh
Trail. The propery included two cabin-
like structures known as "Double Cabins." Group tours of the house, museum,
and property can also be arranged by
appointment.

Hostess: Mrs. Douglas Hollberg
Rooms: 3 (2PB; 1SB)
Full Breakfast
Credit Cards: none
Notes: 2, 5, 7

HELEN

Chattahoochee Ridge Lodge and Cabins

PO Box 175, 500 Ridge Road, 30545
(706) 878-3144; (800) 476-8331
FAX (706) 878-4032

Alone on a woodsy mountain above a
waterfall, the Lodge has five new rooms
and suites (kitchens and fireplaces) with
private entrances, TV, air-conditioning,
free phones, and jacuzzi; plus double
insulation and back up solar for stew-
ards of the earth. In the lodge and cabins you'll like the quiet seclusion, large
windows, and deep-rock water. We'll
help you plan great vacation days. Decor includes wide-board knotty pine,
brass beds, full carpeting, and paddle fans.

Hosts: Mary and Bob Swift
Rooms: 5 + cabins (PB) $50-85
Credit Cards: A, B, C, D
Notes: 2, 5, 7, 8, 9, 10

---

5 Open all year; 6 Pets welcome; 7 Children welcome; 8 Tennis nearby; 9 Swimming nearby;
10 Golf nearby; 11 Skiing nearby; 12 May be booked through travel agent.

Habersham Hollow Bed and Breakfast and Cabins

Route 6, Box 6208, **Clarksville** 30523
(706) 754-5147; FAX (706) 754-1842

Nestled in the northeast Georgia mountains, this elegant country B&B features king beds, fireplace, private baths, and TVs in each room. Nearby on the secluded wooded grounds are cozy fireplace cabins with fully equipped kitchens, TV, and deck with BBQ grills where well-mannered pets are welcome.

Hosts: C.J. and Maryann Gibbons
Rooms: 4 (PB) $85-145
Full Breakfast
Credit Cards: A, B
Notes: 2, 5, 6, 8, 9, 10, 11

HEPHZIBAH

Into the Woods Bed and Breakfast

176 Longhorn Rd., 30815
Office: 11205 Country Club Road,
Waynesboro, PA 17268
(706) 554-1400; **Office** (717) 762-8525

Relax in a completely restored B&B built in the late 1800s. All guest rooms have firm, good beds to assure you a good, restful night. Guests can take a short drive to Augusta for a lovely Riverwalk along the Savannah River, or visit the restaurants and shops. You'll enjoy breakfast, in the morning, in our sunny dining room.

Hosts: Robert and Twila Risser
Rooms: 4 (2PB; 2SB) $65-85
Full Breakfast
Credit Cards: A, B, D
Notes: 2, 5, 7, 10, 12

PEACHTREE CITY

Everhill Manor

114 Kirton Turn, 30269
(770) 631-4369

Everhill Manor is located 40 minutes from the heart of Atlanta with its many attractions. Our Colonial style home offers antique furnishings in two large guest rooms, private or shared baths, and breakfast buffet in our dining room or on the screened porch overlooking the garden. Our unique community is noted for its 65 miles of recreational paths for walking, biking, or driving a golf cart to shopping areas, fishing ponds, playgrounds, or quiet parks beside the lake.

Hosts: Janet and David Hendry
Rooms: 2 (1PB; 1SB) $55-65
Full Buffet Breakfast
Credit Cards: none
Notes: 5, 7, 8, 9, 10

Goodbread Inn

NOTES: Credit cards accepted: A Master Card; B Visa; C American Express; D Discover; E Diners Club; F Other; 2 Personal checks accepted; 3 Lunch available; 4 Dinner available;

ST. MARYS

Goodbread Inn Bed and Breakfast

209 Osborne Street, 31558
(912) 882-7490

This 1875 Victorian inn is in the historic district of a quaint fishing village nine miles east of I-95, halfway between Jacksonville, FL, and Brunswick, GA. Each antique-filled room has its own bath, fireplace, ceiling fan, and air-conditioning. Restaurants and Cumberland Island ferry are within walking distance.

Hosts: Betty and George Krauss
Rooms: 4 (PB) $55-65 + tax
Full Breakfast
Credit Cards: none
Notes: 2, 5, 10, 12

SAUTEE

The Stovall House Country Inn and Restaurant

1526 Highway 225 N., 30571
(706) 878-3355

Our 1837 Victorian farmhouse, restored in 1983, is listed on the National Register of Historic Places. Located on 26 acres in the historic Sautee Valley, the Inn has views of the mountains in all directions. The recipient of several awards for its attentive restorations, the Inn is furnished with family antiques and decorated with hand-stenciling. The restaurant, open to the public, features regional cuisine prepared with a

fresh difference and served in an intimate, yet informal, setting. It's a country experience!

Host: Hamilton (Ham) Schwartz
Rooms: 5 (PB) $64-80
Continental Breakfast
Credit Cards: A, B
Notes: 2, 4, 5, 7, 8, 9, 10

SAVANNAH

Eliza Thompson House

5 West Jones Street, 31401
(912) 236-3620; (800) 348-9378;
FAX (912) 238-1920

Built in 1847, our elegant inn is in the heart of Savannah's historic district. Our 23 lovely guest rooms offer four poster beds, antiques, and private baths. Enjoy breakfast and evening wine and cheese in our beautiful courtyard, as well as desert after dinner in our parlor.

Hosts: Carol and Steve Day
Rooms: 23 (PB) $89-159
Extended Continental Breakfast
Credit Cards: A, B, C
Notes: 2, 5, 9, 10, 12

Joan's on Jones Bed and Breakfast

17 West Jones Street, 31401
(912) 234-3863; (800) 407-3863
FAX (912) 234-1455

In the heart of the historic district, two charming bed and breakfast suites grace the garden level of this three-story Victorian, private home. Each suite has a private entry, off-street parking, bedroom, sitting room, kitchen, bath, pri-

---

5 Open all year; 6 Pets welcome; 7 Children welcome; 8 Tennis nearby; 9 Swimming nearby; 10 Golf nearby; 11 Skiing nearby; 12 May be booked through travel agent.

vate phone, and cable TV. Note the original heart pine floors, period furnishings, and Savannah gray brick walls. Innkeepers Joan and Gary Levy, restauranters, live upstairs and invite you for a tour of their home if you're staying two nights or more.

Hosts: Joan and Gary Levy
Rooms: 2 suites (PB) $115-130
Continental Breakfast
Credit Cards: none
Notes: 2, 5, 6 (dogs in garden suite only), 7, 8, 9, 10, 12

Lion's Head Inn

120 E. Gaston Street, 31401
(912) 232-4580; (800) 355-5466;
FAX (912) 232-7422

The stately 19th century mansion is situated in a quiet neighborhood just north of picturesque Forsyth Park. This lovely 9,200 square-foot home is exquisitely appointed with four-poster beds, private baths, period furnishings, fireplaces, TVs, and telephones. Each morning enjoy a deluxe continental breakfast, and in the evening enjoy wine and cheese on the sweeping veranda over-

Lion's Head Inn

looking the marbled courtyard.

Hostess: Christy Dell'Orco
Rooms: 5 (PB) $90-170
Continental Deluxe Breakfast
Credit Cards: A, B, C, D
Notes: 2, 5, 7, 8, 9, 10, 12

SENOIA

Culpepper House Bed and Breakfast

35 Broad Street, 30276
(770) 599-8182

Step back 120 years to casual Victorian elegance at the Culpepper House. Enjoy a four-poster canopy bed next to a fireplace, with sounds of the night coming through the window. . . . Wake to a gourmet breakfast then take a tandem bike ride through the historic town, visit area shops and picturesque countryside, or just sit on the porch and rock. Only 30 minutes from Atlanta.

Hostess: Maggie Armstrong
Rooms: 3 (PB) $85
Full Gourmet Breakfast
Credit Cards: A, B, C
Notes: 2, 5, 6 (limited), 8, 9, 10, 12

THOMSON

1810 West Inn

254 N. Seymour Drive, 30824
(706) 595-3156; (800) 515-1810

Historic, restored farmhouse, circa 1810, and accompanying renovated country houses on twelve landscaped acres. All rooms have private baths, central air/heat, antique furnishings, and fireplaces. Enjoy the country kitchen,

1810 West Inn

screened veranda, strolling peacocks, and nature trails. Continental breakfast. Business retreats. Featured in *Country Inns* magazine. Convenient to I-20 and Augusta; 2 hours from Atlanta. AAA

Hostess: Virginia White
Rooms: 10 (PB) $60-79
Extended Continental Breakfast
Credit Cards: A, B, C, D, F
Notes: 2, 5, 8, 9, 10, 12

VILLA RICA

Twin Oaks Bed and Breakfast, Cottages, and Reservations

9565 E. Liberty Road, 30180
(770) 459-4374; (800) 459-4374

A uniquely intimate bed and breakfast located on a 23-acre farm only thirty minutes from Atlanta. There are two exquisite guest cottages ideal for honeymoons or celebrating anniversaries. There are also two private suites on the property. All accommodations have hot tubs or jacuzzis, fireplaces, private bathrooms, queen size beds, TV, VCR, refrigerators, microwaves, and coffee makers. There is a swimming pool on

the property, walking trails, horseback riding, and lots of exotic animals for feeding and viewing. Near Six Flags Over Georgia and the projected Gone With the Wind Theme Park.

Hosts: Earl and Carol Turner
Rooms: 2 suites; 2 cottages (PB) $85-120
Full Breakfast
Credit Cards: C
Notes: 2, 5, 9, 10, 12

WARM SPRINGS

Hotel Warm Springs

47 Broad Street, PO Box 351, 31830
(706) 655-2114; (800) 366-7616;
FAX (706) 655-2771

Relive history and the Roosevelt Era in our 1907 hotel, ice cream parlor, and gift shops. Authentically restored and beautifully decorated with Roosevelt furniture and family antiques. Featuring our cozy honeymoon suite with king bed, suspended canopy, Victorian antiques, red heart tub, gold fixtures, breakfast in bed, flowers, champagne, and chocolates. Our large living and dining room with Queen Anne furniture, Oriental rugs, and crystal teardrop chandelier is ideal for group meetings. Nestled in quaint Warm Springs Village—a shopper's paradise, home of FDR's Little White House, 14 miles from Callaway Gardens, and one hour from Atlanta.

Hostess: Geraldine (Gerrie) Thompson
Rooms: 14 (PB) $60-160
Southern Breakfast Feast
Credit Cards: A, B, C, D
Notes: 2, 5, 7, 8, 9, 10, 12

---

5 Open all year; 6 Pets welcome; 7 Children welcome; 8 Tennis nearby; 9 Swimming nearby; 10 Golf nearby; 11 Skiing nearby; 12 May be booked through travel agent.

HAWAII

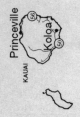

Hawaii

Pacific-Hawaii Bed and Breakfast and Vacation Rentals

99-1661 Aiea Heights Dr., **Aiea, Oahu** 96701
(808) 487-1228 or (808) 486-8838 (voice + FAX)
(800) 999-6026 (voice + FAX)
(808) 889-0500 (Big Island Hawaii phone)

Carefully selected and inspected 400 plus listings on all islands of Hawaii. From moderate to luxurious, we offer B&Bs, studios in private homes, cottages, homes, and fabulous estates. Oceanfront or hideaways. Get to know Hawaii as locals know it! From $55 for two guests to $1,000. Travel agents welcome.

Shipman House

HAWAII—HILO

Shipman House Bed and Breakfast Inn

131 Kaʻiulani Street, 96720
(808) 934-8002; (800) MAP-THIS

Gracious, unpretentious hospitality . . . Built in 1899 and renovated in 1996, Hilo's Shipman House is one of Hawaii's most unique bed and breakfast inns. The first Shipmans arrived in Hawaii in 1854 as Congregational missionaries. The hostess is Rev. Shipman's great-great-granddaughter. Located on the lush green side of Hawaii Island, the B&B overlooks a deep fern-lined gorge and is just five blocks to historic downtown Hilo. One guest room in the main house; two in the 1910 guesthouse. An expanded continental breakfast buffet on the lanai features local fruits, delicious breads, and more.

Hosts: Barbara Ann and Gary Andersen
Rooms: 3 (PB) $130
Continental Plus Breakfast
Credit Cards: A, B
Notes: 2, 5, 9, 10, 12

NOTES: Credit cards accepted: A Master Card; B Visa; C American Express; D Discover; E Diners Club; F Other; 2 Personal checks accepted; 3 Lunch available; 4 Dinner available; 5 Open all year; 6 Pets welcome; 7 Children welcome; 8 Tennis nearby; 9 Swimming nearby; 10 Golf nearby; 11 Skiing nearby; 12 May be booked through travel agent.

HAWAII—KAMUELA

Kamuela Inn

PO Box 1994, 96743
(808) 885-4243; (800) 555-8968;
FAX (808) 885-8857

Comfortable, cozy rooms and suites
with private baths, with or without
kitchenettes, and all with cable, color
television. Complimentary continental
breakfast served in our coffee lanai every morning. Situated in a quiet, peaceful setting just off Highway 19. Conveniently located near shops, retail outlets, banks, theaters, parks, tennis
courts, museums, restaurants, and post
office. The big island's famous white
sand beaches, golf courses, horseback
rides, and valley and mountain tours are
only minutes away.

Hostess: Carolyn Cascavilla
Rooms: 31 (PB) $54-165
Continental Breakfast
Credit Cards: A, B, C, D, E
Notes: 2, 5, 7, 8, 9, 10, 11, 12

HAWAII—NORTH KOHALA

Big Sky Ranch

99-1001 Aiea Heights Dr, Aiea, Oahu 96701
(808) 889-0500;
(808) 487-1228 (voice + FAX);
(808) 486-8838; (800) 999-6026 (voice + FAX)

North Kohala, the last frontier where
one still can encounter some of the old
Hawaii. It also is the God Coast of the
Big Island with ideal climates. Within
a short drive there are nice beaches, elegant resorts with great golf courses,
and some small, inexpensive, "hidden
away" courses only the locals know
about. There are many ancient Hawaiian sacred areas as also the early Ha-
waiians treasured North Kohala. The
expansive sky, with its millions of sparkling stars at night, is a rich source for
scientists to discover new worlds on top
of nearby Maunakea. We offer: At a
luxurious gated community with ten-
acre estates, a fabulous 7,000 square
foot family home, swimming pool, and
magnificent unobstructed ocean vews.
A one bedroom guest apartment with
complete kitchen, bath, TV, and king
bed. A short walk to the ocean (not a
swimming beach) and great hiking
trails.

Hostess: Doris Reichert
Rooms: 1 (PB) $100
Breakfast fixings included
Credit Cards: A, B
Notes: 2, 5, 7, 9, 10, 12

HAWAII—PA'AUILO

Sud's Acres Bed and Breakfast

PO Box 277, 43-1973 Paauilo Mauka Rd, 96776
(808) 776-1611 (voice and FAX); (800) 735-3262

Our cozy two-bedroom cottage, with
complete kitchen and microwave oven,
comfortably sleeps a family of five and
is situated on a Macadamia nut farm at
1800 foot elevation on the slopes of
Mauna Kea. In our main house we have
additional accomodations and wheelchair accessibility. We are 40 miles
north of Hilo airport, 20 miles from
Waimea, and 30 miles from some of

NOTES: Credit cards accepted: A Master Card; B Visa; C American Express; D Discover;
E Diners Club; F Other; 2 Personal checks accepted; 3 Lunch available; 4 Dinner available;

Hawaii's best beaches.

Hosts: "Suds" and Anita Suderman
Rooms: 3 (PB) $65
Continental Breakfast
Credit Cards: A, B, D, E
Notes: 5, 7, 9, 10, 12

KAUAI—KOLOA

Island Home

1707 Kelaukia Street, 96756
(808) 742-2839 (voice and FAX)

Enjoy Kauai's sunny south shore at Island Home in Poipu. Just minutes to walk to great snorkeling and swimming beaches, turtle watching, restaurants, and the beautiful Hyatt Regency. Our units offer private entrances, lanai or deck, TVs, VCRs, telephones, compact refrigerators, microwaves, beach and picnic gear with laundry facilities available. Queen- or king-size beds are offered. Inquire about special rates for those in ministry. Three night minimum.

Hosts: Michael and Gail Beeson
Rooms: 2 (PB) $80
Tropical Continental Breakfast
Credit Cards: none
Notes: 2 (and travelers'), 5, 8, 9, 10, 12

KAUAI—PRINCEVILLE

Hale 'Aha
"House of Gathering"

3875 Kamehameha Dr., P.O. Box 3370, 96722
(808) 826-6733; (800) 826-6733;
FAX (808) 826-9052

VACATION, HONEYMOON, or RETREAT in this peaceful resort setting on the golf course, overlooking the ocean and majestic mountains of the Garden Isle. On one side enjoy Hanalei, where "South Pacific" was filmed, with one beach after another leading you to the famous, lush, Napoli Coast hiking trails. Hale' Aha has been written about in many books and magazines, but only a brochure can tell it all. Enjoy bananas, papayas, and pineapple from your host's garden.

Hosts: Herb and Ruth Bockelman
Rooms: 2 + 2 suites (PB) $85-210
"More Than" Continental Breakfast
Credit Cards: A, B
Notes: 2, 5, 8, 9, 10, 12

MAUI—KULA

Elaine's Up Country Guest Rooms

2112 Noalae Road, 96790
(808) 878-6623; FAX (808) 878-2619

Quiet country setting. Splendid ocean and mountain views. All rooms have private baths, full kitchens, and sitting room privileges. Guests are welcome to cook breakfast or whatever meals they like. Next to our main house is a delightful cottage made to order for a family. One bedroom with queen-size bed and twin beds in the loft. Large kitchen. We ask that our guests do not smoke or drink.

Hosts: Elaine and Murray Gildersleeve
Rooms: 3 + a cottage (PB) $55-110 + tax
No Breakfast served
Credit Cards: F
Notes: 2, 5, 7, 9, 10, 12

---

5 Open all year; 6 Pets welcome; 7 Children welcome; 8 Tennis nearby; 9 Swimming nearby; 10 Golf nearby; 11 Skiing nearby; 12 May be booked through travel agent.

IDAHO

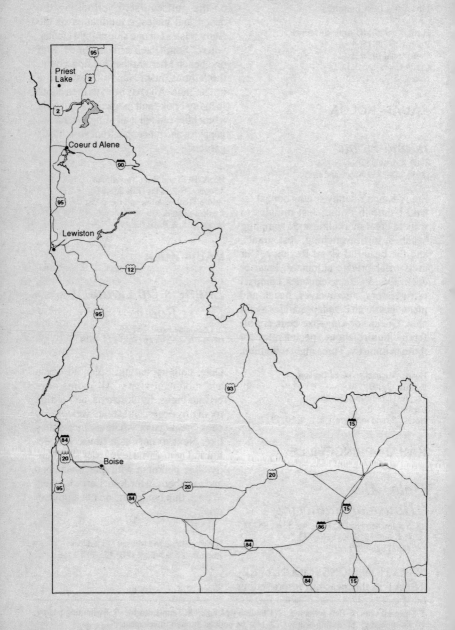

Idaho

BOISE

The J.J. Shaw House Bed and Breakfast Inn

1411 W. Franklin Street, 83702
(208) 344-8899; FAX (208) 344-6677

The J.J. Shaw House is a 1907 Queen Anne Victorian, fully restored and accented throughout with original leaded glass and interesting bay windows. Living area available for guests use include the parlor with fireplace, sitting room where a player piano awaits, sun porch, and formal dining room. Guest rooms include queen beds, phones, and air-conditioning. Located in the quiet, yet convenient north end of downtown Boise, within walking distance of fine restaurants and shops.

Hosts: Michael and Ruthie White
Rooms: 5 (PB) $79-109
Full Gourmet Breakfast
Credit Cards: A, B, D
Notes: 2 (local only), 5, 11

COEUR D'ALENE

Gregory's McFarland House Bed and Breakfast

601 Foster Avenue, 83814
(208) 667-1232

Surrender to the elegance of this award-winning historical home, circa 1905. The full breakfast is gourmet to the last crumb. Guests will be delighted by an ideal blending of beauty, comfort, and clean surroundings. Jerry Hulse, travel editor for *The Los Angeles Times* wrote, "Entering Gregory McFarland's House is like stepping back 100 years to an unhurried time when four posters were

Gregory's McFarland House

NOTES: Credit cards accepted: A Master Card; B Visa; C American Express; D Discover; E Diners Club; F Other; 2 Personal checks accepted; 3 Lunch available; 4 Dinner available; 5 Open all year; 6 Pets welcome; 7 Children welcome; 8 Tennis nearby; 9 Swimming nearby; 10 Golf nearby; 11 Skiing nearby; 12 May be booked through travel agent.

in fashion and lace curtains fluttered at the windows." Private baths, air-conditioning, non-smoking house. If planning a wedding, our resident minister and professional photographer are available to make your special day beautiful.

Hosts: Winifred, Carol, and Stephen Gregory
Rooms: 5 (PB) $85-125 + tax
Full Gourmet Breakfast
Credit Cards: A, B
Notes: 2, 5, 8, 9, 10, 11, 12

Katie's Wild Rose Inn

E. 5150 Couer d'Alene Lake Drive, 83814
(208) 765-WISH (9474) (voice and FAX)
Web site: http://www.dmi.net/idaho_bandb/

Looking through the pine trees to Lake Coeur d'Alene, Katie's Wild Rose Inn is a haven for the weary traveler. Only 6/10 mile from the public dock and beach, the inn has four cozy rooms, one with its own jacuzzi. Guests can relax in the family room beside the fireplace or enjoy a game of pool. A full breakfast is served on the deck or in the dining room where you can admire the view.

Hosts: Joisse and Lee Knowles
Rooms: 4 (2PB; 2SB) $55-95
Full Breakfast
Credit Cards: A, B
Notes: 2, 5, 8, 9, 10, 11

LEWISTON

Shiloh Rose
Bed and Breakfast

3414 Selway Drive, 83501
(208) 743-2482

The Shiloh Rose, decorated in warm,

country Victorian style, offers a spacious three-room suite as your home away from home. Lace curtains, fragrant potpourri and fresh roses in season invite you to linger. Have your morning coffee in the sitting room with a real wood-burning stove. Browse through the overflowing bookshelves, enjoy the TV/VCR ... or the grand piano. A complete gourmet breakfast is served in the dining room or on the deck overlooking the valley. The views are fantastic. Join us. You'll love it!

Hostess: Dorthy Mader
Rooms: 1 3-room suite (PB) $75 + tax
Full Breakfast
Credit Cards: A, B
Notes: 2, 5, 8, 9, 10, 11

PRIEST LAKE

Whispering Waters
Bed and Breakfast

HCR 5, Box 125 B, 83856
(208) 443-3229

Located on the secluded shores of Priest Lake's Outlet Bay. Just minutes away from golf course, hiking, cross-country skiing and snowmobiling trails, gift shops, resorts, and restaurants. Three guest rooms; each has private bath, sitting area with parlor stove, view, outside access, and covered patio. Early morning juice or coffee delivered to the rooms.

Hosts: Lana and Ray Feldman
Rooms: 3 (PB) $85
Full Breakfast
Credit Cards: A, B
Notes: 2, 5, 9, 10, 11 (cross country), 12

NOTES: Credit cards accepted: A Master Card; B Visa; C American Express; D Discover; E Diners Club; F Other; 2 Personal checks accepted; 3 Lunch available; 4 Dinner available;

Illinois

ALGONQUIN

Victorian Rose Garden Bed and Breakfast

314 Washington Street, 60102
(847) 854-9667; (888) 854-9667;
FAX (847) 854-3236

Built in 1886, the Victorian Rose Garden invites guests to relax on its wraparound porch, read by the fireplace, play the baby grand piano, and enjoy the old-fashioned barber corner. Bedrooms are individually decorated with antiques and collectibles. A delicious breakfast is served formally in the dining room. Nearby are golf courses, antiques, bike trail, restaurants, and dinner boat. Chicago is only one hour away. Non-smoking, non-alcoholic, animal-free residence. Let us pamper you!

Hosts: Don and Sherry Brewer
Rooms: 5 (3PB; 2SB) $55-135
Full Breakfast
Credit Cards: A, B, C
Notes: 2, 5, 7, 10, 12

ARCOLA

Curly's Corner Bed and Breakfast

425 E. Country Road 200 N., 61910
(217) 268-3352

This ranch-style, centrally air-conditioned farmhouse is located in the heart of a prairie farmland, quiet Amish community. Your hosts Warren and Maxine are dedicated to cordial hospitality and will gladly share information about the area and provide a suggested tour of Amish businesses. Curly's Corner has four lovely and comfortable bedrooms, queen-size beds, TVs, etc. In the morning enjoy a wonderful breakfast of homemade biscuits, fresh country sausage, bacon, eggs, etc.! Curly's Corner is one-half mile north of beautiful Rockome Gardens; also close to three universities and historical sites.

Hosts: Warren and Maxine Arthur
Rooms: 3 (2PB; 1SB) $50-60
Full Breakfast
Credit Cards: none
Notes: 2, 5, 7 (over 10), 8, 9, 10

---

5 Open all year; 6 Pets welcome; 7 Children welcome; 8 Tennis nearby; 9 Swimming nearby; 10 Golf nearby; 11 Skiing nearby; 12 May be booked through travel agent.

ILLINOIS

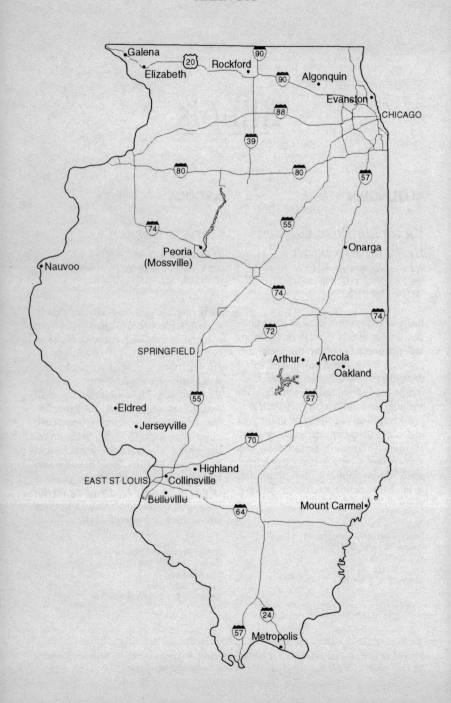

ARTHUR

Heart and Home

137 E. Illinois Street, 61911
(217) 543-2910

Heart of Illinois Amish country. Built in 1911, Victorian filled with warmth of oak floors and stained glass windows. Large front porch and second story sunporch for your relaxation. Three nice guest rooms; one with pull-out Murphy bed ideal for an additional guest. All rooms upstairs; we are not handicap accessible. Smoke and alcohol free. Two blocks from downtown. Central air. Open Thursdays, Fridays, and Saturdays, April through October.

Hosts: Don and Amanda Miller
Rooms: 3 (1PB; 2SB) $50-60
Full Breakfast
Credit Cards: none
Notes: 2, 8

BELLEVILLE

Swans Court Bed and Breakfast

421 Court Street, 62220
(618) 233-0779

Swans Court Bed and Breakfast is located in a Federal historic district. Built in 1883, the house was restored in 1995. The house, furnished in period antiques, reflects the gracious lifestyle of an earlier time without sacrificing modern amenities. Swans Court is within walking distance of shops, restaurants, and historical houses. Besides the many nearby attractions of Southwestern Illinois, it is an easy 20-minute drive to the recreational attractions of downtown St. Louis.

Hostess: Monty Dixon
Rooms: 4 (2PB; 2SB) $65-80
Full Breakfast
Credit Cards: A, B
Notes: 2, 5, 10, 12

Swans Court

CHICAGO

Amber Creek's Chicago Connection

1260 N. Dearborn, Chicago
Mail: PO Box 5, Galena, IL 61036
(800) 781-9530; FAX (815) 777-9476

A delightful one-bedroom apartment on the Gold Coast of Chicago in a quiet, secure building. Tastefully decorated with antiques and comfortable furniture. Spacious, light-filled living room with nice views, including the lake. Full kitchen and full bath. Romantic bedroom with king bed, down quilts, and extra pillows. Linens and towels provided. Walk to lake, Water Tower, and

---

NOTES: Credit cards accepted: A Master Card; B Visa; C American Express; D Discover; E Diners Club; F Other; 2 Personal checks accepted; 3 Lunch available; 4 Dinner available; 5 Open all year; 6 Pets welcome; 7 Children welcome; 8 Tennis nearby; 9 Swimming nearby; 10 Golf nearby; 11 Skiing nearby; 12 May be booked through travel agent.

Michigan Avenue shopping. Half block to airport limousine service, and public transportation. Parking garage next door. Ideal for one couple. Queen-sized futon provides sleeping for additional guests.

Hosts: Kate Freeman
Rooms: 1 (PB) $95-125
Continental Breakfast
Credit Cards: A, B, C, D, E
Notes: 2, 3, 4, 7, 9, 12

COLLINSVILLE

Maggie's Bed and Breakfast
2102 N. Keebler, 62234
(618) 344-8283

Beautiful, quiet, country setting just minutes from downtown St. Louis. Near hospitals, restaurants, and shopping. Cooking with natural ingredients. Antiques and art objects collected in worldwide travels. Games, cable TV, and hot tub with terrycloth robes and house slippers.

Hostess: Maggie Leyda
Rooms: 5 (4PB; 1SB) $35-80
Full Breakfast
Credit Cards: none
Notes: 2, 5, 6, 7 (by arrangement), 8, 9, 10, 12

ELDRED

Bluffdale Vacation Farm
Route 1, 62027
(217) 983-2854

Our new hideaway cottage in the woods is secluded and luxurious. Soak in the whirl pool while you watch the sun set or gaze at the stars, then pop on a robe and enter your room where the fireplace is blazing. Located at the base of the bluffs, you'll have 200 acres of woodlands to explore by foot, horse, or boat. Whatever your recreational and culinary desires, your find them at Bluffdale in the warmth and hospitality of your hosts.

Hosts: Bill and Lindy Hobson
Rooms: 8 (PB) $65-82
Full Breakfast
Credit Cards: none
Notes: 2, 3, 4, 5, 7, 9, 10, 12

Bluffdale Vacation Farm

EVANSTON

The Margarita European Inn
1566 Oak Avenue, 60201
(847) 869-2273; FAX (847) 869-2353

The romantic at heart will truly enjoy this charming European-style inn located next door to Chicago in Evanston, the home of Northwestern University.

NOTES: Credit cards accepted: A Master Card; B Visa; C American Express; D Discover; E Diners Club; F Other; 2 Personal checks accepted; 3 Lunch available; 4 Dinner available;

Relax in the grand parlor with breakfast and the morning paper or in the roof garden at sunset. Explore the numerous antique and specialty shops nearby. On rainy days, curl up with a novel from the wood-paneled English library, or indulge in a culinary creation from our award-winning regional Italian ristorante, Va Pensiero. Facilities for weddings and meetings are also available.

Hosts: Barbara and Tim Gorham
Rooms: 40 (16PB; 34SB) $65-115
Continental Breakfast
Credit Cards: A, B, C
Notes: 2, 3, 4, 5, 7, 8, 9, 10, 12

GALENA

Amber Creek's Eagle's Nest

PO Box 5, 61036
(800) 781-9530; FAX (815) 777-9476

A quaint, charming Federal brick cottage built in 1842 and tucked into a private wooded hillside in Galena's historic district, within walking distance of shops and restaurants. It has been faithfully restored and furnished with antiques of the period. Living room with fireplace, master bedroom with queen bed, second bedroom with double bed. Fully equipped kitchen, bath with shower and double whirlpool, TV, stereo, deck, and grill. Crib available. Linens and towels provided. Perfect for history and antique buffs and those who appreciate authenticity. Ideal for one couple, but will also comfortably accommodate two couples or a small family.

Hostess: Kate Freeman
Rooms: $99-159 per night
Continental Breakfast
Credit Cards: A, B, C, D, E
Notes: 2, 5, 6, 7, 12

Avery Guest House

606 S. Prospect Street, 61036
(815) 777-3883

This Pre-Civil War home located near Galena's main shopping and historic buildings is a homey refuge after a day of exploring. Enjoy the view from our porch swing, feel free to watch TV, or join a table game. Sleep soundly on comfortable queen beds. Our delicious full breakfast is served in our sunny dining room with a bay window overlooking the valley. Mississippi riverboats nearby.

Hosts: Gerry and Armon Lamparelli
Rooms: 3 (1PB; 2SB) $65-85
Full Breakfast
Credit Cards: A, B, D
Notes: 2, 5, 8, 9, 10, 11

Avery Guest House

---

5 Open all year; 6 Pets welcome; 7 Children welcome; 8 Tennis nearby; 9 Swimming nearby; 10 Golf nearby; 11 Skiing nearby; 12 May be booked through travel agent.

Belle Aire Mansion Guest House

11410 Route 20 West, 61036
(815) 777-0893

Belle Aire Mansion guest house is a pre-Civil War Federal home surrounded by eleven well-groomed acres that include extensive lawns, flowers, and a block-long, tree-lined driveway. We do our best to make our guests feel they are special friends.

Hosts: Jan and Lorraine Svec
Rooms: 5 (PB) $70-155
Full Breakfast
Credit Cards: A, B, D
Notes: 2, 7, 8, 10, 12

Bielenda's Mars Avenue Guest Home

515 Mars Avenue, 61036
(815) 777-2808

Bielenda's Mars Avenue Guest Home was built in 1855. It is a Federal style home in the historic district of Galena. Three guest suites with private baths. Country and antiques throughout the home. The unique customized stenciling adds a special touch. Fireplace in livingroom, and large porch with swing Breakfast is full and plenty. Coffee served to guest rooms an hour before breakfast. Cookies and desserts are available in afternoon and evening.

Hosts: Joanne and Michael Bielenda
Rooms: 3 (PB) $85-95
Full Breakfast
Credit Cards: A, B, D
Notes: 2, 5

Brierwreath Manor

Brierwreath Manor Bed and Breakfast

216 N. Bench Street, 61036
(815) 777-0608

Brierwreath Manor, circa 1884, is just one block from Galena's Main Street and has a dramatic and inviting wrap-around porch that beckons to you after a hard day. The house is furnished in an eclectic blend of antique and early American. You'll not only relax but feel right at home. Two suites offer gas-log fireplaces. Central air-conditioning, ceiling fans, and cable TV add to your enjoyment.

Hosts: Mike and Lyn Cook
Rooms: 3 (PB) $85-105
Full Breakfast
Credit Cards: none
Notes: 2, 5, 8, 9, 10, 11

Forget-Me-Not Bed and Breakfast

1467 N. Elizabeth Scales Mound Road,
Elizabeth 61028
(815) 858-3744 (voice and FAX; call first)

Each guest room features a queen-size bed, private bath, patio, and air-condi-

---

NOTES: Credit cards accepted: A Master Card; B Visa; C American Express; D Discover; E Diners Club; F Other; 2 Personal checks accepted; 3 Lunch available; 4 Dinner available;

tioning and heat control. Rooms are spacious and romantically decorated to suit any occasion . . . birthdays, honeymoons, anniversaries, etc. Relax in a large comfortable great room decorated with imported German furnishings. Gaze at deer and turkeys from your guest room window overlooking miles of countryside. Fifteen minutes from historic Galena and Apple Canyon Lake. Five minutes from Eagle Ridge Territory. Very scenic routes.

Hosts: Christa and Richard Grunert
Rooms: 3 (PB) $65-85
Full Breakfast
Credit Cards: A, B
Notes: 2, 5, 7 (12 and older), 8, 9, 10, 11

Forget-Me-Not Bed and Breakfast

Park Avenue Guest House

208 Park Avenue, 61036
(815) 777-1075

1893 Queen Anne Painted Lady. Wraparound screened porch, gardens, and gazebo for summer. Fireplace and opulent Victorian Christmas in winter. One suite sleeps three, and there are three antique-filled guest rooms, all with queen-size beds and fireplaces. Located in quiet residential area, it is only a short walk to Grant Park or across footbridge to Main Street shopping and restaurants.

Hosts: John and Sharon Fallbacher
Rooms: 4 (PB) $70-105
Hearty Continental Breakfast
Credit Cards: A, B, D
Notes: 2, 5, 9, 10, 11

Pine Hollow Inn

4700 N. Council Hill Road, 61036
(815) 777-1071

Pine Hollow is located on a secluded 120 acre Christmas tree farm just one mile from Main Street Galena. Roam around the grounds and enjoy the wildlife or simply put your feet up, lean back and enjoy the country from our front porch. We provide all the comforts of home in a beautiful country setting. Each of our rooms is decorated in a country style with four poster queen-size beds, fireplaces, and private bath. Whirlpool bath suites are available.

Hosts: Sally and Larry Priske
Rooms: 5 (PB) $75-115
Continental Breakfast
Credit Cards: A, B, D
Notes: 2, 5, 8, 9, 10, 11, 12

HIGHLAND

Tibbetts House Bed and Breakfast

801 Ninth Street, 62249
(618) 654-4619; FAX (618) 654-8355

Higland, known as "Neu-Schweizerland," is located just 30 minutes east of St. Louis. The inn was built around the turn of the century and is close to the town square, stores, shops, and restaurants. In the square is a gazebo where festivals and music concerts are held in the summer. At Christmastime, the square and gazebo are decorated for the season. Points of interest include Latzer Homestead, Lindendale Park/Fairgrounds, Wicks Organ Company, and other fascinating landmarks. Each guest room is uniquely decorated. Smoking only on the deck and no alcoholic beverages permitted.

Hostess: Ruth Ann Ernst
Rooms: 5 (3PB; 2SB) $59-69
    ($40 business rate Sun. eve to Thurs. eve)
Hearty Continental Breakfast
Credit Cards: A, B, C
Notes: 2, 5, 8, 9, 10

JERSEYVILLE

The Homeridge Bed and Breakfast

1470 North State Street, 62052
(618) 498-3442

Beautiful, warm, brick 1867 Italianate Victorian private home on 18 acres in a comfortable, country atmosphere. Drive through stately iron gates and pine tree-lined driveway to 14-room historic estate of Senator Theodore Chapman. Expansive pillared front porch; hand-carved, curved stairway to spacious guest rooms and third floor. 20' by 40' swimming pool. Central air-conditioning. Located between Springfield, IL, and St. Louis, MO.

Hosts: Sue and Howard Landon
Rooms: 4 (PB) $65
Full Breakfast
Credit Cards: A, B, C
Notes: 2, 5, 7 (over 14), 8, 9 (on grounds), 10

METROPOLIS

Park Street House

310 Park Street, 62960
(618) 524-5966; (800) 524-5916

Graced with original oak woodwork, antiques, and private collections, each room has unique character. This circa 1910 home is ideally located in a small rivertown within walking distance to shops, restaurants, riverfront and the Superman museum. Minutes away from Fort Massac State Park, the American Quilt Museum, antique shops, and many scenic parks with hiking trails. Enjoy breakfast in the dining room or on the veranda overlooking Washington Park. Resident, bent willow furniture craftsman.

Hosts: Ron and Melodee Thomas
Rooms: 2 (PB) $35-65
Full Breakfast
Credit Cards: A, B
Notes: 2, 5, 7, 8, 10

MOUNT CARMEL

The Poor Farm Bed and Breakfast

Poor Farm Road, 62863
(618) 262-HOME (4663); (800) 646-FARM (3276); FAX (618) 262-8199

From 1857 to 1949 the Wabash Country Poor Farm served as home for the homeless. Today the Poor Farm B&B is a home for the traveler who enjoys a warm friendly atmosphere and a gracious glimpse of yesteryear. Located

---

NOTES: Credit cards accepted: A Master Card; B Visa; C American Express; D Discover; E Diners Club; F Other; 2 Personal checks accepted; 3 Lunch available; 4 Dinner available;

next to a 25-acre park with a well-stocked lake; within walking distance from perhaps the finest 18-hole municipal golf course in Illinois; and a 15-minute drive lands you in the spectacular 270-acre Beall Woods Conservation Area and Nature Preserve!

Hosts: Liz and John Stelzer
Rooms: 5 (2 suites and 3 doubles) (PB) $49-89
Full Country Breakfast
Credit Cards: A, B, C, D
Notes: 2, 3 and 4 (for groups of 10-30), 5, 7, 8, 9, 10, 12

NAUVOO

Mississippi Memories Bed and Breakfast
1 Riverview Terrace, 62354
(217) 453-2771

Located on the banks of the Mississippi, this gracious home offers peaceful lodging and elegantly served, all homemade, full breakfast. Each room features fresh fruit and flowers. In quiet, wooded surroundings, it's just two miles from historic Nauvoo with 30 restored Mormon, era homes and shops. Two decks offer spectacular sunsets, drifting barges, bald eagle watching, piano, two fireplaces, and library. AAA three-diamond rated. No smoking, alcohol, or pets will interrupt you stay.

Hosts: Marge and Dean Starr
Rooms: 4 (2 PB; 2 SB) $59-89
Full Breakfast
Credit Cards: A, B
Notes: 2, 5, 10

OAKLAND

Johnson's Country Home Bed and Breakfast
109 E. Main Street, 61943
(217) 346-3274

Located amidst Lincoln Land and Amish Country in the historic town of Oakland, standing on the corner of Main and Hazel. Reece and June Johnson bought this sadly neglected property in 1970 and began extensive renovation. Today it is again a lovely home. Listed in the Coles County Register of Historic Places. "When you visit our home you will hear about the furnishings, the bridal staircase, and the rich history of each room."

Hostess: June Johnson
Rooms: 2 (SB) $45
Continental Breakfast
Credit Cards: none
Notes: 2, 7, 8, 9, 10

ONARGA

Dairy on the Prairie
RR #2, Box 185, 60955-9505
(815) 683-2774

Among miles of corn and soybean fields

on God's prairie is this recently remodeled homestead that has been "in the family" for 103 years. (1892) Two tall silos and Holstein cows await you at the modern dairy/grain family farm. Enjoy their piano, organ, or keyboard along with hearty food, "down on the farm" hospitality, and a Christian atmosphere.

Hosts: Kenneth and Martha Redeker
Rooms: 3 (SB) $40-60
Full Breakfast (Continental on request)
Credit Cards: none
Notes: 2, 5, 7, 8, 9, 10

PEORIA

Old Church House Inn Bed and Breakfast
1416 East Mossville Road, **Mossville** 61552
(309) 579-2300

Come take sanctuary in our lovingly restored 1869 "country church." Enjoy afternoon tea curled up by a wood-burning fire or on a bench among a riot of garden flowers. Nestled on Peoria's north side, the Inn combines warm elegance, comfort, and pampering ameni-

ties with turn-of-the-century splendor.

Hosts: Dean and Holly Ramseyer and Family
Rooms: 2 (1PB; 1SB) $69-99
Gourmet Continental Plus Breakfast
Credit Cards: A, B
Notes: 2, 5, 8, 9, 10, 11, 12

ROCKFORD

The Barn of Rockford
6786 Guilford Road, 61107
(815) 395-8535

Come experience country living within the city limits of Illinois' second largest city. We are just minutes from a wide variety of shopping, fine dining, and one of the Midwest's best selections of antiques. Relax and explore our 110-year-old restored and converted barn. Enjoy a walk through the perrenial gardens or a swim in the indoor pool. Then start your day with a sure-to-delight breakfast!

Hosts: Ken and Karen Sharp
Rooms: 4 (1PB; 3SB) $65-95
Full Breakfast
Credit Cards: A, B
Notes: 2, 5, 8, 9, 10, 11

Dairy on the Prairie

Indiana

AUBURN

Hill Top Country Inn

1733 County Road 28, 46706
(219) 281-2111

The Hill Top Country Inn offers a quiet and beautiful setting with country porches, wicker furniture, walking areas, small fish pond with fountain, and distinctive bed chambers and sitting room. Our rooms are decorated with a variety of quilts, stenciling, country antiques, a formal dining room, and farm kitchen with an old fashioned cook stove. Places to visit in the area include antique shops, car museum, lakes, and parks.

Hosts: Chuck and Becky Derrow
Rooms: 4 (1PB; 3SB) $45-60
Full Breakfast
Credit Cards: none
Notes: 2, 5, 7, 12

Yawn to Dawn B&B

211 W. 5th Street, 46706
(219) 925-2583; FAX (219) 927-1202

Enjoy the friendly atmosphere of a 1900s home decorated with touches of antiques and collectibles. Within the Auburn area you'll find the Auburn Cord Duesenberg Museum, The National Auto and Trucks Railroad and Art Museums, shopping malls, theaters, Pokagon State Park, fine dining, golf courses, and a beautiful children's zoo, all located five to 30 minutes from Yawn to Dawn. Whether traveling I-69 or the IL/IN/OH toll road, Yawn to Dawn is your place to rest.

Hosts: Don and Shirley Quick
Rooms: 3 (SB) $45
Full Breakfast
Credit Cards: none
Notes: 2, 5, 8, 9, 10, 11

BRISTOL

Tyler's Place

19560 State Route 120, 46507
(219) 848-7145

Tyler's Place is located in the heart of Amish country. Hoosier hospitality, on a 27-hole golf course, water garden, hot tub, air conditioning, and full breakfast. Enjoy a back-roads tour of Amish country. Three miles from I80-90 toll road and 14 miles from the Shipshewana Flea Market.

Hostess: Esther Tyler
Rooms: 4 (2PB; 2SB) $50-65
Full Breakfast
Credit Cards: A, B
Notes: 2, 5, 7, 8, 9, 10, 11

5 Open all year; 6 Pets welcome; 7 Children welcome; 8 Tennis nearby; 9 Swimming nearby; 10 Golf nearby; 11 Skiing nearby; 12 May be booked through travel agent.

INDIANA

COVINGTON

Green Gables Bed and Breakfast

504 Fancy Street, 47932
(317) 783-7164

Covington's first bed and breakfast offers three guest rooms, each with private bath, including the spacious loft with two queen-size beds. Each room has a television; the entire house is air-conditioned. Home-cooked breakfasts are served by the private in-ground pool or by one of two fireplaces in this hilltop home near I-74 in western Indiana. Only five miles from Indiana's finest steakhouse. Art Fest in May and Apple Fest in October; both are held on the courthouse lawn.

Hosts: Bill and Marsha Wilkinson
Rooms: 3 (PB) $65 + tax
Full Breakfast
Credit Cards: A, B, C
Notes: 2, 5, 8, 9, 10

CRAWFORDSVILLE

Sugar Creek Queen Anne Bed and Breakfast

901 W. Market, Box 726, 47933
(317) 362-4095; (800) 392-6293

Sugar Creek's decor is Victorian with a French Provincial touch. The turn-of-the-century home has two guest rooms with private baths and a honeymoon suite complete with a private sitting room and a private bath. Behind the house is a beautiful rose garden and a fourth guest room with private bath and a jacuzzi and fitness center. The house has been newly remodeled with originality and creativity. Sugar Creek Bed and Breakfast is a member of the Indiana Bed and Breakfast Association. No smoking or alcohol permitted in the building.

Hosts: Mary Alice and Hal Barbee
Rooms: 4 (PB) $55
Full Breakfast
Credit Cards: A, B
Notes: 2, 5, 7, 8, 9, 10, 12

FRANKLIN

Oak Haven Bed and Breakfast

4975N Hurricane Road, 46131-9519
(317) 535-9491

A 1913 home nestled among stately trees that give a feeling of tranquillity

---

NOTES: Credit cards accepted: A Master Card; B Visa; C American Express; D Discover; E Diners Club; F Other; 2 Personal checks accepted; 3 Lunch available; 4 Dinner available; 5 Open all year; 6 Pets welcome; 7 Children welcome; 8 Tennis nearby; 9 Swimming nearby; 10 Golf nearby; 11 Skiing nearby; 12 May be booked through travel agent.

to our country setting. Beautifully decorated rooms, family keepsakes, and oak woodwork throughout our "haven." Play the player piano or relax on the old porch swing. Perfect get-away for those with romance in their hearts or peaceful seclusion on their minds. Full country breakfast is served. Easy to find and 25 minutes south of Indianapolis. Close to shopping and golf. Come experience our country hospitality!

Hosts: Alan and Brenda Smith
Rooms: 4 (3PB; 1SB) $45-70
Full Breakfast
Credit Cards: A, B
Notes: 2, 5, 7, 10

Indian Creek Bed and Breakfast

GOSHEN

Indian Creek Bed and Breakfast

20300 County Road 18, 46526
(219) 875-6606; FAX (219) 875-3968

Come and enjoy our newly built country Victorian home in the middle of Amish country. It is decorated with family antiques. Walk back to the woods or sit on the deck to watch for deer. Also enjoy the great room, game room, and family room. Full breakfast. Children welcome. Handicap accessible.

Hosts: Herman and Shirley Hochstetler
Rooms: 4 (PB) $65
Full Breakfast
Credit Cards: A, B, D
Notes: 2, 5, 7, 9, 10, 12

Coterie Bed and Breakfast

66083 State Road 15, 46526
(219) 533-8961

You will find us just two miles south of Goshen College and one hour's drive south of Notre Dame. We are also near the Shipshewana World's Famous Flea Market and clost to Amish Acres. We have two large bedrooms with private baths. One bedroom overlooks our backyard which is home to Canadian geese and ducks. We have air-conditioned rooms summer and a fireplace for winter evenings. We serve a full breakfast in our formal dining room.

Hosts: Dean and Kathy Sheeley
Rooms: 2 (PB) $50 + tax
Full Breakfast
Credit Cards: none
Notes: 2, 5, 7, 8, 9, 10, 11

Timberidge Bed and Breakfast

16801 State Route #4, 46526
(219) 533-7133

The Austrian chalet, white pine log home is nestled in the beauty of the quiet woods, just two miles from Goshen and near many local points of interest. Our guests enjoy the privacy of a master

NOTES: Credit cards accepted: A Master Card; B Visa; C American Express; D Discover; E Diners Club; F Other; 2 Personal checks accepted; 3 Lunch available; 4 Dinner available;

suite. A path through the woods is frequented by birds, squirrels, and deer. Nearby are Amish farms where field work is done by horse drawn equipment. Timberidge offers the best of city and country—close to town, yet removed to the majestic beauty of the woods that evokes a love of nature and a reverence for God's creation. Air-conditioning and TV.

Hosts: Edward and Donita Brookmyer
Rooms: 1 (PB) $60-70
Continental Breakfast
Credit Cards: none
Notes: 2

HUNTINGTON

Purviance House
Bed and Breakfast
326 South Jefferson Street, 46750
(219) 356-4218

Built in 1859, this beautiful home is on the National Register of Historic Places. It features a winding, cherry staircase, ornate ceilings, unique fireplaces; and parquet floors and has been lovingly restored and decorated with antiques and period furnishings to create a warm, inviting atmosphere. Amenities include TV in rooms, snacks, beverages, kitchen privileges, and library. Near recreational areas with swimming, boating, hiking, and bicycling. Historic tours available. One-half hour from Fort Wayne; two hours from Indianapolis.

Hosts: Bob and Jean Gernand
Rooms: 4 (2PB; 2SB) $40-65
Full Breakfast
Credit Cards: A, B, D
Notes: 2, 5, 7, 8, 9, 10, 12

INDIANAPOLIS

Carriage House
Bed and Breakfast
6440 N. Michigan Road, 46268
(317) 255-2276 (voice and FAX)

Relax and enjoy all the comforts of home in your own private suite. Located within 15 to 20 minutes of most Indianapolis events. Can accommodate groups of eight. Upstairs suite includes large whirlpool bath. Our facilities are smoke free and, please, no alcohol on the premises.

Hosts: David and Sue Wilson
Rooms: 2 (PB) $65-200
Full Breakfast
Credit Cards: none
Notes: 2, 5, 10

The Old Northside Bed and Breakfast

The Old Northside
Bed and Breakfast
1340 N. Alabama Street, 46202
(317) 635-9123; (800) 635-9127 reservations only; FAX (317) 635-9243

An 1885 luxurious Victorian mansion in historic downtown, convenient to I-

---

5 Open all year; 6 Pets welcome; 7 Children welcome; 8 Tennis nearby; 9 Swimming nearby;
10 Golf nearby; 11 Skiing nearby; 12 May be booked through travel agent.

65, I-70, and city attractions. The city's finest example of Romanesque Revival architecture with an elegant European turn-of-the-century decor. Themed rooms with jacuzzi tubs in private baths, two with fireplaces. Exercise room, conference room, and corporate services. A personal coffee service delivered to your room before your full gourmet breakfast, complimentary snack, and exceptional service.

Hostess: Susan Berry
Rooms: 5 (PB) $85-145
Full Gourmet Breakfast with beverage service
Credit Cards: A, B, C, D
Notes: 2, 5, 8, 9, 10, 12

KNIGHTSTOWN

Old Hoosier House
Bed and Breakfast

7601 S. Greensboro Pike, 46148
(317) 345-2969; (800) 775-5315

Central Indiana's first and favorite country bed and breakfast located in historic Knightstown, midway between Indianapolis and Richmond. Ideally situated for sightseeing and shopping Indiana's "Antique Alley." Golf on the adjoining eighteen hole Royal Highlands golf course. Golf package available. Handicap accessible. Member of Indiana Bed and Breakfast Association and American Historic Inn, Inc.

Hosts: Tom Lewis and Jean Lewis
Rooms: 4 (PB) $60-70 + tax
Full Breakfast
Credit Cards: none
Notes: 2, 5, 7, 8, 9, 10, 12

LAOTTO

Tea Rose
Bed and Breakfast

7711 E. 500 South, 46763
(219) 693-2884

Enjoy a home-style breakfast on the spacious deck while watching the birds. Our air-conditioned country log home features a large great room, comfortable bedroom, and front porch. Short drive to St. Park, zoo, Auburn Cord Dusenberg Museum, and Shipshewanna. Take a country drive to a quiet and more serene lifestyle. Stop and smell the roses or sit on the porch awhile.

Hosts: Adrian and Anne Ledger
Rooms: 1 (PB) $55
Full Breakfast
Credit Cards: none
Notes: 2, 5, 7, 9, 10

LEESBURG

Prairie House
Bed and Breakfast

495E 900N, 46538
(219) 658-9211 (voice and FAX)

Come enjoy a peaceful farm atmosphere. Four tastefully decorated rooms with air, TV, VCR, and fans available. Close to Grace College, Wagon Wheel Playhouse, Shipshewana Flea Market, Amish Acres, antique browsing, the Old Bay Factory at Goshen, swimming, skiing, boating, and golfing. Excellent dining in the area. Tours of the farm available. Prepare to be pampered!

Hosts: Everett and Marie Tom
Rooms: 4 (2PB; 2SB) $55-65
Full Breakfast
Credit Cards: A, B
Notes: 2, 5, 7, 8, 9, 10

Schussler House

MADISON

Schussler House B&B

514 Jefferson Street, 47250
(812) 273-2068; (800) 392-1931

Experience the quiet elegance of a circa 1849 Federal/Greek Revival home tastefully combined with today's modern amenities. In Madison's historic district, antique shops, historic sites, restaurants, and churches are within a pleasant walk. This gracious home offers spacious rooms decorated with antiques and reproductions and carefully selected fabrics and wall coverings. A sumptuous breakfast in the sun-filled dining room begins your day.

Hosts: Judy and Bill Gilbert
Rooms: 3 (PB) $90 + tax (10%)
Full Breakfast
Credit Cards: A, B, D
Notes: 2, 5, 8, 9, 10, 11, 12

METAMORA

The Thorpe House Country Inn

PO Box 36, 19049 Clayborne Street, 47030
(317) 647-5425

Visit the Thorpe House in historic Metamora where the steam engine still brings passenger cars and the grist mill still grinds cornmeal. Spend a relaxing evening in this 1840 canal town home. Rooms are tastefully furnished with antiques and country accessories. Enjoy a hearty breakfast before visiting more than 100 shops in this quaint village. Our family-style dining room is also open to the public.

Hosts: Mike and Jean Owens
Rooms: 4 + 2 room suite (PB) $70-125
Full Breakfast
Credit Cards: A, B, C, D
Notes: 2, 3, 6, 7, 10, 12

MIDDLEBURY

Bee Hive B&B

Box 1191, 46540
(219) 825-5023 (voice and FAX)

Come visit Amish country and enjoy Hoosier hospitality. The Bee Hive is a two-story, open floor plan with exposed, hand-sawed, red oak beams and

Bee Hive Bed and Breakfast

5 Open all year; 6 Pets welcome; 7 Children welcome; 8 Tennis nearby; 9 Swimming nearby; 10 Golf nearby; 11 Skiing nearby; 12 May be booked through travel agent.

a loft. Enjoy our collection of antique farm machinery and other collectibles. Snuggle under handmade quilts and wake to the smell of freshly baked muffins. A guest cottage is available. Be one of many of our return guests, and become a friend.

Hosts: Herb and Treva Swarm
Rooms: 4 (1PB; 3SB) $52-70
Full Breakfast
Credit Cards: A, B
Notes: 2, 5, 7, 8, 9, 10, 11

The Country Victorian

435 South Main Street, 46540
(219) 825-2568

Come celebrate 100 years of lovely Victorian living. Our large home is a fully updated Victorian with lots of charm and original style. Located in the heart of Amish country, relax on the porch and watch buggies drive by or sit in the hot tub in our old fashioned garden. In colder months, sit by the fireplace to chat or curl up with a good book. We offer evening refreshments and full breakfasts. Get pampered and experience the loving family atmosphere where children are a pleasure! Hot tub and honeymoon suite with jacuzzi. Bicycle rental. Special packages available. Very accessible to Indiana's toll road (I-80/90) and close to Shipshewana. Other local attractions include Amish-style restaurants and crafters, community festivals, University of Notre Dame, and Goshen College.

Hosts: Mark and Becky Potterbaum
Rooms: 5 (PB) $60-105
Full Breakfast
Credit Cards: A, B, D
Notes: 5, 6 (limited), 7, 8, 10, 11, 12

A Laber of Love Bed and Breakfast by Lori

11030 CR 10, 46540
(219) 825-7877

Cape Cod home located in northern Indiana Amish farm country on three acres, two of which are wooded. Screened-in gazebo in woods is ideal for quiet time or just relaxing. Queen-size beds and private baths. Common game/sitting room available for guests use. Air-conditioned. (Guest rooms are located upstairs.) Close to large flea market open from May to October on Tuesdays and Wednesdays. Lots of shopping in Middlebury and Shipshewana. Home-baked cinnamon rolls highlight continental breakfast. Smoke free.

Hostess: Lori Laber
Rooms: 2 (PB) $55
Continental Breakfast
Credit Cards: none
Notes: 2, 5, 10, 12

Yoder's Zimmer mit Frühstück Haus

PO Box 1396, 504 S. Main, 46540
(219) 825-2378

We enjoy sharing our Amish-Mennonite heritage in our spacious Crystal Valley home. The rooms feature handmade quilts and antiques. Antiques and collectibles can be seen throughout the home. Three of our rooms can accommodate families. There are several common rooms available for relaxing, reading, TV, games, or socializing. Facilities are also available for pastor-elder retreats. Air-conditioned, play-

---

NOTES: Credit cards accepted: A Master Card; B Visa; C American Express; D Discover; E Diners Club; F Other; 2 Personal checks accepted; 3 Lunch available; 4 Dinner available;

ground, swimming pool.

Hosts: Wilbur and Evelyn Yoder
Rooms: 5 (SB) $52.50
Full Breakfast
Credit Cards: A, B
Notes: 2, 5, 7, 8, 9, 10, 11, 12

MIDDLETOWN

Country Rose
Bed and Breakfast

5098 N. Mechanicsburg Road, 47356
(317) 779-4501; (800) 395-6449

A small town bed and breakfast looking out on berry patches and flower garden. Awake early or late to a delicious full breakfast. Fifty minutes to Indianapolis, twenty minutes to Anderson and Ball State Universities.

Hosts: Rose and Jack Lewis
Rooms: 2 (1 suite and 1SB) $55-75
Full Breakfast
Credit Cards: none
Notes: 2, 5, 7, 8, 10, 12

NAPPANEE

Market Street Guest House

253 East Market Street, 46550
(219) 773-2261; (800) 497-3791

Three-story Georgian Colonial built in 1922. Olde English decor. Forty-five minutes from Notre Dame and Shipshewana Flea Market. Within two miles of Amish Acres and Borkholder Dutch Village. Walking distance to many antique shops. Experience an evening meal with an Amish family (reservations only). Wake up to a full breakfast in the breakfast room, or have

breakfast served in your room (available only in one room).

Hostess: Sharon Bontrager
Rooms: 5 (PB) $60-75
Full Breakfast
Credit Cards: A, B, D
Notes: 2, 4, 5, 7, 8, 9, 10, 12

Victorian Guest House

302 E. Market Street, 46550
(219) 773-4383

Antiques, stained glass windows, and pocket doors highlight this 1887 Historical Register mansion. Nestled amongst the Amish Countryside where antique shops abound. A warm welcome awaits as you return to gracious living with all the ambiance of the 1800s. Everything has been designed to make your "Bed and Breakfast" stay a memorable one. Close to Notre Dame and Shipshewana. Two hours from Chicago. Complimentary evening tea and sweets. "Prepare for a memory."

Hosts: Bruce and Vickie Hunsberger
Rooms: 6 (PB) $49-84
Full Breakfast
Credit Cards: A, B, D
Notes: 2, 5, 8, 9, 10

NASHVILLE

Day Star Inn

Box 361, 87 E. Main Street, 47448
(812) 988-0430

Day Star Inn is in downtown Nashville in beautiful Brown County. There are over 200 shops and restaurants, art galleries, country music shows, drama theaters, and more. We are two miles from scenic Brown County State Park, and many churches for worship. We require no smoking, alcohol, or pets. All rooms have private baths and cable TV.

Host: Edwin K. Taggart
Rooms: 5 + parlor (PB) $80-95
Continental Plus Breakfast
Credit Cards: A, B, D
Notes: 2, 5, 7, 8, 9, 10, 11, 12

Wraylyn Knoll B&B

2008 Greasy Creek Road, PO Box 481, 47448
(812) 988-0733

Wraylyn Knoll B&B is a family-owned and operated, Brown County, hilltop country guest house. Seven guest rooms with king or queen beds, private baths, and exceptional views. Lots of common areas. Romantic garden with fountain and awesome view of the stars. Plus swimming pool, fishing pond, 12 acres for hiking, croquet, and porch swing. Help yourself to evening refreshments, cool breezes, and warm welcomes! We welcome small groups, too.

Hostess: Marci Wray
Rooms: 7 (PB) $50-75
Full Breakfast (weekends in May to Nov.);
Continental Breakfast (weekdays and off season)
Credit Cards: A, B
Notes: 2, 5, 7, 8, 9, 10, 11, 12

NEW ALBANY

Honeymoon Mansion Bed and Breakfast Inn and Wedding Chapel

1014 East Main Street, 47150
(812) 945-0312; (800) 759-7270

Our mansion and chapel are a national historic landmark built in 1850. Our chapel seats 70 guests and we have an ordained minister on our staff. We are opened 9 to 9 year-round. We have six suites (three with marble jacuzzis) and each has a private bath. We are AAA approved, listed in Mobil Oil's travel guide, and members of the Indiana B&B Association. The tourism division of the State of Indiana has designated Honeymoon Mansion as "a hidden treasure."

Hosts: Franklin and Beverly Dennis
Rooms: 6 (PB) $69.95-139.95
Full Country Breakfast
Credit Cards: A, B
Notes: 2, 5, 7 (over 12), 8, 9, 10, 11, 12

Rosewood Mansion Inn

PERU

Rosewood Mansion Inn

54 North Hood Street, 46970
(317) 472-7151; FAX (317) 472-5575

The Rosewood is a lovely Victorian home in downtown Peru, IN. A welcome change from impersonal hotel accommodations, we offer the warmth and friendliness of a private home, with the privacy and elegance of a fine hotel, for a truly unique experience. Consider the Rosewood Mansion for your next romantic getaway, anniversary, party, business meeting, or corporate retreat. Whether business or pleasure brings you to Peru, the Rosewood rewards you with a wonderful experience at a moderate price.

Hosts: Lynn and Dave Hausner
Rooms: 12 (PB) $70-85
Full Breakfast
Credit Cards: A, B, C, D
Notes: 2, 5, 7, 8, 9, 10, 12

RICHMOND

Philip W. Smith B&B

2039 East Main Street, 47374
(317) 966- 8972; (800) 966-8972

Elegant Queen Anne Victorian family home located in East Main-Glen Miller Park Historic District, right on the IN-OH border off I-70. Built in 1890 by Philip W. Smith, the two and a half story brick has Romanesque details and features stained glass windows and ornate-carved wood. Four distinctive guest rooms: two with full-size beds, two with queen-size beds. Unwind in the evening with homemade snacks, coffee, and tea. Awaken to a breakfast highlighting fresh, regional ingredients. Stroll through four historic districts, listen to outdoor concerts in the park, hike Whitewater River Gorge, relax in the garden at the B&B, and shop the unique shops of Richmond and "Antique Alley." AAA and ABBA approved.

Hosts: Chip and Chartley Bondurant
Rooms: 4 (PB) $65-75
Full Breakfast
Credit Cards: A, B
Notes: 2, 5, 7, 8, 10, 11, 12

Philip W. Smith Bed and Breakfast

ROCKPORT—SEE OWENSBORO, KENTUCKY

SHIPSHEWANA

Morton Street Bed and Breakfast, Inc.

PO Box 775, 46565
(219) 768-4391; (800) 447-6475;
FAX (219) 768-7468

Three old homes located on Morton Street, in the heart of Amish country in Shipshewana. Experience the comfort of country, antique, or Victorian stylings. You will find yourself within walking distance of the town's country quilt and craft shops and the famous Shipshewana flea market. Special winter and weekend rates available.

Hosts: Joel and Kim Mishler with Esther Mishler
Rooms: 10 (PB) (call for rates)
Full Breakfast (Continental on Sundays)
Credit Cards: A, B, D
Notes: 2, 5, 7, 10, 11, 12

5 Open all year; 6 Pets welcome; 7 Children welcome; 8 Tennis nearby; 9 Swimming nearby; 10 Golf nearby; 11 Skiing nearby; 12 May be booked through travel agent.

SHIRLEY

Sweet's Home Sweet Home

402 Center Street, 47384
(317) 737-6357; (800) 418-2076

Large comfortable home specializing in small town hospitality. Large yard with rose garden and within walking distance of the historic district. Centrally located within an easy drive to several attractions. Each room is special: Have Christmas year-round in the Christmas Room, see all the treasures in Papaw's Treasure Room, sleep in Greatma's antique feather bed, or lounge in bow's and lace in the lovely Jo-lia-Reneé Room.

Hosts: Jeanie and Ray Sweet
Rooms: 4 (SB)
Continental Breakfast and evening snack
Credit Cards: none
Notes: 2, 4, 5, 7

SOUTH BEND

Queen Anne Bed and Breakfast Inn

420 W. Washington, 46601
(219) 234-5959; (800) 582-2379

An 1893 Victorian house with antiques, original Frank Loyd Wright bookcases, silk cloth wall covering, and beautiful tiger oak staircase. Abundant breakfast, afternoon tea, and snacks provided. Near downtown, Notre Dame, local attractions, and good restaurants. Relax

circa 1893
Queen Anne Bed and Breakfast Inn

and relive earlier days. Step back into the past.

Hosts: Robert and Pauline Medhurst
Rooms: 6 (PB) $70-105
Full Breakfast
Credit Cards: A, B, C
Notes: 2, 5, 7, 8, 9, 10, 11, 12

TIPPECANOE

Bessinger's Hillfarm Wildlife Refuge B&B

4588 State Road 110, 46570
(219) 223-3288

This cozy log home overlooks 265 acres of rolling hills, woods, pasture fields, and marsh with 31 islands. It is ideal for geese and deer year-round. This farm features hiking trails with beautiful views, picnic areas, and benches tucked away in a quiet area. Varied seasons make it possible to canoe, swim, fish, bird watch, hike, and cross-country ski. Start with a country breakfast and be ready for an unforgettable table experience.

Hosts: Wayne and Betty Bessinger
Rooms: 3 (PB) $55-65
Full Breakfast
Credit Cards: none
Notes: 2, 5, 9, 10, 11

NOTES: Credit cards accepted: A Master Card; B Visa; C American Express; D Discover; E Diners Club; F Other; 2 Personal checks accepted; 3 Lunch available; 4 Dinner available;

WARSAW

Candlelight Inn

503 E. Ft. Wayne Street, 46580
(219) 267 2906; (800) 352 0640;
FAX (219) 269-4646

An 1860 Italiante home renovated by Bill and Debi Hambright. The Inn features eleven foot ceilings, natural woodwork, a grand stairway, marble fireplace, antique-filled rooms, and large porch. Whirlpool tubs available along with queen and king beds, phones, and cable TV in each room. Our Victorian home offers all the Old World charm with today's modern comforts.

Rooms: 11 (PB) $69-135
Full Home-cooked Breakfast
Credit Cards: A, B, C, E
Notes: 2, 5, 8, 9, 10, 12 (no commission)

White Hill Inn

2513 E. Center Street, 46580
(219) 269-6933; FAX (219) 268-1936

This restored English Tudor mansion is situated on the highest land in Warsaw. Surrounded by whispering trees, the Inn is a retreat into the elegants of yesteryear. Only minutes from fine dining, shopping, lake recreation, and the business community. The accommodations include telephones, TVs, private baths, and desks. The suite has a double wide jacuzzi. Full breakfast is served on the porch and a formal dining room is being added to the mansion.

Hosts: Carm and Zoyla Henderson
Rooms: 8 (PB) $70-120
Full Breakfast
Credit Cards: A, B, C, D
Notes: 2, 5, 6, 7 (over 12), 8, 9, 10, 11 (water and cross-country), 12

WEST BADEN SPRINGS

Rhodes House Bed and Breakfast

Box 7, 47469-0007
(812) 936-7378

Relax in homey luxury of an 1890s Victorian home fill with beautiful carved wood and stained glass. Rock on one of the wraparound porches and enjoy the peaceful view of the town park or the famed, historic West Baden domed hotel. Enjoy Hoosier hospitality with a home-grown, home-cooked breakfast of your choice. There is plenty of rolling Indiana scenery soaked with history, and sports will find plenty of Joe Lewis and Larry Bird trivia.

Hosts: Marlene and Frank Sipes
Rooms: 3 (PB) $40-45
Guests' Preference Breakfast
Credit Cards: A, B
Notes: 2, 5, 6 (housed separate), 7, 8, 9, 10, 11

---

5 Open all year; 6 Pets welcome; 7 Children welcome; 8 Tennis nearby; 9 Swimming nearby; 10 Golf nearby; 11 Skiing nearby; 12 May be booked through travel agent.

IOWA

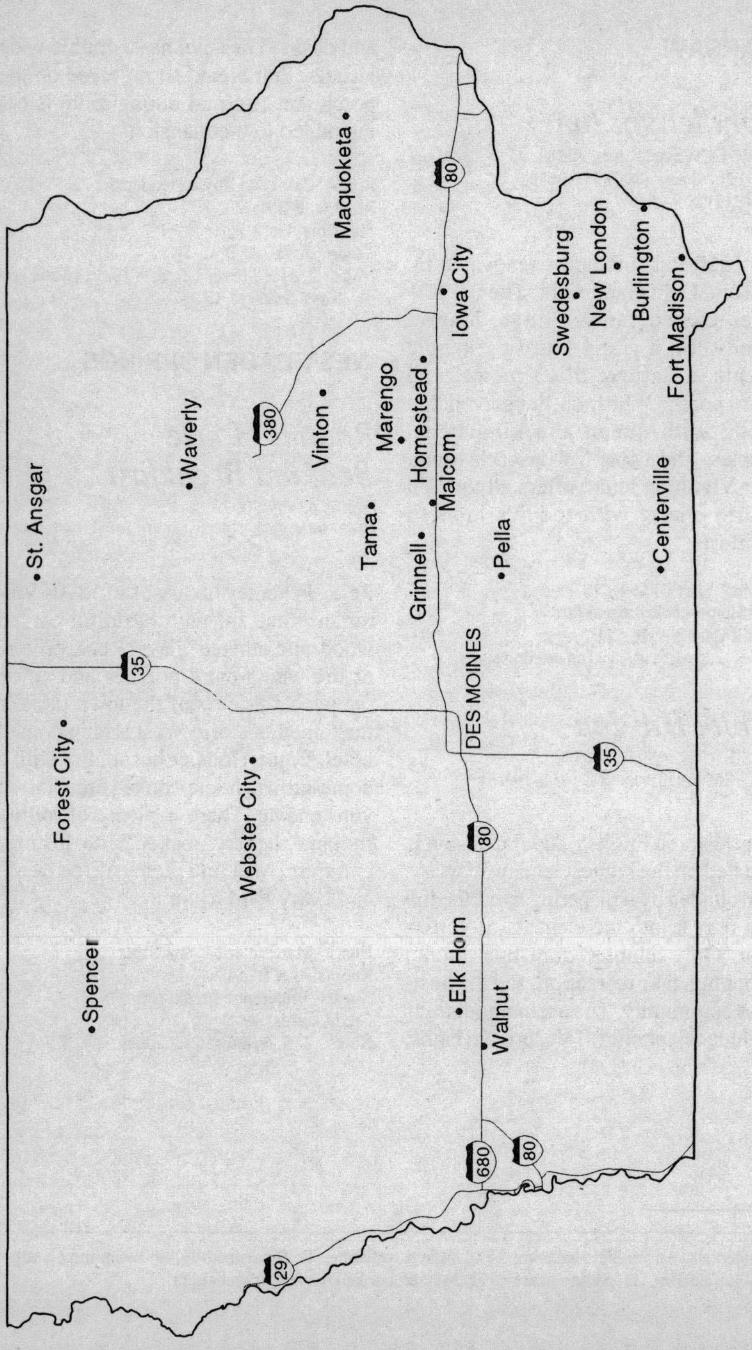

Maquoketa •

[80]

Iowa City

Swedesburg
New London
Burlington
Fort Madison

• Waverly

[380]

Vinton •

Marengo
Homestead •

• St. Ansgar

Tama •
Grinnell •

Malcom

• Pella

• Centerville

DES MOINES

[35]

Forest City •

Webster City •

[35]

[80]

• Spencer

Elk Horn

• Walnut

[680] [80]

[29]

Iowa

BURLINGTON

Lakeview
Bed and Breakfast

11351 60th Street, 52601
(319) 752-8735; (800) 753-8735;
FAX (319) 752-5126

Built from the ruins of the county's third oldest home, this elegant country home stands where stagecoach passengers once slept. Now your retreat to Lakeview is a mix of the old and the new on 30 acres of magnificent country charm. The house features crystal chandeliers, antiques, collectibles, and a circular staircase. Outdoors your can enjoy a swim in our pool; fishing in our three-acre lake stocked with catfish, bass, crappie, and bluegill; or just spend time making friends with our family of miniature horses. Guests can also take advantage of our large video library of noted Christian speakers. A video studio is available for recording and small conferences.

Hosts: Jack and Linda Rowley
Rooms: 4 (PB) $45-60
Expanded Continental Breakfast
Credit Cards: A, B
Notes: 2, 5, 8, 9, 10, 12

CENTERVILLE

One of a Kind

314 W. State, 52544
(515) 437-4540 (voice and FAX)

One of a Kind is a stately three-story brick home built in 1867 and situated in one of Iowa's delightful small communities. You will be within walking distance of antique shops, the town square, city park with tennis courts, swimming pool, etc. Twelve-minute drive to Iowa's largest lake.

Hosts: Jack and Joyce Stufflebeem
Rooms: 5 (2PB; 3SB) $35-60
Full Breakfast
Credit Cards: A, B
Notes: 2, 3, 4, 5, 8, 9, 10, 11, 12

ELK HORN

Joy's Morning Glory
Bed and Breakfast

4308 Main Street, Box 12, 51531
(712) 764-5631; (888) 764-5631

Be special guests in our beautiful, refurbished, 1912 home. As our guest, you will be greeted by an abundant ar-

---

NOTES: Credit cards accepted: A Master Card; B Visa; C American Express; D Discover; E Diners Club; F Other; 2 Personal checks accepted; 3 Lunch available; 4 Dinner available; 5 Open all year; 6 Pets welcome; 7 Children welcome; 8 Tennis nearby; 9 Swimming nearby; 10 Golf nearby; 11 Skiing nearby; 12 May be booked through travel agent.

Joy's Morning Glory Bed and Breakfast

ray of flowers that line our walkways. Inside, your choice of floral decorated bedrooms await you as well. Breakfast is prepared on Joy's antique cookstove and served in the dining room, front porch, or flower-filled backyard. Elk Horn community is home to the largest rural Danish settlement in the United States. The town has a working windmill and is home to the National Danish Immigrant Museum and the Tivoli Festival.

Hosts: Joy and Merle Petersen
Rooms: 3 (SB) $50
Full Breakfast
Credit Cards: none
Notes: 2, 7 (over 10), 8, 9, 10

FOREST CITY

The 1897 Victorian House

306 S. Clark Street, 50436
(515) 582-3613

Offering you hospitality in this turn-of-the-century Queen Anne Victorian home. As a guest in the 1897 Victorian House, you may choose from four beautifully decorated bedrooms, each with private bath. Breakfast, included in your room rate, is served every morning in our dining room, and we specialize in homemade food. An antique shop is located on premises. Gift certificates are available. Come play our 1923 baby grand player piano, play crochet in the yard, and relax in Forest City, a quiet yet progressive rural community.

Hosts: Richard and Doris Johnson
Rooms: 5 (PB) $60-90
Full Breakfast
Credit Cards: A, B
Notes: 2, 3 and 4 (by reservation), 5, 9, 10, 12

The 1897 Victorian House

FORT MADISON

Kingsley Inn

707 Avenue H, 52627
(319) 372-7074; (800) 441-2327;
FAX (319) 372-7096

Experience complete relaxation in 1860's Victorian luxury. Fourteen spacious rooms are furnished in period antiques with today's modern comforts. Awaken to the aroma of "Kingsley Blend" coffee and enjoy the specialty breakfast in the elegant Morning Room.

NOTES: Credit cards accepted: A Master Card; B Visa; C American Express; D Discover; E Diners Club; F Other; 2 Personal checks accepted; 3 Lunch available; 4 Dinner available;

Stroll to replica of 1808 Fort, museum, parks, shops, Catfish Bend Casino, and antique malls. Fifteen minutes from historic Nauvoo, Illinois. Treat yourselves to a unique lunch or dinner at Alpha's on the Riverfront, right off our lobby. Private baths (some whirlpools), CATV, air-conditioning, and telephones. Non-smoking facility.

Hostess: Myrna M. Reinhard
Rooms: 14 (PB) $70-115
Continental Plus Breakfast
Credit Cards: A, B, C, D, E
Notes: 2, 3, 4, 5, 7 (limited), 9, 10, 12

GRINNELL

Carriage House Bed and Breakfast

1133 Broad Street, 50112
(515) 236-7520

Beautiful Queen Anne style Victorian home with relaxing wicker furniture and a swing seat on the front porch. Several fireplaces to be enjoyed in the wintertime. Gourmet breakfast with fresh fruit, quiche, and Irish soda bread fresh from the griddle. Local shopping, nearby lake and hiking, excellent restaurants. One block from Grinnell College, one hour from Des Moines and Iowa City. Member of Iowa Bed and Breakfast Innkeepers Association, Iowa Lodging Association, and Grinnell Area Chamber of Commerce.

Hosts: Ray and Dorothy Spriggs
Rooms: 5 (3PB; 2SB) $45-60
Full Breakfast
Credit Cards: none
Notes: 2, 5, 8, 9, 10, 11, 12

Clayton Farms Bed and Breakfast

621 Newburg Road, 50112
(515) 236-3011

Extra nice contemporary farm home on 320 acres of livestock and grain operation. Fishing and boating on farm pond with place for campfire in season. Family room with fireplce, TV, VCR, library of movies, and kitchenette stocked with beverages and snacks. Family style country breakfast. Group packages for pheasant hunters and hunters of antiques and collectibles. Seven miles from Grinnell College; one hour from Des Moines, Iowa City, and Cedar Rapids. 45 minutes from the Amana Colonies; 20 miles from casino. Air-conditioned. Smoke restricted to outdoors. State licensed and inspected. Brochures available—specify general, hunting, or antiquing.

Hosts: Ron and Judie Clayton
Rooms: 4 (1PB; 3SB) $52.50-57.75
Full Breakfast
Credit Cards: A, B
Notes: 2, 7, 8, 9, 10, 11

Clayton Farms

---

5 Open all year; 6 Pets welcome; 7 Children welcome; 8 Tennis nearby; 9 Swimming nearby; 10 Golf nearby; 11 Skiing nearby; 12 May be booked through travel agent.

HOMESTEAD (AMANA COLONIES)

Die Heimat Country Inn

Main Street, 52236
(319) 622-3937

Die Heimat, "the home place," has 19 rooms furnished with Amana walnut and cherry furniture, TVs, and air-conditioning. Amana walnut canopy beds are the specialty of this—the oldest and largest—bed and breakfast in the Colonies. A nature trail, wineries, woolen mills, and restaurants are all nearby.

Hosts: Warren and Jacki Lock
Rooms: 19 (PB) $45.95-69.95
Full Breakfast
Credit Cards: A, B, D
Notes: 2 (preferred), 6, 7, 8, 9, 10

IOWA CITY

Bella Vista Place Bed and Breakfast

2 Bella Vista Place, 52245
(319) 338-4129

Daissy has furnished her lovely, air-conditioned, 1920s home with antiques and artifacts she has acquired on her travels in Europe and Latin America. Conveniently located on Iowa City's historical northside with a beautiful view of the Iowa River. The Hoover Library, the Amana Colonies, and the Amish center of Kalona are all nearby. A full breakfast, with Daissy's famous coffee, is served in the dining room's unique setting. Daissy is fluent in Spanish and speaks some French. From I-80: take Dubuque St. Exit 244, turn left on Brown St., then first left on Linn St. one block to #2 Bella Vista Place.

Hosts: Daissy P. Owen
Rooms: 4 (2PB; 2SB) $45-75
Full Breakfast
Credit Cards: none
Notes: 2, 5, 7 (over 10), 8, 9, 12

Haverkamps' Linn Street Homestay Bed and Breakfast

619 N. Linn Street, 52245
(319) 337-4363

Enjoy the warmth and hospitality in our 1908 Edwardian home filled with heirlooms and collectibles. Only a short walk to downtown Iowa City and the University of Iowa main campus, and a short drive to the Hoover Library in West Branch, to the Amish in Kalona, and to seven Amama Colonies.

Hosts: Clarence and Dorothy Haverkamp
Rooms: 3 (SB) $35-45
Full Breakfast
Credit Cards: none
Notes: 2, 5, 7, 8, 9, 12

Haverkamps' Linn Street Homestay

NOTES: Credit cards accepted: A Master Card; B Visa; C American Express; D Discover; E Diners Club; F Other; 2 Personal checks accepted; 3 Lunch available; 4 Dinner available;

Pleasant Country Bed and Breakfast

MALCOM

Pleasant Country B&B

4386 110th Street, 50157
(515) 528-4925

Eugene and Mary Lou are a third generation farm family, living in their home which was built in 1896. It is filled with antiques and country deco. The home is a working farm and tours are available. Enjoy a full country breakfast with homemade specialties. We have a pond for fishing and pheasant hunting in season. Rest and relax in the quietness of the countryside.

Hosts: Mary Lou and Eugene Mann
Rooms: 4 (SB) $50-55
Full Breakfast
Credit Cards: none
Notes: 2, 5, 7, 8, 9, 10, 11, 12

MAQUOKETA

Squiers Manor B&B

418 W. Pleasant Street, 52060
(319) 652-6961

Squiers Manor Bed and Breakfast is located in the West Pleasant Street His-

toric District. This 1882 Queen Anne mansion features walnut, cherry, and butternut woods throughout. Enjoy period furnishings, queen-size beds, in-room phone and TV, private baths, as well as single and double jacuzzis. Come hungry and enjoy delicious, candlelight evening desserts and breakfast (more like brunch) served in the elegant dining room. Virl's and Kathy's goal is to make your stay as pleasant and enjoyable as possible. Give us a call today!

Hosts: Virl and Kathy Banowetz
Rooms: 8 (PB) $75-185
Full Breakfast
Credit Cards: A, B, C
Notes: 2, 5, 8, 9, 10, 11, 12

MARENGO

Loy's Farm B&B

2077 KK Avenue, I-80 Exit 216 N., 52301
(319) 642-7787

This beautiful, modern home is on a working grain and hog farm with quiet and pleasant views of rolling countryside. A farm tour is offered with friendly hospitality. Pheasant hunting can be enjoyed. The large recreation room includes a pool table, table tennis, and shuffleboard. Swing set and sand pile are in the large yard. Close to the Amana Colonies, Tanger Mall, Kalona, Iowa City, West Branch, and Cedar Rapids. I-80, Exit 216 North one mile.

Hosts: Loy and Robert Walker
Rooms: 3 (1PB; 2SB) $55 + tax
Full Breakfast
Credit Cards: none
Notes: 2, 4 (by reservation), 5, 6 (caged), 7, 8, 9, 10 (4 courses), 12

---

5 Open all year; 6 Pets welcome; 7 Children welcome; 8 Tennis nearby; 9 Swimming nearby; 10 Golf nearby; 11 Skiing nearby; 12 May be booked through travel agent.

Old Brick Bed and Breakfast

NEW LONDON

Old Brick Bed and Breakfast

2759 Old Hwy. 34, 52645
(319) 367-5403

This 1860s Italianate-style brick farm house, comfortably furnished with family pieces, beckons guests with welcome candles in each window. Our working grain farm offers an opportunity to view current farming techniques, equipment, and speciality crops. Enjoy peaceful surroundings, walk down a country road, visit area antique shops, sit on one of the porches, or relax in spacious guest rooms with queen-size beds and private baths. Full breakfast and arrival refreshments served.

Hosts: Jerry and Caroline Lehman
Rooms: 2 (PB) $50
Full Breakfast
Credit Cards: none
Notes: 2, 4, 5, 7, 8, 9, 10

PELLA

Avondgloren (Sunset View) Bed and Breakfast

984 - 198th Place, 50219-7845
(515) 628-1578; (800) 648-1578;
FAX (515) 628-2401

Our motto is "A home away from home." Our charming brick home is ideally situated 1½ miles southwest of Pella and 1½ miles northwest of Red Rock Dam. It is an acreage with a view of both the sunset and sunrise. It has decorating accents of live plants inside for your year-round enjoyment, as well as flower gardens outside true to the Dutch heritage. Also, a family room with TV and fireplace is available for your use. Central air-conditioning. A back deck with a lovely country view can also be used for your leisure time enjoyment. Pella has a character all its own with its history and Dutch heritage well preserved with many points of interest.

Hosts: Henry and Luella M. Bandstra
Rooms: 3 (SB) $47-57
Full Dutch Breakfast
Credit Cards: A, B, D
Notes: 2, 5, 9, 10

ST. ANSGAR

Blue Belle Inn Bed and Breakfast

PO Box 205, 513 W. Fourth Street, 50472
(515) 736-2225

Rediscover the romance of the 1890s while enjoying the comfort and conve-

NOTES: Credit cards accepted: A Master Card; B Visa; C American Express; D Discover; E Diners Club; F Other; 2 Personal checks accepted; 3 Lunch available; 4 Dinner available;

nience of the 1990s in one of six distinctively decorated guest rooms at the Blue Belle Inn. The festive Victorian Painted Lady features air-conditioning, fireplaces, and Jacuzzis. Lofty tin ceilings, gleaming maple woodwork, stained glass, and crystal chandeliers set in bay and curved window pockets create a shimmering interplay of light and color. Enjoy breakfast on the balcony or gourmet dining by candlelight.

Hostess: Sherrie C. Hansen
Rooms: 6 (5PB; 1SB) $50-130
Full Breakfast
Credit Cards: A, B, D
Notes: 2, 3, 4, 5, 7, 9, 10, 12

Hannah Marie Country Inn

SPENCER

Hannah Marie Country Inn

4070 Hwy. 71, 51301
(712) 262-1286; (800) 792-1286;
FAX (712) 262-3294

JOURNEY HERE. The Romance of Country is enjoyed in this pretty place. Themed guestrooms, loved and comfortable, are very much romantic places: in-room double whirlpools in romantic alcoves, private commodes, queen feather beds, down comforters, softened water, air-conditioning. Candleligt full breakfasts, or request a lite breakfast basket in your room, on the veranda, or under the apple trees. Parasol stroll among the fragrant herbs, vibrant wildflowers, and vegetables. Candlelight dinners available. Nurture your spirit. COME.

Hostess: Mary Nichols
Rooms: 5 (PB) $70-105
Full Breakfast
Credit Cards: A, B, C, D
Notes: 2, 3, 4, 6 (outside), 7, 8, 9, 10, 12 (10%)

SWEDESBURG

The Carlson House

105 Park Street, 52652
(319) 254-2451

Accommodations have an Old World charm in this stylishly decorated home in a Swedish-American country village. Guests enjoy the candlelight breakfast with Swedish treats, historical mementos, and gracious hosts. Guest facilities include a sitting room with TV, extensive reading materials, and wide porches for relaxation. The pleasant grounds of the Carlson House are next to the buildings of the Swedish-American Museum of Swedesburg.

Hosts: Ruth and Ned Ratekin
Rooms: 2 (PB) $50
Full Breakfast
Credit Cards: A, B
Notes: 2, 5

5 Open all year; 6 Pets welcome; 7 Children welcome; 8 Tennis nearby; 9 Swimming nearby; 10 Golf nearby; 11 Skiing nearby; 12 May be booked through travel agent.

TAMA

Hummingbird Haven
A Bed and Breakfast

1201 Harding Street, 52339
(515) 484-2022

We hope you will join us at Hummingbird Haven and get a taste of Central Iowa's hospitality. The B&B offers two guest rooms with a large shared bath. Guests have use of the home, laundry services are available, and the home has central air and heat. Tama's central location makes our B&B a perfect home base for seeing many of Iowa's attractions. Ten minutes from Tama County Museum and Mesquaki Bingo and Casino; 30 minutes from Mashalltown, County Lake with water sports, Opera House in Brooklyn, and Grinnell College and Museum. One hour from much more. Please no pets or smoking.

Hostess: Bernita Thomsen
Rooms: 2 (SB) $38-50
Full Breakfast
Credit Cards: none
Notes: 2, 3, 4, 5, 7, 9, 10

VINTON

The Lion and The Lamb

913 Second Avenue, 52349
(319) 472-5086; (800) 808-LAMB (5262);
FAX (319) 472-9115

Experience elegant accommodations in this newly restored 1892 Queen Anne Victorian Mansion. This "Painted Lady" features elaborate woodwork, seven fireplaces, stained glass windows, parquet floors, and a dusting porch.

Each of our guest rooms have air-conditioning, queen-size beds, and TV. One room has a private bath. We're located between Cedar Rapids and Waterloo. Evening dessert is also provided.

Hosts: Richard and Rachel Waterbury
Rooms: 3 (1PB; 2SB) $55-75
Full Breakfast
Credit Cards: A, B
Notes: 2, 4, 5, 7, 8, 9, 10, 12

WALNUT

Antique City Inn B&B

400 Antique City Dr., PO Box 584, 51577
(712) 784-3722; (800) 714-3722

This 1911 Victorian home has been restored and furnished to its original state. Enjoy a nostalgic experience of simplicity of life, craftsmanship of yesterday, quiet living, and small town hospitality. One block from malls and stores with 250 antique dealers. Home has beautiful woods, dumb waiter icebox, French doors, and wraparound porch.

Hostess: Sylvia Reddie
Rooms: 5 (1PB; 4SB) $42 (includes tax)
Full Breakfast
Credit Cards: A, B, C, D
Notes: 2, 3, 4, 5

Antique City Inn

Clark's Country Inn Bed and Breakfast

701 Walnut Street, PO Box 533, 51577
(712) 784-3010

Iowa's antique capital, one mile south of I-80 between Omaha and Des Moines. Six malls, individual shops, over 200 dealers, open all year. 1912 two-story home with oak interior, antiques, newly remodeled guest rooms, private baths, king/queen beds, central air, and full breakfast. Mastercard/Visa deposit required. No smoking.

Host: Ron and Mary Lou Clark
Rooms: 3 (PB) $52
Full Breakfast
Credit Cards: A, B
Notes: 2, 5, 7 (over 12), 8, 9, 10, 12

WAVERLY

Villa Fairfield

401 Second Avenue SW, 50677
(319) 352-0739

Built in 1876, this totally restored Italianate Victorian bed and breakfast is designed as the perfect get-away spot. The house is furnished with many family antiques and keepsakes, as well as with various articles collected by innkeeper Inez Boevers-Christensen during the years which she presided in Brazil. All rooms are uniquely decorated with their own charm and character and have ceiling fans, air-conditioning, and queen-size beds. Come to the Villa Fairfield to enjoy the rest and relaxation of a bygone era.

Hostess: Inez Boevers-Christensen
Rooms: 4 (2PB; 2SB) $55-75
Full Breakfast
Credit Cards: A, B
Closed January and February
Notes: 2, 10, 12

WEBSTER CITY

Centennial Farm Bed and Breakfast

1091 220th Street, 50595
(515) 832-3050

Centennial Farm is a bed and breakfast homestay located on a farm that has been in the family since 1869. Tom was born in the house. Guests may take a ride in the 1929 Model A pickup truck, if desired. In a quiet location near several good antique shops. Member of Iowa Bed and Breakfast Innkeepers Association, Inc. Air-conditioned. Twenty-two miles west of I-35 at Exit 142 or Exit 144.

Hosts: Tom and Shirley Yungclas
Rooms: 2 (SB) $35
Full Breakfast
Credit Cards: none
Notes: 2, 5, 7, 8, 9, 10

---

5 Open all year; 6 Pets welcome; 7 Children welcome; 8 Tennis nearby; 9 Swimming nearby; 10 Golf nearby; 11 Skiing nearby; 12 May be booked through travel agent.

KANSAS

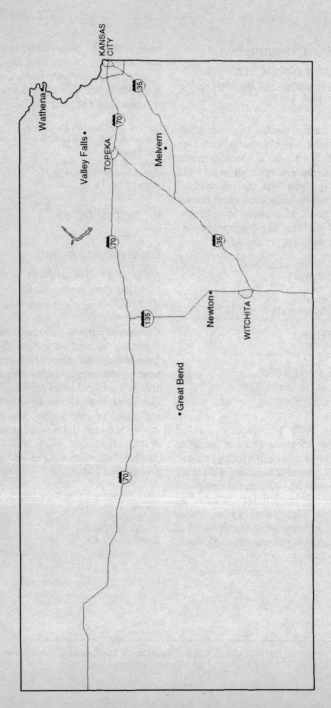

Kansas

GREAT BEND

Peaceful Acres Bed and Breakfast
Route 5, Box 153, 67530
(316) 793-7527

Enjoy a mini-farm and sprawling, tree-shaded, old farmhouse furnished with some antiques. If you like quiet and peace, chickens, goats, guineas, kittens in the springs, and old-fashioned hospitality, you need to come and visit us. Breakfast will be fixed from home-grown products. We are near historical areas: Sante Fe Trail, Ft. Larned, Cheyenne Bottoms, zoo, and tennis courts. Member of the Kansas Bed and Breakfast Association.

Hosts: Dale and Doris Nitzel
Rooms: 3 (1 PB; 2 SB) $30
Full Breakfast
Credit Cards: none
Notes: 2, 3, 4, 5, 7, 8, 9, 10, 12

MELVERN

Schoolhouse Inn
122 SE. Beck, 66510
(913) 549-3473

Two-story, limestone building built in 1870 sets on a one-and-a-half acre lawn. In 1986 it was entered in Kansas Historic Places. The Inn is a place you need to come visit. The guests can visit in a parlor with antique furniture or sit around a large table in the dining room and enjoy playing games. Four large bedrooms upstairs furnished with antiques and contemporary furnishings where guests can relax while reading a

Schoolhouse Inn

NOTES: Credit cards accepted: A Master Card; B Visa; C American Express; D Discover; E Diners Club; F Other; 2 Personal checks accepted; 3 Lunch available; 4 Dinner available; 5 Open all year; 6 Pets welcome; 7 Children welcome; 8 Tennis nearby; 9 Swimming nearby; 10 Golf nearby; 11 Skiing nearby; 12 May be booked through travel agent.

good book or looking at magazines. Enjoy this B&B for celebrating your anniversary or just a quiet getaway to our small town of Melvern. Member of Kansas B&B Association.

Hosts: Rudy and Alice White
Rooms: 4 (2PB; 2SB) $50-60
Full Breakfast
Credit Cards: A, B
Notes: 2, 5, 7, 9

NEWTON

Hawk House
Bed and Breakfast
307 W. Broadway, 67114
(316) 283-2045; (800) 500-2045

This elegant 1914 home has original light fixtures, wallpaper from Europe, and stained glass windows awaiting your arrival. Three blocks from downtown, where quaint shops and antiques can be found. Close to bike paths, historical sites, outlet mall (2 miles), and good restaurants. Guest rooms offer queen-size beds and antique furniture. Facility is available for meetings, retreats, weddings, and receptions. Member Kansas B&B Association.

Hosts: Lon and Carol Buller
Rooms: 4 (1PB; 3SB) $50-60
Full Breakfast
Credit Cards: A, B
Notes: 2, 5, 7, 8, 9, 10

Old Parsonage
Bed and Breakfast
330 East Fourth Street, 67114
(316) 283-6808

Located in Newton's oldest neighborhood, this charming home once served as the parsonage for First Mennonite Church. It features a cozy yet spacious atmosphere filled with antiques and family heirlooms. The Old Parsonage is a short walk away from the historical Warkentin House and Warkentin Mill which are listed on the National Register of Historic Places. Two miles from Bethel College. Dine in one of Newton's fine ethnic eateries, or browse quaint antique and craft shops.

Hosts: Karl and Betty Friesen
Rooms: 3 (1PB; 2SB) $48
Continental Breakfast
Credit Cards: A, B
Notes: 2, 5, 7

VALLEY FALLS

The Barn
Bed and Breakfast Inn
RR2 Box 87, 66088
(913) 945-3225; FAX (913) 945-3226

In the rolling hills of northeast Kansas, this 101-year-old barn has been converted into a bed and breakfast. Sitting high on a hill with a beautiful view, it has a large indoor heated pool, fitness room, three living rooms, and king or queen beds in all rooms. We serve you

---

NOTES: Credit cards accepted: A Master Card; B Visa; C American Express; D Discover; E Diners Club; F Other; 2 Personal checks accepted; 3 Lunch available; 4 Dinner available;

supper, as well as a full breakfast, and have three large meeting rooms available.

Hosts: Tom and Marcella Ryan
Rooms: 20 (PB) $75-85
Full Breakfast and Supper
Credit Cards: A, B, C, D
Notes: 2, 3, 4, 5, 7, 8, 9, 10, 12

WATHENA

Carousel Bed and Breakfast
Route 1 Box 124, 66090
(913) 989-3537

The Carousel Bed and Breakfast, an eary 1900 two-story Victorian house,

sits on top a hill overlooking the beautiful countryside of the glacial hills, bluffs, and forest of Doniphan County, Kansas. The house is wall papered throughout. Four sets of bay windows with lace curtains, area rugs, and period antiques reflect the elegant Victorian style. A large front porch overlooks beautiful terraced lawns. Personalized decor in each guest room.

Hosts: Jack and Betty Price
Rooms: 3 (1PB; 2SB) $45-65
Full Breakfast
Credit Cards: A, B
Notes: 2, 5, 7, 9, 10, 11

---

5 Open all year; 6 Pets welcome; 7 Children welcome; 8 Tennis nearby; 9 Swimming nearby; 10 Golf nearby; 11 Skiing nearby; 12 May be booked through travel agent.

KENTUCKY

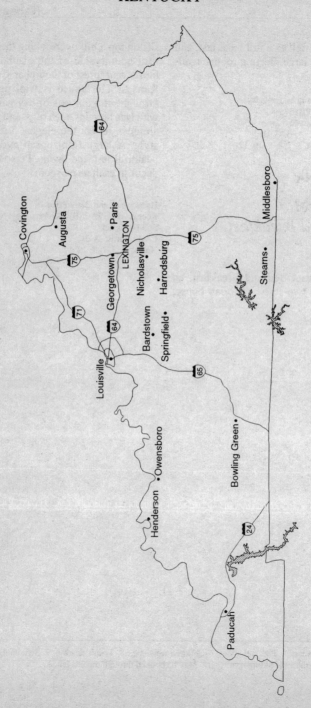

Kentucky

AUGUSTA

Augusta Ayre Bed and Breakfast

201 West Second Street, 41002
(606) 756-3228

Built in 1840, this Federal house (a designated Kentucky landmark) takes you back to a simpler time. Located one block from antique and gift shops, art galleries, restaurants, parks, and the Ohio River. Amenities include fireplaces, ceiling fans, central air/heat, and a sitting room with cable TV/VCR. Children and pets are welcome. Gift certificates and deluxe packages are available.

Host: Maynard Krum
Rooms: 2 (SB) $50-90
Full Breakfast
Credit Cards: D
Notes: 2, 5, 6, 7, 8, 9, 10 (20 miles)

Augusta Bed and Breakfast Association

PO Box 31, 41002
FAX (606) 756-3228; also see individual inn's numbers

Steeped in history, Augusta is the quintessential river town. Stroll along the river and tree lined streets as you leave the hustle and bustle of the big city behind. Ride the ferry and view the varied architectural styles as you step back in time.

Explore the antique and gift shops and art galleries as you hunt for that special find. Then dine in one of Augusta's fine restaurants before retiring for the evening at a cozy bed and breakfast.

Let us host your next retreat, conference, or group outing. Facilities are available for meetings and meals. Murder Mysteries with professional actors can be arranged. Augusta hospitality is without equal and your visit is welcome.

Association members:

Augusta Ayre 201 West Second St. (606) 756-3228	*Doniphan House* 302 East Fourth St. (606) 756-2409
Augusta Landing 206 East Riverside Dr. (606) 756-2510	*The Lamplighter Inn* 103 West Second St. (606) 756-2603
Augusta White House Inn 307 Main St. (606) 756-2004	

NOTES: Credit cards accepted: A Master Card; B Visa; C American Express; D Discover; E Diners Club; F Other; 2 Personal checks accepted; 3 Lunch available; 4 Dinner available; 5 Open all year; 6 Pets welcome; 7 Children welcome; 8 Tennis nearby; 9 Swimming nearby; 10 Golf nearby; 11 Skiing nearby; 12 May be booked through travel agent.

Augusta White House Inn Bed and Breakfast

307 Main Street, 41002
(606) 756-2004

Augusta White House Inn is a beautifully restored two-story brick structure (c. 1830) retaining its early Victorian era style and elegance coupled with true Southern hospitality. Comfortable rooms with flowered wallpaper and high crown molded ceilings as a reminder of yesteryear, but with modern convenience.

Hostess: Rebecca Spencer
Rooms: 5 (2PB; 3SB) $59-79
Full Breakfast
Credit Cards: A, B, C, D
Notes: 8, 9, 10

BARDSTOWN

Beautiful Dreamer B&B

440 E. Stephen Foster Avenue, 40004
(502) 348-4004, (800) 811-8312

Federal design home (circa 1995) in historic district. Fully A/C rooms. Cherry furniture, antiques, and all rooms available with queen-sized beds: Beautiful Dreamer (w/double jacuzzi), Stephen Foster (handicapped accessible), and Captain's (fireplace-single jacuzzi). Enjoy a hearty breakfast then relax on our porches with a beautiful view of my Old Kentucky Home.

Hostess: Lynell Ginter
Rooms: 3 (PB) $79-99
Full Breakfast
Credit Cards: A, B
Notes: 2, 5, 7 (over 8), 8, 9, 10, 12

Jailer's Inn

111 W. Stephen Foster Avenue, 40004
(502) 348-5551; (800) 948-5551;
FAX (502) 348-1852

We pamper our "prisoners!" Come "spend time" in jail and unlock an adventure in history. Large, spacious rooms, beautifully decorated in antiques and heirlooms. All rooms have private baths so "escape" to our Victorian, Colonial, Library, Garden, or 1819 room. The 1819 and Colonial rooms have double jacuzzis. Deluxe continental breakfast served in lovely courtyard in summertime. Located in center of Historic Bardstown. Rated AAA, Mobile Oil, American B&B Association. The Jailer's Inn is a "captivating experience."

Host: Paul McCoy
Rooms: 6 (PB) $65-95
Full Breakfast
Credit Cards: A, B, C, D
Notes: 2, 7, 8, 9, 10, 12

Kenmore Farms Bed and Breakfast

1050 Bloomfield Road, 40004
(502) 348-8023; (800) 831-6159;
FAX (502) 348-0617

Drop your hurried ways and enjoy the charm and warmth of days gone by. This beautifully restored 1860s Victorian home features antiques, Oriental rugs, gleaming poplar floors, and a cherry stairway. Air-conditioned guest rooms are furnished with Lincoln or poster beds and lovely linens, including period pieces. Large, private baths and spacious vanities. A hearty country breakfast served—all home

NOTES: Credit cards accepted: A Master Card; B Visa; C American Express; D Discover; E Diners Club; F Other; 2 Personal checks accepted; 3 Lunch available; 4 Dinner available;

cooked—a real treat! The decor and our brand of hospitality create a relaxing and enjoyable atmosphere. AAA approved.

Hosts: Dorothy and Bernie Keene
Rooms: 4 (PB) $80-90
Full Breakfast
Credit Cards: none
Notes: 2, 5, 7 (over 12), 8, 9, 10

Kenmore Farms

BOWLING GREEN

Alpine Lodge

5310 Morgantown Road, 42101
(502) 843-4846; (888) 444-3791

Alpine Lodge is a spacious, Swiss chalet-style home that has over 6,000 square feet and is located on eleven and a half acres. The furnishings are mostly antiques. A typical Southern breakfast of eggs, sausage, biscuits, gravy, fried apples, grits, coffee cake, coffee, and orange juice starts your day. There are grounds and nature trails to stroll through. We also have a swimming pool, gazebo, and outdoor spa. All the rooms have phones and cable TV (three movie channels). The Lodge is near many popular attractions. Your hosts are retired musicians who might be per-

suaded to play something for the guests.

Hosts: Dr. and Mrs. David Livingston
Rooms: 5 (3PB; 2SB) $45-65; suites $75-90
Full Breakfast
Credit Cards: A, B, C, D, E
Notes: 2, 3, 4, 5, 6, 7, 9, 10, 12

COVINGTON

The Licking-Riverside Historic B&B 8/13/98

516 Garrard Street, 41011
(606) 291-0191; (800) 483-7822;
FAX (606) 291-0939

An historic home in the historic district along the Licking River. Famous jacuzzi suite with river view, Victorian decor, fireplace, sitting area, TV, VCR; deluxe queen rooms with private baths. Courtyard with decks overlooking wooded area with river frontage. Enjoy a short walk to the Ohio River and get a marvelous view of the Cincinnati skyline. Many year-round activities, as well as our beautiful riverfront. Packages available include Reds, Bengals, and the Arts!

Hostess: Lynda L. Freeman
Rooms: 3 (PB) $69-129 $99 - 149
Continental Breakfast
Credit Cards: C
Notes: 2, 5, 7, 8, 9, 10, 12

GEORGETOWN

Pineapple Inn B&B

645 S. Broadway, 40324
(502) 868-5453 (voice and FAX)

Located in beautiful Georgetown, Kentucky, our beautiful home, built in 1876, is on the National Register. Country,

5 Open all year; 6 Pets welcome; 7 Children welcome; 8 Tennis nearby; 9 Swimming nearby; 10 Golf nearby; 11 Skiing nearby; 12 May be booked through travel agent.

French dining room, and large living room. Three bedrooms with private baths upstairs: Grandma's Country Room with full bed, Victorian Room also with full bed, and Americana Room with twin beds. Main Floor Derby Room with queen-sized, canopied bed and private bath with hot tub. The home is furnished with antiques and very beautifully decorated. Full breakfast is served.

Hosts: Muriel and Les
Rooms: 4 (PB) $65-85 (includes tax)
Full Breakfast
Credit Cards: A, B
Notes: 2, 5, 7, 8, 9, 10, 12

HARRODSBURG

Canaan Land Farm B&B

4355 Lexington Road, 40330
(606) 734-3984

Step back in time to a house over 200 years old. Canaan Land B&B is a historic home, c.1795. Rooms feature antiques, collectibles, and feather beds. Full breakfast included and true Southern hospitality. This is a working sheep farm with lambing spring and fall. Large swimming pool and hot tub. Your host is a shepherd/attorney, and you hostess is a handspinner/artist. Farm is secluded and peaceful. Close to Shaker Village. Also, an historic log cabin (c. 1815) with three additional rooms, including private baths. This is a nonsmoking B&B.

Hosts: Theo and Fred Bee
Rooms: 7 (6PB;1SB) $75-105
Full Breakfast
Credit Cards: none
Notes: 2, 5, 7 (12 and older), 9 (on-site), 10, 12

HENDERSON

L&N Bed and Breakfast

327 North Main Street, 42420
(502) 831-1100; FAX (502) 826-0075

Two-story, Victorian home located in downtown Henderson, near the Ohio River and within walking distance of three city parks. Rooms are comfortable and beautifully decorated with private baths. Home has central heat and air. Guests can be lulled to sleep by passing trains.

Hosts: Mary Elizabeth and Norris Priest
Rooms: 4 (PB) $75
Continental Breakfast
Credit Cards: none
Notes: 2, 5, 8, 10

The Victorian Secret

LOUISVILLE

The Victorian Secret Bed and Breakfast

1132 S. First Street, 40203
(502) 581-1914; (800) 449-4691 pin #0604

"Step inside and step back 100 years in time" describes this three-story,

---

NOTES: Credit cards accepted: A Master Card; B Visa; C American Express; D Discover; E Diners Club; F Other; 2 Personal checks accepted; 3 Lunch available; 4 Dinner available;

Victorian brick mansion in historic Louisville. Recently restored to its former elegance, the 100-year-old structure offers spacious accommodations, high ceilings, and original woodwork. The Louisville area, rich in historic homes, will also tempt railbirds and would-be jockeys to make a pilgrimage to the famous tack at Churchill Downs, Home of the Kentucky Derby.

Hosts: Nan and Steve Roosa
Rooms: 6 (2PB; 4SB) $58-89
Continental Breakfast
Credit Cards: none
Notes: 5, 7, 8, 9, 10, 11, 12

MIDDLESBORO

The RidgeRunner B&B

208 Arthur Heights, 40965
(606) 248-4299

Nestled in the Cumberland Mountains of southeast Kentucky sits an 1894 Victorian mansion emphasizing a view, friendly atmosphere, and the peace of yesteryear. "It combines the elegance of Victorian craftsmanship with the warmth of family gatherings." View the spectacular spring and fall mountian foliage from the 60-foot front porch. A family-style home-cooked breakfast is served each morning in the dining room. Enjoy the beauty and history of nearby Cumberland Gab. The facilities are also available for parties and family gatherings.

Hostess: Susan Richards
Rooms: 4 (2PB; 2SB) $55-65
Full Breakfast
Credit Cards: none
Notes: 2, 5, 7 (over 12), 8, 9, 10, 12

The RidgeRunner

NICHOLASVILLE

Sandusky House and The O'Neal Cabin B&B

1626 Delaney Ferry Road, 40356
(606) 223-4730

A tree-lined drive to the Sandusky House is just a prelude to a wonderful visit to the Bluegrass. A quiet ten-acre country setting amid horse farms yet close to downtown Lexington, Kentucky, Horse Par, and Shakertown. The Greek Revival Sandusky House was built circa 1850 from bricks fired on the farm. A 1780, one-thousand-acre land grant from Patrick Henry, governor of Virginia, given to Revolutionary War soldier, Jacob Sandusky. In addtition to the Sandusky House we also have an 1820s, reconstructed, two-story, two-bedroom, authentic log cabin with full kitchen and whirlpool bath. Large stone fireplace, AC, and located in a wooded area close to main house. A get-a-way that is ideal for the entire family! Please call for a brochure.

Hosts: Jim and Linda Humphrey
Rooms: 3 (PB) $69 main house, $85 cabin
Full Breakfast
Credit Cards: A, B
Notes: 2, 5, 7 (over 12 in main house; all in cabin)

---

5 Open all year; 6 Pets welcome; 7 Children welcome; 8 Tennis nearby; 9 Swimming nearby; 10 Golf nearby; 11 Skiing nearby; 12 May be booked through travel agent.

OWENSBORO

Trails End B&B

5931 Highway 56, 42301
(502) 771-5590; FAX (502) 771-4723

Trail's End offers several options in two different locations across state lines. The "Barn Cottage" is named for its location next to the Ramey Riding Stables three miles west of Rockport, Indiana, and ten minutes north of Owensboro on Hwy. #45. This lovely country condo cottage is finely appointed with antiques and furnished patio overlooking the countryside and horse pastures. It has three bedrooms and laundry room with shower and separate tub. Refrigerator is stocked with breakfast "fixin's." Only 45 minutes to Holiday World and less to Lincoln homestead. Overnight stabling also available. "Red House" in Kentucky is adjacent to an indoor tennis club where Ramey Tennis Schools camps are held in season. It sits next to an apple orchard and has horses in the pasture field behind. It has three bedrooms, one queen and two with two bunk beds. A former tenant house, the quaint country cottage has in addition a sitting room, laundry room, and bath with shower and separate tub. Breakfast is served in the clubhouse. An out door pool, tennis courts, playground, and running creek are also on the premises, and two mobile homes are available at a lower rate.

Hostess: Joan G. Ramey
Cottages: 2 (PB) $50-75
Full Southern Breakfast
Credit Cards: A, B
Notes: 2, 5, 6, 7, 8, 9 (outdoor)

PADUCAH

The 1857's Bed and Breakfast

127 Market House Square, 42001-7771
(Mail: PO Box 7771, 42002-7771)
(502) 444-3960 (voice and FAX);
(800) 264-5607

The 1857's Bed and Breakfast is in the center of Paducah's historic downtown on Market House Square. The three-story building was built in 1857 and is on the National Register of Historic Places. The first floor is Cynthia's Ristorante. The second floor guest rooms have been renovated in Victorian Era-style and period furnishings abound. Also available for guest enjoyment on the third floor is a game room with a view of the Ohio River. The game room features an elegant mahogany billiards table. Hot tub also on the second floor, outside deck. Advance reservations advised.

Hostess: Deborah Bohnert
Rooms: 3 (1PB; 2SB) $65-85
Continental Plus Breakfast
Credit Cards: A, B
Notes: 2, 5, 8, 9, 10, 11, 12

Ehrhardt's B&B

285 Springwell Lane, 42001
(502) 554-0644

Our brick Colonial ranch home is located just one mile off I-24, which is noted for its lovely scenery. We hope to make you feel at home in antique-filled bedrooms and a cozy den with a fireplace. Nearby are the beautiful Kentucky and Barkley Lakes and the fa-

---

NOTES: Credit cards accepted: A Master Card; B Visa; C American Express; D Discover; E Diners Club; F Other; 2 Personal checks accepted; 3 Lunch available; 4 Dinner available;

mous Land Between the Lakes area.

Hosts: Eileen and Phil Ehrhardt
Rooms: 2 (SB) $45
Full Breakfast
Credit Cards: none
Notes: 2, 7 (over 6), 8, 9, 10

Paducah Harbor Plaza Bed and Breakfast

201 Broadway, 42001
(502) 442-2698 (voice and FAX);
(800) 719-7799

Paducah Harbor Plaza B&B guests thrive on the attention and hospitality of their innkeeper. On the first floor, guests will find the buildings' original copper ceilings, marble columns, ceramic tile floors, and stained glass windows restored to their original beauty. Four guest rooms are located on the second floor. Each is comfortably furnished with early 20th century antique furniture and warm, handmade quilts. The air-conditioned rooms feature ten foot ceilings, original windows, ceiling fans, and tongue-and-groove painted floors. Historic downtown Paducah offers many attractions, fine restaurants, and cultural events.

Hostess: Beverly McKinley
Rooms: 4 (SB) $65-125
Continental Plus Breakfast
Credit Cards: A, B, C
Notes: 2, 5, 7, 8, 9, 10, 11, 12

Trinity Hills Farm Bed and Breakfast Home

10455 Old Lovelaceville Road, 42001
(800) 488-3998

Trinity Hills Farm, a 17-acre country retreat, provides exceptional service and accommodations. Designed for romantic getaways or family gatherings. Handicap accessible. Features include stained-glass windows, vaulted ceilings, fireplaces, spacious commons areas, and suites with whirlpool or private spa. Outdoors guest may fish, boat, birdwatch, hike, visit the farm animals and peacocks, or relax in the large spa near our water gardens. No smoking.

Hosts: Mike and Ann Driver (owners)
  and Jim and Nancy Driver (Mike's parents)
Rooms: 5 (PB) $60 (2 suites $70-90)
Full Country or Gourmet Breakfast
Credit Cards: A, B, D
Notes: 2, 5, 6 (with prior notice), 7, 12

Trinity Hills Farm

PARIS

Rosedale B&B

1917 Cypress Street, 40361
(606) 987-1845; (800) 644-1862

Nestled on three secluded acres, complete with flower and herb gardens, benches, hammock, and lawn games. The 14-room 1862 Italianate brick home is furnished with comfortable antiques. Guests are welcome to peruse the shelves of the mahogany library with its cozy firplace. The screened

---

5 Open all year; 6 Pets welcome; 7 Children welcome; 8 Tennis nearby; 9 Swimming nearby;
10 Golf nearby; 11 Skiing nearby; 12 May be booked through travel agent.

porch, overlooking some of the gardens, is a picturesque setting for breakfast, reading, and relaxing. Less than 20 miles from I-64 and I-75, and 18 miles NE of Lexington in the heart of Bluegrass thoroughbred horse country. Paris and the surrounding area offers outstanding antique shopping and a number of specialty shops. The Kentucky Horse Park is just 15 minutes away, and Keeneland Race Course, Rupp Arena, and the University of Kentucky are less than 30 minutes away.

Hosts: Katie and Jim Haag
Rooms: 4 (2PB; 2SB) $65-85
Full Breakfast
Credit Cards: A, B
Notes: 2, 5, 7 (12 and up), 8, 10

SPRINGFIELD

Maple Hill Manor Bed and Breakfast

2941 Perryville Road, 40069
(606) 366-3075; (800) 886-7546

Listed on the National Register of Historic Places, we are located on 14 tranquil acres in the scenic Bluegrass region. It took three years to build, circa 1851, has ten-foot doors, 13½-foot ceilings, nine-foot windows, cherry spiral staircase, stenciling in foyer, three brass and crystal chandeliers, and nine fireplaces. The honeymoon hideaway has canopy bed and jacuzzi. One hour from Louisville and Lexington. No smoking.

Hosts: Bob and Kay Carroll
Rooms: 7 (PB) $65-90
Full Breakfast
Credit Cards: A, B
Notes: 2, 5, 7, 8, 9, 10, 12

The Marcum-Porter House

STEARNS

The Marcum-Porter House

PO Box 369, 42647
(606) 376-2242; (606) 748-9070;
(502) 223-3368

Located in the heart of the Big South Fork National Recreation Area, this charming early 20th century house offers gracious accommodations for discriminating guests with interests in history and unspoiled scenic beauty. Homemade gourmet breakfast served in formal dining room. Spacious grounds. Nearby attractions include the Big South Fork Scenic Railway, nine-hole golf course, local history museum, hiking, whitewater rafting and fishing on wild rivers and streams, and Cumberland Falls State Park.

Hosts: Pat Porter Newton/Charles and Sandra Porter
Rooms: 4 (1PB; 3SB) $45-65
Gourmet Breakfast
Credit Cards: A, B
Notes: 2, 7, 10

NOTES: Credit cards accepted: A Master Card; B Visa; C American Express; D Discover; E Diners Club; F Other; 2 Personal checks accepted; 3 Lunch available; 4 Dinner available;

Louisiana

ALSO SEE RESERVATION SERVICES UNDER MISSISSIPPI

Milbank Historic House

JACKSON

Milbank Historic House

PO Box 1000, 3045 Bank Street, 70748
(504) 634-5901

Located in the beautiful Felicianas of Louisiana, Milbank is a massive, romantic antebellum mansion. It has a varied and interesting history. Rooms are furnished with authentic antique furniture of the late 1800s. Persian rugs, ormolu clocks, carved settees, poster beds, armoires, and much more. Upstairs galleries to stand on and enjoy scenic large backyard. Delicious breakfast; friendly hosts. Owners are Mr. and Mrs. M. L. Harvey.

Hosts: Paul and Margurite Carter
Rooms: 3 (PB) $75
Full Breakfast (Continental available on request)
Credit Cards: A, B
Notes: 5 (except holidays), 7 (12 and up), 10

LAYFETTE/CARENCRO

La Maison de Compagne, Lafayette, B&B

825 Kidder Road, **Carencro** 70520
(318) 896-6529; (800) 895-0235;
FAX (318) 896-1494

Beautiful country Victorian home (c. 1871) with nine acres of quiet countryside easily accessible from I-10 and I-49. Pool in season. Children 12 and older accepted. Alcoholic beverages prohibited on premises and smoking outdoors only. Five minutes from three best known Cajun restaurants. Antiques throughout; owern occupied. Attractions included within a 30 mile radius are Ante-bellum homes, churches, fishing, boating, swamp tours, golf, gardens, museums, festivals, food, Cajun

---

5 Open all year; 6 Pets welcome; 7 Children welcome; 8 Tennis nearby; 9 Swimming nearby; 10 Golf nearby; 11 Skiing nearby; 12 May be booked through travel agent.

LOUISIANA

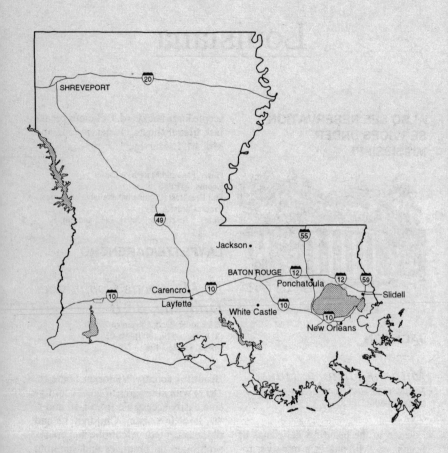

music, and fun—all here in the heart of Cajun Country.

Hosts: Joeann and Fred McLemore
Rooms: 4 (PB) $95-105
Full Breakfast
Credit Cards: A, B, C, D
Notes: 2, 5, 9, 10, 12

NEW ORLEANS

The Dusty Mansion

2231 Gen Pershing, 70115
(504) 895-4576; FAX (504) 891-0049

Charming turn-of-the-century home, cozy and affordable. Sundeck, game room, hot tub. Close to St. Charles Ave. Street Car, easy access to French Quarter, Aquarium, Zoo, and Botanical Gardens.

Hostess: Cynthia Tomlin Riggs
Rooms: 4 (2PB; 2SB) $50-75
Continental Breakfast
Credit Cards: A, B, C, D
Notes: 2, 5, 7, 8, 10, 12

Essem's House "New Orleans First Bed and Breakfast"

3660 Gentilly Boulevard, 70122
(504) 947-3401; (888) 240-0070;
FAX (504) 838-0140

Tree-shaded boulevards, direct transport to French Quarter (15-20 min.), safe, convenient area of stable family homes. This ten room brick home has three bedrooms. One king with private bath. Two doubles with a shared bath.

Separate cottage efficiency (one king or two singles with private bath.) Guests enjoy the solarium, the living room, and the back garden.

Hostess: Sarah Margaret Brown
Rooms: 4 (2PB; 2SB) $55-85
Continental Breakfast
Credit Cards: A, B, C, D
Notes: 2, 5, 7, 8, 9, 10

New Orleans Bed and Breakfast Accommodations

PO Box 8163, 70182
(504) 838-0071; FAX (504) 838-0140

If you appreciate crystal chandeliers, hardwood floors, antiques, Oriental rugs, interesting architecture, or simple traditional elegance, call us. If you want private hide-aways, condominiums, private apartments, or cozy rooms in New Orleans neighborhoods, call us. Whatever your choice, you will find gracious hospitality, knowledgeable hosts who are concerned about your safety, comfort, and pleasure. We are also familiar with bed and breakfast plantations, homes, or cottages throughout Louisiana. Call us, too, for referrals to other states, England, Israel, or a villa in Mallorca. Sarah-Margaret Brown, owner.

The Prytania Inns

1415 Prytania Street, 70131
(504) 566-1515; FAX (504) 566-1518

Built in the 1850s as a private home with slave quarters, Prytania Inn was

---

NOTES: Credit cards accepted: A Master Card; B Visa; C American Express; D Discover; E Diners Club; F Other; 2 Personal checks accepted; 3 Lunch available; 4 Dinner available; 5 Open all year; 6 Pets welcome; 7 Children welcome; 8 Tennis nearby; 9 Swimming nearby; 10 Golf nearby; 11 Skiing nearby; 12 May be booked through travel agent.

actually used as an inn at the turn of the century. Having undergone an award-winning restoration in 1984 with all its original, splendid architecatural features intact, it is once again open to visitors appreciative of the authentic Old New Oreleans atmosphere it evokes. Close by are the Prytania Inn II and III, both are historic mansions in the romantic Neo-classical plantation style and decorated comfortably with antiques. The recently renovated St. Vincent's, an old orphange, also has guest rooms available. The Inns are five minutes from the French Quarter by street car.

Hosts: Peter and Sally Schreiber
Rooms: average 20 per building; $30-69
Full Breakfast
Credit Cards: A, B, C, D, E
Notes: 2, 3, 5, 6, 7, 8, 9, 10

The Prytania Inns

PONCHATOULA

The Bella Rose Mansion
255 N. Eighth Street, 70454
(504) 386-3857 (voice and FAX)
HTTP://cimarron.net/usa/la/bella/html

"When only the best will do." Bella Rose is on the National Historical Register in the heart of America's Antique City and Plantations. Thirty five minutes from New Orleans International Airport and 45 minutes from Baton Rouge. Romantic heart-shaped jacuzzi suites and unique rooms; exquisite hand-carved mahogany, spiral staircase crowned with a stained glass dome is the finest in the South. Guests enjoy a silver service breakfast of eggs Benedict, Banana Foster crepes, Mimosas, and New Orleans blend coffee in a marble walled solarium with a fountain of Bacchus. Georgian in style, the mansion consists of over 12,000 square feet. Indoor terrazzo shuffleboard court, an extensive library, and a heated Olympia style swimming pool are only a few of the magnificent features the await you at the Bella Rose Mansion. Available for functions.

Hostess: Rose James
Rooms: 2 jacuzzi suites + 4 rooms (PB)
Full Breakfast
Credit Cards: A, B
Notes: 5, 8, 9, 10, 12

SLIDELL

Salmen-Fritchie House Bed and Breakfast
127 Cleveland Avenue, 70458
(504) 643-1405; (800) 235-4168;
FAX (504) 643-2251

This magnificent 1895 Victorian home is listed in the "*The Best Places to Stay in the South.*" Just 30 minutes from New Orleans famous French Quarter or the Mississippi Gulf Coast. Easy access from I-10 Expressway. Family owned

NOTES: Credit cards accepted: A Master Card; B Visa; C American Express; D Discover; E Diners Club; F Other; 2 Personal checks accepted; 3 Lunch available; 4 Dinner available;

for 100 years, it now offers comfortable lodging for personal and business travelers. Home sits on a four and one half acre city block with 300 year old live oaks, and is listed on the National Historic Register. Home has five guest rooms in the main house and one cottage with a living room, kitchen combo, laundry facility, private bedroom, screened porch with courtyard, and marble jacuzzi for two.

Hosts: Sharon and Homer Fritchie
Rooms: 5 (PB) $85-95; cottage $225
Full Breakfast
Credit Cards: A, B, C
Notes: 2, 5, 7 (over 10), 8, 9, 10, 11, 12

Salmen-Fritchie House Bed and Breakfast

WHITE CASTLE

Nottoway Plantation Inn and Restaurant

PO Box 160, 30970 Highway 405, 70788
(504) 545-2730 or (504) 545-9167;
FAX (504) 545-8632

Built in 1859 by John Randolph, a wealthy sugar cane planter, Nottoway is a Neo-classical mansion. Nottoway is the largest remaining plantation home in the South. Its guest rooms are individually decorated with period furnishings. Wake up with juice, coffee, and homemade muffins served to your room. Full breakfast served downstairs.

Hostess: Cindy Hidalgo
Rooms: 10 +, 3 suites (PB) $125-250
Full Breakfast
Credit Cards: A, B, C, D
Notes: 2, 3, 4, 5, 7, 8, 9, 10, 12

---

5 Open all year; 6 Pets welcome; 7 Children welcome; 8 Tennis nearby; 9 Swimming nearby; 10 Golf nearby; 11 Skiing nearby; 12 May be booked through travel agent.

MAINE

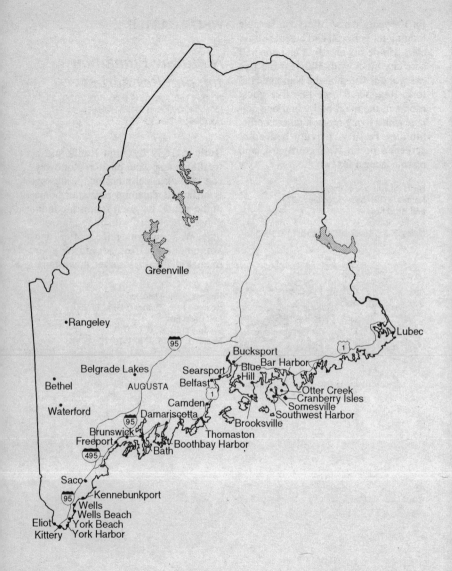

Maine

BAR HARBOR

The Atlantic Oakes
The Willows

PO Box 3, Eden Street, 04609
(207) 288-5801; (800) 33 MAINE;
FAX (207) 288-8402
Web site: http://barharbor.com/oakes.html

We have restored the Sir Harry Oakes
mansion/summer cottage on our
grounds. This charming house was
named *The Willows* after the willow
trees on the entrance drive. About 200
summer cottages were built in Bar Harbor from 1880 to 1890. *The Willows*
was built in 1913, one of the last estates built. The large wooden hotels
(now gone) were built from 1865-1885.
No matter how large and ostentatious
the summer homes were, they were always called "cottages." *The Willows* is
located on the ground of the Atlantic
Oakes By-The-Sea. There are four tennis courts and indoor and outdoor pools
available for use by B&B guests.

Hosts: The Coughs
Rooms: 9 (PB) $65-250
Continental or Full Breakfast
Credit Cards: A, B, C
Notes: 5, 8, 9, 10, 12

Black Friar Inn

10 Summer Street, 04609
(207) 288-5091; FAX (207) 288-4197

Black Friar Inn is a completely rebuilt
and restored inn incorporating beautiful woodwork, mantels, windows, and
bookcases from old mansions and
churches on Mount Desert Island.
Gourmet breakfast includes homemade
breads, pastry, and muffins; fresh fruit;
eggs du jour; etc. Afternoon refreshments are provided. All rooms have
queen beds; the suite has a king bed.
Within walking distance of the waterfront, restaurants, and shops, with

Black Friar Inn

NOTES: Credit cards accepted: A Master Card; B Visa; C American Express; D Discover;
E Diners Club; F Other; 2 Personal checks accepted; 3 Lunch available; 4 Dinner available;
5 Open all year; 6 Pets welcome; 7 Children welcome; 8 Tennis nearby; 9 Swimming nearby;
10 Golf nearby; 11 Skiing nearby; 12 May be booked through travel agent.

ample parking available. Short drive to Acadia National Park.

Hosts: Perry and Sharon, Risley and Falke
Rooms: 7 (PB) $90-140
Full Breakfast
Credit Cards: A, B
Notes: 2, 5, 7 (over 11), 8, 9, 10, 11 (x-country)

BATH

Fairhaven Inn

RR 2, Box 85, N. Bath Road, 04530
(207) 443-4391

A 1790 Colonial nestled on the hillside overlooking the Kennebec River on 20 acres of country sights and sounds. Beaches, golf, and maritime museum nearby, plus cross-country ski trails and wood fires. Gourmet breakfast is served year-round. Candlelight dinners available in winter.

Hosts: Susie and Dave Reed
Rooms: 8 (6PB; 2SB) $70-100
Full Breakfast
Credit Cards: A, B
Notes: 4 (weekend package), 5, 6 and 7 (by arrangement), 8, 9, 10, 11 (x-country)

BELFAST

The Jeweled Turret Inn

40 Pearl Street, 04915
(207) 338-2304; (800) 696-2304

This grand lady of the Victorian era, circa 1898, offers many unique architectural features and is on the National Register of Historic Places. The Inn is named for the grand staircase that winds up the turret, lighted by stained and leaded glass panels with jewel-like embellishments. Each guest room is filled with Victoriana and has its own bath. A gourmet breakfast is served. Shops, restaurants, and waterfront are a stroll away.

Hosts: Carl and Cathy Heffentrager
Rooms: 7 (PB) $60-95
Full Breakfast
Credit Cards: A, B
Notes: 2, 5, 8, 9, 10, 11,12

BELGRADE LAKES

Wings Hill

Route 27, PO Box 386, 04918
(207) 495-2400; (800) 50 WINGS

The ultimate stop in central Maine. In a class by itself, the Inn is powerfully decorated with oriental, art, and antiques. Large guest rooms with private baths. A great base for all vacation needs. Sensational food and accommodations. Quiet, adult, refined luxury. Renovated 200 year old farm house. Wonderful grounds in a scenic area.

Hosts: Dick Hofmann
Rooms: 8 (PB) $95
Full Breakfast
Credit Cards: A, B, C
Notes: 2, 5, 7, 9, 10, 11, 12

BETHEL

Sunday River Inn and Cross Country Ski Center

R.R. 2, Box 1688, 04217
(207) 824-2410; FAX (207) 824-3181

Sunday River Inn is a small country resort built around winter sports. A nationally renowned cross-country ski

---

NOTES: Credit cards accepted: A Master Card; B Visa; C American Express; D Discover; E Diners Club; F Other; 2 Personal checks accepted; 3 Lunch available; 4 Dinner available;

Sunday River Inn

center is adjacent to the Inn, and Sunday River Ski Resort with eight mountains of alpine skiing is one-half mile away. A wood-fired sauna and hot tub, a skating rink, snowshoe trails, and dogsledding are also available. With all this the guests still return for the *food!*

Hosts: Steve and Peggy Wight
Rooms: 17 (2PB; 15SB) $65-78 prepaid
Full Breakfast and Dinner
Credit Cards: A, B, C, D
Notes: 2, 4, 7, 8, 9, 10, 11, 12

BLUE HILL

Mountain Road House

R.R. 1, Box 2040 Mountain Road, 04614
(207) 374-2794

Located on the only road that traverses the face of Blue Hill Mountain, our 1890s farmhouse offers views of the Bay while only one mile from the village. Choose twin, double, or queen-size bedrooms, each with private bath. Early bird coffee/tea available at 7 AM, the breakfast includes a hot entree, fresh fruit, and coffee cake. Enjoy antiquing, galleries, craft shops, bookstores, musical events, fine dining, hiking, coastal

villages, and of course Acadia National Park. No smoking.

Hosts: Carol and John McCulloch
Rooms: 3 (PB) $55-85
Full Breakfast
Credit Cards: A, B
Notes: 2, 5, 7, 12

BOOTHBAY HARBOR

Admiral's Quarters Inn

Commercial Street, 04538
(207) 633-2474

Commanding an unsurpassed view of the Harbor. This is a large old sea captain's house set on a knoll looking out to sea. Charming rooms, all with private entrances, baths, individual decks, and decorated with a blend of white wicker and antiques. Ceiling fans cool several of the suites when sea breezed aren't working their magic. Each day begins with a hearty homemad breakfast which will fullfill any Admiral's demands. "Way out of the ordinary . . . but not out of the way!"

Hosts: Les and Deb Hallstrom
Rooms: 6 (PB) $65-125
Full Hearty, Homemade Breakfast
Credit Cards: A, B, D
Notes: 2, 5, 8, 9, 10

Admiral's Quarters Inn

5 Open all year; 6 Pets welcome; 7 Children welcome; 8 Tennis nearby; 9 Swimming nearby; 10 Golf nearby; 11 Skiing nearby; 12 May be booked through travel agent.

Anchor Watch
Bed and Breakfast

3 Eames Road, 04538
(207) 633-7565

Our seaside, captain's house welcomes you to Boothbay Region. It's a pleasant walk to unique shops, fine dining, and scenic boat trips. A delicious homemade breakfast is served in the sunny breakfast nook looking out to the sea. Quilts, stenciling, and nautical decor make our four bedrooms comfortable and cozy. Enjoy your afternoon tea in the attractive sitting room facing the ocean. Your host captains the Monhegan and Squirrel Island ferries from nearby Pier 8.

Hostess: Diane Campbell
Rooms: 4 (PB) $75-105
Full Breakfast
Credit Cards: A, B
Notes: 2, 5, 8, 9, 10, 12

Five Gables Inn

Five Gables Inn

PO Box 335 Murray Hill Road, **East Boothbay** 04544
(207) 633-4551; (800) 451-5048

The last of Linekin Bay's turn-of-the-century summer hotels. A beautifully restored inn. Each room has private bath

and a breathtaking view of the Bay. Each morning guests enjoy a full breakfast on our large veranda overlooking the Bay. After a day of whalewatching, sightseeing, or visiting L. L. Bean in Freeport, relax with afternoon tea (including something freshly baked).

Hosts: Mike and De Kennedy
Rooms: 16 (PB) $100-170
Full Breakfast
Credit Cards: A, B
Notes: 2, 9, 10, 12

Harbour Towne Inn
on the Waterfront

71 Townsend Avenue, 04538
(207) 633-4300 (voice and FAX);
(800) 722-4240

THE FINEST B&B ON THE WATERFRONT. Our refurbished Victorian Inn retains turn-of-the-century ambiance while providing all modern amenities. The colorful gardens and quiet, tree-shaded location slopes right to the edge of the beautiful New England harbor. Choose an Inn room with or without an outside deck for scenic views or a Carriage House room with waterfront decks. Our luxurious penthouse is a modern and spacious home that sleeps six people in absolute luxury and privacy. Come stay with us just once and you will know why our guests return year after year. No smoking.

Hosts: E. George Thomas (owner) and Nancy
     McClure (manager)
Rooms: 12 (PB) $49-150 ($79-250 in season)
Continental Breakfast
Credit Cards: A, B, C, D
Notes: 2, 5, 7 (well behaved), 8, 9, 10, 11, 12

NOTES: Credit cards accepted: A Master Card; B Visa; C American Express; D Discover; E Diners Club; F Other; 2 Personal checks accepted; 3 Lunch available; 4 Dinner available;

BROOKSVILLE

Oakland House—Shore Oaks Seaside Inn

RR 1 Box 400, Herrick Road, 04617
(800) 359-RELAX; FAX can be arranged

The Inn was built in 1907 as a private Craftsman / Mission style summer cottage. Victorian pieces are tastefully blended in. There is a living room with stone fireplace, library, dining room, porch, and gazebo / deck extending out onto the water. See loons, seals, and windjammers right off shore. Relax, dream. . . , breakfast, dine (in season). Use Oakland House's dock, rowboats, firewood, salt / freshwater beaches, and climb to grand vistas. Bar Harbor, Acadia National Park, Stonington, Blue Hill, Isle au Haut, and the "Mailboat" are nearby.

Hosts: Jim and Sally Littlefield
Rooms: 10 (7PB; 3SB) $41-172
Seasonal Full or Continental Breakfast
Credit Cards: none
Notes: 2, 3, 4, 9, 10, 12

BRUNSWICK

Harborgate Bed and Breakfast

R.D. 2, Box 2260, 04011
(207) 725-5894

This contemporary redwood home is 40 feet from the ocean. Flower gardens and wooded landscape provide gracious relaxation. Two ocean-facing, first floor bedrooms are separated by a guest living room with patio. Dock for swimming and sunbathing. Close to Bowdoin College, L.L. Bean, and sandy beaches. Wide selection of stores, gift shops, and steak and seafood restaurants. Summer theater, college art museum, Perry McMillan Museum, and historical society buildings and events.

Hostess: Carolyn Bolles
Rooms: 2 (SB) $60
Continental Breakfast
Credit Cards: none
Closed November through April
Notes: 2, 9

BUCKSPORT

Old Parsonage Inn

PO Box 1577, 04416
(207) 469-6477

The Clough family invites you to share their historic Federal home, formerly the Methodist parsonage, located one half mile from coastal Route 1. All rooms are tastefully decorated and retain original architectural features. The third floor houses an 1809 Masonic Hall. Private guest entrance, kitchenette in the breakfast/sitting room. Short walk to waterfront and restaurants. Convenient for day trips to Acadia, both sides of Penobscot Bay, and historic Fort Knox.

Hosts: Judith and Brian Clough
Rooms: 3 (1PB; 2SB) $45
No Breakfast
Credit Cards: A, B
Notes: 2, 5, 7, 8, 9, 10

---

5 Open all year; 6 Pets welcome; 7 Children welcome; 8 Tennis nearby; 9 Swimming nearby; 10 Golf nearby; 11 Skiing nearby; 12 May be booked through travel agent.

CAMDEN

The Owl and Turtle Harbor View Guest Rooms

PO Box 1265, 8 Bay View, 04843
(207) 236-9014

Two of the three rooms immediately overlook the harbor. Air-conditioning, TV, electric heat, phone, private bath, private parking. Continental breakfast served on tray to room. Downstairs is one of the states best book shops. Surrounded by good restaurants and shops. No smoking.

Hosts: The Conrad Family
Rooms: 3 (PB) $50-55 (off season)
    $80-90 (in season) + tax
Continental Breakfast
Credit Cards: A, B
Notes: 2, 5, 7, 8, 9, 10, 11, 12

CRANBERRY ISLES

The Red House

PO Box 164, Main Road, 04625
(207) 244-5297

Enjoy the breathtaking beauty of Maine, while experiencing the relaxing, quiet atmosphere of The Red House on Great Cranberry Island. Situated on a large saltwater inlet, guests need only look outside for beautiful scenery and extraordinary ocean views. At The Red House there are six guest rooms and each is distinctively decorated in traditional style; some with shared baths and some private with baths. Come and share your hosts' island home and ex-

perience the tranquil peace of God's creation.

Hosts: Dorothy and John Towns
Rooms: 6 (3PB; 3SB) $50-80
Full Breakfast
Credit Cards: A, B
Notes: 2, 4, 7 (over 6), 9, 10 (off island)

DAMARISCOTTA

Brannon-Bunker Inn

H.C.R. 64, Box 045B, 04543
(207) 563-5941

Brannon-Bunker Inn is an intimate and relaxed country bed and breakfast situated minutes from sandy beach, lighthouse, and historic fort in Maine's mid-coastal region. Located in a 1920s Cape, converted barn and carriage house, the guest rooms are furnished in themes regarding the charm of yesterday and the comforts of today. Antique shops, too!

Hosts: Jeanne and Joe Hovance
Rooms: 7 (5PB; 2SB) $60-70
Continental Plus Breakfast
Credit Cards: A, B, C
Notes: 2, 5, 7, 8, 9, 10, 12

ELIOT

Farmstead Bed and Breakfast

379 Goodwin Road, 03903
(207) 748-3145

Lovely country inn on three acres. Warm, friendly atmosphere exemplifies farm life of the late 1800s. Guest rooms are Victorian in style. Each has

---

NOTES: Credit cards accepted: A Master Card; B Visa; C American Express; D Discover; E Diners Club; F Other; 2 Personal checks accepted; 3 Lunch available; 4 Dinner available;

Farmstead Bed and Breakfast

mini-refrigerator and microwave for late evening snacks or those special diets. Full breakfast may include blueberry pancakes or french toast, homemade syrup, fruit, and juice. Handicap accessible. Minutes from Kittery Factory Outlets, York Beaches, and Portsmouth, NH, historic sites. One hour from Boston.

Hosts: Meb and John Lippincott
Rooms: 6 (PB) $48-54
Full Breakfast
Credit Cards: A, B, C
Notes: 2, 5, 6, 7, 12

FREEPORT

Captain Josiah Mitchell House Bed and Breakfast

188 Main Street, 04032
(207) 865-3289

Two blocks from L.L. Bean, this house is a few minutes walk past centuries-old sea captains' homes and shady trees to over 120 factory outlet discount shops in town. After exploring, relax on our beautiful, peaceful veranda with antique wicker furniture and "remem-

ber when" porch swing. State inspected and approved. Family owned and operated.

Hosts: Loretta and Alan Bradley
Rooms: 7 (PB) $68-85 (lower winter rates)
Full Breakfast
Credit Cards: A, B
Notes: 2, 5, 8, 9, 10, 11, 12

Country at Heart Bed and Breakfast

37 Bow Street, 04032
(207) 865-0512

Our cozy 1870s home is located off Main Street and only two blocks from L.L. Bean. Park your car and walk to the restaurants and many outlet stores. Stay in one of three country decorated rooms: the Shaker Room, Quilt Room, or the Teddy Bear Room. Our rooms have hand-stenciled borders, handmade crafts, and either antique or reproduction furnishings. There is also a gift shop for guests.

Hosts: Roger and Kim Dubay
Rooms: 3 (PB) $65-85
Full Breakfast
Credit Cards: A, B
Notes: 2, 5, 7, 9, 10, 11, 12

5 Open all year; 6 Pets welcome; 7 Children welcome; 8 Tennis nearby; 9 Swimming nearby; 10 Golf nearby; 11 Skiing nearby; 12 May be booked through travel agent.

GREENVILLE

Greenville Inn

PO Box 1194 Norris Street, 04441
(207) 695-2206 (voice and FAX);
(888) 695-6000

Restored 1895 lumber baron's mansion on a hillside overlooking Moosehead Lake and the Squaw Mountains. A large leaded glass window decorated with a painted spruce tree, gas lights, embossed wall coverings, and carved fireplace mantles grace the Inn. A sumptuous continental breakfast buffet is included with the room. In the evening our restaurant is open to the public. Open year-round.

Hosts: Effie, Michael, and Susie Schnetzer
Rooms: 12 (PB) $75-165
Continental Plus Buffet Breakfast
Credit Cards: A, B, D
Notes: 2, 4, 5, 8, 9, 10, 11, 12

KENNEBUNKPORT

The Captain Lord Mansion

PO Box 800, 04046
(207) 967-3141; FAX (207) 967-3172

The Captain Lord Mansion is an intimate and stylish inn situated at the head of a large village green, overlooking the Kennebunk River. Built during the War of 1812 as an elegant, private residence, it is now listed on the National Historic Register. The large, luxurious guest rooms are furnished with rich fabrics, European paintings, and fine period antiques, yet have modern creature comforts such as private baths and working fireplaces. Christians, as well as gracious hosts and innkeepers, Bev Davis, husband Rick Litchfield and their friendly, helpful staff are eager to make your visit enjoyable. Family style breakfasts are served in an atmospheric, country kitchen. A conference room is also available.

Hosts: Bev Davis / Rick Litchfield
Rooms: 16 (PB) $125-249
Full Breakfast
Credit Cards: A, B, D
Notes: 2, 5, 8, 9, 10, 11 (cross-country)

The Inn on South Street

PO Box 478A, 04046
(207) 967-5151; (800) 963-5151

Now approaching its 200th year, this stately Greek Revival house is in Kennebunkport's historic district. Located on a quiet street, the Inn is within walking distance of restaurants, shops, and the water. There are three beautifully decorated guest rooms and one luxury apartment/suite. Private baths, queen-size beds, fireplaces, a common room, afternoon refreshments, and early morning coffee. Breakfast is always special and is served in the large country kitchen with views of the river and ocean. Rated A[+] and Excellent by ABBA.

Hosts: Jaques and Eva Downs
Rooms: 3 + 1 suite (PB) $85-145; $155-195 suite
Full Breakfast
Credit Cards: A, B
Notes: 2, 8, 9, 10, 11, 12

NOTES: Credit cards accepted: A Master Card; B Visa; C American Express; D Discover; E Diners Club; F Other; 2 Personal checks accepted; 3 Lunch available; 4 Dinner available;

Maine Stay Inn and Cottages

34 Maine Street, PO Box 500A-CBB, 04046
(207) 967-2117; (800) 950-2117;
FAX (207) 967-8757

A grand Victorian inn that exudes charm from its wraparound porch to its perennial flower garden and spacious lawn. The white clapboard house, built in 1860 and listed on the National Historic Register, and the adjoining cottages sit grandly in Kennebunkport's historic district. The Main Stay features a variety of delightful accommodations all with private baths, color cable TV, and air-conditioning. A sumptuous full breakfast and afternoon tea are included. The Inn is an easy walk to the harbor, shops, galleries, and restaurants. AAA 3-diamond and Mobil 3-stars rated.

Hosts: Lindsay and Carol Copelang
Rooms: 17 (PB) $85-210
Full Breakfast
Credit Cards: A, B
Notes: 5, 7, 8, 9, 10, 12

Maine Stay Inn

KITTERY

Enchanted Nights Bed and Breakfast

29 Wentworth Street, Scenic Route 103, 03904
(207) 439-1489

Affordable luxury 75 minutes north of Boston, Coastal Maine. Fanciful and whimsical for the romantic at heart. French and Victorian furnishings with CATVs. Three minutes to historic Portsmouth dining, dancing, concerts in the park, historic homes, theater, harbor cruises, cliff walks, scenic ocean drives, beaches, charming neighboring resorts, water park, and outlet malls. Whirlpool tub for two. Full breakfast, or $12 less, and enjoy a Portsmouth cafe. Pets welcome. No smoking indoors.

Hosts: Nancy Bogenberger / Peter Lamandia
Rooms: 8 (6PB; 2SB) $47-147
Full Breakfast
Credit Cards: A, B, C, D
Notes: 2, 5, 6, 7, 8, 9, 10, 12

LUBEC

Breakers By the Bay

37 Washington, 04652
(207) 733-2487

Visit the unspoiled coast of Maine in this quaint New England fishing village. Breakers By the Bay is one of the oldest home in a town that was founded over 200 years ago. The house features original hand huned floors upstairs and beams visible in the basement, including handmade square nails. The house is furnishedwith antiques, hand quilted bedspreads on antique beds, and hand

---

5 Open all year; 6 Pets welcome; 7 Children welcome; 8 Tennis nearby; 9 Swimming nearby; 10 Golf nearby; 11 Skiing nearby; 12 May be booked through travel agent.

crocheted table clothes. You will enjoy breathtaking views of the bay from your own private deck. Your breakfast is served at your convenience in the formal dining room. Relax under our large old maple trees, one dated to be 300- to 400-years-old. Visit Quaddy Head State Park, The Franklin D. Roosevelt House on Campobello Island, and the lighthouses. You will remember your stay always!

Hostess: Marilyn Elg
Rooms: 5 (PB) $50-70 + tax
Full Breakfast
Credit Cards: none
Notes: 2, 8, 10, 12

MT. DESERT/SOMESVILLE

Long Pond Inn, a B&B
Box 120, 04660
(207) 244-5854

Conveniently located in historic Somesville, the heart of Mt. Desert Island, the Inn offers a peaceful retreat within 15 minutes of all island activities. Our Inn offers warmth and hospitality that reflects an admired tradition associated with New England inns. The Inn was built with dismantled vintage materials from summer estates, country stores, hotels, and cottages. Four guest bedrooms are uniquely furnished featuring a cozy two-room suite with king-size bed, private deck, and jacuzzi tub. We also have three rooms with queen-size beds, private baths, and one with additional jacuzzi tub. Your stay includes a hearty, continental breakfast of fresh seasonal fruit and homemade muffins. After breakfast take a stroll in our gardens or paddle one of our rental canoes on Long Pond. Our rooms are single and double occupancy only.

Hosts: Lois and Brian Hamor
Rooms: 4 (PB) $75-125
Continental Plus Breakfast
Credit Cards: A, B
Notes: 2, 7 (12 and under), 8, 9, 10

OTTER CREEK

Otter Creek Inn
Otter Creek Road, Route 3, PO Box 9, 04665
(207) 288-9422; FAX (207) 288-0325

The Otter Creek Inn offers a variety of friendly, affordable, and convenient accommodations in a location perfect for enjoying the beauty of Acadia National Park. Perfect for outdoor enthusiasts who enjoy hiking, bicycling, rock climbing, and horseback riding as well as travelers who are looking for a quiet setting to marvel at nature's wonders. Our six newly-renovated guest rooms all have private baths, and their are two cabins with full kitchens and housekeeping facilities. Our large two bedroom apartment offers a full kitchen, living room, and dining area that is ideal for two couples or a small family.

Rooms: 9 (PB) $60-125
Credit Cards: A, B
Continental Breakfast
Open May to October
Notes: 2

OTTER CREEK INN
A Bed-and-Breakfast

NOTES: Credit cards accepted: A Master Card; B Visa; C American Express, D Discover; E Diners Club; F Other; 2 Personal checks accepted; 3 Lunch available; 4 Dinner available;

RANGELEY

Northwoods Bed and Breakfast

PO Box 79, Main Street, 04970
(207) 864-2440

An historic 1912 home of rare charm and easy elegance, Northwoods is centrally located in Rangeley Village with spacious rooms, a lakefront porch, expansive grounds, and private boat dock. Northwoods provides superb accommodations. Golf, tennis, water sports, hiking, and skiing are a few of the many activities offered by the region.

Hosts: Carol and Robert Scofield
Rooms: 4 (3PB; 1SB) $60-75 ($70-90 in season)
Full Breakfast
Credit Cards: A, B
Notes: 2, 8, 9, 10, 11, 12

SACO

Crown 'N' Anchor Inn

PO Box 228, 121 N. Street, 04072-0228
(207) 282-3829; (800) 561-8865

Our North Street location places the Crown 'N' Anchor Inn at the hub of local attractions. Delight in this Greek revival two-story house with ornate Victorian furnishings, period antiques, and many collectibles. Guests desiring to take time out from their busy schedules are invited to socialize in our parlor, curl up with a good book in our library, or just relax and enjoy the garden views from the comfort of our front porch. Just minutes from Kennebunkport, Wells, Ogunquit, Kittery, and more.

Hosts: John Barclay and Martha Forester
Rooms: 6 (PB) $60-95
Full Breakfast
Credit Cards: A, B, C
Notes: 2, 5, 6, 7 (by arrangement), 8, 9, 10, 11, 12

SEARSPORT

Brass Lantern Inn

PO Box 407, 81 W. Main St. (US Rt. 1), 04974
(207) 548-0150; (800) 691-0150
Email: brasslan@brasslan.sdi.astate.net

Nestled at the edge of the woods, this gracious Victorian inn, built in 1850 by a sea captain, overlooks Penobscot Bay. Features include an ornate tin ceiling in the dining room, antiques, an extensive doll collection, and a shop on premises specializing in collectible trains. Each guest room has a private bath and is designed for a comfortable stay. Near Penobscot Marine Museum. Open all year, The Brass Lantern will be lit to welcome you!

Hostesses: Pat Gatto and Lee Anne Lee
Rooms: 4 (PB) $75-85
Full Breakfast
Credit Cards: A, B
Notes: 2, 5, 7, 8, 9, 10, 11, 12

Thurston House Bed and Breakfast Inn

8 Elm Street, PO Box 686, 04974
(207) 548-2213; (800) 240-2213; Call about FAX
Email: thurston@accadia.net

This beautiful colonial home, circa 1830, with ell and carriage house was

---

5 Open all year; 6 Pets welcome; 7 Children welcome; 8 Tennis nearby; 9 Swimming nearby; 10 Golf nearby; 11 Skiing nearby; 12 May be booked through travel agent.

built as a parsonage house for Stephen Thurston, uncle of Winslow Homer, who visited often. Now you can visit in a casual environment. The quiet village setting is steps away from Penobscot Marine Museum, beach park on Penobscot Bay, restaurants, churches, galleries, antiques, and more. Relax in one of four guest rooms, one with a bay view, two great for kids, and enjoy the "forget about lunch" breakfasts.

Hosts: Carl and Beverly Eppig
Rooms: 4 (2PB; 2SB) $50-65
Full Breakfast
Credit Cards: A, B
Notes: 2, 5, 7, 8, 9, 10, 11, 12

SOUTHWEST HARBOR

The Island House

PO Box 1006, Clark Point Road, 04679
(207) 244-5180

Relax in a gracious, restful seacoast home on the quiet side of Mt. Desert Island. We serve such Island House favorites as blueberry scones and fresh fruit crepes. A charming, private loft apartment is available. Acadia National Park is only a five-minute drive away. Located across the street from the harbor, near swimming, sailing, biking, and hiking.

Hosts: Ann and Charles Bradford
Rooms: 4 (SB; PB off season) $50-95
Full Breakfast
Credit Cards: A, B (for overseas guests and guarantee of room)
Notes: 2, 5, 7 (over 5, well supervised), 9, 10, 11, 12

Island Watch Bed and Breakfast

PO Box 1359, Freeman Ridge Road, 04679
(207) 244-7229

Wake to the rising sun over Cadillac Mountain and the majestic sea, high atop Freeman Ridge in the heart of Mount Desert Island, on the quiet side. A birdwatcher's paradise where wildlife abounds. A 15 minute walk to Acadia National Park, five minutes to the village center. Superb accommodations includes smoke free atmosphere, private baths, and hearty breakfasts.

Hostess: Maxine Clark
Rooms: 6 (PB) $75-85
Full Breakfast
Credit Cards: none
Notes: 2, 8, 9, 10

Lambs Ear Inn

Lambs Ear Inn

60 Clark Point Road, PO Box 30, 04679
(207) 244-9828

Our old Maine house was built in 1857. It is comfortable and scenic, away from the hustle and bustle. Private baths, comfortable beds with crisp, fresh linens. Sparkling harbor views and a

---

NOTES: Credit cards accepted: A Master Card; B Visa; C American Express; D Discover; E Diners Club; F Other; 2 Personal checks accepted; 3 Lunch available; 4 Dinner available;

breakfast to remember. Come and be a part of this special village and of Mt. Desert Island surrounded by Acadia National Park.

Hostess: Elizabeth Hoke
Rooms: 8 (PB) $75-145
Full Breakfast
Credit Cards: A, B, C, D
Notes: 2 (restricted), 7 (limited), 8, 9, 10, 12

THOMASTON

Cap'n Frost Bed and Breakfast

241 Main Street, 04861
(207) 354-8217

Our 1840 Cape is furnished with country antiques, some of which are for sale. If you are visiting our mid-coastal area, we are a comfortable overnight stay, close to Mohegan Island and a two-hour drive to Acadia National Park. Reservations are helpful.

Hosts: Arlene and Harold Frost
Rooms: 3 (1PB; 2SB) $45-50
Full Breakfast
Credit Cards: none
Notes: 2, 5, 9, 11

WATERFORD

Kedarburn Inn

Rt. 35, Box 61, 04088
(207) 583-6182; FAX (207) 583-6424

Located in historic Waterford Village, a place to step back in time while you enjoy the comforts of today. Charming

bedrooms decorated with warm country touches, including handmade quilts by Margaret, will add pleasure to your visit. Each day will start with a hearty breakfast. In the evening one can relax and enjoy an elegant dinner served daily. Whether you come for outdoor activities or simply to enjoy the countryside, let us pamper you in our relaxed and friendly atmosphere.

Hosts: Margaret and Derek Gibson
Rooms: 6 (4PB; 2SB) $69-88
Full Breakfast
Credit Cards: A, B, C, D
Notes: 2, 5, 6, 7, 9, 10, 11, 12

The Parsonage House Bed and Breakfast

Rice Road, PO Box 116, 04088
(207) 583-4115

Built in 1870 for the Waterford Church, this restored historic home overlooks Waterford Village, Keoka Lake, and Mt. Tirem. It is located in a four-season area providing a variety of opportunities for the outdoor enthusiast. The Parsonage is a haven of peace where Christ is honored. Three double guest rooms are tastefully furnished. Weather permitting, we feature a full breakfast on the screened porch. Guests love our large New England farm kitchen and its glowing wood-burning stove.

Hosts: Joe and Gail St. Hilaire
Rooms: 3 (1PB; 2SB) $60-85
Full Breakfast
Credit Cards: none
Notes: 2, 3, 5, 7, 9, 10, 11

WELLS

Purple Sandpiper Guest House

1058 Post Road (Rt. 1), 04090
(207) 646-7990

Year-round bed and breakfast, just one mile from Wells Beach. All six rooms have private baths and entrances, color cable TV, and refrigerators. We also have an inground pool and barbecue area. In-season trolley service. Continental breakfast includes fresh-baked muffins, pastry, breads, cereal, juice, and coffee. Enjoy Wells's beaches, antique shops, and fine seafood restaurants. Conveniently located minutes from Kennebunkport, Ogunquit Village, York Harbor's lighthouse, and Kittery's shopping outlets.

Hosts: Stephen and Amy Beauregard
Rooms: 6 (PB); $35-75
Continental Breakfast
Credit Cards: A, B
Notes: 5, 7, 8, 9, 10

Sand Dollar Inn B&B on the Beach

WELLS BEACH

Sand Dollar Inn Bed and Breakfast on the Beach

50 Rachel Carson Lane, 04090
(207) 646-2346

Come, renew your spirit at our 1920s oceanfront beach house. The roll of the ocean waves, smell of salt air breezes, the majesty of a starlit sky are simple creations of God accented by bountiful breakfasts and warm hospitality that will place you in a state of peace and tranquility. Join us.

Hosts: Bob and Carolyn Della Pietra
Rooms: 5 (3PB; 2SB) $75-135
Full Breakfast
Credit Cards: A, B
Notes: 2, 4 (occasionally), 5, 9, 10

YORK BEACH

Homestead Inn Bed and Breakfast

PO Box 15, 03910
(207) 363-8952

Friendly, quiet, and homey—four rooms in an old (1905) boardinghouse converted to our home in 1969. Panoramic view of ocean and shore hills. Walk to two beaches, shops, and Nubble Lighthouse. Great for small, adult groups. Fireplace in living room. Breakfast served in barn board dining room and outside on private sun deck.

Hosts: Dan and Danielle Duffy
Rooms: 4 (SB) $54-64
Continental Plus Breakfast
Credit Cards: none
Notes: 2, 8, 9, 10, 12

Homestead Inn

YORK HARBOR

Bell Buoy
Bed and Breakfast
570 York St., PO Box 445 (Route 1A), 03911
(207) 363-7264

At the Bell Buoy, there are no strangers, only friends who have never met. Located minutes from I-95 and US 1, minutes from Kittery outlet malls, or a short walk to sandy beaches or you may want to stroll the marginal way along the ocean shore just minutes away. Fireplace and cable TV. Homemade bread or muffins are served with breakfast in the dining room each morning or on the front porch.

Hosts: Wes and Kathie Cook
Rooms: 5 (2PB; 3SB) $65-85
Full Breakfast
Credit Cards: none
Notes: 2, 5, 7 (over 6), 8, 9, 10

5 Open all year; 6 Pets welcome; 7 Children welcome; 8 Tennis nearby; 9 Swimming nearby; 10 Golf nearby; 11 Skiing nearby; 12 May be booked through travel agent.

MARYLAND

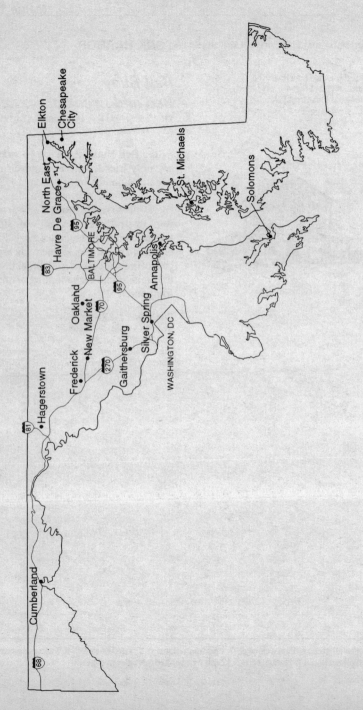

Maryland

ALSO SEE LISTINGS UNDER DISTRICT OF COLUMBIA.

ANNAPOLIS

The Barn on Howard's Cove

500 Wilson Road, 21401
(410) 266-6840; FAX (410) 266-7293

The Barn on Howard's Cove welcomes you with warm hospitality to a converted 1850's horse barn overlooking a beautiful cove of the Severn River. You will be located just outside the hub-bub of Annapolis and convenient to both Baltimore and Washington, D.C. Begin the day with choice of full breakfasts served in dining area, on a sunny deck, or a solarium—all overlooking the river. Enjoy beautiful gardens, rural setting, antiques, quilts, Oriental rugs, antiques, and a charming Noah's ark collection. Two guest rooms, both with private bathrooms, await you. One room has a sleeping loft and private deck on the river. Both guest rooms overlook the river. Docking in deep water provided.

Hosts: Graham and Libbie Gutsche
Rooms: 2 (PB) $85-90
Full or Continental Breakfast
Credit Cards: none
Notes: 2, 5, 7, 8, 10, 12 (10%)

Chesapeake B&B

408 Cranes Roost, 21401
(410) 757-7599; call for FAX

Comfortable, English country town home nestled in wooded community near Chesapeake Bay and Magothy River. Furnished in antiques, Orientals, and contemporaries. Bedroom choices include a king, queen, and a single. Perfect for family vacation or couple's getaway. Guest space has private living room. Marked nature trail. Hostess was local restaurant critic and can recommend dining choices. Only ten minutes from historic Annapolis, the U.S. Naval Academy, St. John's College, boating, and other marine adventures. Prefer a two night minimum.

Hostess: Carolyn Curtis
Rooms: 3 (1PB; 2SB) $60-80
Continental Breakfast
Credit Cards: none
Notes: 2, 5, 7, 8, 10

NOTES: Credit cards accepted: A Master Card; B Visa; C American Express; D Discover; E Diners Club; F Other; 2 Personal checks accepted; 3 Lunch available; 4 Dinner available; 5 Open all year; 6 Pets welcome; 7 Children welcome; 8 Tennis nearby; 9 Swimming nearby; 10 Golf nearby; 11 Skiing nearby; 12 May be booked through travel agent.

Chez Amis
Bed and Breakfast

85 East Street, 21401
(410) 263-6631; (800) 474-6631;
FAX (410) 295-7889

Around 1900 Chez Amis "House of Friends" was a grocery store. Still evident are the original oak display cabinet, tin ceiling, and pine floors. One half block from Capital, one block from the harbor, and minutes by foot to the Naval Academy. "European Country" decor with antiques and quilts. Four guest rooms with two private baths. King and queen brass beds, TVs, central air-conditioning, terry robes, coffee service, and down comforters in every room. Don is a retired Army lawyer; Mickie a former D.C. tour guide. They welcome you with true "Southern" Christian hospitality!

Hosts: Don and Mickie Deline
Rooms: 4 (2PB; 2SB) $75-95 + tax
Full Breakfast
Credit Cards: A, B
Notes: 2, 5, 12

Duke and Duchess Bed and Breakfast

Duke and Duchess
Bed and Breakfast

151 Duke of Gloucester Street, 21401
(401) 268-6323

A beautifully renovated 1850 home located in the Historic District of Annapolis. Just a short walk to the US Naval Academy, City Dock, restaurants, and shops. Furnished tastefully with antiques and artwork, guests can relax and enjoy an atmosphere of cozy elegance. The B&B offers clean, comfortable accommodations with modern conveniences, including central air-conditioning. A full, complimentary breakfast is served. Advance reservations by phone. Special weekday and off-season rates.

Hostess: Doris Marsh
Rooms: 2 (PB) $75-150
Full Breakfast
Credit Cards: A, B
Notes: 2, 5, 6, 7, 10

CHESAPEAKE CITY

Inn at the Canal

104 Bohemia Ave., PO Box 187, 21915-0187
(410) 885-5995; FAX (410) 885-3585

Located in a state historic district on the banks of the Chesapeake and Delaware Canal is this grand Victorian built in 1868. Architectural details which bespeak the wealth and grandeur still remain today. Twelve-foot ceilings showcase the original handpainted designs. Enter through a grand, solid walnut door to see a center hall with winding staircase. Waterside porches offer best views

---

NOTES: Credit cards accepted: A Master Card; B Visa; C American Express; D Discover; E Diners Club; F Other; 2 Personal checks accepted; 3 Lunch available; 4 Dinner available;

of ships and pleasure craft as well as summer concerts.

Hosts: Mary and Al Ioppolo
Rooms: 6 (PB) $75-105
Full Breakfast
Credit Cards: A, B, C, D, E
Notes: 2, 5, 8, 9, 10, 12

Inn at the Canal

CUMBERLAND

The Inn at Walnut Bottom
120 Greene Street, 21502
(301) 777-0003; (800) 286-9718;
FAX (301) 777-8288

Classic country inn in downtown Cumberland, consisting of twelve rooms and family suites each with a telephone and color cable TV. Rooms are charmingly decorated with period reproductions and antique furniture. Afternoon refreshments and full breakfast included with lodging. Cozy parlor stocked with games and puzzles. Excellent restaurant on premises. The Inn is within walking distance of the Western

Maryland Scenic Railroad, the historical district, and several antique shops. Extraordinary hiking, biking, and sightseeing close by. AAA 3-diamond.

Hosts: Grant M. Irvin and Kirsten O. Hansen
Rooms: 10 + 2 suites (8PB; 4SB) $75-115
Full Breakfast
Credit Cards: A, B, C, D
Notes: 2, 3, 4, 5, 7, 9, 10, 11, 12

ELKTON

Garden Cottage at Sinking Springs Herb Farm
234 Blair Shore Road, 21921
(410) 398-5566; FAX (410) 392-2389

With an early plantation house, including a 400 year old sycamore, the garden cottage nestles at the edge of a meadow flanked by herb gardens and a historic barn with a gift shop. It has a sitting room with fireplace, bedroom, bath, air-conditioning, and electric heat. Freshly ground coffee and herbal teas are offered with the country breakfast. Longwood Gardens and Winterthur Museum are 50 minutes away. Historic Chesapeake City is nearby with excellent restaurants. Sleeps three in two rooms. Third person pays only $25. Entrance at Elk Forest Road.

Hosts: Bill and Ann Stubbs
Rooms: 1 (PB) $85-88
Full Breakfast
Credit Cards: A, B
Notes: 2, 5, 6, 7, 8, 10, 12

---

5 Open all year; 6 Pets welcome; 7 Children welcome; 8 Tennis nearby; 9 Swimming nearby; 10 Golf nearby; 11 Skiing nearby; 12 May be booked through travel agent.

FREDERICK

Middle Plantation Inn

9549 Liberty Road, 21701-3246
(301) 898-7128

From this rustic inn built of stone and log, drive through horse country to the village of Mt. Pleasant. The Inn is located several miles east of Frederick on 26 acres. Each room is furnished with antiques and has a private bath, air-conditioning, and TV. The keeping room, a common room, has stained glass and a stone fireplace. Nearby are antique shops, museums, and many historic attractions. Located within 40 minutes of Gettysburg, Pennsylvania, Antietam Battlefield, and Harper's Ferry.

Hosts: Shirley and Dwight Mullican
Rooms: 4 (PB) $95-110
Continental Breakfast
Credit Cards: A, B
Notes: 2, 5, 8, 9, 10, 12

GAITHERSBURG

Gaithersburg Hospitality Bed and Breakfast

18908 Chimney Place, 20879
(301) 977-7377

This luxury host home just off I-270 with all amenities, including private parking, is located in the beautifully planned community of Montgomery Village, near churches, restaurants, and shops, and is ten minutes from D.C. Metro Station or a convenient drive south to Washington, D.C., and north

to historic Gettysburg, PA, and Harper's Ferry. This spacious bed and breakfast has two rooms with private baths, one has a queen bed. Also offered are a large, sunny third room with twin beds, and a fourth room with a single bed. Hosts delight in serving full, home cooked breakfasts with your pleasure and comfort in mind.

Hosts: Suzanne and Joe Danilowicz
Rooms: 4 (2PB; 2SB) $50-60
Full Breakfast
Credit Cards: none
Notes: 2, 7, 8, 9, 10, 12

Lewrene Farm

HAGERSTOWN

Lewrene Farm Bed and Breakfast

9738 Downsville Pike, 21740
(301) 582-1735

Enjoy our quiet, Colonial country home on 125 acres near I-70 and I-81, a home away from home for tourists, business people, and families. We have room for family celebrations. Sit by the fireplace or enjoy the great outdoors. Antietam Battlefield and Harper's Ferry are nearby; Washington, DC, and Balti-

NOTES: Credit cards accepted: A Master Card; B Visa; C American Express; D Discover; E Diners Club; F Other; 2 Personal checks accepted; 3 Lunch available; 4 Dinner available;

more are one and one half hours away. Quilts for sale.

Hosts: Irene and Lewis Lehman
Rooms: 5 (3PB; 2SB) $55-95
Full Breakfast
Credit Cards: A, B
Notes: 2, 5, 7, 8, 9, 10, 11

Sunday's B&B

39 Broadway, 21740
(301) 797-4331; (800) 221-4828

This elegant 1890 Queen Anne Victorian home is situated in the historic north end of Hagerstown. Relax in any of the many public rooms and porches or explore the many historic attractions, antique shops, golf courses, museums, shopping outlets, and ski areas that are nearby. You'll experience special hospitality and many personal touches at Sunday's. A full breakfast, afternoon tea and desserts, evening refreshments, fruit baskets, fresh flowers, special toiletries, and late night cordial and chocolate are just some of the offerings at Sunday's. We are located less than 90 minutes from Baltimore and Washington, D.C.

Host: Bob Ferrino
Rooms: 3 (PB) $75-90 ($85-100 weekends)
Full Breakfast
Credit Cards: A, B, E
Notes: 2, 4, 5, 7 (10 and older), 8, 9, 10, 11, 12

HAVRE DE GRACE

Currier House

800 South Market Street, 21078
(410) 939-7886
Email: janec@currier_bb.com
URL:http://www.currier_bb.com

Casual comfort located in the histori-

cal, residental district of Havre de Grace, overlooking the Chesapeake Bay. One block to lighthouse, museums, and park. Full renovated house dating from 1800. Four guest rooms, each with a queen-size bed and private bath. Central air-conditioning. Full "waterman's" breakfast might include sauteed oysters and Maryland stewed tomatoes, when in season, of course.

Hosts: Jane and Paul Belbot
Rooms: 4 (PB) $85-95
Full Waterman's Breakfast
Credit Cards: A, B
Notes: 2, 5, 10, 12

Currier House

NEW MARKET

National Pike Inn

9 W. Main Street, PO Box 229, 21774
(301) 865-5055

The National Pike Inn, Federal 1796-1804, offers five air-conditioned rooms beautifully decorated in different themes. Our Colonial sitting room is perfect for meditation. The private enclosed, courtyard is wonderful for a quiet retreat outdoors where you can enjoy our beautiful gardens and birds.

---

5 Open all year; 6 Pets welcome; 7 Children welcome; 8 Tennis nearby; 9 Swimming nearby; 10 Golf nearby; 11 Skiing nearby; 12 May be booked through travel agent.

National Pike Inn

New Market, founded in 1793, offers more than 30 antique shops all in historic homes along Main Street. Dining excellence is provided by Mealey Restaurant for dinner and The Village Tea Room for lunch, all within easy walking distance.

Hosts: Tom and Terry Rimel
Rooms: 5 (4PB; 1SB in 2-room suite) $75-125
 (suite $160)
Full Breakfast
Credit Cards: A, B
Notes: 2, 5 (by reservation), 7(over 10), 8, 10

NORTH EAST

Chesapeake Lodge at Sandy Cove

PO Box B, 21901
(410) 287-5433; (800) 234-COVE (2683);
FAX (410) 287-3196

Peaceful, relaxing, and breathtaking is how guests describe Sandy Cove. Nestled among 200 acres of unspoiled woodland, overlooking the headwaters of the Chesapeake Bay, and located only one hour from Baltimore and Philadelphia. Discounts are available for Sunday through Thursday stays.

Our self contained eight year old lodge and conference center includes 152 deluxe guest rooms, twelve air-conditioned meeting rooms with largest meeting room seating 1,100, banquet capacity of 550. Call for a list of Christian conferences held at Sandy Cove.

Host: Sandy Cove Ministries
Rooms: 152 (PB) $49-89
Full Breakfast
Credit Cards: A, B, D
Notes: 2, 3, 4, 5, 7, 8, 9, 10

OAKLAND

The Oak and Apple Bed and Breakfast

208 N. Second St., 21550
(301) 334-9265

Circa 1915, this restored Colonial Revival sits on a beautiful large lawn with mature trees and includes a large, columned front porch, enclosed sun porch, parlor with fireplace, and cozy gathering room with television. Awaken to fresh continental breakfast served fireside in the dining room or on the sun porch. The quaint town of Oakland offers a wonderful small-town atmosphere, Deep Creek Lake, Wisp Ski Resort, and state parks with hiking, fishing, swimming, bicycling, boating, and skiing are nearby.

Hostess: Jana Brown
Rooms: 5 (3PB; 2SB) $60-85
Expanded Continental Breakfast
Credit Cards: A, B
Notes: 2, 5, 8, 9, 10, 11, 12

NOTES: Credit cards accepted: A Master Card; B Visa; C American Express; D Discover; E Diners Club; F Other; 2 Personal checks accepted; 3 Lunch available; 4 Dinner available;

ST. MICHAELS

Kemp House Inn

412 Talbot Street, PO Box 638, 21663
(410) 745-2243

Built in 1807 by Colonel Joseph Kemp, a commander in the War of 1812, this superbly crafted home is one of a collection of large Federal period brick structures in St. Michaels. Each of the rooms are tastefully furnished with period decor. Cozy, antique, four poster, rope beds with patchwork quilts and down pillows, wing-back chairs, low-light sconces, candles, and working fireplaces create an ambiance of the early 19th century.

Hosts: Diane and Steve Cooper
Rooms: 8 (6PB; 2SB) $70-110
Continental Breakfast
Credit Cards: A, B, D
Notes: 2, 5, 7, 8, 9, 10, 12

Parsonage Inn

210 N. Talbot Street, 21663
(410) 745-5519; (800) 394-5519

This late Victorian, circa 1883, was lavishly restored in 1985 with seven guest rooms, private baths, and brass beds with Laura Ashley linens. Fireplaces in three rooms. The parlor and dining room are in the European tradition. Striking architecture! Two blocks to the maritime museum, shops, and restaurants. Mobile and AAA three-star ratings.

Host: Will Workman
Rooms: 8 (PB) $90-145
Full Breakfast
Credit Cards: A, B
Notes: 2, 5, 7, 8, 10, 12

Wades Point Inn on the Bay

PO Box 7, 21663
(410) 745-2500

For those seeking the serenity of the country and the splendor of the bay, we invite you to charming Wades Point Inn, just a few miles from St. Michaels. Complemented by the ever-changing view of boats, birds, and water lapping the shoreline, our 120 acres of fields and woodlands, with one mile walking or jogging trail, provide a peaceful setting for relaxation and recreation on Maryland's eastern shore.

Hosts: Betsy and John Feiler
Rooms: 15 winter, 24 summer (16PB; 8SB) $80-175
Expanded Continental Breakfast
Credit Cards: A, B
Closed January through February
Notes: 2, 8, 9, 10

SILVER SPRING

Varborg Bed and Breakfast

2620 Briggs Chaney Road., 20905-4508
(301) 384-2842; (301) 384-4379

This suburban, Colonial home in the countryside is convenient to Washington, DC, and Baltimore, MD, just off Route 29 and close to Route 95. Three guest rooms with a shared bath are available. Hosts are happy to share their knowledge of good nearby restaurants.

---

5 Open all year; 6 Pets welcome; 7 Children welcome; 8 Tennis nearby; 9 Swimming nearby; 10 Golf nearby; 11 Skiing nearby; 12 May be booked through travel agent.

The specialty of the house is homemade bread.

Hosts: Bob and Pat Johnson
Rooms: 3 (SB) $30-50
Full Breakfast (Continental if desired)
Credit Cards: none
Notes: 5, 7, 8, 9, 10

SOLOMONS

Webster House
A Bed and Breakfast

PO Box 1607, 14364 Sedwick Avenue, 20688
(410) 326-0454

Rest and restoration are yours at this delightful Christian bed and breakfast in Solomons, a quaint Southern Maryland community. A reproduction of the old Webster House that stood on this property for 113 years was built to glorify God. Lovely gardens, a revitaliz- ing hot tub, homemade delights on our screened-in porch, and three charming rooms add a peace that will touch your heart. Your hosts are looking forward to making your stay a wonderful memory. Gift certificates and mid-week specials available.

Hosts: Dr. Peter Prentice and Barbara Prentice
Rooms: 3 (1PB; 2SB) $85-110
Full Breakfast
Credit Cards: A, B
Open from April to November.
Notes: 2, 9, 10

Webster House

Massachusetts

Golden Slumber Accommodations B&B/Inn Reservation Service

640 Revere Beach Boulevard, **Revere** 02151
(617) 289-1053; (800) 892-3231;
FAX (617) 289-9112

Golden Slumber features an unrivaled array of screened accommodations on the seacoast of Massachusetts including Cape Cod, the North and South Shores, and Greater Boston. From sprawling, ocean-front villas to quaint, romantic, country road retreats, our gracious historic residences and unique contemporary properties offer the paramount in revered Yankee hospitality. All boast the finest amenities and several feature incomparable water views, canopy beds, jacuzzis, fireplaces, private entrances, and swimming pools. No reservation fee! Children welcome. Limousine and gift service. Free brochure/directory.

Coordinator: Leah A. Schmidt
Rooms: 150 (90%PB; 10%SB) $55-220
Full and Continental Breakfast
Credit Cards: A, B
Notes: 2, 3, 4, 5, 6, 7, 8, 9, 10, 12

Lamb and Lion Inn

BARNSTABLE (CAPE COD)

Lamb and Lion Inn
2504 Main Street (PO Box 511), 02630
(508) 362-6823

The Inn, an original Cape Cod home built in 1740, sits on a secluded knoll overlooking the Old King's Highway. Over the years, rambling additions have created a central courtyard which is where our swimming pool is located with easy access from every comfortable accommodation. Blending our furnishings from antique to wicker, our piano playing innkeeper strives for an intimate and casual ambiance. An upscale continental breakfast is served in our Colonial kitchen and can be enjoyed poolside or in the dining area. You are

---

5 Open all year; 6 Pets welcome; 7 Children welcome; 8 Tennis nearby; 9 Swimming nearby;
10 Golf nearby; 11 Skiing nearby; 12 May be booked through travel agent.

MASSACHUSETTS

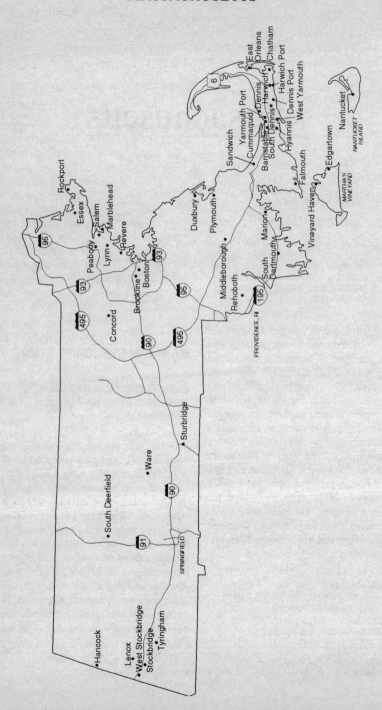

cordially invited to enjoy a most unique, year-round vacation spot. Near all Cape Cod attractions.

Host: Donald P. McKeag
Rooms. (PD) $105 150 ($95 off season)
Continental Breakfast
Credit Cards: A, B, C, D
Notes: 2, 5, 8, 9, 10

BOSTON

A B&B Agency of Boston (and Boston Harbor Bed and Breakfast)

47 Commercial Wharf, 02110
(617) 720-3540; (800) 248-9262;
FAX (617) 523-5761

Downtown Boston's largest selection of guest rooms in historic bed and breakfast homes including Federal and Victorian town houses and beautifully restored 1840s waterfront lofts. Available, nightly, weekly, and/or monthly. Or, choose from the loveliest selection of fully furnished, private studios, one- and two-bedroom condominiums, corporate suites and lofts with all the amenities, including fully furnished kitchens, private baths (some with jacuzzis), TV, and telephones. Exclusive locations include waterfront, Faneuil Hall/Quincy Market, North End, Back Bay, Beacon Hill, Copley Square, and Cambridge.

Hosts: Ferne Mintz
Rooms: 120 (80PB; 40SB) $65-120
Continental Breakfast
Credit Cards: A, B
Notes: 2, 5, 7, 12

Greater Boston Hospitality

PO Box 1142, **Brookline** 02146
(617) 277-5430

Greater Boston Hospitality offers hundreds of Georgians, Federals, Victorians, and Brownstones private homes and condos throughout the greater Boston area. All include breakfast, many include parking. Most are located in historic areas. We provide on call service to both business and pleasure travelers. Discounts available for longer stays. Wide range of accommodatoins from $50 to $125 a night. Call us and we will find the right place for you. Visit Boston as a native. Major credit cards accepted. Lauren Simonelli, owner.

BROOKLINE (BOSTON)

The Beacon Inn

1087 and 1750 Beacon Street, 02146
(617) 566-0088; (800) 726-0088;
FAX (617) 397-9267

Enjoy the warmth and grace of this turn-of-the-century home which has been converted into the most inviting and charming guest house. Located in the hub of the historical and cultural area, minutes awary from major hospitals, universities, sporting events, and downtown Boston on the MBTA Greenline.

Hosts: Scott and Marcy
Rooms: 24 (13PB; 11SB) $49-99
Continental Breakfast
Credit Cards: A, B, C
Notes: 5, 7, 12

NOTES: Credit cards accepted: A Master Card; B Visa; C American Express; D Discover; E Diners Club; F Other; 2 Personal checks accepted; 3 Lunch available; 4 Dinner available; 5 Open all year; 6 Pets welcome; 7 Children welcome; 8 Tennis nearby; 9 Swimming nearby; 10 Golf nearby; 11 Skiing nearby; 12 May be booked through travel agent.

Beacon Plaza

1459 Beacon Street, 02146
(617) 232-6550

The Beacon Plaza has been owned and operated by the Pappas family for almost 40 years. Located on public transportation (MBTA Greenline) and Boston's historic, cultural, business, and other tourist attractions are mere minutes away. Come visit Boston, a truly four-season city. Our turn-of-the-century Brownstone awaits your arrival—a beacon of hospitality for the weary traveler.

Hosts: The Pappas Family
Rooms: 40 (20PB; 20SB) $45-85
No Breakfast
Credit Cards: A, B
Notes: 5, 7, 8, 9, 10

CHATHAM (CAPE COD)

The Cranberry Inn at Chatham

359 Main Street, 02633
(508) 945-9232; (800) 332-4667;
FAX (508) 945-3769

Welcoming Cape Cod visitors since 1830, The Cranberry Inn is ideally located in the heart of Chatham's picturesque historic district! Elegant yet relaxed, the Inn offers 18 delightful guest rooms, each individually decorated with antique and reproduction furnishings. Rooms feature four-poster, brass, or canopy beds, private bath, air-conditioning, telephone, and TV. Many rooms have fireplaces and balconies. Golfing, swimming, boating, and some of the finest shops and restaurants on the Cape are all nearby.

Hosts: Ray and Brenda Raffurty
Rooms: 16 + 2 suites (PB) $85-230 depending
    on season
Full Breakfast Buffet
Credit Cards: A, B, C, D
Notes: 2, 5, 7 (over 8), 8, 9, 10, 12

CONCORD

Hawthorne Inn

462 Lexington Rd., 01742
(508) 369-5610; FAX (508) 287-4949

Fast by the ancient way; that the Minute Men trod to first face the British Regulars, rests this most colorful inn where history and literature gracefully entwine. On earth once claimed by Emerson, Hawthorne, and the Alcotts, the Hawthorne Inn beckons the traveler to refresh the spirit in a winsome atmosphere abounding with antique furnishings and delight the eye exploring rooms festooned with handmade quilts, original artwork, and archaic artifacts.

Hosts: Gregory Burch and Marilyn Mudry
Rooms: 7 (PB) $110-175
Continental Plus Breakfast
Credit Cards: A, B, C, D
Notes: 2, 5, 7, 8, 9, 11

CUMMAQUID (CAPE COD)

The Acworth Inn

PO Box 256, 4352 Old King's Hwy. (Rt. 6A), 02637
(508) 362-3330; (800) 362-6363

The Acworth Inn is a romantic getaway nestled among the trees along the Old

---

NOTES: Credit cards accepted: A Master Card; B Visa; C American Express; D Discover;
E Diners Club; F Other; 2 Personal checks accepted; 3 Lunch available; 4 Dinner available;

King's Highway which winds through the historic, unspoiled north side of Cape Cod. Built in 1860, the Inn is a classic Cape house, completely renovated and outfitted with charming hand-painted pieces and colorful fabrics. It features six bright and airy guest rooms, each with a private bath.

Hosts: Jack and Cheryl Ferrell
Rooms: 6 (PB) $75-95
Bountiful Continental Breakfast
Credit Cards: A, B, C, D
Notes: 2, 5, 8, 9, 10, 12

The Acworth Inn

DEERFIELD-SOUTH

Deerfield's Yellow Gabled House

111 N. Main Street, 01373
(413) 665-4922

Located on the site of an historic battle of 1675 and 1½ miles from the crossroads of I-91, Route 116, and Route 5 and 10 is a picturesque house with gardens and three decorated bed chambers. Sitting room and library for reading and meeting your fellow travelers. Enjoy

early morning coffee in the summer room.

Hostess: Edna Julia Staheler
Rooms: 3 (1PB; 2SB) $75-110
Full Breakfast
Credit Cards: none
Notes: 2, 5, 8, 9, 10, 11, 12

DENNIS

Isaiah Hall B&B Inn

PO Box 1007, 152 Whig Street, 02638
(508) 385-9928; (800) 736-0160;
FAX (508) 385-5879

Enjoy country ambiance and hospitality in the heart of Cape Cod. Tucked away on a quiet historic side street, this lovely 1857 farmhouse is within walking distance of the beach, restaurants, shops, and playhouse. Delightful gardens surround the Inn with country antiques, Oriental rugs, and quilts within. Rooms have private baths, air-conditioning, and most have queen-size beds. Some have balconies or fireplaces. Near biking, golf, and tennis. AAA three-diamond rating and ABBA three crown award.

Hostess: Marie Brophy
Rooms: 10 + 1 suite (PB) $78-117 ($145 suite)
Expanded Continental Breakfast
Credit Cards: A, B, C
Notes: 2, 7 (over 7), 8, 9, 10, 12

DENNIS PORT

The Rose Petal B&B

PO Box 974, 152 Sea Street, 02639
(508) 398-8470

A picturesque, traditional New England

---

5 Open all year; 6 Pets welcome; 7 Children welcome; 8 Tennis nearby; 9 Swimming nearby; 10 Golf nearby; 11 Skiing nearby; 12 May be booked through travel agent.

The Rose Petal Bed and Breakfast

home, complete with picket fence, invites guests to share this historic 1872 residence in a delightful seaside resort neighborhood. Stroll past century-old homes to a sandy beach. Home-baked pastries highlight a full breakfast. A comfortable parlor offers TV, piano, and reading. Enjoy queen-size beds, antiques, hand-stitched quilts, and spacious and bright baths. Convenient to all Cape Cod's attractions. Open all year. AAA-three Diamonds; ABBA-three Crowns.

Hosts: Dan and Gayle Kelly
Rooms: 3 (2PB; 1SB) $52-92
Full Breakfast
Credit Cards: A, B, C
Notes: 5, 7, 8, 9, 10, 12

DUXBURY

The Winsor House Inn
390 Washington Street, 02332
(617) 934-0991; FAX (617) 934-5955

Built in 1803 by sea captain Nathaniel Winsor, this charming antique-filled country inn is located 35 miles south of Boston in the quaint seaside village of Duxbury. The three cozy sunlit bedrooms are complete with canopy beds and fireplaces. Enjoy casual dining in the English-style pub, a gourmet dinner in the flower-filled Carriage House, or a romantic evening in the candlelit dining room. Rates are subject to change.

Hosts: Mr. and Mrs. David M. O'Connell
Rooms: 3 (PB) $ 105-125 + tax
Full Breakfast
Credit Cards: A, B, C, D
Notes: 2, 3 (seasonal), 4 (daily) 5, 8, 9, 10

The Winsor House Inn

EAST ORLEANS

Ivy Lodge
194 Main Street, PO Box 1195, 02643-1195
(508) 255-0119

A guest house since 1910, this smoke-free 1864 Greek Revival home is graced with family photos and antiques. A morning wake-up breakfast basket is found outside each guest room door, to be enjoyed in your room or under a shade tree on the spacious grounds. Located midway between ocean and bay beaches in beautiful, historic Orleans at the elbow of Cape Cod. Walk-

---

NOTES: Credit cards accepted: A Master Card; B Visa; C American Express; D Discover; E Diners Club; F Other; 2 Personal checks accepted; 3 Lunch available; 4 Dinner available;

ing distance to shops and restaurants. Other amenities close by.

Hosts: David and Barbara McCormack
Rooms: 3 (PB) $70-80
Continental Breakfast
Apartment: 1 (PB) $125, no breakfast
Credit Cards: none
Notes: 2, 5, 7 (in apartment), 8, 9, 10

Nauset House Inn

143 Beach Road, PO Box 774, 02643
(508) 255-2195

A real, old fashioned, country inn farmhouse, circa 1810, is located on three acres with an apple orchard, one half mile from Nauset Beach. A quiet romantic getaway. Large common room with fireplace and a brick-floored dining room where breakfast is served. Cozily furnished with antiques, eclectic—a true fantasy.

Hosts: Diane and Al Johnson; John and Cindy
    Vessella
Rooms: 14 (8PB; 6SB) $55-105
Full ($5) or Continental ($3) Breakfast
Credit Cards: A, B
Notes: 2, 8, 9, 10

Ship's Knees Inn

186 Beach Road, PO Box 756, 02643
(508) 255-1312; FAX (508) 240-1351

This 170-year-old restored sea captain's home is a three minute walk to beautiful sand-duned Nauset Beach. Inside the warm, lantern-lit doorways are 19 rooms individually appointed with special Colonial color schemes and authentic antiques. Some rooms feature authentic ship's knees, hand painted

trunks, old clipper ship models, braided rugs, and four-poster beds. Tennis and swimming are available on the premises. Three miles away overlooking Orleans Cove, the Cove House property offers three rooms, a one-bedroom efficiency apartment, and two cottages.

Hosts: Jean and Ken Pitchford
Rooms: 22, 1 efficiency apt., 2 cottages (14PB,
    11SB) $50-100
Continental Breakfast
Credit Cards: A, B
Notes: 2, 5, 7 (Cove House), 8 and 9 (on premises), 10, 12

Ship's Knees Inn

EDGARTOWN—MARTHA'S VINEYARD

The Arbor

222 Upper Main Street, PO Box 1228, 02539
(508) 627-8137

This charming Victorian home was originally built on the island of Chappaquiddick and moved by barge to its present location; a short stroll to the village shops, fine restaurants, and the bustling activity of the Edgartown harbor. The rooms are typically New England, furnished with antiques, and filled with the fragrance of fresh flowers. Central air-conditioning. Peggy will

---

5 Open all year; 6 Pets welcome; 7 Children welcome; 8 Tennis nearby; 9 Swimming nearby;
10 Golf nearby; 11 Skiing nearby; 12 May be booked through travel agent.

gladly direct you to unspoiled beaches, walking trails, fishing, and all the delights of Martha's Vineyard.

Hostess: Peggy Hall
Rooms: 10 (8PB; 2SB) $95-145 (off season rates available)
Continental Breakfast
Credit Cards: A, B
Notes: 2, 7 (over 12), 8, 9, 10, 12

Captain Dexter House of Edgartown

35 Pease's Point Way, PO Box 2798, 02539
(508) 627-7289; FAX (508) 627-3328

Our historic inn offers both charm and hospitality. Enjoy beautiful gardens. Savor a home-baked continental breakfast and evening aperitif. Relax in a four-poster, lace canopied bed in a room with a working fireplace. Stroll to the harbor, town, and restaurants. Bicycle or walk to the beach. Let our innkeepers make your vacation something special!

Hosts: Eric and Pamela
Rooms: 11 (PB) $65-195
Continental Plus Breakfast
Credit Cards: A, B, C, E
Notes: 2, 8, 9, 10, 12

ESSEX

George Fuller House

148 Main Street, 01929
(508) 768-7766

Built in 1830, this handsome Federalist-style home retains much of its 19th century charm, including Indian shutters and a captain's staircase. Three of the guest rooms have working fire-places. Decorations include handmade quilts, braided rugs, and caned Boston rockers. A full breakfast might include such features as Cindy's French toast drizzled with brandy lemon butter. Gordon College and Gordon Conwall Seminary are close by.

Hosts: Cindy and Bob Cameron
Rooms: 5 + 2 suites (PB) $79-109
Full Breakfast
Credit Cards: A, B, C, D, E
Notes: 2, 5, 7, 8, 9, 10, 12

Captain Tom Lawrence House Inn

FALMOUTH

Captain Tom Lawrence House Inn

75 Locust Street, 02540
(508) 540-1445; (800) 266-8139;
FAX (508) 457-1790

1861 whaling captain's residence in historic village close to beach, bikeway, ferries, bus station, ships, and restaurants. Explore entire Cape, Vineyard, and Plymouth by day trips. Six beautiful guest rooms have private baths and firm beds, some with canopies. Fully furnished apartment with kitchenette and air-conditioning sleeps two to four people. Antiques, a Steinway piano, fireplace in sitting room. Homemade, delicious breakfasts include specialties from organic grain. German spoken. All rooms have central air-conditioning. No smoking! AAA and Mobile rated.

Hostess: Barbara Sabo-Feller
Rooms: 6 (PB) $75-125
Full Breakfast
Credit Cards: A, B
Closed January
Notes: 2, 7 (over 12), 8, 9, 10

Inn on the Sound

313 Grand Avenue, 02540
(508) 457-9666; (800) 564-9668;
FAX (508) 457-9631

This oceanfront bed and breakfast offers ten spacious guest rooms, nine with water views, all with serene, casual, and comfortable beachhouse-style atmosphere. Enjoy the magnificent view from the forty-foot deck; sample the full gourmet breakfast; relax with a favorite book in front of the fireplace; or visit the many year-round attractions from our ideally located inn. Walk to the ferry to Martha's Vineyard, bicycle rentals, great restaurants, and, of course, the beach. Reservations recommended, especially in the summer season.

Hosts: Renee Ross and David Ross
Rooms: 10 (PB) $95-140
Full Breakfast
Credit Cards: A, B, C, D
Notes: 2, 5, 8, 9, 10, 12

Village Green Inn

40 Main Street, 02540
(508) 548-5621; (800) 237-1119;
FAX (508) 457-5051

Gracious, old, 1804 Colonial-Victorian is ideally located on Falmouth's historic village green. Walk to fine shops and restaurants; bike to beaches and picturesque Woods Hole along the Shining Sea Bike Path. Enjoy 19th-century charm and warm hospitality amidst elegant surroundings. Four lovely guest rooms and one romantic suite all have private baths and unique fireplaces (two are working). A full gourmet breakfast is served featuring delicious house specialties. Many thoughtful amenities are included.

Hosts: Diane and Don Crosby
Rooms: 5 (PB) $90-140
Full Breakfast
Credit Cards: A, B, C
Notes: 2 (for deposit only), 5, 7 (12 and over), 8, 9, 10

Village Green Inn

FALMOUTH HEIGHTS (CAPE COD)

Grafton Inn

261 Grand Avenue S., 02540
(508) 540-8688; (800) 642-4069;
FAX (508) 540-1861

Oceanfront Victorian, 30 steps to sandy beach, with breathtaking views of Martha's Vineyard. Eleven air-conditioned guest rooms with private baths are furnished with comfortable queen beds and period antiques. Sumptuous, full, gourmet breakfast served at private tables overlooking Nantucket Sound. Thoughtful amenities include, fresh flowers and homemade chocolates. Bicycles, beach chairs, and towels. Late afternoon wine and cheese. Walk to Island Ferry, restaurants, and shops. No smoking. Open all year. AAA and Mobil rated.

Hosts: Liz and Rudy Cvitan
Rooms: 11 (PB) $75-149
Full Breakfast
Credit Cards: A, B, C, D
Notes: 5, 8, 9, 10, 12

The Moorings Lodge

The Moorings Lodge

207 Grand Avenue S., 02540
(508) 540-2370

Captain Frank Spencer built this large, lovely Victorian home in 1905. It is directly across from a sandy beach with lifeguard safety and it is within walking distance of good restaurants and the island ferry. Your homemade, buffet breakfast is served on a glassed-in porch overlooking the island, Martha's Vineyard. Your airy rooms with private baths

add to your comfort. Call us home while you tour the Cape!

Hosts: Ernie and Shirley Benard
Rooms: 8 (PB) $75-105
Full Breakfast
Credit Cards: A, B
Notes: 2, 7, 8, 9, 10, 12

HANCOCK

Kirkmead Bed and Breakfast

Route 43 at state line
Mail: RRI, Box 169A, Stephentown, NY 12168
(413) 738-5420

Former stagecoach inn begun in 1767, the B&B is convenient to Jiminy Peak, Hancock Shaker Village, and Tanglewood. Easy access to a beautiful 30-acre mountain location. Walk along our tree-lined lane or wander on our nature trail beside our babbling brook. Full homemade breakfast featuring family recipes. Each guest room is air-conditioned and has its own private bath. No smoking, please. Two night minumum.

Hosts: Don and Pat Bowman
Rooms: 7 (PB) $60
Full Homemade Breakfast
Credit Cards: none
Notes: 2, 5, 7, 8, 11

HARWICH PORT (CAPE COD)

Augustus Snow House

528 Main Street, 02646
(508) 430-0528; (800) 320-0528;
FAX (508) 432-7995

Romantic Victorian mansion built in 1901, the Augustus Snow House remains one of Cape Cod's most breathtaking examples of Queen Anne Victorian architecture. Today, this turn-of-the-century home with its gabled dormers and wraparound verandah is one of the Cape's most elegant and exclusive inns, catering to a small number of discerning guests. Five exquisite bedrooms with queen or king beds, private baths (some with jacuzzis), fireplaces, color TVs, gourmet breakfast, and afternoon refreshments. The private beach is just a three minute stroll away.

The Inn on Sea Street

Hosts: Joyce and Steve Roth
Rooms: 5 (PB) $105-160
Full Gourmet Breakfast
Credit Cards: A, B, C, D
Notes: 2, 3, 4, 5, 8, 9, 10, 12

Harbor Walk

6 Freeman Street, 02646
(508) 432-1675

This Victorian summer guest house was originally built in 1880 and is furnished with eclectic charm. A few steps from the house will bring you into view of Wychmere Harbor and further along to one of the fine beaches of Nantucket sound. The village of Harwich Port is only one half mile from the Inn and contains interesting shops and some of the finest restaurants on Cape Cod. Harbor Walk offers six comfortable rooms with twin or queen beds. An attractive garden and porch are available for sitting, lounging, and reading. Open May through October.

Hosts: Preston and Marilyn Barry
Rooms: 6 (4PB; 2SB) $45-60
Full Breakfast
Credit Cards: none
Notes: 2, 6 (limited), 7, 8, 9, 10, 12

HYANNIS

The Inn
on Sea Street

358 Sea Street, 02601
(508) 775-8030; FAX (508) 771-0878

The Inn on Sea Streeat is an elegant nine-room Victorian, plus a cottage, just steps from the beach. Antiques, canopy beds, and Persian rugs abound in this friendly, relaxed atmosphere. Gourmet breakfast of fruit and home-baked delights is served with silver, crystal, china, and flowers at individual tables. One night stays welcome.

Hosts: Lois Nelson and J.B. Whitehead
Rooms: 9 (7PB; 2SB) $78-105
Cottage: 1(PB) $115
Full Breakfast
Credit Cards: A, B, C, D
Notes: 2, 8, 9, 10

Sea Breeze Inn

397 Sea Street, 02601
(508) 771-7213; FAX (508) 862-0663

Sea Breeze is a fourteen room quaint bed and breakfast. It is just a three

5 Open all year; 6 Pets welcome; 7 Children welcome; 8 Tennis nearby; 9 Swimming nearby;
10 Golf nearby; 11 Skiing nearby; 12 May be booked through travel agent.

minute walk to the beach and 20 minutes to the island ferries. Restaurants, night-life, shopping, golf and tennis are within a ten minute drive. Some rooms have ocean views. An expanded continental breakfast is served between 7:30 and 9:30 each morning. All rooms are air-conditioned.

Hosts: Patricia and Martin Battle
Rooms: 14 (PB) $55-115
Expanded Continental Breakfast
Credit Cards: A, B, C, D
Notes: 2, 5, 7, 8, 9, 10, 12

LENOX

Garden Gables Inn

135 Main Street, PO Box 52, 01240
(413) 637-0193; FAX (413) 637-4554

220-year-old charming and quiet inn located in historic Lenox on five wooded acres dotted with gardens. 72-foot swimming pool. Some rooms have fireplaces, and sitting rooms are furnished with antiques and a Steinway grand piano. All rooms have private baths and air-conditioning, and some rooms also have whirlpool tubs and private porches. Breakfast is included. In-room phones are provided and the famous Tanglewood festival is only one mile away. Restaurants are all within walking distance.

Hosts: Mario and Lynn Mekinda
Rooms: 18 (PB) $70-220
Full Breakfast
Credit Cards: A, B, C, D
Notes: 2, 5, 7 (over 12), 8, 10, 11

Seven Hills Country Inn and Restaurant

40 Plunkett Street, 01240
(413) 637-0060; (800) 869-6518;
FAX (413) 637-3651

Lovely 27-acre country property featuring beautiful terraced lawns and gardens, huge swimming pool, two hard surface tennis courts, banquet and meeting facilities, and outstanding restaurant with wonderful and creative cuisine. Many rooms furnished with antiques, all have private bath and air-conditioning. We are a romantic spot and do weddings like no one else can. Also popular resort and vacation destination, but business travelers love us, too. Lodging/food packages and tie-in discounts available. Near Tanglewood, summer home of the Boston Symphony Orchestra, and Jacob's Pillow, featuring the world's finest dance troupes. Lose yourself in time and come visit!!!

Hosts: Patricia and Jim Eder
Rooms: 52 (PB) $85-250
Full High Season Breakfast (Continental off season)
Credit Cards: A, B, C, D, E, F
Notes: 2, 4, 5, 6, 7, 8, 9, 10, 11, 12

LYNN

Diamond District Bed and Breakfast

142 Ocean Street, 01902
(617) 599-4470; (800) 666-3076;
FAX (617) 595-2200

This 17 room Architect (Thomas M. James designed the Schubert Theater of Boston), designed Georgian clapboard

---

NOTES: Credit cards accepted: A Master Card; B Visa; C American Express; D Discover; E Diners Club; F Other; 2 Personal checks accepted; 3 Lunch available; 4 Dinner available;

mansion was built in 1911 for a Lynn shoe manufacturer. Features include a gracious foyer and a grand staircase winding up the three floors, a spacious fireplace living room with ocean view finished in Mexican mahogany, French doors leading to an adjacent large 36x14 veranda that overlooks the gardens and ocean. 300 feet of a three mile sandy beach for swimming, walking, and jogging. Walk to local restaurants. Home-cooked, plentiful breakfast, vegetarian and low fat available.

Hosts: Sandra and Jerry Caron
Rooms: 9 (5PB; 4SB) $65-120
Full Home-cooked Breakfast
Credit Cards: A, B, C, D, E, F
Notes: 5, 7, 8, 9, 10, 12

MARBLEHEAD

Harborside House

23 Gregory Street, 01945
(617) 631-1032

An 1850 Colonial overlooks picturesque Marblehead Harbor, with water views from the paneled living room with a cozy fireplace, period dining room, sunny breakfast porch, and third-story deck. A generous breakfast includes juice, fresh fruit, home-baked goods, and cereals. Antique shops, gourmet restaurants, historic sites, and beaches are a pleasant stroll away. The owner is a professional dressmaker and a nationally ranked competitive swimmer. No smoking.

Hostess: Susan Livingston
Rooms: 2 (SB) $65-80
Expanded Continental Breakfast
Credit Cards: none
Notes: 2, 5, 7 (over 10), 8, 9

Pineywood Farm Bed and Breakfast

MARION

Pineywood Farm Bed and Breakfast

599 Front Street, PO Box 322, 02738
(508) 748-3925; (800) 858-8084

A charming, 1815 farmhouse with carriage house, which has been completely restored, yet retains the warmth and ambiance of a bygone era . . . complete with wide plank, white pine floors; four working fireplaces; a large screened porch; and a "good morning" staircase. We offer spacious rooms with air-conditioning, cable TV, paddle fans, and private baths, overlooking a lovely perennial garden and private swimming pool. Located on a three-arce estate 1½ miles from Tabor Academy. The town beach is at the end of our street. We are open year round.

Hosts: Beverly and George McTurk
Rooms: 3 + a two-bedroom suite (PB) $85-125
Gourmet Continental Breakfast
Credit Cards: none
Notes: 2, 5, 8, 9, 10

---

5 Open all year; 6 Pets welcome; 7 Children welcome; 8 Tennis nearby; 9 Swimming nearby; 10 Golf nearby; 11 Skiing nearby; 12 May be booked through travel agent.

MIDDLEBORO

Zachariah Eddy House Bed and Breakfast

51 South Main Street, 02346
(508) 946-0016

1831 historic home located in the heart of the historic and antique district. Features many interesting architectural details, including unique "Chapel Bath." Easy highway access (one mile). Front door bus service to Boston. "101 Things to See and Do Within 35 Miles" (call for list). Ideal touring headquarters for Boston, Plymouth, Cape Cod, Newport, and Providence. Summer offers "Catch of the Day Trips"—enjoy pulling lobsters, digging clams, shore dinners, clam chowder, and Cape Cod Canal moonlight cruise.

Hosts: Bradford and Cheryl Leonard
Rooms: 3 (1PB; 2SB) $49-75 off season;
    $75-105 in season
Full and Continental Breakfast
Credit Cards: A, B, D
Notes: 3, 4, 5, 7 (over 12), 8, 9, 10, 12

NANTUCKET

Martin House Inn

61 Centre Street, PO Box 743, 02554
(508) 228-0678

In a stately 1803 mariner's home in Nantucket's historic district, a romantic sojourn awaits you a glowing fire in a spacious, charming living/dining room; large, airy guest rooms, three with fireplaces, with authentic period pieces and four-poster beds; a lovely yard and veranda for peaceful summer afternoons. Our complimentary breakfast includes inn-baked breads and muffins, fresh fruit, and homemade granola.

Hosts: Channing and Ceci Moore
Rooms: 13 (9PB; 4SB) $65-155
Expanded Continental Breakfast
Credit Cards: A, B, C
Notes: 2, 5, 7 (over 5), 8, 9, 10

House of the Seven Gables

NANTUCKET ISLAND

House of the Seven Gables

32 Cliff Road, 02554
(508) 228-4706; (800) 905-5005

Built in the 1880s as an anex for one of Nantucket's oldest hotels, before its destruction, this house is one of the few and finest examples of architecture during that period. Located a ten minute walk from Main Street, the house overlooks the mouth of the harbor and faces north across Nantucket Sound towards Hyannis Port, 20 miles away. This

---

NOTES: Credit cards accepted: A Master Card; B Visa; C American Express; D Discover; E Diners Club; F Other; 2 Personal checks accepted; 3 Lunch available; 4 Dinner available;

quiet, informal guest house features ten guest rooms that are nicely furnished with period antiques. The complimentary continental breakfast is served in your room on trays set with fresh flowers and include home-baked delights.

Hostess: Sue Walton
Rooms: 10 (8PB; 2SB) $85-175
Continental Breakfast
Credit Cards: A, B, C
Notes: 2, 8, 9

PEABODY

Joan's
Bed and Breakfast

R210 Lynn Street, 01960
(508) 532-0191

Located 25 miles from Boston, 10 miles from historic Salem, and 25 miles from quaint Rockport. We have wonderful restaurants in the area, also two large shopping malls and a terrific summer theater. Also enjoy our in-ground pool!

Hostess: Joan Hetherington
Rooms: 3 (1PB; 2SB) $50-65
Continental Plus Breakfast and afternoon tea
Credit Cards: none
Notes: 2, 5, 7, 9 (on-site), 10, 12

PLYMOUTH

Remembrance
Bed and Breakfast Home

265 Sandwich Street, 02360
(508) 746-5160

Remembrance is an old center-chimney

Cape, delightfully decorated with antiques, wicker, art, plants, and flowers. Rooms, with antique brass bedsteads, are cozy yet bright and airy. Provision for one older child. Delicious full breakfast is served in the greenhouse overlooking a pretty walled garden and bird feeders. Guests feel they are visiting a friend. Special diets accommodated. Tea time. Gentle resident pets. Books and magazines in abundance. Air-conditioned, non-smoking, central location.

Hostess: Beverly Bainbridge
Rooms: 2 (SB) $165
Full Breakfast
Credit Cards: none
Notes: 2, 5, 7, 8, 9, 10, 12

REHOBOTH

Gilbert's Tree Farm
Bed and Breakfast

30 Spring Street, 02769
(508) 252-6416

Our 150-year-old home is special in all seasons. The in-ground pool refreshes weary travelers, and the quiet walks through our 100 acres give food for the soul. Guests also enjoy the horses. We praise God for being allowed to enjoy the beauty with others. No smoking inside the house.

Hosts: Jeanne and Martin Gilbert
Rooms: 3 (SB) $45-50
Full Breakfast
Credit Cards: none
Notes: 2, 5, 6 (horses only), 7, 8, 9, 10, 12 (10%)

---

5 Open all year; 6 Pets welcome; 7 Children welcome; 8 Tennis nearby; 9 Swimming nearby; 10 Golf nearby; 11 Skiing nearby; 12 May be booked through travel agent.

ROCKPORT

The Inn on Cove Hill

37 Mt. Pleasant Street, 01966
(508) 546-2701

A friendly atmosphere with the option
of privacy is available in this painstakingly restored, 200-year-old Federal
home in a perfect setting two blocks
from the harbor and shops. Cozy bedrooms are meticulously appointed with
antiques; some have canopy beds. Wake
up to the aroma of hot muffins and enjoy breakfast at the unbrella tables in
the pump garden.

Hosts: John and Marjorie Pratt
Rooms: 11 (9PB; 2SB) $48-104
Continental Breakfast
Credit Cards: A, B
Notes: 2, 9

Lantana Guest House

22 Broadway, 01966
(508) 546-3535; (800) 291-3535

An intimate guest house in heart of historic Rockport, Lantana House is close
to Main Street, the T-Wharf, and the
beaches. There is a large sundeck reserved for guests, as well as, TV, games,
magazine, and books, a guest refrigerator, and ice service. Nearby you will
find a golf course, tennis courts, picnic
areas, rocky bays, and inlets. Boston is
one hour away by car. No smoking.

Hostess: Cynthia A. Sewell
Rooms: 7 (5PB; 2SB) $60-80
Continental Plus Breakfast
Credit Cards: A, B, D
Notes: 2, 5, 7, 8, 9, 10

Linden Tree Inn

Linden Tree Inn

26 King Street, 01966
(508) 546-2494; (800) 865-2122

The Inn is located on one of Rockport's
many picturesque streets and offers a
haven for a restful and relaxing vacation. We are a leisurely 800-foot walk
to the sandy beach, restaurants, art galleries, unique shops, and the train station. Inside our Victorian-style home
you will find 14 individually decorated
guest rooms, all with private baths.
Guests enjoy the Inn's formal living
room, sun porch, the bay and pond
views from the cupola, the spacious
yard, and Dawn's "made from scratch"
continental breakfast served buffet-style
in the dining room.

Hosts: Jon and Dawn Cunningham
Rooms: 18 (PB) $73-95
Hearty Homemade Continental Breakfast
Credit Cards: A, B
Notes: 2, 5, 7, 9, 10, 12

SALEM

Amelia Payson House

16 Winter Street, 01970
(508) 744-8304

Built in 1845, 16 Winter Street is one

NOTES: Credit cards accepted: A Master Card; B Visa; C American Express; D Discover;
E Diners Club; F Other; 2 Personal checks accepted; 3 Lunch available; 4 Dinner available;

of Salem's finest examples of Greek Revival architecture. Elegantly restored and beautifully decorated, each room is furnished with period antiques, and warmed by a personal touch. Comfort amenities include private baths, air-conditioning, and cable TV. Located in the heart of Salem's historic district, a five-minute stroll finds downtown shopping, historic houses, museums, and Pickering Wharf's water-front dining. The seaside towns of Rockport and Gloucester are a short drive up the coast; downtown Boston is only 30 minutes away by car or easily reached by train or bus. Color brochure available. No smoking.

Hosts: Ada and Donald Roberts
Rooms: 4 (PB) $65-95
Continental Plus Breakfast
Credit Cards: A, B, C
Notes: 5, 9, 10

Amelia Payson House

The Salem Inn

7 Summer Street, 01970
(508) 741-0680; (800) 446-2995;
FAX (508) 744-8924

The Salem Inn is an upscale thirty one room inn which is located in the heart of the downtown McIntire Historic Dis-

trict. The Inn comprises two renovated and restored sea captain's homes on the National Register: the West House and the Curwen House. The ambiance in this unique setting includes working fireplaces, canopy beds, antique furnishings, and period details, as well as the modern day convenience of whirlpool baths, cable TV, telephones, in-room coffee makers, and air-conditioning. This full service inn features an excellent on-site restaurant and a unique gift shop, The Enchanted Forest. Special Packages! For a corporate meeting or special functions the perfect choice is The Salem Inn. The Inn offers private, exclusive meeting space, full catering, on-site parking, deluxe guest rooms, complete line of audio visual equipment, FAX machine, and computer hook ups. We supply the staff, service, and the spirit for the most successful meeting and special occasions.

Hosts: Diane and Richard Pabich
Rooms: 31 (PB) $99-175
Continental Breakfast
Credit Cards: A, B, C, D, E
Notes: 2, 4, 5, 6, 7, 9, 10, 12

SANDWICH

Captain Ezra Nye House

152 Main Street, 02563
(508) 888-6142; (800) 388-CAPT;
FAX (508) 833-2897

Whether you come to enjoy summer on Cape Cod, a fall foliage trip, or a quiet winter vacation, the Captain Ezra Nye House is a great place to start. Located 60 miles from Boston, 20 miles from Hyannis, and within walking distance of many noteworthy attractions, including Heritage Plantation, Sandwich Glass Museum, and the Cape Cod Canal. Award winning Readers Choice, Best B&B Upper Cape, *Cape Cod Life* magazine, and named one of the Top Fifty Inns in America by *Inn Times*.

Hosts: Elaine and Harry Dickson
Rooms: 7 (PB) $85-100
Full Breakfast
Credit Cards: A, B, C, D
Notes: 2, 5, 7 (over 6), 8, 9, 10, 12

The Cranberry House Bed and Breakfast

50 Main Street, 02563
(508)888-1281

The Cranberry House is a friendly place to stay on Cape Cod. A full continental breakfast is served in the dining room or on the deck. Relax in the den overlooking the beautifully landscaped yard. Hosts offer cable TV and complimentary drinkd. Sandwich, the Cape's oldest town, has many shops, restaurants, museums, gardens, and beaches. The Cape Cod Canal has walking and biking trails. No smoking inside.

Hosts: John and Sara Connolly
Rooms: 3 (1PB; 2SB) $50-75
Continental Deluxe Breakfast
Credit Cards: none
Notes: 2 (and travelers'), 5, 7 (over 10), 8, 9, 10

The Summer House

158 Main Street, 02563
(508) 888-4991

This exquisite 1835 Greek Revival home, featured in *Country Living* magazine, is located in the heart of historic

The Summer House

Sandwich village and features antiques, working fireplaces, hand-stitched quilts, flowers, large sunny rooms, and English-style gardens. We are within strolling distance of dining, museums, shops, pond, and the boardwalk to the beach. Bountiful breakfasts and afternoon tea in the garden.

Hosts: Marjorie and Kevin Huelsman
Rooms: 5 (1PB; 4SB) $55-75
Full Breakfast
Credit Cards: A, B, C, D
Notes: 2, 5, 7 (over 5), 8, 9, 10, 12

SOUTH DARTMOUTH

The Little Red House

631 Elm Street, 02748
(508) 996-4554

A charming gambrel Colonial home located in the lovely coastal village of Padanaram. This home is beautifully furnished with country accents, antiques, lovely living room with fireplace, and luxuriously comfortable four-poster or brass-and-iron beds. A full homemade breakfast in the roman-

NOTES: Credit cards accepted: A Master Card; B Visa; C American Express; D Discover; E Diners Club; F Other; 2 Personal checks accepted; 3 Lunch available; 4 Dinner available;

tic, candlelit dining room is a delectable treat. Close to the harbor, beaches and historic sites; a short distance to New Bedford, Newport, Plymouth, Bøston, and Cape Cod. Martha Vineyard's ferry is just 10 minutes away.

Hostess: Meryl Zwirblis
Rooms: 3 (1PB; 2SB) $55-75
Full Breakfast
Credit Cards: none
Notes: 2, 5, 9, 10, 12

Captain Nickerson Inn

SOUTH DENNIS

Captain Nickerson Inn
333 Main Street, 02660
(508) 398-5966; (800) 282-1619

Delightful, Victorian sea captain's home built in 1828 and changed to its present Queen Anne style in 1879. Comfortable front porch is lined with white wicker rockers and tables. Five guest rooms decorated with period four poster or white iron queen beds and Oriental or hand woven rugs. The living and dining rooms have fireplaces and stained glass windows. The Inn, which is situated on a bike path, offers bicycles to guests for a small fee. The

Cape Cod 20-plus-mile bike Rail Trail is only one half mile from the Inn. Area attractions include championship public golf courses, world class beaches, paddle boats, horseback riding, museums, Cape Playhouse, fishing, craft and antique shops, and a local church which houses the oldest working pipe organ in the country. Full Breakfast is satisfying with homemade muffins and a hot entree. Smoking is restricted to the front porch.

Hosts: Pat and Dave York
Rooms: 5 (3PB; 2SB) $60-90
Full Breakfast
Credit Cards: A, B, D
Notes: 2, 4 (weekends only), 5, 7, 9, 10, 12

STOCKBRIDGE

Arbor Rose Bed and Breakfast
Box 114, 8 Yale Hill, 01262
(413) 298-4744

Lovely, old, New England mill house with pond, gardens, and mountain view. Walk to Berkshire Theater and Stockbridge Center. Beautiful rooms, comfy, good beds, antiques, paintings, and sunshine. Fireplace and TV in common room. Home-baked mmm . . . breakfast.

Hostess: Christina Alsop
Rooms: 4 (2PB; 2SB) $55-150
Home-baked Continental; Full Breakfast on weekends
Credit Cards: A, B, C
Notes: 2, 5, 7, 8, 9, 10, 11, 12

---

5 Open all year; 6 Pets welcome; 7 Children welcome; 8 Tennis nearby; 9 Swimming nearby; 10 Golf nearby; 11 Skiing nearby; 12 May be booked through travel agent.

STURBRIDGE

The Colonel Ebenezer Crafts Inn

Fiske Hill Road, 01566
(508) 347-3313; (800) PUBLICK;
FAX (508) 347-5073

The Colonel Ebenezer's Crafts Inn built in 1786 on the summit of Fiske Hill, offers a sensational panoramic view. Accommodations at the magnificently restored inn are enchanting and historically captivating. There are canopy beds, as well as poster beds. Guests may relax by the pool or unwind in the sunroom, take afternoon tea, or simply enjoy sweeping views of the countryside.

Host: Albert Cournoyer
Rooms: 8 (PB) $65-155
Continental Breakfast
Credit Cards: A, B, C
Notes: 2, 5, 7, 9

STURBRIDGE (WARE)

Antique 1880 Bed and Breakfast

14 Pleasant Street, Ware 01082
(413) 967-7847

Built in 1876, this Colonial style has pumpkin and maple hardwood floors, beamed ceilings, six fireplaces, and antique furnishings. Afternoon tea is served by the fireplace; breakfast is served in the dining room or on the porch, weather permitting. It is a short, pretty, country ride to historic Old Sturbridge Village and Old Deerfield Village; hiking and fishing are nearby.

Midpoint between Boston and the Berkshires, this is a very comfortable bed and breakfast.

Hostess: Margaret Skutnik
Rooms: 5 (2PB; 3SB) $40-65
Full Breakfast
Credit Cards: none
Notes: 2, 5, 8, 9, 10, 11, 12

TYRINGHAM

The Golden Goose

123 Main Road, Box 336, 01264
(413) 243-3008

Warm, friendly, circa 1800 bed and breakfast nestled in a secluded valley. Near to Tanglewood, Stockbridge, skiing, and hiking. All homemade jams, applesauce, and biscuits, fresh fruit in season, and hot and cold cereals. Open all year.

Hosts: Lilja and Joseph Rizzo
Rooms: 7 (5PB; 2SB) $80-125
Semi-Full Breakfast
Credit Cards: A, B, C, D
Notes: 2, 5, 7, 8, 9, 10, 11, 12

VINEYARD HAVEN (MARTHA'S VINEYARD)

Captain Dexter House of Vineyard Haven

100 Main Street, PO Box 2457, 02568
(508) 693-6564; (508) 693-8448

Your perfect country inn! Built in 1840, the house has been meticulously restored and exquisitely furnished to reflect the charm of that period. You will be surrounded by flowers from our garden and pampered by innkeepers who

NOTES: Credit cards accepted: A Master Card; B Visa; C American Express; D Discover; E Diners Club; F Other; 2 Personal checks accepted; 3 Lunch available; 4 Dinner available;

Captain Dexter House of Vineyard Haven

believe in old-fashioned hospitality. The inn's eight romantic guest rooms are distinctively decorated. Several rooms have working fireplaces (as does the parlor) and four-poster canopy beds. Stroll to town and harbor.

Hosts: Lori and Mike
Rooms: 8 (PB) $55-195
Continental Plus Breakfast
Credit Cards: A, B, C, E
Notes: 2, 8, 9, 10, 12

WEST STOCKBRIDGE

Card Lake Inn

29 Main Street, 01266
(413) 232-0272 (voice and FAX)

Minutes from Tanglewood, the Norman Rockwell museum, and the Butternut Ski Area. Fine dining and lodging at reasonable prices. Rooms are Colonially furnished, many with brass beds. Fully air-conditioned. Restaurant and rooms are smoke-free.

Hosts: Ed and Lisa Robbins
Rooms: 7 (5PB; 2SB) $45-135
Continental Breakfast
Credit Cards: A, B, C, D
Notes: 2, 3, 4, 5, 7, 9, 10, 11, 12

WEST YARMOUTH

The Manor House Bed and Breakfast

57 Maine Avenue, 02673
(508) 771-3433; (800) 9-MANOR-9

The Manor House is a lovely, 1920s, six-bedroom, Dutch Colonial bed and breakfast overlooking Lewis Bay. Each room has a private bath and all are decorated differently and named after special little touches of Cape Cod. We are ideally located mid-Cape on the southern side, with easy access to virtually everything the Cape has to offer. We offer a bountiful breakfast, afternoon tea and friendly hospitality.

Hosts: Rick and Liz Latshaw
Rooms: 6 (PB) $74-118
Full Breakfast
Credit Cards: A, B, C
Notes: 2, 5, 8, 9, 10, 12

The Manor House

---

5 Open all year; 6 Pets welcome; 7 Children welcome; 8 Tennis nearby; 9 Swimming nearby; 10 Golf nearby; 11 Skiing nearby; 12 May be booked through travel agent.

YARMOUTH PORT

The Colonial House Inn
277 Main Street, Route 6A, 02675
(508) 362-4348; (800) 999-3416;
FAX (508) 362-8034

The Colonial House Inn

This registered historical landmark has antique appointed guest rooms, private baths, and air-conditioning. It features gracious hospitality, old world charm, and traditional New England cuisine. Full liquor license, fine wines, and an indoor heated swimming pool. Lovely grounds, large deck, TV room, and Victorian living room. Close to nature trails, golf, tennis, antique shops, beaches, and shopping.

Host: Malcolm Perna/Tony Malcolm
Rooms: 21 (PB) $50-85
Continental Breakfast
Credit Cards: A, B, C, D
Notes: 2, 3, 4, 5, 6, 7, 8, 9, 10, 11, 12

NOTES: Credit cards accepted: A Master Card; B Visa; C American Express; D Discover; E Diners Club; F Other; 2 Personal checks accepted; 3 Lunch available; 4 Dinner available;

Michigan

BAY CITY

Clements Inn

1712 Center Avenue, 48708
(517) 894-4600; (800) 442-4605;
FAX (517) 895-8535

This 1886 Queen Anne-style Victorian · home features six fireplaces, magnificent woodwork, oak staircase, amber-colored glass windows, working gas lamps, organ pipes, and two clawfoot tubs. Each of the seven bedrooms includes cable TV, telephone, private bath, and air-conditioning. Special features include in-room gas fireplaces, in-room whirlpool tubs, and the 1,200 square foot Ballroom Suite, including fireplace, whirlpool, and furnished kitchen.

Hosts: Brian and Karen Hepp
Rooms: 7 (PB) $70-140
Continental Breakfast
Credit Cards: A, B, C, D, E
Notes: 2, 5, 7, 8, 10, 11, 12 (10%)

BELLAIRE

Grand Victorian B&B Inn

402 N. Bridge Street, 49615
(616) 533-6111; (800) 336-3860;
FAX (616) 533-8197

1895 Victorian gingerbread mansion

built by lumber baron Henri Richardi. Listed on National Register, the Inn features antiques throughout, three fireplaces, etched glass, exquisite woodwork, and wicker-filled front porch/balconies overlooking a park. Minutes to golf/skiing (Shanty/Schuss). Tandem town bike for shopping. Elegant breakfast experience. No smoking. Four rooms each with private bath. Featured on *June Midwest Living* cover.

Hosts: George and Jill Watson
Rooms: 4 (PB) $85-108
Full Breakfast
Credit Cards: A, B, C
Notes: 2, 8, 9, 10, 11, 12

BOYNE CITY

Deer Lake Bed and Breakfast

00631 East Deer Lake Road, 49712
(616) 582-9039

A beautiful comtemporary waterfront B&B is nestled in an all-season resort area, conveniently located on Deer Lake between Boyne Falls and Boyne City. There are five charming and comfortable rooms, each with a private bath. Individual heat and AC. Two of the

---

5 Open all year; 6 Pets welcome; 7 Children welcome; 8 Tennis nearby; 9 Swimming nearby; 10 Golf nearby; 11 Skiing nearby; 12 May be booked through travel agent.

MICHIGAN (UPPER PENINSULA)

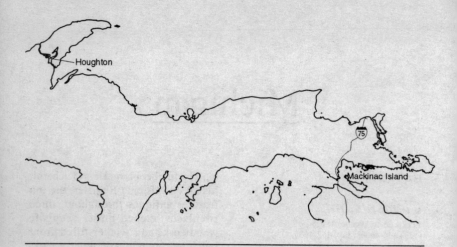

MICHIGAN

Deer Lake Bed and Breakfast

rooms have private balconies overlooking the lake and pond. Three room share a 40-foot balcony. Jewelry case available.

Hosts: Shirley and Glenn Piepenburg
Rooms: 5 (PB) $80-95
Full Breakfast
Credit Cards: A, B, D
Notes: 2, 5, 7, 8, 9, 10, 11, 12

CHARLOTTE

Schatze Manor Bed and Breakfast

1281 W. Kinsel Hwy., 48813
(517) 543-4170; (800) 425-2244

Come, stay, and enjoy quiet elegance in our Victorian Oak Suite with red Oriental soaking tub, or enjoy sleeping in our 1948 Chevy Woody Room, or feel like a celebrity and relax in our Movie Star Room. All with private baths, distinctive hand carved woodwork, unique

decorating, full breakfast, evening dessert, and a non-smoking atmosphere. Golf packages and dinner/theater packages available. Lansing 20 miles.

Hosts: Donna and Paul Dunning
Rooms: 3 (PB) $60-105
Full Breakfast
Credit Cards: A, B, C
Notes: 2, 5, 8, 9, 10

CLIO

Chandelier Guest House

1567 Morgan Road, 48420
(810) 687-6061

Relax in our country home. Enjoy bed and breakfast comforts including choice of rooms with twin, full, or queen beds. You may wish to be served full breakfast in bed, beneath the beautiful crystal chandelier, or on the sun porch with a view of surrounding woods. Located minutes from Clio Amphitheater, Flint Crossroad Village, Birch Run Manufacturer's Marketplace, Frankenmuth, and Chesaning. Senior citizen discount. Call for directions. Hospitality Award Winner in Flint and Genesee County, Michigan.

Hosts: Alfred and Clara Bielert
Rooms: 2 (1SB) $50-55
Full Country Breakfast
Credit Cards: none
Notes: 2, 5, 7, 10, 12

NOTES: Credit cards accepted: A Master Card; B Visa; C American Express; D Discover; E Diners Club; F Other; 2 Personal checks accepted; 3 Lunch available; 4 Dinner available; 5 Open all year; 6 Pets welcome; 7 Children welcome; 8 Tennis nearby; 9 Swimming nearby; 10 Golf nearby; 11 Skiing nearby; 12 May be booked through travel agent.

Cinnamon Stick B&B

12364 N. Genesee Road, 48420
(810) 686-8391

Large, country farm home on 50 rolling acres. Walking trails, stocked pond for fishing, and tennis court on site. Guest facilities includes four bedrooms, great room with fieldstone fireplace, dining room, and patio flower-garden area. Minutes to Frankenmuth, Birch Run Outlet Mall, Crossroads Village and Huckleberry Rail Road, and Genesee Bell paddle boat. Open all year.

Hosts: Brian and Carol Powell
Rooms: 4 (2PB; 2SB) $60-80
Full Breakfast
Credit Cards: A, B
Notes: 2, 5, 7, 8 (on-site), 9, 10

Cinnamon Stick Bed and Breakfast

COLDWATER

Bativa Inn
Bed and Breakfast

1824 W. Chicago Road, US 12, 49036
(517) 278-5146

This 1872 Italiante, country inn has original massive woodwork, high ceilings, and restful charm. Seasonal decorations are a specialty. Christmas festival of trees. Located near recreation and discount shopping. In-ground pool, cross-country skiing, and 15 acres of wildlife trails. Guest pampering is the innkeepers' goal with treats and homemade breakfast. Perfect for small retreats.

Host: Fred Marquardt
Rooms: 5 (PB) $64-79
Full Breakfast
Credit Cards: A, B, D
Notes: 2, 5, 8, 9, 11

ELK RAPIDS

Cairn House
Bed and Breakfast

8160 Cairn Highway, PO Box 866, 49629
(616) 264-8994

Elegant Colonial style home in beautifully landscaped surroundings, 15 miles north of Traverse City. Minutes from the bay. Delicious full breakfasts. Excellent area for year-round sports, gourmet dining, and shopping. Available for family celebrations and retreats. Children welcome. Boat parking available. Your comfort is our priority. Special midweek prices.

Hosts: Roger and Mary Vandervort
Rooms: 3 (PB) $60
Full Breakfast
Credit Cards: none
Notes: 2, 5, 7, 8, 9, 10, 11, 12

FENNVILLE

The Kingsley House B&B

626 W. Main Street, 49408
(616) 561-6425

This elegant, Queen Anne Victorian was built by the prominent Kingsley

NOTES: Credit cards accepted: A Master Card; B Visa; C American Express; D Discover; E Diners Club; F Other; 2 Personal checks accepted; 3 Lunch available; 4 Dinner available;

family in 1886 and selected by *Inn Times* as one of the 50 best bed and breakfasts in America. It was also featured in *Insider* magazine. Near Holland, Saugatuck, Allegan State Forest, sandy beaches, and cross-country skiing. Bicycles available, three rooms with whirlpool baths and fireplaces, and a getaway honeymoon suite. Enjoy the beautiful surroundings and family antiques. Breakfast is served in the formal dining room.

Hosts: Gary and Kari King
Rooms: 8 (PB) $75-150
Full Breakfast (weekends); Continental Plus (weekdays)
Credit Cards: A, B, C, D
Notes: 2, 5, 8, 9, 10, 11, 12

The Kingsley House

Ridgeland

6875-126th Avenue, 49408
(616) 857-1633

Take a walk back in time to the turn of the century and experience a stay in one of the original guest homes of the Lakeshore area. We are a family oriented bed and breakfast with antique furnishings. Located near the Saugatuck

Douglas area in a rural setting by Lake Michigan. See wildlife in its natural setting; have a private bath and jacuzzi. Non-smoking.

Hosts: Carl and Michele Nicholson
Rooms: 3 (PB) $75-85
Full Breakfast
Credit Cards: A, B
Notes: 2, 5, 7, 9, 10, 11

FLINT AND FRANKENMUTH— SEE ALSO CLIO

FRANKENMUTH

Bavarian Town Bed and Breakfast

206 Beyerlein Street, 48734
(517) 652-8057

Beautifully decorated Cape Cod dwelling with central air-conditioning and private half baths in a peaceful, residential district of Michigan's most popular tourist town, just three blocks from Main Street. Bilingual hosts are descendants of original German settlers. Will serve as tour guide of area, including historic St. Lorenz Lutheran Church. Color TV with comfortable sitting area in each room. Shared kitchenette. Leisurely served full breakfasts with homemade, baked food. Shared recipes. Superb hospitality.

Hosts: Louie and Kathy Weiss
Rooms: 2 (P½B, shower is shared) $55-65
Full Breakfast
Credit Cards: none
Notes: 2, 5, 7, 8, 9, 10

---

5 Open all year; 6 Pets welcome; 7 Children welcome; 8 Tennis nearby; 9 Swimming nearby; 10 Golf nearby; 11 Skiing nearby; 12 May be booked through travel agent.

Bed and Breakfast at the Pines

Bed and Breakfast at the Pines

327 Ardussi Street, 48374
(517) 652-9019

Welcome to our friendly, "non-smoking," ranch-style home in a quiet residential neighborhood within walking distance of main tourist areas and famous restaurants. Hosts offer sight-seeing ideas and suggestions of the area, along with Michigan travel tips. Bedrooms furnished with heirloom quilts, ceiling fans, and fresh flowers; shared shower with terry robes provided. A family-style breakfast of house specialties served in the dining area. Favorite recipes shared with guests. No smoking.

Hosts: Richard and Donna Hodge
Rooms: 2 (1PB; 1SB) $40-50
Modified Continental Breakfast
Credit Cards: none
Notes: 2, 3, 6, 7

GRAND HAVEN

Boyden House Inn B&B

301 South 5th, 49417
(616) 846-3538

Built in 1874, our charming Victorian

inn is decorated with treasures from far-away places, antiques, and original art. Enjoy the comfort of air-conditioned rooms with private baths and two whirlpool baths. Some rooms feature fireplaces or balconies. Relax in our common room and veranda surrounded by a beautiful perennial garden. Full, homemade breakfast served in our lovely dining room. Walking distance to board walk beaches, shopping, and restaurants.

Hosts: Corrie and Berend Snoeyer
Rooms: 6 (PB) $65-110
Full Breakfast
Credit Cards: A, B, C, D
Notes: 2, 5, 7, 8, 9, 10, 11, 12

Seascape Bed and Breakfast

20009 Breton, **Spring Lake** 49456
(616) 842-8409

On a private, Lake Michigan beach. Relaxing lakefront rooms. Enjoy the warm hospitality and "Country Living" ambiance of our nautical lakeshore home. Full, homemade breakfast served in gathering room with fieldstone fireplace or on the sun deck. Either offers a panoramic view of Grand Haven Harbor. Stroll or cross-country ski on dune land nature trails. Open all year around, offering a kaleidoscope of scenes with the changing of the seasons. Stay Sunday-Thursday and get one night free!

Hostess: Susan Meyer
Rooms: 3 (PB) $75-125
Full Breakfast
Credit Cards: A, B
Notes: 2, 5, 8, 9, 10, 11, 12 (no commission)

NOTES: Credit cards accepted: A Master Card; B Visa; C American Express; D Discover; E Diners Club; F Other; 2 Personal checks accepted; 3 Lunch available; 4 Dinner available;

Village Park Bed and Breakfast

60 W. Park Street, **Fruitport** 49415-9668
(616) 865-6289; (800) 469-1118

Overlooking the welcoming waters of Spring Lake and Village Park where guests can picnic, play tennis, or use pedestrian bike paths and boat launch. Spring Lake has access to Lake Michigan. Relaxing common area with fireplace; guests may also relax on decks or in outdoor hot tub. Historic setting of Mineral Springs Health Resort. Tradition continues with "Wellness Weekend" special package; also Romantic Getaway and B&B Vacation Week packages available. Serving Grand Haven and Muskegon areas; Hoffmaster Park with Gillette Sand Dune Nature Center nearby; also close to Maranatha Bible Conference Center.

Hosts: John Hewett (and B&B ange, Virginia)
Rooms: 6 (PB) $60-90
Continental/Full Breakfast
Credit Cards: A, B
Notes: 2, 5, 7, 8, 9, 10, 11 (cross-country), 12

HOLLAND

Dutch Colonial Inn

560 Central Avenue, 49423
(616) 396-3664; FAX (616) 396-0461

Relax and enjoy a gracious 1928 Dutch Colonial. Your hosts have elegantly decorated their home with family heirloom antiques and furnishings from the 1930s. Guests enjoy the cheery sun porch, honeymoon suites, fireplaces, or rooms with whirlpool tubs for two. Festive touches are everywhere during the Christmas holiday season. Nearby are Windmill Island, wooden shoe factory, Delftware factory, tulip festival, Hope College, Michigan's finest beaches, bike paths, and cross-country ski trails. Corporate rates are available for business travelers.

Hosts: Bob and Pat Elenbaas, Ellen Moes
Rooms: 5 (PB) $75-150
Full Breakfast
Credit Cards: A, B, C, D
Notes: 2, 5, 8, 9, 10, 11, 12

North Shore Inn of Holland

North Shore Inn of Holland

686 North Shore Drive, 49424
(616) 394-9050; FAX (616) 392-1389

Water views, three-course gourmet breakfasts, and personalized service are hallmarks of the North Shore Inn. This elegantly restored 1920s lakeside B&B is in a tranquil setting yet close to area attractions. The cozy bedrooms, decorated with quilts and antiques, feature private baths and king or queen beds. The North Shore Inn is open year-round. Relax in the wicker chaise on the screened porch in summer or enjoy the comfortable sofa in front of the fire-

5 Open all year; 6 Pets welcome; 7 Children welcome; 8 Tennis nearby; 9 Swimming nearby;
10 Golf nearby; 11 Skiing nearby; 12 May be booked through travel agent.

place in winter.

Hosts: Beverly and Kurt Van Genderen
Rooms: 3 (2PB; 1SB) $100-120
Full 3-Course Breakfast
Credit Cards: none
Notes: 2, 5, 8, 9, 10, 12 (no commision)

HOUGHTON

Charleston House Historic Inn

918 College Avenue, 49931
(906) 482-7790; (800) 482-7404;
FAX (906) 482-7068

Turn-of-the-century historic Georgian house with double veranda, ceiling fans, and wicker furniture. The Inn features ornate woodwork, leaded and beveled glass windows, library with fireplace, and grand interior staircase. Comfortable period reproduction and antique furnishings with king canopy and twin bed. All private baths, air-conditioning, cable color TV, and telephones. Full buffet breakfast. Near the university. Smoking limited to the garden.

Hosts: John and Helen Sullivan
Rooms: 9 (PB) $90-180
Full Breakfast
Credit Cards: A, B, C
Notes: 2, 5, 7 (12 and older), 8, 9, 10, 11, 12

Charleston House Historic Inn

INTERLOCHEN

Sandy Shores Bed and Breakfast

4487 State Park Highway, 49643
(616) 276-9763

Your "home away from home." Large living room, glassed-in porch, decking. Rooms tastefully furnished. Guests have access to all facilities including yard and private, sandy beach on Duck Lake. Convenient to summer/winter activities, shopping, and dining. Within walking distance of Interlochen Arts Academy. 17 miles SW of Traverse City.

Hostess: Sandra E. Svec
Rooms: 3 (SB) $70-80
Continental Plus Breakfast
Credit Cards: none
Notes: 2, 5, 9, 10, 11, 12

IONIA

Union Hill Inn

306 Union Street, 48846
(616) 527-0955

Enjoy a peaceful getaway amongst pre-Victorian splendor. You can relax in our historic 1868 home as if you were at Grandma's or Grandpa's. Rooms decorated with antiques. TVs and air-conditioning. You may walk the hills in our town or simply enjoy the beautiful view from the porches, which Union Hill is noted for. Wonderful antiquing area and World's largest free fair. "Home away from home" for business guests. Cor-

---

NOTES: Credit cards accepted: A Master Card; B Visa; C American Express; D Discover; E Diners Club; F Other; 2 Personal checks accepted; 3 Lunch available; 4 Dinner available;

porate rates available. Located midway between Lansing and Grand Rapids.

Hosts: Tom and Mary Kay Moular
Rooms: 6 (1PB; 5SB) $50-75
Full Breakfast
Credit Cards: none
Notes: 2, 5, 7, 8, 9, 10, 11, 12

Union Hill Inn

JACKSON

Summit Place Bed and Breakfast
1682 W. Kimmel Road, 49201
(517) 787-0468

Enjoy warmth and elegance where the past blends with the present in a beautiful, quiet countryside. We specialize in service, comfort, and a full breakfast, served in our formal dining room and prepared the old-fashioned way—from scratch. Bedrooms are lovely and comfortable with reading chairs, desk, color cable TV, extra quilts, and phones. Tea with treats served in afternoons and wake-up coffee and muffins are delivered to your door. Take in the many area attractions, including MIS Speedway,

Michigan Space Center, museums, malls, antique shops, and fine dining.

Hosts: Marlene and Douglas Laing
Rooms: 2 (SB) $50-65
Full Breakfast
Credit Cards: A, B
Notes: 2, 5, 7, 9

LAKE CITY

Bed and Breakfast in the Pines
1940 S. Schneider Street, 49651
(616) 839-4876

A quaint chalet nestled among the pines on shimmering Sapphire Lake. Each bedroom has its own outside door leading to its own deck facing the lake. Enjoy our large fireplace and warm hospitality. Handicap ramp. Thirteen miles east of Cadillac. No alcohol, smoking, or pets. Enjoy downhill or cross-country skiing, fishing, swimming, hiking, biking, and boating. By two-week advance reservation only.

Hostess: Reggie Ray
Rooms: 1 (PB) $70
Suites: 1 (PB) $75-100
Full Breakfast
Credit Cards: none
Notes: 2, 5, 8, 9, 10, 11

LELAND

Manitou Manor
PO Box 864, 49654
(616) 256-7712

A century-old farmhouse makes staying in the Leelanau Lake region a peace-

---

5 Open all year; 6 Pets welcome; 7 Children welcome; 8 Tennis nearby; 9 Swimming nearby; 10 Golf nearby; 11 Skiing nearby; 12 May be booked through travel agent.

ful experience. Manitou Manor is a historical bed and breakfast, open year-round, which boasts private baths and family-style breakfasts. From weddings to quiet getaways, it's a perfect place to celebrate the seasons.

Hosts: Sandy, Mike, and Chris Lambdin
Rooms: 6 (5PB; 1SB) $75-110
Full Breakfast
Credit Cards: A, B
Notes: 2, 5, 7, 8, 9, 10, 11, 12

Doll House Inn

LUDINGTON

Doll House Inn Historical B&B

709 E. Ludington Avenue, 49431
(616) 843-2286; (800) 275-4616

Gracious 1900 American Foursquare, seven rooms including bridal suite with whirlpool tub for two. Enclosed porch. Smoke and pet free adult accommodations. Full, heart-smart breakfast. Air-conditioning, corporate rates, bicycles, cross-country skiing, walk to beach and town, and special weekend and murder/mystery packages fall and winter.

Transportation to and from car ferry/airport.

Hosts: Joe and Barb Gerovac
Rooms: 7 (PB) $60-110
Full Breakfast
Credit Cards: A, B
Closed Dec. 20-Jan. 3
Notes: 2, 5, 8, 9, 10

The Inn at Ludington

701 E. Ludington Avenue, 49431
(616) 845-7055; (800) 845-9170

The charm of the past with the comfort of today. No stuffy hands-off museum atmosphere here—our vintage furnishings invite you to relax ans feel at home. The bountiful breakfast will sustain you for a day of beachcombing, biking, or antiqueing. In winter, cross-country skiing awaits at Ludington State Park. Looking for something different? Murder mysteries are a specialty. Make this your headquarters for a Ludington/Lake Michigan adventure. Just look for the "painted lady" with the three-story turret. Non-smoking.

Hosts: Diane Shields/David Nemitz
Rooms: 6 (PB) $65-85
Full Buffet Breakfast
Credit Cards: A, B, C
Notes: 2, 3 (picnic), 5, 7, 8, 9, 10, 11, 12

Snyder's Shoreline Inn

903 W. Ludington Avenue, PO Box 667, 49431
(616) 845-1261; FAX (616) 843-4441

Snyder's Shoreline Inn ranks among the finest in Western Michigan with glorious Lake Michigan sunsets from private balconies. Luxurious suites, some with

NOTES: Credit cards accepted: A Master Card; B Visa; C American Express; D Discover; E Diners Club; F Other; 2 Personal checks accepted; 3 Lunch available; 4 Dinner available;

Snyder's Shoreline Inn

in-room spas. Delightful handicapped rooms available. Antique lover's delight. Heavenly beds in rooms graced with stenciled walls and hand-stitched quilts. Outdoor pool and spa. Miles of white sand beaches nearby. Walking distance to shopping and restaurants. Smoke free. Packages available. Cater to groups (ex. Bible studies, retreats, etc.). AAA two-diamond and ABBA three-crown ratings. Call eary for reservations.

Hosts: Tom, Sharon, and Angie Snyder
Rooms: 44 (PB) $65-229
Continental Breakfast
Credit Cards: A, B, C, D
Notes: 8, 9, 10

MACKINAC ISLAND

Haan's 1830 Inn

PO Box 123, 49757
(906) 847-6244; winter (847) 526-2662

The earliest Greek Revival home in the Northwest Territory, this inn is on the Michigan Historic Registry and is completely restored. It is in a quiet neighborhood three blocks around Haldiman Bay from bustling 1800s downtown and Old Fort Mackinac. It is also adjacent to historic St. Anne's Church and gardens. Guest rooms are furnished with antiques. Enjoy the island's 19th century ambiance of horse drawn buggies and wagons.

Hosts: Nicholas and Nancy Haan
Rooms: 7 (5PB; 2SB) $80-145
Deluxe Continental Breakfast
Credit Cards: none
Closed late October to mid May
Notes: 2, 7, 8, 10

Pine Cottage Bed and Breakfast

PO Box 1890, 49757
(906) 847-3820

Constructed in 1890 forever preserving the Victorian era, Pine Cottage B&B is a quaint getaway for those that want to remember a time gone by. This bed and breakfast offers private and semi-private baths, cable TV, and an abundance of warm hospitality. Come relax and enjoy the quiet, friendly atmosphere of mystical Mackinac Island which offers indoor and outdoor fun for everyone.

Hosts: Greg and Peggy Woodard
Rooms: 15 (5PB; 10SB) $50 (winter); $74-125
   (in season)
Continental Breakfast
Credit Cards: A, B
Notes: 2, 6, 7, 8, 10, 11 (cross-country)

---

5 Open all year; 6 Pets welcome; 7 Children welcome; 8 Tennis nearby; 9 Swimming nearby;
10 Golf nearby; 11 Skiing nearby; 12 May be booked through travel agent.

MUSKEGON

Port City Victorian Inn

1259 Lakeshore Drive, 49441
(616) 759-0205 (voice and FAX);
(800) 274-3574

1877 romantic Victorian getaway on the bluffs overlooking Muskegon Lake. Five bedrooms with air-conditioning, two featuring expansive suites with lake views and double whirlpool baths, and three with private baths. Rooftop balcony, cozy TV/VCR room, fireplace in parlor, and a sunroom. Open year-round.

Hosts: Frederick and Barbara Schossau
Rooms: 5 (PB) $95-125
Full Breakfast
Credit Cards: A, B, C, D, E, F
Notes: 2, 5, 7, 8, 9, 10, 11, 12

Port City Victorian Inn

ONEKAMA

Lake Breeze House

5089 Main Street, 49675
(616) 889-4969

Our two-story frame house on Portage Lake is yours with a shared bath, living room, and breakfast room. Each room has its own special charm with family antiques. Come, relax, and enjoy our back porch and the sounds of the babbling creek. By reservation only. Boating and charter service available.

Hosts: Bill and Donna Erickson
Rooms: 3 (1P½B; 2SB) $55
Full Breakfast
Credit Cards: none
Notes: 2, 7, 8, 9, 10, 11

OWOSSO

R & R Ranch

308 E. Hibbard Road, 48867
(517) 723-2553

A newly remodeled farmhouse from the 1900s, the ranch sits on 130 acres overlooking the Maple River Valley. A large concrete, circle drive with white board fences leads to stables of horses and cattle. The area's wildlife includes deer, fox, rabbits, pheasant, quail, and songbirds. Observe and explore from the farm lane, river walk, or outside deck. Country-like accents adorn the interior of the farmhouse, and guests are welcome to use the family parlor,

---

NOTES: Credit cards accepted: A Master Card; B Visa; C American Express; D Discover; E Diners Club; F Other; 2 Personal checks accepted; 3 Lunch available; 4 Dinner available;

garden, game room, and fireplace. Newly installed central air-conditioning.

Hosts: Carl and Jeanne Rossman
Rooms: 3 (SB) $45
Continental Breakfast
Credit Cards: none
Notes: 2, 5, 6, 7, 10

PENTWATER

Historic Nickerson Inn

262 Lowell, PO Box 986, 49449
(616) 869-6731; FAX (616) 369-6151

The Historic Nickerson Inn has been serving guests with "special hospitality" since 1914. Our inn was totally renovated in 1991. All our rooms have private baths and air-conditioning. We have two jacuzzi suites with fireplaces and balconies overlooking Lake Michigan. Two short blocks to Lake Michigan beach, and three blocks to shopping district. New ownership. Open all year. Casual, fine dining in our 80-seat restaurant. Excellent for retreats, workshops, and year-round recreation.

Hosts: Gretchen and Harry Shiparski
Rooms: 10 (PB) $85-100
Suites: 2 (PB) $160-185
Full Breakfast
Credit Cards: A, B
Notes: 2, 4, 5, 7 (over 12), 8, 9, 10, 11 (cross-country), 12

Pentwater "Victorian" Inn

180 E. Lowell, PO Box 98, 49449
(616) 869-5909; FAX (616) 869-7002

This beautiful Victorian inn, built in the 1800s, has attractive gingerbread exterior and stained-glass windows which have been lovingly preserved. Located a short walk from the village shops, fine dining, and Lake Michigan Beach with its spectacular sunsets. This popular B&B inn provides comfort and hospitality from the personal greeting by your hosts and evening snack, to the elegant three-course breakfast made all from scratch and served in the dining room. Each of the five bedrooms is tastefully decorated with British and American antiques that the hosts collected while living in England. Three porches grace the Inn and the back porch is enclosed with a hot tub room. No smoking.

Hosts: Quintus and Donna Renshaw
Rooms: 5 (PB) $65-85
Full Breakfast
Credit Cards: A, B
Notes: 2, 5, 7, 8, 9, 10, 11 (cross-country), 12

Pentwater "Victorian" Inn

PETOSKEY

Terrace Inn

PO Box 266, 216 Fairview, 49770
(616) 347-2410; (800) 530-9898

The Terrace Inn is a charming historic B&B inn, built in 1911 and designated a National Historic Landmark. It is located in the center of Bay View, a fairytale Victorian village of over 400 Victorian cottages, adjacent to Petoskey in Northwest Michigan. The Inn is family owned and operated. Each guest room has private bath and original antique furnishings. Breakfast served in the spectacular dining room or on our large scenic porch. Guests have use of a private beach, tennis courts, and country club. Hiking, biking, and cross-country ski trails are at our doorstep. Packages, specialty weekends, and group facilities available. Smokefree!

Hosts: Tom and Denise Erhart
Rooms: 44 (PB) $44-99
Coninental Breakfast
Credit Cards: A, B, C
Notes: 2, 3, 4, 5, 7, 8, 9, 10, 11, 12

The 1882 John Crispe House

PLAINWELL

The 1882 John Crispe House Bed and Breakfast

404 East Bridge Street, 49080
(616) 685-1293

Enjoy museum-quality Victorian el-

egance on the Kalamazoo River just off US 131 on Michigan 89, the John Crispe House is close to some of western Michigan's finest gourmet dining, golf, skiing, and antique shops. Air-conditioned. No smoking or alcohol. Gift certificates are available.

Hosts: Nancy E. Lefever and Joel T. Lefever
Rooms: 3 (PB) $75-110
Full Breakfast
Credit Cards: A, B
Notes: 2, 5, 7, 8, 10, 11

ROCKFORD

Heaven Sent II

7134 Northland Drive NE, 49341
(616) 866-8595 (voice and FAX);
(616) 866-9375

With a flavor of the country and a touch of the city, Heaven Sent II is close to the quaint Rockford area just on the north side of Grand Rapids and with lots to do in the vicinity. Close to golf courses, ski areas, mountian biking, swimming, boating, and a number of shopping malls. Grand Rapids and surrounding areas have a number of ethnic festivals and art fairs through many of the seasons. Minutes away from fitness clubs.

Hostess: Maria DeLugt Kocsis
Rooms: 1 (PB) $75-95
Suites: 1 (PB) $100-125
Either Full or Continental Breakfast
Credit Cards: none
Notes: 5, 7, 8, 9, 10, 11

NOTES: Credit cards accepted: A Master Card; B Visa; C American Express; D Discover; E Diners Club; F Other; 2 Personal checks accepted; 3 Lunch available; 4 Dinner available;

South Cliff Inn

ST. JOSEPH

South Cliff Inn B&B

1900 Lakeshore Drive, 49085
(616) 983-4881; FAX (616) 983-7391

South Cliff Inn B&B is an English country home overlooking Lake Michigan. Beautiful decor with many antiques and custom designed furnishings. Fireplaces and whirlpool tubs available in some of our guest rooms. Homemade breakfast served in the lakeside sunroom. Private beach is only a five-minute walk. Shops, restaurants, beaches, antiques and many attractions nearby. Downtown is only one mile away. Voted best B&B in Southwestern Michigan in 1994.

Host: Bill Swisher
Rooms: 7 (PB) $68-150
Continental Plus Breakfast (sometimes Full)
Credit Cards: A, B, C, D
Notes: 5, 8, 9, 10, 11, 12

SAUGATUCK

The Maplewood Hotel

PO Box 1059, 428 Butler Street, 49423
(616) 857-1771; (800) 650-9790;
FAX (616) 857-1773

The Maplewood Hotel architecture is unmistakably Greek Revival. Some rooms have fireplaces and double jacuzzi tubs. Other areas include a library, a glass enclosed porch where you can enjoy a gourmet breakfast, and a full-sized lap pool. Situated in downtown Saugatuck, within walking distance to all shops and restaurants.

Hostesses: Catherine Simon (owner) and Jenna
 Schaeffer (manager)
Rooms: 15 (PB) $85-155
Full Gourmet Breakfast
Credit Cards: A, B, C
Notes: 2, 5, 7, 8, 9, 10, 11, 12

The Maplewood Hotel

Twin Gables Country Inn

900 Lake Street, PO Box 881, 49453
(616) 857-4346; (800) 231-2185

Overlooking Kalamazoo Lake, the State Historic Inn, central air-conditioned throughout, features 14 charming guest rooms with private baths and furnished in antiques and country. Cross-country skiiers relax in the large indoor hot tub and cozy up to a warm crackling fireplace, while summer guests may take a refreshing dip in the outdoor pool and enjoy glorious sunsets on the front ve-

---

5 Open all year; 6 Pets welcome; 7 Children welcome; 8 Tennis nearby; 9 Swimming nearby; 10 Golf nearby; 11 Skiing nearby; 12 May be booked through travel agent.

randa. Three separate one- and two-room cottages are also available.

Hosts: Michael and Denise Simcik
Rooms: 14 (PB)
Continental Plus Breakfast
Credit Cards: A, B, C, D
Notes: 2, 5, 7, 8, 9, 10, 11, 12

SHELBY

The Shepherd's Place Bed and Breakfast

2200 32nd Avenue, 49455
(616) 861-4298

Enjoy a peaceful retreat in a country atmosphere yet close to Lake Michigan beaches, dunes, fishing, golfing, and horseback riding. Choose between our comfortable and cozy accommodations with queen-size bed or twin beds, both with private baths. Full breakfast is served in our dining room or porch overlooking bird haven. No smoking allowed.

Hosts: Hans and Diane Oehring
Rooms: 2 (PB) $55-60
Full Breakfast
Credit Cards: none
Open May through October
Notes: 2, 9, 10

The Seymour House

SOUTH HAVEN

The Seymour House

1248 Blue Star Highway, 49090
(616) 227-3918 (voice and FAX)

An 1862 Victorian mansion on eleven acres encourages relaxation with wide open spaces, an acre pond for fishing, trails through the woods, and a garden patio. Minutes to popular Saugatuck/South Haven beaches, restaurants, galleries, horseback riding, golf, and orchards. Five individually decorated guest rooms with private baths, some with fireplaces or jacuzzi. Beautifully presented gourmet breakfast included. Two-bedroom guest log cabin with fireplace. Central AC in cabin and B&B.

Hosts: Tom and Gwen Paton
Rooms: 5 (PB) $69-129
Full Breakfast
Credit Cards: A, B
Notes: 2, 5, 9, 10, 11, 12

UNION PIER

The Inn at Union Pier

9708 Berrien, PO Box 222, 49129
(616) 469-4700; FAX (616) 469-4720

Just 75 minutes from Chicago and 200 steps to the beach, the Inn blends casual elegance with barefoot informality. Choose from 16 charming, spacious guest rooms, most featuring antique Swedish woodburning fireplaces and porches overlooking the landscaped

---

NOTES: Credit cards accepted: A Master Card; B Visa; C American Express; D Discover; E Diners Club; F Other; 2 Personal checks accepted; 3 Lunch available; 4 Dinner available;

grounds. Take one of the Inn's bicycles out for a spin on a quiet country road, unwind in the outdoor hot tub and sauna or enjoy Michigan wines and popcorn served every evening in the Great Room. A bountiful breakfast and afternoon refreshments are included. The Inn at Union Pier also hosts corporate retreats in a productive environment.

Hosts: Joyce Erickson Pitts and Mark Pitts
Rooms: 16 (PB) $115-185
Full Gourmet Breakfast
Credit Cards: A, B, D
Notes: 2, 5, 8, 9, 10, 11

The Inn at Union Pier

YPSILANTI

The Parish House Inn

103 S. Huron Street, 48197
(313) 480-4800; (800) 480-4866;
FAX (313) 480-7472

This former parsonage of the First Congregational Church is a totally restored Queen Anne style house. The nine guest rooms all have antique furniture, Victorian colors and wallpaper, and, yet, offer guests all the modern conveniences. Awake to the aroma of freshly brewed coffee, baking breads, and sizzling bacon. The location is ideal for travelers on I-94 and US 23 who are going to the University of Michigan, E.M.U., an area event, or local business.

Hostess: Mrs. Chris Mason
Rooms: 9 (PB) $65-115
Full Breakfast
Credit Cards: A, B, C
Notes: 2, 5, 8, 9, 10, 11, 12

5 Open all year; 6 Pets welcome; 7 Children welcome; 8 Tennis nearby; 9 Swimming nearby; 10 Golf nearby; 11 Skiing nearby; 12 May be booked through travel agent.

MINNESOTA

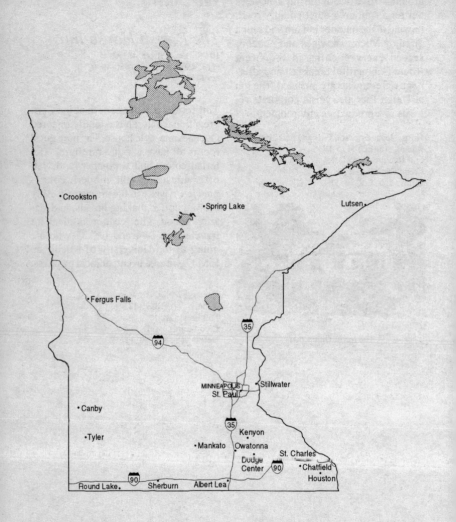

• Crookston

• Spring Lake

Lutsen

• Fergus Falls

35

94

MINNEAPOLIS • Stillwater
St. Paul

• Canby

35

Kenyon
• Mankato Owatonna

• Tyler

Dodge St. Charles
Center • Chatfield
Houston

90 90
Round Lake. Sherburn Albert Lea

Minnesota

ALBERT LEA

Victorian Rose Inn

609 W. Fountain Street, 56007
(507) 373-7602; (800) 252-6558

Queen Anne Victorian home (1898) in virtually original condition, with fine woodwork, stained glass, gingerbread, and antique light fixtures. Antique furnishings, down comforters. Spacious rooms, one with fireplace. Air-conditioned. Full Breakfast. Business/extended-stay rates; gift certificates. Children by arrangement; no pets; no smoking.

Hosts: Darrel and Linda Roemmich
Rooms: 4 (PB) $40-70
Full Breakfast
Credit Cards: A, B
Notes: 2, 5, 7, 8, 10, 12

CANBY

Eaton's Victorian Rose

201 Fourth Street W., 56220
(888) 212-ROSE; FAX (507) 223-5474

Eaton's Victorian Rose is a romantic, restored late 1800s Queen Anne. Relax, read, or have a quiet conversation in many public rooms furnished with antiques, beautiful wallpapers, and accent pieces. Breakfast or homemade dessert served on a sunny porch or in the spacious dining room. Like going home to Grandma's.

Hostess: Flora A. Emery-Hiese
Rooms: 3 (PB) $60-65
Full Breakfast
Credit Cards: A, B
Notes: 2, 3, 4, 5, 8, 9, 10, 11

CHATFIELD

Lund's Guest Houses

218 SE Winona Street, 55923
(507) 867-4003

These charming 1920s homes are decorated in the 1920s and 1930s style and located only 20 minutes from Rochester, at the gateway to beautiful Bluff country. Each house has screened porches, kitchen, dining room, living room, four bedrooms, private baths, TVs, electric or pump organs, and microwave. Rent the whole house or one bedroom.

Hosts: Shelby and Marion Lund
Rooms: 8 (PB) $65
Continental Breakfast
Credit Cards: none
Notes: 2, 6 and 7 (restricted), 8, 9, 10, 11

NOTES: Credit cards accepted: A Master Card; B Visa; C American Express; D Discover; E Diners Club; F Other; 2 Personal checks accepted; 3 Lunch available; 4 Dinner available; 5 Open all year; 6 Pets welcome; 7 Children welcome; 8 Tennis nearby; 9 Swimming nearby; 10 Golf nearby; 11 Skiing nearby; 12 May be booked through travel agent.

Elm Street Inn

CROOKSTON

Elm Street Inn

422 Elm Street, 56716
(218) 281-2343; (800) 568-4476;
FAX (218) 281-1756

Georgian Revival (1910) home with
antiques, hardwood floors, and stained
and beveled glass. Wicker-filled sun
porch, old fashioned beds, quilts, fresh
flowers. Memorable candlelight full
breakfast. Bicycles, limo to casino.
Community pool next door. Children by
arrangement; no pets; no smoking.

Hosts: John and Sherry Winters
Rooms: 4 (PB) $65
Full Breakfast
Credit Cards: A, B, C
Notes: 2, 5, 8, 9, 10, 12

DODGE CENTER

Pfeifer's Eden
Bed and Breakfast

RR 1, Box 215, 55927
(507) 527-2021

An 1898 Victorian home with peaceful
surroundings just a few miles from the
historic town of Mantorville and 25
miles from the Mayo Clinic in Rochester. Many antique furnishings are yours
to enjoy. Guests are intrigued by old-
fashioned pastimes: playing the eight-
foot pump organ, touring the world in
stereographic cards, pedaling the player
piano, or just relaxing on the open and
screened porches on mild days or by the
fireplace in autumn and winter.

Hosts: Mike and Debbie Pfeifer
Rooms: 4 (2 PB, 2SB) $45-55
Full Breakfast
Credit Cards: none
Notes: 2, 5, 7, 8, 9, 10, 11

FERGUS FALLS

Bakketopp Hus

RR 2, Box 187 A, 56537
(218) 739-2915; (800) 739-2915

Quiet, spacious, lake home with vaulted
ceilings, fireplaces, private spa, flower
garden patio, and lakeside decks. Antique furnishings from family homestead; four poster, draped, French
canopy bed; and private baths. Here you
can listen as loons call to each other
across the lake in the still of dusk, wit-
ness the falling foliage splendor, relax
by the crackling fire, or sink into the
warmth of the spa after a day of hiking
or skiing. Near antique shops and
Maplewood State Park. Ten minutes off
I-94. Gift certificates available. Reservation with deposit.

Hosts: Dennis and Judy Nims
Rooms: 3 + loft area (PB) $65-95
Full Breakfast
Credit Cards: A, B, D
Notes: 2, 5, 7, 8, 9, 10, 11

NOTES: Credit cards accepted: A Master Card; B Visa; C American Express; D Discover;
E Diners Club; F Other; 2 Personal checks accepted; 3 Lunch available; 4 Dinner available;

HOUSTON

Addie's Attic B&B

117 S. Jackson, PO Box 677, 55943
(507) 896-3010

Beautiful turn-of-the century home,
circa 1903; cozy front parlor with
curved glass window. Games, TV, and
player piano available. Guest rooms
decorated and furnished with "attic
finds." Hearty, country breakfast served
in dining room. Near hiking, biking,
cross-country skiing trails, canoeing,
and antique shops. Week-day rates.

Hosts: Fred and Marilyn Huhn
Rooms: 4 (SB) $45-50
Full Breakfast
Credit Cards: none
Notes: 2, 5, 8, 9, 10, 11

Addie's Attic

KENYON

Grandfather's Woods Bed and Breakfast

3640 450th Street, 55946
(507) 789-6414

"Grandfather's Woods" fifth generation, working farm, charming 1860's
home showcases family antiques and
old-fashioned comfort. Hearty breakfast;
private or shared baths. Horse-drawn
hay/sleigh rides, hiking, cross-country
skiing through 65 wooded acres to river.
Near, and an integral part of the history,
of Holden Lutheran Church, "birthplace" of St. Olaf College founded in
1860 by Rev. B.J. Muus. Near state park
and bike trail. Half-way between Rochester and St. Paul/Minneapolis. Reservations preferred. No smoking.

Hosts: Judy and George Langemo
Rooms: 3 (2PB; 2SB) $60-99
Full and/or Continental Breakfast
Credit Cards: none
Notes: 2, 4, 5, 7 (supervised), 9, 10, 11

LUTSEN

Lindgren's Bed and Breakfast

C.R. 35, PO Box 56, 55612-0056
(218) 663-7450

1920s log home in Superior National
Forest on walkable shoreline of Lake
Superior. Knotty cedar interior decorated with wildlife trophies. Massive
stone fireplaces, Finnish sauna, whirlpool, baby grand piano, and TV's/
VCR's/CD. In center of area known for
skiing, golf, stream and lake fishing,
skyride, mountain biking, snowmobiling, horseback riding, alpine slide,
fall colors, Superior Hiking Trail, and
near Boundary Waters Canoe Area entry point. Spacious, manicured grounds.
One-half mile off Highway 61 on the

5 Open all year; 6 Pets welcome; 7 Children welcome; 8 Tennis nearby; 9 Swimming nearby;
10 Golf nearby; 11 Skiing nearby; 12 May be booked through travel agent.

Lake Superior Circle Tour.

Hostess: Shirley Lindgren
Rooms: 4 (PB) $85-125
Full Hearty Breakfast
Credit Cards: A, B
Notes: 2, 5, 7 (over 12), 8, 9, 10, 11, 12

MANKATO

Butler House Bed and Breakfast

704 S. Broad, 56001
(507) 387-5055; FAX (507) 388-5462

An English-style (1905) mansion is elegantly furnished and includes palatial porch, beautiful suites, canopy beds, whirlpool, fireplace, and private baths. Features include hand-painted murals, Steinway grand, windowseats, artist studio, and a conference room. No smoking. Near state trail, biking, skiing, golfing, and antiquing. Come join us for an escape into a world of comfort and relaxation.

Hosts: Ron and Sharry Tschida
Rooms: 5 (PB) $55-115 (deposit required)
Full Breakfast weekends; Continental weekdays
Credit Cards: A, B, C
Notes: 2, 5, 9, 10, 11, 12

Butler House

OWATONNA

The Northrop-Oftedahl House Bed and Breakfast

358 E. Main Street, 55060
(507) 451-4040; FAX (507) 451-2752

This 1898 Victorian with stained glass is three blocks from downtown. It has pleasant porches, grand piano, six-foot footed bathtub and souvenirs (antiques and collectibles from the estate). Northrop, family-owned and operated, is one of twelve historical homes in the area, rich in local history with an extensive reading library, backgammon, croquet, badminton, bocce, and more. Near hiking and biking trails, tennis, parks, snowmobiling, and 35 miles to Mayo Clinic. Special group rates for retreats. NEW—Bikers' Bunks.

Hosts: Jean and Darrell Stewart/Gregory Norhrop
Rooms: 5 (SB) $35-62.50
Continental Breakfast; Full Breakfast on request
Credit Cards: none
Notes: 2, 3 and 4 (by reservations), 5, 6 (by arrangement), 7, 8, 9, 10, 11

ROUND LAKE

The Prairie House on Round Lake

RR 1 Box 105, 56167-9601
(507) 945-8934

Built in 1879 by a prominent Chicago businessman as part of a 2,500 acre estate, this farmhouse is a retreat from the bustle of city life. It is a working horse

---

NOTES: Credit cards accepted: A Master Card; B Visa; C American Express; D Discover; E Diners Club; F Other; 2 Personal checks accepted; 3 Lunch available; 4 Dinner available;

farm. American paint horses roam the pasture and three barns house both young stock in training and show horses that are exhibited all over the world. A cupola rising from the central stairway is circled by four dormer bedrooms on the second floor. Antique furniture accented with equine touches that reflect the spirit of the farm. Fishing, hiking, swimming, boating, and tennis are at the doorstep.

Hosts: Ralph and Virginia Schenck
Rooms: 4 (2PB; 2SB) $45-55
Full Breakfast
Credit Cards: none
Notes: 2, 5, 6, 7, 8 (on site), 9, 10

ST. CHARLES

Thoreson's Carriage House Bed and Breakfast

606 Wabasha Avenue, 55972
(507) 932-3479

Located near beautiful Whitewater State Park with its swimming, trails, and demonstrations by the park naturalist. We are also in Amish territory and minutes from the world-famous Mayo Clinic. Piano and organ are available for added enjoyment. Please write for free brochure.

Hostess: Moneta Thoreson
Rooms: 2 (SB) $40-45
Full Breakfast
Credit Cards: none
Notes: 2, 5, 7, 8, 9, 10

ST. PAUL

Desoto at Prior's Bed and Breakfast

1522 Desoto Street, 55101-3253
(612) 774-2695

Elegant, newly constructed home in quiet residential area. Sunny, cheerful rooms with private tub and enclosed shower baths. Air-conditioning. Full gourmet breakfast with homemade caramel rolls or scones. Dietary preferences honored. Breakfast recipe chosen for "1994 Lake States' Best Bed and Breakfasts" publication. Easy drive to Minneapolis, St. Paul, Mall of America, and other major attractions. Guests tell us they feel comfortable here being able to pray before breakfast if they wish.

Hosts: Dick and Mary Prior
Rooms: 2 (PB) $69-79
Full Gourmet Breakfast
Credit Cards: none
Notes: 2, 5, 8, 9, 10, 12

Desoto at Prior's Bed and Breakfast

---

5 Open all year; 6 Pets welcome; 7 Children welcome; 8 Tennis nearby; 9 Swimming nearby; 10 Golf nearby; 11 Skiing nearby; 12 May be booked through travel agent.

SHERBURN

Four Columns Inn

Route 2, Box 75, 56171
(507) 764-8861

Enjoy Scandinavian hospitality in an antique-filled, loving remodeled, Greek Revival inn. Four antique-filled bedrooms, clawfoot tubs, and working fireplaces welcome guests. A library, circular stairway, living room with a grand piano, and a solarium with jacuzzi make a stay here memorable. A hide-away bridal suite has access to a roof deck with a super view of the country-side is perfect for honeymooners or an-niversary couples. A hearty breakfast is served in the formal dining room, on the balcony, in the gazebo, or in the kitchen by the fireplace. Near lakes, antiques, amusement park, and live summer theater. Two miles north of I-90 between Chicago and the Black Hills. Call for brochure. No Smoking. Children by arrangement.

Hosts: Norman and Pennie Kittleson
Rooms: 4 (3PB) $50-70
Full Breakfast
Credit Cards: none
Notes: 2, 5, 7 (by arrangement), 9, 10, 11, 12.

SPRING LAKE

Anchor Inn

HCD 1, Box 260, 56680
(218) 798-2718

Lodge in the Chippewa National For-est on the Bigfork Canoe Trail; built in the early 1920s and originally used by duck hunters. Decorated with antique furniture and memorabilia. Shared bath. Delicious breakfast. State parks, historic sites, and restaurants nearby. Boats and motors available. Reservations. No smoking!

Hosts: Charles and Virginia Kitterman
Rooms: 4 (SB) $30-60
Full Breakfast
Credit Cards: A, B
Open May through October.
Notes: 2, 7, 8, 9, 10

STILLWATER

James A. Mulvey Residence Inn

622 W. Churchill Street, 55082
(612) 430-8008

This is an enchanting place. Built in 1878 by lumberman, James A. Mulvey, the Italianate residence and stone car-riage house grace the most visited his-toric rivertown in the upper Midwest. Exclusively for you are the grand par-lor, formal dining room, Victorian sun porch, and five fabulously decorated

James A. Mulvey Residence Inn

NOTES: Credit cards accepted: A Master Card; B Visa; C American Express; D Discover; E Diners Club; F Other; 2 Personal checks accepted; 3 Lunch available; 4 Dinner available;

guest rooms filled with art and antiques. Four-course breakfast, double-whirlpools, fireplaces, mountain bikes, and air-conditioning. Welcome refreshments. Grace-filled service from innkeepers who care.

Hosts: Rev. Truett and Jill Lawson
Rooms: 5 (PB) $99-159
Full 4-Course Breakfast
Credit Cards: A, B, D
Notes: 2, 5, 8, 9, 10, 11, 12

TYLER

Babette's Inn

308 S. Tyler Street, 56178
(507) 537-1632

Babette's Inn

Well known for great breakfasts and beautiful suites, this Inn welcomes guests to enjoy the Danish Village of Tyler. The 1914 red brick, historic home offers privacy, book and foreign film libraries, bicycles, on-premises antique shop, porch swings, and gardens. A very good value in luxury accommodations. "4-star" *Venture Magazine*. *Minneapolis Tribune* "Reader's Favorite."

Hosts: Jim and Alicia Johnson
Rooms: 3 suites (PB) (2 with fireplace) $65-79
Full Gourmet Breakfast
Credit Cards: A, B, D
Notes: 2, 5, 7 (with approval), 8, 9, 10, 11, 12

---

5 Open all year; 6 Pets welcome; 7 Children welcome; 8 Tennis nearby; 9 Swimming nearby; 10 Golf nearby; 11 Skiing nearby; 12 May be booked through travel agent.

MISSISSIPPI

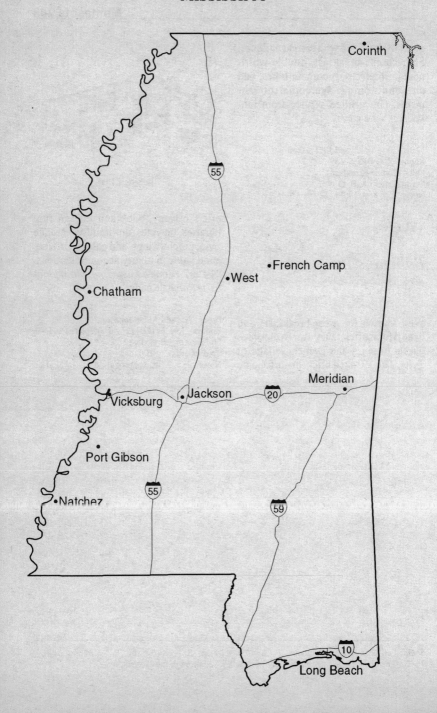

Mississippi

CHATHAM

Mount Holly Plantation Inn
HC63 Box 140, 38731
(601) 827-2652; (601) 827-5661

Mount Holly is located between Greenville and Vicksburg on beautiful Lake Washington and sits on six acres surrounded by cotton fields. Built of slave-made bricks with 14-foot ceilings and two-foot thick walls, Mount Holly is the most outstanding historic mansion in the Delta. An antebellum mansion restored in 1980 by the present owners and led by the Holy Spirit. Christ is honored in this home. No smoking permitted.

Hosts: Ann and T.C. Woods
Rooms: 6 (3PB; 3SB) $75-100
Full Breakfast
Credit Cards: A, B
Notes: 2, 5, 8, 9, 10, 12

CORINTH

The Generals' Quarters
924 Fillmore Street, 38834
(601) 286-3325; FAX (601) 287-8188

The General's Quarters is a beautifully restored , Victorian home located in the historic district of the old Civil War town. The rooms are decorated with period antiques and contemporary pieces; and all rooms have private baths, cable TV and telephones; and the suite boasts a 140-year-old, four poster canopy bed. There is a second floor lounge with veranda, beautiful parlor and porch on the first floor, and lovely gardens to relax in after a day of sightseeing, antiquing, playing golf, or touring the various Civil War sights in Corinth and the outlaying areas. Our resident chef prepares a delicious full breakfast and evening snack. We are close to Shiloh National Military Park and the Tennessee-Tombigbee Waterway. The General's

---

Quarters provides some of the best hospitality that the South has to offer.

Hosts: Luke Doehner and Charlotte Brandt
Rooms: 4 + 1 suite (PB) $75-85
Full Breakfast
Credit Cards: A, B, D
Notes: 5, 8, 10, 12

FRENCH CAMP

French Camp Bed and Breakfast Inn

1 Bluebird Lane, PO Box 120, 39745
(601) 547-6482; FAX (601) 547-6790

The Inn is located on the historic Natchez Trace National Parkway halfway between Jackson and Tupelo, Mississippi. It has been constructed from two restored, authentic hand-hewn log cabins, each more than 100 years old. Indulge in Southern cooking at its finest: sorghum-soaked "scratch" muffins, creamy grits, skillet fried apples, fresh cheese, scrambled eggs, crisp slab bacon, and lean sausage, with two kinds of homemade bread and three kinds of homemade jellies. Life doesn't get any better!

Hosts: Ed and Sallie Williford
Rooms: 5 (PB) $60
Full Breakfast
Credit Cards: B
Notes: 2, 3, 4, 5, 6, 7, 8, 9, 12

Fairview Inn

JACKSON

Fairview Inn

734 Fairview Street, 39202
(601) 948-3429; (888) 948-1908;
FAX (601) 948-1203

Colonial Revival mansion on the National Historic Register. The Inn offers elegant and comfortable ambiance accented by fine fabrics and antiques in an historic neighborhood. Near churches, shopping, two colleges, and major medical complexes. AAA four-diamond award; Top Inn of 1994 award by *Country Inns* magazine.

Hosts: Carol and Bill Simmons
Rooms: 8 (PB) $115-165
Full Breakfast
Credit Cards: A, B, C, D
Notes: 2, 4 (by reservation), 5, 8, 9, 10, 12

LONG BEACH

Red Creek Inn, Vineyard, and Racing Stable

7416 Red Creek Road, 39560
(601) 452-3080 (voice and FAX);
(800) 729-9670

Raised French cottage built in 1899 by a retired, Italian sea captain to entice his young bride away from her parents' home in New Orleans. Red Creek Inn, Vineyard, and Racing Stable is situated on eleven acres with ancient live oaks and fragrant magnolias, and delights itself in peaceful comforts. With a 64-foot porch, including porch swings, our inn is furnished in antiques for our guests'

NOTES: Credit cards accepted: A Master Card; B Visa; C American Express; D Discover; E Diners Club; F Other; 2 Personal checks accepted; 3 Lunch available; 4 Dinner available;

Red Creek Inn, Vineyard, and Racing Stable

enjoyment. Ministerial discount of 10%.

Hosts: Karl and "Toni" Mertz
Rooms: 5 (3PB; 2SB) $49-79
Continental Plus Breakfast
Credit Cards: none
Notes: 2, 3 and 4 (advance request only), 5, 7, 9,
    10, 12 (10%)

MERIDIAN

Lincoln Ltd.; Bed and Breakfast Mississippi

PO Box 3479, 39303
(601) 482-5483; (800) 633-MISS
FAX (601) 693-7447

Service offers B&B accommodations in historic homes and inns in the whole state of **Mississippi**, also southeast **Louisiana**, **Western Tennessee**, and **Alabama**. One phone call convenience for your B&B reservations and trip planning through Mississippi. Experience history from Natchez to Memphis, including the Gulf Coast and the Natchez Trace Parkway. We offer antebellum mansions, historic log houses, and contemporary homes. Also, there is a B&B suite on the premises. Call for details

and brochure. $65-175; major credit cards welcome. Barbara Lincoln Hall, coordinator.

NATCHEZ

The Bed and Breakfast Mansions of Natchez

PO Box 347, 200 State Street, 39121
(601) 446-6631; (800) 647-6742;
FAX (601) 446-8687

Over 30 magnificent B&B inns offer exquisite accommodations in pre-Civil War mansions, country plantations, and charming Victorian elegance. Situated on high buffs overlooking the Mississippi River, historic Natchez offers visitors year-round tours of historic homes, horse-drawn carriage tours, plus the famous spring and fall pilgrimages featuring some of America's most splendid historic homes.

Hosts: Natchez Pilgrimage Tours
Rooms: Over 100 (PB) starting at $75
Full Southern Style Breakfast (at most inns)
Credit Cards: A, B, C, D
Notes: 2, 12

Dunleith

84 Homochitto, 39120
(601) 446-8500; (800) 433-2445

Dunleith is listed on the National Register of Historic Places and is a national landmark. It is located on 40 acres near downtown Natchez. Eleven rooms, three in main house and eight in courtyard wing. Full Southern breakfast served in Poultry House. All rooms have

5 Open all year; 6 Pets welcome; 7 Children welcome; 8 Tennis nearby; 9 Swimming nearby;
10 Golf nearby; 11 Skiing nearby; 12 May be booked through travel agent.

private baths and working fireplaces. No children. Reservations required.

Owner: W.F. Heins, III
Rooms: 11 (PB) $85-130
Full Breakfast
Credit Cards: A, B, D
Notes: none

NATCHEZ TRACE AREA

Natchez Trace Bed and Breakfast Reservation Service

PO Box 193, **Hampshire, TN** 38461
(615) 285-2777; (800) 377-2770

This reservation service is unusual in that all the homes listed are close to the Natchez Trace, the delightful National Parkway running from Nashville, Tennessee, to Natchez, Mississippi. Kay Jones can help you plan your trip along the Trace, with homestays in interesting and historic homes along the way. Locations of homes include Coumbia, FairView, Franklin, Hohenwald, and Nashville, **Tennessee;** Florence, and Cherokee, **Alabama**; and Church Hill, Corinth, French Camp, Kosciusko, Loeman, Natchez, and Vicksburg, **Mississippi.** Rates $60-125.

PORT GIBSON

Oak Square Plantation

1207 Church Street, 39150
(601) 437-4350; (800) 729-0240;
FAX (601) 437-5768

This restored antebellum mansion of the Old South is in the town General U.S. Grant said was "too beautiful to burn." On the National Register of Historic Places, it has family heirloom antiques and canopied beds and is air-conditioned. Your hosts' families have been in Mississippi for 200 years. Christ is the Lord of this house. "But as for me and my house, we will serve the Lord," Joshua 24:15. On U.S. Highway 61, adjacent to the Natchez Trace Parkway.

Hosts: Mr. and Mrs. William Lum
Rooms: 12 (PB) $75-95; (special family rates)
Full Breakfast
Credit Cards: A, B, C, D
Notes: 2, 5, 7

Annabelle Bed and Breakfast

VICKSBURG

Annabelle Bed and Breakfast

501 Speed Street, 39180
(601) 638-2000; (800) 791-2000;
FAX (601) 636-5054

Featured in 1996 in *Southern Living, Country Inns,* and *Foder's:* "The South's Best B&Bs", this stately Victorian-Italianate residence was built on a bluff above the Mississippi River circa. 1868. Here elegance with Southern charm and hospitality blend into making your stay a truly memorable experience. Relax in the beautiful parlor, by the sparkling pool, or in the romantic old courtyard, shaded by crepe myrtles and giant magnolia and pecan trees. AAA three-diamond award.

Hosts: George and Carolyn Mayer
Rooms: 6 + 1 suite (PB) $80-125
Full Breakfast
Credit Cards: A, B, C, D, E
Notes: 2, 5, 8, 9 (pool on-site), 10, 12

WEST

The Alexander House
210 Green Street, PO Box 187, 39192
(601) 967-2266; (800) 350-8034

The Alexander House

Step inside the front door of the Alexander House Bed and Breakfast and go back in time to a more leisurely and gracious way of life. Victorian decor at its prettiest and country hospitality at its best is guaranteed to please your senses. Captain Alexander, Dr. Joe, Ulrich, Annie, and Miss Bealle are all rooms waiting to cast their spell over those who visit. Day trips to historic or recreational areas may be charted or chartered. Located just three miles off I-55.

Hosts: Ruth Ray and Woody Dinstel
Rooms: 5 (3PB; 2SB) $65
Full Breakfast
Credit Cards: A, B, C, D
Notes: 2, 4, 5, 12

5 Open all year; 6 Pets welcome; 7 Children welcome; 8 Tennis nearby; 9 Swimming nearby; 10 Golf nearby; 11 Skiing nearby; 12 May be booked through travel agent.

MISSOURI

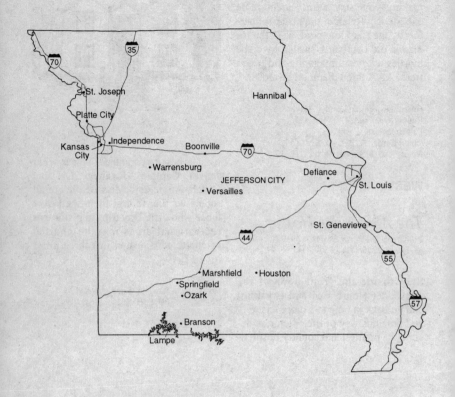

Missouri

Ozark Mountain Country B&B Service

PO Box 295, **Branson**, 65615
(417) 335-8134 (voice and FAX);
(800) 695-1546

Ozark Mountain Country has been arranging accommodations for guests in **southwest Missouri** and **northwest Arkansas** since 1982. Our services are free. In the current list of over 100 homes and small inns, some locations offer private entrances, fantastic views, guest sitting areas, swimming pools, jacuzzis, and/or fireplaces. Most locations are available all year. Personal checks accepted. Some homes welcome children; a few welcome pets (even horses). Write for complimentary host brochure describing B&Bs available, listing, and discount coupons. Coordinator: Kay Cameron. $35-145; major credit cards welcomed.

BOONVILLE

Morgan Street Repose Bed and Breakfast

611 E. Morgan Street, 65233
(816) 882-7195; (800) 248-5061

1869 national historic registered Home delightfully restored for a romantic, gracious, and hospitable stay. Filled with heirlooms, antiques, books, games, and curiosities to delight you. Our extravagant breakfasts are formally served in one of three dining rooms or Secret Garden. Situated one block to antique/specialty shops, restaurants, and Katy biking/hiking trail. Rental bikes available. Afternoon tea served.

Hostess: Doris Shenk
Rooms: 3 (PB) $68-95
Full Gourmet Breakfast
Credit Cards: none
Notes: 2, 5, 7 (older), 12

Morgan Street Repose

NOTES: Credit cards accepted: A Master Card; B Visa; C American Express; D Discover; E Diners Club; F Other; 2 Personal checks accepted; 3 Lunch available; 4 Dinner available; 5 Open all year; 6 Pets welcome; 7 Children welcome; 8 Tennis nearby; 9 Swimming nearby; 10 Golf nearby; 11 Skiing nearby; 12 May be booked through travel agent.

BRANSON

Cameron's CRAG

PO Box 295, 65615
(417) 335-8134 (voice and FAX);
(800) 933-8529

Located high on a bluff overlooking Lake Taneycomo and the valley, three miles south of Branson, enjoy a spectacular view from a new spacious, detached, private suite with whirlpool tub, kitchen, living, and bedroom area. Two room suite with indoor hot tub and private bath. A third room has a great view of the lake and a private hot tub on the deck. All rooms have king-size beds, hot tubs, private entrances, TV/VCR's, and a video library.

Hosts: Glen and Kay Cameron
Rooms: 3 (PB) $75-95
Full Breakfast
Credit Cards: A, B, C, D
Notes: 2, 4, 5, 12

Josie's Peaceful Getaway

HCR 1 Box 1104 Indian Point, 65616
(417) 338-2978, (800) 289-4125

Pristine, gorgeous lakefront scenery on Table Rock Lake where sunsets and moonlit nights lace the sky. Contemporary design featuring cathedral ceilings and stone fireplaces mingled with a Victorian flair. Cozy wood burning fireplaces, lavish jacuzzi spas, candlelight, and fresh flowers abound. Dine in luxury as you enjoy breakfast served on china and crystal. Celebrate your honeymoon or anniversary in style. Eight miles to Branson and music shows; five minutes to Silver Dollar City/Marina. Smoke-free environment.

Hosts: Bill and JoAnne Coats
Rooms: 3 (PB) $65-110
Full Breakfast
Credit Cards: A, B, C, D
Notes: 2, 5, 7 (with restrictions), 9, 10, 12

Lakeshore Bed and Breakfast

HC#1 Box 935, 65616
(417) 338-2698 (voice and FAX);
(800) 285-9739

A peaceful place on beautiful Table Rock Lake, two miles from Silver Dollar City. Great for family or church groups up to 12 people, also honeymoon and anniversaries. A contemporary home with boat dock and swim deck, covered patio with picnic table and grill, glider swing. Two units have private entrance, queen beds, hide-a-beds, coffee bar, refrigerator, microwave, TV, VCR, A/C, private bath with showers, and one with whirlpool tub. One unit has double bed and private bath. A nutritious, hearty breakfast.

Hostess: Gladys Lemley
Rooms: 3 (PB) $50-75
Full Breakfast
Credit Cards: none
Notes: 2, 5, 7, 8, 9, 10, 11, 12

Lakeshore Bed and Breakfast

NOTES: Credit cards accepted: A Master Card; B Visa; C American Express; D Discover; E Diners Club; F Other; 2 Personal checks accepted; 3 Lunch available; 4 Dinner available;

The Parsons House

DEFIANCE

The Parsons House Bed and Breakfast

211 Lee Street, PO Box 38, 63341
(314) 798-2222; (800) 355-6878;
FAX (314) 798-2220

Restored, 1842 Federal-style home overlooks the Missouri River Valley. Listed in the Historic Survey, it features fireplaces, walnut staircase, and many antiques. For your enjoyment: an organ, piano, garden, large library, and porches. Closeby are the Katy Bike Trail, Daniel Boone Home; and Missouri wineries, yet downtown St. Louis is only 35 miles away. Breakfast in the parlor, gardens, or on one of the porches. Resident dog, cat, computer consultant, and artist.

Hosts: Al and Carol Keyes
Rooms: 3 (PB) $70-90
Full Breakfast
Credit Cards: A, B
Notes: 2, 5 (except Christmas), 7 (limited), 10

HANNIBAL

Fifth St. Mansion Bed and Breakfast Inn

213 South Fifth Street, 63401
(573) 221-0445; (800) 874-5661;
FAX (573) 221-3335

Built in 1858 in Italianate style by friends of Mark Twain, antique furnishings complement the stained glass, ceramic fireplaces, and original gaslight fixtures of the house. Two parlors, dining room, and library with hand-grained walnut paneling, plus wraparound porches provide space for conversation, reading, TV, games. Walk to Mark Twain historic district, shops, restaurants, riverfront. The mansion blends Victorian charm with plenty of old-fashioned hospitality. The whole house is available for reunions and weddings.

Hosts: Mike and Donalene Andreotti
Rooms: 7 (PB) $65-90
Full Breakfast
Credit Cards: A, B, C, D
Notes: 2, 5, 7, 8, 9, 10, 12

Fifth St. Mansion

---

5 Open all year; 6 Pets welcome; 7 Children welcome; 8 Tennis nearby; 9 Swimming nearby;
10 Golf nearby; 11 Skiing nearby; 12 May be booked through travel agent.

Windstone House

HOUSTON

Windstone House Bed and Breakfast

539 Cleveland Road, 65483
(417) 967-2008

Windstone House is a large two-story home with a spacious wraparound porch and balcony, setting in the middle of more than 80 acres that provide a breathtaking view of the Ozarks countryside. The home has been tastefully furnished with a collection of antiques. In warm weather, breakfast is served on the balcony overlooking a spectacular panorama of meadows and woodland. If you are bent on unwinding, then this is the place for you.

Hostess: Barbara Kimes
Rooms: 3 (1PB; 2SB) $60
Full Breakfast
Credit Cards: none
Notes: 2, 5, 7, 9, 10

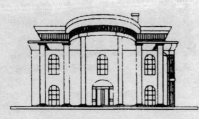

The Mansion House

INDEPENDENCE

The Mansion House

2121 S. Sterling Avenue, 64052
(816) 254-5413 or (816) 254-5416

The integrity of this beautiful historical plantation home, which is very deserving, has been kept intact. Built in 1832, it boasts many interesting stories connected with people and the quantrills. This is one of Missouri's best kept secrects, and comes with four exquistely decorated Victorian bedrooms and baths, all with their own unique setting. You will find yourself surrounded with the elegance of long-ago era, which is the harmony this home so richly deserves. You will wake up to a freshly-cooked breakfast in our formal dining room.

Hosts: Dave and Paula Swayne
Rooms: 4 (PB) $75-100
Full Breakfast
Credit Cards: A, B
Notes: 2, 5, 8, 9

KANSAS CITY

Basswood Country Inn Resort

15880 Interurban Rd., **Platte City** 64079-9185
(816) 858-5556 (voice and FAX);
(800) 242-2775

Have a Basswood experience at Kansas City's doorstep! Choose a Country French suite, lakeside cottage, or two-bedroom suites, all with mini or full kitchens. Some have jacuzzi and/or fireplace. Wooded walking trails, fishing

---

NOTES: Credit cards accepted: A Master Card; B Visa; C American Express; D Discover; E Diners Club; F Other; 2 Personal checks accepted; 3 Lunch available; 4 Dinner available;

lakes, and outdoor pool. Write or call for a brochure. Reservations only.

Hosts: Don and Betty Soper
Rooms: 10 (PB) $69-131
Continental Breakfast
Credit Cards: A, B, D
Notes: 2, 5, 7, 9, 10, 11, 12

Bed and Breakfast Reservations for Kansas City

PO Box 14781, **Lenexa, KS** 66285
(913) 888-3636

Accommodations in Kansas City (Missouri), Weston, Liberty, Independence, and St. Joseph. 35 inns and home-stays range from circa 1845 to a contemporary Geodesic dome in the woods. Amenities available include hot tubs, jacuzzis, queen and king beds, private baths, and full gourmet breakfasts. Prices range $50 to $150. Major credit cards welcome at the individual inns. Edwina Monroe, coordinator.

Hotel Savoy Bed and Breakfast

219 W. 9th, 64105
(816) 842-3575 (voice and FAX);
(800) 728-6922

Kansas City's oldest and most historic hotel (c. 1888) is located in the heart of the convention and business district. The hotel offers beautifully appointed guest suites filled with antiques and personal amenities. Our breakfast has over 32 items to choose from. Start your day with lobster bisque, smoked salmon with caviar, medallions of beef, or a light continental breakfast. A truly memorable experience for your next business trip, special getaway, or catered affairs. The surrounding area has many places of historic value to visit that are within a few blocks walk or just minutes by car.

Host: Larry Green
Rooms: 22 (PB) $79-150
Full Gourmet Breakfast
Credit Cards: A, B, C, D, E, F
Notes: 2, 3, 4, 5, 7, 8, 9, 10, 12

Hotel Savoy Bed and Breakfast

Southmoreland on the Plaza

116 E. 46th Street, 64112
(816) 531-7979; FAX (816) 531-2407

Classic New England Colonial mansion located between renowned Country Club Plaza (shopping/entertainment district) and Nelson-Atkins and Kemper Museums of Art. Elegant B&B ambiance with small hotel amenities. Rooms with private decks, fireplaces, or jacuzzi baths. Special services for business travelers. Sport / dining privileges at nearby historic private club. Mobil Travel

5 Open all year; 6 Pets welcome; 7 Children welcome; 8 Tennis nearby; 9 Swimming nearby; 10 Golf nearby; 11 Skiing nearby; 12 May be booked through travel agent.

Guide Four-star winner since 1993. Only B&B to receive Midwest Travel Writers' "Gem of the Midwest" award.

Hostesses: Penni Johnson and Susan Moehl
Rooms: 12 (PB) $105-150
Full Breakfast
Credit Cards: A, B, C
Notes: 2, 5, 8, 9, 10, 12

LAMPE

Grandpa's Farm

Box 476, HCR 1, 65681
(417) 779-5106; (800) 280-5106

A real old-time, 16-acre Ozark Mountain farm with plenty of friendly animal life. Luxurious Honeymoon suite with spa, Red Bud suite with large whirlpool tub, Dogwood suite with kitchenette, and Mother Hen room. Near Branson, MO and Eureka Springs, AR. Big, country breakfast served on screened in porch. Secret hideout lofts for children. Visit our web site at http://iaswww.com/grandpa.html

Hosts: Keith and Pat Lamb
Rooms: 4 (PB) $65-85
Full Breakfast
Credit Cards: A, B, D
Notes: 2, 5, 7, 9, 12

MARSHFIELD

Dickey House Bed and Breakfast Inn

331 South Clay Street, 65706
(417) 468-3000; FAX (417) 859-5478

The stately, three-story Ante-bellum

Mansion situated on one acre of park-like grounds, is one of Missouri's finest bed and breakfast inns. Four antique-filled guest rooms with private baths, plus two spectacular suites with luxuriously appointed decor, double jacuzzi, fireplace, and cable TV. The Inn and dining room are enhanced by a display of fine American and European art and antiques. A gourmet breakfast is served in true Victorian style, amid fine china, silver, and crystal.

Hosts: William and Dorothy Buesgen
Rooms: 6 (PB) $55-95
Full Breakfast
Credit Cards: A, B, D
Notes: 2, 5, 7 (well behaved), 8, 9, 10, 12

Dear's Rest Bed and Breakfast

OZARK

Dear's Rest Bed and Breakfast

1408 Capp Hill Ranch Road, 65721
(417) 581-3839; (800) 588-2262

Slip away from worldly stress and relax surrounded by nature "with a view." Our Amish built cedar home waits for "only you" (up to six) where hiking thru

---

NOTES: Credit cards accepted: A Master Card; B Visa; C American Express; D Discover; E Diners Club; F Other; 2 Personal checks accepted; 3 Lunch available; 4 Dinner available;

the forest or stream snorkeling in the clear, spring-fed Bull Creek are just part of the fun. The fireplace and homey antiques give Dear's Rest a peaceful feeling of bygone days. If shopping for antiques or Branson shows gets too strenuous, try our hot tub "under the stars."

Hosts: Linda and Allan Schilter
Rooms: 1 suite (PB) $75
Full Country Breakfast
Credit Cards: A, B, D
Notes: 2, 5, 7, 9, 12

ST. GENEVIEVE

Inn at St. Gemme Beauvais

78 N. Main, 63670
(573) 883-5744; (800) 818-5744;
FAX (573) 883-3899

Inn at St. Gemme Beauvais

Jacuzzis, hors d'oeuvres, and private suites filled with antiques only begin your pampering stay in Missouri's oldest, continually operating bed and breakfast. The romantic dining room, complete with working fireplace, is the perfect setting for an intimate breakfast. The Inn has been recently redecorated and is walking distance to many shops and historical sites. Packages available for that special occasion, as well as picnics to take on hiking trails.

Hostess: Janet Joggerst
Rooms: 7 (PB) $69-125
Full Breakfast
Credit Cards: A, B
Notes: 2, 3, 5, 7, 8, 9, 10

ST. JOSEPH

Harding House B&B and Miss Annie's B&B

219 N. 20th Street, 64501
(816) 232-7020

Gracious turn-of-the-century home. Elegant, oak woodwork and pocket doors. Antiques and beveled, leaded glass windows. Historic area near museums, churches, and antique shops. Four unique guest rooms. Eastlake has a romantic wood-burning fireplace and queen-size bed; Blue room has an antique water lily quilt on the wall. Children welcome. Full breakfast with homemade pastry.

Hosts: Glen and Mary Harding
Rooms: 2 + a 2-room suite (1PB; 3SB) $45-55
Full Breakfast
Credit Cards: A, B, C, D
Notes: 2, 5, 7, 8, 10, 12

---

5 Open all year; 6 Pets welcome; 7 Children welcome; 8 Tennis nearby; 9 Swimming nearby; 10 Golf nearby; 11 Skiing nearby; 12 May be booked through travel agent.

Lafayette House Bed and Breakfast

ST. LOUIS

Lafayette House B&B

2156 Lafayette Avenue, 63104
(314) 772-4429; (800) 641-8965;
FAX (314) 664-2156

This 1876 Victorian mansion with modern amenities is in the center of things to do in St. Louis and on a direct bus line to downtown. It is air-conditioned and furnished with antiques and traditional furniture. Many collectibles and large, varied library to enjoy. Families welcome. Resident cats and dog.

Hosts: Bill Duffield, Nancy Buhr, and Anna Millet
Rooms: 4 + 1 suite (2PB; 3SB) $55-85
Full Breakfast
Credit Cards: A, B
Notes: 2, 5, 7, 8, 9, 10, 12

SPRINGFIELD

Virginia Rose Bed and Breakfast

317 E. Glenwood, 65807
(417) 883-0693; (800) 345-1412

This two-story farmhouse, built in 1906,

offers country hospitality right in town. Situated in a tree-covered acre, our home is furnished with early 1900 antiques, quilts on queen-sized beds, and rockers on the porch. Relax in the parlor with a book, puzzle, or game, or watch a movie on the TV/VCR. Only minutes from BASS Pro Outdoor World, restaurants, shopping, antique shops, and miniature golf, and only 40 miles from Branson.

Hosts: Jackie and Virginia Buck
Rooms: 3 + 2 suites (PB) $50-100
Full Breakfast
Credit Cards: A, B
Notes: 2, 5, 7, 9, 10, 12

VERSAILLES

The Hilty Inn Bed and Breakfast

206 E. Jasper, 65084
(573) 378-2020; (800) 667-8093

The Hilty Inn, northwest of the Lake of Ozarks where the Ozark Hills meet the

The Hilty Inn

NOTES: Credit cards accepted: A Master Card; B Visa; C American Express; D Discover; E Diners Club; F Other; 2 Personal checks accepted; 3 Lunch available; 4 Dinner available;

prairie, is an 1877 Victorian home with sitting porches and pine floors. Guests enjoy private baths, a parlor, dining room, Gift Shoppe, and sitting room with TV and phone. Nearby is the historical Morgan County Courthouse, the Martin Hotel Museum, and the Royal Theatre with monthly musicals, plays, and performers. Relax and enjoy friendly hospitality and comfort while you are away from home.

Hostess: Doris Hilty
Rooms: 4 (PB) $55-95
Full or Continental Breakfast
Credit Cards: A, B, C
Notes: 7 (inquire first), 9, 10

WARRENSBURG

The Camel Crossing Bed and Breakfast

210 East Gay, 64093
(816) 429 2973; FAX (816) 429 2722
Email: camelx@iland.net

Take a magic carpet to this bed and breakfast that is homey in atmosphere but museum-like in its decor. Brass, copper, hand tied carpets, and furnishings from the Far East will captivate your imaginations. An oasis for mind and body, if you come a stranger, you'll leave as a friend.

Hosts: Ed and Joyce Barnes
Rooms: 4 (2PB; 2SB) $55-65
Full Breakfast
Credit Cards: A, B
Notes: 2, 5, 7, 8, 9, 10

5 Open all year; 6 Pets welcome; 7 Children welcome; 8 Tennis nearby; 9 Swimming nearby; 10 Golf nearby; 11 Skiing nearby; 12 May be booked through travel agent.

MONTANA

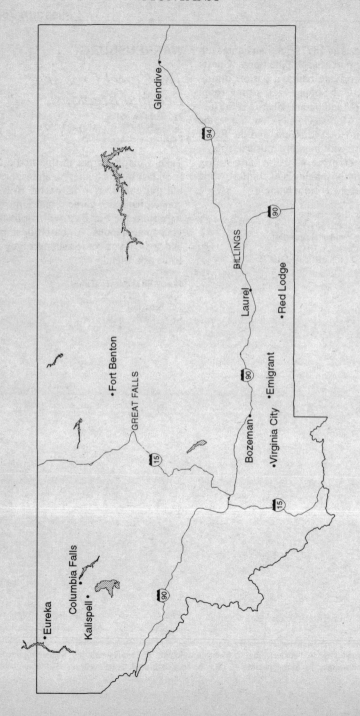

Montana

BOZEMAN

The Fox Hollow Bed and Breakfast at Baxter Creek

545 Mary Road, 59715
(406) 582-8440 (voice and FAX);
(800) 431-5010

Our country setting is in the heart of the Gallatin River Valley. Enjoy panoramic views of majestic mountain ranges from the hot tubs on our wrap-around deck. Our 1993, country style home offers spacious guest rooms, all with private baths. Wake to full country breakfasts every morning. Easy access from interstate and minutes from airport or town.

Hosts: Nancy and Michael Dawson
Rooms: 5 (PB) $75-98
Full Breakfast
Credit Cards: A, B, C, D
Notes: 2, 5, 8, 9, 10, 11, 12

COLUMBIA FALLS

Park View Inn B&B

904 Fourth Avenue W., PO Box 567, 59912
(406) 892-PARK (7275) voice and FAX

Park View Inn is located in a small town setting with views of Glacier National Park and our own city park across the street, which is complete with swimming pool, basketball court, and children's play area, as well as beautiful trees and picnic areas. We know you'll enjoy our two-story Victorian home with two suites and two luxury rooms or one of our three cabins, especially our honeymoon cabin featuring jacuzzi and four-poster bed.

Hosts: Gary and Jayne Hall
Rooms: 7 (3PB; 4SB) $45-95
Full and Continental Breakfast available
Credit Cards: A, B
Notes: 2, 5, 6 (in cabins only), 7, 8, 9, 10, 11

Park View Inn

NOTES: Credit cards accepted: A Master Card; B Visa; C American Express; D Discover; E Diners Club; F Other; 2 Personal checks accepted; 3 Lunch available; 4 Dinner available; 5 Open all year; 6 Pets welcome; 7 Children welcome; 8 Tennis nearby; 9 Swimming nearby; 10 Golf nearby; 11 Skiing nearby; 12 May be booked through travel agent.

EMIGRANT (NEAR NORTH ENTRANCE TO YELLOW-STONE NATIONAL PARK)

Paradise Gateway Bed and Breakfast and Log Guest Cabin

PO Box 84, 59027
(406) 333-4063; (800) 541-4113
Web site: http://www.wtp.net/go/paradise

Paradise Gateway B&B, just minutes from Yellowstone National Park, offers quiet, charming, comfortable guest rooms in the shadow of the majestic Rocky Mountains. As day breaks, enjoy a country, gourmet breakfast by the banks of the Yellowstone River, a noted blue ribbon trout stream. A "cowboy treat tray" is served in the afternoon. Enjoy summer and winter sports. Only entrance open to Yellowstone year 'round. Call for reservations. Plus Emigrant Peak Log Cabin located on 25 acres of Yellowstone River frontage next to the bed and breakfast. Modern two-bedroom log cabin with laundry services and complete kitchen. Decorated in country charm and extremely private. $125 a night for two—additional $20 per person above two—sleeps six. Continental breakfast served.

Hosts: Pete and Carol Reed
Rooms: 3 + 2-room cabin $125 (PB) $85-95
Full Breakfast in B&B; Continental in cabin
Credit Cards: A, B
Notes: 2, 5, 8, 9, 10, 11, 12

EUREKA

Huckleberry Hannah's Montana B&B

3100 Sophie Lake Road, 59917
(888) 889-3381 Toll Free

Nearly 6,000 square feet of old-fashioned, country-sweet charm, it is the answer to vacationing in Montana. The B&B sits on 50 wooded acres, and bordering a fabulous trout-filled lake with glorious views of the Rockies. This bed and breakfast depicts a quieter time in our history when the true pleasures of life represented a walk in the woods or a moonlight swim. Or maybe just a little early morning relaxation in a porch swing, sipping a fresh cup of coffee, and watching a colorful sunrise. The surrounding area is 91% public lands, perfect for hiking, biking, hunting, fishing, and swimming. It's a cross-country skiers dream in winter, also easy driving distance to downhill skiing in Whitefish. And, don't forget those comfortable sunny rooms and all that wonderful home-cooked food. The B&B is owned and operated by the author of one of the Northwest's Best-Selling Cookbooks "Huckleberry Hannah's Country Cooking Sampler." Questions cheerfully answered. Ask about kids and pets and Senior Discounts! Local airport nearby. Free brochure.

Hosts: Jack and Deanna Doying
Rooms: 5 + lake cottage (PB) $50-75
Full Breakfast (Continental upon request)
Credit Cards: A, B, D
Notes: 2, 3, 4, 5, 6 (some), 7, 8, 9, 11, 12

FORT BENTON

Long's Landing Bed and Breakfast

PO Box 935, 1011 17th Street, 59442
(406) 622-3461

Forty minutes north of Great Falls, just off Highway 87, Long's Landing B&B is nestled close to the Missouri River in the birthplace of Montana. Three charming guest rooms await the traveler. Enjoy two museums, golf course, Old Fort Park, river trips, and other nearby points of interest. Open Memorial weekend through October 15th. No smoking. Come as a traveler and leave as a friend.

Hostess: Amy Long
Rooms: 3 (1PB; 2SB) $45
Continental Breakfast
Credit Cards: none
Notes: 2, 7 (over 10), 8, 9, 10, 12

GLENDIVE

The Hostetler House Bed and Breakfast

113 N. Douglas Street, 59330
(406) 365-4505; FAX (406) 365-8456

Located two blocks from downtown shopping and restaurants, The Hostetler House is a charming, 1912 historic home with two comfortable guest rooms, sitting room, sun porch, deck, gazebo, and hot tub. Full gourmet breakfast is served on Grandma's china. On I-94 and the Yellowstone River, we are close to parks, swimming pool, tennis courts, golf course, antique shops, and churches. Craig and Dea invite you to "Arrive as a guest and leave as a friend."

Hosts: Craig and Dea Hostetler
Rooms: 2 (SB) $50
Full Gourmet Breakfast
Credit Cards: A, B, D
Notes: 2, 5, 8, 9, 10, 11 (cross-country), 12

KALISPELL

Stillwater Inn

206 Fourth Avenue E., 59901
(406) 755-7080; (800) 398-7024;
FAX (406) 756-0020

Relax in this lovely, historic home built in 1900, decorated to fit the period, and furnished with turn-of-the-century antiques. Four guest bedrooms, two with private baths. Full gourmet breakfast. Walking distance to churches, shopping, dining, art galleries, antique shops, Woodland Park, and the Conrad Mansion. Short drive to Glacier National Park, Big Mountain skiing, six golf courses, excellent fishing, and hunting. Please, no smoking in the house. Come, enjoy our hospitality.

Hosts: Pat and Jane Morison
Rooms: 4 (2PB; 2SB) $60-85
Full Breakfast
Credit Cards: A, B
Notes: 2, 5, 7, 8, 9, 10, 11, 12

LAUREL

Riverside B&B

2231 Theil Road, 59044
(406) 628-7890; (800) 768-1580;
FAX (406) 656-8306

Just off I-90, fifteen minutes from Billings, on a main route to skiing and Yellowstone National Park. Fly fish the Yellowstone from our backyard; soak away stress in the hot tub; llinger and llook at the lloveable llamas; take a spin on our bicycle built for two; enjoy a peaceful sleep, a friendly visit, and a fantastic breakfast.

Hosts: Lynn and Nancy Perey
Rooms: 2 (PB) $65
Full Breakfast
Credit Cards: A, B, C
Notes: 2, 5, 7 (over 10), 10, 11, 12

RED LODGE

Willows Inn

224 S. Platt Avenue, PO Box 886, 59068
(406) 446-3913

Nestled beneath the majestic Beartooth Mountains in a quaint historic town, this delightful turn-of-the-century Victorian, complete with picket fence and porch swing, awaits you. A light and airy atmosphere with warm, cheerful decor greets the happy wanderer. Five charming guest rooms, each unique, are in the main inn. Two delightfully nostalgic cottages with kitchen and laundry are also available. Home-baked pastries are a specialty. Videos, books, games, afternoon refreshments, and sun deck.

Hosts: Kerry, Carolyn, and Elven Boggio
Rooms: 5 + 2 cottages (3PB; 2SB) $55-75
Continental Plus Breakfast
Credit Cards: A, B, D
Notes: 2, 5, 7 (restricted), 8, 9, 10, 11, 12

Stonehouse Inn

VIRGINIA CITY

Stonehouse Inn

Box 202, 306 E. Idaho, 59755
(406) 843-5504

Located on a quiet street only blocks away from the historic section of Virginia City, this Victorian stone home is listed on the National Register of Historic Places. Brass beds and antiques in every room give the Inn a romantic touch. Five bedrooms share two baths. Full breakfasts are served each morning, and smoking is allowed on our porches. Skiing, snowmobiling, golfing, hunting, and fly fishing nearby.

Hosts: John and Linda Hamilton
Rooms: 5 (SB) $50 + tax
Full Breakfast
Credit Cards: A, B, D
Notes: 2, 4, 5, 7, 8, 10, 12

NOTES: Credit cards accepted: A Master Card; B Visa; C American Express; D Discover; E Diners Club; F Other; 2 Personal checks accepted; 3 Lunch available; 4 Dinner available;

Nebraska

BERWYN

1909 Heritage House at Berwyn

PO Box 196, 101 Curran, 68819
(308) 935-1136

A warm welcome awaits you in this lovely three-story Victorian/Country home with air-conditioned rooms. Heritage House is located in Central Nebraska, on Highway Two, which is one of the most scenic highways in America. Enjoy a country breakfast served in an elegant dining room, country kitchen, sunroom, or Garden Room. Relax in therapy spa. Visit country chaple and gift shop in Heritage House Park.

Hosts: Meriam and Dale Thomas
Rooms: 5 (1PB; 4SB) $40-85
Full Breakfast
Credit Cards: none
Notes: 2, 3, 4, 5, 8, 9, 10

CRETE

The Parson's House

638 Forest Avenue, 68333
(402) 826-2634

Enjoy warm hospitality in a restored

four square home built at the turn of the century, furnished with many antiques and a modern whirlpool bathtub. Located near Doane College and its beautiful campus. A full breakfast is served in the formal dining room.

Hostess: Sandy Richardson
Rooms: 2 (SB) $40
Full Breakfast
Credit Cards: none
Notes: 2, 5, 8, 9

The Parson's House

ELGIN

Plantation House

RR2 Box 17, 68636-9301
(402) 843-2287

Experience a quieter, gentler era in our

---

5 Open all year; 6 Pets welcome; 7 Children welcome; 8 Tennis nearby; 9 Swimming nearby; 10 Golf nearby; 11 Skiing nearby; 12 May be booked through travel agent.

NEBRASKA

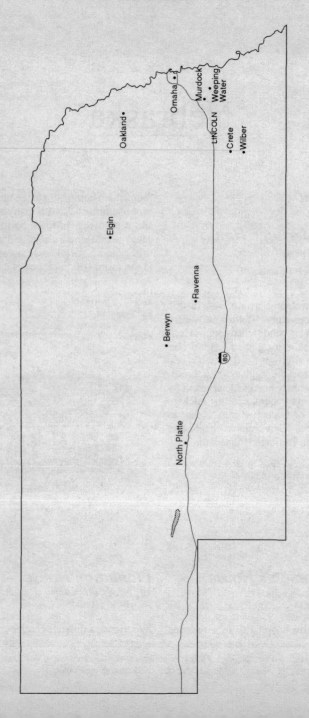

MURDOCK

Plantation House

Greek-Revival mansion at the edge of a small town in rural Northeast Nebraska. Share the home's unique history with your hosts in the luxurious formal living room, then relax in the lower level family room with greenhouse windows and a wood-burning stove/fireplace. Visit the lovely city park, just across the street, or venture on to explore historic Neligh Mills and Ashfall Fossil Beds, less than an hour away.

Hosts: Merland and Barbara Clark
Rooms: 5 + 1 cottage (2PB; 3SB) $35-55 + tax
Full Breakfast
Credit Cards: none
Notes: 2, 5, 7, 8, 9, 10, 12

Farm House

32617 Church Road, 68407
(402) 867-2062

Originally built in 1896, The Farm House provides a glimpse back to country life of the past, complete with expansive ten-foot ceilings, wood floors, an oak spindle staircase, antiques, and even a front porch swing. Room decor and furnishings throughout provide a feeling of comfortable, country elegance with many quilts and Pat's collection of angels. Air-conditioned. Half hour from Lincoln and Omaha.

Hosts: Mike and Pat Meierhenry
Rooms: 3 (1PB; 2SB) $35-45
Full Breakfast
Credit Cards: none
Notes: 2, 5, 6, 7, 8, 9, 10

NORTH PLATTE

KNOLL's Country Inn

6132 South Range Road, 69101
(800) 337-4526

KNOLL's Country Inn is a modern home in the country where it is peaceful and quiet. Take a walk and enjoy a beautiful sunset across the prairie. Relax in a whirlpool bath tub or under the stars in our outdoor spa. During the winter months you can snuggle up in front of the fireplace. After a wonderful, refreshing night's sleep, you will

Farm House

NOTES: Credit cards accepted: A Master Card; B Visa; C American Express; D Discover; E Diners Club; F Other; 2 Personal checks accepted; 3 Lunch available; 4 Dinner available; 5 Open all year; 6 Pets welcome; 7 Children welcome; 8 Tennis nearby; 9 Swimming nearby; 10 Golf nearby; 11 Skiing nearby; 12 May be booked through travel agent.

wake to the aroma of a home-cooked breakfast.

Hostess: Arlene Knoll
Rooms: 5 (1PB; 4SB) $30-75
Full Breakfast
Credit Cards: none
Notes: 2, 5, 7 (12 + over), 9, 10, 11

OAKLAND

Benson Bed and Breakfast

402 N. Oakland Avenue, 68045
(402) 685-6051

Located in the center of a small town. Benson B&B is beautifully decorated with a breakfast you won't soon forget, served in a dining room with all its finery. Large collection of soft drink collectibles, a library full of books, beautiful garden room to relax in, and a large whirlpool tub with color TV on the wall. All rooms are on the second level. Craft and gift shops on the main floor. Three blocks west of Hwy 77. No smoking!

Hosts: Stan and Norma Anderson
Rooms: 3 (SB) $50-55
Full, Elegant Breakfast
Credit Cards: none
Notes: 2, 5, 8, 9, 10, 12

OMAHA

The Jones'

1617 S. 90th Street, 68124
(402) 397-0721

Large, private residence with large deck and gazebo in the back. Fresh cinnamon rolls are served for breakfast. Your hosts' interests include golf, travel,

needlework, and meeting other people. Located five minutes from I-80.

Hosts: Don and Theo Jones
Rooms: 3 (1PB; 2SB) $25
Continental Breakfast
Credit Cards: none
Notes: 2, 5, 6, 7, 8

RAVENNA

Aunt Betty's Bed and Breakfast

804 Grand Avenue, 68864
(308) 452-3739

Enjoy the peacefulness of a small, central Nebraska town while staying at Aunt Betty's three-story Victorian Bed and Breakfast. Four bedrooms furnished in antiques and decorated with attention to detail. Relax in the sitting room while awaiting a delicious, full breakfast including Aunt Betty's "Sticky Buns" and homemade goodies. Flower garden area with fish pond for relaxing. Accommodations for hunters in the hunter's loft. Antique shop part of the B&B. Golf and tennis nearby. One-half hour from I-80.

Hosts: Harvey and Betty Shrader
Rooms: 4 (SB) $45-55
Full Breakfast
Credit Cards: A, B
Notes: 2, 3 and 4 (by appointment), 5, 7, 8, 9, 10

WEEPING WATER

Lauritzen's Danish-American B&B

1002 E. Eldora Avenue, 68463
(402) 267-3295

Lauritzen's turn-of-the-century home is

Lauritzen's Danish-American B&B

WILBER

Hotel Wilber
Bed and Breakfast Inn

W. Second and S. Wilson Streets
Second and Wilson Streets, PO Box 641, 68465
(402) 821-2020; (800) 609-4663

furnished in Danish keepsakes and American antiques and has a beautiful landscaped yard. Enjoy either The Prairie Rose Room which has a private balcony to enjoy the stars or an early morning cup of coffee, or The Lily of the Valley Room, a peaceful first floor room; both with comfortable queen beds. Breakfast includes Danish and American specialties, imported Danish jams, fresh fruit, gourmet coffee, and juice. While in historic Weeping Water, enjoy the small town atmosphere and wonderful museums of early American small town life, or visit Ken's farm where you can get a feel for the crop and cattle operations or take a wildlife/nature tour.

Hosts: Ken and Alice Lauritzen
Rooms: 2 (PB)
Full Breakfast
Credit Cards: none
Notes: 2, 4, 5, 9, 10, 12

Escape to tranquility and warm hospitality at this restored 1895 Victorian in the nation's Czech Capital. Soothing antique-furnished rooms await, each with cable TV and personally controlled heating and air. Relax in the pub, garden, lobby, or dining room featuring traditional Czech and American cuisines. Three churches, several shops, a museum, and pool are all within four blocks. Great place for winter retreats! Ask about group discount. Forty minutes to Lincoln; ninty to Omaha.

Hostess: Frances L. Erb
Rooms: 10 (SB) $42.95-69.95
Full Breakfast
Credit Cards: A, B
Notes: 2, 3, 4, 5, 7, 8, 9, 10, 12

Historic 1895
Hotel Wilber

---

5 Open all year; 6 Pets welcome; 7 Children welcome; 8 Tennis nearby; 9 Swimming nearby; 10 Golf nearby; 11 Skiing nearby; 12 May be booked through travel agent.

NEVADA

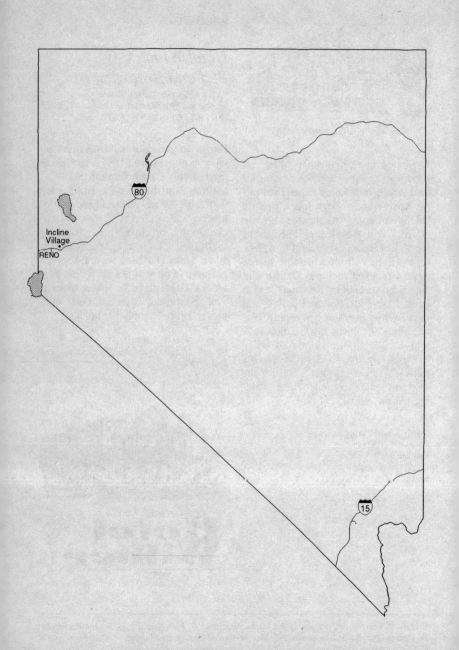

Nevada

Mi Casa Su Casa
Bed and Breakfast
Reservation Service

PO Box 950, **Tempe,** AZ 85280-0950
(602) 990-0682; (800) 456-0682 (reservations);
FAX (602) 990-3390

Over 160 inspected and approved homestays, guest cottages, ranches, and inns in Arizona, Utah, New Mexico, and Nevada. In **Arizona,** listings include Ajo, Apache Junction, Bisbee, Cave Creek, Clarkdale, Dragoon, Flagstaff, Mesa, Page, Patagonia, Payson, Pinetop, Phoenix, Prescott, Scottsdale, Sedona, Sierra Vista, Tempe, Tombstone, Tucson, Yuma, and other cities. In **New Mexico,** we have included Albuquerque, Algodones, Chimayo, Los Cruces, Silver City, Sante Fe, and Taos. In **Utah,** listings include Moab, Monroe, Salt Lake City, Springdale, St. George, and Tropic. In **Nevada,** we list Las Vegas. Rooms with private and shared baths range from $40-175. Credit cards welcomed. Full or continental breakfast. A book with individual descriptions, rates, and pictures is available for $9.50. Ruth Young, coordinator.

INCLINE VILLAGE

Haus Bavaria

593 N. Dyer Circle, PO Box 9079, 89452
(702) 831-6122; (800) 731-6222;
FAX (702) 831-1238

This European-style residence in the heart of the Sierra Nevadas, is within walking distance of Lake Tahoe. Each of the five guest rooms open onto a balcony, offering lovely views of the mountains. Breakfast, prepared by your host Bick Hewitt, includes a selection of home-baked goods, fresh fruit, juices, freshly ground coffee, and teas. A private beach and swimming pool are available to guests. Ski at Diamond Peak, Mt. Rose, Heavenly Valley, and other nearby areas.

Host: Bick Hewitt
Rooms: 5 (PB) $145
Full Breakfast
Credit Cards: A, B, C, D
Notes: 2, 5, 8, 9, 10, 11, 12

NOTES: Credit cards accepted: A Master Card; B Visa; C American Express; D Discover; E Diners Club; F Other; 2 Personal checks accepted; 3 Lunch available; 4 Dinner available; 5 Open all year; 6 Pets welcome; 7 Children welcome; 8 Tennis nearby; 9 Swimming nearby; 10 Golf nearby; 11 Skiing nearby; 12 May be booked through travel agent.

NEW HAMPSHIRE

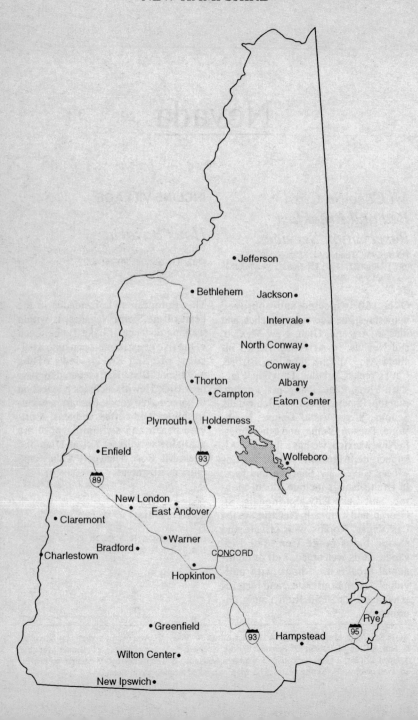

New Hampshire

ALBANY

Kancamagus Swift River Inn

Route 112 Kancamagus Highway., 03818
(603) 447-2332

This is a quality inn with that Old World flavor in a stress-free environment. Located in the White Mountains of New Hampshire in the Mt. Washington Valley on the most beautiful highway in the state, the Kancamagus Highway, one and a half miles off Route 16. We are only minutes from all factory outlets, attractions, and fine restaurants.

Hosts: Joseph and Janet Beckenbach
Rooms: 10 (PB) $40-90
Continental Breakfast
Credit Cards: A, B, D
Notes: 2, 5, 7, 8, 9, 10, 11, 12

Kancamagus Swift River Inn

BETHLEHEM

The Mulburn Inn

2370 Main Street, Route 302, 03574
(603) 869-3389; (800) 457-9440;
FAX (603) 869-5633

A charming B&B on the historic Woolworth Estate, hosted by the Skeels family. Seven warm and comfortable rooms, all with private bath. King-, queen-, and full-size beds available. Port-a-cribs provided on request. Full breakfast by the fire. Cheery common rooms with easy chairs for reading and relaxing. Cable TV and guest phone in the common room. Spacious grounds for children to play. Four season attractions; hiking, biking, skiing, golfing on two local PGA rated courses, fishing, swimming, Storyland, Santa's Village, and Six-Gun City. Minutes away from the scenic beauty of Franconia Notch, Crawford Notch, and Mt. Washington. Children welcome. No smoking. No pets. AAA and Mobile approved and rated. Golf and ski packages available.

Hosts: The Skeels Family
Rooms: 7 (PB) $55-90
Full Breakfast
Credit Cards: A, B, C, D
Notes: 2, 4 (groups only), 5, 7, 8, 9, 10, 11, 12

NOTES: Credit cards accepted: A Master Card; B Visa; C American Express; D Discover; E Diners Club; F Other; 2 Personal checks accepted; 3 Lunch available; 4 Dinner available; 5 Open all year; 6 Pets welcome; 7 Children welcome; 8 Tennis nearby; 9 Swimming nearby; 10 Golf nearby; 11 Skiing nearby; 12 May be booked through travel agent.

Candlelite Inn

BRADFORD

Candlelite Inn
Bed and Breakfast

5 Greenhouse Lane, 03221
(603) 938-5571

An 1857 country Victorian inn nestled on three acres in the Lake Sunapee Region. We serve a full breakfast—down to dessert—in our Sun Room which overlooks the pond. Relax on the gazebo porch while sipping lemonade on a lazy summer day, or curl up in the living room in front of the corner fireplace. Within minutes to skiing, hiking, antiquing, and restaurants. We are a non-smoking inn.

Hosts: Marilyn and Les Gordon
Rooms: 6 (PB) $65-85
Full Breakfast
Credit Cards: A, B, C, D
Notes: 2, 5, 7, 8, 9, 10, 11, 12

CAMPTON

Mountain-Fare Inn

Mad River Road, PO Box 553, 03223
(603) 726-4283

In New Hampshire's White Mountains.

Lovely 1840's village home with the antiques, fabrics, and feel of country cottage living. Gardens in summer; foliage in fall; a true skier's lodge in winter. Accessible, peaceful, warm, friendly, affordable. Hearty breakfasts. Unspoiled beauty from Franconia Notch to Squam Lake. Four-season sports, soccer field, music, and theater. Wonderful family vacationing.

Hosts: Susan and Nick Preston
Rooms: 10 (7 PB; 3 SB) $50-90
Full Breakfast
Credit Cards: A, B, D, E
Notes: 2, 5, 7, 8, 9, 10, 11, 12

MapleHedge Bed and Breakfast Inn

CHARLESTOWN

MapleHedge
Bed and Breakfast Inn

355 Main Street, Route 12, 03603
(603) 826-5237; (800) 9 MAPLE 9;
FAX (603) 826-5237

Rather than just touring homes two-and-a-half centuries old, make one your "home away from home" while visiting western New Hampshire or Eastern Vermont. MapleHedge offers five dis-

---

NOTES: Credit cards accepted: A Master Card; B Visa; C American Express; D Discover; E Diners Club; F Other; 2 Personal checks accepted; 3 Lunch available; 4 Dinner available;

tinctly different bedrooms with private baths and antiques chosen to compliment the individual decor. It has very tastefully added all modern day amenities such as central air-conditioning, fire sprinkler system, and queen beds. Enjoy a gourmet breakfast in the grand dining room of this magnificent home that is on the National Register and situated among 200 year old maples and lovely gardens.

Hosts: Joan and Dick DeBrine
Rooms: 5 (PB) $85-100
Full three-Course Breakfast
Credit Cards: A, B
Notes: 2, 5, 7 (over 12), 8, 9, 10, 11, 12

CLAREMONT

Goddard Mansion
Bed and Breakfast

25 Hillstead Road, 03743
(603) 543-0603; (800) 736-0603;
FAX (603) 543-0001

Circa 1905, this mansion with adjacent garden tea house is set amid acres of lawns and gardens with panoramic mountain views. This beautifully restored English manor style, 18-room mansion, with expansive porches, has ten uniquely decorated guest rooms. The living room has fireplace and window seats for cuddling up with a good book and enjoying a vintage baby grand piano. A 1939 Wurlitzer jukebox lights up a corner of the walnut panelled dining room where a full, natural breakfast awaits guests each morning. Four-season activities, historic sites, cultural events, fun, and

"fine" dining are nearby. The area is an antique buff's adventureland! Brochere available. Families welcome.

Hostess: Debbie Albee
Rooms: 10 (3PB; 7SB) $65-105
Full Breakfast
Credit Cards: A, B, C, D, E
Notes: 2, 5, 7, 8, 9, 10, 11

Goddard Mansion

CONWAY

The Inn
at Crystal Lake

Route 153, PO Box 12, **Eaton Center** 03832
(603) 447-2120; (800) 343-7336;
FAX (603) 447-3599

Unwind in the comforts of our 1884 Victorian Inn, nestled in peaceful Eaton village, just six miles south of Conway. Eleven tastefully decorated guest rooms furnished with antiques, all with private baths. Begin each day with a full country breakfast served in old-fashioned elegance at your own private table. A short drive down a country road will bring you to all the activities of the Mt. Washington Valley. Shopping, dining, and five major ski areas will keep you happily entertained, or just relax here and enjoy our historic village, beautiful Crystal Lake, and the hospitality of your hosts. Experience New England in a country inn.

Hosts: Richard and Janice Octeau
Rooms: 11 (PB) $60-100 (foliage season $100-130)
Full Breakfast
Credit Cards: A, B, C, D
Notes: 2, 5, 7, 8, 9, 10, 11, 12

The Inn at Crystal Lake

EAST ANDOVER

Highland Lake Inn
PO Box 164, Maple Street, 03231
(603) 735-6426; FAX (603) 735-5355

A 1767 classic building on twelve acres in a Currier and Ives setting with lake and mountain views. Secluded beach, fishing, boating, hiking, downhill and cross-country skiing, ice-skating, championship golf, and antiquing. Spacious guest rooms, private baths, elegantly decorated with antiques, fine bedding, and fireplaces. Full sumptuous breakfasts.

Hosts: The Petras Family
Rooms: 10 (PB) $85-100
Full Breakfast
Credit Cards: A, B, C, D
Notes: 5, 8, 9, 10, 11, 12

ENFIELD

Boulder Cottage on Crystal Lake
RR 1 Box 257, 03748
(603) 632-7355

A turn-of-the-century Victorian cottage owned by our family for 73 years. Our home faces beautiful Crystal Lake, a small, private lake centrally located in the Dartmouth-Sunapee Region. We promise our guests an unspoiled environment with classic views of the lake and mountains. Our guests can enjoy swimming, canoeing, boating, fishing, hiking, or just relaxing on our comfortable screened porch or sunny decks. Weekly rates can be arranged. Children are welcome. Non-smoking home.

Hosts: Harry and Barbara Reed
Rooms: 4 (2PB; 2SB) $45-65
Full Country Breakfast
Credit Cards: none
Notes: 2, 7, 9, 10, 12

Mary Keane House
Box 5 Lower Shaker Village, 03748
(603) 632-4241

Late Victorian house in historic Shaker village setting on Lake Mascoma. Lasalette Chapel and Shrine next door. Mary Keane House has light-filled, spacious one- and two-room suites furnished with period antiques and accented with old linens, large screened porch, and balconies with a view of the lake. Swim or boat from our own private beach. Relax by the fire in the evening. Close to Dartmouth College

---

in Hanover, many fine restaurants, museums, and cultural events.

Hosts: David and Sharon Carr
Rooms: 7 (PB) $89-119
Expanded Continental Breakfast
Credit Cards: A, B, C
Notes: 2, 5, 6, 7, 9, 10, 11, 12

GREENFIELD

The Greenfield Bed and Breakfast Inn

Box 400, Forest Road, 03047
(603) 547-6327; (800) 678-9199;
FAX (603) 547-2418 (call first)

Bob Hope and his wife Dolores have visited twice because it is romance in Victorian splendor. The Inn offers a sleep-six hayloft suite with kitchen, a sleep-six cottage with kitchen and three bathrooms, plus a sleep two to three suit with kitchen. Breakfast with crystal, china, and Mozart. In a quiet valley surrounded by mountains and big veranda views. Only 90 minutes from Boston or 40 minutes from Manchester airports.

Hosts: Barbara and Vic Mangini
Rooms: 9 (7PB; 2SB) $49-99; + 2 suites and a cottage
Full Breakfast
Credit Cards: A, B, C
Notes: 2 (preferred), 5, 7 (restrictions), 8, 9, 10, 11, 12

Stillmeadow Bed and Breakfast at Hampstead

HAMPSTEAD

Stillmeadow Bed and Breakfast at Hampstead

PO Box 565, 545 Main Street, 03841
(603) 329-8381; FAX (603) 329-4075

Historic home built in 1850 with five chimneys, three staircases, hardwood floors, Oriental rugs, and wood stoves. Set on rolling meadows adjacent to professional croquet courts. Single, doubles, and suites, all with private baths. Families are welcome, with amenities such as fenced-in play yard and children's playroom. Easy commute to Manchester, NH, and Boston, MA. Complimentary refreshments and the cookie jar is always full. Formal dining and living rooms; expanded Continental breakfast.

Hosts: Lori and Randy Offord
Rooms: 4½ (4PB) $60-90
Expanded Continental Breakfast
Credit Cards: A, B, C
Notes: 2, 5, 6 (with advance approval), 7, 8, 9, 10, 11, 12 (non-commissionable)

HOLDERNESS

The Inn on Golden Pond

Route 3, PO Box 680, 03245-0680
(603) 968-7269; FAX (603) 968-9226

An 1879 Colonial home is nestled on 50 wooded acres offering guests a traditional New England setting where you can escape and enjoy warm hospitality and personal service of the resident hosts. Rooms are individually decorated with braided rugs and country curtains and bedspreads. Hearty, home-cooked

---

5 Open all year; 6 Pets welcome; 7 Children welcome; 8 Tennis nearby; 9 Swimming nearby; 10 Golf nearby; 11 Skiing nearby; 12 May be booked through travel agent.

breakfast features farm fresh eggs, muffins, homemade bread, and Bonnie's most requested rhubarb jam.

Hosts: Bonnie and Bill Webb
Rooms: 8 (PB) $95-130
Full Breakfast
Credit Cards: A, B, C
Notes: 2, 5, 8, 9, 10, 11, 12

HOPKINTON

The Country Porch Bed and Breakfast

281 Moran Road, 03229
(603) 746-6391

Situated on 15 peaceful acres of lawn, pasture, and forest, this B&B is a reproduction of an 18th century Colonial. Sit on the wraparound porch and gaze out over the meadow, bask in the sun, and then cool off in the pool. The comfortably appointed rooms have a Colonial, Amish, or Shaker theme and have king or twin beds. Summer and winter activities are plentiful and fine country dining is a short drive away. "Come and sit a spell." No smoking.

Hosts: Tom and Wendy Solomon
Rooms: 3 (PB) $75-80
Full Breakfast
Credit Cards: A, B
Notes: 2, 5, 9, 10, 11

JACKSON

Ellis River House

Rt. 16, PO Box 656, 03846
(603) 383-9339; (800) 233-8309;
FAX (603) 383-4142

Sample true New England hospitality at this enchanting, small hotel and country inn within a short stroll of the village. The Ellis River House has eighteen comfortable king-and queen-size guest rooms decorated with Laura Ashley prints, some with fireplaces and two person jacuzzis, cable TV, scenic balconies, and period antiques, all with individually controlled heat and air-conditioning. Two-room and family suites, river front cottage, hot tub, sauna, and heated pool, siting and game rooms, delightful sundeck overlooking the pristine Ellis River. Enjoy a full country breakfast with homemade breads, or a delicious trout dinner. Afterwards relax with libations and billiards in the pub.

Hosts: Barry and Barbara Lubao
Rooms: 18 (15PB; 3SB) $59-229
Full Country Breakfast
Credit Cards: A, B, C, D, E
Notes: 2, 4, 5, 6 + 7 (limited), 8, 9, 10, 11, 12

JEFFERSON

Applebrook

Route 115A, 03583-0178
(603) 586-7713; (800) 545-6504

Taste our mid-summer raspberries while enjoying spectacular mountain views. Applebrook is a comfortable, casual bed and breakfast in a large Victorian farmhouse with a peaceful, rural setting. After a restful night's sleep, you will enjoy a hearty breakfast before venturing out for a day of hiking, fishing, antique hunting, golfing, swimming, or skiing. Near Santa's Village and Six-Gun City. Dormitory available for groups. Brochures available. Hot tub

NOTES: Credit cards accepted: A Master Card; B Visa; C American Express; D Discover; E Diners Club; F Other; 2 Personal checks accepted; 3 Lunch available; 4 Dinner available;

Applebrook

under the stars.

Hosts: Sandra Conley and Martin Kelly
Rooms: 12 + dormitory (5PB; 7SB) $40-75
Full Breakfast
Credit Cards: A, B
Notes: 2, 5, 6, 7, 8, 9, 10, 11, 12

NEW IPSWICH

The Inn at New Ipswich

11 Porter Hill Road, PO Box 208, 03071
(603) 878-3711

Relax a while in a graceful 1790 Colonial amid stone walls and fruit trees. With cozy fireplaces, front porch rockers, and large guest rooms furnished country-style, you'll feel right at home. Breakfasts are bountiful! Situated in New Hampshire's Monadnock Region, activities abound: hiking, band concerts, antique auctions, maple sugaring, apple picking, unsurpassed autumn color, and cross-country and downhill skiing. No smoking. Children over

eight welcome.

Hosts: Ginny and Steve Bankuti
Rooms: 6 (PB) $75
Full Breakfast
Credit Cards: A, B
Notes: 2, 5, 7 (over 8), 10, 11

NEW LONDON

Pleasant Lake Inn

125 Pleasant Street, PO Box 1030, 03257-1030
(603) 526-6271; (800) 626-4907

Our 1790, lakeside, country inn is nestled on the shore of Pleasant Lake with Mt. Kearsarge as its backdrop. The panoramic location is only one of the many reasons to visit. All four seasons offer activities from our doorway: lake swimming, fishing, hiking, skiing, or just plain relaxing. Dinner is available. Call or write for brochure.

Hosts: Margaret and Grant Rich
Rooms: 11 (PB) $80-100
Full Breakfast
Credit Cards: A, B
Notes: 2, 4, 5, 7 (over 7), 8, 9, 10, 11, 12

5 Open all year; 6 Pets welcome; 7 Children welcome; 8 Tennis nearby; 9 Swimming nearby;
10 Golf nearby; 11 Skiing nearby; 12 May be booked through travel agent.

The 1785 Inn

NORTH CONWAY

The 1785 Inn

PO Box 1785, 03860-1785
(603) 356-9025; (800) 421-1785;
FAX (603) 356-6081

The 1785 Inn is a relaxing place to vacation at any time of the year. The 1785 Inn is famous for its views and food. Located at the Scenic Vista, popularized by the White Mountain School of Art, its famous scene of Mt. Washington is virtually unchanged from when the Inn was built over 200 years ago. The Inn's homey atmosphere will make you feel right at home, and the food and service will make you eagerly await your return.

Hosts: Becky and Charlie Mallar
Rooms: 17 (12PB; 5SB) $59-169
Full Breakfast
Credit Cards: A, B, C, D, E
Notes: 2, 4, 5, 7, 8, 9, 10, 11, 12

Buttonwood Inn

PO Box 1817, Mt. Surprise Road, 03860
(603) 356-2625; (800) 258-2625 (U.S.A.);
FAX (603) 356-3140

Visit our secluded 1820s cape on Mt.

Surprise, only two miles from North Conway village. Nine guest rooms allow us time to pamper you with personal service; one room has a gas fireplace. Stroll five acres of lawns and award-winning gardens. Swim in our pool, surrounded by on old granite barn foundation. Rock on the front porch or sit in an adirondack chair and see if you can spy a hummingbird. Hike or cross-country ski from our door. Lipsmacking breakfasts keep guests returning.

Hosts: Claudia and Peter Needham
Rooms: 9 (5PB; 4SB) $70-150
Full Breakfast
Credit Cards: A, B, C, D, E
Notes: 2, 5, 7, 8, 9, 10, 11, 12

Peter & Carol Watson
Innkeepers

Eastman Inn

Eastman Inn

PO Box 882 Main Street, 03860
(603) 356-6707; (800) 626-5855

Upscale 1797 Colonial Inn located in the heart of North Conway. Walking distance to outlet shopping, scenic railroad, and downtown shops and restaurants. Just minutes to all major attractions. We offer beautifully decorated sitting areas, fireplaced living room, and recreation room with wood stove. Experience the romantic environment of a 1797 Colonial inn, where you enter a stranger and leave a friend. Fourteen spacious bedrooms all with private bath, TV, A/C, and full country breakfast.

Hosts: Peter and Carol Watson
Rooms: 14 (12PB; 2SB) $60-150
Full Country Breakfast
Credit Cards: A, B, D
Notes: 5, 8, 9, 10, 11

The Forest, A Country Inn

PO Box 37, **Intervale** 03845
(603) 356-9772; (800) 448-3534;
FAX (603) 356-5652

Step back to quieter times at our 1890 Victorian B&B. With only 11 charming guest rooms, you are assured of personal friendly attention. Beautifully served breakfasts, fireplaced rooms, a romantic stone cottage with fireplace, antiques, pool, lovely gardens, and veranda/sunroom. Cross-country ski from our back door. Minutes to hiking, biking, skiing, and golfing.

Hosts: Bill and Lisa Guppy
Rooms: 11 (9PB; 2 SB) $65-169
Full Breakfast
Credit Cards: A, B, C, D
Notes: 2, 5, 7, 8, 9, 10, 11, 12

Merrill Farm Resort

428 White Mountain Highway, 03860
(603) 447-3866; (800) 445-1017;
FAX (603) 447-3867

100 year old accommodation with modern amenities and country warmth and hospitality. Fireplaced units and whirlpool units. Free "rise and shine" breakfast. Children 12 and under stay free (up to two per room). Heated outdoor pool and recreation. Handy to 10 major ski areas. Right on Saco River—free canoeing. Fully air-conditioned. Canadian cash at par most of year. Senior discounts. AAA Rated, 10% discount.

Innkeeper: Lynn McArdle
Rooms: 60 (PB) $39-149
Rise and Shine Breakfast
Credit Cards: A, B, C, D, E
Notes: 5, 7, 8, 10, 11, 12

The Victorian Harvest Inn

28 Locust Lane, PO Box 1763, 03860
(just off White Mountian Hwy., Route 16/302)
(603) 356-3548; (800) 642-0749;
FAX (603) 356-8430

Non-smokers delight in your comfortable elegant B&B home at the edge of quaint North Conway Village. Explore unique shoppes, outlets, and the AMC trails. Our 1850s multi-gabled Victorian find comes with six large comfy rooms, all with mountain views. Start your romantic adventure with a bounteous breakfast experience and classic New England hospitality. Relax by the fireplace or snuggle with a literary treasure in our elegant library. Private baths, lovely in-ground pool, and full air conditioning to add to your comfort. AAA three-diamond award. American Bed and Breakfast Association: rated "A" three-crowns. Cross-country skiing from the door, and 3-10 minutes to downhill skiing. "We welcome all God's people."

Hosts: Linda and Robert Dahlberg
Rooms: 4 + 1 two-room suite (4PB; 2SB in suite) $70-115 (higher rates in foliage season)
Full Breakfast
Credit Cards: A, B, C, D
Notes: 2, 4 (Sat. night group only), 5, 7 (over 6), 8, 9, 11, 12

---

5 Open all year; 6 Pets welcome; 7 Children welcome; 8 Tennis nearby; 9 Swimming nearby; 10 Golf nearby; 11 Skiing nearby; 12 May be booked through travel agent.

PLYMOUTH

Colonel Spencer Inn

RR #1, Box 206, 03264
(603) 536-3438

A 1764 center-chimney Colonial with antique furnishings, wide pine floor boards, hand-hewn beams, and Indian shutters. Seven antique-appointed bedrooms with private baths welcome quests. A full country breakfast is served in a fireplaced dining room. The Inn is convenient to lake and mountain attractions, at Exit 27, off I-93, one-half miles south on Route 3.

Hosts: Carolyn and Alan Hill
Rooms: 7 (PB) $45-65
Full Breakfast
Credit Cards: none
Notes: 2, 5, 7, 8, 9, 10, 11, 12

Colonel Spencer Inn

RYE

Rock Ledge Manor
Bed and Breakfast

1413 Ocean Boulevard, Route 1-A, 03870
(603) 431-1413

A gracious, traditional, seaside, manor home with an excellent location that offers an ocean view from all rooms. It is central to all New Hampshire and southern Maine seacoast activities; six minutes to historic Portsmouth and Hampton; 20 minutes to the University of New Hampshire; 15 minutes to Exeter Academy. Reservations are advised.

Hosts: Norman and Janice Marineau
Rooms: 4 (2PB; 2SB) $70-90
Full Breakfast
Credit Cards: none
Notes: 2, 5, 7 (12 and older), 8, 9, 10, 11

THORNTON

Amber Lights Inn
Bed and Breakfast

RR1 Box 828, **Campton** 03223
(603) 726-4077

Amber Lights Inn B&B is a beautifully restored, 1815 Colonial in the heart of the White Mountains in Thornton, NH, a quiet country setting. We have five meticulously clean guest rooms, all appointed with luxurious queen-size beds, handmade quilts, and antiques. In the early evening join in a conversation with your lively innkeeper Carola over nightly hors d'oeuvres. We are conveniently located between Loon Mountain and Waterville Valley, close to all White Mountains attractions. Ask about our murder mystery weekends.

Hosts: Paul Sears and Carola Warnsman
Rooms: 5 (4PB; 1SB) $75-96
Suites: 2 (3 rooms each for 2-6 people) $96-165
Full Breakfast
Credit Cards: A, B, C, D
Notes: 2, 5, 6, 7, 8, 9, 10, 11, 12

NOTES: Credit cards accepted: A Master Card; B Visa; C American Express; D Discover; E Diners Club; F Other; 2 Personal checks accepted; 3 Lunch available; 4 Dinner available;

WARNER

Jacob's Ladder Bed and Breakfast

69 E. Main Street, 03278
(603) 456-3494

Situated in the quaint village of Warner, Jacob's Ladder is conveniently located between exits 8 and 9 off I-89. The early 1800s home is furnished predominantly with antiques, creating a tasteful country atmosphere. Cross-country ski and snowmobile trail on site with three downhill ski areas within 20 miles. Lakes, mountains, covered bridges, arts and crafts, and more nearby. No smoking.

Hosts: Marlon and Deb Baese
Rooms: 3 (1PB; 2SB) $45-55
Full Breakfast
Credit Cards: D
Notes: 2, 5, 7, 8, 9, 10, 11

WILTON CENTER

Stepping Stones Bed and Breakfast

6 Bennington Battle Trail, 03086
(603) 654-9048

Stepping Stone is owned by a garden designer and weaver. Display gardens surround the 19th century house set in the quiet, rural Monadnock region. A scrumptious breakfast is served on the porch or terrace in summer and in the solar garden room year-round. Enjoy good reading, stereo, and TV in the cozy living room, or watch active weaver and gardener at work in a serene and civilized atmosphere. Summer theaters, chamber music, hiking, and antiquing all nearby.

Hostess: Ann Carlsmith
Rooms: 3 (1PB; 2SB) $50-55
Full Breakfast
Credit Cards: none
Notes: 2, 5, 6, 7, 9, 10, 11

WOLFEBORO

The Tuc' Me Inn Bed and Breakfast

118 N. Main Street, PO Box 657, 03894
(603) 569-5702

Our 1850, Colonial, Federal is located within walking distance of the lake and the quaint village of Wolfeboro, "The oldest summer resort in America." Family antiques in country, Victorian style. Relax in our music room, parlor, screened-in porches, or our cozy reading room. Complimentary breakfast bar. We are a non-smoking inn. For your comfort, all bedrooms are air-conditioned.

Hosts: Ernie, Terry, and Tina Foultz and Idabel Evans
Rooms: 7 (3PB; 4SB) $55-85
Breakfast Bar
Credit Cards: A, B
Notes: 2, 5, 7, 8, 9, 10, 11, 12

---

5 Open all year; 6 Pets welcome; 7 Children welcome; 8 Tennis nearby; 9 Swimming nearby; 10 Golf nearby; 11 Skiing nearby; 12 May be booked through travel agent.

NEW JERSEY

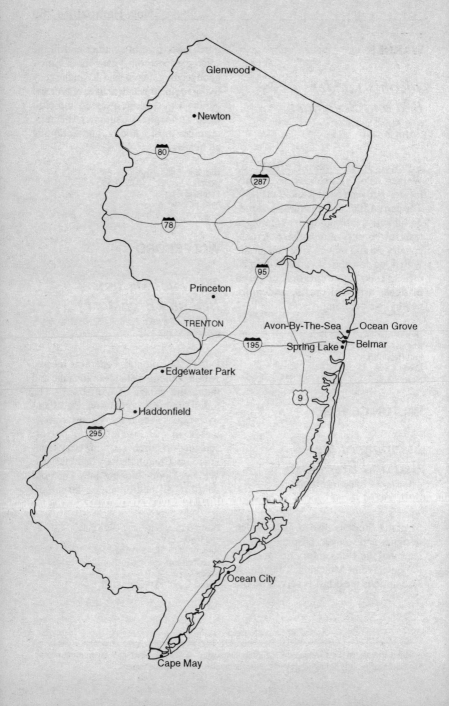

New Jersey

AVON-BY-THE-SEA

Cashelmara Inn

22 Lakeside Avenue, 07717
(908) 776-8727; (800) 821-2976;
FAX (908) 988-5819

A tastefully restored turn-of-the-century
inn rests on the bank of a swan lake and
the Atlantic Ocean. This desirable setting offers a unique opportunity to smell
the fresh salt air, to feel the ocean
breeze, and to hear the sounds of the
surf and the sea gulls from the privacy
of your seaside room. Hearty breakfasts
are a tradition at the Cashelmara Inn.

Hosts: Mary Wiernasz and Martin Mulligan
Rooms: 13 (PB) $75-150 (suite $225-250)
Full Breakfast
Credit Cards: A, B, C, D
Notes: 2, 5, 7, 8, 9, 10

The Inn at the Shore

BELMAR

The Inn at the Shore

301 Fourth Avenue, 07719
(908) 681-3762; FAX (201) 945-2822
Web site: www.bbianj.com/innattheshore

The Inn is located within sight of the
Atlantic Ocean and Belmar's wide
beautiful beaches and boardwalk, and
just steps away from serene Silver Lake,
home to the first flock of swans bred in
America. Guests will enjoy the Inn's casual, Victorian-style ambiance on our
expansive wraparound porch, where
relaxing in a rocking chair takes you
back to the seashore of days gone by.
Visitors make themselves comfortable
in our spacious common areas including a cafe style brick patio ready for

---

NOTES: Credit cards accepted: A Master Card; B Visa; C American Express; D Discover;
E Diners Club; F Other; 2 Personal checks accepted; 3 Lunch available; 4 Dinner available;
5 Open all year; 6 Pets welcome; 7 Children welcome; 8 Tennis nearby; 9 Swimming nearby;
10 Golf nearby; 11 Skiing nearby; 12 May be booked through travel agent.

barbecues or refreshing beverages after a day of reflection, our large living room with its lovely stone fireplace and state-of-the-art entertainment center, and the grand dining room and library are perfect for quiet moments of reading, writing, or just unwinding by our tranquil aquarium. We serve a generous continental breakfast consisting of home-baked muffins, croissants, fresh fruits, cereals, juices, etc.

Hosts: Rosemary and Tom Volker
Rooms: 12 (3PB; 9SB) $45-110
Continental Breakfast
Credit Cards: A, B, C
Notes: 2, 5, 7, 8, 9, 10, 12

CAPE MAY

The Albert Stevens Inn

127 Myrtle Avenue, 08204
(609) 884-4717; (800) 890-CATS

Built in 1898 by Dr. Albert G. Stevens as a wedding gift for his bride, Bessie, the Inn is just a ten minute walk to the beach and two blocks from Victorian shopping. The guest rooms are furnished with antiques and have private baths and air-conditioning. A 102-degree, six-person jacuzzi is privately scheduled for guests' comfort. Home of the original Cat's Garden Tea and Tour, the Inn is known for its comfort, privacy, and gourmet breakfasts. Resident pet cats.

Hosts: Curt and Diane Diviney-Rangen
Rooms: 9 (PB) $90-165
Full Breakfast
Credit Cards: A, B, C, D
Notes: 2, 4, 8, 9, 10, 12

Bedford Inn

805 Stockton Avenue, 08204
(609) 884-4158; FAX (609) 884-0533

Fully restored Victorian B&B—romantic and elegant. All rooms and "honeymoon" suites are furnished with authentic antiques and have private bath, TV, and air-conditioning; many with queen beds. Parlor with fireplace and two porches. Rates include gourmet breakfast and afternoon tea and treats, beach passes, beach chairs, and on-site parking. Great location—very close to beach and town center.

Hosts: Alan and Cindy Schumucker
Rooms: 11 (PB) $85-180
Full Breakfast
Credit Cards: A, B, C
Notes: 8, 9, 10

Captain Mey's Inn

Captain Mey's Inn

202 Ocean Street, 08204
(609) 884-7793

The Inn is an 1890 Colonial Revival Victorian named after the Dutch explorer, Captain Cornelius Mey. The Dutch heritage is evident from the Persian rugs on the tabletops to the Delft

Blue china collection. The wraparound veranda is furnished with wicker furniture, hanging ferns, and Victorian wind curtains. A full breakfast is served by candlelight with classical music in the formal dining room; in the summer breakfast is served on the veranda.

Hosts: George and Kathleen Blinn
Rooms: 8 (PB) $75-210 (deluxe)
Full Breakfast
Credit Cards: A, B, C
Notes: 5, 7 (over 8), 8, 9, 10, 12 (off season and midweek only)

Duke of Windsor Inn
817 Washington Street, 08204
(609) 884-1355

This grand 1890 Victorian home offers gracious, relaxing accommodations furnished with period antiques, high-backed beds, and marble-topped tables and dressers. Two octagon rooms in our 40-foot turret are particularly fun and romantic. The dining room has five chandeliers and an elaborate plaster ceiling. We are within walking distance of the beach, historical attractions, tennis, and shopping.

Hosts: Bruce and Fran Prichard
Rooms: 9 (8PB; 1SB) $65-165
Full Breakfast
Credit Cards: A, B (for deposit only)
Open February to December.
Notes: 2, 8, 9, 10

The Inn on Ocean
25 Ocean Street, 08204
(609) 884-7070; (800) 304-4477;
FAX (609) 884-1384

An intimate, elegant, Victorian inn. Fanciful Second Empire style with an exuberant personality. Beautifully restored. King and queen beds. Private baths. Fireplaces. Fully air-conditioned. Full breakfasts. Wicker-filled ocean view porches. Billiard room. Open all seasons. Free on-site parking. Guest says, "A magical place!," "Second visit is as lovely as first!," and "Compliments to the chef!"

Hosts: Jack and Katha Davis
Rooms: 5 (PB) $99-195 (by season)
Full Breakfast
Credit Cards: A, B, C, E
Notes: 2, 5, 8, 9, 10, 12

The Kings Cottage

The Kings Cottage
9 Perry Street, 08204
(609) 884-0415

This three-story "Stick Style" Victorian Cottage is an exquisite example of the work done by noted architect Frank Furness. Taking full advantage of its location, the rooms, all with private baths and the two wicker-filled verandas optimize the ocean views. The interior has been lovingly restored and furnished in true Victorian fashion to

---

5 Open all year; 6 Pets welcome; 7 Children welcome; 8 Tennis nearby; 9 Swimming nearby; 10 Golf nearby; 11 Skiing nearby; 12 May be booked through travel agent.

reflect the grandeur of that period. Antiques abound, especially in the parlor and formal dining room where a full breakfast is served utilizing fine china, crystal, and silver, all the trappings that make life that much more enjoyable. You may enjoy afternoon tea on the veranda or in the formal garden.

Hosts: Pat and Tony Marino
Rooms: 9 (PB) $95-195
Full Breakfast
Credit Cards: A, B
Notes: 5, 8, 9, 10, 12

The Mooring

The Mooring

801 Stockton Avenue, 08204
(609) 884-5425; FAX (609) 884-1357

Built in 1882, The Mooring is one of Cape May's original guest houses. Enjoy the comfortable elegance of this classic Second Empire inn, with its grand entrance hall and wide spiral staircase leading to spacious guest rooms—each with period furnishings, private bath, and ceiling fan; most with air-conditioning. Full breakfast and afternoon tea served in the dining room at tables for two. A block to the beach; easy walking distance to shops and restaurants. Free on-site parking; low weekday rates off-season.

Hostess: Leslie Valenza
Rooms: 12 (PB) $75-150
Full Breakfast
Credit Cards: A, B
Notes: 2, 7 (over 5), 8, 9, 10, 12

Windward House

24 Jackson Street, 08204
(609) 884-3368

An elegant Edwardian, seaside inn has an entry way and staircase that are perhaps the prettiest in town. Spacious, antique-filled guest rooms have queen beds, air-conditioners, and TVs. With three sun and shade porches, cozy parlor fireplace, and Christmas finery, the Inn is located in the historic district, one-half block from the beach and shopping mall. Rates include homemade breakfast, afternoon refreshments, beaches passes, and parking. Midweek discounts all year; off-season weekend packages.

Hosts: Sandy and Owen Miller
Rooms: 8 (PB) $80-150
Full Breakfast
Credit Cards: A, B (deposit only)
Notes: 2, 5, 7 (over 8), 8, 9, 10, 12

The Wooden Rabbit Inn

609 Hughes Street, 08204
(609) 884-7293; FAX (609) 898-0842

Charming country inn in the heart of Cape May, surrounded by Victorian cottages. Cool, shady street, the prettiest in Cape May. Two blocks to beautiful, sandy beaches, one block to shops and fine restaurants. Guest rooms are air-conditioned, have private baths, TV, and comfortably sleep two to four. Decor is country, with relaxed family atmosphere. Delicious breakfasts and afternoon tea time. Three pet cats to fill your laps. Open year round. Families welcome.

Hosts: Greg and Debby Burow
Rooms: 4 (PB) $160-190
Breakfast
Credit Cards: A, B, D
Notes: 2, 5, 7, 8, 9, 10, 12

The Wooden Rabbit Inn

EDGEWATER PARK/BEVERLY

Historic Whitebriar Bed and Breakfast

1029 Cooper Street, 08010
(609) 871-3859

Historic Whitebriar is a German Salt Box style home that has been added on to many times since it was the home of John Fitch, Steam Ship Inventory 1787. The latest addition is an English Conservatory, built in Beverly, England, from a 200-year-old design and shipped to Beverly, New Jersey, just a few years ago. The Conservatory is on the east side of the house, and breakfast is served here overlooking the season pool and spa. Whitebriar is a living history farm with animals to be tended, and guests are welcome to collect the eggs, brush the ponies, and pick the raspberries. Located just 30 minutes from historic Philadelphia, three hours from Washington, and one and one half hours from The Big Apple, just off interstates.

Hosts: Carole and Bill Moore
Rooms: 2 + apartments (SB) $50-85
Full Breakfast
Credit Cards: none
Notes: 2, 5, 6, 7 (additional charge), 9

GLENWOOD

Apple Valley Inn

Corner of Rt. 517 and Rt. 565, PO Box 302, 07418
(210) 764-3735

Elegantly appointed B&B in the early American tradition. Colonial mansion circa 1831. Pool, trout stream, apple orchard, antique shop, Old Grist Mill, skiing, water-park, Appalachian Trail, West Point, NJ, Botanical Gardens, two state parks, and Hudson Valley attractions within a short drive. Holidays. Two night minimum. Reduced rates for six plus day stay. Special events weekends.

Hostess: Mitzi Durham
Rooms: 7 (2PB; 5SB) $70-90
Full Breakfast
Credit Cards: none
Notes: 2, 3 (picnic), 5, 7 (over 13), 8, 9 (on-site), 10, 11, 12

---

5 Open all year; 6 Pets welcome; 7 Children welcome; 8 Tennis nearby; 9 Swimming nearby; 10 Golf nearby; 11 Skiing nearby; 12 May be booked through travel agent.

HADDONFIELD

Queen Anne Inn

44 West End Avenue, 08033
(609) 428-2195

The only accommodations in South Jersey within walking distance to the high-speed train line (17 minutes to center city Philadelphia, less to the Aquarium or Rutgers Camden). No car required. Close to Philadelphia Airport. Walk to shops and restaurants. Stay in this fully restored Victorian (on the National Register) in elegant residential neighborhood. Relax on big beautiful porch or in the common rooms. Fully air-conditioned, cable TV, and phones.

Hosts: Nancy Lynn/Fred Charpita
Rooms: 8 (3PB; 5SB) $79-99
Continental Plus Breakfast
Credit Cards: A, B, C, D
Notes: 2, 5, 8, 9, 10, 12

NEWTON

The Wooden Duck

140 Goodale Road, 07860
(201) 300-0395; FAX (201) 300-0141

The Wooden Duck is a secluded, 17-acre mini-estate about an hour's drive from New York City. Located on a country road in rural Sussex County, it is close to antiques, golf, the Delaware Water Gap, Waterloo Village, and winter sports. The rooms are spacious with private baths, television, VCR, phone, and desks. There is central air-conditioning, an in-ground pool, game room, and living room with see-through fireplaces. Antique furnishings and reproductions. Biking and hiking are at the doorstep with a 1,000-acre state park across the street and a "Rails to Trails" (abandoned railway maintained for hiking and biking) running behind the property. Wildlife abounds in the area.

Hosts: Bob and Barbara Hadden
Rooms: 5 (PB) $90-110
Full Breakfast
Credit Cards: A, B, C, D
Notes: 2, 5, 8, 9, 10, 11

Delancey Manor

OCEAN CITY

Delancey Manor

869 Delancey Place, 08226
(609) 398-9831

A turn-of-the-century summer house just 100 yards to a great beach and our 2.45 mile boardwalk. Summer fun for families and friends at "America's greatest family resort." Two breezy porches with ocean view. Walk to restaurants, boardwalk fun, and the Tabernacle with its renowned speakers. Located in a residential neighborhood

---

NOTES: Credit cards accepted: A Master Card; B Visa; C American Express; D Discover; E Diners Club; F Other; 2 Personal checks accepted; 3 Lunch available; 4 Dinner available;

in a dry town. Larger family rooms available. Breakfast optional for a small charge. Advance reservations recommended.

Hosts: Stewart and Pam Heisler
Rooms: 7 (3PB; 4SB) $45-75
Expanded Continental Breakfast
Credit Cards: none
Notes: 2, 7, 8, 9, 10

New Brighton Inn

519 Fifth Street, 08226
(609) 399-2829; FAX (609) 398-7786

This charming 1880 Queen Anne Victorian has been magnificently restored to its original beauty. All rooms and common areas (living room, library and, sun porch) are elegantly and comfortably furnished with antiques. The front veranda is furnished with rockers and a large swing. Rates include beach tags and use of bicycles.

Hosts: Daniel and Donna Hand
Rooms: 6 (PB) $85-115
Full Breakfast
Credit Cards: A, B, C, D
Notes: 2, 8, 9, 10

Ocean City Guest and Apartment House
Referral Service

Ocean City Guest and Apartment House Referral Service

PO Box 356, 08226
(609) 399-8894 (9AM to 9PM)

An association of 30 apartment, B&B, and guest home owners will provide you with a free brochure or our telephone referral service. A wide range of accommodations throughout Ocean City, NJ, "America's greatest family resort," from the beach to the bay to the boardwalk. Call or write us for information.

Scarborough Inn "An 1895 Bed and Breakfast"

720 Ocean Avenue, 08226
(609) 399-1558; (800) 258-1558;
FAX (609) 399-4472

The Scarborough Inn, invitingly adorned in colors of wedgewood, rose, and soft creme, lends its special character to the neighborhood where it stands, just one and one half short blocks from the Atlantic Ocean. The Scarborough affords visitors a vacation residence reminiscent of an old-fashioned European-style inn—small enough to be intimate, yet large enough to offer privacy. Featured in *Country Inns* magazine.

Hosts: Gus and Carol Bruno
Rooms: 26 (PB) $70-120
Continental Plus Breakfast
Credit Cards: A, B, C, D
Notes: 7, 8, 9, 10, 12

5 Open all year; 6 Pets welcome; 7 Children welcome; 8 Tennis nearby; 9 Swimming nearby; 10 Golf nearby; 11 Skiing nearby; 12 May be booked through travel agent.

OCEAN GROVE

Cordova

26 Webb Avenue, 07756
(908) 774-3084 (summer); (212) 751-9577
(winter); FAX (212) 207-4720

Ocean Grove was founded as a religious
retreat center at the turn of the century.
This flavor has lasted in the quiet,
peaceful atmosphere. Constant religious
programs for the family, as well as
popular music, are arranged in the 7,000
seat Great Auditorium. The Cordova
has "Old World" charm. Rooms are furnished with antiques. Friendliness, hospitality, cleanliness, and quiet one block
from the magnificent white sand beach
and boardwalk. The Cordova was recently featured in the travel guide, "O'
New Jersey." Also listed in the *New
Jersey* magazine as one of the "Seven
best on the Jersey shore." The porches
have an ocean view. Call about the
"Murder Mystery" weekends. Midweek
specials; also seven nights for the price
of five. Saturday night refreshments.

Hostess: Doris Chernik
Rooms: 15 (5PB; 10SB) $45-80
Continental Breakfast
Credit Cards: none
Notes: 2, 7, 8, 9, 12

PRINCETON

Bed and Breakfast
of Princeton

PO Box 571, 08542
(609) 924-3189; FAX (609) 921-6271
Internet: 71035.757@compuserve.com

BBOP offers "homestay" accommodations in a small group of private homes.
Some accommodations are within walking distance of the town center while
others are minutes away by automobile
or public transportation. Most homes
are non-smoking. Rate begin at $40
single and $50 double occupancy and
include a continental breakfast. There
is a two-night minimum stay require-
ment. John Hurley, coordinator.

Hamilton House Inn

SPRING LAKE

Hamilton
House Inn

15 Mercer Avenue, 07762
(908) 449-8282; FAX (908) 449-0206

The aroma of fresh-baked bread beckons you to our cheery dining room for
full breakfast served at intimate tables.
Sip iced tea by our backyard pool, enjoy the ocean view from out front porch,
stroll the boardwalk, or spend the day
on the white sandy beaches of the Atlantic just a few steps away. Relax in
our spacious parlor—central air in summer and the warmth of cozy fireplaces

---

NOTES: Credit cards accepted: A Master Card; B Visa; C American Express; D Discover;
E Diners Club; F Other; 2 Personal checks accepted; 3 Lunch available; 4 Dinner available;

during cooler seasons. Hospitality in the Old World tradition.

Hosts: Bud and Anne Benz
Rooms: 8 (PB) $95-225
Full Breakfast
Credit Cards: A, B, C, D, E
Notes: 2, 5, 8, 9 (on premises), 10

White Lilac Inn

414 Central Avenue, 07762
(908) 449-0211

White Lilac Inn

We are shore region! The White Lilac Inn, circa 1888, with its triple-tiered porches, reflects the graciousness of a Southern style that allows guests to relax and enjoy the simple life of an earlier time. Sit by the fire and enjoy friendly hospitality. Breakfast is full, leisurely, homemade, and served at tables for two in our Garden Room and enclosed porch. Come discover the romance at the end of each day.

Host: Mari Kennelly Slocum
Rooms: 10 (8PB; 2SB) $79-109 off-season;
$99-139 in-season
Full Breakfast served 8:30-10AM
Credit Cards: A, B, C, D
Closed January 1st through February 10th
Notes: 2, 7 (14 and older), 8, 9, 10, 12 (Innviews)

---

5 Open all year; 6 Pets welcome; 7 Children welcome; 8 Tennis nearby; 9 Swimming nearby; 10 Golf nearby; 11 Skiing nearby; 12 May be booked through travel agent.

NEW MEXICO

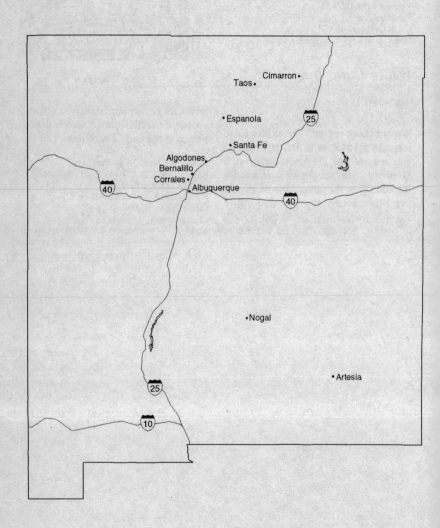

New Mexico

Mi Casa Su Casa Bed and Breakfast Reservation Service

PO Box 950, **Tempe**, AZ 85280-0950
(602) 990-0682; (800) 456-0682 (reservations);
FAX (602) 990-3390

Over 160 inspected and approved homestays, guest cottages, ranches, and inns in Arizona, Utah, New Mexico, and Nevada. In **Arizona**, listings include Ajo, Apache Junction, Bisbee, Cave Creek, Clarkdale, Dragoon, Flagstaff, Mesa, Page, Patagonia, Payson, Pinetop, Phoenix, Prescott, Scottsdale, Sedona, Sierra Vista, Tempe, Tombstone, Tucson, Yuma, and other cities. In **New Mexico**, we have included Albuquerque, Algodones, Chimayo, Los Cruces, Silver City, Sante Fe, and Taos. In **Utah**, listings include Moab, Monroe, Salt Lake City, Springdale, St. George, and Tropic. In **Nevada**, we list Las Vegas. Rooms with private and shared baths range from $40-175. Credit cards welcomed. Full or continental breakfast. A book with individual descriptions, rates, and pictures is available for $9.50. Ruth Young, coordinator.

ALBUQUERQUE

Bottger Mansion Bed and Breakfast in Old Town

110 San Felipe NW, 87104
(505) 243-3639 (voice and FAX)

Walk to everything! Museums, galleries, fine restaurants, historic structures and sights, plus unlimited shopping. Experience a stay in a historic, elegant Victorian. Seven gracious bedrooms all have private baths, one jacuzzi. Relax in shaded grass and marble courtyards, and enjoy our 24-hour soda fountain and coffee/tea bar. Wake up each morning to a full specialty breakfast, and look forward to our evening social hour with wine and hors d'oeuvres.

Hostesses: Patsy Garcia and Jo Ivey
Rooms: 7 (PB) $89-129
Full Breakfast
Credit Cards: A, B, C
Notes: 2, 5, 7, 8, 9, 10, 11, 12

NOTES: Credit cards accepted: A Master Card; B Visa; C American Express; D Discover; E Diners Club; F Other; 2 Personal checks accepted; 3 Lunch available; 4 Dinner available; 5 Open all year; 6 Pets welcome; 7 Children welcome; 8 Tennis nearby; 9 Swimming nearby; 10 Golf nearby; 11 Skiing nearby; 12 May be booked through travel agent.

Enchanted Vista Bed and Breakfast

10700 Del Rey NE, 87122
(505) 823-1301

A southwest villa on a one-acre estate, totally fenced for privacy with parking in rear by private entrance to all suites. Spacious suites with decks and verandas that offer spectacular views. Continental breakfast served at your convenience in your suite. Suites include micro-kitchens, perfect for extended stays. Just 20 minutes from airport and 45 minutes to Sante Fe. Just minutes from ski slopes, and only five minutes from the "tram."

Hosts: Tillie and Al Gonzales
Rooms: 2 (PB) $62-74
Continental Breakfast
Credit Cards: none
Notes: 2, 3, 5, 6, 7, 8, 9, 10, 11, 12

ALGODONES/SANTA FE

Hacienda Vargas Bed and Breakfast Inn

PO Box 307 (1431 E. Camino Real) 87001
(505) 867-9115; (800) 261-0006;
FAX (505) 867-1902

Located on the historic El Camino Real, Hacienda Vargas occupies a site of historical significance in the saga of New Mexico. It has been a stagecoach stop, an Indian trading post, and U.S. Post Office. During the renovation great care was taken to preserve the original structure. The oldest part dates to the 1840s. The Inn has two bedrooms and five suites with private entrances, baths, and fireplaces. Four suites have jacuzzi tubs. A large barbecue area and hot tub available for guests' enjoyment. A full country breakfast is served in the main dining room. Conviently located in the village of Algodones, approximately 30 minutes south of Santa Fe and 15 minutes north of Albuquerque. The innkeepers are well-traveled, former bankers who speak Spanish. AAA three diamond rated.

Hosts: Paul and Jule De Vargas
Rooms: 2 + 5 suites (PB) $79-139
Full Breakfast
Credit Cards: A, B
Notes: 5, 7 (over 12), 8, 9, 10, 11, 12

Heritage Inn

ARTESIA

Heritage Inn

209 W. Main, 88210
(505) 748-2552; (800) 594-7392;
FAX (505) 746-3407

New country/Victorian atmosphere will take you back in time and warm your heart and soul. Spacious rooms with private baths, room phones, color TV, continental breakfast, computer modem hookups for business travelers and out-

---

NOTES: Credit cards accepted: A Master Card; B Visa; C American Express; D Discover; E Diners Club; F Other; 2 Personal checks accepted; 3 Lunch available; 4 Dinner available;

side patio and deck for relaxation. Very secure second floor, downtown location convenient to excellent restaurants. Smoke free. No pets. AAA three diamond rated.

Hosts: James and Wanda Maupin
Rooms: 8 (PB) $55
Continental Breakfast
Credit Cards: A, B, C, D
Notes: 5, 9, 10

BERNALILLO

La Hacienda Grande

21 Baros Lane, 87004
(505) 867-1887; (800) 353-1887;
FAX (505) 867-4621
Email: lhg@swcp.com
http:\\www.vwa.com\nm\lahaci..html

At La Hacienda Grande, a 1996 *Country Inns* choice for "Top 6 Best Buys" and "Top 24 Inns in the US," offers Southwestern casual elegance in a magnificent 250 year old Spanish hacienda built around a central courtyard. Originally it was part of a Spanish land-grant of 100 square miles given to Elena Gallegos in 1711. It later became one of the first stagecoach stops between Albuquerque and Sante Fe. Today it has been fully restored while maintaining all the charm of two-foot thick adobe walls, wood ceilings, and floors of tile, stone, or brick. The guest rooms are very well appointed with handmade furnishings and original artwork. We offer a full gourmet breakfast, and coffee is served to your room at wake up. Afternoon refreshments are available. We offer romance packages with intimate dinners for two by pre-arrangement, and

massage therapy by appointment. We are available for weddings, family reunions, retreats, business meetings, parties, and special luncheons, picnics, receptions and company Christmas parties. AAA three diamond rated.

Hostess: Shoshana Zimmerman
Rooms: 6 (PB) $89-109 (subject to change)
Full Breakfast
Credit Cards: A, B, C
Notes: 4 (by arrangement), 5, 6 (limited), 7, 9, 10, 11, 12

CIMARRON

Casa Del Gavilan

Highway 21 South, PO Box 518, 87714
(505) 376-2246; (800) GAVILAN;
FAX (505) 376-2247

A place of spirit where hawk and eagle soar. Secluded turn-of-the-century adobe villa nestled in the foothills of the Sangre de Cristo Mountains. Enjoy elegant hospitality and breathtaking views in a historic setting. Four guest rooms with private baths, plus a two-room suite. In the shadow of the Tooth of Time, the Casa is adjacent to Philmont Scout Ranch and the Santa Fe Trail. Villa Vidale recreation area, Kit Carson's home and several fine museums are nearby. Eagle Nest Lake, Angel Fire and Red River ski resorts, and Taos are all within easy driving distance.

Hosts: Bob and Helen Hittle
Rooms: 4 + suite (PB) $ 70-100
Full Breakfast
Credit Cards: A, B, C, D
Notes: 2, 5, 7, 12

---

5 Open all year; 6 Pets welcome; 7 Children welcome; 8 Tennis nearby; 9 Swimming nearby; 10 Golf nearby; 11 Skiing nearby; 12 May be booked through travel agent.

CORRALES

Corrales Inn
Bed and Breakfast

58 Perea Road, PO Box 1361, 87048
(505) 897-4422; (800) 897-4410;
FAX (505) 890-5244

Southwestern Territorial, large library/ living room with fireplace invites guests to peruse 2,000 volumes of regional travel and art books. Colorful Southwestern art, Navajo rugs, pueblo pottery, and Mexican collectibles immerse the visitor in New Mexico's diversity. Six distinctively decorated rooms with private baths, individual heating and cooling, and TV. Courtyard with flowers, fountain, hot tub, and hummingbirds; afternoon snacks; port or sherry in library; and "wonder-full" breakfasts. 200 yards to restaurants, galleries, and shops. Walk past apple orchards, horse farms, and ancient adobes to the cottonwood forests of Rio Grande.

Hosts: Pat and Ron Moffat
Rooms: 6 (PB) $75-85
Full Breakfast
Credit Cards: A, B, C
Notes: 2, 5, 8, 9, 10, 11, 12

Corrales Inn

ESPANOLA

The Inn
of La Mesilla

Rt. 1, Box 368A, 87532
(505) 753-5368 (voice and FAX)

Beautiful Pueblo style home, the Inn is rural elegance in the heart of the Eight Northern Indian Pueblos and high on a hill with fabulous views. Quiet. Full breakfast and afternoon tea. Hot tub jacuzzi on large redwood deck with views. Two rooms both with private full bath, color TVs, and ceiling fans. 23 miles to downtown Sante Fe. Two English Springer Spaniels; Pork Chop and Te-Bon!!

Hostess: Yolanda F. Hoemann (Pork Chop and Te-Bon)
Rooms: 2 (PB) $80 (include tax)
Full Breakfast
Credit Cards: none
Notes: 2

NOGAL

Monjeau Shadows

HC 67, Box 87, 88341
(505) 336-4191

Four-level Victorian farmhouse located on ten acres of beautiful, landscaped grounds. Picnic area, nature trails. King and queen beds; honeymoon suite. Furnished with antiques. Just minutes from Lincoln National Park and White Mountain Wilderness. Cross-country skiing, fishing, and horseback riding. For fun or just relaxing. Enjoy the year-round comfort of Monjeau Shadows.

Hosts: J.R. and Kay Newton
Rooms: 5 (4PB; 1SB) $65-75
Full Breakfast
Credit Cards: A, B
Notes: 2, 5, 7, 9, 10, 11

Alexanders Inn

SANTE FE

Alexanders Inn

529 E. Palace Avenue, 87501
(505) 986-1431; FAX (505) 982-8572

This award-winning historic inn, located near the Plaza and Canyon Road, is lovingly decorated with antiques, lace, stenciling, and fresh flowers. In the morning, savor the aroma of gourmet, fresh-brewed coffee as you snuggle under down comforters. Then treat yourself to our scrumptious breakfast buffet, complete with delicious home-made granola and baked goodies. Relax on the veranda, overlooking our bountiful flower garden, munching on freshly-baked cookies. Enjoy a luxurious soak under the stars in our back-yard hot tub. Personal service is our specialty. When you stay with us you'll experience the warmth of staying with good friends along with all the comforts

of a fine hotel.

Hostess: Carolyn Lee
Rooms: 8 (6PB; 2SB) $75-150
Continental Plus Breakfast
Credit Cards: A, B
Notes: 2, 5, 6, 7, 8, 9, 10, 11, 12

TAOS

Orinda Bed and Breakfast

Box 4451, 81571
(505) 758-8581; (800) 847-1837;
FAX (505) 751-4895
Internet: Orinda.

A 50 year old adobe home, dramatic pastoral setting on two acres. View of Taos Mountains, surrounded by elm and cottonwood trees. Decorated in south-western design. Original art presented in rooms and common areas. Kiva fire-places in suites. Quiet, on a private road, but only 15-minute walk to galleries , plaza, and restaurants.

Hosts: Cary and George Pratt
Rooms: 4 (3PB; 1SB) $70-85
Full Breakfast
Credit Cards: A, B, C, D
Notes: 2, 5, 7, 8, 9, 10, 11, 12

Orinda Bed and Breakfast

---

5 Open all year; 6 Pets welcome; 7 Children welcome; 8 Tennis nearby; 9 Swimming nearby; 10 Golf nearby; 11 Skiing nearby; 12 May be booked through travel agent.

The Willows Inn

NDCBU 6560 (Corner of Kit Carson Road and
Dolan Street) 87571
(505) 758-2558; (800) 525-TAOS (8267);
FAX (505) 758-5445

The Willows Inn is a B&B located on a
secluded acre lot just a short walk to
the Taos Plaza. Listed on the National
Historic Registry, the property was the
home and studio of E. Martin Hennings.
Hennings was a member of the revered
Taos Society of Artists, the group that
established Taos as an artist colony in
the 1920s. Scrumptious, full breakfasts
are served family style in the dining
rooms. Guests enjoy homemade snacks
and beverages in the late afternoon on
the flagstone courtyard in summer or by
the fire in the cooler seasons. Each guest
room has smooth adobe walls with *kiva*
fireplaces, open beam (*viga*) ceilings,

The Willows Inn

and Douglas Fir floors with various
decor themes which highlight cultures
significant to the Taos area. The
grounds and courtyards form a park-like
oasis with flowers, fountains, and two
of America's largest living willow trees.

Hosts: Doug and Janet Camp
Rooms: 5 (PB) $95-130 + tax
Full Breakfast
Credit Cards: A, B
Notes: 2, 5, 7, 9, 10, 11, 12

New York

ALSO SEE RESERVATION SERVICES UNDER NEW JERSEY

American Country Collection of B&B

1353 Union Street, **Schenectady**, 12308
(518) 370-4948

This reservation service provides reservations for eastern **New York**, western **Massachusetts**, and all of **Vermont**. Just one call does it all. Relax and unwind at any of our over 100 immaculate, personally inspected bed and breakfasts and country inns. Many include fireplace, jacuzzi, and/or Modified American Plan. We have budget-minded to luxurious accommodations in urban, suburban, and rural locations. $50-200. Gift certificates available and major credit cards accepted. Carol Matos, coordinator.

ALBION

Friendship Manor

349 S. Main Street, 14411
(716) 589-7973

This historic house, dating back to 1880, is surrounded by lovely roses, an herb garden, and lots of shade trees. A swimming and tennis courts are provided for your pleasure. The intimate interior is an artful blend of Victorian-style furnishings with antiques throughout. Enjoy a breakfast of muffins, breads, fruit, juice, coffee, or tea in the formal dining room served buffet style for your convenience. Friendship Manor is central to Niagara Falls, Buffalo, or Rochester. For traveling through or just a getaway.

Hosts: John and Marylin Baker
Rooms: 4 (1PB; 3SB) $55 + tax
Continental Plus Breakfast
Credit Cards: none
Notes: 2, 5, 7, 10

AVERILL PARK

Ananas Hus Bed and Breakfast

148 South Road, 12018
(518) 766-5035

The Tomlinsons invite you to share the beautiful, tranquil, smoke-free, and pet-free environment of their hillside home on 30 acres with a panoramic view of the Hudson River Valley. Ananas Hus serves breakfast by the fireplace in win-

---

5 Open all year; 6 Pets welcome; 7 Children welcome; 8 Tennis nearby; 9 Swimming nearby;
10 Golf nearby; 11 Skiing nearby; 12 May be booked through travel agent.

NEW YORK

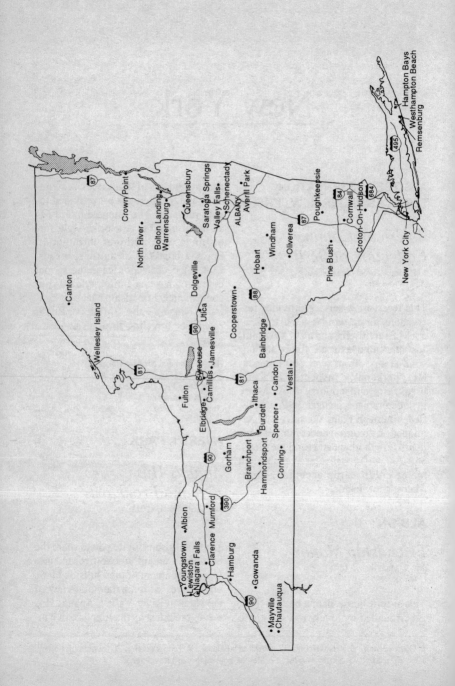

ter and, weather permitting, under the roofed patio. If it becomes necessary on days of high humidity, the air-conditioning is turned on. Ananas Hus rests 8/10 of a mile off Rout 43 on County Road 23 in West Stephenton, convenient to Western Massachusetts and the Capitol District of New York state, which abounds with cultural, natural, historical, and sports attractions. Great ski country—both cross-country and down hill.

Hosts: Clyde H. Tomlinson and Thelma Olsen
    Tomlinson
Rooms: 3 (SB) $60
Full Homemade Breakfast
Credit Cards: C
Notes: 2, 5, 7 (over 12), 9, 10, 11, 12

Ananas Hus Bed and Breakfast

BAINBRIDGE

Berry Hill Gardens Bed and Breakfast

RD 1, Box 128, Ward-Loomis Road, 13733
(607) 967-8745 (voice and FAX);
(800) 497-8745

This restored 1820s farmhouse on a hilltop is surrounded by extensive herb and perennial gardens and 180 acres where you can hike, swim, bird-watch, skate, cross-country ski, or sit on the wraparound porch and watch nature parade. Our rooms are furnished with comfortable antiques. A ten-minute drive takes you to restaurants, golf, tennis, auctions, and antique centers. You can also buy plants, dried flowers, and wreaths grown and hand-crafted on the farm to take home with you. Cooperstown and most local colleges are only 45 minutes away. Three hours to New York City.

Hosts: Jean Fowler and Cecilio Rios
Rooms: 1 (pB) $95
Full Breakfast
Credit Cards: A, B, C
Notes: 2, 5, 7, 8, 9, 10, 11, 12

BOLTON LANDING

Hilltop Cottage Bed and Breakfast

PO Box 186 Lakeshore Drive, 12814
(518) 644-2492

A clean, comfortable, renovated farmhouse is near Lake George in the beautiful eastern Adirondack Mountains. Walk to beaches, restaurants, and marinas. Enjoy a quiet, home atmosphere with hearty breakfasts. In the summer, this is a busy resort area. Autumn offers fall foliage, hiking, skiing. There is a wood-burning stove for use in winter. A brochure is available.

Hosts: Anita and Charles Richards
Rooms: 4 (2PB; 2SB) $50-70
Full Breakfast
Credit Cards: A, B
Notes: 2, 5

NOTES: Credit cards accepted: A Master Card; B Visa; C American Express; D Discover; E Diners Club; F Other; 2 Personal checks accepted; 3 Lunch available; 4 Dinner available; 5 Open all year; 6 Pets welcome; 7 Children welcome; 8 Tennis nearby; 9 Swimming nearby; 10 Golf nearby; 11 Skiing nearby; 12 May be booked through travel agent.

BURDETT

The Red House Country Inn

4586 Picnic Area Road, 14818-9716
(607) 546-8566; FAX (607) 546-4105 (call first)
Email: redhsinn@aol.com

The Inn is located in the beautiful 13,000-acre Finger Lakes National Forest with 28 miles of maintained hiking and cross-country ski trails. Six award winning wineries are within ten minutes from the completely restored 1840s farmstead on five acres of groomed lawns and flower gardens. Enjoy beautifully appointed rooms, country breakfasts, in-ground pool, and a fully equipped kitchen. Twelve minutes from Ithaca; 30 minutes from Corning.

Hostesses: Joan Martin and Sandy Schmanke
Rooms: 5 (SB) $60-85
Full Breakfast
Credit Cards: A, B, C, D
Notes: 2, 4 (Nov-Apr), 5, 7 (over 12), 8, 9 (on premises), 10, 11, 12

CAMILLUS

The Re Family Bed and Breakfast

4166 Split Rock Road, 13031
(315) 468-2039

100 year old early American farmhouse featuring log-style den, country kitchen, side deck utilized for fair weather breakfasts, 40-foot pool, lawns, two guest rooms with queen-size brass beds and orthopedic mattresses, and pedestal sink in each room. Next to garden-style bathroom with walk-in tile shower, vanity

with double sinks, and full-mirrored back wall. Also one room with full bed and captain's bed for two singles or for children. Stress-free environment close to Syracuse.

Hosts: Joseph and Terry Re
Rooms: 3 (SB) $55-75
Continental Breakfast
Credit Cards: none
Notes: 2, 5, 7, 8, 9, 10, 11, 12

CANDOR

The Edge of Thyme, A Bed and Breakfast Inn

6 Main Street, PO Box 48, 13743
(607) 659-5155; (800) 722-7365 (out of NY)

Featured in Historic Inns of the Northeast. Located in this quiet rural village is a large gracious Georgian home—leaded glass windowed porch, marble fireplaces, period sitting rooms, gardens, and pergola. Epicurean breakfast served in genteel manner. Central to Cornell, Ithaca College, Corning, Elmira, Watkins Glen, and wineries. Gift Shoppe; High Tea by appointment.

Hosts: Eva Mae and Frank Musgrave
Rooms: 4 + a suite (3PB; 2SB) $65-125
Full Breakfast
Credit Cards: A, B
Notes: 2, 5, 7 (well-behaved), 8, 9, 10, 11 (cross-country), 12

The Edge of Thyme

NOTES: Credit cards accepted: A Master Card; B Visa; C American Express; D Discover; E Diners Club; F Other; 2 Personal checks accepted; 3 Lunch available; 4 Dinner available;

White Pillars Bed and Breakfast

CANTON

White Pillars Bed and Breakfast

395 Old State Road, PO Box 185, 13630
(315) 386-2353 (voice and FAX);
(800) 261-6292

Experience classic antiquity and modern living in this beautifully renovated 1850s homestead. Guest room luxuries include whirlpool tub, marble floor, air-conditioning, cable TV, and expansive windows, overlooking 100 acres of meadows. This quiet rural setting is only six miles from Canton, the county seat and home of several colleges. Summer guests are invited to use the facilities of their hosts' seven-acre trout lake, 20 minutes away, for swimming, canoeing, and fishing.

Hosts: John and Donna Clark
Rooms: 4 (2PB; 2SB) $50-65
Full Breakfast
Credit Cards: A, B, C
Notes: 2, 5, 7, 8, 9, 10, 11, 12

CLARENCE

Asa Ransom House

10529 Main Street, (Route 5), 14031
(716) 759-2315; FAX (716) 759-2791

Warmth, comfort, and hospitality are our main attractions. Nine guest rooms have antique and period furnishings, seven of these have fireplaces. Many rooms have a porch or balcony. We also have a library, gift shop, and herb garden on a two acre lot in the village. The original building housing the library, gift shop, and tap room dates back to 1853, built by Asa Ransom who received the land from the Holland Land Company in 1799.

Hosts: Robert Lenz; Judy Lenz
Rooms: 9 (PB) $85-145
Full Breakfast
Credit Cards: A, B, D
Closed January
Notes: 2, 4, 7, 8, 9, 10

COOPERSTOWN

Berrywick II

RD 2, Box 486, 13326
(607) 547-2052

Located six miles from Cooperstown, home of the Baseball Hall of Fame, the Farmer's Museum, and the New York State Historical Association—Fenimore House and the Glimmerglass Opera House. All beautifully situated around nine mile long Otsego Lake. Berrywick II is a renovated 19th century farmhouse with separate entrance for guests to con-

---

5 Open all year; 6 Pets welcome; 7 Children welcome; 8 Tennis nearby; 9 Swimming nearby; 10 Golf nearby; 11 Skiing nearby; 12 May be booked through travel agent.

verted, two-bedroom apartment. Queen, double, and twin-bedded rooms with kitchen/sitting room and bath perfectly suited for a couple of couples or families with well-behaved children. Sorry, no pets and no smoking.

Hosts: Helen and Jack Weber
Rooms: 3 (1SB) $75
Continental or Full Breakfast
Credit Cards: none
Notes: 2, 5, 7, 9, 10

1865 White Birch Bed and Breakfast

CORNING

1865 White Birch Bed and Breakfast

69 E. First Street, 14830
(607) 962-6355

The White Birch, Victorian in structure but decorated in country, has a been refurbished to show off its winding staircase, hardwood floors, and wall window in the dining room that overlooks the backyards. We are located in a residential area, two blocks from restored historic Market Street and six blocks from the Corning Museum of Glass. A warm fire during the colder months welcomes guests in the common room where TV and great conversation are available. A full, gourmet breakfast is served each morning.

Hosts: Kathy and Joe Donahue
Rooms: 4 (2PB; 2SB) $65-80
Full Home-baked Breakfast
Credit Cards: A, B, C
Notes: 2, 5, 7, 8, 9, 10, 11 (cross-country)

Delevan House

188 Delevan Avenue, 14830
(607) 962-2347

This Southern Colonial house sits on a hill overlooking Corning. It is charming, graceful, and warm in quiet surroundings. Delicious breakfast served from 8-9 AM. Check-in time 3 PM, check-out time 10:30 am. Free transportation from airport. Two minutes from Market Street and Glass Center by car. TV in all rooms. Very private. Enjoy a cool refreshment on lovely screened-in porch.

Hostess: Mary M. De Pumpo
Rooms: 3 (1PB; 1½SB) $65-85
Full Breakfast
Credit Cards: none
Notes: 2, 5, 7 (over 10), 10, 11, 12

CORNWALL

Cromwell Manor Inn

Angola Road, 12518
(914) 534-7136

Built in 1820, Cromwell Manor Inn is a fully-restored, romantic, country estate. Set on seven landscaped acres overlooking a 4,000-acre, mountain, forest preserve. The 6,000 square foot manor is fully furnished with period antiques and fine furnishings. Enjoy a full breakfast served on the veranda, or in our country breakfast room, at your own private table. 1764 restored cottage is also available for larger groups; sleeps eight. We are located 55 minutes north of New York City and five miles from historic West Point. Fireplaces and romance. Visit nearby wineries, restorations, Woodbury Commons, and hike the majestic Hudson Valley.

Hosts: Dale and Brenda Ohara
Rooms: 13 (12PB; 1SB) $120-150;
Suites: $220-250
Full-Served Breakfast
Credit Cards: A, B
Notes: 5, 8, 9, 10, 11, 12

Cromwell Manor Inn

CROTON-ON-HUDSON

Alexander Hamilton House

49 Van Wyck Street, 10520
(914) 271-6737; FAX (914) 271-3927

The Alexander Hamilton House, circa 1889, is a sprawling Victorian home situated on a cliff overlooking the Hudson. The home has many period antiques and collections and offers a queen bedded suite with fireplaced sitting room, two large rooms with queen beds (one with an additional daybed),

and a bridal chamber with king bed, jacuzzi, entertainment center, pink marble fireplace, and lots of skylights. The master suite, with queen bed, fireplace, picture windows, stained glass, full entertainment center, jacuzzi, skylight, and winding river views was furnished last year. A one bedroom apartment with double bed, living room and kitchen on one wall, private bath, and separate entrance is also available for longer stays. Nearby attractions include West Point, the Sleepy Hollow Restorations, Lyndhurst, Boscobel, the Rockefeller mansion, hiking, biking, and sailing. New York City under an hour away by train or car. No smoking or pets. All rooms have air conditioning, private bath, cable TV, and phone. Off-street parking. Weekly and monthly rates available on request. Credit card guarantee required. Seven day cancellation policy.

Hostess: Barbara Notarius
Rooms: 7 (PB) $95-250 + tax and gratuity
Full Breakfast
Credit Cards: A, B, C, D
Notes: 2, 5, 7, 9, 10, 12

CROWN POINT

Crown Point B&B "The Wyman House"

Route 9N, Main Street., PO Box 490, 12928
(518) 597-3651; FAX (518) 597-4451

The "Wyman House" is an elegant "painted lady," Victorian Manor house on five and one half acres. Its gracious interior is filled with period antiques. Each of five bed chambers is distinctively decorated and has its own ambiance and private bath. The house boasts

5 Open all year; 6 Pets welcome; 7 Children welcome; 8 Tennis nearby; 9 Swimming nearby; 10 Golf nearby; 11 Skiing nearby; 12 May be booked through travel agent.

woodwork panels of six types of wood. Outside there are three porches and a fountain amidst blooming gardens. Breakfast is all homemade. Near Lake Champlain, the area has museums, historical sites, and antiques.

Hosts: Hugh and Sandy Johnson
Rooms: 5 (PB) $60-120
Continental Plus Breakfast
Credit Cards: A, B
Notes: 2, 5, 7, 8, 9, 10, 11, 12

DOLGEVILLE

Adrianna B&B

44 Stewart Street, 13329
(315) 429-3249; (800) 335-4233

Rural, Little Falls area near I-90 exit 29A. Cozy residence blending antique and contemporary furnishings. Convenient to Saratoga, Cooperstown, historic sites, and snowmobile, cross-country and hiking trails. Four guest rooms, two with private bath; full breakfast. Smoking restricted. Air-conditioning.

Hostess: Adrianna Naizby
Rooms: 3 (1PB; 2SB) $55-65 + tax
Full Breakfast
Credit Cards: A, B
Notes: 2, 5, 6 (well-behaved), 7 (over 5), 9, 10, 11, 12

FULTON

Battle Island Inn

2167 State Route 48, 13069
(315) 593-3699

Battle Island Inn is a pre-Civil War farm estate that has been restored and furnished with period antiques. The Inn is across the road from a golf course that also provides cross-country skiing. Guest rooms are elegantly furnished with imposing high back beds, TVs, phones, and private baths. Breakfast is always special in the 1840s dining room.

Hosts: Richard and Joyce Rice
Rooms: 5 (PB) $60-85
Full Breakfast
Credit Cards: A, B, C, D
Notes: 2, 5, 7, 10, 11

The Gorham House

GORHAM

The Gorham House

PO Box 43, 4752 E. Swamp Road, 14461-0043
(719) 526-4402

Built before the turn of the century, this 14-room country Colonial-style farmhouse is decorated with family treasures and special finds. You will never forget: The two elegant common rooms. The intimate library and its cozy parlor divided by large pocket doors. Spacious, beautifully-appointed guest rooms each have their own seating and reading areas. The kitchen contains a large collection of advertising tins, while the eat-in pantry features framed Cream of Wheat advertisements from the 1900s. Warm yourself by the wood stove after skiing. Walk the five acres and explore the many different wildflowers, berry bushes, fruit trees, and Nancy's herb garden. Relax on one of three porches.

Hosts: Nancy and Al Rebmann
Rooms: 4 (1PB; 3SB) $60-80
Credit Cards: none
Notes: 2, 5, 7 (over 12), 8, 9, 10, 11, 12

GOWANDA

The TEEPEE

14396 Four Mile Level Road, 14070
(716) 532-2168

The TEEPEE is operated by full-blooded Seneca Indians on the Cattaraugus Indian Reservation. Max is of the Turtle Clan and Phyllis is of the Wolf Clan. Tours of the reservation are available and also tours of the nearby Amish community. Good base when visiting Niagara Falls.

Hosts: Phyllis and Max Lay
Rooms: 4 (SB) $50
Full Breakfast
Credit Cards: none
Notes: 2, 5, 7, 8, 9, 10, 11

HAMBURG

Sharon's Lake House Bed and Breakfast

4862 Lakeshore Road, 14075
(716) 627-7561

Built on the shore of Lake Erie, both rooms and sitting room offer a magnificent view of Buffalo city skyline and the Canadian border only fifteen minutes west of the city. Rooms are new and beautifully decorated with waterfront view. All prepared food is gourmet quality style. New hot tub room and widow's watch overlooking Lake Erie available. Reservations and two night minimum stay required.

Hostess: Sharon DiMaria
Rooms: 2 (1PB; 1SB) $55-110
Full Gourmet Breakfast
Credit Cards: none
Notes: 2, 3, 4, 5, 7 (by reservation), 9, 10, 11

Gone With the Wind on Keuka Lake

HAMMONDSPORT

Gone With the Wind on Keuka Lake

453 W. Lake Road, **Branchport,** 14418
(607) 868-4603

The name paints the picture—1887 stone Victorian, on 14 acres overlooking our quiet lake cove adorned by an inviting picnic gazebo. Feel the magic of total relaxation and peace of mind in the solarium hot tub; gather your gifts of imagination on our nature trails; unlock your creative powers to see your dreams accomplished. Fireplaces, delectable breakfasts, private beach and dock. Reserve "The Sequel," a log haven, for small retreats, gatherings, or business meetings. One hour south of Rochester in the Fingerlakes on New York.

Hosts: Linda and Robert Lewis
Rooms: 6; $75-125
Full Breakfast
Credit Cards: none
Notes: 2, 5, 8, 9, 10, 11

HAMPTON BAYS

House on the Water

Box 106; 11946
(516) 728-3560

Quiet waterfront residence in Hampton Bays surrounded by two acres of gardens on Shinnecock Bay. A pleasant neighborhood on a peninsula, good for jogging and walking. Two miles to ocean beaches. Seven miles to Southampton. Kitchen facilities, bicycles, boats, lounges, and umbrellas. A full breakfast from 8 am to 12 pm is served on the terrace overlooking the water. Watch the boats and swans go by. Adults only. No pets. Rooms have water views and private baths and entrances. German, French, and Spanish spoken.

Hostess: Mrs. UTE
Rooms: 3 (2PB; 1SB) $75-95 (less off-season, midweek, and specials)
Full Breakfast
Credit Cards: none
Notes: 2, 8, 9, 10, 12 (10%)

HOBART

Breezy Acres Farm Bed and Breakfast

R.D. 1, Box 191, 13788
(607) 538-9338

For a respite from your busy, stressful lives, come visit us. We offer cozy accommodations with private bath in our circa 1830's farmhouse. You'll awaken refreshed to wonderful aromas from the kitchen. A full, homemade breakfast will be served to you while you plan your day. You could spend a week here leisurely exploring the museums, Howe Caverns, and Baseball Hall of Fame; leaving some time each day to roam our 300 acres, or to sit in a wicker swing on our old-fashioned pillared porches soaking in the view of meadows, pastures, and rolling hills. Or make use of golfing, tennis, fishing, and skiing facilities; all nearby.

Hosts: Joyce and David Barber
Rooms: 3 (PB) $60-75
Full Homemade Breakfast
Credit Cards: A, B, C
Notes: 2, 5, 7 (some restrictions), 8, 9, 10, 11

ITHACA

A Slice of Home

178 N. Main Street, **Spencer,** 14883
(607) 589-6073

Newly remodeled,150-year old farmhouse with four bedrooms. Country cooking with hearty breakfasts. Located in the Fingerlakes Winery area just 20 minutes to Ithaca and Watkins Glen.

Hiking, tenting, bicycle tours, and cross-country skiing. Hospitality is our specialty.

Hosts: Beatrice Brownell
Rooms: 4 (1PB; 2SB) $45-75
Full Breakfast
Credit Cards: none
Notes: 2, 5, 6 (outside), 7 (over 12), 12

Log Country Inn Bed and Breakfast of Ithaca

PO Box 581, 14851
(607) 589-4771; (800) 274-4771;
FAX (607) 589-6151

Escape to the rustic charm of a log house at the edge of 7,000 acres of state forest in the Finger Lakes region. Modern accommodations provided in the spirit of international hospitality. Awaken to the sound of birds and explore the peaceful surroundings. Enjoy full Eastern European breakfasts with blintzes or Russian pancakes and comfortable rooms with private baths. Sauna and afternoon tea available during the fall and winter months. Easy access to hiking and cross-country trails. Families with children are welcome and we will also find a place for your pet. Our Inn provides a perfect place for spiritual retreats or family reunions. Cornell University, Ithaca College, Corning Glass Center, wineries, and antique stores close by. Your hostess is a biologist (former profession), and her husband Slawomir is a documentary filmmaker.

Hostess: Wanda Grunberg
Rooms: 3 (1PB; 2SB) $45-65
Full Breakfast
Credit Cards: A, B, C
Notes: 2, 5, 6, 7, 9, 11, 12

JAMESVILLE

High Meadows B&B

3740 Eager Road, 13078
(315) 492-3517

Enjoy country hospitality at High Meadows, high in the hills 10 miles south of Syracuse. We have two guest room with a shared bath, a private suite, and a furnished bedroom apartment. Enjoy a plant-filled solarium, wraparound deck with a magnificient 50-mile view. A continental breakfast, featuring fresh fruit, muffins, and homemade jams, can be served on the deck, weather permitting. Explore scenic, lush Central New York with its many lakes, nature centers, and vineyards.

Hosts: Al and Nancy Mentz
Rooms: 3 + furnished apartment (1PB; 2SB) $55-90
Continental Breakfast
Credit Cards: none
Notes: 2, 5, 7, 9, 10, 11, 12

The Village Inn

MAYVILLE (CHAUTAUQUA)

The Village Inn B&B

111 S. Erie Street (Route 394), 14757
(716) 753-3583

Turn-of-the-century Victorian home located near the shores of Lakes

---

5 Open all year; 6 Pets welcome; 7 Children welcome; 8 Tennis nearby; 9 Swimming nearby; 10 Golf nearby; 11 Skiing nearby; 12 May be booked through travel agent.

Chautauqua and Erie, three miles from Chautauqua Institution, and less than 30-minute drive from Peek'n Peak and Cockaigne ski centers. We offer comfort in both single and double rooms in a home furnished with many antiques and trimmed in woodwork crafted by European artisians. In the morning enjoy a breakfast of homemade waffles, nut kuchen, in-season fruit, coffee, and juice in our sunny breakfast room.

Host: Dean Hanby
Rooms: 3 (3SB) $45-55
Full Breakfast
Credit Cards: C
Notes: 2, 5, 6, 7, 8, 9, 10, 11, 12

MUMFORD

The Genesee Country Inn

948 George Street, 14511
(716) 538-2500; (800) NYSTAYS (reservations only); FAX (716) 538-4565

Classic, but cozy. Historic stone mill. Nine room B&B inn with all private baths, some fireplaces, canopy beds, A/C, and TV. Serenity and privacy just one mile from Genesee Country Village Museum and 30 minutes from downtown. Woods, watherfalls, and trout fishing on the property. Gourmct breakfasts. Recommended by AAA-3, Mobile-3, and Independent Innkeepers Association. No smoking. Pets in residence.

Hostess: Glenda Barcklow
Rooms: 9 (PB) $85-140
Full Breakfast
Credit Cards: A, B, C, D
Notes: 2, 5, 8, 9, 10, 11

NEW YORK

Alma Mathews House

275 W. 11th Street, 10014
(212) 691-5931 or 5932; FAX (212) 727-9746

Alma Mathews House is a pleasant, but inexpensive, guest house/conference center for persons who are in New York for non-profit business. Located in a quiet corner of Greenwich Village, this splendid facility is offered as an act of stewardship by the Women's Division of the General Board of Global Ministries of the Methodist Church. It accommodates up to 35 persons overnight in 19 rooms—12 doubles, six singles, and one sofa couch room. Ideal for meetings—two conference rooms for 35-40 persons each, a common TV lounge, two formal parlors, plus laundry and kitchenette facilities. No meals are served; however, delicatessen arrangements can be made for groups who are meeting. Handicapped accessible. Convenient to public transportation and numerous neighborhood restaurants and shops.

Hosts: Alison A. Proft, manager, and Victor M. Fontanez, assistant manager
Rooms: 19 (3PB; 16SB) $90
Credit Cards: A, B
Notes: 2, 5

NIAGARA FALLS

The Cameo Manor North

3881 Lower River Road, **Youngstown** 14174
(716) 745-3034

Located just seven miles north of Niagara Falls, our English manor house

---

NOTES: Credit cards accepted: A Master Card; B Visa; C American Express; D Discover; E Diners Club; F Other; 2 Personal checks accepted; 3 Lunch available; 4 Dinner available;

is the perfect spot for that quiet getaway you have been dreaming about. Situated on three secluded acres, the manor offers a great room with fireplaces, solarium, library, and an outdoor terrace for your enjoyment. Our beautifully appointed guest rooms include suites with private sun rooms and cable TV. A breakfast buffet is served daily.

Hosts: Greg and Carolyn Fisher
Rooms: 5 (3PB; 2SB) $65-130
Full Breakfast
Credit Cards: A, B, D
Notes: 5, 7, 8, 9, 10, 11, 12

The Country Club Inn

5170 Lewiston Road, **Lewiston** 14092
(716) 285-4869 (voice and FAX)

Located just minutes from Niagara Falls, The Country Club Inn is a non-smoking bed and breakfast. Three large and beautifully-decorated guest rooms with private bath, queen-size bed, and cable TV. A great room with pool table, leads to a covered patio overlooking the golf course. A full breakfast is served at our guests' convenience in our elegant dining room. Conveniently lo-cated near the NYS thruway and bridges to Canada.

Hosts: Barbara Ann and Norman Oliver
Rooms: 3 (PB) $75-90
Full Breakfast
Credit Cards: none
Notes: 2, 5, 7, 9, 10

Manchester House

653 Main Street, 14301
(716) 285-5717; (800) 489-3009;
FAX (716) 282-2144

This brick and shingle residence was built in 1903 and was used as a doctor's residence and office for many years. After extensive renovation, Manchester House opened and a bed and breakfast in 1991. Carl and Lis received a Niagara Falls Beautification award for their work. Manchester House is within easy walking distance of the Falls, the Aquarium, and the Geological Museum. Plenty of off-street parking is available.

Hosts: Lis and Carl Slenk
Rooms: 3 (PB) $60-80
Full Breakfast
Credit Cards: A, B
Notes: 5, 7, 12

The Country Club Inn

5 Open all year; 6 Pets welcome; 7 Children welcome; 8 Tennis nearby; 9 Swimming nearby; 10 Golf nearby; 11 Skiing nearby; 12 May be booked through travel agent.

NORTH RIVER

Garnet Hill Lodge

13th Lake Road, 12856
(518) 251-2444; (800) 497-4207;
FAX (518) 251-3089

Garnet Hill Lodge is a four season destination resort located in New York's Adirondack mountains. Walking into Garnet Hill's main lodge, "The Log House," you're greeted by the spaciousness of a great hotel, the warmth of a rustic mountain lodge, and the friendly charm of a country inn. Garnet Hill has 27 guest rooms in four buildings. Summer guests enjoy hiking, tennis, and a private beach on pristine 13th Lake. In winter, Garnet Hill is transformed into a complete cross-country ski resort. In any season a stay at Garnet Hill Lodge is complemented by a variety of delicious meals from hearty breakfasts to full-course dinners.

Hosts: George and Mary Heim
Rooms: 27 (24PB; 3SB)
Credit Cards: A, B
Notes: 2, 3, 4, 5, 7, 8, 9, 10, 11, 12

OLIVEREA

Slide Mountain Forest House

805 Oliverea Road, 12410
(914) 254-5365

Nestled in the Catskill Mountains State Park, our inn offers the flavor and charm of the old country. Come and enjoy our beautiful country setting, superb lodging, fine dining, and chalet rentals. Family-run for over 60 years, we strive to give you a pleasant and enjoyable stay. German and continental cuisine, lounge, pool, tennis, hiking, fishing, antiquing, and more available for your pleasure.

Hosts: Ursula and Ralph Combe
Rooms: 21 (17PB; 4SB) $50-70
Full Breakfast
Credit Cards: A, B, D
Notes: 4, 5 (chalets only), 7, 8, 9, 10, 11

PINE BUSH

The Milton Bull House

1065 Route 302, 12566
(914) 361-4770

The Milton Bull House is a traditional bed and breakfast. The historic house has nine rooms furnished with antiques. The house is Federal in style. There are two large, airy guest rooms sharing a full bath. Located in the Hudson Valley, there are wonderful opportunities for hiking, rock climbing, shopping, and visits to local wineries and churches nearby. Rates include an old-fashioned farm breakfast with home baking.

Hosts: Graham and Ellen Jamison
Rooms: 2 (1PB; 2SB) $64.35
Full Breakfast
Credit Cards: none
Notes: 2, 5, 8, 9, 10, 11

POUGHKEEPSIE

Inn at the Falls

50 Red Oaks Mill Road, 12603
(914) 462-5770; (800) 344-1466;
FAX (914) 462-5943

Inn at the Falls in Dutchess County combines the most luxurious elements

---

NOTES: Credit cards accepted: A Master Card; B Visa; C American Express; D Discover; E Diners Club; F Other; 2 Personal checks accepted; 3 Lunch available; 4 Dinner available;

of a modern hotel with the ambiance and personal attention of a country home. Complimentary European-style breakfast delivered to your room each morning. Twenty-two hotel rooms and fourteen suites all individually decorated for those who demand the finest in overnight accommodations.

Hosts: Arnold and Barbara Sheer
Rooms: 36 (PB) $110-150
Continental Breakfast
Credit Cards: A, B, C, D, E
Notes: 5, 7, 8, 9, 10, 11, 12

QUEENSBURY (ADIRONDACK AREA)

Crislip's Bed and Breakfast

693 Ridge Road, 12804
(518) 793-6869

Located in the Adirondack area just minutes from Saratoga Springs and Lake George, this landmark Federal home provides spacious accommodations complete with period antiques, four-poster beds, and down comforters. The country breakfast menu features buttermilk pancakes, scrambled eggs, and sausages. Your hosts invite you to relax on their porches and enjoy the mountain view of Vermont.

Hosts: Ned and Joyce Crislip
Rooms: 3 (PB) $55-75
Full Breakfast
Credit Cards: A, B
Notes: 2, 5, 6 (sometimes), 7, 8, 9, 10, 11, 12

REMSENBURG

Pear Tree Farm Bed and Breakfast

96 S. Country Road, PO Box 268, 11960
(516) 325-1443; (800) 291-4121

Pear Tree Farm, a 200 year old charming farm house nestled among many historic homes in the beautiful hamlet of Remsenburg Long Island, offers a romantic getaway with gracious, warm hospitality. Surrounded by beautiful flower/herb gardens, this country estate on two acres, offers warmth and beauty, filled with antiques and country charm. There is a pool, outdoor sauna, and two private guest cottages. Fully air-conditioned. A short drive to the Atlantic Ocean. The Hamptons and Montauk Pt. are some of the nearby attractions. ABBA 3 crown rated.

Hostess: Barbara Genco
Rooms: 3 (2PB; 1SB) $95-150 (off season $65-110)
Continental Gourmet Breakfast
Credit Cards: A, B
Notes: 2, 3, 5, 6, 7, 8, 9, 10

SARATOGA SPRINGS

The Inn on Bacon Hill

PO Box 1462, 12866
(518) 695-3693

Relax in the peacefulness of elegant country living in this spacious, recently restored, 1862 Victorian just twelve

The Inn on Bacon Hill

minutes from historic Saratoga Springs and its racetracks. Four air-conditioned bedrooms overlook fertile farmland. A baby grand piano adorns the Victorian Parlor Suite. Enjoy our lovely gardens, extensive library, comfortable guest parlor, and the many architectural features unique to the Inn. An inn where you come as strangers and leave as friends! Off season, an innkeeping workshop is offered.

Hostess: Andrea Collins-Breslin
Rooms: 4 (2PB; 2SB) $75-95 (racing season higher)
Full Country Breakfast
Credit Cards: A, B
Notes: 2, 5, 7 (over 12), 8, 9, 10, 11, 12

Six Sisters
Bed and Breakfast

149 Union Avenue, 12866
(518) 583-1173; FAX (518) 587-2470

1880 Victorian beckons you with its relaxing veranda. Within walking distance of museums, city park, downtown, specialty shops, antiques, and restaurants. Spacious rooms, private baths, king/queen beds, and a full home-cooked breakfast. Mineral bath and

massage package: November-May. Rec. by *NY Times* and *Gourmet*.

Hostess: Kate Benton
Rooms: 4 (PB) $60-125 (except racing season)
Full Breakfast
Credit Cards: A, B, C
Notes: 2, 5, 7 (over 10), 8, 9, 10, 11, 12

SYRACUSE

Giddings Garden B&B

290 W. Seneca Turnpike, 13207
(315) 492-6389; (800) 377-3452

An early morning stroll through the luscious gardens, with the sounds of birds singing and waterfalls, enhances your appetite for the full gourmet breakfast to come. We are an upscale, historic B&B, circa 1810. We have three rooms all with exquisite private baths with marble and mirrored walls. Queen poster beds, fireplaces, color cable TV, and air-conditioning. Choose your favorite mood: The Honey Room—romantic; The Executive—masculine; The Country Garden—flowery.

Hosts: Pat and Nancie Roberts
Rooms: 3 (3PB) $75-105
Full Gourmet Breakfast
Credit Cards: none
Notes: 2, 5, 7, 8, 9, 10, 11, 12

Giddings Garden Bed and Breakfast

NOTES: Credit cards accepted: A Master Card; B Visa; C American Express; D Discover; E Diners Club; F Other; 2 Personal checks accepted; 3 Lunch available; 4 Dinner available;

SYRACUSE AREA— SKANEATELES

Elaine's Bed and Breakfast Selections

Mailing address: 4987 Kingston Road, **Elbridge** 13060-9773
(315) 689-2082 (after 10AM)

Elaine's is a reservation service presently listing B&Bs in **New York** State in the following towns: Baldwinsville, Cincinnatus, Cleveland on Oneida Lake, DeWitt, Durhamville, Edmeston (near Cooperstown), Elbridge, Fayetteville, Geneva, Glen Haven, Gorham, Groton, Homer, Jamesville, Lafayette, Liverpool, Lyons, Marathon (near Binghamton and Ithaca), Marcellus, Naples, Ovid, Owasco Lake, Pompey, Port Ontario, Pulaski, Rome, Sheldrake-on-Cayuga, Skaneateles, Sodus Bay (on Lake Ontario), South Otselic, Spencer, Syracuse, Tully, Vernon, and Vesper. Elaine N. Samuels, coordinator.

UTICA

The Iris Stonehouse Bed and Breakfast

16 Derbyshire Place, 13501-4706
(315) 732-6720

Enjoy city charm close to everything, three miles south of I-90, Exit 31. This stone Tudor house has leaded glass windows that add charm to the eclectic decor of the four guest rooms. A guest sitting room offers a comfortable area for relaxing, reading, watching TV, or socializing in a smoke-free atmosphere. Central air-conditioning.

Hosts: Shirley and Roy Kilgore
Rooms: 4 (2PB; 2SB) $45-75
Full Breakfast
Credit Cards: A, B, C, D
Notes: 2, 5, 7 (over 8), 10, 11, 12

VALLEY FALLS

Maggie Towne's B&B

351 Phillips Road, 12185
(518) 663-8369 or (518) 686-7331

This lovely old Colonial is located amid beautiful lawns and trees. Enjoy a cup of tea or glass of wine before the huge fireplace in the family room. Use the music room or curl up with a book on the screened-in porch. Mornings, your host serves home-baked goodies. She will gladly prepare a lunch for you to take on tour or enjoy at the house. It's 20 miles to historic Bennington, Vermont, and 30 to Saratoga.

Hostess: Maggie Towne
Rooms: 3 (SB) $45
Full Breakfast
Credit Cards: none
Notes: 3, 5, 6 (sometimes), 7 (crib available), 8, 9, 10, 11

VESTAL (BINGHAMTON)

Strawberry Hill B&B Inn

564 Jones Road, 13850
(607) 785-5058; FAX (607) 785-6282

Country hospitality awaits you in our

---

5 Open all year; 6 Pets welcome; 7 Children welcome; 8 Tennis nearby; 9 Swimming nearby; 10 Golf nearby; 11 Skiing nearby; 12 May be booked through travel agent.

century-old farmhouse filled with comfortable antiques. We warmly extend an invitation to you to relax on the wide verandas and enjoy the panoramic view of the gently rolling hills and quiet meadows. Master suite and jacuzzi, inground pool, full breakfast, fireplaces, and country French decor. Weekday, corporate, and senior discounts.

Hostess: H. Hope Cormack
Rooms: 5 (2PB; 3SB) $85-125
Full Breakfast
Credit Cards: A, B, D
Notes: 2, 5, 7, 8, 9, 10, 11, 12

WARRENSBURG

White House Lodge
53 Main Street, 12885
(518) 623-3640

An 1847 Victorian home in the heart of the queen village of the Adirondacks, an antiquer's paradise. The home is furnished with many Victorian antiques which send you back in time. Five minutes to Lake George, Fort William Henry, and Great Escape. Walk to res-

taurants and shopping. Enjoy air-conditioned TV lounge for guests only. Wicker rockers and chairs on front porch. Window and Casablanca fans.

Hosts: Jim and Ruth Gibson
Rooms: 3 (SB) $85
Continental Breakfast
Credit Cards: A, B
Notes: 5, 7 (over 8), 9, 10, 11

WELLESLEY ISLAND

Hart House
21979 Club Road, PO Box 70, 13640
(315) 482-LOVE (5683)

Hart House, a grand cottage before Boldt Castle, features four exquisite suites with canopy beds, decorator sheeting, whirlpools, fine antiques, and a whisper-quiet peace for your restorations of body, mind, and spirit. A five-course, candlelight breakfast perfectly begins your day in the wonderful 1000 Islands. Only a five-minutes drive from I-81 and the Canadian border. We are redefining hospitality.

Hosts: Rev. Dudley and Kathy Danielson
Rooms: 4 (PB) $95-155
Full Five-Course, Gourmet Breakfast
Credit Cards: none
Notes: 2, 5, 7, 8, 9, 10, 11, 12

WESTHAMPTON BEACH

1880 House
Bed and Breakfast
2 Seafield Lane, PO Box 648, 11978
(516) 288-1559; (800) 346-3290;
FAX (516) 288-0721

The Seafield House is a hidden, 100-

NOTES: Credit cards accepted: A Master Card; B Visa; C American Express; D Discover; E Diners Club; F Other; 2 Personal checks accepted; 3 Lunch available; 4 Dinner available;

year-old country retreat perfect for a romantic hideaway, a weekend of privacy, or just a change of pace from city life. Only 90 minutes from Manhattan, Seafield House is ideally situated on Westhampton Beach's exclusive Seafield Lane. The estate includes a swimming pool and a tennis court and is a short, brisk walk to the ocean beach. The areas offers outstanding restaurants, shops, and opportunities for antique hunting. Indoor tennis, Guerney's International Health Spa, and Montauk Point are nearby.

Hostess: Elsie Collins
Rooms: 3 suites (PB) $100-195
Full Breakfast
Credit Cards: A, B, C
Notes: 2, 5, 8, 9, 10, 12

Ballycove

7 Cox Cove Road, 11978
(516) 288-6774; FAX (516) 288-3546

Ballycove is a quiet, relaxed bed and breakfast overlooking Quantuck Bay. We are part of the "Hamptons," Long Island. We are a short walk to a charming village and a beautiful Atlantic Ocean beach. Two beautiful, large rooms with private bath and TV. One room with whirlpool bath, couch, refrigerator, table, and chairs. The other overlooks a sixty-foot pool with wonderful landscaping.

Hostess: Phyllis Noonan
Rooms: 3 (2PB; 1SB)
Full Breakfast
Credit Cards: none
Notes: 2, 5, 7, 10, 12

WINDHAM

Albergo Allegria

Route 296, 12496
(518) 734-5560; (800) 6-ALBERGO;
FAX (518) 734-5570

Italian for the "Inn of Happiness," Albergo Allegria seeks to pamper all that walk through her doors. This sprawling Queen Anne mansion (c. 1876) features full private baths, a master suite with a sunken double jacuzzi, two spacious living room area, video library, period wallpaper, and antiques. Nestled in the Catskill Forest Preserve, there are outdoor activities for all ages and preferences. Convenient to Catskill Moutain House, Kaaterskill Falls, Woodstock, Howe Caverns, and Albany. Rated AAA 3-diamonds and Mobil 3-stars.

Hosts: Vito and Lenore Radelich
Rooms: 21 (PB) $55-195
Full Gourmet Breakfast
Credit Cards: A, B
Notes: 2 (NY residents only), 4, 5, 7, 8, 9, 10, 11, 12

Albergo Allegria

---

5 Open all year; 6 Pets welcome; 7 Children welcome; 8 Tennis nearby; 9 Swimming nearby; 10 Golf nearby; 11 Skiing nearby; 12 May be booked through travel agent.

Country Suite Bed and Breakfast

PO Box 700, 12496
(518) 734-4079

Lovely 100-year-old farmhouse, furnished with family heirlooms and antiques, nestled in the Catskill Mountains on 10.5 acres of land. Renovated by current owners to accommodate guests seeking the quiet charm and ambiance of country life and relaxation. Open year-round for those who need "to get away."

Hostesses: Sondra Clark and Lorraine Seidel
Rooms: 9 (3PB; 6SB) $55-75
Full Complimentary Breakfast
Credit Cards: C
Notes: 2, 5, 7 (well-behaved), 8, 9, 10, 11, 12

YOUNGSTOWN

The Mill Glen Inn

1102 Pletcher Road., 14174
(716) 754-4085

You will enjoy a relaxing stay in a quiet country home with fresh flowers and early morning trays in each guest room.

The Mill Glen Inn

Breakfast is served in the Wagner Dining Room or, in season, on the covered porch with a view of our lovely gardens. Our renovated farmhouse was built in 1886 and has been designated a historic property by the town of Lewiston's Historic Society. Great shopping and restaurants nearby.

Hosts: Peter and Milly Brass
Rooms: 3 (1PB; 2SB) $45-65
Continental Plus Breakfast
Credit Cards: none
Notes: 2, 5, 7, 8, 9, 10, 11, 12

North Carolina

ASHEBORO

The Doctor's Inn
716 S. Park Street, 27203
(910) 625-4916 or (910) 625-4822

The Doctor's Inn is a home filled with antiques. It offers its guests the utmost in personal accommodations. Amenities include a gourmet breakfast served on fine china and silver, fresh flowers, terry-cloth robes and slippers, and ice cream parfaits. Nearby are over 60 potteries, and the North Carolina Zoo (five miles).

Hosts: Marion and Beth Griffin
Rooms: 2 (1PB; 1SB) $75-85
Full Breakfast
Credit Cards: none
Notes: 2, 5, 8, 9, 10

The Doctor's Inn

ASHEVILLE

Albemarle Inn
86 Edgemont Road, 28801
(704) 255-0027; (800) 621-7435

A distinguished Greek Revival mansion with exquisite carved oak staircase, balcony, paneling, and high ceilings. Beautiful residential area. On the National Register of Historic Places. Spacious, tastefully decorated, comfortable guest rooms with TV, telephones, air-conditioning, and private baths with clawfoot tubs and showers. Delicious full breakfast served in our dining room and sun porch. Swimming pool. Unmatched hospitality. AAA 3-Diamond rated.

Hosts: Kathy and Dick Hemes
Rooms: 11 (PB) $90-150
Full Breakfast
Credit Cards: A, B, D
Notes: 2, 5, 7 (over 13), 8, 9, 10, 12

Cairn Brae
217 Patton Mountain Road, 28804
(704) 252-9219

A mountain retreat on three secluded acres above Asheville features beautiful views, walking trails, and a large

---

5 Open all year; 6 Pets welcome; 7 Children welcome; 8 Tennis nearby; 9 Swimming nearby; 10 Golf nearby; 11 Skiing nearby; 12 May be booked through travel agent.

NORTH CAROLINA

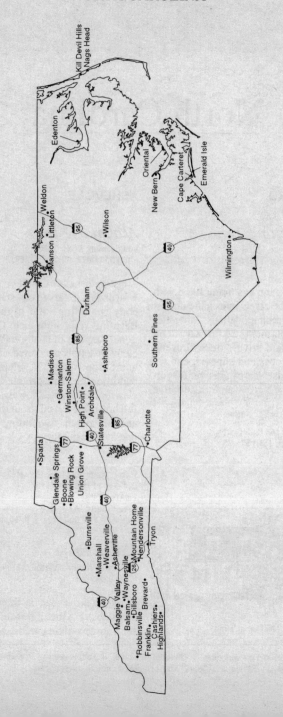

terrace overlooking Beaver Dam Valley. Homemade full breakfast. Quiet, away from traffic, and only minutes from downtown.

Hosts: Edward and Milli Adams
Rooms: 3 (PB) $90-105
Full Breakfast
Credit Cards: A, B
Open April through Nov.
Notes: 2, 3, 7 (over 10), 8, 9, 10

Cedar Crest Victorian Inn

674 Biltmore Avenue, 28803
(704) 252-1389; (800) 252-0310;
FAX (704) 253-7667

This 1890 Queen Anne mansion is listed on the National Register of Historic Places. One of the largest and most opulent residences surviving Asheville's 1890s boom period. A captain's walk, projecting turrets, and expansive veranda's welcome guests to lavish interior woodwork and stained glass. All rooms are furnished with antiques, with satin and lace trappings.

Hosts: Jack and Barbara McEwan
Rooms: 11 (PB) $115-170
Full Breakfast
Credit Cards: A, B, C, D, E
Notes: 2, 5, 7 (over 10), 12

Reed House

119 Dodge Street, 28803
(704) 274-1604

This comfortable Queen Anne Victorian with rocking chairs and swings on the porch also has a rocking chair in every room. Breakfast features homemade muffins, rolls, and jams and is served on the porch. Listed on the National Register of Historic Places; near Biltmore Estate. Open May 1 through November 1.

Hostess: Marge Turcot
Rooms: 2 (SB) $50; 2BR family cottage $95;
Suite: 1 (PB) $70
Continental Breakfast
Credit Cards: A, B
Notes: 2, 7, 8, 9, 10, 11

BALSAM

Balsam Mountain Inn

7 Springs Road, PO Box 40, 28707
(704) 456-9498; (800) 224-9498;
FAX (704) 456-9298

Nestled on 26 acres near the crest of the Great Balsam Mountains, the Inn is enveloped by spectacular peaks rising to more than 6,00 feet. You can relish good food and revel in the comfort of plump pillows and thick comforters.

Hosts: Merrily Teasley/George Austin
Rooms: 50 (PB) $90-150
Full Breakfast
Credit Cards: A, B, D
Notes: 2, 3, 4, 5, 7, 8, 9, 10, 11, 12

Balsam Mountain Inn

NOTES: Credit cards accepted: A Master Card; B Visa; C American Express; D Discover; E Diners Club; F Other; 2 Personal checks accepted; 3 Lunch available; 4 Dinner available; 5 Open all year; 6 Pets welcome; 7 Children welcome; 8 Tennis nearby; 9 Swimming nearby; 10 Golf nearby; 11 Skiing nearby; 12 May be booked through travel agent.

The Inn at Ragged Gardens

BLOWING ROCK

The Inn
at Ragged Gardens
203 Sunset Drive, 28605
(704) 295-9703

Set amidst an acre of rock-walled lawn
and gardens, our inn occupies a quiet
corner in the heart of the village. We
offer six guest rooms and two suites all
with private baths and fireplaces, some
with private balconies and some with
whirlpool baths. Relax in the spacious
living room with its granite rock fireplace. Breakfast in the chestnut panelled
dining room or on the covered porch.
A non-smoking inn, we are open year-
round and look forward to making your
stay a great one. We offer a 20% discount for clergy, Sunday through Thursday.

Hosts: Lee and Jama Hyett
Rooms: 6 + 2 suites (PB) $105-150
Full Breakfast
Credit Cards: A, B
Notes: 2, 5, 7, 8, 9, 10, 11, 12

BOONE

The Gragg House
Kalmia Acres, 210 Ridge Point Drive, 28607
(704) 264-7289; FAX (704) 265-0031

Ten minutes from the Blue Ridge Parkway and blessed with mountain views,
The Gragg House opens to a lush landscape of native wildflowers and rhodo-
dendron. Where bird songs are nearly
the only sound to break the silence of
this secluded getaway. The Gragg
House hospitality is an important
supplement to its glorious setting. The
hosts offer friendly little touches without imposing too much activity or attention on guests who would rather be
alone. A sumptuous breakfast can always truly be the unexpected.

Hosts: Judy Gragg and Robert Gragg
Rooms: 3 (1PB; 2SB) $75-95
Full Gourmet Breakfast
Credit Cards: none
Notes: 2, 5, 7 (by prior arrangement), 8, 9, 10,
11, 12 (no commissions)

BREVARD

The Red House Inn
412 Probart Street, 28712
(704) 884-9349

The Red House was built in 1851 and
has served as a trading post, a railroad
station, the county's first courthouse,
and the first post office. It has been lovingly restored and is now open to the
public. Charmingly furnished with turn-
of-the-century antiques. Convenient to

NOTES: Credit cards accepted: A Master Card; B Visa; C American Express; D Discover;
E Diners Club; F Other; 2 Personal checks accepted; 3 Lunch available; 4 Dinner available;

the Blue Ridge Parkway, Brevard Music Center, and Asheville's Biltmore Estate.

Hostess: Marilyn Ong
Rooms: 6 (4PB; 2SB) + 1 cottage (PB) $45-79
Full Breakfast
Credit Cards: A, B
Closed January through March
Notes: 2, 8, 9, 10, 12

The Red House Inn

Womble Inn

301 W. Main Street, 28712
(704) 884-4770

The Womble Inn invites you to relax in a welcoming, comfortable atmosphere. Each of the six guest rooms is especially furnished in antiques and decorated to make you feel cared for. All of the guest rooms have private baths and air-conditioning. Your breakfast will be served to you on a silver tray or you may prefer to be seated in the dining room. The Inn is one-half mile from the exciting Brevard Music Center.

Hosts: Steve and Beth Womble
Rooms: 6 (PB) $52-62
Continental Breakfast (full available for fee)
Credit Cards: A, B, D
Notes: 2, 3, 5, 7, 8, 9, 10, 11

BURNSVILLE

A Little Bit of Heaven B&B

937 Bear Wallow Road, 28714
(704) 675-5379; FAX (704) 675-0364

Getaway from the day to day routine for awhile and enjoy "A Little Bit of Heaven." This B&B offers a charming home with spectacular mountain views all around. The four guests rooms are beautifully decorated and furnished with queen or twin beds and private baths. While guests visit they can enjoy an abundance of activities in the area or just relax around the house and be pampered by the warm hospitality of their hosts.

Hosts: John and Shelley Johnson
Rooms: 4 (PB) $60-75
Full Breakfast
Credit Cards: none
Notes: 2, 5, 7, 8, 9, 10, 11

The NuWray Inn

PO Box 156, Town Square, 28714
(704) 682-2329; (800) 368-9729

Historic country inn . . . since 1833. Nestled in the Blue Ridge Mountains in a quaint town square setting. Thirty miles northeast of Asheville. Close to Mt. Mitchell, Blue Ridge Parkway, Grandfather Mountain, antiques, golf, crafts, hiking, and fishing, or just relax on the porch. Room rates include a hearty country breakfast and afternoon refreshments, with our nationally famous family style dinners also available.

Hosts: Chris and Pam Strickland
Rooms: 26 (PB) $75-110
Full Breakfast
Credit Cards: A, B, C, D
Notes: 2, 4, 5, 7, 8, 9, 10, 11, 12

5 Open all year; 6 Pets welcome; 7 Children welcome; 8 Tennis nearby; 9 Swimming nearby; 10 Golf nearby; 11 Skiing nearby; 12 May be booked through travel agent.

CAPE CATERET

Harborlight Guest House Bed and Breakfast

332 Live Oak Drive, 28584
(919) 393-6868 (voice and FAX);
(800) 624-VIEW

The Harborlight, located on the central North Carolina coast, is situated on a peninsula with water on three sides; thus, all suites offer panoramic water views. All suites also offer private entrances and private baths; luxury suites feature two-person jacuzzis, fireplaces, and in-room breakfast. The guest house is minutes from area beaches, secluded island excursions, and the outdoor drama "Worthy is the Lamb"—a passion play that depicts the life of Christ.

Hosts: Bobby and Anita Gill
Rooms: 9 (PB) $75-175
Full Breakfast
Credit Cards: A, B, C
Notes: 5, 8, 9, 10

CASHIERS

Millstone Inn

Hwy. 64 W., PO Box 949, 28717
(704) 743-2737; (888) MILLSTONE (645-5786); FAX (704) 743-0208

Selected by *Country Inns* magazine as one of the best twelve inns, Millstone Inn has breathtaking views of the Nantahala forest. The exposed beams are complemented by the carefully selected antiques and artwork. Enjoy a gourmet breakfast in our glass enclosed dining room overlooking Whiteside

Mountain. Located at 3,500 feet, it's always cool for a hike to the nearby Silver Slip Falls, or enjoy the nearby golf, tennis, restaurants, and antique shops.

Hosts: Paul and Patricia Collins
Rooms: 11 (PB) $99-159
Full Breakfast
Credit Cards: A, B, C, D
Notes: 2, 8, 9, 10, 11, 12

The Elizabeth Bed and Breakfast

CHARLOTTE

The Elizabeth Bed and Breakfast

2145 E. 5th Street, 28204
(704) 358-1368

This 1927 lavender "lady" is located in historic Elizabeth, Charlotte's second oldest neighborhood. European country-style rooms are beautifully appointed with antiques, ceiling fans, decorator linens, and unique collections. All rooms have central air and private baths; some have TV and phones. Enjoy a generous full or continental breakfast, then relax in our garden courtyard, complete with charming gazebo, or stroll beneath giant oak trees to convenient restaurants and shopping. Nearby attractions include the Mint Museum of

NOTES: Credit cards accepted: A Master Card; B Visa; C American Express; D Discover; E Diners Club; F Other; 2 Personal checks accepted; 3 Lunch available; 4 Dinner available;

Art, Blumenthal Performing Arts Center, Discovery Place, and professional sporting events.

Hostess: Joan Mastny
Rooms: 4 (PB) $55-88
Full or Continental Breakfast
Credit Cards: A, B
Notes: 2, 5, 9, 12

The Homeplace Bed and Breakfast

5901 Sardis Road, 28270
(704) 365-1936; FAX (704) 366-2729

Restored 1902 country Victorian with wraparound porch and tin roof is nestled among two and one-half wooded acres. Secluded "cottage style" gardens with a gazebo, brick walkways, and a 1930's log barn further enhance this nostalgic oasis in southeast Charlotte. Experienced innkeepers offer a full breakfast. Opened in 1984, the Homeplace is a "reflection of the true bed and breakfast."

Hosts: Peggy and Frank Dearien
Rooms: 2 + 1 suite with sitting room (PB) $98-125
Full Breakfast
Credit Cards: A, B, C
Notes: 2, 5, 7 (over 10), 12 (10%)

The Homeplace Bed and Breakfast

McElhinney House

McElhinney House

10533 Fairway Ridge, 28277
(704) 846-0783 (voice and FAX)

A two-story, traditional home located in popular southeast Charlotte, 15 minutes from Charlotte-Douglas Airport. Close to fine restaurants, museums, Carowinds Park, and many golf courses. A lounge area with cable TV, a hot tub, laundry facilities, and barbecue are available. Families are welcome. A continental breakfast is served in the lounge or on the deck.

Hosts: Mary and Jim McElhinney
Rooms: 2 (PB) $55-65
Continental Breakfast
Credit Cards: A, B
Notes: 2, 5, 7, 8, 9, 10

Victorian Villa

10925 Windy Grove Road, 28208
(704) 394-5545

A beautifully restored Victorian home located on Lake Wylie. Victorian Villa has three fireplaces, stained-glass windows, and a relaxing sunporch. Unwind

---

5 Open all year; 6 Pets welcome; 7 Children welcome; 8 Tennis nearby; 9 Swimming nearby;
10 Golf nearby; 11 Skiing nearby; 12 May be booked through travel agent.

by the pool and jacuzzi, drop a lin in by the dock, or enjoy a breathtaking sunset overlooking the lake. Gracious guest rooms and suites decorated with 18th century antiques, each designed with your comfort in mind. There are domestic pets on the premises. Conveniently located to the airport, coliseum, panther stadium, and convention center. Easily accessible to all interstates.

Hosts: Chan and Nancy Thompson
Rooms: 5 (PB) $89-199
Continental Breakfast on weekdays; Full on Saturday and Sunday
Credit Cards: A, B, C
Notes: 5, 7 (12 and older), 9

DILLSBORO

Applegate Inn
163 Hemlock Street, 28725
(704) 586-2397

The "Gateway" to country charm, relaxation, and Southern hospitality at it's best. Situated in the village of Dillsboro, we are located on Scott's Creek, a footbridge from the Great Smoky Mountain Depot and Dillsboro's 50 unique shops. A quaint country home—families and seniors appreciate our one level. Private baths and queen beds, and efficiencies with kitchen facilities. Full country breakfast. Let us make you the apple of our eye! Proverbs 3:24, 26.

Hosts: Emil and Judy Milkey
Rooms: 6 (5PB; 1SB) $55-75
Full Breakfast
Credit Cards: A, B, D
Notes: 2, 5, 7, 8, 12

Arrowhead Inn

DURHAM

Arrowhead Inn
106 Mason Road, 27712
(919) 477-8430 (voice and FAX);
(800) 528-2207

The 1775 Colonial manor house is filled with antiques, quilts, samplers, and warmth. Located on four rural acres, Arrowhead features fireplaces, original architectural details, air-conditioning and homemade breakfasts. A two-room log cabin is also available. Easy access to restaurants, Duke University, University of North Carolina-Chapel Hill, Raleigh, and historic sites, including Duke Homestead Tobacco Museum and Bennett Place. Near I-85.

Hosts: Barb, Jerry, and Cathy Ryan
Rooms: 8 (PB) $80-175
Full Breakfast
Credit Cards: A, B, C, E
Notes: 2, 5, 7, 8, 9, 10, 12

EDENTON

Albemarle House
204 W. Queen Street, 27932
(919) 482-8204

Enjoy welcoming refreshments on the porch or in the parlor of our circa 1900

NOTES: Credit cards accepted: A Master Card; B Visa; C American Express; D Discover; E Diners Club; F Other; 2 Personal checks accepted; 3 Lunch available; 4 Dinner available;

country Victorian home. Located in Edenton's historic district, we are just two blocks from the Albemarle Sound. Our home is furnished with antiques and reproductions, stenciling, artwork, quilts, and collections. Bicycles. Sailing cruises offered. Full breakfast. Three spacious rooms with private baths including a family suite.

Hosts: Marijane and Reuel Schappel
Rooms: 3 (PB) $75
Full Breakfast
Credit Cards: none
Notes: 2, 5, 7 (over 10), 8, 9, 10

Captain's Quarters Inn

Captain's Quarters Inn

202 W. Queen Street, 27932
(919) 482-8945; (800) 482-8945

The Inn is a seventeen-room, circa 1907 home in the Edenton historic district with a 65-foot wraparound front porch (swings and rockers). Eight charming bedrooms with modern, private baths (seven queen beds, two twin beds). We serve plenty of gourmet food, including welcome refreshments, continental breakfast, and a full three-course breakfast, as well as gourmet dinner on weekends. Sailing offered spring, summer, and fall; mystery weekends in fall, winter, and spring.

Hosts: Bill and Phyllis Pepper
Rooms: 8 (PB) $35095
Continental and Full Breakfast
Credit Cards: A, B
Notes: 2, 5, 7, 8, 9, 10, 12

EMERALD ISLE

Emerald Isle Inn Bed and Breakfast

502 Ocean Drive, 28594
(919) 354-3222 (voice and FAX)

Located at the ocean, this jewel of a Crystal Coast inn is truly a treasure to be discovered. A peaceful haven to all who seek a quiet, restful, and sun-filled getaway. Your stay includes a full gourmet breakfast with freshly-ground coffee and other tempting samplings. Suites include Victorian, French country, tropical, and our new luxury suite. Swings and porches with ocean and sound views add to your enjoyment. With direct beach access, you are only steps away from discovering the gentle shoreline treasures. We are only minutes from antiquing, fine restaurants, historic sites and the outdoor drama passion play "Worthy is the Lamb." Come to your home away from home for a visit you'll always remember!

Hosts: A.K. and Marilyn Detwiller
Rooms: 5 (4PB; 2SB) $75-150
Full Gourmet Breakfast
Credit Cards: none
Notes: 2, 5, 7, 8, 9, 10

5 Open all year; 6 Pets welcome; 7 Children welcome; 8 Tennis nearby; 9 Swimming nearby; 10 Golf nearby; 11 Skiing nearby; 12 May be booked through travel agent.

FRANKLIN

Lullwater Retreat

88 Lullwater Road, 28734
(704) 524-6532; FAX (704) 369-7879

The 120 year old farmhouse and cabins are located on a river and creek in a peaceful mountain cove. Hiking trails, river swimming, tubing, and other outdoor activities are on the premises. It serves as a retreat center for church groups and family reunions. Guests cook their own meals or visit nearby restaurants. Chapel, rocking chairs, wonderful views, and indoor and outdoor games. Christian videos and reading materials are supplied.

Hosts: Robert and Virginia Smith
Rooms: 10 (5PB; 5SB) $39-50
Self-serve Breakfast
Credit Cards: none
Notes: 2, 5, 7, 9, 10, 11, 12

GLENDALE SPRINGS

Mountain View Lodge and Cabins

Blue Ridge Parkway MP 256, PO Box 90, 28629
(910) 982-2233; (800) 209-8142 (PIN# 0595)

Located on the beautiful Blue Ridge Parkway in the cool North Carolina mountains. Feel right at home with "Texas-mountainbilly" hospitality, live music, and silly wild turkeys! Seren deer regularly attend "recitals" at the lodge front windows. Lodge suites with fireplaces; one or two bedroom cabins. Close to world-famous churches of the Frescoes and the New River, second oldest river in the world. Bring your camera and pets!

Hosts: Elton and JoAnn Derden
Rooms: 15 (13PB; 2SB) $50-75
Full Breakfast (for lodge folks)
Credit Cards: A, B
Notes: 2, 3 + 4 (arranged), 5, 6, 7, 9, 10, 11, 12

HENDERSONVILLE

Apple Inn

1005 White Pine Drive, 28739
(704) 693-0107; (800) 615-6611

There's no place like home, unless it's the Apple Inn! Only two miles from downtown Hendersonville, the Inn is situated on three acres featuring charmingly comfortable rooms, each with modern private baths that await your arrival. Delicious home-cooked breakfasts, fresh flowers, and antiques compliment the ambiance of this turn-of-the-century home. Enjoy billards, tennis, swimming, hiking, antiquing, birdwatching, or just plain relaxing. Create tomorrow's memories amidst yesterday's charm!

Hosts: Bob and Pam Hedstrom
Rooms: 5 (PB) $79-89
Full Breakfast
Credit Cards: A, B
Notes: 2, 5, 7, 8, 9, 10, 12

Apple Inn

The Claddagh Inn

755 N. Main Street, 28792
(704) 697-7778; (800) 225-4700;
FAX (704) 697-4700

The Claddagh Inn at Hendersonville is a recently renovated, meticulously clean bed and breakfast that is eclectically furnished with antiques and a variety of collectibles. The Inn is located two blocks from the main shopping promenade of beautiful, historic downtown Hendersonville. The friendly, homelike atmosphere is complemented by a safe and secure feeling guests experience while at this lovely inn. The Claddagh Inn is listed on the National Register of Historic Places. No smoking rooms available. AAA approved.

Hosts: Vicki and Dennis Pacilio
Rooms: 12 + 2 suites (PB) $63-99
Full Breakfast
Credit Cards: A, B, C, D
Notes: 2, 5, 7, 8, 9, 10, 12

The Waverly Inn

783 N. Main, 28792
(704) 693-9193; (800) 537-8195;
FAX (704) 692-1010
Email: jsheiry@aol.com

Listed on the National Register, this is the oldest inn in Hendersonville. Recently renovated, there is something for everyone including claw foot tubs, king and queen canopy beds, a suite, telephones, rocking chairs, sitting rooms, and all rooms have private baths. Enjoy our complimentary soft drinks and fresh baked goods. Walk to exceptional restaurants, antique stores, and shopping. Biltmore Estate, Blue Ridge Parkway, and Connemara are nearby. Full country breakfast included in rates. Rated as one of 1993s top ten bed and breakfasts in the USA by *INNovations*.

Hosts: John and Diane Sheiry, Darla Olmstead
Rooms: 15 (PB) $79-139
Full Breakfast
Credit Cards: A, B, C, D
Notes: 2, 5, 7, 8, 9, 10, 12

HIGHLANDS

Long House Bed and Breakfast

PO Box 2078, 28741
(704) 526-4394; (800) 833-0020

Long House B&B offers a comfortable retreat in the scenic mountains of western North Carolina. Guests enjoy the beauty and charm of the quaint town and scenic wonders of the Nentahala National Forest. This rustic mountain B&B offers all the comforts with country charm and warm hospitality. A hearty breakfast is served family-style and is one of the many highlights of everyone's visit!

Hosts: Lynn and Valerie Long
Rooms: 4 (PB) $55-95
Very Full Breakfast
Credit Cards: A, B
Notes: 2, 7, 8, 9, 10, 11

HIGHPOINT

The Bouldin House

4332 Archdale Road, **Archdale** 27263
(910) 431-4909 (voice and FAX);
(800) 739-1816

Our finely-crafted and lovingly restored historic bed and breakfast sits on three

5 Open all year; 6 Pets welcome; 7 Children welcome; 8 Tennis nearby; 9 Swimming nearby; 10 Golf nearby; 11 Skiing nearby; 12 May be booked through travel agent.

acres of a former tobacco farm. Quiet, country atmosphere; casual and relaxed, yet elegant. Warmly decorated rooms combine old and new, each with spacious, modern, private baths. Awaken to early morning coffee/tea service. Follow the aroma of our generous, home-cooked breakfast to the oak-paneled dining room. America's largest concentration of furniture showrooms are only minutes away. Come, indulge yourself.

Hosts: Ann and Larry Miller
Rooms: 4 (PB) $85-95
Full Gourmet Breakfast
Credit Cards: A, B, D
Notes: 2, 5, 8, 10, 12

KILL DEVIL HILLS

Cherokee Inn Bed and Breakfast

500 N. Virginia Dare Trail, 27948
(919) 441-6127; (800) 554-2764;
FAX (919) 441-1072

Our beach house, located at Nags Head Beach on the outer banks of North Carolina, is 600 feet from the ocean. Fine food, history, sports, and adventure galore. We welcome you for a restful, active, or romantic getaway. Enjoy the cypress walls, white ruffled curtains, and wraparound porch.

Hosts: Bob and Kaye Combs
Rooms: 6 (PB) $60-95
Continental Breakfast
Credit Cards: A, B, C
Notes: 2, 8, 9, 10, 12

LITTLETON (LAKE GASTON)

Littleton's Maplewood Manor

120 College Street, PO Box 1165, 27850
(919) 586-4682

Littleton's Manor is a small hometown B&B, offering you a nice clean, spacious room with a king or twin beds, shared bath, and a full breakfast. There are books, games, videos, CD's, and tapes, all for you to enjoy. There will be tea in the afternoon and wine and crackers in the evening. The grounds are park-like and for you to enjoy. There are also benches and chairs placed around for the use of our guests. The screened porch is another great place for relaxation. Multi-night discounts.

Hosts: Helen and Alan Burtchell
Rooms: 2 (SB) $55
Full Breakfast
Credit Cards: A, B
Notes: 5, 9, 10

MADISON

The Boxley Bed and Breakfast

117 E. Hunter Street, 27025
(910) 427-0453; (800) 429-3516;
FAX (910) 427-4154

The Greek, Federal-style home, built in 1825, is located in the historic district of Madison. Boxwoods adorn the long front walk and the gardens in the rear. The porch, connecting the main house to the dining room and kitchen, is a wonderful place to sit in and relax, and enjoy the peacefulness and serenity the 19th century setting. JoAnn and Monte want you to make yourself at home.

Hosts: JoAnn and Monte McIntosh
Rooms: 4 (PB) $70
Full Breakfast
Credit Cards: A, B, C
Notes: 2, 5, 7, 8, 10

MAGGIE VALLEY

The Ketner Inn and Farm

190 Jonathan Creek Rd. (PO Box 1628), 28751
(704) 926-1511; (800) 714-1397

A relaxed, quiet, turn-of-the-century vacation awaits you. Built in 1898 the Inn has been restored and is decorated entirely with Victorian and country antiques. Five bedrooms have private baths and cable TV, central air and heat. Located in the heart of the Smoky Mountains on 27 rolling acres, the front and back porches offer magnificent views, hiking, cattle, antique farm equipment, and an outdoor hot tub.

Hosts: Randall and Sara McCrory
Rooms: 5 (PB) $50-65
Full Breakfast
Credit Cards: A, B
Notes: 2, 5, 7, 8, 9, 10, 11, 12

Kimball Oaks

MANSON

Kimball Oaks

Route 1, Box 158, 27553
(919) 456-2004 (voice and FAX)

1800's home on Kerr Lake–800 mile shore line an hour north of Research Triangle, two hours south of Richmond, and 3½ hours south of Washington. Comfortable home tastefully decorated in a quiet nature-filled setting near Kimball Point. Lawn games and comfortable chairs under massive oaks. Modern baths. Home-baked breads. Refreshments on arrival. Proprietors hosting skills honed by years of military and diplomatic living in Brussels, Geneva, Verona, Rome, and Washington. Italian and French spoken.

Hosts: Colonel and Mrs. Allen Kimball
Rooms: 3 (1PB; 2 SB) $60-100
Full Breakfast
Credit Cards: A, B
Notes: 2, 3, 4, 5 (closed Christmas),7 (over 12), 9, 10

MARSHALL

Marshall House B&B

5 Hill Street, PO Box 865, 28753
(704) 649-9205; FAX (704) 649-2999

Built in 1903, the inn overlooks the peaceful town of Marshall and the waters of the French Broad River. This country inn, listed on the National Historic Register, is decorated with fancy chandeliers, antiques, and pictures. Four fireplaces, formal dining room, parlor, and upstairs TV/reading room. Storytelling about the house, the town, the people, and the history. Loving

5 Open all year; 6 Pets welcome; 7 Children welcome; 8 Tennis nearby; 9 Swimming nearby; 10 Golf nearby; 11 Skiing nearby; 12 May be booked through travel agent.

house pets, the toot of a choo-choo train, and good service make your visit a unique experience.

Hosts: Ruth and Jim Boylan
Rooms: 9 (2PB; 7SB) $39.50-75
Continental Plus Breakfast
Credit Cards: A, B, C, D, E
Notes: 3, 4, 5, 6, 7, 9, 10, 11, 12

Mountain Home Bed and Breakfast

MOUNTAIN HOME

Mountain Home Bed and Breakfast

PO Box 234, 10 Courtland Boulevard, 28758
(704) 697-9090; (800) 397-0066

Between Asheville and Hendersonville, and near the airport, antiques and Oriental-style rugs grace this English-style home. Large, Tennessee, pink marble porch and rocking chairs to relax the day or night away. Cable TV and telephones in all rooms. Some rooms with private entrance. Full candlelight breakfast. Convenient to Biltmore Estate (on their preferred lodging list), Chimney Rock, Pisgah National Forest, Carl Sandburg Home, and much more. Wheelchair accessible ramp to front and one room.

Hosts: Blake, Tammie, and Judy
Rooms: 7 (PB) $85-195
Full Breakfast
Credit Cards: A, B
Notes: 2, 5, 8, 10, 12

NAGS HEAD

First Colony Inn®

6720 S. Virginia Dare Trail, 27959
(919) 441-2343; (800) 368-9390;
FAX (919) 441-9234

Enjoy Southern hospitality at the only historic B&B inn on the Outer Banks (National Register). Enjoy our individual rooms, continental breakfast buffet and afternoon tea, private walk to the beach, pool, and croquet. Or visit the Wright Brothers Memorial, lighthouses, and Fort Raleigh (site of the Lost Colony). The only AAA Four Diamond rating in Eastern North Carolina.

Hosts: The Lawrences
Rooms: 26 (PB) $80 (low winter)-250 (high summer)
Continental Plus Buffet Breakfast
Credit Cards: A, B, D
Notes: 2 (30 days in advance), 5, 7, 8, 9 (pool on premises), 10, 12

NEW BERN

Harmony House Inn

215 Pollock Street, 28560
(919) 636-3810; (800) 636-3113;
FAX (919) 636-3810
Email: harmony@nternet.net

Enjoy comfortable elegance in an unusually spacious Greek Revival inn built circa 1850 with final additions circa 1900. Guests enjoy a parlor, front porch with rocking chairs and swings, antiques and reproductions, plus a full breakfast in the dining room. Soft drinks and juice available throughout stay. All rooms have fully private, modern bath-

NOTES: Credit cards accepted: A Master Card; B Visa; C American Express; D Discover; E Diners Club; F Other; 2 Personal checks accepted; 3 Lunch available; 4 Dinner available;

rooms. Located in the historic district near Tryon Palace, shops, and restaurants. No smoking!

Hosts: Ed and Sooki Kirkpatrick
Rooms: 10 (PB) $85-95
Full Breakfast
Credit Cards: A, B, D
Notes: 2, 5, 7, 8, 9, 10, 12

King's Arms Colonial Inn

212 Pollock Street, 28560
(919) 638-4409; (800) 872-9306;
FAX (919) 638-2191

The King's Arms Inn, named for an old New Bern tavern said to have hosted members of the First Continental Congress, upholds a heritage of hospitality as New Bern's winner of the "Best of the Best" award for bed and breakfast accommodations. Spacious rooms with comfortable four-poster, canopied, or brass beds; all modern amenities; and elegant decor harbor travelers who want to escape the present and steep themselves in Colonial history. Home-baked breakfasts feature piping hot specialty ham and cheese and seasonal fruit muffins from our exclusive recipe; fresh fruit, juice, and coffee or tea delivered to your room by candlelight with the morning paper. The inviting third floor Mansard Suite offers a view of the Neuse River and features unique open gables and the tongue and groove paneling added to this 1848 Greek Revival during the last part of the 19th century.

Hosts: Richard and Pat Gulley
Rooms: 7 + 1 suite (PB) $85-125
Continental Plus Breakfast
Credit Cards: A, B, C
Notes: 2, 5, 7, 8, 9, 10, 12

Magnolia House Bed and Breakfast

315 George Street, 28562
(916) 633-9488 (voice and FAX); (800) 601-9488

We invite you to romance yourselves with a stay at New Bern's Magnolia House. You may choose from three uniquely decorated guest room, each with private bath. Located two doors from Tryon Place, once home to the Royal Governor of North Carolina, you will find Magnolia House to be centrally located in the heart of the historic district. Fine restaurants, quaint shops, museums, and antiqueing are within walking distance. Magnolia House is furnished with local estate antiques and family pieces. A full breakfast is served at your convenience. You may choose to have it served under the magnolia tree for which the inn is named. Honeymoon and anniversary packages are our specialty. Gift certificates are available.

Hosts: Kim and John Trudo
Rooms: 3 (PB) $65-90
Full Breakfast
Credit Cards: A, B, C, D
Notes: 2, 5, 10, 12

ORIENTAL

Tar Heel Inn

508 Church Street, PO Box 176, 28571
(919) 249-1078

The Tar Heel Inn is over 100 years old and has been restored to capture the atmosphere of an English country inn. Guest rooms have four-poster or canopy king and queen beds. Patios and bi-

5 Open all year; 6 Pets welcome; 7 Children welcome; 8 Tennis nearby; 9 Swimming nearby;
10 Golf nearby; 11 Skiing nearby; 12 May be booked through travel agent.

Tar Heel Inn

cycles are for guest use. Five churches are within walking distance. Tennis, fishing, and golf are nearby. This quiet fishing village is known as the sailing capital of the Carolinas. Sailing cruises can be arranged, and there are great restaurants. Smoking on porch and patios only. Three-diamond AAA rating.

Hosts: Shawna and Robert Hyde
Rooms: 8 (PB) $70-90
Full Breakfast
Credit Cards: A, B
Notes: 2, 7 (by arrangement), 8, 9, 10, 12

ROBBINSVILLE

Snowbird Mountain Lodge

275 Santeetlah Road, 28771
(704) 479-3433; FAX (704) 479-3473

Once you have been here, it's easy to see why you would return. No developments mar these mountains and no convenience stores clog the narrow roads. What you will find is absolutely spectacular scenery and an oasis called The Snowbird, the quintessential mountain inn. The two-story lodge building, completed in 1941, is nestled on almost 100 acres of undisturbed hilltop. Distinquished by a cathedral ceiling with hand-cut solid chestnut beams,

butternut paneling, a 2,500 volume library, and two massive stone fireplaces, the main lodge area invites you to relax in peaceful comfort. The Wolfe and Smith Cottages are also waiting to welcome you through the Snowbird's season that starts in April and extends through November. Your innkeepers plan many lodge activities—including hikes, cooking seminars, fly fishing programs, and more—or explore the local offerings at your own pace.

Hosts: Karen and Robert Rankin
Rooms: 22 (PB) $120-130
Full Breakfast (American Plan)
Credit Cards: A, B
Notes: 2, 3, 4, 7 (over 12), 8, 9

Knollwood House

SOUTHERN PINES

Knollwood House

1495 W. Connecticut Avenue, 28387
(910) 692-9390; FAX (910) 692-0609

The English manor house stands among five acres of longleaf pines, dogwoods, azaleas, towering holly trees, and 40-foot magnolias. From a terrace where Glenn Miller's orchestra once gave a concert, Knollwood's lawns roll down to the 15th fairway of a famous Donald Ross golf course. Furnished with late

---

NOTES: Credit cards accepted: A Master Card; B Visa; C American Express; D Discover; E Diners Club; F Other; 2 Personal checks accepted; 3 Lunch available; 4 Dinner available;

18th century/early 19th century antiques, both suites and guest rooms are available. Special golf package rates are available on request.

Hosts: Dick and Mimi Beatty
Rooms: 4 (PB) $80-150
Full Breakfast
Credit Cards: A, B
Notes: 2, 5, 7 (over 10), 8, 9, 10, 12

SPARTA

Turby Villa

2075 NC Highway 18 N., 28675
(910) 372-8490

At an altitude of 3,000 feet, this contemporary two-story home is the centerpiece of a 20-acre farm located two miles from town. The house is surrounded by an acre of trees and manicured lawn with a lovely view of the Blue Ridge Mountains. Breakfast is served either on the enclosed porch with white wicker furnishings or in the more formal dining room with Early American furnishings. Mrs. Mimi Turbiville takes justifiable pride in her attractive, well-maintained bed and breakfast.

Hostess: Maybelline R. Turbiville
Rooms: 3 (PB) $35 (single) $50 + tax
Full Breakfast
Credit Cards: none
Notes: 2, 5, 7, 8, 10

STATESVILLE

Cedar Hill Farm B&B

778 Elmwood Road, 28677
(704) 873-4332; (800) 948-4423

An 1840 farmhouse and private cottages

on a 32-acre sheep farm in the rolling hills of North Carolina. Antique furnishings, air-conditioning, cable TV, and phones in rooms. After your full country breakfast, swim, play badminton, or relax in a porch rocker or hammock. For a busier day, visit two lovely towns with historic districts, Old Salem, or two larger cities in a 45-mile radius. Convenient to restaurants, shopping, and three interstate highways.

Hosts: Brenda and Jim Vernon
Rooms: 3 (PB) $60-95
Full Breakfast
Credit Cards: A, B
Notes: 2, 5, 6 (limited), 7, 9, 10, 12

Cedar Hill Farm

Madelyn's in the Grove

PO Box 298, 1836 West Memorial Hwy, **Union Grove** 28689
(704) 539-4151; (800) 948-4473;
FAX (704) 539-4080
Email: mhill@i-america.net

Listen to the birds and unwind. We have moved our B&B to Union Grove, only 15 minutes north of Statesville and I-40, and only two minutes from I-77, exit 65. There are many things to see and to do. After a fun-filled day, come back and have cheese and crackers and a glass of lemonade. Sit on one of the

---

5 Open all year; 6 Pets welcome; 7 Children welcome; 8 Tennis nearby; 9 Swimming nearby; 10 Golf nearby; 11 Skiing nearby; 12 May be booked through travel agent.

porches or the gazebo, watch the stars, and be glad that you are at Madelyn's in the Grove.

Hosts: Madelyn and John Hill
Rooms: 3 (PB) $65-75
Full Gourmet Breakfast
Credit Cards: A, B, C
Notes: 2, 5, 7, 10, 12

TRYON

Fox Trot Inn

PO Box 1561, 800 Lynn Rd., (Rt. #108), 28782
(704) 859-9706

This lovingly restored residence, circa 1915, is situated on six wooded acres within the city limits. It is convenient to everything, yet secluded with a quietly elegant atmosphere. Full gourmet breakfast, heated swimming pool, fully furnished guest house with two bedrooms, kitchen, living room, fireplace, deck, and mountain views. Two guest rooms have sitting rooms. Inn and guest house are fully air-conditioned.

Host: Wim Woody
Rooms: 4 (PB) $80-125;Guest House: $550 weekly
Full Breakfast
Credit Cards: none
Notes: 2, 5, 6 (in guest house), 7, 8, 9, 10, 12

Fox Trot Inn

WAYNESVILLE

Wynne's Creekside Lodge Bed and Breakfast

Route 2, Box 365, 28786
(704) 926-8300 (voice and FAX);
(800) 849-4387

Situated on trout-stocked Jonathan Creek in the scenic western North Carolina mountains, Wynne's Creekside Lodge lies on two and a half country acres five minutes outside Maggie Valley. The Inn, a 1926 two-story farmhouse, was recently raised and set upon a wood and stone contemporary addition. Six-person jacuzzi, mountain bike rentals, and fishing. A full country breakfast includes homemade bread, jams, or pastry. Complimentary cappuccino or refreshments served. Three rooms and one suite in a Christian atmosphere.

Hosts: Les and Gail Wynne
Rooms: 4 (PB) $55-60
Full Breakfast
Credit Cards: A, B
Notes: 2, 5, 6 (separate facilities), 7, 8, 9, 10, 11

WEAVERVILLE

Dry Ridge Inn

26 Brown Street, 28787
(704) 658-3899; (800) 839-3899

This casually elegant bed and breakfast is quietly removed ten minutes north of Asheville's many attractions. Country-style antiques and contemporary art enhance this unique 1800s village farmhouse. A full breakfast is served with individual seating. Relax in our outdoor

---

NOTES: Credit cards accepted: A Master Card; B Visa; C American Express; D Discover; E Diners Club; F Other; 2 Personal checks accepted; 3 Lunch available; 4 Dinner available;

Dry Ridge Inn

spa or with quality, spiritual reading after enjoying a day of mountain adventure.

Hosts: Paul and Mary Lou Gibson
Rooms: 7 (PB) $80-110
Full Breakfast
Credit Cards: A, B, C, D
Notes: 2, 5, 7 (older), 10, 11, 12

WELDON

Weldon Place Inn

500 Washington Avenue, 27890
(919) 536-4582; (800) 831-4470;
FAX (919) 536-4708

Your home away from home is only two miles from I-95 Exit 173 halfway between New York and Florida. Sleep in canopy beds, wake to singing sparrows, stroll through our cozy historic hometown, and savor a gourmet breakfast. At the Weldon Place Inn, your peace of mind begins with antiques and country elegance. Personal attention is provided to ensure you the ultimate in solitude and relaxation. Select the Romantic Retreat Package and you'll enjoy flowers, sparkling cider, a whirlpool tub and breakfast in bed. Local sites include

state historic site, early canal system, river overlook of the rapids, and the railroad.

Hosts: Angel and Andy Whitby
Rooms: 4 (PB) $65-89
Full Breakfast
Credit Cards: A, B, C
Notes: 5, 8, 12

WILMINGTON

The Curran House

312 S. Third Street, 28401
(910) 763-6603; (800) 763-6603

In historic downtown Wilmington, three blocks from the Cape Fear River and 15 minutes from our great Atlantic beaches. Two king and one queen room available, each uniquely decorated with amenities such as guest robes, hair dryers, cable TV/VCRs, telephones, and private baths. Badminton and ping-pong are set up outside and ready to play. We are within walking distance to some great restaurants, antique shopping, museums, as well as carriage and riverboat rides.

Hosts: Vickie and Greg Stringer
Rooms: 3 (PB) $60-95
Full Breakfast
Credit Cards: A, B
Notes: 2, 5, 7 (12 + older), 10

James Place Bed and Breakfast

9 South Fourth Street, 28401
(910) 251-0999; (800) 303-9444;
FAX (910) 251-1150
Email: jamesinn@wilmington.net

Our inn, in Wilmington's Historic Dis-

---

5 Open all year; 6 Pets welcome; 7 Children welcome; 8 Tennis nearby; 9 Swimming nearby; 10 Golf nearby; 11 Skiing nearby; 12 May be booked through travel agent.

trict, is minutes from some of Carolina's finest beaches. A carefully restored cira 1909 home with a large front porch for rocking and reminiscing. The Renewal Room has a special intimacy with a two-person jacuzzi bath, queen bed, and personal balcony. The Nesting Suite has a queen canopy bed, sitting area, and private bath. The Shaker Room has queen and twin beds plus a private bathroom. Enjoy relaxing in the courtyard hot tub.

Miss Betty's B&B Inn

Hosts: Tony and Maureen Spataro
Rooms: 3 (PB) $70-95
Full Breakfast
Credit Cards: A, B
Notes: 2, 5, 7, 8, 9, 10, 12

Taylor House Inn

14 N. Seventh Street, 28401
(910) 763-7581; (800) 382-9982

Neoclassic built in 1905 in Historic District and blessed with vast ceilings, enormous rooms, rich oak woodwork, parquet floors, stained glass windows, and a magnificent open staircase. Guest rooms are artfully appointed with antiques, hand-decorated furniture, canopies, ceiling fans, and beautiful linens. A full gourmet breakfast is served on White China.

Hosts: Glenda Moreadith
Rooms: 5 (PB) $95-110
Full Breakfast
Credit Cards: A, B, C
Notes: 2, 5, 8, 9, 10

WILSON

Miss Betty's Bed and Breakfast Inn

600 West Nash Street, 27893-3045
(919) 243-4447; (800) 258-2058

Selected as one of the **"best places to stay in the South"** Miss Betty's is ideally located midway between Maine and Florida along the main North-South route, I-95. Comprised of three beautifully restored structures in the downtown historic section; the National Registered Davis-Whitehead-Harriss House (circa 1858), the adjacent Riley House (circa 1900), and Rosebud (circa 1942) are a recapture of the elegance and style of days gone by and where quiet Victorian charm abounds in an atmosphere of all modern-day conveniences. Guests can browse for antiques in the Inn or visit any of the numerous antique shops that have given Wilson the title "Antique Capital of North Carolina." A quiet eastern North Carolina town known for its famous barbecue, Wilson also has four beautiful golf courses and numerous tennis courts.

Hosts: Betty and Fred Spitz
Rooms: 10 including 3 king suites (PB) $60-75
Full Breakfast
Credit Cards: A, B, C, D, E
Notes: 2, 5, 8, 9, 10

WINSTON-SALEM

Lady Anne's Victorian Bed and Breakfast
612 Summit Street, 27101
(910) 724-1074

Warm, southern hospitality surrounds you in this 1890 Victorian home, listed on the National Register of Historic Places. An aura of romance touches each suite or room, all individually decorated with period antiques, treasures, and modern luxuries. Some rooms have two-person whirlpools, cable TV, HBO, stereo, telephone, coffee, refrigerator, private entrances, and balconies. An evening dessert and full breakfast are served. Lady Anne's is ideally located near downtown attractions, performances, restaurants, shops, and Old Salem Historic Village. Smoking only on the porch!

Hostess: Shelley Kirby
Rooms: 4 (PB) $55-155
Full Breakfast
Credit Cards: A, B, C
Notes: 5, 8, 9, 10, 12 (no commission)

WINSTON-SALEM— GERMANTON

MeadowHaven Red and Breakfast
NC Highway 8, PO Box 222, 27019-0222
(910) 593-3996; FAX (910) 593-3138

A contemporary retreat on 25 country acres along Sauratown Mountain in the Blue Ridge Foothills. Meadowhave offers a choice of romantic rooms, a new log cabin with mountain view, or a mountain-top cottage with two bedrooms. All provide private luxury baths, TV/VCR with movies, hair dryer, and plush bathrobes. "Luv Tubs" for two, fireplace, spa, and sauna available. Heated indoor pool, hot tubs, game room, fishing pond, pedal boats, game room, and more on the property. Convenient to Hanging Rock and Pilot Mountain State Parks, Old Salem, and the Dan River. Plan a "Lovebirds' Retreat" to Meadow-Haven!

Hosts: Sam and Darlene Fain
Rooms: 5 (PB) $70-175
Full Breakfast
Credit Cards: A, B, C, D
Notes: 2, 5, 8, 9, 10, 12

MeadowHaven Bed and Breakfast

---

5 Open all year; 6 Pets welcome; 7 Children welcome; 8 Tennis nearby; 9 Swimming nearby; 10 Golf nearby; 11 Skiing nearby; 12 May be booked through travel agent.

NORTH DAKOTA

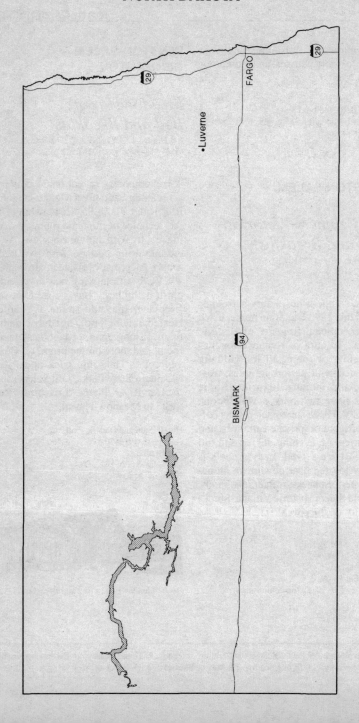

North Dakota

LUVERNE

Volden Farm
Bed and Breakfast

R.R. 2, Box 50, 58056
(701) 769-2275

This weathered redwood farmhouse is a 1926/1978 built home—two in one—if you please. Relaxation is the theme.

Hiking through the native prairie down to the Sheyenne River is an option, along with reading in a comfortable spot on the porch or deck. Antiques and collectibles surround you and the food is good!

Hosts: Jim and JoAnne Wold
Rooms: 4 + cottage (2PB; 2SB) $50-95
Full Breakfast
Credit Cards: none
Notes: 2, 3, 4, 5, 7, 8, 9, 10, 11, 12

NOTES: Credit cards accepted: A Master Card; B Visa; C American Express; D Discover; E Diners Club; F Other; 2 Personal checks accepted; 3 Lunch available; 4 Dinner available; 5 Open all year; 6 Pets welcome; 7 Children welcome; 8 Tennis nearby; 9 Swimming nearby; 10 Golf nearby; 11 Skiing nearby; 12 May be booked through travel agent.

OHIO

Ohio

The Albany House

ALBANY

The Albany House Bed and Breakfast

9 Clinton Street, 45710
(614) 698-6311

Enjoy today's comfort in yesterday's atmosphere at The Albany House. A 150-year-old house, renovated for a B&B in the village of Albany, seven miles west of Athens and Ohio University. Enjoy antiques, quilts, Oriental rugs, and family heirlooms, plus modern amenities of air-conditioning, indoor heated pool, fireplace, and guest living room with TV/VCR. Resident cat.

Hosts: Sally and Ted Hutchins
Rooms: 6 (PB) $75-100
Continental Plus Breakfast
Credit Cards: B
Notes: 2, 5, 7 (over 8), 8, 9 (indoor pool), 10, 12

BERLIN

Donna's Bed and Breakfast and Cottages

PO Box 307 (East Street), 44610
(330) 893-3068; (800) 320-3338

Beautifully appointed country decor rooms, log cabin, honeymoon/anniversary cottages, elegant and luxurious

Donna's Country Bed and Breakfast

NOTES: Credit cards accepted: A Master Card; B Visa; C American Express; D Discover; E Diners Club; F Other; 2 Personal checks accepted; 3 Lunch available; 4 Dinner available; 5 Open all year; 6 Pets welcome; 7 Children welcome; 8 Tennis nearby; 9 Swimming nearby; 10 Golf nearby; 11 Skiing nearby; 12 May be booked through travel agent.

chalets. Most accommodations have heart-shaped water fall jacuzzi, fireplace, cathedral wood ceiling with skylights, deck, ketchenette, cable TV, VCR, stereo—all rooms have private bath and air. Member of OBBA, BBB, and featured on TV 27 & TV 8.Call for full color brochure.

Hosts: Johannes and Donna Marie Schlabach
Rooms: 3, 1 log cabin, 2 cottages, + 2 chalets
   (8PB) $55-225
Inquire about breakfast plan.
Credit Cards: A, B, D
Notes: 2, 5, 7, 8, 9, 10, 12

Main Street Bed and Breakfast

4895 W. Main Street, PO Box 158, 44610
(330) 763-2025; (800) 763-2101;
FAX (330) 893-2100

In the heart of Berlin shops. Featuring three newly-remodeled, luxury rooms with waterfall jacuzzi, queen-size beds, private baths, satellite TV, kitchenettes, and authentic Amish-crafted furniture and quilts. Full breakfast at local restaurant.

Hosts: Elvin and Laura Coblentz
Rooms: 3 (PB) $95
Full Menu Breakfast
Credit Cards: A, B, D
Notes: 2, 5, 7, 12

The Oaks Bed and Breakfast

4752 US 62, PO Box 421, 44610
(330) 893-3061

Nestled in the small town of Berlin in picturesque Holmes County, The Oaks Bed and Breakfast is "your home away from home." We offer three rooms, including a lofted master suite complete with skylights, whirlpool, and its own sitting room—a total private get away! Sit back and relax on the screened porch or deck surrounded by the large oak trees, or take a stroll uptown to the many craft shops, furniture stores, and eating establishments. Fully air-conditioned and smoke free.

Hosts: Duane and Carol Miller
Rooms: 2 plus 1 suite (PB) $65-95
Continental Breakfast
Credit Cards: A, B, D
Notes: 2, 5, 7, 8, 9, 10, 12

BLUE ROCK

McNutt Farm II / Outdoorsman Lodge

6120 Cutler Lake Road, 43720
(614) 674-4555

Country bed and breakfast for overnight travelers in rustic quarters on a working farm in the quiet of the Blue Rock hill country. Only eleven miles from I-70, 35 miles from I-77, and 60 miles from I-71. B&B guests enjoy their own private kitchen, living room with fireplace or woodburner, private bath, porch with swing, and a beautiful view with forests and pastured livestock. Choose either the log cabin or the carriage house. For those who want more than an overnight stay, please ask about our log cabin by the week or weekend. A cellar-house cabin is also available, although it is somewhat primitive. Sleep to the sounds of the whippoorwills and tree frogs. Awake to the ever-crowing rooster, the wild turkey calling,

NOTES: Credit cards accepted: A Master Card; B Visa; C American Express; D Discover; E Diners Club; F Other; 2 Personal checks accepted; 3 Lunch available; 4 Dinner available;

and sometimes the bleating of a new-born fawn can be heard. We welcome you by reservation and deposit.

Hosts: Don R. and Patty L. McNutt
Rooms: 2 suites (PB) $40-100
Continental Breakfast
Credit Cards: none
Notes: 2 (deposit, cash for balance), 5, 6 and 7 (prearranged), 9, 10

BOWLING GREEN

Pine Ridge Bed and Breakfast

14543 Sand Ridge Road, 43402
(419) 352-2064

Pine Ridge offers comfortable accommodations and warm hospitality in a Victorian style farmhouse dating from 1878. Two guest rooms and bath on the second floor overlook woods, well kept lawn and gardens, and fertile farms. Breakfast is served in the spacious living/dining room or sunny porch, and often includes homemade breads or coffee cakes and fruits from the orchard or garden.

Hosts: Bill and Sue Rock
Rooms: 2 (SB) $50 ($35 single)
Full Breakfast
Credit Cards: none
Notes: 2, 7

BRYAN

The Elegant Inn B&B

215 North Walnut Street, 43506
(419) 636-2873; (800) 577-2873

The Inn is a large Victorian home built in the late 1800s within walking distance from the courthouse square. On the porch guests can enjoy the swing while being shaded bya a large, old buckeye tree. Stroll the tree-lined streets of the city enjoying the sights and sounds of a small town in northwest Ohio.

Hosts: Martha and Ted Cline
Rooms: 4 (1PB; 3SB) $45-55
Full Breakfast
Credit Cards: none
Notes: 2, 5, 8, 9 (public pool), 10

The Elegant Inn

CALDWELL

The Harkins House Inn

715 West Street, 43724
(614) 732-7347

When passing through the beautiful countryside of southeastern Ohio take a moment to relax in the comfort of the Harkins House, a newly restored 1905 home. The home was built by V.E. Harkings. His son, Donald and his wife Bea lived there until 1991. Jeff and

5 Open all year; 6 Pets welcome; 7 Children welcome; 8 Tennis nearby; 9 Swimming nearby; 10 Golf nearby; 11 Skiing nearby; 12 May be booked through travel agent.

Stacey are their descendants. There are presently two guest rooms with private baths. One in country blue and sunny yellow floral wallpaper. The other in red rose buds with touches of green and ivory.

Hosts: Jeff and Stacey Lucas
Rooms: 2 (PB) $53
Full Breakfast
Credit Cards: A, B, C
Notes: 2, 5, 7, 8, 9, 10

Pleasant Valley Bed and Breakfast

CAMDEN

Pleasant Valley Bed and Breakfast
7343 Pleasant Valley Road, 45311
(513) 787-3800

Our bed and breakfast is a sixteen room Victorian brick with a center hall design, matching pocket doors, rich woodwork, fireplaces, and a third floor attic ballroom. There is also a summer kitchen and carriage house. We have a billiard room as well as a game room for puzzles, reading, board games, or card playing. Fishing, volleyball, horse shoes, or a leisurely stroll are a welcome pastime on our ten acres with colorful birds, butterflies, herbs, and wildflowers.

Hosts: Tim and Peg Lowman
Rooms: 4 (2PB; 2SB) $50-60
Full Breakfast
Credit Cards: none
Notes: 2, 3, 4, 6, 7, 8, 9, 10, 11 (water)

CHARM

Charm Countryview Inn
PO Box 100, 44617
(330) 893-3003

Traveling on State Route 557 past Amish buggies and farms on your way to the Charm Countryview Inn, you'll notice the calm atmosphere, the lovely trees and meadows, the winding drive over our bridge, and up the hill to the Inn's peaceful setting at the edge of the woods. Each guest room is individually decorated and has been named after members of our family. The comfortably furnished rooms feature handmade quilts on queen-size beds and beautiful solid oak furniture. There's no limit to the amount of time you may spend relaxing in a rocker on our spacious front porch simply enjoying the beautiful view and the fresh country air.

Innkeepers: Paul and Naomi Miller
Rooms: 15 (PB) $65-95
Full Breakfast; (Sunday) Continental
Credit Cards: A, B
Notes: 2, 5

Guggisberg Swiss Inn
5025 S.R. 557, PO Box 1, 44617
(216) 893-3600

New quaint, peaceful, little inn, nestled snuggly in the hills of the world's largest Amish settlement–close to shops and attractions. Each room has two double beds with all the comforts of home; local TV channels plus HBO, TNT, etc. Enjoy a horse-drawn carriage or sleigh ride (seasonal–at small additional charge) or sit outside and watch the farmers work their fields. Enjoy visiting with the other guests in front of the fireplace in the lobby. Swiss breakfast includes cheese, meat, bread, cereal, fruit, danish, coffee, and orange juice.

Hosts: Eric and Julia Guggisberg
Rooms: 23 + 1 suite (PB) $79-129
Credit Cards: A, B, C, D, E
Notes: 2, 5, 7 (no children on top floor), 8, 9, 10, 11

Shamrock Bed and Breakfast

COLUMBUS

Shamrock Bed and Breakfast

5657 Sunbury Road, **Gahanna** 43230-1147
(614) 337-9849

The Shamrock B&B is one half mile from I-270, close to the airport, and 15 minutes from downtown. The B&B is handicapped accessible and it is all on one floor. There are one and one fourth acres of landscaped gardens, trees, patio, and arbor for enjoyment. For entertainment guests can choose from the

large library of books, videos, and CDs or just relax in front of the fireplace. There is easy access to downtown activities like Polaris Amphitheater, shopping, parks, gardens, galleries, and country. Entirely air-conditioned and special smoking rooms available.

Host: Tom McLaughlin
Rooms: 2 (PB) $50-60 (discount for 3 or more days)
Full Irish Breakfast with menu
Credit Cards: none
Notes: 2, 3, 5, 7, 8, 9, 10, 11

DAYTON

Candlewick Bed and Breakfast

4991 Bath Road, 45424
(513) 233-9297

This tranquil Dutch Colonial home sits atop a hill on five rolling acres. George, a retired engineer, and Nancy, a retired teacher, invite you to spend a peaceful night in comfortable rooms containing a blend of antiques and Colonial and country furnishings. Full breakfast includes fresh fruit and juice, choice homemade pastries, and freshly brewed coffee. Weather permitting, enjoy breakfast on the screened porch overlooking a largee pond often visited by wild ducks and geese. Convenient to the Air Force Museum and major universities, Candlewick is a perfect retreat for either business or pleasure.

Hosts: Nancy and George Thompson
Rooms: 2 (SB) $55-60 (includes tax)
Full Breakfast
Credit Cards: none
Notes: 2, 5

---

5 Open all year; 6 Pets welcome; 7 Children welcome; 8 Tennis nearby; 9 Swimming nearby; 10 Golf nearby; 11 Skiing nearby; 12 May be booked through travel agent.

DEFIANCE

Sanctuary Ministries

20277 Schick Road, 43512
(419) 658-2069

Sanctuary Ministries is a quiet getaway
in a Christian atmosphere. A two-story
cedar-sided home with air-conditioning,
a six-acre lake, a pond, and five acres
of woods make for a peaceful getaway.
This is a favorite fishing hole for many
with row boat and canoe. Picnicking
and bird-watching from porch swings
add to the tranquil atmosphere.

Hosts: Emil and Barbara Schoch
Rooms: 2 (SB) $35-50
Full Breakfast
Credit Cards: none
Notes: 2, 5, 7, 9, 10

DELLROY

Candleglow Bed and Breakfast

4247 Roswell Road SW, 44620
(330) 735-2407

Today's comfort in yesterday's Victorian atmosphere. Romantic, casual elegance. Three spacious guest rooms
with king or queen beds. Private baths
with clawfoot or whirlpool tubs. Full
breakfast, afternoon tea, and snack in
room. Atwood Lake Resort Area.
Swimming, boating, hiking, horseback
riding, tennis, golf, and antique shops
are all close by.

Hostess: Audrey Genova (innkeeper)
Rooms: 3 (PB) $90 (summer call for winter rates)
Full Breakfast
Credit Cards: none
Notes: 2, 5, 8, 9, 10

Mowrey's Welcome Home B&B

DOVER

Mowrey's Welcome Home B&B

4489 Dover-Zoar Road NE, 44622
(330) 343-4690

Hills, 120 species of native trees, and
country hospitality provide the setting
for this inviting home, modern in design and comfort, but traditional in ambiance. Explore woods and creek, or
enjoy views from the porches. Converse
or read from hundreds of books
throughout the house. Guests are treated
like favorite cousins and invited to play
the grand piano, parlor organ, or old
victrola. Antique furnishings, fireplaces,
and family handiwork add to the welcome feel of home.

Hosts: Paul and Lola Mowrey
Rooms: 3 + suite (1PB; 2SB) $45-80
Continental Plus Breakfast
Credit Cards: none
Notes: 2, 5, 7 (over 9), 8, 9, 10, 12

Olde World Bed and Breakfast

2982 SR 516 NW, 44622
(330) 343-1333; (800) 447-1273

Welcome back to the 1880s. Our restored Victorian-style farmhouse nestled among the hills of Tuscarawas Valley is your escape from it all. Only one mile from I-77, we are centrally located to Amish Country and historic sites. Our five suites are uniquely decorated to include Victorian, Parisian, Oriental, Alpine, and Mediterranean. The parlor is equipped with game table and TV; hot tub and veranda are always available to guests. Complete packages available including romance getaways and special winter rates.

Hostess: Jonna Sigrist
Rooms: 5 (PB) $70-85
Full Breakfast
Credit Cards: A, B, D
Notes: 2, 3, 5, 9, 10, 12

Hill View Acres

EAST FULTONHAM

Hill View Acres
7320 Old Town Road, 43735
(614) 849-2728

Old World hospitality and comfort await each of our guests. During your visit, wander over the 21 acres, relax on the deck or patio, use the pool and year-round spa, or cuddle up by the fireplace in cooler months. A hearty, country breakfast with homemade breads, jams, and jellies is served. We are located ten miles southwest of Zanesville.

Hosts: Jim and Dawn Graham
Rooms: 2 (SB) $40.25-45.50 (including tax)
Suite: 1"very private" (PB) $70 + tax
Full Breakfast
Credit Cards: A, B, C
Notes: 2, 3, 4 (by arrangement), 5, 7, 9, 10

FAYETTE

Red Brick Inn
206 W. Main Street, 43521
(419) 237-2276

Guests will enjoy a visit to our 120 year old Victorian home filled with antique furnishings—many are family heirlooms. There are three bedrooms available, each with private bath. Two of the rooms have a private porch and baths are handicap accessible. We are located in northwest Ohio near Harrison Lake State Park and Fayette's historic opera house. Corner of S.R. 66 and S.R. 20.

Hosts: Don and Jane Stiriz
Rooms: 3 (PB) $55
Full Breakfast
Credit Cards: none
Notes: 2, 5, 8, 9, 10

FREDERICKSBURG

Gilead's Balm Manor Bed and Breakfast
8690 CR 201, 44627
(330) 695-3881

Nestled among the Amish farms of Holmes County, 12 minutes north of Berlin, Ohio, you will find five land-

---

5 Open all year; 6 Pets welcome; 7 Children welcome; 8 Tennis nearby; 9 Swimming nearby; 10 Golf nearby; 11 Skiing nearby; 12 May be booked through travel agent.

scaped acres of Amish country elegance. We have added four luxurious and spacious suites with 12-foot ceilings to our Manor House. Each suite includes two-person jacuzzi, fireplace/gas logs, kitchen, private bath, satellite TV, air-conditioner, and double French doors with round top windows overlooking our 2 1/2 acre lake. Just minutes from shops and restaurants. Our guests say, it's like experiencing the luxurious accommodations of an estate in Europe overlooking a lake. Your hosts, David and Sara Mae Stutzman are both from Amish and Mennonite backgrounds.

Hosts: David and Sara Mae Stutzman
Rooms: 4 (PB) $125 (Sunday through Thrusday)
   $155-165 (Friday + Saturday)
Continental (fresh fruit + pastry bar) Breakfast
Credit Cards: A, B, C, D
Notes: 2, 5, 7, 8, 9, 10, 12

FREDERICKTOWN

Owl Creek B&B
11821 Yankee Street, 43019
(614) 694-4164

Nestled in five acres of one hundred year old trees on a beautiful ravine by a peaceful stream. We specialize in ro-

mantic weekend getaways. We offer two suites with private baths, queen-size beds, AC, 16-foot ceiling in gathering room with fireplace, 20 feet of french doors open out the back on to a 40-foot deck, and a 20-foot screened porch. Weekend packages can include dinner by candlelight, full country breakfast, wagon ride through the countryside, picnic lunch at a covered bridge, and a Lyon Falls Trail hike. Located just one hour north of Columbus off I-71.

Hosts: Gary and Shirley Hannahs
Rooms: 2 (PB) $85-105
Full Breakfast
Credit Cards: none
Notes: 2, 4, 5, 8, 9, 10, 11, 12

FRESNO

Valley View Inn of New Bedford
32327 SR 643, 43824
(330) 897-3232; (800) 331-8439

The panoramic view from the back of the Inn is nothing short of breathtaking and is enhanced only by the changing seasons. Guests can enjoy the coziness of the fireplace in the living room or relax in the family room. A player pi-

Owl Creek Bed and Breakfast

NOTES: Credit cards accepted: A Master Card; B Visa; C American Express; D Discover; E Diners Club; F Other; 2 Personal checks accepted; 3 Lunch available; 4 Dinner available;

ano, checkers, ping-pong table, chess, or a comfortable Lazy Boy chair await you. No TVs to interrupt the serenity that abounds as one enjoys gazing at the surrounding fields and farms, woods, and wildlife. The Inn is located between Roscoe Village and Sugarcreek and within minutes from all Amish shopping places. We're in the heart of Amish Country and in the service of God's people. No smoking. Handicap accessible.

Hosts: Dan and Nancy Lembke
Rooms: 10 (PB) $75-105
Full Breakfast; Continental (Sun.)
Credit Cards: A, B
Notes: 2, 5, 7 (13 and older), 10

GENEVA-ON-THE-LAKE

The Otto Court Bed and Breakfast

5653 Lake Road, 44041
(216) 466-8668; FAX (216) 466-0106

Otto Court B&B is a family-run business situated on two acres of lakefront property. There are eight cottages and a 19-room hotel overlooking Lake Erie. Besides a small game room, there is a horse shoe pit, a volleyball court, picnic tables, and beach with area for a bonfire. Within walking distance is the Geneva State Park and Marina. The Old Firehouse winery, Geneva-on-the-Lake Amusement Center, and the Jennie Munger Museum are also nearby.

Hostess: Joyce Otto
Rooms: 12 (8PB; 4SB) $48-63
Full Breakfast
Credit Cards: A, B, D
Notes: 2, 4, 5, 7, 8, 9, 10, 11, 12

GEORGETOWN

Bailey House Bed and Breakfast

112 N. Water Street, 45121
(513) 378-3087

The Bailey House is on the National Register of Historic Places. The three-story Greek Revival home is furnished in antiques and features three bedrooms with washstands and anique beds. Bailey House is a half block from U. S. Grant's boyhood home and private tours are available.

Hostesses: Nancy Purdy and Jane Sininger
Rooms: 3 (SB)
Full Breakfast
Credit Cards: none
Notes: 2, 5, 6, 7, 8, 9, 10

GREEN SPRINGS

Cloverhill Bed and Breakfast, Inc.

401 North Clay Street, 44836
(419) 639-3515

Cloverhill sits on a hill overlooking the community of Green Springs located in northern Ohio between Fremont and Tiffin on State Route 19—an area rich with history. Nice quiet stay in a small village. 15 minutes from Tiffin University and Seneca Caverns; 30 minutes from Lake Erie and Cedar Point.

Hostess: Carolyn Young
Rooms: 4 (SB) $50
Continental Breakfast
Credit Cards: none
Notes: 2, 5, 7

5 Open all year; 6 Pets welcome; 7 Children welcome; 8 Tennis nearby; 9 Swimming nearby; 10 Golf nearby; 11 Skiing nearby; 12 May be booked through travel agent.

GREENVILLE

The Waring House

304 W. Third Street, 45331
(513) 937-2682; FAX (937) 548-3448

The Waring House is an 1869 Victorian home restored to reflect the elegance of this romanitic era. The ten-room Italianate includes a double parlor, library, four bedrooms and guest bath, formal dining room, kitchen, along with a lovely garden and inground pool. Your hosts individualize the accommodations to insure a memorable stay. A highlight of a visit includes a home-cooked breakfast served in the formal dining room.

Hosts: Mike and Judy Miller
Rooms: 3 (SB) $50
Full Breakfast
Credit Cards: D
Notes: 2, 5, 7, 8, 9, 10

HAMILTON

Eaton Hill Bed and Breakfast

1951 Eaton Road, 45013
(513) 856-9552

Eaton Hill has a country feel although it is officially part of Hamilton. The white Colonial home is surrounded by fields, trees, and flower beds. Only ten miles from the Miami University campus and conveniently situated for parents, guests, and friends of the University and Butler County residents. Two double bedrooms with shared bath will provide you with a quiet night's rest amid antique furnishings. Children welcome ($10 each). A portable crib and high chair are available.

Hostess: Mrs. Pauline K. Zink
Rooms: 2 (SB) $50 + tax
Full Breakfast
Credit Cards: none
Notes: 2, 5, 6 (caged), 7, 8, 9, 10

HOLMES COUNTY (AMISH COUNTRY)

SEE—BERLIN, CHARM, DOVER, FREDERICKSBURG, FRESNO, MILLERSBURG, NEW PHILADELPHIA, ORRVILLE, STRASBURG, SUGARCREEK, WILMOT, AND WOOSTER

LEBANON

Hexagon House

419 Cincinnati Avenue, 45036-2123
(513) 932-9655

Built in the mid 1850s, Hexagon House is located 30 miles north of Cincinnati; easy to reach from interstates and convenient to local attractions. The house is listed on the National Register of Historic Places due to its unique six-sided exterior and its interesting interior floor plan. Rooms are spacious, comfortable, and tastefully decorated. The objective of your full-time hostess is to provide each guest with a pleasantly memorable experience.

Hosts: Lois Duncan Hart and husband Ron
Rooms: 3 (1PB: 2SB) $60-75
Full Breakfast
Credit Cards: none
Notes: 2, 5, 7 (over 12), 10

NOTES: Credit cards accepted: A Master Card; B Visa; C American Express; D Discover; E Diners Club; F Other; 2 Personal checks accepted; 3 Lunch available; 4 Dinner available;

LIMA

Market Street Inn

1069 W. Market Street, 45805
(419) 228-5777; FAX (419) 228-8613

Built in 1907, the Inn features a blend
of country and antique furnishings.
Guests are invited to socialize in our
parlor and sitting rooms, or enjoy a classic movie in the TV room. Relax in the
garden patio in summer or in front of a
blazing fire in the cold of winter. Just a
short walk from beautiful wooded
parks, 20 minutes from the Neil
Armstrong Space Museum.

Hosts: Pamela and Jason Moore
Rooms: 4 (1PB; 3SB) $55-65
Full Breakfast
Credit Cards: A, B
Notes: 2, 5, 8, 10, 12

MILAN

Gastier Farm Bed and Breakfast

1902 Strecker Road, 44846
(419) 499-2985

The farm homestead has been in the
family for over 100 years. Now the
farmhouse is available for sharing with
travelers. Located two miles west of the
Ohio Turnpike exit 7, next to the Norfolk Southern Railroad between Toledo
and Cleveland. No pets or smoking.
Reservations required.

Hosts: Ted and Donna Gastier
Rooms: 3 (SB) $50
Continental Plus Breakfast
Credit Cards: A, B
Notes: 2, 5, 7, 8, 9, 10

Gastier Farm

MILLERSBURG

Berlin House Bed and Breakfast

4460 SR 39 East, 44654
(330) 674-1140

A quiet and peaceful B&B on the east
edge of Berlin village, in the heart of
the world's largest Amish community.
Convenient to all area attractions and
Amish-cooking restaurants. Delicious
continental breadfast features homemade bread and granola and locally-
made Swiss cheese. Three rooms with
king- or queen-size beds, cozy living
room with gas fireplace, kitchen, and
dining area. Relaxing outdoor patio and
backyard. A/C; no smoking. Rent one
room or the whole house—nightly or
weekly. Amish-Mennonite hosts.

Hosts: David and Erma Troyer, Karen Zook, and
    Wilma Dveck
Rooms: 3 (1PB; 2SB) $39-89
Continental Breakfast
Credit Cards: A, B
Notes: 2, 5, 7

---

5 Open all year; 6 Pets welcome; 7 Children welcome; 8 Tennis nearby; 9 Swimming nearby;
10 Golf nearby; 11 Skiing nearby; 12 May be booked through travel agent.

Bigham House Bed and Breakfast and English Tea Room

151 S. Washington Street, 44654
(330) 674-2337; (800) 689-6950

A 19th century B&B is located on a quiet street in the historic district of Millersburg, Ohio in the heart of the largest Amish settlement in the world. All rooms with private baths, queen-size beds, air-conditioning, and cable TV. Guest rooms are furnished with a mix of antiques and reproductions. Price includes a full, hearty breakfast.

Hosts: John and Janice Ellis
Rooms: 4 (PB) $55-75
Full Breakfast
Credit Cards: A, B, C, D
Notes: 2, 3, 5, 7, 9, 10, 12

Indiantree Farm Bed and Breakfast

5488 SR 515, 44654
(216) 893-2497

Peaceful lodging a in guest house on a picturesque hilltop farm in the heart of Amish Country, a mile from Walnut Creek. Large front porch, farming with horses, hiking trails. Apartments, with kitchen and bath, for the price of a room. An oasis where time slows and the mood is conversation, not television.

Hosts: Larry D. Miller
Rooms: 3 (PB) $60-75
Continental Breakfast
Credit Cards: none
Notes: 2, 5, 11

NEW PHILADELPHIA

Concetta's B&B

121 Beaver Avenue NE, 44663
(330) 343-7382; FAX (330) 339-7243

Concetta's is a charming, warm, newly renovated 1900 Victorian home, convenient to Amish Country, eight challenging golf courses, scenic Atwood an Tappan Lakes Region, and numerous other activities. We are also close to the Tuscarawas branch of Kent State University, Tuscarawas County courthouse, and New Philadelphia city square. Directory and information provided for your choice of worship services. Full home-cooked breakfast included.

Hostess: Vicki L. Maurer
Rooms: 3 (SB) $75
Full Breakfast
Credit Cards: 2, 5, 8, 9, 10
Notes: 2, 5, 8, 9, 10

OXFORD

The Duck Pond Bed and Breakfast

6391 Morning Sun Road, S.R. 732 N
Mail: PO Box 504, 45056
(513) 523-8914

An 1863 farmhouse situated three miles north of Miami University and uptown Oxford, and two miles south of Hueston Woods State Park, which has an 18-hole golf course, nature trails, boating, swimming, and fishing. Antiquing is just 15 miles away. Come and enjoy the quaintness that only a B&B can offer. Be our guest and enjoy our famous Hawaiian French toast. Reservations are required,

---

NOTES: Credit cards accepted: A Master Card; B Visa; C American Express; D Discover; E Diners Club; F Other; 2 Personal checks accepted; 3 Lunch available; 4 Dinner available;

so please call in advance. The Duck Pond is a member of OBBA (Ohio Bed and Breakfast Association) and has met OBBA standards inspection.

Hosts: Don and Toni Kohlstedt
Rooms: 4 (1PB; 3SB) $50-70 ($10 for extra person)
Full Country Breakfast
Credit Cards: none
Notes: 2, 5, 7 (over 12), 8, 9, 10

PLAIN CITY

Yoder's Bed and Breakfast

8144 Cemetery Pike, 43064
(614) 873-4489

Located on a 107-acre farm northwest of Columbus. Big Darby Creek runs along the front yard. Excellent bird-watching and fishing in the creek. The house is air-conditioned. Rooms have king and queen beds. We are within minutes of two Amish restaurants, gift shops, cheese house, chocolate house, Amish furniture store, bookstores, and antiques shops. Only about 30 minutes from downtown Columbus. No smoking.

Hosts: Claribel and Loyd Yoder
Rooms: 4 (1PB; 3SB) $55-65
Full Breakfast
Credit Cards: none
Notes: 2, 5, 9, 10

POLAND

Inn at the Green

500 S. Main Street, 44514
(330) 757-4688

An 1876 classic Victorian townhouse sharing village green with a Presbyte-rian church founded in 1802. The Inn retains 12-foot ceilings, large moldings, five working Italian marble fireplaces, interior window shutters, and poplar floors. The Inn is decorated with antiques, American art, and Oriental rugs. Poland is a preserved western reserve village in which President William McKinley grew up from age 8 to 24.

Hosts: Ginny and Steve MeLoy
Rooms: 4 (PB) $60
Continental Breakfast
Credit Cards: A, B, D
Notes: 2, 5, 7, 8, 9, 10, 12

Inn at the Green

SANDUSKY

The 1890 Queen Anne Bed and Breakfast

714 Wayne Street, 44870
(419) 626-0391

Spacious accommodations with charm and elegance await guests at the 1890 Queen Anne B&B in downtown Sandusky. Built of native limestone, this 100-year-old Victorian homelands ambiance and romance for its guests. Three large air-conditioned rooms offer tranquil luxury for relaxation. Beauty abounds in the regal outdoors as viewed from a screened-in porch where continental plus breakfasts are enjoyed. Easy access abounds to beaches, Lake Erie island boat trips, Cedar Point, shopping, and other recreational opportunities. Brochure available upon request.

Hosts: Robert and Joan Kromer
Rooms: 3 (PB) $75-85
Continental Plus Breakfast
Credit Cards: A, B, D
Notes: 2, 5, 8, 9, 10

SIDNEY

GreatStone Castle

429 N. Ohio Avenue, 45365
(513) 498-4728; FAX (513) 498-9950

GreatStone Castle, registered with the National Historical Society, is a 100-year-old mansion on two beautiful acres. The Castle is constructed of 18-inch limestone with three turrets and is finished with rare, imported hardwood. Antique furniture, fireplaces, and fine furnishings help complete the elegant setting. Deluxe continental breakfast served in conservatory.

Hosts: Frederick and Victoria Keller
Rooms: 5 (3PB; 2SB) $60-90
Deluxe Continental Breakfast
Credit Cards: A, B, C
Notes: 2, 5, 6, 9, 10, 11, 12

STRASBURG

Ellis's Bed and Breakfast

104 Fourth Street SW, 44680
(330) 878-7863

Our turn-of-the-century home is com-

fortably furnished for your "home away from home." A big screen TV in the sunken living room and a secluded patio are for your relaxation. A tasty, complete breakfast, different each morning, is served in the dining room using our best china, silver, etc. We are conveniently located for Zoar, Amish Country, Dover/New Philadelphia, and Canton. Antiques, flea markets, gift shops, and restaurants abound. No smoking, please.

Hosts: Tom and Grace Ellis
Rooms: 3 (SB) $50 ($35 single)
Full Breakfast
Credit Cards: none
Notes: 2, 5, 7

SUGARCREEK

Breitenbach Bed and Breakfast

307 Dover Road, 44681
(330) 343-3603; (800) THE WINE (inside Ohio only); FAX (330) 343-8290

Splendid accommodations in a quaint Swiss village in the heart of Amish country. This home is artistically furnished with a mixture of antiques, ethnic treasures, and local arts and crafts. Nearby Amish restaurants, cheese houses, flea markets, antique malls, and quilt and craft shops. Evening refresh-

Breitenbach Bed and Breakfast

NOTES: Credit cards accepted: A Master Card; B Visa; C American Express; D Discover; E Diners Club; F Other; 2 Personal checks accepted; 3 Lunch available; 4 Dinner available;

ments and a full gourmet breakfast.

Hostess: Deanna Bear
Rooms: 4 (PB) $65-85
Full Breakfast
Credit Cards: A, B, C
Notes: 2, 5, 8, 10

Hickory Bend Bed and Breakfast

SUGAR GROVE

Hickory Bend Bed and Breakfast

7541 Dupler Road SE, 43155
(614) 746-8381

Nestled in the Hocking Hills of south-eastern Ohio on ten wooded acres. "So peaceful, we got to go out to watch the car go by on Sunday afternoon," says Pat. Patty is a spinner and a weaver. The cozy, private room with private bath is located outside the home in the midst of dogwood, poplar, and oak trees. Guests come to the home for breakfast and conversation. Heated in the winter and cooled in the summer. Write for brochure.

Hosts: Pat and Patty Peery
Rooms: 1 (PB) $50
Full Breakfast
Credit Cards: none
Notes: 2, 8, 9, 10

TIPP CITY

The Willowtree Inn

1900 West Street Route 571, 45371
(513) 667-2957 (voice and FAX)

Nestled on five country acres and surrounded by rolling fields. The Willowtree Inn is the perfect getaway. An ancient willow tree drowses by a spring-fed pond while ducks lazily paddle by. It's a place to relax, kick your shoes off, and enjoy good old-fashioned hospitality. Built in 1830, our 6,000 square-foot historic estate has been fully restored. The original wide plank, ash floors and built-in book-shelves add elegance to the front parlor, where guests gather for complimentary evening refreshments.

Hosts: Charles H. Sell, II and Jolene K. Sell
Rooms: 3 (PB) $65-85
Full Breakfast
Credit Cards: A, B
Notes: 2, 5, 7, 10, 12

URBANA

At Home in Urbana Bed and Breakfast

301 Scioto Street, 43078-2129
(513) 653-8595; (800) 800-0970;
FAX (513) 652-4400

Restored 1842 home in historic district. Furnished in Victorian period pieces and family antiques. Two blocks away from downtown shops and restaurants. All rooms are air-conditioned and have

5 Open all year; 6 Pets welcome; 7 Children welcome; 8 Tennis nearby; 9 Swimming nearby; 10 Golf nearby; 11 Skiing nearby; 12 May be booked through travel agent.

private baths. Non-smoking guests only.

Hosts: Grant and Shirley Ingersoll
Rooms: 3 + 1 suite (PB) $60-90
Full Breakfast
Credit Cards: A, B, C, D
Notes: 2, 5, 10, 11

WAKEMAN

Melrose Farm

727 Vesta Road, 44889
(419) 929-1867 (voice and FAX)

Situated halfway between Ashland and Oberlin, Melrose Farm is a peaceful country retreat. Each of the three lovely guestrooms in the 125-year-old brick house has its own private bath. Guests will enjoy the tennis court, stocked pond, perennial gardens, and quiet rural setting. Thirty miles from Cedar Point, one hours drive from Cleveland or Toledo, and two hours from Columbus. Old-fashioned relaxed hospitality.

Hosts: Abe and Eleanor Klassen
Rooms: 3 (PB) $75
Full Breakfast
Credit Cards: none
Notes: 2, 3, 5, 7, 8 (on-site), 9, 10

Hasseman House Inn

WILMOT

Hasseman House Inn

925 US 62, PO Box 215, 44689
(330) 359-7904; FAX (330) 359-7159

Situated at the door to Ohio's Amish country is the Hasseman House Inn. This charming and warm, early 1900 Victorian inn invites you to unpack your bags and relax. Furnished with antiques, the Hassman House Inn is indeed a step back into a bygone era. The Inn features four cozy rooms complete with private baths and air-conditioning. You will fall in love with the intricate woodwork and original stained glass. Walk-ins are welcome!

Hosts: Milo and Kathryn Miller
Contact: Debbie Schlabach
Rooms: 4 (PB) $69-110
Full Breakfast (Continental on Sunday)
Credit Cards: A, B, D
Notes: 2, 5, 9

Raber's Tri County View

PO Box 155, 44689
(330) 359-5189

Located in the world's largest Amish settlement, with lots of rolling hills and fields all around. Each room has its own unique, peaceful atmosphere and decor, with a private bath, queen-size beds, central heating and air, microwave, refigerator, and coffee pot. A garden swing where you can relax and enjoy the view of three different counties. No smoking inside. One mile from Wilmot, ten miles from Berlin, Walnut Creek, and Kidron of Amish Country. Lots of quilts, antiques, and craft shops, cheese

NOTES: Credit cards accepted: A Master Card; B Visa; C American Express; D Discover; E Diners Club; F Other; 2 Personal checks accepted; 3 Lunch available; 4 Dinner available;

houses, furniture stores, and the best restaurants in the state.

Hosts: Ed and Esther Raber
Rooms: 3 + 1 suite (PB) $55-85
Full Breakfast
Credit Cards: A, B
Notes: 2, 5, 7, 8, 9, 10

WINTERSVILLE

The Lamp Post Bed and Breakfast

372 Canton Road, 43952
(614) 264-0591

Your home away from home, decorated in country style with stained-glass windows, lamps, and sun catchers. Much of the decor is handmade with loving care to add to the country look. Just a short 15 minutes from Franciscian University, which boasts of having students from 50 states and 43 foreign countries. The mall is 10 minutes from our house, along with dining establishments from fast food to sit-down dinners.

Hosts: Bill and Peggy Duncan
Rooms: 2 (SB) $46
Full Breakfast
Credit Cards: none
Notes: 2

WOOSTER

Historic Overholt House Bed and Breakfast

1473 Beall Avenue, 44691
(330) 263-6300 (voice and FAX); (800) 992-0643

Elegantly decorated, "Stick Style Vic-

torian," historic home with a rare solid walnut "flying staircase," is located at the gateway to Amish Country and adjacent to the College of Wooster campus. Romantic packages, mystery evening, and gift certificates available. Enjoy a full breakfast with homemade breads and goodies. Hot tub available for guests. AAA approved.

Hostesses: Sandy Pohalski and Bobbie Walton
Rooms: 3 (PB) $63-70
Full Breakfast
Credit Cards: A, B, D
Notes: 2, 5; 7, 8, 9, 10

Millenium Classic Bed and Breakfast

1626 Beall Avenue, 44691
(330) 264-6005; (800) 937-4199;
FAX (330) 264-5008

Millennium Classic Bed and Breakfast is centrally located right in the heart of Wooster. Close to College of Wooster, hospital, shopping mall, restaurants, grocery store, and the bus stops in front of house. A Post Victorian architectural style exterior home, following traditional, classic theme in the interior. Lots of decks, porches, quiet sitting areas, and shade trees. A friendly, homelike atmosphere.

Innkeeper: John Byler
Rooms: 5 (3PB; 1SB) $45-95
Continental Breakfast
Credit Cards: A, B
Notes: 2, 5, 7, 8, 9, 10, 12

---

5 Open all year; 6 Pets welcome; 7 Children welcome; 8 Tennis nearby; 9 Swimming nearby; 10 Golf nearby; 11 Skiing nearby; 12 May be booked through travel agent.

OKLAHOMA

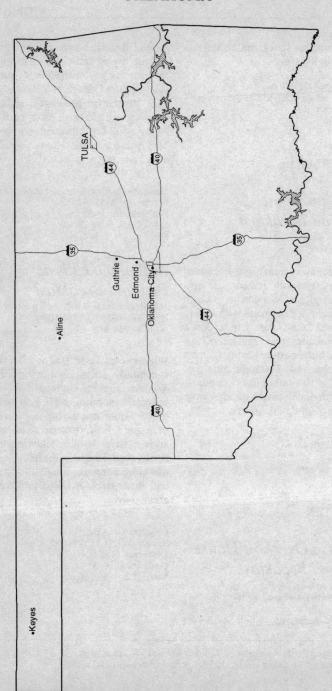

Oklahoma

ALINE

Heritage Manor

R.R. 3, Box 33, 73716
(405) 463-2563 or (405) 463-2566;
(800) 295-2563

Heritage Manor is a country getaway on 80 acres that was settled in the 1893 Land Run in northwest Oklahoma. Two pre-statehood homes have been joined together and restored by innkeepers using a Victorian theme. Beautiful sunrises, sunsets, and stargazing from rooftop deck and relaxing in the hot tub or reading a book from the 5,000-volume library. Ostriches, donkeys, and Scotch Highland cattle roam a fenced area. Close to Selenite Crystal digging area and several other attractions.

Hosts: A.J. and Carolyn Rexroat
Rooms: 4 (1 PB; 3SB) $50-150
Full Breakfast
Credit Cards: none
Notes: 2, 3 and 4 (by reservation), 5, 6 and 7 (by arrangement), 9, 10 (30 miles)

EDMOND

The Arcadian Inn

328 E. First Street, 73034
(405) 340-7486; (800) 299-6347

With angels watching over you, you are ministered peace and relaxation. The Arcadian Inn is a step back in time to the era of Christian love, hospitality, and family values. The historical home of Dr. Ruhl, the inn has five luxurious Victorian guests rooms with tubs, fireplaces, canopy beds, and sunrooms. Sumptuous homemade breakfast served in the sunny dining room beneath cherub paintings. Perfect for romantic getaways, business travelers, or old-fashioned family gatherings. Jacuzzi and outdoor spa available.

Hosts: Martha and Gary Hall
Rooms: 6 (PB) $85-195
Full Breakfast
Credit Cards: A, B, C, D
Notes: 2, 5, 8, 9, 10, 12

NOTES: Credit cards accepted: A Master Card; B Visa; C American Express; D Discover; E Diners Club; F Other; 2 Personal checks accepted; 3 Lunch available; 4 Dinner available; 5 Open all year; 6 Pets welcome; 7 Children welcome; 8 Tennis nearby; 9 Swimming nearby; 10 Golf nearby; 11 Skiing nearby; 12 May be booked through travel agent.

Victorian Rose Bed and Breakfast

GUTHRIE

Victorian Rose
Bed and Breakfast

415 E. Cleveland, 73044
(405) 282-3928

The 100-year-old Queen Anne-style home, built in 1894, mixes the charm of the past with the comforts of the present. Located on a brick street and features a wraparound porch with gingerbread accents, with porch swing and garden area. Lovely restoration with quality workmanship are displayed with beautiful oak floors, exquisite original beveled windows, gleaming brass light fixtures, and antiques. Located three blocks from historic downtown (the largest urban historical fistrict in the U.S.). Three beautiful Victorian guest rooms offer queen-size beds and private baths. Full, comple-mentary, gourmet breakfast. Family rates and gift certificates available.

Hosts: Linda and Foy Shahan
Rooms: 3 (PB) $74-84
Full Gourmet Breakfast
Credit Cards: A, B, D
Notes: 2, 5, 7, 8, 9, 10, 12

KEYES

Cattle Country Inn

HCR 1, Box 34, 73947
(405) 543-6458

We are truly country located. If you like wide open spaces where you can see for miles and not be in hearing distance of any highway traffic, you are welcome to stay with us. Located in the pan-handle between Guymon and Boise City, the Inn is a nice stopping place on the way to or from the Rockies. Come experience the hospitality and hearty cookin' served up by your host in the beautiful, spacious, and very modern ranch-style home. Located 38 miles west of Guymon on Hwy. 64 then eight and one half miles south on dirt roads. Cimaron County, the last county west, has many points of interest, as well as plenty of good prairie dog and pheas-ant hunting.

Hosts: Lane and Karen Sparkman
Rooms: 6 (3SB) $45-65
Full Breakfast
Credit Cards: A, B, C
Notes: 2, 3, 4, 5, and 7 (all by reservation)

NOTES: Credit cards accepted: A Master Card; B Visa; C American Express; D Discover; E Diners Club; F Other; 2 Personal checks accepted; 3 Lunch available; 4 Dinner available;

OKLAHOMA CITY

The Grandison Bed and Breakfast

1841 NW 15th, 73106
(405) 521-0011 (voice and FAX);
(800) 240-INNS

This three-story, country Victorian sits on a large double lot with beautifully landscaped gardens, trees taller than the house, and a gazebo. Built in 1912, the home has all the original brass and crystal chandeliers and stained glass windows. It is furnished throughout with antiques from the turn-of-the-century. There is a jacuzzi in the third-floor suite. Just ten minutes from Myriad Gardens and Convention Center, State Fairgrounds, Remington Park Raceway, Oklahoma City Zoo, The National Cowboy Hall of Fame, and many wonderful restaurants and shopping facilities.

Hosts: Claudia and Bob Wright
Rooms: 5 (PB) $55-125
Full Breakfast
Credit Cards: A, B, C, D
Notes: 2, 3, 4, 5, 6 and 7 (by reservation)

The Grandison at Maney Park

1200 N. Shartel, 73103
(405) 232-8778; (800) 240-4667;
FAX (405) 521-0011

Nine bedrooms featuring antique furnishings, queen- and king-size beds, private baths with double jacuzzi and shower, gas fireplaces. Built in 1904 and moved to its present locations in 1909, the home features carved mahogany woodwork, massive entry with curved staircase, original stained glass and brass fixtures—charming details at every turn. We offer both romantic getaways and executive services. TV and phone in rooms on request, refreshment bar, work-out room, and gift shop.

Hosts: Bob and Claudia Wright
Rooms: 9 (PB) $65-150
Full Breakfast on weekends (Continental breakfast on weekdays)
Credit Cards: A, B, C, D
Notes: 2, 5, 6, 7, 12

---

5 Open all year; 6 Pets welcome; 7 Children welcome; 8 Tennis nearby; 9 Swimming nearby; 10 Golf nearby; 11 Skiing nearby; 12 May be booked through travel agent.

OREGON

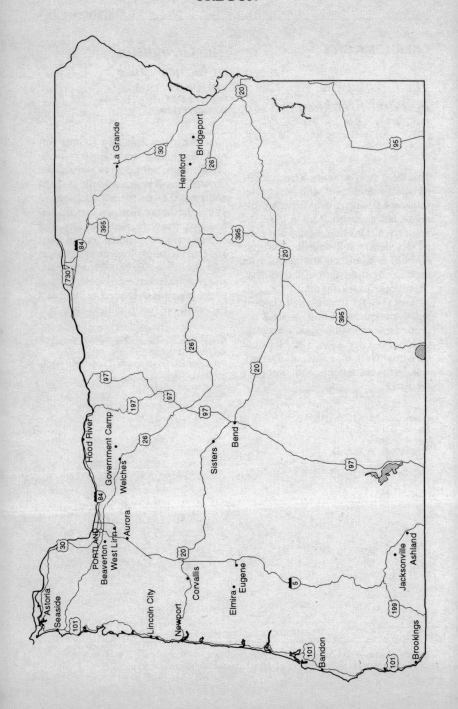

Oregon

ASHLAND

Cowslip's Belle B&B

159 N. Main Street, 97520
(541) 488-2901; (800) 888-6819;
FAX (541) 482-6138

Teddy bears, chocolate truffles, cozy down comforters, and scrumptious breakfasts. A delightful 1913 Craftsman bungalow and carriage house in the heart of Ashland's historic district. A nationally recognized award-winner, featured in *McCall's* a one of the "Most Charming Inns in America", *Country Accents* magazine, "Northwest Best Places," "The Best Places to Kiss in the Pacific Northwest," and "Weekends for Two in the Pacific Northwest—50 Romantic Getaways."

Hosts: Jon and Carmen Reinhardt
Rooms: 4 (PB) $75-120
Full Breakfast
Credit Cards: A, B
Notes: 2, 5, 8, 9, 10, 11, 12

Mt. Ashland Inn

550 Mt. Ashland Ski Road, 97520
(541) 482-8707; (800) 830-8707;
FAX (541) 482-8707

Beautifully handcrafted log lodge and sauna/spa terrace command spectacular views from mountain ridge just south of Ashland. Rock fireplace, Oriental rugs, and antique furnishings create warm, luxurious atmosphere. Hike or ski the Pacific Crest Trail from the front door. Quality snowshoes and mountain bikes available at no charge. "A magical mountian retreat,." says *Country Home*; *** Northwest Best Places; AAA; Mobil; "A retreat for all seasons …promises renewal, relaxation, and adventure!" *Country Livin*g magazine.

Hosts: Chuck and Laurel Biegert
Rooms: 5 (PB) $76-180
Full Breakfast
Credit Cards: A, B, C, D
Notes: 2, 5, 8, 9, 10, 11, 12

Mt. Ashland Inn

NOTES: Credit cards accepted: A Master Card; B Visa; C American Express; D Discover; E Diners Club; F Other; 2 Personal checks accepted; 3 Lunch available; 4 Dinner available; 5 Open all year; 6 Pets welcome; 7 Children welcome; 8 Tennis nearby; 9 Swimming nearby; 10 Golf nearby; 11 Skiing nearby; 12 May be booked through travel agent.

The Redwing Bed and Breakfast

115 N. Main Street, 97520
(541) 482-1807; (800) 461-6743;
FAX (541) 488-1433

The Redwing, nestled in Ashland's charming historic district, is a 1911 craftsman-style home with its original lighting fixtures, beautiful wood, and comfortable decor. Each of our inviting guest rooms enjoy its own distinctive intimacy, queen-size beds, and private bath. We are located one city block from the Shakespeare Festival, Lithia Park, restaurants, and gift shops. In addition, downhill and cross-country skiing, river rafting, and fishing are nearby. July 1994, *Bon Appetit.*

Hosts: Mike and Judi Cook
Rooms: 3 (PB) $70-125
Full Breakfast
Credit Cards: A, B, D
Notes: 2, 5, 8, 9, 10, 11

ASTORIA

Columbia River Inn Bed and Breakfast

1681 Franklin Avenue, 97103
(503) 325-5044; (800) 953-5044

Columbia River Inn is charming in every way. Built in 1870, this beautiful "Painted Lady" Victorian has a gazebo for weddings and parties in the beautifully landscaped garden. Come see the "stairway to the stars," a unique terraced garden view of the celebrated Columbia River. The Inn offers four elegantly furnished rooms, all with private baths,

and one with a working fireplace and jacuzzi tub. Many memories are discovered and the experience will last forever. My specialty is hospitality, "Home is where the heart is. . ." Off-street parking available.

Hostess: Mrs. Karen N. Nelson
Rooms: 4 (PB) $75-125
Full Breakfast
Credit Cards: A, B
Notes: 2, 5, 7, 10

Columbia River Inn

Franklin Street Station Bed and Breakfast Inn

1140 Franklin Street, 97103
(503) 325-4314; (800) 448-1098

Featured in the *Los Angeles Times* travel section and recipient excellent ratings in many B&B guide books, this Victorian home is decorated beautifully and reflects the early years of Astoria with its ornate craftsmanship. We are close to downtown and walking distance to museums and restaurants. Our accommodations include five rooms, three which have views of the Columbia River and two are two-room suites. Our full complimentary breakfast includes our specialty of Belgium Waffles, sausage, fresh fruit, juice, and coffee. We will make your stay a memorable one and know you'll return again.

Hostess: Reneé Caldwell
Rooms: 5 (PB) $63-115
Full Breakfast
Credit Cards: A, B, C, D
Notes: 2, 5, 7, 8, 9, 10, 12

Inn-Chanted Bed and Breakfast

707 Eighth Street, 97103
(503) 325-5223; (800) 455-7018

The historic Fulton House, built in 1883, is beautifully decorated with silk brocade wallpaper, crystal chandeliers, and ornately painted medallions and columns. Guest rooms have magnificent views of the Columbia River, private baths, queen-size beds, and TVs. Full gourmet breakfasts. Dolls and trains displayed. Within walking distance to historic buildings, town, and antique shops.

Hosts: Richard and Dixie Swart
Rooms: 3 (PB) $70-100
Full Breakfast
Credit Cards: A, B, C, D
Notes: 2, 5, 7, 8, 12

AURORA

The Inn at Aurora

15109 NE Second Street, 97002
(503) 678-1932

Designed and furnished to reflect the simplicity of the Old Aurora Colony, this new home is located in the National Historic District near The Ox Barn Museum and numerous antique shops. Hand-crafted items by local artists are also available. Seasonal fresh fruits, berries, nuts, and vegetables are treasures of this area together with unique places to dine. Champoeg State Park by the Willamette River and Silver Falls State Park are nearby for hiking and biking. All rooms have king beds, private baths, air-conditioning, cable TV, phone, and refrigerator. The suite is hearthside with a spa tub. Upper room balconies offer pleasant views of Aurora and the natural landscape.

Hostess: Elizabeth Heininge
Rooms: 4 (PB) $69-105
Full Breakfast
Credit Cards: A, B
Notes: 5, 6 (by prior arrantement), 7, 10, 12

The Inn at Aurora

BANDON

Sea Star Guesthouse

370 First Street, 97411
(503) 347-9632; FAX (503) 347-9533

Consider a visit to a uniquely designed coastal getaway in historic Old Town Bandon's waterfront offering of the

5 Open all year; 6 Pets welcome; 7 Children welcome; 8 Tennis nearby; 9 Swimming nearby; 10 Golf nearby; 11 Skiing nearby; 12 May be booked through travel agent.

harbor and beachlands. Sleeping rooms or full suites have private baths, queen beds, cable TV, coffee/tea servie, and optional continental breakfast. Suites have fully equipped kitchens and a sofa bed or futon in living room. No smoking.

Hostess: Eileen Sexton
Rooms: 4 (PB) $40-90
Full or Continental Breakfast
Credit Cards: A, B, C
Notes: 3, 4, 5, 7, 9, 10

BEAVERTON

The Yankee Tinker Bed and Breakfast

5480 SW 183rd Avenue, 97007
(503) 649-0932; (800) 846-5372

"A hand-crafted New England experience in the heart of Northwest Oregon." Located ten miles west of Portland in a peaceful residential neighborhood. From here, visit wineries, farmers' markets, historical sites as well as the dramatic Columbia River Gorge and grand Oregon beaches. Three distinctive guest rooms with comfortable beds are graced by handmade quilts, antiques, family heirlooms, and include A/C. Guest sitting room features a fireplace and TV; private yard has spacious deck and gardens. Memorable breakfasts, served alfresco weather permitting, are designed to accommodate special dietary needs and your schedule. The mouthwatering choices might include blueberry pancakes or muffins, peaches 'n cream French toast, or herbed omelets. Benefit from "all the extras" that make your business or leisure travel successful.

The *Yankee Tinker's* warmth and hospitality will convince you to linger an extra day or two as well as to plan a return visit.

Hosts: Jan and Ralph Wadleigh
Rooms: 3 (2PB; 2SB) $60-70
Full Breakfast
Credit Cards: A, B, C, D, E
Notes: 2, 5, 9, 10, 12

BEND

Gazebo Bed and Breakfast

21679 Obsidian Avenue, 97702
(541) 389-7202

Come visit our country home with a panoramic view of the Cascades from Mt. Hood to Mt. Bachelor. Relax among our antique furnishings or in the rock garden and gazebo. Enjoy nearby skiing, hiking, fishing, rafting, and the best golfing in Oregon. Minutes from town. Family-style breakfast. Smoking outdoors only.

Hosts: Gale and Helen Estergreen
Rooms: 2 (1PB; 1SB) $50-60
Full Breakfast
Credit Cards: none
Notes: 2, 5, 7, 9, 10, 11

BRIDGEPORT

Bruno Ranch Bed and Breakfast and Primitive Campground

PO Box 51, 97819
(541) 446-3468

Plenty of wildlife, peace, and quiet! Come and enjoy Old World hospitality

---

NOTES: Credit cards accepted: A Master Card; B Visa; C American Express; D Discover; E Diners Club; F Other; 2 Personal checks accepted; 3 Lunch available; 4 Dinner available;

and New World country charm at a ranch that adjoins the Wallowa-Whitman National Forest—rural Oregon at its best! Just 25 miles south of Baker, the surrounding land abounds with opportunities for good fishing, hunting, hiking, and scenic driving. Plan a few days with us to rest and recharge! Two rooms available year-round.

Hostess: Maria Bruno
Rooms: 2 (SB) $30
Full Breakfast
Credit Cards: none
Notes: 3, 4, 5, 7

Bruno Ranch

BROOKINGS

Chetco River Inn
21202 High Prairie Road, 97415
(541) 469-8128; (800) 327-2688

35 wooded acres of privacy and tranquillity on the river. Modern facility using alternate energy. Full country breakfast included. Dinners available with prior arrangements. Hiking, fishing, swimming, star gazing, nature watching, and relaxing are waiting for

you. Coastal town and Kalmiopsis Wilderness Area are close by. Great for retreats and small groups.

Hostess: Sandra Brugger
Rooms: 4 (3PB; 1SB) $95-105
Full Breakfast
Credit Cards: A, B
Notes: 2, 4, 5, 7, 9, 12

CORVALLIS

Abed and Breakfast at Spark's Hearth
2515 SW 45th Street., 97333
(541) 757-7321; FAX (541) 753-4332

Critque passing golfers from our back deck or spoil yourself in the outdoor spa—we furnish plush body towels and robes, you bring a suit. Visit on red velvet Victorian furnishings and Oriental carpets in the living room, or crash in comfort in the TV/reading room. Sleep in country quiet on a king bed in a king-sized bedroom. Awake to a full breakfast including fresh fruit compote, hot entree, and homemade pie and served on china and crystal. Life is good!

Hosts: Neoma and Herb Sparks
Rooms: 4 (2PB; 2SB) $65-78
Full Breakfast
Credit Cards: A, B, C, D
Notes: 2, 5, 7 (over 8), 8, 9, 10, 12

ELMIRA

McGillivray's Log Home Bed and Breakfast
88680 Evers Road, 97437-9733
(541) 935-3564

Fourteen miles west of Eugene, on the

---

5 Open all year; 6 Pets welcome; 7 Children welcome; 8 Tennis nearby; 9 Swimming nearby; 10 Golf nearby; 11 Skiing nearby; 12 May be booked through travel agent.

McGillivray's Log Home

way to the coast, you will find the best of yesterday and the comforts of today. King beds, air-conditioning, and quiet. Old-fashioned breakfasts are usually prepared on an antique, wood-burning cookstove. This built-from-scratch 1982 log home is near Fern Ridge Lake.

Hostess: Evelyn McGillivray
Rooms: 2 (PB) $70-80
Full Breakfast
Credit Cards: A, B
Notes: 2, 5

EUGENE

Camille's Bed and Breakfast

3277 Onyx Place, 97405
(541) 344-9576; FAX (541) 345-9970

Camille's Bed and Breakfast is a 60s contemporary home in quiet, woodsy neighborhood furnished with American country antiques. Rooms have wonderfully comfortable queen beds, with work space. Cozy guest sitting room with phone and TV. Full hearty breakfast. Located just over a mile south of the University of Oregon, downtown is just minutes away. Bike path and park

with major jogging path nearby. Excellent restaurant within walking distance. One hour drive to Oregon coast.

Hosts: Bill and Camille Kievith
Rooms: 2 (1PB; 2SB) $55-70
Full Breakfast
Credit Cards: none
Notes: 2, 5, 8, 9, 10

The Campbell House, A City Inn

252 Pearl Street, 97401
(541) 343-1119; (800) 264-2519;
FAX (541) 343-2258

Splendor and romance in the tradition of a fine European hotel. Each of the elegant rooms feature private bath, TV/VCR, telephone, and robes. Selected rooms feature a four-poster bed, fireplace, and jetted or clawfoot tub. Take pleasure from the Old World ambiance of the parlor and library with a fine selection of books and videos to choose from. Walking distance to restaurants, theaters, museums, and shops. Two blocks from nine miles of riverside bike paths and jogging trails.

Hostess: Mrya Plant
Rooms: 20 (PB) $79-450
Full Breakfast
Credit Cards: A, B, C, D
Notes: 3, 7, 9, 10, 12

Kjaer's House in the Woods Bed and Breakfast

814 Lorane Highway, 97405
(541) 343-3234

This 1910 Craftsman home in a park-like setting provides urban convenience

---

NOTES: Credit cards accepted: A Master Card; B Visa; C American Express; D Discover; E Diners Club; F Other; 2 Personal checks accepted; 3 Lunch available; 4 Dinner available;

and suburban tranquillity. The grounds have both wildflowers and landscaped shrubs, colorful in the spring but peaceful throughout the year; wildlife is abundant. The home is furnished with antiques, Oriental carpets, a square rosewood grand piano, an extensive music library, and a plate collection. A full breakfast is served featuring local cheeses, nuts, and fruits. In operation since 1984 this B&B is inspected by the Eugene Area B&B Association and the Oregon B&B Guild. Hosts are long time Eugene residents who take pleasure in sharing their knowledge of the area with guests.

Hosts: George and Eunice Kjaer
Rooms: 2 (PB) $55-75
Full Breakfast
Credit Cards: none
Notes: 2, 5, 7, 8, 9, 10, 12

Fort Reading Bed and Breakfast

HEREFORD

Fort Reading Bed and Breakfast

HCR 86 Box 140, 97837
(541) 446-3478 (voice and FAX); (800) 573-4285

We are a working cattle ranch located 40 miles southwest of Baker City, in the Burnt River Valley. While you're with us, enjoy a stroll around the ranch, the country charm of your own two-bedroom cottage, amd a ranch-style breakfast in the ranch house breakfast room. Squirrel, deer, and elk hunts can be arranged. There are also streams and lake nearby for fishing. No smoking.

Hosts: Daryl and Barbara Hawes
Rooms: 2 (SB) $40-75
Full Ranch-style Breakfast
Credit Cards: none
Open April through September
Notes: 2, 3, 4, 6, 7

HOOD RIVER

The Upper Rooms on Avalon

3444 Avalon Drive, 97031
(503) 386-2560; (888) 386-3941
Email: upperrooms@moriah.com

Down home charm in our renovated Avalon farmhouse on the Heights in Hood River. Just minutes from skiing, windsurfing, and other outdoor recreation. Cozy neighborhood with little traffic noise and yet just bordering city limits. Deck and large upstairs bedrooms with views of Mt. Adams. Relaxed friendly atmosphere. Family style breakfast. Barbeque available. Reasonable rates.

Hosts: Jim and Dorothy Tollen
Rooms: 2 (SB) $65
Full Breakfast
Credit Cards: A, B
Notes: 5, 7, 8, 9, 10, 11, 12

---

5 Open all year; 6 Pets welcome; 7 Children welcome; 8 Tennis nearby; 9 Swimming nearby;
10 Golf nearby; 11 Skiing nearby; 12 May be booked through travel agent.

JACKSONVILLE

The Touvelle House

455 N. Oregon Street, PO Box 1891, 97530
(541) 899-8938

Stang Manor Inn

Judge Touvelle's wife designed this stately 1916 Craftsman-style mansion which stands on one and a half acres two blocks from Jacksonville's main street. Six charming bedrooms each have their own bathrooms, and the Inn also features a great room, a library, a sunroom, and a dining room. Outside there are two spacious covered verandas, a pool, and a spa. Come stay with us to be pampered and spoiled like hotel guests were at the turn of the century. We serve a complete breakfast and refreshments are available.

Hosts: Carolee and Dennis Casey
Rooms: 6 (PB) $70-105
Full Breakfast
Credit Cards: A, B, C, D
Notes: 2, 5, 9 (on-site), 10, 11, 12

LA GRANDE

Stang Manor Inn

1612 Walnut, 97850
(503) 963-2400 (voice and FAX); (888) 286-9463

Capturing the romance and elegance of a former era, Stang Manor is a lovingly preserved, Georgian Colonial home which beckons even the casual traveler to bask in its comfort and hospitality. One of the rooms adjoins a balcony overlooking the rose garden. The suite features a large fireplace in its comfortable sitting room. Extraordinary woodwork throughout the house serves as a reminder that the original owner, Au-

gust Stange, spared no expense to make this 1920s mansion a masterpiece. Full breakfast in the formal dining room sparkles with silver, crystal, candles, and conversation.

Hosts: Marjorie and Pat McClure
Rooms: 4 (PB) $70-90 (includes tax)
Full Breakfast
Credit Cards: A, B, D
Notes: 2, 5, 10, 11, 12

LINCOLN CITY

Brey House "OCEAN VIEW" B&B Inn

3725 NW Keel Avenue, 97367
(541) 994-7123

The ocean awaits you just across the street. Enjoy whale-watching, storm-watching, or just beach-combing. We are conveniently located a short walking distance away from local restaurants and retail shops. Four beautiful rooms to choose from, all with private baths and queen beds. Flannel sheets and electric blankets in all rooms. Enjoy Milt and Shirley's talked-about breakfast. Three-story, Cape Code style house.

Hosts: Milt and Shirley Brey
Rooms: 4 (PB) $70-135
Full Breakfast
Credit Cards: A, B, D
Notes: 2, 5, 9, 10, 12

NOTES: Credit cards accepted: A Master Card; B Visa; C American Express; D Discover; E Diners Club; F Other; 2 Personal checks accepted; 3 Lunch available; 4 Dinner available;

Pacific Rest B&B

1611 NE 11th Street, 97367
(541) 994-BEDS (2337)

Newer home on hillside within walking distance to shops, restaurants, and beach. Offering large rooms, private baths, covered decks, and large gathering room for visiting and relaxing. Family operated with gracious hospitality and personal service. Christian counseling available. Books for inspiration and. enjoyment. Small pets and children welcome. Partial ocean view from rooms. One unit sleeps five; the other unit sleeps three. Full gourmet breakfast and evening dessert.

Hosts: Ray and Judy Waetjen
Rooms: 2 (PB) $75
Full Breakfast
Credit Cards: none
Notes: 2, 5, 6, 7, 8, 9, 10, 12

Pacific Rest

MOUNT HOOD AREA (SEE ALSO WELCHES)

Falcon's Crest Inn

PO Box 185, 87287 Government Camp Loop
Hwy., **Government Camp** 97028
(503) 272-3403; (800) 624-7384 (reservations);
FAX (503) 272-3454

Falcon's Crest Inn is a beautiful mountain lodge/chalet-style house, architecturally designed to fit into the quiet natural forest and majestic setting of the Cascades. Conveniently located at the intersection of Highway 26 and the Government Camp Loop Highway, it is within walking distance to Ski Bowl, a year-round playground featuring downhill skiing in the winter and the Alpine Slide in the summer! The Inn has five suites, all with private baths. Each guest room is individually decorated with interesting and unique collectibles and views of mountains and forest. Telephones are available for guest use in each suite. Smoking restricted. Fine dining restaurant on premises and ski packages available! Multiple nights discounts available.

Hosts: B.J. and Melody Johnson
Rooms: 5 (PB) $95-179
Full Breakfast
Credit Cards: A, B, C, D
Notes: 2, 4, 5, 9, 10, 11, 12

NEWPORT

Oar House Bed and Breakfast

520 SW Second Street, 97365
(541) 265-9571; (800) 252-2358

A Lincoln County historic landmark built in 1900, renovated and expanded in 1993. Centrally located in the picturesque Nye Beach area. Lighthouse tower provides 360° views of the ocean, local lighthouses, mountains, romantic sunsets, whales, and winter storms. Commodious guest common areas. Art, books, periodicals, daily newspapers. Unique guest rooms with ocean view

5 Open all year; 6 Pets welcome; 7 Children welcome; 8 Tennis nearby; 9 Swimming nearby; 10 Golf nearby; 11 Skiing nearby; 12 May be booked through travel agent.

and queen beds. Seated breakfast at 9AM in the dining room. Deck sheltered from wind. Off-street parking.

Hostess: Jan LeBrun
Rooms: 4 (PB) $90-120
Full Breakfast
Credit Cards: A, B, D
Notes: 2, 5, 8, 9, 10

SEASIDE

10th Avenue Inn Bed and Breakfast

125 10th Avenue, 97138
(503) 738-0643 (voice and FAX);
(800) 569-1114

Enjoy this 1908 ocean view home just steps from the beach and a short walk on the promenade to restaurants and shopping. Light, airy guest rooms are decorated in soft colors, sprinkled in antiques, and include TVs. Full breakfast. Please no smoking or pets. Vacation rental available; sleeps seven.

Hosts: Francie and Vern Starkey
Rooms: 4 (PB) $55-70 + tax
Full Breakfast
Credit Cards: A, B
Notes: 2, 5, 7 (over 9), 8, 9, 10

Sand Dollar Bed and Breakfast

Sand Dollar B&B

606 N. Holladay Drive, 97138
(503) 738-3491; (800) 738-3491

Historic Craftsman bungalow includes two upstairs bedrooms with private baths and comfy beds, or you may prefer our cottage with its spectacular view and full kitchen. Children are always welcome. Only a short walk to the beach, shops, or restaurants. Hosts are retired minister and wife. No smoking.

Hosts: Bob and Nita Hempfling
Rooms: 3 (PB) $55-100
Full Breakfast
Credit Cards: A, B, C, D
Notes: 2 ,5 ,7, 8, 9, 10, 12

SISTERS

Cascade Country Inn

15870 Barclay Drive, 97759
(541) 549-4666; (800) 316-0089

With a panoramic view of the snow-capped Cascades, Cascade Country Inn is an elegant, yet homey retreat for those who are looking for the best. Antiques, hand-painted murals, delicate stenciling and custom stained glass greet you from sun-filled rooms. Handmade quilts, overstuffed sofas, and afghans throughout create the feeling of coming home. Celebrate weddings, honeymoons, anniversaries, birthdays, family reunions, or just "time away." Fly in and taxi to an open door of country charm; or drive in. Come create a memory with us!

Hostesses: Judy and Victoria Tolonen
Rooms: 7 (PB) $100-125
Full Breakfast
Credit Cards: A, B
Notes: 2, 5, 7, 8, 10, 11

NOTES: Credit cards accepted: A Master Card; B Visa; C American Express; D Discover; E Diners Club; F Other; 2 Personal checks accepted; 3 Lunch available; 4 Dinner available;

Cascade Country Inn

Conklin's Guest House

69013 Camp Polk Road, 97759
(541) 549-0123; (800) 549-4262

Conklin's Guest House is surrounded by a sprawling meadow with a panoramic backdrop of snow-capped peaks. Rich in history, the near century-old homesite gives evidence that early settlers chose the most beautiful sites first! Modern conveniences and attention to detail ensure a comfortable and restful stay. The house offers guests a truly peaceful environment within walking distance of the bustling shops and restaurants of Sisters. Guests are welcome to use the barbecue, swimming pool, laundry facilities, and to otherwise *be at home!* The ponds are stocked with trout for catch and release fishing. The Sisters area has something for everyone from rafting and rock climbing to dining and shopping and much more, all the time!

Hosts: Marie and Frank Conklin
Rooms: 5 (PB) $90-110
Full Breakfast
Credit Cards: none
Notes: 2, 5, 7 (over 5), 8, 9 (heated pool on B&B grounds), 10, 11

WELCHES (MT. HOOD AREA)

Doublegate Inn B&B

26711 E. Welches Road, 97067
(503) 622-4859 (voice and FAX)

The house, which has now become the Doublegate Inn B&B, has been a landmark in the Mt. Hood area since it was built in the 1920s. Commonly referred to as "the house with the rock wall" and located just one block from a golf course, the B&B sits serenely atop a cedar treed knoll with a view of the Salmon River behind. The beautifully decorated Inn filled with crafts and antiques, features four distinctly styled guest rooms, each with private baths and some with spa tubs. The Doublegate Inn is quietly yet conveniently located near the many diverse activities found on and around scenic Mt. Hood. Be spoiled and refreshed and find the romance in "God's Country" just off the Oregon Trail! Sumptuous "no lunch" breakfasts served "en suite" on the deck or fireside in the dining room.

Hosts: Gary and Charlene Poston
Rooms: 4 (PB) $80-115
Full Breakfast
Credit Cards: none
Notes: 2, 5, 7 (over 12), 8, 9, 10, 11

---

5 Open all year; 6 Pets welcome; 7 Children welcome; 8 Tennis nearby; 9 Swimming nearby; 10 Golf nearby; 11 Skiing nearby; 12 May be booked through travel agent.

Old Welches Inn

Old Welches Inn Bed and Breakfast

26401 E. Welches Road, 97067
(503) 622-3754

The oldest building in the Mt. Hood area, the Inn was built in 1890 and is traditionally styled, reminiscent of the fine old homes of the Old South. Light-filled rooms with large French windows let the surrounding vistas of mountains and rivers greet you daily. Start you day with a full breakfast in our dining room which overlooks the patio and the Salmon River. Spend your evenings by the fireplace with a selection from our library or visiting with new friends. Your hosts work hard to insure a com-

fortable and memorable stay.

Hosts: Judith and Ted Mondun
Rooms: 4 (1PB; 3SB) $75-130
Full Breakfast
Credit Cards: A, B, C, D
Notes: 2, 5, 6 (in cottage), 7 (over 12), 9, 10, 11, 12 (2 night min.)

WEST LINN

Swift Shore Chalet

1190 Swift Shore Circle, 97068
(503) 650-3853 (voice and FAX)

"The perfect getaway . . . a time to relax in the quietness of a beautiful home, surrounded by a panoramic view of hillsides covered with trees, a garden filled with the fragrance of flowers, and songs of birds. A full breakfast, beautifully served on the deck or in the dining room, includes warm scones, cinnamon rolls, fruit sorbets, waffles, pancakes, quiches, and much more. Let yourself be pampered and served with quiet attention to detail. Just minutes to downtown Portland or many outlying attractions."

Hosts: Nancy and Horace Duke
Rooms: 2 (PB) $70 + tax
Full Breakfast
Credit Cards: A, B, C, D
Notes: 2, 5, 7, 10, 11

NOTES: Credit cards accepted: A Master Card; B Visa; C American Express; D Discover; E Diners Club; F Other; 2 Personal checks accepted; 3 Lunch available; 4 Dinner available;

Pennsylvania

ALSO SEE RESERVATION
SERVICES UNDER
DELAWARE AND NEW JERSEY

A Bed and Breakfast Connection (B&B of Philadelphia)

PO Box 21, **Devon** 19333
(610) 687-3565; (800) 448-3619;
FAX (610) 995-9524
Email: bnbphila@aol.com

From elegant townhouses in history-filled **Center-City** to a manor house in scenic **Bucks County**; from an elegant home-within-a-barn in the **suburbs** to charming Victorian inns in **York**, Bed and Breakfast Connections/Bed and Breakfast of Philadelphia offers a wide variety of styles and locations in its scores of inspected homes, guesthouses and inns. For example—choose from accommodations just three blocks from "America's most historic square mile," **Independence National Historical Park**; or within easy distance of **Valley Forge Park**; or in the heart of the **Brandywine Valley** area with its magnificent historic estates and museums. Stay on a working farm in the Amish country of **Lancaster County**. Our accommodations range in price from $30 to $200 per night; we offer houses with one guest room and inns with many rooms. We cover seven counties in the southeastern corner of Pennsylvania. Peggy Gregg and Mary Alice Hamilton, co-owners. Major credit cards accepted.

Rest and Repast Bed and Breakfast Reservations

PO Box 126, **Pine Grove Mills** 16868
(814) 238-1484 or (814) 861-6566;
FAX (814) 234-9890
Internet: http://iul.com/business/bnbinpa

Since 1982, Rest and Repast has represented inspected B&Bs in central PA, including the Penn State University area plus a fine selection of inns statewide. The sixty plus properties include scenic farms near famous fly fishing streams, estates on the National Register, private apartments, cottages, and lodges as well as a variety of contemporary homes. Several sites appropriate for small wedding receptions, family reunions, and corporate retreats. Visit our web site for a more complete list and additional details on many of the properties represented. $55-100, corpo-

---

5 Open all year; 6 Pets welcome; 7 Children welcome; 8 Tennis nearby; 9 Swimming nearby; 10 Golf nearby; 11 Skiing nearby; 12 May be booked through travel agent.

PENNSYLVANIA

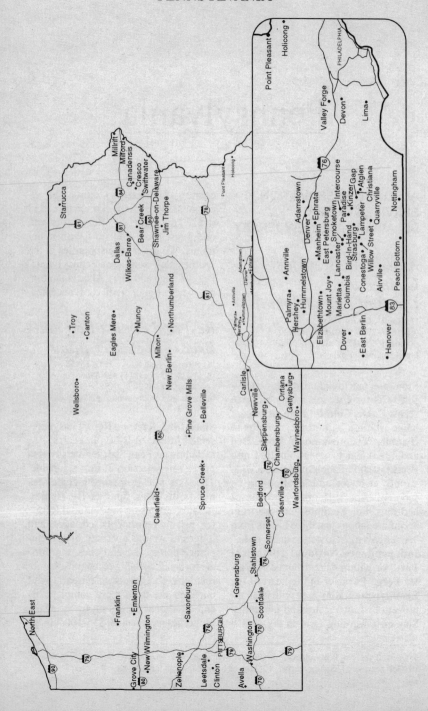

rate and long term rates available. Deposit required, cash or check only. Free brochure available.

ADAMSTOWN

Adamstown Inn
62 W. Main Street, 19501-0938
(717) 484-0800; (800) 594-4808

Experience simple elegance in a Victorian home resplendent with leaded-glass windows and door, magnificent chestnut woodwork, and Oriental rugs. All six guest rooms are decorated with family heirlooms, handmade quilts, lace curtains, and many distinctive touches. Accommodations range from antique to king beds. Four rooms have jacuzzis for two, and two rooms feature gas fireplaces. The Inn is located in a small town brimming with antique dealers and only minutes from Reading and Lancaster.

Hosts: Tom and Wanda Berman
Rooms: 6 (PB) $65-105
Expanded Continental Breakfast
Credit Cards: A, B, D
Notes: 2, 5, 8, 9, 10, 12

AIRVILLE

Spring House
1264 Muddy Creek Forks Road, 17302
(717) 927-6906

Built in 1798 of warm fieldstone, Spring House is a fine example of Colonial architecture with original stenciling that overlooks a river valley. Now on the National Register of Historic Places, the Spring House has welcomed guests from around the world who seek a historic setting, tranquillity, and access to Amish Country and Gettysburg with scenic railroad soon to be open to the public. Regional breakfast specialties and Amish cheeses welcome the traveler. Country luxuries abound: featherbeds and woodstoves in the winter, large porch with porch swing for summer breezes. Also, creek swimming, hiking and biking trails, and horseback riding nearby.

Hosts: Ray Constance Hearne and, husband, Michael Schuster
Rooms: 4 (3PB; 1SB) $60-95
Full Breakfast
Credit Cards: none
Notes: 2, 5, 7, 8, 9, 10, 11, 12

ANNVILLE

Swatara Creek Inn
Box 692 RD 2, 17003
(717) 865-3259

1860s Victorian mansion situated on four acres in the peaceful country. All rooms have private baths, canopied

---

NOTES: Credit cards accepted: A Master Card; B Visa; C American Express; D Discover; E Diners Club; F Other; 2 Personal checks accepted; 3 Lunch available; 4 Dinner available; 5 Open all year; 6 Pets welcome; 7 Children welcome; 8 Tennis nearby; 9 Swimming nearby; 10 Golf nearby; 11 Skiing nearby; 12 May be booked through travel agent.

Swatara Creek Inn

queen-size beds, air-conditioning, and include a full breakfast. Sitting room, dining room, and gift shop on the first floor. Wheelchair accessible. Close to Hershey, Mt. Hope Winery, Mt. Gretna, Reading outlets, and Lancaster Amish area. Close to a lot of historical sites: Cornwall Mines, Ephrata Cloisters, Gettysburg, etc. No smoking in house.

Hosts: Dick and Jeannette Hess
Rooms: 10 (PB) $55-80
Full Breakfast
Credit Cards: A, B, C, D, E
Notes: 2, 5, 7 (well behaved), 8, 9, 10, 12

ATGLEN

Highland View

Box 1546 Highland Road, 19310
(610) 593-5066

This country home is in a peaceful setting surrounded by Amish farms. An Amish craft shop is next door. This ranch-style home has central air and a large sunroom to enjoy a full breakfast with this Mennonite couple. Two guest rooms, king and queen, share a bath. We are located in an area ideal for touring Pennsylvania Dutch Country and only

twenty miles from Longwood Gardens. The village of Intercourse is just 15 minutes away. Stop by for coffee and shoofly pie, a Dutch treat. Dried apple arrangements are Cora's hobbies.

Hosts: Sam and Cora Umble
Rooms: 2 (1PB; 2SB) $40-45
Full Breakfast
Credit Cards: none
Notes: 2, 4, 5, 7, 10, 12

AVELLA

Weatherbury Farm

1061 Sugar Run Road, 15312
(412) 587-3763; FAX (412) 587-0125

Award-winning bed and breakfast on working farm — meadows, gardens, cows, sheep, and tranquility! Four guest rooms located in the 1870s farmhouse and summer kitchen are lovingly furnished with country charm; each with private bath and air-conditioning. Heated pool. Bountiful farm breakfast. Great hiking, biking, boating, and fishing nearby. Visit Meadowcroft Museum of Rural Life, historic Southwest Pennsylvania, and Pittsburgh. Children welcome.

Hosts: Dale, Marcy, and Nigel Tudor
Rooms: 4 (PB) $65
Full, Bountiful Farm Breakfast
Credit Cards: A, B, C, D
Notes: 2, 5, 7, 8, 9, 10, 12

BEAR CREEK

Bischwind

One Coach Road, 18602
(717) 472-3820

The elegance and country ambience of

NOTES: Credit cards accepted: A Master Card; B Visa; C American Express; D Discover; E Diners Club; F Other; 2 Personal checks accepted; 3 Lunch available; 4 Dinner available;

the Theodore Roosevelt era is reflected in Bishchwind's hospitality. T.R. was one of two presidents to visit Bischwind, built by lumber baron Albert Lewis in 1886. This Tudor manor house is upscale and tenderly treats its guests with distinction. Our brunches are most appreciated. Come and share a memorable moment.

Hosts: Barbara and Alfred Von Dran
Rooms: 8 (6PB; 2SB)
Full Breakfast
Credit Cards: A, B, C, D
Notes: 5, 8, 9, 10, 11, 12

BEDFORD

Conifer Ridge Farm

R.D. #2, Box 202 A, **Clearville** 15535
(814) 784-3342

Conifer Ridge Farm has 126 acres of woodland, pasture, Christmas trees, and crops. There is a one-acre pond with a pier for swimming, fishing, and boating. The home's rustic exterior opens to a spacious contemporary design of exceptional beauty. You'll feel its country character in the old barn beams and brick walls that collect the sun's warmth for solar heat. Near Bedford, Bedford Village, Raystown Lake, and Rocky Gap State Park in Maryland.

Hosts: Dan and Myrtle Haldeman
Rooms: 2 (PB) $55; cabin for 4 people $30
Full Breakfast
Credit Cards: none
Notes: 2, 4, 5, 7, 9, 10, 11

BELLEVILLE

Twin Oaks Bed and Breakfast

73 S. Dryhouse Road, 17004
(717) 935-2026

In the heart of the Kishacoquillas Valley only 30 minutes from Penn State. Norman and Sarah welcome their guests to a new facility with clean, spacious rooms. In a quiet country setting with a panoramic view of Stone and Jacks mountains. A full breakfast is served. Children are welcome. Open all year.

Hosts: Norman and Sarah Glick
Rooms: 4 (1PB; 3SB) $40-50
Full Breakfast
Credit Cards: none
Notes: 2, 5, 7, 12

BIRD-IN-HAND

The Village Inn of Bird-in-Hand

2695 Old Philadelphia Pike, PO Box 253, 17505
(800) 914-2473; FAX (717) 768-1117

Listed on the National Historic Register, our inn is located on Route 340, five miles east of Lancaster in the heart of the Pennsylvania Dutch Country. Each room features its own private bath and includes a continental plus breakfast, free use of indoor and outdoor pools, tennis courts located within walking distance, and a complimentary two-hour tour of the surrounding Amish farm-

---

5 Open all year; 6 Pets welcome; 7 Children welcome; 8 Tennis nearby; 9 Swimming nearby; 10 Golf nearby; 11 Skiing nearby; 12 May be booked through travel agent.

lands. Reservations suggested. Package available.

Hosts: Richmond and Janice Young
Rooms: 11 (PB) $75-144
Continental Breakfast
Credit Cards: A, B, C, D
Notes: 5, 7, 8, 9, 10, 12

CANADENSIS

Brookview Manor B&B

Route 447, R.R. #1, Box 365, 18325
(717) 595-2451; (800) 585-7974;
FAX (717) 595-5065

Situated on four picturesque acres, the inn offers the traveler an ideal retreat from the workaday world. Enjoy the simple pleasures of hiking trails or a cozy porch glider on a spacious wrap-around porch. Each room offers a pan-oramic view of the forest, mountains, and stream, and all have private baths. Breakfast is served in our cheery din-ing room and includes fruits, juices, fresh muffins, and a hearty main entree.

Hostess: Mary Anne Buckley
Rooms: 10 (PB) $100-150
Full Breakfast
Credit Cards: A, B, C, D, E
Notes: 2, 5, 7 (over 12), 8, 9, 10, 11, 12

Brookview Manor Bed and Breakfast

Dreamy Acres

Route 447 and Seese Hill Rd., Box 7, 18325-0007
(717) 595-7115

Esther and Bill Pickett started Dreamy Acres as a bed and breakfast inn in 1959, doing bed and breakfast before it was in style. Situated on three acres with a stream and a pond, Dreamy Acres is in the heart of the Pocono Mountains vacationland, close to stores, churches, gift shops, and recreational facilities. Guest rooms have air-conditioning and color cable TV, and some have VCRs.

Hosts: Esther and Bill Pickett
Rooms: 6 (4PB; 2SB) $38-55
Expanded Continental Breakfast
Credit Cards: none
Notes: 2, 5, 8, 9, 10, 11

CANTON

M-mm Good Bed and Breakfast

R.D. 1, Box 71, 17724
(717) 673-8153

Located along Route 414, three miles east of Canton, in a quiet country set-ting in the center of the Endless Moun-tains. Enjoy clean, comfortable rooms and a full breakfast including muffins or sticky buns. Hiking and fishing closeby and picnic tables under maple trees.

Hosts: Melvin and Irene Good
Rooms: 3 (SB) $27.50
Full Breakfast
Credit Cards: none
Notes: 2, 5, 7

NOTES: Credit cards accepted: A Master Card; B Visa; C American Express; D Discover; E Diners Club; F Other; 2 Personal checks accepted; 3 Lunch available; 4 Dinner available;

CARLISLE

Line Limousin Farmhouse Bed and Breakfast

2070 Ritner Highway, 17013
(717) 243-1281

Relax and unwind in an 1864 brick and stone farmhouse on 100 acres, two miles off I-81, Exit 12. French Limousin cattle are raised here. Enjoy antiques, including a player piano, and the use of a golf driving range. Join us for worship at our historic First Presbyterian Church. Two rooms having comfortable king beds and private bath. Two rooms with shared bath. Non-smokers, please.

Hosts: Bob and Joan Line
Rooms: 4 (2PB; 2SB) $58.30-79.50
Full Breakfast
Credit Cards: none
Notes: 2, 5, 7 (over 8), 10

Pheasant Field Bed and Breakfast

Pheasant Field B&B

150 Hickorytown Road, 17013
(717) 258-0717 (voice and FAX)
Email: pheasant@pa.net

Stay in a homey, old, brick farmhouse in quiet surroundings. Wake up to a full, cooked breakfast including homemade bread or muffins. We have four air con-

ditioned guest rooms, two with private bath. There is a tennis court on the grounds and overnight horse boarding is available. "Come Home to the Country." AAA—three star rating.

Hosts: Denise (Dee) Fegan and Chuck DeMarco
Rooms: 4 (2PB; 2SB) $65-95
Full Breakfast
Credit Cards: A, B, C
Notes: 2, 5, 7 (over 8), 8 (on-site), 9, 10, 11, 12

CHAMBERSBURG

Falling Spring Inn B&B

1838 Falling Spring Road, 17201
(717) 267-3654; FAX (717) 267-2584

Enjoy country living only two miles from I-81, Exit 6 and Route 30, on a working farm with animals and Falling Spring, a nationally renowned, freshwater trout stream. A large pond, lawns, meadows, ducks, and birds all make a pleasant stay. Historic Gettysburg is only 25 miles away. Relax in our air conditioned rooms with queen beds. One room with spa. One room wheelchair accessible.

Hosts: Adin and Janet Frey
Rooms: 5 (PB) $49-89
Full Breakfast
Credit Cards: A, B
Notes: 2, 5, 7, 8, 9, 10, 11, 12

CHRISTIANA

Georgetown Bed and Breakfast

1222 Georgetown Road, 17509
(717)786-4570

Once a miller's home, the original struc-

---

5 Open all year; 6 Pets welcome; 7 Children welcome; 8 Tennis nearby; 9 Swimming nearby; 10 Golf nearby; 11 Skiing nearby; 12 May be booked through travel agent.

ture was converted to a bed and breakfast for the enjoyment of guests in a relaxing home away from home. Entrance to the house is by a brick walkway. The herb garden on the left lets guests smell the lavender and mint that are just two of the herbs used to garnish morning breakfasts. There is a choice of three bedrooms decorated with antiques and collectibles. Lancaster County Amish, a unique group of people who travel in horse-drawn carriages, pass in front of the Georgetown. Visit the local Strasburg Train Museum.

Hostess: Doris W. Woerth
Rooms: 3 (1PB; 2SB) $40-50
Full Breakfast
Credit Cards: none
Notes: 2, 5, 9, 10

Victorian Loft

CLEARFIELD

Victorian Loft Bed and Breakfast

216 S. Front Street, 16830
(814) 765-4805; (800) 798-0456;
FAX (814) 765-9596

Elegant 1894 Victorian, riverfront home in historic district. Memorable breakfast, air-conditioned rooms, skylights, balcony, private kitchen and dining, guest entertainment center, family movies, and whirlpool bath. Weaving/sewing studio; spinning demonstrations by request. Hosts are Bible college graduates. Perfect stop on I-80—three miles off Exit 19 in rural West Central PA. Also, completely equipped three-bedroom cabin on eight forested acres, two miles from Parker Dam and Elliot State Parks with swimming, fishing, boating, and numerous outdoor activities.

Hosts: Tim and Peggy Durant
Rooms: 2 (SB) $45-75; suite (PB) $85-100; cabin
    $60-100
Full Breakfast
Credit Cards: A, B, C, D
Notes: 2, 5 (call ahead), 6 (limited), 7, 8, 9, 11, 12

CLINTON

Country Road B&B

Moody Road, Box 265, 15026
(412) 899-2528

A peaceful, quiet, farm setting just five miles from Gr. Pittsburgh Airport with pick-up service available, and 20 minutes from downtown. A restored 100-year-old farmhouse with trout pond, in-ground pool, and screened-in front porch. Recently a cottage, once a springhouse, and 200-year-old log cabin were restored and made available to guests. Golf course within walking distance, and air tours available in vintage, Piper restored aircraft.

Hosts: Janice and David Cornell
Rooms: 5 (4PB; 1SB) $55-85
Full Breakfast
Credit Cards: A, B, D
Notes: 2, 5, 7, 9, 10

CONESTOGA

Mellinger Manor

1300 Breneman Road, 17516
(717) 871-0699

Mellinger Manor was completed in 1894 by one of Manor Township's wealthiest families Its Victorian/Edwardian architecture is unique to the township. The setting is a hamlet called Cresswell, surrounded by farmland and small lovely homes. Lancaster city is 20 minutes away, the Amish and a large outlet shopping center are 30 to 40 minutes away, Gettysburg is about one hour away, and Hershey is about 45 minutes away. Cyclists are aboundant in the area due to the scenic Susquehanna River being just over the hill. There is golfing in nearby Millersville, home of Millersville University, and there is a scenic hiking trail less than half a mile away that wanders around the river.

Hosts: Bob and Barb VanderPlate
Rooms: 4 (1PB; 3SB) $70-100
Full Breakfast
Credit Cards: A, B
Notes: 2, 5, 8, 10

LaAnna Guest House

CRESCO

LaAnna Guest House

RR 2, Box 1051, 18326
(717) 676-4225

The 111-year-old Victorian is furnished with Victorian and Empire antiques and has spacious rooms, quiet surroundings, and a trout pond. Walk to waterfalls, mountain views, and wildlife.

Hostess: Kay Swingle
Rooms: 3 (SB) $35
Continental Breakfast
Credit Cards: none
Notes: 2, 5, 7, 8, 9, 10, 11

DENVER

Cocalico Creek Bed and Breakfast

224 S. 4th Street, 17517
(717) 336-0271; (888) 208-7334

Located in Northern Lancaster County. Casual elegance in a country setting. Four tastefully decorated bedrooms, each with private bath; one room offers a private balcony. Air-conditioning for summer comfort and heated beds with down comforters for winter chills. Explore the history, culture, and rural scenic beauty. Reading and Lancaster outlets nearby. Antique capital of USA minutes away. Convenient to Hershey Park, Dutch Wonderland, and many other attractions. No smoking policy.

Hostess: Charlene Sweeney
Rooms: 4 (PB) $60-85
Full Breakfast
Credit Cards: none
Notes: 2, 5, 7, 9, 10

5 Open all year; 6 Pets welcome; 7 Children welcome; 8 Tennis nearby; 9 Swimming nearby; 10 Golf nearby; 11 Skiing nearby; 12 May be booked through travel agent.

DOVER

Detter's Acres Bed and Breakfast

6631 Old Carlisle Road, 17315
(717) 292-3172

This is a 76-acre working farm with Colonial type home. Raise beef cattle. Social room with fireplace. All rooms air-conditioned and have TV. Full home-cooked breakfast. Short driving distance to Lancaster Amish, Gettysburg Military Park, Hershey Amusement Park, and York Interstate Fairgrounds. Lorne is a salesman, farmer and entertainer. Ailean is an artist and has an art gallery on the premises. Horse and Amish buggy rides available at nominal fee. Golf cart for guests to use on farm.

Hosts: Lorne and Ailean Detter
Rooms: 3 (1PB; 2SB) $55-60
Full Breakfast
Credit Cards: none
Notes: 2, 5, 9, 10, 11

EAGLES MERE

Shady Lane, A Bed and Breakfast Inn

PO Box 314, Allegheny Avenue, 17731
(717) 525-3394; (800) 524-1248

Surrounded by tall trees on a mountaintop with a mesmerizing view of the Endless Mountains. A five minute walk to swimming, boating, canoeing, and fishing on the gorgeous mile-long, springfed lake (with groomed path around the perimeter). Minutes' walk to craft and gift shops in small village. All in a Victorian "town that time forgot," a resort town since the late 1800s, with summer theater and winter cross-country skiing, ice-skating, and famous toboggan slide.

Hosts: Pat and Dennis Dougherty
Rooms: 7 (PB) $75
Full Breakfast
Credit Cards: none
Notes: 2, 5, 8, 9, 10, 11, 12

EAST BERLIN

Bechtel Mansion Inn

400 West King Street, 17316
(717) 259-7760; (800) 331-1108
Internet UHL: www.bed-net.com/bechtel.html

This charming Victorian mansion has been tastefully restored and furnished with antiques, period furniture, Oriental carpets, and lace curtains. Located eighteen miles east of Gettysburg in the East Berlin National Historic District,

Bechtel Mansion Inn

NOTES: Credit cards accepted: A Master Card; B Visa; C American Express; D Discover; E Diners Club; F Other; 2 Personal checks accepted; 3 Lunch available; 4 Dinner available;

the Inn is on the western frontier of the 18th Century Pennsylvania Dutch Country. It is ideal for a relaxing getaway, a golf or bicycling retreat, a honeymoon location, or a birthday or anniversary celebration. Visit Gettysburg or Lancaster. Gift certificates are available.

Hosts: Charles and Mariam Bechtel with Ruth Spangler
Rooms: 9 (PB) $75-145
Full Breakfast
Credit Cards: A, B, C, D, E
Notes: 2, 5, 8, 10, 11, 12 (10% commission)

EAST PETERSBURG

George Zahm House Bed and Breakfast

6070 Main Street, 17520
(717) 569-6026

The George Zahm House, built in 1854, is a restored Federal period home in beautiful Lancaster County, Pennsylvania. The inn features three bedrooms with private baths and a first floor suite that includes a sitting room, bedroom, and private bath. The inn has ten-foot ceilings throughout and is furnished with an eclectic collection of antiques. Breakfast is served in the dining room and features homemade muffins, breads, Belgian waffles, granolas, and seasonal fresh fruit.

Hosts: Robyn Kemple-Keeports, Jeff Keeports, and Daneen Kemple
Rooms: 4 (PB) $65-85
Continental Plus Breakfast
Credit Cards: A, B
Notes: 2, 5, 7 (over12), 8, 9, 10

ELIZABETHTOWN

Apples Abound Inn B&B

518 S. Market Street, 17022
(717) 367-3018

A refreshing bite of hospitality, rest, and romance in a 1907 Victorian home in Lancaster County centrally located near Hershey, York, and Lancaster. The three guest rooms are a delightful treat to simple elegance and understated charm. Your stay will be like biting into a crisp red apple; refreshing, delicious, and appetite quenching. A visit will fill all your senses. Come and be tempted among our apples.

Hosts: Jennifer and Jon Sheppard
Rooms: 3 (1-2PB; 2SB) $70-80
Full Breakfast (Continental on weekdays)
Credit Cards: A, B
Notes: 2, 5, 7, 8, 10, 11, 12

West Ridge Guest House

West Ridge Guest House

1285 West Ridge Road, 17022
(717) 367-7783; FAX (717) 367-8468

Tucked midway between Harrisburg and Lancaster, this European manor can be found four miles off Route 283 at Rheems-Elizabethtown exit. Nine guest rooms with private baths, phones, and

---

5 Open all year; 6 Pets welcome; 7 Children welcome; 8 Tennis nearby; 9 Swimming nearby; 10 Golf nearby; 11 Skiing nearby; 12 May be booked through travel agent.

TV. Some rooms have fireplaces and whirlpool tubs. Two are two-room suites. An exercise room with hot tub and large great room is in an adjacent guest house. You may relax on one of the decks or gazebo and enjoy the restful view and quiet country setting. Twenty to forty minutes to local attractions, including Hershey Park, Lancaster County Amish Community, outlet shopping malls, Masonic homes, and Harrisburg, the state capital. Four star rated by ABBA.

Historic Smithton Inn

Hostess: Alice P. Heisey
Rooms: 9 (PB) $60-100
Full Breakfast
Credit Cards: A, B, C
Notes: 2, 5, 7, 8, 10, 12

EMLENTON

Whippletree Inn and Farm

RD 3, Box 285, Big Bend Road, 16373
(412) 876-9543

The Inn is a restored, turn-of-the-century home on a cattle farm. The house, barns, and 100 acres of pasture sit on a hill above the Allegheny River. A pleasant trail leads down to the river. Guests are welcome to use the one-half mile racetrack for horses and carriages. Hiking, biking, cross-country skiing, canoeing, hunting, and fishing are nearby. Emlenton offers antique and craft shopping in the restored Old Mill. A/C.

Hosts: Warren and Joey Simmons
Rooms: 4 (2PB; 2SB) $50-60
Full Breakfast
Credit Cards: B
Notes: 2, 5, 7, 9, 10

EPHRATA

Historic Smithton Inn

900 W. Main Street, 17522
(717) 733-6094

Smithton Inn originated prior to the Revolutionary War. The Inn is a romantic and picturesque place located in Lancaster County. Its big, square rooms are bright and sunny. Each room has its own working fireplace and can be candlelighted during evening hours. There is a sitting area in each guest room with comfortable leather upholstered chairs, reading lamps, soft goose down pillows, and bright, handmade Pennsylvania Dutch quilts. Smithton's Dahlia Gardens feature a striking display of blossoms that are grown from tubers that were all winners in American Dahlia Society competitions. Mannerly children and pets are welcome, but please make prior arrangements. Smoking is prohibited.

Hostess: Dorthy R. Graybill
Rooms: 8 (PB) $75-150; suites $145-175
Full Breakfast
Credit Cards: A, B, C
Notes: 2, 5, 6 (prior arrangement), 7, 8, 9, 10, 12

NOTES: Credit cards accepted: A Master Card; B Visa; C American Express; D Discover; E Diners Club; F Other; 2 Personal checks accepted; 3 Lunch available; 4 Dinner available;

The Inns at Doneckers

318-324 N. State Street, 17522
(717) 738-9502; FAX (717) 738-9554

Relax in country elegance in historic Lancaster County. Four inns of 40 distinctive rooms, decorated in fine antiques, some fireplace/jacuzzi suites. A few steps from The Doneckers Community, a 35-year-old family owned business of exceptional fashion store for the family and the home, award-winning gourmet restaurant, art/craft/quilt galleries and artists' studios, and farmers' market. Minutes from antique and collectible markets. "An oasis of sophistication in PA Dutch Country"—*Country Inns* magazine.

Host: H. William Donecker (owner)
Rooms: 40 (38PB; 2SB) $59-185
Continental Breakfast
Credit Cards: A, B, C, D, E, F
Notes: 2, 3, 4, 5, 7, 8, 9, 10

Martin House

265 Ridge Avenue, 17522
(717) 733-6804; (888) 651-8418
Email: vmartin@prolog.net
Web site: http://www.martin-house.com

The curving driveway leads to our contemporary home which has a spacious deck overlooking the tranquil semi-secluded grounds. Located in Pennsylvania Dutch Country, close to antique markets, shopping malls, Hershey Park, and golf courses. For your comfort we offer king- and queen-size beds in tastefully decorated rooms. The master bedroom comes with a hot tub for your enjoyment. Efficiency apartment that sleeps two to six is also available.

Hosts: Moses and Vera Martin
Rooms: 3 (2PB; 1-2SB) $55-115
Full Breakfast
Credit Cards: none
Notes: 2, 5, 7, 9, 10

FRANKLIN

Quo Vadis Bed and Breakfast

1501 Liberty Street, 16323
(814) 432-4208; (800) 360-6598

A stately home, accented with terra cotta tile, Quo Vadis is an 1867, eclectic, Queen Anne house. It is located in an historic district listed on the National Register with a walking tour. The high-ceilinged, spacious rooms, parquet floors, detailed woodworking, moldings, and friezes are from a time of caring craftsmanship and Victorian elegance. The furniture is mahogany,

Martin House

5 Open all year; 6 Pets welcome; 7 Children welcome; 8 Tennis nearby; 9 Swimming nearby; 10 Golf nearby; 11 Skiing nearby; 12 May be booked through travel agent.

rosewood, oak, walnut, and wicker and has been acquired by the same family for four generations. The quilts, embroidery, and lacework are the handiwork of two beloved ladies. Restaurants, museums, antiques, Barrow-Civic Theater, DeBonce Antique Music World, bicycle paths, train trip, fishing, Allegheny River Valley are all nearby to enjoy. Smoking allowed only on the porch. Approved: AAA, ABBA, Mobil, and PTC.

Hosts: Cherie and David
Rooms: 6 (PB) $60-80
Full Breakfast
Credit Cards: A, B, C
Notes: 2, 5, 7, 12

Quo Vadis Bed and Breakfast

GAP

Ben Mar Farm Bed and Breakfast

5721 Old Phila Pike, 17527
(717) 768-3309

Come stay with us on our working dairy farm. We are located in the heart of famous "Amish Country." Experience quiet country life while staying in the large, beautifully decorated rooms of our 200 year old farmhouse. Our efficiency apartment is a favorite including a full kitchen and queen and double beds with private bath. Enjoy a fresh continental breakfast brought to your room. Air-conditioned.

Hosts: Herb and Melanie Benner
Rooms: 3 (PB) $40-50
Continental Plus Breakfast
Credit Cards: none
Notes: 2, 5, 7, 8

GETTYSBURG (SEE ALSO EAST BERLIN)

The Brafferton Inn

44 York Street, 17325
(717) 337-3423

In the town of historic Gettysburg the Brafferton Inn is one of its gracious landmarks. The elegant 1786 fieldstone home, listed on the National Registry of Historic Places, has been fully restored to include a private bath for each of the ten guestrooms. Featured in *Country Living,* the Inn has exquisite antiques and original artistry throughout. The Inn combines elegance and ease. Warm colored Orientals, comfortable wingbacks, and a tall 1800 grandfather clock grace the living room. The dining room boasts a stunning folk art mural. Other surprising nooks and crannies, a deck and in-town garden provide getaway spots. The spirit of an earlier time pervades.

Hosts: Jane and Sam Back
Rooms: 10 (PB) $80-125
Full Breakfast
Credit Cards: A, B, C, D
Notes: 2, 5, 7 (over 7), 8, 9, 10, 11, 12

NOTES: Credit cards accepted: A Master Card; B Visa; C American Express; D Discover; E Diners Club; F Other; 2 Personal checks accepted; 3 Lunch available; 4 Dinner available;

The Doubleday Inn
104 Doubleday Avenue, 17325
(717) 334-9119

Located directly on the Gettysburg
Battlefield, this beautifully restored
Colonial country inn enjoys splendid
views of historic Gettysburg and the
battlefield. Guests enjoy candlelight
country breakfasts, afternoon refreshments, and the cozy comfort of a centrally air-conditioned inn surrounded by
lovely antiques and Civil War memorabilia. Free presentations by battlefield
historians on selected evenings.

Hosts: Ruth Anne and Charles Wilcox
Rooms: 9 (5PB; 4SB) $84-104
Full Breakfast
Credit Cards: A, B, D
Notes: 2, 5, 8, 10, 11, 12

Keystone Inn
231 Hanover Street, 17325
(717) 337-3888

The Keystone Inn is a large, brick, Victorian home built in 1913. The high-
ceilinged rooms are decorated with lace
and flowers, and a handsome chestnut
staircase rises to the third floor. The
guest rooms are bright, cheerful, and air-
conditioned. Each has a reading nook
and writing desk. Choose your own
breakfast from our full breakfast menu.
One suite available.

Hosts: Wilmer and Doris Martin
Rooms: 5 + 1 suite (3PB; 2SB) $59-100
Full Breakfast
Credit Cards: A, B, D
Notes: 2, 5, 7, 8, 9, 10, 11

GREENBURG

Huntland Farm Bed and Breakfast
RD 9, Box 21, 15601
(412) 834-8483; FAX (412) 838-8253

Nestled in the foothills of the Allegheny Mountains, the 100-acre Huntland
Farm is three miles northeast of
Greensburg. The house, built in 1848
and listed in *Historic Places in Western PA*, is furnished with antiques. A
large living room, as well as porches
and gardens are available for guests'
use. Four, large, corner bedrooms make
it comfortable for up to eight people.
Nearby are many scenic and historical
places, walking trails, hot air ballooning, and shops.

Hosts: Robert and Elizabeth Weidlein
Rooms: 4 (SB) $75
Full Breakfast
Credit Cards: A, B
Notes: 2, 5, 7 (over 12), 10, 12

GROVE CITY

Snow Goose Inn B&B
112 East Main Street, 16127
(412) 458-4644; (800) 317-4644

The Snow Goose Inn is a large turn-of-
the-century home, circa 1895 and formerly a doctor's home. It has a large
wraparound front porch with an old-
fashioned porch swing. We offer comfortable, air-conditioned guest rooms
with private baths and each decorated
with antiques and touches of country.

5 Open all year; 6 Pets welcome; 7 Children welcome; 8 Tennis nearby; 9 Swimming nearby;
10 Golf nearby; 11 Skiing nearby; 12 May be booked through travel agent.

A full breakfast is served, along with homemade muffins and other home-baked breakfast rolls, etc.

Hosts: Orvil and Dorothy McMillen
Rooms: 4 (PB) $65
Full Breakfast
Credit Cards: A, B
Notes: 2, 5, 7, 8, 9, 10, 11, 12

HANOVER

Beechmont Inn

315 Broadway, 17331
(717) 632-3013; (800) 553-7009

An elegant, 1834 Federal period inn with seven guest rooms, all private baths, fireplaces, air-conditioning, after-noon refreshments, and gourmet breakfast. One large suite has a private whirlpool tub, canopy beds, and fireplaces. Gettysburg Battlefield, Lake Marburg, golf, and great antiquing nearby. Convenient location for visits to Hershey, York, or Lancaster. Weekend and golf packages and romantic honeymoon or anniversary packages offered. Picnic baskets available. Great area for biking and hiking. AAA and Mobil approved.

Hosts: William and Susan Day
Rooms: 7 (PB) $80-135
Full Breakfast
Credit Cards: A, B, C, D
Notes: 2, 3, 5, 8, 9, 10, 11, 12

HERSHEY

Mottern's B&B

28 East Main Street, **Hummelstown** 17036
(717) 566-3840; FAX (717) 566-3780

Enjoy small town hospitality only five minutes from Hershey. Private apart-ment in a restored 1860s limestone home can be your "home away from home." Bedroom with queen-sized bed, living room with sofa bed, kitchen, dining room, bath with shower, central air, color cable TV, large patio, and gas grill. Private off-street parking. We are located in the center of our small town, walking distance to churches, shops, restaurants, banks, and the public park. No smoking. Private Hershey tours.

Hostesss: Susan Mottern
Rooms: 1 (private 5-room apartment) $85-100
   (Additional $10 per person over 5 years old)
Continental Breakfast
Credit Cards: A, B
Notes: 2, 5, 7, 8, 9, 10, 11

Pinehurst Inn Bed and Breakfast

50 Northeast Drive, 17033
(717) 533-2603; (800) 743-9140;
FAX (717) 534-2639

Spacious brick home surrounded by lawns and countryside. There is a warm, welcoming, many-windowed living room and old-fashioned porch swing. All this within walking distance of all Hershey attractions: Hershey Museums, Rose Gardens, Hersheypark, and Chocolate World. Less than one hour's drive to Gettysburg and Lancaster County. Each room welcomes you with a queen-size bed and a Hershey Kiss on each pillow.

Hosts: Roger and Phyllis Ingold
Rooms: 15 (2PB; 13SB) $45-72
Complete Breakfast
Credit Cards: A, B
Notes: 2, 5, 7, 8, 9, 10, 12

Shepherd's Acres Bed and Breakfast

R.D. 3, Box 370, Bell Road, **Palmyra** 17078
(717) 838-3899

Welcome to the Hershey-Lancaster area! You'll enjoy it more if you stay on our 20-acre farmette overlooking the scenic Lebanon Valley. Our new and spacious Cape-Cod home is filled with Margy's hand-sewn quilts and wall-hangings, with some antique furniture accenting the "country theme" as well. The eat-in enclosed porch area is a great place to enjoy both beauty and tranquillity as you watch the sheep in the pasture or the deer in the fields.

Hosts: Jerry and Margy Allebach
Rooms: 3 (1PB; 2SB) $45-60
Full Breakfast
Credit Cards: none
Notes: 2, 5, 8, 9, 10, 11

Barley Sheaf Farm

HOLICONG

Barley Sheaf Farm

PO Box 10 (Route 202), 18928
(215) 794-5104

Barley Sheaf is an early Bucks County farm, comfortably situated on 30 acres

at the end of a long tree-lined drive. Once owned by the playwright George S. Kaufmann, it was the gathering place in the 30s and 40s for some of Broadway's brightest illuminaries (ie. Dorothy Parker, Mose Hart, the Marx brothers, etc.). A park-like setting provides beauty and seclusion ideally suited for a romantic getaway. Lovely guest rooms, gracious common rooms, exceptional hospitality and an outstanding breakfast are Barley Sheaf hallmarks.

Hosts: Veronika and Peter Suess
Rooms: 10 (PB) $105-255
Full Breakfast
Credit Cards: A, B, C
Notes: 2, 5, 8, 9, 10, 11, 12

JIM THORPE

The Inn at Jim Thorpe

24 Broadway, 18229
(717) 325-2599; (800) 329-2599;
FAX (717) 325-9145

The Inn rests in a unique and picturesque setting in the heart of historic Jim Thorpe. Our elegant, restored guest rooms are complete with private baths, color TV/HBO, and air-conditioning. Our stunning Victorian suite is available for that very special occasion. While in town take in the sights including mansion tours, museum, art galleries, and quaint shops, or go mountain biking and whitewater rafting. It's all right outside our doors!

Host: David Drury
Rooms: 29 (PB) $65-250
Continental Breakfast
Credit Cards: A, B, C, D, E
Notes: 3, 4, 5, 7, 9, 11, 12

5 Open all year; 6 Pets welcome; 7 Children welcome; 8 Tennis nearby; 9 Swimming nearby; 10 Golf nearby; 11 Skiing nearby; 12 May be booked through travel agent.

KINZERS

Sycamore Haven Farm

35 S. Kinzer Road, 17535
(717) 442-4901

We have approximately 40 milking cows and many young cattle and cats for children to enjoy. Our farmhouse has three guest rooms, all with double beds and one single. We also have cots and a playpen. Located 15 miles east of Lancaster on Route 30.

Hosts: Charles and Janet Groff
Rooms: 3 (SB) $30-40
Continental Breakfast
Credit Cards: none
Notes: 2, 5, 6, 7, 8, 9, 10

LAMPETER (LANCASTER)

Australian Walkabout Inn

837 Village Road, PO Box 294, 17537
(717) 464-0707; FAX (717) 464-2501

This 1925 brick, Mennonite farmhouse features large wraparound porches, balconies, English gardens, and antique furnishings. The Inn takes its name from the Australian word which means to go out and discover new places. Australian born host Richard will help you explore the Amish country surrounding the home. An elegant, full breakfast is served by candlelight. The honeymoon and anniversary rooms/suites are beautiful and include fireplaces and hot tubs. AAA—three-diamonds.

Hosts: Richard and Margaret Mason
Rooms: 6 (PB) $89-139
Suites: 2 (PB) $129-199
Full Breakfast
Credit Cards: A, B, C, D
Notes: 2, 3, 4, 5, 7, 8, 9, 10, 12

Country Living Inn

LANCASTER

Country Living Inn

2406 Old Philadelphia Pike, 17602
(717) 295-7295

Just like "HOME!" Warm inviting hospitality. Country decor with quilts on the full, queen, or king beds. New shaker furniture, glider rockers, or sofas in the deluxe suite or queen rooms. Romantic suite with a whirlpool for two. Amish farms on the north and west side. Coffee, tea, and hot chocolate served daily. Pastries served weekends (May to October on the front porch. The front

Australian Walkabout Inn

NOTES: Credit cards accepted: A Master Card; B Visa; C American Express; D Discover; E Diners Club; F Other; 2 Personal checks accepted; 3 Lunch available; 4 Dinner available;

porches have rockers and benches for visiting, relaxing, or watching Amish buggies go by.

Hosts: Bill and Judy Harnish
Rooms: 34 (PB) $43-130
Continental Breakfast
Credit Cards: A, B
Notes: 5, 10, 12

Flowers and Thyme Bed and Breakfast

238 Strasburg Pike, 17602
(717) 393-1460

Our 1941 brick German-style house with wraparound porch is bordered by farmland. The landscaped gardens feature a variety of perennials, herbs, and flowering annuals. Rooms are cozy, furnished with aniques, quilts, and ceiling fans. One room features a jacuzzi. Breakfasts are served in the vaulted ceiling, glass-windowed gathering room and may include potato quiche, overnight french toast, and other homemade specialties. We are only minutes from outlets and one mile from Route 30.

Hosts: Don and Ruth Harnish
Rooms: 3 (2PB; 1SB) $65-95
Full Breakfast
Credit Cards: none
Notes: 2, 5, 7 (over 12), 8, 9, 10

Gardens of Eden Bed and Breakfast

1894 Eden Road, 17601
(717) 393-5179; FAX (717) 393-7722

Victorian iron master's home built circa 1860 on the banks of the Conestoga River is three miles northeast of Lancaster. Antiques and family collections of quilts and coverlets fill the three guest rooms, all with private baths. The adjoining guest cottage (restored summer kitchen) features a walk-in fireplace, dining room, bedroom, and bath on second floor. Marilyn's floral designs are featured and for sale. The three acres of gardens feature herbs, perennials, and wildflowers among the woodsy trails. Local attractions are personalized by a tour guide service and dinner in a young Amish couple's home. Canoe and row boat available. Two bike trails pass the house.

Hosts: Marilyn and Bill Ebel
Rooms: 4 (PB) $75-120
Full Breakfast
Credit Cards: A, B
Notes: 2, 5, 7 (in guest house), 8, 9, 10, 12

The King's Cottage

The King's Cottage, A Bed and Breakfast Inn

1049 East King Street, 17602
(717) 397-1017; (800) 747-8717;
FAX (717) 397-3447

Recently named to American Historic Inns' "Top 10 List." All rooms offer traditionally-styled elegance, modern comfort, and warm hospitality in Amish

---

5 Open all year; 6 Pets welcome; 7 Children welcome; 8 Tennis nearby; 9 Swimming nearby; 10 Golf nearby; 11 Skiing nearby; 12 May be booked through travel agent.

Country. King and queen beds, private baths, gourmet breakfasts, and personal service create a gracious friendly atmosphere at this Spanish-style mansion. "The Carriage House" features a private fireplace and over-sized jacuzzi. Relax by the fire and enjoy afternoon tea in the library while getting directions to restaurants and attractions. Amish dinners or personal tours arranged. Near farmers' markets, Gettysburg, and Hershey. On National Register; AAA and Mobile listed EXCELLENT!

Hosts: Karen and Jim Owens
Rooms: 9 (PB) $69-180
Full Breakfast
Credit Cards: A, B, D
Notes: 2, 5, 7 (12 and over), 8, 9, 10, 12

Lincoln Haus Inn Bed and Breakfast

1687 Lincoln Highway East, 17602
(717) 392-9412

Lincoln Haus Inn is the only inn in Lancaster County with a distinctive hip roof. It is furnished with antiques and rugs on gleaming, hardwood floors, and it has natural oak woodwork. I am a member of the Old Amish Church, serving family-style breakfast with a homey atmosphere. Convenient location, close to Amish farmlands, malls, historic Lancaster; five minutes from Route 30 and Pennsylvania Dutch Visitors' Bureau.

Hostess: Mary K. Zook
Rooms: 6 (PB) $49-75; 2 apartments (PB)
Full Breakfast
Credit Cards: none
Notes: 2, 4, 5, 7, 8, 9, 10, 12

New Life Homestead

New Life Homestead Bed and Breakfast

1400 East King Street (Rt. 462), 17602
(717) 396-8928

Stately, brick Victorian in the heart of Amish Country. Each room is fashioned with heirlooms and antiques. Air-condition, private baths, full breakfast, and evening refreshments add to your comfort. Highlight of your stay is the answers to all your questions about our area's "Plain People." Details given on out of the way places to go. Privacy when you want it, company when you need it. A traditional family value Mennonite home. See us on the net: http//padutch.welcome.com/newlife.html

Hosts: Carol and Bill Giersch
Rooms: 3 (2PB; 1SB) $60-80
Full Family-style Breakfast
Credit Cards: none
Notes: 2, 5, 7 (limited), 8, 9, 10, 12

O'Flaherty's Dingeldein House Bed and Breakfast

1105 East King Street, 17602
(717) 293-1723; (800) 779-7765;
FAX (717) 293-1947

Enjoy genuine warmth and hospitality

NOTES: Credit cards accepted: A Master Card; B Visa; C American Express; D Discover; E Diners Club; F Other; 2 Personal checks accepted; 3 Lunch available; 4 Dinner available;

in the friendly atmosphere of our home. Our Dutch Colonial home is traditionally appointed for your comfort, two fireplaces in the fall and winter and A/C when needed to provide a restful, relaxing stay in beautiful Lancaster County. Conveniently located near downtown Lancaster attractions and just a short, scenic ride to the Amish farmland, outlet shopping, and antique area. Amish dining arranged. Personalized maps prepared. Our breakfast guarantees you won't go away hungry. AAA approved, three diamonds.

Hosts: Jack and Sue Flatley
Rooms: 4 (2PB; 2SB) $70-80
Full Breakfast
Credit Cards: A, B, D
Notes: 2, 5, 7, 8, 9, 10

Whitman's Tavern— Historic 1725 Inn and Museum
2014 Old Philadelphia Pike, 17602
(717) 299-5305

Lancaster's oldest, only pre-Revolutionary War inn still lodging travelers in the original building. Reflects rural and historic flavor of the area. Restored to the simple, authentic, pioneer style that was familiar to European immigrants who joined the Conestoga wagon trains being provisioned at the Inn for the western and southern treks into the wilderness areas. Fresh flowers, working fireplaces, antique quilts, and antiques in all the romantic rooms. Pandora's Antique Shop is on the premises. Bird-in-Hand and Intercourse villages, other antique shops, and auc-

tions just beyond. Valley Forge, Hershey, Gettysburg, Winterthur, Chadds Ford, and New Hope all within a 90-minute drive. On the National Register of Historic Places and a national landmark. Beautiful park across the street; Amish cow pasture in the rear.

Host: Brant Hartung
Rooms: 7 (2PB; 5SB) $60-90
Continental Plus Breakfast
Credit Cards: none
Notes: 2, 5, 8, 9, 10, 11, 12

LANCASTER COUNTY (PENNSYLVANIA DUTCH COUNTRY) SEE ALSO—ATGLEN, BIRD-IN-HAND, CHRISTIANA, CONESTOGA, DENVER, EAST PETERSBURG, ELIZABETHTOWN, EPHRATA, GAP, KINZERS, LANCASTER, MANHEIM, MARIETTA, MOUNT JOY, NOTTINGHAM, PARADISE, PEACH BOTTOM, SMOKETOWN, AND QUARRYVILLE)

The Apple Bin Inn B&B
2835 Willow Street Pike, **Willow Street** 17584
(717) 464-5881; (800) 338-4296;
FAX (717) 464-1818

Southern Lancaster County's finest bed and breakfast. Minutes from Lancaster's oldest home, The Hans Herr House, Amish, historic buildings, shopping outlets, and antiques. Bring your bike and see the area at a slow pace—we offer storage. Picnic lunches available (additional cost). Don't forget the wonder-

The Apple Bin Inn

ful food of the area. We will help you plan your visit wisely. Color cable TV and phones in guest rooms. Come enjoy your home away from home. Spend the weekend and join us for church Sunday morning following breakfast.

Hosts: Barry and Debbie Hershey
Rooms: 5 (3PB; 2SB) $60-95; Carriage House
   $135
Full Breakfast
Credit Cards: A, B, C
Notes: 2, 5, 8, 9, 10

Bed and Breakfast— The Manor

830 Village Road, PO Box 416, **Lampeter** 17537
(717) 464-9564; (800) 461-6BED

This cozy farmhouse is minutes away from Lancaster's historical sites and attractions. Guests delight in Mary Lou's homemade breakfasts featuring Eggs Mornay, crepes, stratas, fruit cobblers, and homemade breads and jams. A swim in our pool and a nap under a shade tree is the perfect way to cap your day of touring. Dinner, an overnight stay, and a buggy ride with an Old Order Amish family can be arranged.

Amish waitresses. Children welcome.

Hostesses: Mary Lou Paolini and Jackie Curtis
Rooms: 6 (4PB; 2SB) $79-99
Gourmet Buffet-style Breakfast
Credit Cards: A, B
Notes: 2, 3, 4, 5, 7, 8, 9, 10

Carriage Corner Bed and Breakfast

3705 E. Newport Road, PO Box 371,
Intercourse 17534
(717) 768-3059

"A comfortable bed, a hearty breakfast, a charming village, and friendly hosts" has been used to describe our B&B. We have five comfortable rooms with country decor, Amish quilt hangings, and private baths. Our bed and breakfast offers a relaxing country atmosphere with hand-crafted touches of folk-art and country. Rooms are air conditioned. We are centered in the heart of beautiful farms and a culture which draws many to nearby villages of Intercourse, Bird-in-Hand, and Paradise. Amish dinners arranged. There is much to learn from these calm and gentle people.

Hosts: Gordon and Gwen Schuit
Rooms: 4 (2PB; 2SB) $40-70
Full Breakfast
Credit Cards: A, B
Notes: 2, 5, 7, 12

The Columbian, A Bed and Breakfast Inn

360 Chestnut Street, **Columbia** 17512
(717) 684-5869; (800) 422-5869

Circa 1897. Centrally located in the small historic river town of Columbia, The Columbian, a brick Colonial Re-

---

NOTES: Credit cards accepted: A Master Card; B Visa; C American Express; D Discover; E Diners Club; F Other; 2 Personal checks accepted; 3 Lunch available; 4 Dinner available;

vival mansion, features an ornate stained glass window, magnificent tiered staircase, and unique wraparound porches. Large, air-conditioned rooms offer queen-size beds, private baths, and CATV. Suite with balcony and rooms with fireplaces available. Come relax and unwind in our lovely home and browse through the nearby antique shops, art galleries, outlets, and museums only a brief stroll away.

Hosts: Becky and Chris Will
Rooms: 6 (SB) $70-89
Full Breakfast
Credit Cards: A, B
Notes: 2, 5, 7, 8, 9, 10, 11

The Columbian

Homestead Lodging

184 East Brook Road (Route 896), **Smoketown** 17576
(717) 393-6927; FAX (717) 393-6927

Welcome to Homestead Lodging in the heart of the Pennsylvania Dutch Amish farmlands. Listen to the clippity-clop of horse and buggies go by or stroll down the lane to the scenic farmlands around us. Within walking distance of restaurants and minutes from farmers' markets; quilt, antique, and craft shops; museums; and auctions. Tours avail-

able. Family-operated B&B with clean, country rooms, each with private bath, cable color TV with remote/radio, refrigerator, air-conditioning, and heat. Microwave available.

Hosts: Robert and Lori Kepiro
Rooms: 4 (PB) $37-56
Continental Breakfast
Credit Cards: A, B, C, D
Notes: 2 (deposit only), 5, 7, 8, 9, 10, 11

The Inn at Hayward Heath

2048 Silver Lane, **Willow Street** 17584
(717) 464-0994

The Inn is located in gently rolling hills of Lancaster County. Our country farmhouse, built in 1887, has been beautifully restored to replicate Colonial living. You may reflect on America's past in our Shaker-style room with queen-sized canopy bed or enjoy the romantic touch of our spacious country garden room with queen-sized bed, sitting area, and attached private bath with a two-person whirlpool. Our charming first floor rose bedroom features a queen-sized bed and a large private bath. A two-bedroom suite is also available for friends or family who are traveling together. Our guests are invited to use the large liv-

The Inn at Hayward Heath

---

5 Open all year; 6 Pets welcome; 7 Children welcome; 8 Tennis nearby; 9 Swimming nearby; 10 Golf nearby; 11 Skiing nearby; 12 May be booked through travel agent.

ing room for visiting, reading, or viewing TV. A sumptuous breakfast is served in the formal dining room every morning. We are close to historic areas, tourist attractions, outlet shopping malls, Amish farms, and craft, antique, and quilt shops.

Hosts: Joan and David Smith
Rooms: 4 (PB) $65-95
Full Breakfast
Credit Cards: A, B, D
Notes: 2, 5, 8, 10

Hamanassett Bed and Breakfast

LEETSDALE

The Whistlestop Bed and Breakfast

195 Broad Street, 15056
(412) 251-0852

A quaint brick Victorian built in 1888 by the Harmonist Society, a Christian communal group similar to the Shakers. It features the "Upper Berth," a third floor suite with a small kitchen and a dining area, and the "Lower Berth" with a sofa bed and private entrance. Kids stay free with parents. Your hostess is well known for her country cooking, specializing in breads, muffins, pastries, and jams. Leetsdale is located on the Ohio River, 12 miles west of Pittsburgh —airport is 20 minutes away—and close to the classic American village of Sewickley where fine examples of historic architecture are well maintained. The home is smoke free.

Hosts: Steve and Joyce Smith
Rooms: 3 (PB) $60-70
Full Country Breakfast
Credit Cards: D
Notes: 2, 5, 7, 10

LIMA

Hamanassett Bed and Breakfast

PO Box 129, 19037
(610) 459-3000 (voice and FAX)

Early 19th century mansion on 48 secluded, peaceful acres of woodlands, gardens, and trails in the Brandywine Valley: Winterthur, Hagley, Nemours, Brandywine (Wyeth) Museums, and Longwood Gardens. Well-appointed rooms prevail with queens, doubles, twins, canopied king beds, private baths, TV and amenities. Beautiful Federalist living room and extensive library. Full country breakfast—sophisticated cuisine. Near tennis, golf, and excellent dining. An elegant, quiet, weekend escape along US Route 1 corridor and a world away. Two night minimum. No smoking.

Hostess: Evelene H. Dohan
Rooms: 8 (6PB; 2SB) $90-125
Full Breakfast
Credit Cards: none
Closed July 15 to August 30
Notes: 2, 8, 10

NOTES: Credit cards accepted: A Master Card; B Visa; C American Express; D Discover; E Diners Club; F Other; 2 Personal checks accepted; 3 Lunch available; 4 Dinner available;

MANHEIM

The Inn at Mt. Hope

2232 East Mt. Hope Road, 17545-0155
(717) 664-4708; (800) 644-4708;
FAX (717) 272-7042

An 1850s stone home with high ceilings and magnificent pine floors. The Inn sits on four and one half acres of woodland and grass bordered by a stream. Convenient to all Lancaster County attractions as well as Hershey and adjacent to the Mt. Hope Winery and Pennsylvania Renaissance Faire. Ideal setting for a small couples retreat or getaway. Screened porch and family TV room are available for relaxation.

Hosts: Bob and Nancy Ladd
Rooms: 5 (2PB; 3SB) $60-110
Full Breakfast
Credit Cards: A, B
Notes: 2, 5, 7, 9, 10

The Inn at Mt. Hope

The Loft Inn

1263 South Colebrook Road, 17545
(717) 898-8955

Nestled in the heart of Pennsylvania Dutch Country, The Loft is a contemporary private suite located in the former loft of a 100-year-old tobacco barn and is complete with full kitchen, large master bedroom, bath, living room, and air-conditioning. A delicious continental breakfast is delivered to your door each morning. Centrally located with excellent shopping in Lancaster County, the Reading outlets, and Philadelphia nearby, and quality dining of every variety minutes away.

Hosts: Miriam and Herb Nachbar
Rooms: 1 (PB) $65-75
Continental Breakfast
Credit Cards: none
Notes: 2, 5, 7, 10

Wenger's Bed and Breakfast

571 Hossler Road, 17545
(717) 665-3862

Relax and enjoy your stay in the quiet countryside of Lancaster County. Our ranch-style house is within walking distance of our son's 100-acre dairy farm. The spacious rooms will accommodate families. You can get a guided tour through the Amish farmland. Hershey, the chocolate town, Pennsylvania's state capital at Harrisburg, and the Gettysburg battlefield are all within one hour's drive.

Hosts: Arthur D. and Mary K. Wenger
Rooms: 2 (PB) $40-45
Full Breakfast
Credit Cards: none
Notes: 2, 5, 7

---

5 Open all year; 6 Pets welcome; 7 Children welcome; 8 Tennis nearby; 9 Swimming nearby; 10 Golf nearby; 11 Skiing nearby; 12 May be booked through travel agent.

MARIETTA

Historic Linden House

606 E. Market Street, 17547
(717) 426-4697; (800) 416-4697;
FAX (717) 426-4136

The Historic Linden House is a Federal style home built in 1806 and listed on the National Historic Register. When they built it, it was considered one of the finest mansions in south-central PA, costing between $16,000 and $17,000 to build. A charming town situated along the Susquehanna River, which TIME HAS FORGOTTEN with 48% of its buildings in the historic district. The home historically is known for its staircase, being the longest, original preserved continuous handrail staircase in Lancaster County. Guests enjoy queen-size beds and private baths. Fresh flowers in seasons. Spend a relaxing evening in the parlor by the two crackling fireplaces. The house contains a total of sixteen fireplaces. Special packages and discounts available.

Hosts: Henry, Jeanene, and David Hill
Rooms: 6 (PB) $50-75
Expanded Continental Breakfast (weekdays); Full (weekends)
Credit Cards: A, B
Notes: 2, 5, 7

Vogt Farm
Bed and Breakfast

1225 Colebrook Road, 17547
(717) 653-4810; (800) 854-0399

Comfortable accommodations located in our 1868 home on a 26-acre cattle and sheep farm. You can enjoy the country and the quiet from one of our three porches. Each room is filled with our treasures—some old, some new—for your pleasure. We have been hosting guests from around the world for over 20 years. We will be pleased to share maps and hints for touring beautiful Lancaster County. We are centrally located between Harrisburg, Hershey, Lancaster, and York.

Hosts: Keith and Kathy Vogt
Rooms: 3 (1PB; 2SB) $60-100
Full Breakfast
Credit Cards: A, B, C, D, E
Notes: 2, 5, 7, 8, 9, 10, 12

MILFORD

Black Walnut B&B
Country Inn

509 FireTower Road, 18337
(717) 296-6322

Tudor-style stone house with historic marble fireplace and 12 charming guest rooms plus one suite with antiques and brass beds. A 160-acre estate, it is quiet and peaceful and convenient to horseback riding, antiquing, golf, skiing, rafting, and canoeing on the Delaware River. Serving the finest cuisine in a beautiful country setting overlooking a five-acre lake just outside of Milford.

Host: Stewart Schneider
Rooms: 12 (8PB; 4SB) $53-100
Continental Breakfast
Credit Cards: A, B, C
Notes: 4, 5, 7, 9, 10, 11, 12

NOTES: Credit cards accepted: A Master Card; B Visa; C American Express; D Discover; E Diners Club; F Other; 2 Personal checks accepted; 3 Lunch available; 4 Dinner available;

Cliff Park Inn and Golf Course

RR 4, Box 7200, 18337
(717) 296-6491; (800) 225-6535;
FAX (717) 296-3982

Historic country inn on secluded 600-acre estate. Spacious rooms with private bath, telephone and climate control. Victorian-style furnishings. Fireplaces. Golf at the door on one of America's oldest golf courses (1913). Hike or cross-country ski on seven miles of marked trails. Golf and ski equipment rentals. Golf school. Full service restaurant rated three stars by Mobil Guide. MAP or B&B plans available. Specialists in business conferences and country weddings.

Host: Harry W. Buchanan III
Rooms: 18 (PB) $90-155
Full Breakfast
Credit Cards: A, B, C, D, E
Notes: 2, 3, 4, 5, 7, 8, 9 (on premises), 10, 11, 12

MILL RIFT

Bonny Bank Bungalow Bed and Breakfast

PO Box 481, 18340
(717) 491-2250

Let the rush of the rapids lull you to sleep in this cozy bungalow perched on the banks of the Upper Delaware National Scenic and Recreational River. Located on a dead-end road in a small town. Private entrance and private bath. TV available, if you can take your eyes off the view. River access area for swimming and tubing (tubes available at no charge). Canoe/raft rentals and hiking on public lands nearby.

Hosts: Doug and Linda Hay
Rooms: 1 (PB) $45
Full Breakfast
Credit Cards: none
Notes: 2, 8, 9

MILTON

Pau-Lyn's Country Bed and Breakfast (A Restful Haven)

RD 3, Box 676, 17847
(717) 742-4110

The beautiful Susquehanna Valley of Central PA is unique. Truly a variety of pleasant experience await persons who desire being in touch with God's handiwork and observing agriculture, scenic mountains, rivers and valleys. Recreational activities also abound. Guests experience "a Restful Haven" as the innkeepers with their generous hospitality provide nostalgic memories throughout the antique furnished, 1850 Victorian brick house, two miles from I-80. Comfortable, air-conditioned bedrooms add to the relaxing atmosphere.

Hosts: Paul and Evelyn Landis
Rooms: 7 (4PB; 3SB) $45-55
Full Breakfast
Credit Cards: none
Notes: 2, 5, 7, 8, 9, 10, 11, 12

MOUNT JOY

Cedar Hill Farm

305 Longenecker Road, 17552
(717) 653-4655

This 1817 stone farmhouse overlooks

---

5 Open all year; 6 Pets welcome; 7 Children welcome; 8 Tennis nearby; 9 Swimming nearby; 10 Golf nearby; 11 Skiing nearby; 12 May be booked through travel agent.

a peaceful stream and was the birthplace of the host. Stroll the acreage or relax on the wicker rockers on the large front porch. Enjoy the singing of the birds and serene countryside. A winding staircase leads to the comfortable rooms, each with a private bath and centrally air-conditioned. A room for honeymooners offers a private balcony. Breakfast is served daily by a walk-in fireplace. Located midway between the Lancaster and Hershey areas where farmers' markets, antique shops, and good restaurants abound. Gift certificates for anniversary or holiday giving. Open all seasons.

Hosts: Russel and Gladys Swarr
Rooms: 5 (PB) $70-75
Continental Plus Breakfast
Credit Cards: A, B, C, D
Notes: 2, 5, 7, 8, 10

Green Acres Farm B&B

1382 Pinkerton Road, 17552
(717) 653-4028; FAX (717) 653-2840

Our 1830 farmhouse is furnished with antiques and offers a peaceful haven for your getaway. The rooster, chickens, Pigmy goats, lots of kittens, pony, and

1,000 hogs give a real farm atmosphere on this 160-acre grain farm. Children love the pony cart rides and the 8' x 10' playhouse, and everyone enjoys the trampoline and swings. We offer tour information about the Amish Country and can arrange your dinner with an Amish family.

Hosts: Wayne and Yvonne Miller
Rooms: 7 (PB) $70 (+ $6 per child)
Full Breakfast
Credit Cards: A, B
Notes: 2, 5, 6, 7, 8, 9, 10

Hillside Farm Bed and Breakfast

607 Eby Chiques Road, 17552
(717) 653-6697; (717) 653-5233 (call first)

Quiet, secluded 1863 brick farm homestead overlooking Chiques Creek, dam, and waterfall. Located 10 miles west of downtown Lancaster and entirely surrounded by farmland. Comfortable, cozy, country furnishings including dairy antiques and milk bottles. Close to Amish, Hershey, antique shops, flea markets, auctions, wineries, and trails for hiking and biking. Bike trail maps available. Dinner arranged in advance

Green Acres Farm

Hillside Farm

with Amish. Strictly non-smoking. Air-conditioned.

Hosts: Gary and Deb Lintner
Rooms: 5 (3PB; 2SB) $50-62.50 + 6% tax
Full Country Breakfast served Family-style
Credit Cards: none
Notes: 2, 5, 7 (10 and older), 8, 9, 10, 11, 12

MUNCY

The Bodine House
307 South Main Street, 17756
(717) 546-8949

The Bodine House, featured in the December 1991 issue of *Colonial Homes* magazine, is located on tree-lined Main Street in the historic district. Built in 1805, the House has been authentically restored and is listed on the National Register of Historic Places. Most of the furnishings are antiques. The center of Muncy, with its shops, restaurants, library, and churches, is a short walk down the street. No smoking.

Hosts: David and Marie Louise Smith
Rooms: 4 (PB) $55-75; Carriage House (up to six guests) $125
Full Breakfast
Credit Cards: A, B, C, D
Notes: 2, 5, 7 (over 6), 8, 9, 10, 11, 12

NEW BERLIN

The Inn at Olde New Berlin
321 Market Street, 17855-0390
(717) 966-0321; FAX (717) 966-9557

"A luxurious base for indulging in a clutch of quiet pleasures" is *The Philadelphia Inquirer's* most apt description for this elegantly appointed Victorian inn. The superb dining opportunities at Gabiel's Restaurant (on-site) coupled with the antique-filled lodging accommodations provide romance and ambiance. An upscale experience in a rural setting, only one hour north of Harrisburg. Guests relay that they depart feeling nurtured, relaxed, yet, most of all, inspired. Gifts, herb garden, air- conditioning. AAA approved.

Hosts: Nancy and John Showers
Rooms: 6 (PB) $85-100
Full Breakfast
Credit Cards: A, B
Notes: 2, 3, 4, 5, 7, 8, 9, 10

NEW WILMINGTON

Beechwood Inn
175 Beechwood Drive, 16142
(412) 946-2342

Civil War home with Victorian decor offers three porches with lovely views. All rooms enjoy private baths, queen beds, room keys, central air, and conversation areas. A common parlor is upstairs with cable TV, couch, and kitchen. A covered balcony stretches the width of the house and looks into our

---

5 Open all year; 6 Pets welcome; 7 Children welcome; 8 Tennis nearby; 9 Swimming nearby; 10 Golf nearby; 11 Skiing nearby; 12 May be booked through travel agent.

peaceful village park. Very close to many shops and restaurants. Ten minutes to Routes 80, 60, 19, and 18. Full breakfast included. Non-smoking.

Hosts: Tom and Janet Hartwell
Rooms: 3 (PB) $60 includes tax
Full Breakfast
Credit Cards: A, B
Notes: 2, 5, 7, 8, 9, 10

Behm's Bed and Breakfast

166 Waugh Avenue, 16142
(412) 946-8641; (800) 932-3315

Located but one block from Westminster College campus, Behm's 100 year old B&B is comfortably furnished with family, primitive, and collected antiques. Located within walking distance of shops and restaurants, Behm's is surrounded by rural, Old Order Amish. Nationally recognized water-colorist Nancy Behm's gallery on site.

Hosts: Bob and Nancy Behm
Rooms: 5 (1PB; 4SB) $50-65
Full Hearty Breakfast
Credit Cards: A, B
Notes: 2, 5, 7, 8, 9, 10

Behm's Bed and Breakfast

NEWVILLE

Nature's Nook Farm

740 Shed Road, 17241
(717) 776-5619

Nature's Nook Farm is located in a quiet, peaceful setting along the Blue Mountains. Warm Mennonite hospitality and clean, comfortable lodging await you. Enjoy freshly brewed, garden tea and fresh fruit in season. Homemade cinnamon rolls, muffins, or coffee cake are a specialty. Perennial flower garden. Close to Colonel Denning State Park with hiking trails, fishing, and swimming. Two hours to Lancaster, one hour to Harrisburg, anf one and a half hours to Gettysburg and Hershey. Wheelchair accessible.

Hosts: Don and Lois Leatherman
Rooms: 1 (PB) $50
Continental Breakfast
Credit Cards: none
Notes: 2, 4, 5, 7, 8, 9, 10

NORTH EAST

Vineyard Bed and Breakfast

10757 Sidehill Road, 16428
(814) 725-5307

Your hosts would like to welcome you to the "Heart of Grape Country" on the shores of Lake Erie where you are surrounded by vineyards and orchards. Our turn-of-the-century farmhouse is quiet and peaceful with rooms furnished with queen or king beds and tastefully decorated to complement our home.

Hosts: Clyde and Judy Burnham
Rooms: 4 (2PB; 2SB) $55-65
Full Breakfast
Credit Cards: A, B
Notes: 2, 5, 7, 9, 10, 11

NORTHUMBERLAND

Campbell's Bed and Breakfast

707 Duke Street, 17857-1709
(717) 473-3276

Campbell's Bed and Breakfast, a turn-of-the-century inn built in 1859, has three large bedrooms await your occupancy. Enjoy a refreshing swim in the large in-ground pool surrounded by the rose garden, or relax by the fire in the spacious living room during the cool months.

Hosts: Bob and Millie Campbell
Rooms: 3 (2PB; 1SB) $50-60
Full Breakfast
Credit Cards: none
Notes: 2, 5, 7 (cal first), 8, 9 (on-site), 10, 12

NOTTINGHAM

Little Britain Manor

20 Brawn Rd., (Village of Little Britain), 19362
(717) 529-2862

We are a farm B&B surrounded by Amish and Mennonite farms in beautiful Southern Lancaster County. Relax in our quiet, restful, country home away from noise, busy crowds, and city traffic. Gather in the large farm kitchen to enjoy a full country breakfast and experience the warmth of heartfelt hospitality. Nicely located to do Lancaster Amish attractions, antiques, crafts, Longwood Gardens, and Baltimore Inner Harbor.

Hosts: Fred and Evelyn Crider
Rooms: 4 (SB) $50
Full Country Breakfast
Credit Cards: none
Notes: 2, 7

ORRTANNA

Hickory Bridge Farm

96 Hickory Bridge Road, 17353
(717) 642-5261

Only eight miles west of historical Gettysburg. Unique country dining and B&B. Cozy cottages with wood stoves and private baths located in secluded wooded settings along a stream. Lovely rooms available in the farmhouse with antiques, private baths, and whirlpool tubs. Full, farm breakfast served at the farmhouse which was built in the late 1700s. Country dining offered on Fridays, Saturdays, and Sundays in a 130-year-old barn decorated with many antiques. Family owned and operated for over 15 years.

Hosts: Robert and Mary Lynn Martin
Rooms: 7 (6PB; 1SB) $79-89
Full Breakfast
Credit Cards: A, B
Notes: 2, 4 (on weekends), 5, 7, 9, 10, 11

---

5 Open all year; 6 Pets welcome; 7 Children welcome; 8 Tennis nearby; 9 Swimming nearby; 10 Golf nearby; 11 Skiing nearby; 12 May be booked through travel agent.

PARADISE

Maple Lane Farm Bed and Breakfast

505 Paradise Lane, 17562
(717) 687-7479

This 200-acre, family owned dairy farm is situated in the heart of Amish Country with nearby quilt and craft shops, museums, farmers' markets, antique shops, outlets, and auctions. The large front porch overlooks spacious lawn, green meadows, and rolling hills with no busy highways. Pleasantly furnished rooms have quilts, crafts, canopy and poster beds, TV, and air-conditioning. Victorian parlor for guest use. Breakfast served daily. Featured in several national magazines.

Hosts: Ed and Marion Rohrer
Rooms: 4 (2PB; 2SB) $45-58
Complimentary Breakfast
Credit Cards: none
Notes: 2, 5, 7, 8, 9, 10

Parson's Place in Paradise B&B

37 Leacock Road, 17562
(717) 687-8529

Mid 1700s stone house with stone patio overlooking flower gardens and picturesque road traveled by horse-drawn buggies to the Amsh village-mecca of "Intercourse" (the tourist center of Lancaster county) three miles to the East. Share this charming home furnished with country decor with former pastor and wife.

Parson's Place

Hosts: Parson Bob and Margaret Bell
Rooms: 3 (2PB; 1SB) $50-70
Full Menu Breakfast
Credit Cards: A, B
Notes: 2, 5

PEACH BOTTOM

Pleasant Grove Farm Bed and Breakfast

368 Pilottown Road, 17563
(717) 548-3100

Located in beautiful, historic Lancaster County, this 160-acre dairy farm has been a family run operation for 110 years, earning the title of Century Farm by the Pennsylvania Department of Agriculture. As a working farm, It provides guests the opportunity to experience daily life in a rural setting. Built in 1814, 1818, and 1820, the house once served as a country store and post office. Full country breakfast served by candlelight.

Hosts: Charles and Labertha Tindall
Rooms: 4 (SB) $45-60
Full Breakfast
Credit Cards: none
Notes: 2, 5, 7, 9

NOTES: Credit cards accepted: A Master Card; B Visa; C American Express; D Discover; E Diners Club; F Other; 2 Personal checks accepted; 3 Lunch available; 4 Dinner available;

PHILADELPHIA—SEE VALLEY FORGE

POCONO MOUNTAINS
(SEE ALSO—CANADENSIS, CRESCO, AND SWIFTWATER)

Eagle Rock Lodge Bed and Breakfast

PO Box 265, River Road, **Shawnee on Delaware** 18356
(717) 421-2139

This century-old, eight-bedroom inn is located on 10.5 Delaware River acres adjacent to the scenic Delaware Water Gap National Recreation Area and the Pocono Mountains. Breakfast is served on an 80-foot Screened porch overlooking the river. Enjoy a step back in time to a more relaxed by-gone era. Consider group rentals.

Hosts: Jane and Jim Cox
Rooms: 8 (1PB; 6SB) $60-95
Full Breakfast
Credit Cards: C
Notes: 2, 5, 7, 8, 9, 10, 11, 12

Eagle Rock Lodge

POINT PLEASANT (NEW HOPE)

Tattersall Inn

PO Box 569, Cafferty and River Road, 18950
(215) 297-8233; (800) 297-4988

This 18th century, plastered, fieldstone home with its broad porches and manicured lawns recalls the unhurried atmosphere of a bygone era. Enjoy the richly wainscoted entry hall, formal dining room with marble fireplace, and a collection of vintage phonographs. Step back in time when you enter the Colonial common room with beamed ceiling and walk-in fireplace. The spacious, antique-furnished guest rooms are a joy. Air-conditioned. Private baths.

Hosts: Gerry and Herb Moss
Rooms: 6 (PB) $70-115
Full Breakfast
Credit Cards: A, B, C, D
Notes: 2, 5, 7, 8, 9, 12

QUARRYVILLE

Runnymede Farm Guest House Bed and Breakfast

1030 Robert Fulton Highway, 17566
(717) 786-3625

Enjoy our comfortable farmhouse in southern Lancaster County. The rooms are clean and air-conditioned, and the lounge has a TV. Close to tourist attractions, but not in the mainstream. Country breakfast is optional.

Hosts: Herb and Sara Hess
Rooms: 3 (SB) $35-40
Full Breakfast
Credit Cards: none
Notes: 2, 5, 7, 8, 9, 10

5 Open all year; 6 Pets welcome; 7 Children welcome; 8 Tennis nearby; 9 Swimming nearby;
10 Golf nearby; 11 Skiing nearby; 12 May be booked through travel agent.

SAXONBURG

The Main Stay B&B

PO Box 507, 214 Main Street, 16056
(412) 352-9363

This 150-year-old country home is located in Saxonburg, in the heart of farm country in southern Butler County of Pennsylvania, about 30 miles from Pittsburgh. Its a fine place to get away from the stress and strains of everyday life or to spend the night enroute east or west. Saxonburg is not a large place but it boasts some fine shops to browse and an excellent restaurant to enjoy.

Hosts: Barbara and Ivan Franson
Rooms: 4 (PB) $60 (includes tax)
Full Breakfast
Credit Cards: A, B, C
Notes: 2, 5, 7, 10

SCOTTDALE

Pine Wood Acres B&B

Route 1, Box 634, 15683
(412) 887-5404

Experience gracious hospitality in our 1880 farm house. Enjoy the changes each season brings to the landscape of our tranquil country setting. Antiques, quilts, herb and perennial gardens, bountiful breafasts, and afternoon tea. Near Wright's Fallingwater. Only ten miles south of the junction of I-70 and 76 at New Stanton.

Hosts: Ruth and James Horsch
Rooms: 3 (2PB; 1SB) $68.90-79.50
Full Breakfast
Credit Cards: none
Notes: 2, 5, 6, 7, 8, 9, 10, 11, 12

Zephyr Glen

Zephyr Glen B&B

205 Dexter Road, 15683
(412) 887-6577; FAX (412) 887-6177 (call first)

Our 1822 Federal style Mennonite farm house is nestled on three wooded acres. The house is filled with antiques, old quilts, and seasonal decorations. We feature caring Christian hospitality, warm country decor, afternoon tea, bed turn down, and a heart breakfast. Sit by the fireplace, rock on the wide porch, or stroll through herb, flower, and fruit gardens. Antiques, Fallingwater, hiking, biking, white water, and historic sites are nearby. We'll help you find your favorite. Come and enjoy!

Hosts: Glen and Noreen McGurl
Rooms: 3 (PB) $70-75
Full Breakfast
Credit Cards: A, B, D
Notes: 2, 5, 7 (over 12), 8, 10, 11, 12

SHIPPENSBURG

Wilmar Manor Bed and Breakfast

303 West King Street, 17257
(717) 532-3784

A beautiful Victorian mansion built in

NOTES: Credit cards accepted: A Master Card; B Visa; C American Express; D Discover; E Diners Club; F Other; 2 Personal checks accepted; 3 Lunch available; 4 Dinner available;

1898 in the heart of Shippensburg. You can stroll down Main Street of our historic village or enjoy the serenity of our spacious landscaped gardens. The air-conditioned guest rooms are comfortably furnished with antiques. Your choice of private or shared baths at reasonable rates. Enjoy a delicious breakfast served in our formal Victorian dining room.

Hosts: Marise and Wilton Banks
Rooms: 7 (2PB; 5SB) $52-60
Full Breakfast
Credit Cards: A, B
Notes: 2, 5, 7, 9, 10, 11, 12

SMOKETOWN

Smoketown Lodging and Carriage House B&B

190 East Brook Road, 17576
(717) 397-6944

Nestled on three beautiful acres of an original Amish homestead. Our guests call it their "home away from home." Enjoy a walk down the lane to our Amish neighbors or by the stream to feed the ducks. Relax on our two patios or in our non-smoking lounge, or enjoy a game of tennis on our new court. Restaurants including a family-style restaurant, within walking distance; buggy rides; farmers and flea markets, and outlets just a short distance. All rooms have full bath, AC, CA/TV, clock radio, and refrigerator.

Hosts: Don and Phyllis Ringuette
Rooms: 17 (PB) $34-80
Continental Breakfast
Credit Cards: A, B
Notes: 2, 5, 7, 8 (on premises), 9, 10, 12

SOMERSET

H.B.'s Cottage

231 West Church Street, 15501
(814) 443-1204; FAX (814) 443-4313

H.B.'s Cottage, an exclusive and elegant B&B located within the Borough of Somerset, is a stone and frame 1920s cottage with an oversize fireplace in the living room. It is furnished in the traditional manner with accent pieces from the innkeepers' overseas travels—a retired Naval Officer and his wife—and collectible Teddy Bears from the hostess' extensive collection. The guest rooms are warmly and romantically decorated, and one has a private porch. Downhill and cross-country skiing, mountain biking, and tennis are specialties of the hosts. Located close to Seven Springs Mountain Resort, Falling Water Hidden Valley Resort, biking and hiking trails, and white water sports. Advance reservations are suggested.

Hosts: Hank and Phyllis Vogt
Rooms: 2 (PB) $60-75
Full Breakfast
Credit Cards: A, B
Notes: 2, 6 (limited), 8, 9, 10, 11

H.B.'s Cottage

5 Open all year; 6 Pets welcome; 7 Children welcome; 8 Tennis nearby; 9 Swimming nearby; 10 Golf nearby; 11 Skiing nearby; 12 May be booked through travel agent.

Quill Haven Country Inn

1519 North Center Avenue, 15501
(814) 443-4514; FAX (814) 445-1376

Experience the elegant yet relaxed atmosphere of this newly remodeled 1918 "Gentleman's" farm house furnished with antiques and fine reproductions. Four uniquely decorated guest rooms with private baths and TVs; a common room with fireplace, VCR, and games; and a sunroom where breakfast is served. Ample off-street parking. Centrally located near Hidden Valley and Seven Springs Ski Resorts, Frank Lloyd Wright's Fallingwater, the Youghiogheny Reservoir, and Ohiopyle for hiking, biking, and white water sports. Outlet mall, state parks, golf courses, festivals, and antique shops in the area. One mile from the PA Turnpike, Exit 10.

Hosts: Carol and Rowland Miller
Rooms: 4 (PB) $75-95
Full Breakfast
Credit Cards: A, B
Notes: 2, 5, 7 (over 5), 9, 10, 11

SPRUCE CREEK

The Dell's B&B at Cedar Hill Farm

HC-01, Box 26, Route 45 E., 16683
(814) 632-8319

This early 1800s farmhouse is located in Huntingdon County on an active livestock farm. Individual and family activities are available at Old Bedford Village, Horse Shoe Curve, Bland's Park, Raystown Lake, Lincoln and Indian Caverns, and Penn State University. Member of the Pennsylvania Farm Vacation Association. Fishing and hunting available on private and state game lands during stated seasons; proper licenses required.

Hosts: Sharon and Tim Dell
Rooms: 4 (SB) $35-50
Full Breakfast
Credit Cards: A, B
Notes: 2, 5, 7, 11

STAHLSTOWN

Thorn's Cottage B&B

RD 1, Box 254, 15687
(412) 593-6429

Our location is in the Ligonier Valley area of the scenic Laurel Mountains, eight miles from the PA Turnpike, 50 miles east of Pittsburgh. This area abounds in history and nature with hiking trails, the beautiful town of Ligonier, and Idlewild Amusement Park. Your cottage offers homey woodland privacy, A/C, stereo, cable TV, Christian tape library, full kitchen, host's sunporch, and herb garden. Breakfast served at the cottage includes fresh home-baked muffins and scones.

Hosts: Larry and Beth Thorn
Rooms: 1 three-room cottage (PB) $55
Full Breakfast
Credit Cards: none
Notes: 2, 5, 7, 9, 10, 11

STARRUCCA

Nethercott Inn

PO Box 26 Starrucca Creek Road, 18462
(717) 727-2211; FAX (717) 727-3811

This lovely, 1893 Victorian home is

The Decoy

nestled in a small village in the Endless Mountains and furnished in a pleasing mixture of country and antiques. All rooms have queen-size beds and private baths. A full breakfast is included. Located three and one half hours from New York City and Philadelphia, and eight hours from Toronto, Canada.

Hosts: Charlotte and John Keyser
Rooms: 5 (PB) $75 (midweek discounts available)
Full Breakfast
Credit Cards: A, B, C, D
Notes: 2, 5, 7, 10, 11, 12 (10%)

STRASBURG

The Decoy Bed and Breakfast

958 Gisenberger Road, 17579
(717) 687-8585 (voice and FAX);
(800) 726-2287

This former Amish home is set in farmland with spectacular views and an informal atmosphere. Craft shops and attractions are nearby. We are part of an "inn to inn" tour. We host quilting seminars (yours or ours), a fabric store tour, family reunions, and church retreats. We can arrange dinner with an

Amish family. Two cats in residence.

Hosts: Debby and Hap Joy
Rooms: 5 (PB) $53.00-74.20
Full Breakfast
Credit Cards: none
Notes: 2, 5, 7, 8, 10, 12

SWIFTWATER

Holiday Glen Resort

PO Box 96, Bush Road, 18370
(717) 839-7015

Does the hectic pace of civilization make you long for tranquillity? Come to the Holiday Glen, a quiet little country resort tucked away in the scenic Paradise Valley of the Poconos. On our 17 acres, wooded trails lead you into a quiet forest and a world of peace, or fish in our pond and stream. Cottages have queen beds, air-conditioning, mini-fridges, TVs, and fireplaces. A country breakfast is served compliments of your Scottish host, Sarah.

Hostess: Sarah Caulfield
Cabins: 9 (PB) $75-90
Full Breakfast
Credit Cards: A, B
Notes: 5, 7, 8, 9, 10, 11

---

5 Open all year; 6 Pets welcome; 7 Children welcome; 8 Tennis nearby; 9 Swimming nearby; 10 Golf nearby; 11 Skiing nearby; 12 May be booked through travel agent.

TROY

Golden Oak Inn Bed and Breakfast

196 Canton Street, 16947
(800) 326-9834

Experience Victorian elegance in the heart of the Endless Mountains of northern Pennsylvania. This Queen Anne style home, circa 1901, is graced with Vcitorian decor, antiques, and heirlooms. It captures the history of the Civil War with a collection of artwork, artifacts, and a library filled with history books. Gourmet breakfasts are prepared by Richard, Culinary Institute of America graduate, and served amidst a romantic atmosphere of candlelight and music.

Hosts: Richard and Sharon Frank
Rooms: 4 (SB) $55-65
Candlelight Gourmet Breakfast
Credit Cards: A, B, D
Notes: 2, 5, 8, 9, 10, 11

Golden Oak Inn

VALLEY FORGE

Association of Bed and Breakfasts in Philadelphia, Valley Forge, and Brandywine

PO Box 562, 19481
(610) 783-7838; (800) 344-0123;
FAX (610) 783-7783

There is a B&B for you!—whether business, vacation, getaways, or relocating. Also serving **Bucks** and **Lancaster Counties**. Over 500 rooms available in historic city/country inn, town houses, unhosted estate cottages, and suites. Request a free brochure, family plan, jacuzzi, fireplace, pool, or descriptive directory ($3). Special services include gift certificates, dinner reservations, wedding/special occasions/photography at unique B&Bs, personal attention, and gracious hospitality. No fee for reservations. Featured in *Philadelphia Magazine*. Rates range from $35 to $135. Major credit cards accepted. Carolyn J. Williams, coordinator.

WAYNESBORO

The Shepherd and Ewe Bed and Breakfast

11205 Country Club Road, 17268
(717) 762-8525; (888) 937-4393;
FAX (717) 762-5880

Renowned for its rich shepherding heritage, The Shepherd and Ewe extends that same nurturing tradition to its guests who are invited to unwind in one

---

NOTES: Credit cards accepted: A Master Card; B Visa; C American Express; D Discover; E Diners Club; F Other; 2 Personal checks accepted; 3 Lunch available; 4 Dinner available;

The Shepherd and Ewe Bed and Breakfast

of four guest rooms or the spacious master suite. Filled with Victoriana and lovingly restored and collected antiques, each room is clean and inviting. Full country breakfast with homemade breads, muffins, and other delights. Located high atop lush acres of rolling farmland, the B&B is a short drive to Gettysburg and Mercersburg, PA, Sharpsburg, MD, fine restaurants, state parks, hiking trails, art galleries, and antique shops.

Hosts: Twila and Robert Risser
Rooms: 5 (2PB; 3SB) $65-85
Full Country Breakfast
Credit Cards: A, B, C, D
Notes: 7 (well behaved)

WARFORDSBURG

Buck Valley Ranch
Route 2, Box 1170, 17267
(717) 294-3759

Buck Valley Ranch is located in the Appalachian Mountains of southern PA's Fulton County. We are surrounded by 2000 acres of PA State game lands, which allows for hours of horseback riding. Experience true peace and quiet of country life where you can still sit on the porch on a summer's night and

listen to whipporwills. Meals are prepared from home-grown vegetables, homemade desserts, and locally raised meats. Memebers of PA Farm Vacation Association. Rate includes all meals, lodging, and horseback riding for two people for two days and one night.

Hosts: Nadine and Leon Fox
Rooms: 4 (SB) $250
Full Breakfast
Credit Cards: A, B, D
Notes: 2, 3, 4, 5, 7, 8, 9 (on premises), 10, 11, 12

WASHINGTON

Rush House
810 E. Maiden Street, 14301
(412) 223-1890

Rush House is a 100-year-old Victorian style house built to accomodate Catfish Creek, which flows through a tunnel under the house. The bedrooms are decorated with antique pieces and antique clocks abound throughout the house. A buffet breakfast is served each morning in the spacious dining room.

Hosts: Jim and Judy Wheeler
Rooms: 4 (PB) $75-110
Full Breakfast
Credit Cards: A, B
Notes: 2, 5, 8, 9

WELLSBORO

Kaltenbach's Bed and Breakfast
RD #6 Box 106A, Stony Fork Road (Kelsey Street), 16901
(717) 724-4954; (800) 722-4954

This sprawling, country home with

room for 32 guests offers visitors comfortable lodging, home-style breakfasts, and warm hospitality. Set on a 72-acre farm, Kaltenbach's provides ample opportunity for walks through meadows, pastures, and forests; picnicing; and watching the sheep, pigs, rabbits, and wildlife. All-you-can-eat country breakfasts are served. Honeymoon suites have tub or jacuzzi for two. Hunting and golf packages are available. Pennsylvania Grand Canyon. Kaltenbach's was awarded a three- Crown rating from the American Bed and Breakfast Association for its accommodations and hospitality. Professional Association of Innkeepers International Inn Member.

Host: Lee Kaltenbach
Rooms: 10, 2 suites (9PB) $60-125
Full Breakfast
Credit Cards: A, B
Notes: 2, 3, 4, 5, 7, 8, 9, 10, 11

WILKES-BARRE

Ponda-Rowland Bed and Breakfast Inn

RR 1, Box 349, **Dallas** 18612
(717) 639-3245; (800) 854-3286;
FAX (717) 639-5531

Circa 1850 inn on large scenic farm in the Endless Mountains of PA. King beds, private baths, air-conditioning, beamed ceilings, ceiling fans, Completely furnished with museum quality country antiques. Mountain views, 34-acre private wildlife sanctuary with trails, and ponds. Fishing, canoeing,

tobogganing, ice-skating, hay rides, horses, sheep, goats, turkeys, pot-bellied pig, llama, and more to see, do, and touch. Refreshments afternoon and evening. Large stone fireplace. Breakfast by candlelight. Nearby are air tours, swimming, horseback riding, downhill skiing, and fine restaurants. Approved by AAA, AB&BA, and Mobil.

Hosts: Jeanette and Cliff Rowland
Rooms: 5 (PB) $70-95
Full Breakfast
Credit Cards: A, B, C, D
Notes: 2, 5, 7, 10, 11, 12

ZELIENOPLE

Historic Benvenue Manor Bed and Breakfast

160 Manor Drive, 16063
(412) 452-1710

"Benvenue" original name of our 1816 stone manor home means a "Good Welcome." Enjoy a spectacular view, relax by the open fire, feast on a gourmet breakfast, four Victorian bedrooms, two private baths, guest livingroom, gracious hospitality. High tea at 3pm on Tuesday and Thursday afternoons and Saturday by special arrangement. Hosting birthday parties and showers. Children welcome, 35 minutes downtown Pittsburgh.

Hostess: Margo L. Hogan
Rooms: 4 (2PB; 2SB) $60-75
Full Breakfast
Credit Cards: none
Notes: 2, 3, 4, 5, 7, 8, 9, 10

NOTES: Credit cards accepted: A Master Card; B Visa; C American Express; D Discover;
E Diners Club; F Other; 2 Personal checks accepted; 3 Lunch available; 4 Dinner available;

Rhode Island

BLOCK ISLAND

The Rose Farm Inn

Roslyn Road - Box E, 02807
(401) 466-2034 or 2021 (both voice and FAX)

Experience the romance of the Victorian era. Treat yourself to a romantic room beautifully furnished with antiques and king- or queen-size bed. Enjoy the peaceful tranquillity of the farm from shaded decks cooled by gentle breezes. Gaze at the ocean from your window or share a whirlpool bath for two. Awaken to a light buffet breakfast served in our charming porch dining room with an ocean view.

Hostess: Judith B. Rose
Rooms: 19 (17PB;2SB) $95-179
Continental Plus Breakfast
Credit Card: A, B, C, D
Notes: 2, 7 (over 11), 8, 9

MIDDLETOWN

Inn at Shadow Lawn

120 Miantonomi Avenue, 02842
(401) 849-1298; (800) 828-0000;
FAX (401) 849-1306

Finnegan's Inn is one of Newport County's finest B&B inns, set on two acres of beautifully landscaped lawns and gardens. This 1850's Victorian mansion, with its crystal chandeliers and stained-glassed windows, has eight large bedrooms each with private bath, TV, refrigerator, and air-conditioning. Five rooms also have attached kitchens. Come and enjoy a bottle of complimentary wine.

Hosts: Randy and Selma Fabricant
Rooms: 8 (PB) $79-135
Continental Plus Breakfast
Credit Cards: A, B
Notes: 5, 7 (over 12), 8, 9, 10, 12

Lindsey's Guest House

Lindsey's Guest House

6 James Street, 02842
(401) 846-9386

Walk to beaches and restaurants. Five minutes to Newport's famous mansions, Ocean Drive, Cliff Walk, boat and bus

---

5 Open all year; 6 Pets welcome; 7 Children welcome; 8 Tennis nearby; 9 Swimming nearby;
10 Golf nearby; 11 Skiing nearby; 12 May be booked through travel agent.

RHODE ISLAND

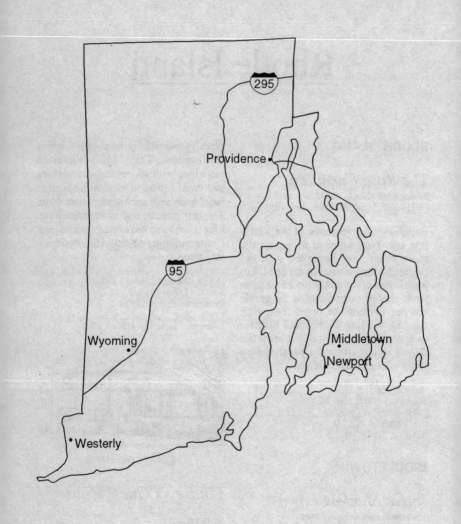

tours, and bird sanctuary. Quiet residential neighborhood with off-street parking. Large yard and deck with hostess available for information about events and discounts. Split-level, owner-occupied home with expanded continental breakfast. One room is wheel chair accessible for 28-inch wheelchair.

Hostess: Anne Lindsey
Rooms: 4 (2PB;2SB) $45-85
Full Breakfast
Credit Cards: A, B
Notes: 2, 5, 7, 8, 9, 10, 12

NEWPORT

Brinley Victorian Inn

23 Brinley Street, 02840
(401) 849-7649; (800) 999-8523;
FAX (401) 845-9634

Romantic year round, the Inn becomes a Victorian Christmas dream come true. Comfortable antiques and fresh flowers fill every room. Easy walking to most attractions with off-road parking on site. Friendly, unpretentious, service AAA rated.

Hosts: John and Jennifer Sweetman (owners)
Rooms: 17 (13 PB, 4 SB) $55-149
Credit Cards: A, B, C
Notes: 2, 5, 7 (over 8), 8, 9, 10, 12

Cliffside Inn

2 Seaview Avenue, 02840
(401) 847-1811; (800) 845-1811;
FAX (401) 848-5850

Nestled upon a quiet neighborhood street just steps away from the historic Cliff Walk, the Cliffside Inn displays the grandure of a Victorian manor with the warmth and comfort of a home. A full breakfast, consisting of homemade muffins, granola, fresh fruit, and a hot entree, such as eggs benidect or whipped cream topped French toast, is served each morning in the spacious parlor. Victorian teas is served from 4:30 to 5:30PM; A morning coffee and juice service is available from 7 to 9AM. There are thirteen guest rooms, each uniquely decorated in period Victorian antiques blended with luxurious Laura Ashley linens and drapes. Each room contains a telephone and private bath, some with working fireplaces and jacuzzis or steambaths. Smoking is permitted on the large front veranda, furnished with wicker furniture and covered with floral cushions. All rooms are air-conditioned.

Hosts: Stephen Nicolas
Rooms: 13 (PB) $165-325
Full Hot Gourmet Breakfast
Credit Cards: A, B, C, D, E
Notes: 2, 5, 7 (14 and over), 8, 9, 10, 12

Halidon Hill Guest House

Halidon Avenue, 02840
(401) 847-8318

Georgian Colonial home with large deck area and inground pool. Located near restaurants, shops, mansions, and yacht clubs. Spacious, beautifully decorated rooms with TV, phone, and small

---

NOTES: Credit cards accepted: A Master Card; B Visa; C American Express; D Discover; E Diners Club; F Other; 2 Personal checks accepted; 3 Lunch available; 4 Dinner available; 5 Open all year; 6 Pets welcome; 7 Children welcome; 8 Tennis nearby; 9 Swimming nearby; 10 Golf nearby; 11 Skiing nearby; 12 May be booked through travel agent.

refrigerator. Full breakfast served. Suites also available.

Hosts: Helen and Paul Burke
Rooms: 2 + a 2-bedroom apartment (PB)
    $55-150
Full Breakfast
Credit Cards: C, D, E
Notes: 2, 5, 7, 8, 9 (pool on-site), 10

The Willows of Newport, Romantic Inn & Garden

8 and 10 Willow St. Historic Point, 02840-1927
(401) 846-5486

Built in the 1700s, the Inn exemplifies all the charm and elegance of the pre-Revolutionary peroid. Your hostess pampers her guests with cut flowers, turned-down brass canopy beds, breakfast in bed, and A/C. Stroll three blocks to downtown/waterfront, or enjoy our Secret Garden. Mobil three star award, Best Garden Award '94-'95, and AB&BA award of excellence. Listed in "Best Places to Kiss."

Hostess: Pattie Murphy
Rooms: 5 (PB) $85-185
Continental Breakfast
Credit Cards: none
Notes: 2, 8, 9, 10, 11, 12

The Willows of Newport

PROVIDENCE

Old Court Bed & Breakfast

144 Benefit Street, 02903
(401) 751-2002; FAX (401) 272-4830

The Old Court is filled with antique furniture, chandeliers, and memorabilia from the nineteenth century, with each room designed to reflect period tastes. All rooms have private baths, and the antique, Victorian beds are comfortable and spacious. Just a three-minute walk from the center of downtown Providence, near Brown University and Rhode Island School of Design.

Hosts: David "Dolby" Dolbashian
Rooms: 10 + 1 suite (PB) $85-250
Full Breakfast
Credit Cards: A, B, D
Notes: 2, 5, 8, 9, 12

State House Inn

43 Jewett Street, 02908
(401) 351-6111; FAX (401) 351-4261

A country inn usually means peace and quiet, friendly hosts, comfort and simplicity, with beautiful furnishings. The State House Inn has all of these qualifications, but just happens to be located in the city of Providence. Our inn has fireplaces, hardwood floors, Shaker or Colonial furnishings, canopy beds, and modern conveniences such as FAX, TV, and phone. Located near downtown and local colleges and universities.

Hosts: Frank and Monica Hopton
Rooms: 10 (PB) $89-109
Full Breakfast
Credit Cards: A, B, C
Notes: 2 (with CC for ID), 5, 7, 8, 10, 12

NOTES: Credit cards accepted: A Master Card; B Visa; C American Express; D Discover; E Diners Club; F Other; 2 Personal checks accepted; 3 Lunch available; 4 Dinner available;

WESTERLY

The Villa
Bed and Breakfast

190 Shore Road, 02891
(401) 596-1054; (800) 722-9240;
FAX (401) 596-6268

Leave the pressures behind! Treat yourself to an award-winning private hide-a-way. Romantic jacuzzi suites, fireplace suites, and outdoor hot tub and pool. Excellent restaurants nearby. All rooms have color cable TV, refrigerators, and private baths. Breakfast is served in our dining area, in your private room, or poolside, in season. Approved by Mobile, *** AB&BA, selected by Fodor's.

Host: Jerry Maiorano
Rooms: 7 (PB) $75-195
Breakfast Buffet
Credit Cards: A, B, C
Notes: 2, 5, 6, 8, 9, 10, 12

Woody Hill

Woody Hill
Bed and Breakfast

149 South Woody Hill Road, 02891
(401) 322-0452

This Colonial reproduction is set on a hilltop overlooking 20 acres of informal gardens, woods, and fields. Antiques, wide-board floors, handmade quilts, and fireplaces create an early American atmosphere. A full breakfast and use of secluded 40-foot, in-ground pool are included. Close to Newport, Block Island, Mystic, and Casino.

Hostess: Dr. Ellen L. Madison
Rooms: 4 (3PB; 2 SB) $650-115
Full Breakfast
Credit Cards: none
Notes: 2, 5, 7, 8, 9, 10, 12

WYOMING

The Cookie Jar
Bed and Breakfast

64 Kingstown Road (Exit 3A off I-95), 02898
(401) 539-2680; (800) 767-4262

The heart of our home, the living room, was built in 1732 as a blacksmith's shop. Later, the forge was removed and a large granite fireplace was built by an American Indian stonemason. The original wood ceiling, hand-hewn beams, and granite walls remain today. The property was called the Perry Plantation, and, yes, they had two slaves who lived above the blacksmith's shop. We offer friendly, home-style living in a comfortable, country setting. New: All rooms now have a private bath, private sitting room, color TV and are air-conditioned. On Route 138 just off I-95.

Hosts: Dick and Madelein Sohl
Rooms: 3 (PB) $75
Full Breakfast
Credit Cards: none
Notes: 2, 5, 7, 8, 9, 10, 12

---

5 Open all year; 6 Pets welcome; 7 Children welcome; 8 Tennis nearby; 9 Swimming nearby; 10 Golf nearby; 11 Skiing nearby; 12 May be booked through travel agent.

SOUTH CAROLINA

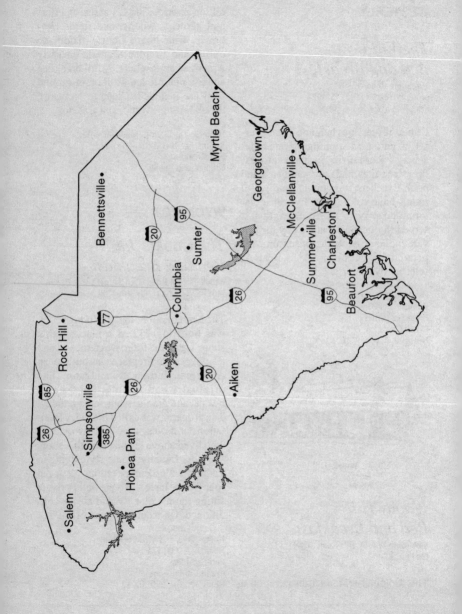

South Carolina

AIKEN

Holley Inn

235 Richland Avenue, 29801
(803) 648-4265 (voice and FAX)

A beautiful older Southern inn in recently renovated elegance. Located in the center of the historic city, we have six restaurants within one block; we also have a restarant. Near shops and movies. Enjoy our pool, courtyard, and lounge.

Host: Forrest Holley
Rooms: 35 (PB) $45-75
Continental Breakfast (Full available)
Credit Cards: A, B, C, D, E
Notes: 2, 3, 4, 5, 6 (some), 7, 8, 9 (on premises), 10, 12

BEAUFORT

TwoSuns Inn
Bed and Breakfast

1705 Bay Street, 29902
(803) 522-1122; (800) 532-4244;
FAX (803) 522-1122

Enjoy the charm of a small, resident host B&B in a remarkably beautiful Nationally Landmarked Historic District about midway between Charleston and Savannah—complete with a panoramic bayview verandah, individually appointed king or queen guestrooms, an informal afternoon "Tea and Toddy Hour," and sumptuous breakfasts. The setting is idyllic, the atmosphere is ca-

Holley Inn

NOTES: Credit cards accepted: A Master Card; B Visa; C American Express; D Discover; E Diners Club; F Other; 2 Personal checks accepted; 3 Lunch available; 4 Dinner available; 5 Open all year; 6 Pets welcome; 7 Children welcome; 8 Tennis nearby; 9 Swimming nearby; 10 Golf nearby; 11 Skiing nearby; 12 May be booked through travel agent.

sually elegant—a restored 1917 grand home with modern baths and amenities accented with collectibles and antiques. Carrol and Ron are gracious.

Hosts: Carrol and Ron Kay
Rooms: 5 (PB) $105 and up
Full Breakfast
Credit Cards: A, B, C, D
Notes: 2, 5, 8, 9, 10, 12

The Breeden Inn and Carriage House

BENNETTSVILLE

The Breeden Inn and Carriage House

404 East Main Street, 29512
(803) 479-3665; FAX (803) 479-1040

Built in 1886, this romantic Southern mansion is situated on two acres in Bennettsville's historic district. Beautiful decor and comfortable surroundings will capture your interest and inspire your imagination. A haven for antique lovers. Listed on the National Register of Historic Places, the Inn is located 25 minutes from I-95 — a great halfway point between Florida and New York. Our porches and grounds . . . truly a Southern tradition can be enjoyed at both guest houses. Swings, rockers, wicker, cast iron, adirondacks, and even

ceiling fans await to play a part in helping you unwind. Curl up with a book under the old magnolia tree . . . sun by the pool—there's a comfy spot for everyone. Come . . . we have some peace, quiet, and comfort for you. No smoking. Owned and operated by a Christian family.

Hosts: Wesley and Bonnie Park
Rooms: 7 (PB) $65
Full Breakfast
Credit Cards: A, B, D
Notes: 2, 5, 7, 9, 10, 12

CHARLESTON

1837 Bed and Breakfast

126 Wentworth Street, 29401
(803) 723-7166

Enjoy accommodations in a wealthy cotton planter's home and brick carriage house centrally located in Charleston's historic district. Canopied, poster, rice beds. Walk to boat tours, the old market, antique shops, restaurants, and main attractions. Near the Omni and College of Charleston. Full, gourmet breakfast is served in the formal dining room and

1837 Bed and Breakfast

NOTES: Credit cards accepted: A Master Card; B Visa; C American Express; D Discover; E Diners Club; F Other; 2 Personal checks accepted; 3 Lunch available; 4 Dinner available;

includes sausage pie, Eggs Benedict, ham omelets, and home-baked breads. The 1837 Tea Room serves afternoon tea to our guests and the public. Off-street parking.

Hosts: Sherri Weaver and Richard Dunn, owners
Rooms: 8 (PB) $69-129
Special Winter Rates December - February
Full Breakfast
Credit Cards: A, B, C
Notes: 2, 5, 7, 8, 9, 10, 12

Ashley Inn B&B

201 Ashley Avenue, 29403
(803) 723-1848; FAX (803) 768-1230

Stay in a stately, historic, circa 1835 home. So warm and hospitable, the Ashley Inn offers seven intimate bedrooms featuring canopy beds, private baths, fireplace, and air-conditioning. Delicious breakfasts are served on a grand columned piazza overlooking a beautiful Charleston garden or in the formal dining room. Relax with tea and cookies after touring nearby historic sites or enjoying the complimentary touring bicycles. Simple elegance in a warm, friendly home noted for true Southern hospitality.

Hosts: Sally and Bud Allen
Rooms: 7 (PB) $69-160
Full Breakfast
Credit Cards: A, B, C, D
Notes: 2, 5, 7 (over 12), 8, 9, 10, 12

The Belvedere Bed and Breakfast

40 Rutledge Avenue, 29401
(803) 722-0973

A late 1800s Colonial mansion in the downtown historic district on Colonial Lake has an 1800 Adam interior with mantels and woodwork. Three large bedrooms have antiques, Oriental rugs, and family collections. Easy access to everything in the area.

Hosts: David Spell (innkeeper) and Rick Zender (manager)
Rooms: 3 (PB) $125
Continental Plus Breakfast
Credit Cards: none
Closed December 1-February 15
Notes: 2, 7 (over 8), 8, 9, 10, 12 (no commissions paid)

Cannonboro Inn

184 Ashley Avenue, 29403
(803) 723-8572; FAX (803) 768-1230

This 1853 historic home offers six beautifully decorated bedrooms with antique four poster and canopied beds. A place to be pampered, where you sleep in until the aroma of sizzling sausage and home baked biscuits lure you to a full breakfast on the columned piazza overlooking a low country garden and fountain. After breakfast, tour nearby historic sites on complimentary bicycles and return to more pampering with afternoon sherry, tea, and sumptuous home baked goods. Our private baths, off-street parking, color TV, and air-conditioning along with that very special Southern hospitality, says this is what Charleston is all about!

Hosts: Sally and Bud Allen
Rooms: 6 (PB) $69-150
Full Breakfast
Credit Cards: A, B, C, D
Notes: 2, 5, 7 (over 12), 8, 9, 10, 12

---

5 Open all year; 6 Pets welcome; 7 Children welcome; 8 Tennis nearby; 9 Swimming nearby; 10 Golf nearby; 11 Skiing nearby; 12 May be booked through travel agent.

Country Victorian Bed and Breakfast

105 Tradd Street, 29401-2422
(803) 577-0682

Come relive the charm of the past. Relax in a rocker on the piazza of this historic home and watch the carriages go by. Walk to antique shops, churches, restaurants, art galleries, museums, and all historic points of interest. The house, built in 1820, is located in the historic district south of Broad. Rooms have private entrances and contain antique iron and brass beds, old quilts, antique oak and wicker furniture, and braided rugs over heart-of-pine floors. Homemade cookies will be waiting. Many extras!

Hostess: Diane Deardurff Weed
Rooms: 2 (PB) $75-95
Expanded Continental Breakfast
Credit Cards: none
Notes: 2, 5, 7 (over 10), 8, 9, 10

King George IV Inn

32 George Street, 29401
(803) 723-9339; FAX (803) 727-0065

A 200-year-old, circa 1790, Charleston historic house located in the heart of historic district. The Inn is Federal style with three levels of Charleston side porches. All rooms have 10'-12' ceilings with decorative plaster moldings, wide-planked hardwood floors, old furnishings, and antiques. Private baths, parking, AC, TVs. One minute walk to historic King Street; five-minute walk to historic market. A step back in time!

Hosts: Debbie, Mike, and BJ
Rooms: 10 (8PB; 2SB) $65-145
Continental Plus Breakfast
Credit Cards: A, B
Notes: 2, 5, 6 (by arrangement), 7, 8, 9, 10, 12

The Kitchen House Circa 1732

126 Tradd Street, 29401
(803) 577-6362

Nestled in the heart of the historic district, The Kitchen House is a totally restored 18th Century dwelling. Southern hospitality, absolute privacy, fireplaces, and antiques. Private patio, Colonial herb garden, fish pond, and fountain. Full breakfast, plus concierge service. This pre-Revolutionary home was featured in *Colonial Homes Magazine*, the *New York Times*, and *Best Places to Stay in the South*.

Hostess: Lois Evans
Rooms: 3 (PB) $95-195
Full Breakfast
Credit Cards: A, B
Notes: 2, 5, 7, 8, 9, 10, 12

Rutledge Victorian Inn

114 Rutledge Avenue, 29401
(803) 722-7551; FAX (803) 727-0065

Elegant Charleston house in downtown Historic District. Century-old house with rare decorative Italianate architecture with beautiful ceiling moldings. Rooms have mahogany and oak fire-

---

NOTES: Credit cards accepted: A Master Card; B Visa; C American Express; D Discover; E Diners Club; F Other; 2 Personal checks accepted; 3 Lunch available; 4 Dinner available;

places, 12-foot ceilings, hardwood floors, 10-foot doors and windows, and antiques. Lovely 120-foot porch with rocking chairs and joggling board, overlook the Park and Roman Columns, remains of the Confederate soldiers reunion hall. Relaxed atmosphere, A/C, parking, and TVs. Lovely formal dining rooms where complimentary "Continental Plus" breakfast is served. 5-20 minute walk to historic sights.

Hosts: Lynn, Mike, and BJ
Rooms: 12 (9PB; 3SB) $65-125 (more for suite)
Continental Plus Breakfast
Credit Cards: A, B
Notes: 2, 5, 6 (some), 7, 8, 9, 10, 12

Rutledge Victorian Inn

Villa de La Fontaine Bed and Breakfast

138 Wentworth Street, 29401
(803) 577-7709

Villa de La Fontaine is a columned Greek Revival mansion in the heart of the historic district. It was built in 1838 and boasts a three-quarter-acre garden with fountain and terraces. Restored to impeccable condition, it is furnished with museum-quality furniture and ac-

cessories. The hosts are retired ASID interior designers and have decorated the rooms with 18th-century American antiques. Several of the rooms feature canopied beds. Breakfast is prepared by a master chef who prides himself on serving a different menu every day. Off-street parking. Minimum-stay requirements for weekends and holidays. The inn offers guests a choice between its four rooms and two suites.

Hosts: Bill Fontaine/Aubrey Hancock, A.S.I.D.
Rooms: 4 + 2 suites (PB)
Full Breakfast
Credit Cards: none
Notes: 2, 5, 8, 9, 10

COLUMBIA

Richland Street Bed and Breakfast

1425 Richland Street, 29201
(803) 779-7001

Richland Street Bed and Breakfast is a Victorian home located in the heart of Columbia's Historic District in walking distance of tour homes, restaurants, and downtown shopping. Inside your are

Richland Street Bed and Breakfast

---

5 Open all year; 6 Pets welcome; 7 Children welcome; 8 Tennis nearby; 9 Swimming nearby; 10 Golf nearby; 11 Skiing nearby; 12 May be booked through travel agent.

greeted with a large gathering area, seven oversize guest rooms with private baths, and loads of hospitality. Each room has its own personality, decorated with period antiques. The Bridal Suite with whirlpool tub is especially inviting. You will enjoy the front porches with gazebo and rockers. Special attention given to each guest includes a deluxe continental breakfast served in classic Victorian style. Rated Four-Diamond American Auto Association.

Hosts: Naomi S. Perryman
Rooms: 7 (PB) $79-115; suite $125
Deluxe Breakfast
Credit Cards: A, B, C
Notes: 2 (in advance), 5, 10

The Shaw House

GEORGETOWN

The Shaw House

613 Cypress Court, 29440
(803) 546-9663

A spacious, two-story, Colonial home in a natural setting with a beautiful view overlooking miles of marshland perfect for bird watchers. Within walking distance to downtown and great restaurants on the waterfront. Rooms are large with many antiques and private baths. Breakfast is served at our guests' convenience. Also included are nighttime chocolates on each pillow, turn backs, and some loving extras. Guests always leave with a little gift like prayers, recipes, and/or jellies. AAA, Mobile, and ABBA approved.

Hosts: Mary and Joe Shaw
Rooms: 3 (PB) $50-65
Full Breakfast
Credit Cards: none
Notes: 2, 5, 7, 8, 9, 10

"ShipWrights" Bed and Breakfast

609 Cypress Court, 29440
(803) 527-4475

Three thousand-plus square feet of beautiful, quiet, clean home is yours to use when you stay. It's nautically attired and tastefully laced with family heirlooms. Guests say they feel like they just stayed at their bestfriend's home. The bedrooms and baths are beautiful and very comfortable. You'll never get "Grandma Eicker's Pancakes" anywhere else (the inn is famous for them). There's a great story behind the pancakes! The view from the large porch is breathtaking, perfect for bird-watching. Five minutes from Ocean Beach. AAA approved.

Hosts: Leatrice M. Wright
Rooms: 2 (PB) $55-60
Full Breakfast
Credit Cards: none
Notes: 2, 5, 7, 8, 9, 10

NOTES: Credit cards accepted: A Master Card; B Visa; C American Express; D Discover; E Diners Club; F Other; 2 Personal checks accepted; 3 Lunch available; 4 Dinner available;

Winyah Bay Bed and Breakfast

403 Helena Street, 29440
(803) 546-9051; (800) 681-6176

Enjoy the breezes from the bay as you stroll down the longest private dock in the state. Winyah Bay also offers access to a small island. Each room has a view of the bay. You have a private entrance, sitting area, and breakfast area. The cupboards and refrigerator are stocked so you schedule is your own.

Hosts: Peggy, Diane, and Jason Wheeler
Rooms: 2 (PB) $65-100
Continental Plus Breakfast
Credit Cards: A, B
Notes: 5, 8, 9, 10, 11, 12

HONEA PATH

"Sugarfoot Castle"

211 South Main Street, 29654
(803) 369-6565

Enormous trees umbrella this 19th Century, brick, Victorian home. Fresh flowers grace the 14-inch thick walled rooms furnished with family heirlooms. Enjoy the living room's interesting collections or the library's comfy chairs, TV, VCR, books, fireplace, desk, and game table. Upon arising, guests find coffee and juice outside their doors, followed by breakfast of hot breads, cereal, fresh fruit, and beverages served by candlelight in the dining room. Rock away the world's cares on a screened porch overlooking peaceful grounds. AAA ap-

proved. Two night minimum.

Hosts: Gail and Cecil Evans
Rooms: 3 (PB) $55-59
Heavy Continental Breakfast
Credit Cards: A, B
Notes: 2, 5, 8, 9, 10

MCCLELLANVILLE

Laurel Hill Plantation

8913 N. Hwy. 17, PO Box 190, 29458
(803) 887-3708

A nature lover's delight! Laurel Hill faces the Atlantic Ocean. Wraparound porches provide spectacular views of creeks and marshes. The reconstructed house is furnished with antiques that reflect the Low Country lifestyle. A perfect blend of yesterday's nostalgia and today's comfort in a setting of unparalleled coastal vistas. Located on Highway 17, 30 miles north of Charleston, 25 miles south of Georgetown, and 60 miles south of Myrtle Beach.

Hosts: Jackie and Lee Morrison
Rooms: 4 (PB) $85-95
Full Breakfast
Credit Cards: A, B
Notes: 2, 5, 7 (restricted), 9, 10, 12

Laurel Hill Plantation

---

5 Open all year; 6 Pets welcome; 7 Children welcome; 8 Tennis nearby; 9 Swimming nearby; 10 Golf nearby; 11 Skiing nearby; 12 May be booked through travel agent.

Serendipity Inn

MYRTLE BEACH

Serendipity Inn

407 - 71st Avenue North, 29572
(803) 449-5268; (800) 762-3229

An award-winning, Spanish-style inn—
unique, elegant, and secluded—is just
300 yards from the ocean beach. Heated
pool and hot tub. All rooms have air-
conditioning, TVs, private baths, and refrigerators. Over 70 golf courses nearby,
as well as fishing, tennis, restaurants,
theaters, and shopping. Near all country music theaters. Ninety miles to historic Charleston

Hosts: Terry and Sheila Johnson
Rooms: 14 (PB) $52-110
Continental Breakfast
Credit Cards: A, B
Notes: 7, 8, 9, 10, 12

ROCK HILL

East Main Guest House

600 East Main Street, 29730
(803) 366-1161

Located in the historic district and just

20 minutes from downtown Charlotte,
NC, this B&B offers guest rooms with
queen-size beds, fireplaces, TVs, and
phones. The honeymoon suite has
stained-glass windows, canopy bed, and
a whirlpool bath as well. A sitting/game
room is provided and a fax is available.
Continental breakfast is served in the
gracious dining room or, weather permitting, under the garden pergola. AAA
three-diamond rated.

Hosts: Jerry and Melba Peterson
Rooms: 3 (PB) $59-79
Expanded Continental Breakfast
Credit Cards: A, B
Notes: 2, 5, 8, 9, 10, 11, 12

SALEM

Sunrise Farm Bed and Breakfast

PO Box 164, 325 Sunrise Drive, 29676
(864) 944-0121

This gracious 1890 Victorian farmhouse is set in the scenic foothills of
the Blue Ridge Mountains. Surrounded
by a 74-acre cattle farm and located
near waterfalls, nature trails, and mountain lakes. Well decorated rooms in the
main house and two charming cottages
with kitchens.

Hosts: James and Jean Webb
Rooms: 3 + 2 cottages (PB) $65-95
Continental Plus Breakfast
Credit Cards: A, B
Notes: 2, 5, 7 (over 6), 12

NOTES: Credit cards accepted: A Master Card; B Visa; C American Express; D Discover;
E Diners Club; F Other; 2 Personal checks accepted; 3 Lunch available; 4 Dinner available;

SIMPSONVILLE

Hunter House Antiques and Bed and Breakfast

201 East College Street, 29681
(864) 967-2827; (800) 815-4561

Hunter House is an elegant home wiht 12-foot ceilings, wraparound porch, garden, grand staircase, and stained glass. We also have an antique shop and banquet room. Our rooms are large and feature antiques, and we serve a full breakfast in our formal dining room at our guests' convenience. At Hunter House you will find warm hospitality and gracious surroundings.

Hosts: Dianne and Earl Neely
Rooms: 1 with double bed + 1 suite with queen
    bed (SB) $65-95
Full Breakfast
Credit Cards: none
Notes: 2, 5, 7, 8, 10

SUMMERVILLE

Linwood Historic Home and Gardens

200 South Palmetto Street, 29483
(803) 871-2620

Once the home of a 19th Century plantation owner, gracious hospitality abounds at "LINWOOD," a beautifully restored Victorian home with high ceilings, chandeliers, period antiques, and wide porches. Nestled on two acres of lush gardens, "LINWOOD" is in the center of the charming village of Summerville near shops and restaurants. Famous plantations, golf courses, beaches, and historic Charleston are nearby. Recreation or retreat—we are here to serve you. Recommended by *Southern Living*.

Hosts: Peter and Linda Shelbourne
Rooms: 4 (3PB; 1SB) $75-150
Continental Breakfast and afternoon English tea
    is served.
Credit Cards: B
Notes: 2, 5, 7, 8, 9, 10, 12

SUMTER

The Bed and Breakfast of Sumter

6 Park Avenue, 29150
(803) 773-2903; FAX (803) 775-6943

Charming, 1896 home facing a lush park in the historic district. Large front porch with swing and rocking chairs. Gracious guest rooms with antiques, fireplaces, and all private baths. Formal Victorian parlor and TV sitting area. FAX machine is also available. Gourmet breakfast includes fruit, entree, and homebaked breads. Antiques, Swan Lake, and 15 golf courses closeby.

Hosts: Jess and Suzanne Begley
Rooms: 5 (PB) $65-75
Full Breakfast
Credit Cards: A, B
Notes: 2, 5, 8, 10, 12

---

5 Open all year; 6 Pets welcome; 7 Children welcome; 8 Tennis nearby; 9 Swimming nearby; 10 Golf nearby; 11 Skiing nearby; 12 May be booked through travel agent.

SOUTH DAKOTA

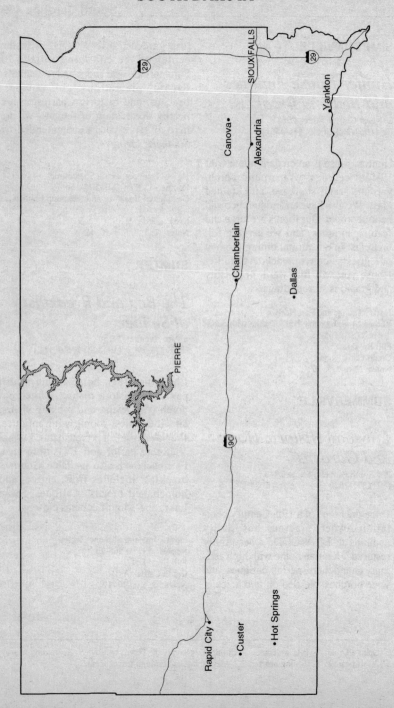

South Dakota

ALEXANDRIA

B's Bed and Breakfast

42027 North Shore Drive, 57311
(605) 239-4671

We invite you to a comfortable home with a covered deck that overlooks Lake Hanson. We are just four miles off I-90 or 16 miles southeast of Mitchell which features the world's only Corn Palace and a fantastic Doll and Baloon Museum. In Alexandria, each June, St. Mary of Mercy Church sponsors a Fatima Family Congress for spiritual renewal. A gas grill and paddleboats are available to guests, as well as beach swimming.

Hosts: Leonard and Marie Bettmeng
Rooms: 3 (SB) $30
Full or Continental Breakfast
Credit Cards: none
Notes: 2, 3, 5, 6 (if chained or penned), 7, 9 and winter sledding

Skoglund Farm

CANOVA

Skoglund Farm

Route 1 Box 45, 57321
(605) 247-3445

Skoglund Farm brings back memories of Grandpa and Grandma's home. It is furnished with antiques and collectibles. A full, home-cooked evening meal and breakfast are served. You can sightsee in the surrounding area, visit Little House on the Prairie Village, hike, or

---

NOTES: Credit cards accepted: A Master Card; B Visa; C American Express; D Discover; E Diners Club; F Other; 2 Personal checks accepted; 3 Lunch available; 4 Dinner available; 5 Open all year; 6 Pets welcome; 7 Children welcome; 8 Tennis nearby; 9 Swimming nearby; 10 Golf nearby; 11 Skiing nearby; 12 May be booked through travel agent.

just relax. Several country churches are located nearby.

Hosts: Alden and Delores Skoglund
Rooms: 5 (SB) $30 each adult; $20 each teen; $15 each child; children 5 and under free.
Full Breakfast
Credit Cards: none
Notes: 2, 3, 4 (included), 5, 6, 7, 8, 9, 10, 12

CHAMBERLAIN

Riverview Ridge

HC 69, Box 82A, 57325
(605) 734-6084

Contemporary home built on a bluff overlooking a scenic bend in the Missouri River. King and queen beds, full breakfast, and secluded country peace and quiet. Three and one half miles north of downtown Chamberlain on Hwy 50. Enjoy outdoor recreation; visit museums, Indian reservations, and casinos; or just relax and make our home your home.

Hosts: Frank and Alta Cable
Rooms: 3 (1PB; 2SB) $50-65
Full Breakfast
Credit Cards: A, B
Notes: 2, 5, 7, 9, 10

Custer Mansion Bed and Breakfast

CUSTER

Custer Mansion Bed and Breakfast

35 Centennial Drive, 57730
(605) 673-3333

Enjoy the nostalgia of an authentic 1891, Victorian Gothic home listed on National Register of Historic Places. Transoms, stained glass, and antiques feature Victorian elegance and country charm with western hospitality. Lovely, individually decorated rooms are named for songs. All-you-can-eat, delicous, home-cooked breakfast. Two honeymoon suites, one with jacuzzi tub. Central to all Black Hills attractions: Mt. Rushmore, Crazy Horse Memorial, Custer State Park, and many more. (Minimum stay of two nights, holidays and peak season.) Reduced rates off season. Recommended by *Bon Appetit*, AAA, and Mobil Travel Guide and member of BBISD.

Hosts: Mill and Carole Seaman
Rooms: 6 (4PB; 2SB) $50-90
Full Breakfast
Credit Cards: none
Notes: 2, 5, 7, 8, 9, 10, 11

DALLAS

Bolton Ranch

Route 2, Box 80, 57529
(605) 835-8960

The Bolton Ranch is a working ranch. Our guests stay in our modern ranch home. Wildlife includes deer, turkey, pheasant, and grouse. There is plenty

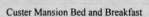

NOTES: Credit cards accepted: A Master Card; B Visa; C American Express; D Discover; E Diners Club; F Other; 2 Personal checks accepted; 3 Lunch available; 4 Dinner available;

to do — fishing, hiking, bicycling, and horseback riding. 7,000 acres to relax on; sit back and listen to the coyotes howl. Member of BB/ISD

Hosts: Brad and Kay Bolton
Rooms: 2 (SB) $50
Full Breakfast
Credit Cards: none
Notes: 2, 3, 4, 5, 6, 7

Bolton Ranch

HOT SPRINGS

The "B and J" Bed and Breakfast

HCR 52, Box 101-B, 57747
(605) 745-4243

Nestled in the Southern Black Hills, this charming 1880 log cabin, decorated in antiques, provides guests with a unique pioneer setting. Enjoy the peaceful mountain scenery while listening to the Fall River that never freezes. Early mornings, deer and wild turkey may be seen. True Western hospitality and a good home-cooked breakfast are always available in Jeananne's kitchen. Nearby, go horseback riding, dine chuck wagon style, and listen to western style music every night. The "B and J" is located one mile south of Hot Springs on US 385/18. In Hot Springs, swim at the historic Evans Plunge where the water is always 87 degrees; visit the Mammoth Site, the world's largest find of Columbian Mammoth bones; fish nearby in Cold Brook Lake; and golf at one of the Midwest's most challenging and beautiful courses. Just minutes to Angostura Lake Recreation area, Wind Cave National Park, and Custer State Park where buffalo, antelope, elk, and prairie dogs roam freely.

Hosts: Bill and Jeananne Wintz
Rooms: one 450 sq. ft. cabin (PB) $95-125
Full Breakfast
Credit Cards: none
Notes: 2, 7, 8, 9, 10, 11

RAPID CITY

Abend Haus Cottages and Audrie's B&B

23029 Thunderhead Falls Road, 57702
(605) 342-7788

The ultimate in charm and Old World hospitality. We are family owned and operated since 1985 and the area's first and finest B&B establishment. Our spacious suites and cottages are furnished in comfortable European antiques. All feature a private entrance, private bath, patio, hot tub, and full Black Hill's style breakfast. Each suite provides a setting that quiets your heart. Our country home, The Cranbury House, has two

---

5 Open all year; 6 Pets welcome; 7 Children welcome; 8 Tennis nearby; 9 Swimming nearby; 10 Golf nearby; 11 Skiing nearby; 12 May be booked through travel agent.

suites. If the past intrigues you, then the Old Powerhouse is for you. Built of brick in 1910, it generated electric from a water flume into the late '30s and now features two suites. Das Abend Haus Cottage (The Evening House) is a restful creekside hideaway, tucked into a mountainside. It has two suites that are designed after a German cottage in the Black forest. The individual log cottages are also reminiscent of Germany. Soak in your private hot tub and watch Rapid Creek flow along. These accommodations are unsurpassed anywhere.

Hosts: Hank and Audry Kuhnhauser
Rooms: 9 (PB) $95-145
Full Breakfast
Credit Cards: none
Notes: 2, 5, 8, 9, 10, 11

Historic Hotel Alex Johnson

523 Sixth Street, 57701
(605) 342-1210; FAX (605) 342-7436

Visit the Hotel Alex Johnson and stay at a historic landmark. 141 newly restored guest rooms. Old World charm combined with award-winning hospitality, this legend offers a piece of Old West history in the heart of downtown Rapid City. Listed on the National Registry of Historic Places.

Rooms: 141 (PB) $58-88
Full Breakfast in Restaurant Setting
Credit Cards: A, B, C, D, E, F
Notes: 2, 3, 4, 5, 7, 8, 10, 12

Historic Hotel Alex Johnson

YANKTON

Mulberry Inn

512 Mulberry Street, 57078
(605) 665-7116

The beautiful Mulberry Inn offers the ultimate in comfort and charm in a traditional setting. Built in 1873, the Inn features parquet floors, six guest rooms furnished with antiques, two parlors with marble fireplaces, and a large porch. Minutes from the Lewis and Clark Lake and within walking distance of the Missouri River, fine restaurants, and downtown. The Inn is listed on the National Register of Historic Places.

Hostess: Millie Cameron
Rooms: 6 (2PB; 4SB) $35-52 May-September;
$32-48 October-April
Continental (Full breakfast extra charge)
Credit Cards: A, B, C
Notes: 2, 5, 7, 8, 9, 10

NOTES: Credit cards accepted: A Master Card; B Visa; C American Express; D Discover; E Diners Club; F Other; 2 Personal checks accepted; 3 Lunch available; 4 Dinner available;

Tennessee

ALSO SEE RESERVATION SERVICES UNDER GEORGIA AND MISSISSIPPI

Natchez Trace Bed and Breakfast Reservation Service

PO Box 193, **Hampshire** 38461
(615) 285-2777; (800) 377-2770

This reservation service is unusual in that all the homes listed are close to the Natchez Trace, the delightful National Parkway running from Nashville, Tennessee, to Natchez, Mississippi. Kay Jones can help you plan your trip along the Trace, with homestays in interesting and historic homes along the way. Locations of homes include Coumbia, FairView, Franklin, Hohenwald, and Nashville, **Tennessee;** Florence, and Cherokee, **Alabama**; and Church Hill, Corinth, French Camp, Kosciusko, Loeman, Natchez, and Vicksburg, **Mississippi.** Rates $60-125.

Woodlawn

ATHENS

Woodlawn

110 Keith Lane, 37303
(423) 745-8211; (800) 745-8213

Woodlawn, an elegant Greek Revival Antibellum home circa 1858, is listed on the National Historic Register. Woodlawn was a uion hospital during the Civil War. It is furnished with gorgeous antique pieces and Oriental rugs that add to its warm feel. Located on five acres in the heart of downtown Athens, a charming historic town filled with antique and specialty shops. Pool on-

---

5 Open all year; 6 Pets welcome; 7 Children welcome; 8 Tennis nearby; 9 Swimming nearby; 10 Golf nearby; 11 Skiing nearby; 12 May be booked through travel agent.

TENNESSEE

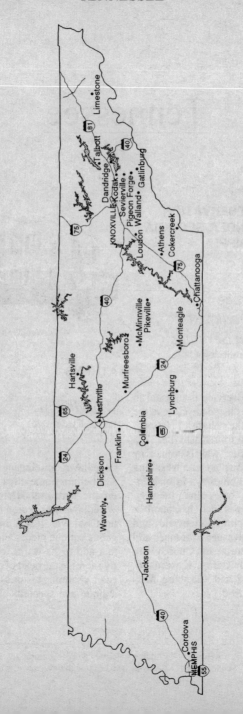

site; golf and tennis nearby; and whitewater rafting on the Ocoee River, 30 minutes away.

Hosts: Barry and Susan Willis
Rooms: 4 (PB)
Full Breakfast
Credit Cards: A, B, D
Notes: 2, 5, 7 (over 6) 8, 9 (on-site), 10, 11, 12

CHATTANOOGA

Adams Hilborne

801 Vine Street, 37403
(423) 265-5000; FAX (423) 265-5555

Cornerstone to Chattanooga's Fort Wood Historic District; mayor's mansion in 1889. Rare Victorian Romanesque design with original coffered ceilings, handcarved oak stairway, beveled glass windows, and ceramic tile embellishments. Old World charm and hospitality in a tree-shaded setting rich with Civil War history and turn-of-the-century architecture. Small European-style hotel accommodations in 15 tastefully restored, exquisitely decorated guest rooms. Private baths, fireplaces, and complimentary breakfast for guests. Fine dining nightly at the Repertoire Restarant and casual dining at Café Alfresco, wine, and liquors available. Ballroom, meeting and reception areas, private dining, and catering available to the public by arrangement. Minutes from Chattanooga museums, fine shops and restaurants, the aquarium,

UTC arena, and other cultural events and attractions. Private off-street parking.

Hosts: Wendy and David Adams
Rooms: 7 + 4 suites (PB) $100-295
Continental Breakfast
Credit Cards: A, B, C
Notes: 2, 3, 4, 5, 7 (by prior arrangement), 8, 9, 10, 12

Alford House Bed and Breakfast

5515 Alford Hill Drive, 37419
(615) 821-7625

This half-century, 15 room house welcomes you! Family owned and operated, in a peaceful Christian atmosphere, the B&B is ten minutes to Tennessee Aquarium, Rock City, and all other attractions. In our Gathering Room there's a piano, and on wintery nights a cozy fire awaits you. Enjoy early morning coffee and breakfast in the dining room or, weather permitting, on the upper deck. Surrounded by tall oaks and bordering the Chicamauga National Park. A large collection of antique glass baskets are displayed for your pleasure, and many antiques throughout our home. You will be blessed with restful sleep on our beauty rest bedding in one of our four guest rooms. Off-season discounts.

Hosts: Rhoda (Troyer) Alford
Rooms: 4 (2PB; 2SB) $65-95
Lite Breakfast
Credit Cards: none
Notes: 8, 9, 10, 11, 12

NOTES: Credit cards accepted: A Master Card; B Visa; C American Express; D Discover; E Diners Club; F Other; 2 Personal checks accepted; 3 Lunch available; 4 Dinner available; 5 Open all year; 6 Pets welcome; 7 Children welcome; 8 Tennis nearby; 9 Swimming nearby; 10 Golf nearby; 11 Skiing nearby; 12 May be booked through travel agent.

Mountian Garden Inn

COKER CREEK

Mountian Garden Inn

PO Box 171, 37314
(423) 261-2689

Luxurious romantic suites and cozy bedrooms; all with private baths and air-conditioning. A stately cypress log inn with wraparound porches and rockers galore. A family-style B&B specializing in reunions — special group rates. Very peaceful setting with a panoramic, three-state view overlooking the Cherokee National Forests of NC, GA, and TN. Adjacent to historic "Trail of Tears," waterfall hiking, gold panning, and horseback riding.

Hosts: The Stewart-Wentworth Family
Rooms: 2 + 2 suites (PB) $40-80
Full Breakfast
Credit Cards: none
Notes: 2, 5, 7

COLUMBIA

Locust Hill Inn

1185 Mooresville Pike, 38401
(615) 388-8531; (800) 577-8264

Beautifully restored, 1840 ante-bellum home, decorated with family antiques. Pamper yourself with morning coffee in your room and evening refreshments at the fireside. Spacious rooms with private baths and comfortable sitting areas. Delicious gourmet breakfasts feature country ham, featherlight biscuits, and homemade jams enjoyed in the dining room or sunroom. Enjoy the fireplaces and relax in the library, flower gardens, or on the three porches. Romantic weekend packages are available; and gourmet dinners also available. French and German spoken.

Hosts: Bill and Beverly Beard
Rooms: 3 (PB) $80-100
Full Breakfast
Credit Cards: A, B, D
Notes: 2, 3, 4, 5, 10, 12

Sugar Fork Bed and Breakfast

DANDRIDGE

Sugar Fork
Bed and Breakfast

743 Garrett Road, 37725
(423) 397-7327; (800) 487-6534

Guests will appreciate the tranquil setting of Sugar Fork, a short distance to the Great Smoky Mountains. Situated on Douglas Lake, the B&B has private

---

NOTES: Credit cards accepted: A Master Card; B Visa; C American Express; D Discover; E Diners Club; F Other; 2 Personal checks accepted; 3 Lunch available; 4 Dinner available;

access and floating dock. Enjoy warm-weather water sports and fishing year-round. Fireplace in common room, quest kitchenette, wraparound deck, swings, and park bench by the lake. A hearty breakfast is served family-style in the dining room or, weather permitting, on the deck. No smoking in guestrooms.

Hosts: Mary and Sam Price
Rooms: 3 (2PB; 2SB) $55 (SB) $65 (PB) + tax
Full Breakfast
Credit Cards: A, B
Notes: 2, 5, 7, 8, 9, 10, 11

DICKSON

East Hills
Bed and Breakfast Inn
100 East Hill Terrace, 37055
(615) 441-9428

Fully restored traditional home with Southern charm, built in the late 40s on four acres with lots of big, tall trees. The home has four bedrooms with private baths and cable TV, a large living room, and library/den with fireplaces. Beautifully decorated and furnished throughout with period antiques. Located on Hwy. 70 near Luther Lake and six miles from Montgomery Bell State Park. Convenient to shopping, hospital, restaurant, and downtown area. Rates include afternoon tea and muffins and a full breakfast in the mornings. No smoking or alcohol allowed.

Hosts: John and Anita Luther
Rooms: 4 (PB) $65-95
Full Breakfast
Credit Cards: A, B, C
Notes: 2, 5, 10

FRANKLIN

Lyric Springs Country Inn
7306 S. Harpeth Road, 37064
(615) 329-3385; (800) 621-7824;
FAX (615) 329-3381

Elegant, antique-filled, creek-side inn featured in *Better Homes and Gardens*, *Country Inns*, *USA Today*, *Fodor's*, and *Women's Wear Daily*. A haven for romance and retreat. Gourmet food. Picnics. Spa services: message, manicure, pedicure, facial. Billiards, fishing, hiking, swimming, biking, horseback riding, board games, and puzzles. Music. Waterfalls. Restricted smoking.

Hostess: Patsy Bruce
Rooms: 4 (PB) $110-115
Full Breakfast
Credit Cards: A, B, C
Notes: 2, 4 (by reservation), 5, 9, 10, 12

Namaste Acres Barn Bed and Breakfast

Namaste Acres Barn
Bed and Breakfast
5436 Leipers Creek Road, 37064
(615) 791-0333; FAX (615) 591-0665

Quiet valley setting. Pool side deck and hot tub, hiking, horseback trails. Country inn offers four theme suites, including the Loft, Bunkhouse, Cabin, and

Franklin. In-room coffee, phone, and refrigerator, TV/VCR (movies). Private entrance and bath. Featured in *Southern Living, Horse Illustrated,* and *Western Horseman*. One mile from Natchez Trace Parkway, 11 miles from historic Franklin, and 23 miles from Nashville. Est. 1993. Reservation requested; weekday discounts. AAA approved.

Hosts: Bill, Lisa, and Lindsay Winters
Rooms: 4 (PB) $80
Full Country Breakfast
Credit Cards: A, B, C, D
Notes: 2, 5, 7 (10 and older), 9, 10, 12

GATLINBURG

Butcher House in the Mountains
1520 Garrett Lane, 37738
(423) 436-9457

Nestled 2,800 feet above the main entrance to the Smokies, Butcher House in the Mountains offers mountain seclusion as well as convenience. The Swiss-like cedar and stone chalet enjoys one of the most beautiful views in the state. Antiques are tastefully placed throughout the house and a guest kitchen is available for coffee and lavish dessert.

Butcher House

European gourmet brunch served. AAA rated three-Diamond; ABBA rated excellent.

Hosts: Hugh and Gloria Butcher
Rooms: 5 (PB) $79-119
Full European Gourmet Breakfast
Credit Cards: A, B, C
Notes: 2, 5, 8, 9, 10, 11, 12

Eight Gables Inn

Eight Gables Inn
219 North Mountain Trail, 37738
(423) 430-3344; (800) 279-5716;
FAX (423) 430-3344

For the perfect bed and breakfast getaway, Eight Gables is the answer. Reserve your accommodations from among ten spacious guest rooms which appeal to even the most discriminating taste. At the foot of the Great Smoky Mountains National Park, Eight Gables Inn's location is easily accessible to all area attractions. The Inn offers bedrooms with private baths and luxurious living space and has an additional covered porch area. AAA approved-Four Diamond. Family owned and operated by Don and Kim Casons.

Hosts: Don and Kim Cason
Rooms: 10 (PB) $99-129
Full Breakfast
Credit Cards: A, B, C, D
Notes: 2, 3 and 4 (available on request), 5, 6, 7, 8, 10, 11, 12

Olde English Tudor Inn

135 West Holly Ridge Road, 37738
(423) 436-7760; (800) 541-3798;
FAX (423) 430-7308

The Olde English Tudor Inn Bed and Breakfast is set on a hillside overlooking the beautiful mountain resort of Gatlinburg. It is ideally located within a few minutes walk to downtown and a few minutes drive to The Great Smoky Mountain National Park. The Inn has seven spacious guest rooms with their own modern bath and cable TV (HBO). Each guest is made to feel at home in the large community room, furnished with TV/VCR and freestanding woodburning stove. Call toll free for a brochure.

Hosts: Larry and Kathy Schuh
Rooms: 7 (PB) $75-105
Full Breakfast
Credit Cards: A, B, C
Notes: 2, 5, 7, 8, 9, 10, 11, 12

HARTSVILLE

Miss Alice's Bed and Breakfast

8325 Hwy. 141 South, 37074
(615) 374-3015 or (615) 444-4401

Relax, enjoy Tennessee's Southern hospitality in a restored early 1900's farmhouse. Walk through the woods, read, play horseshoes, sit on the deck, lie in the hammock, have lemonade in the wellhouse, or draw up a bucket of cool sulfur water for a treat. Wake up with a cup of gourmet coffee and afterwards enjoy a farmer's breakfast. Area attractions include Stones River Battlefield, The Hermitage, Opryland, Cragfont, Vice President Gore's hometown, Cumberland University, and many antique shops.

Hostess: Volene B. Barnes
Rooms: 2 (1PB; 1SB) $65
Full Breakfast
Credit Cards: none
Notes: 2, 5, 9, 10

JACKSON

Highland Place Bed and Breakfast

519 North Highland Avenue, 38301
(901) 427-1472

A stately home of distinct charm, offering comfortable accommodations and Southern hospitality. Highland Place B&B is West Tennessee's 1995 Designers Showplace. Each room, hall, staircase, and even hidden away nooks has have been designed and decorated by the outstanding designers of West TN. Experience the pleasure of sharing the surroundings of one of the state's finest homes. Circa 1911, the inn was totally renovated in early 1995 and reopened in April of 1995.

Hosts: Glenn and Janice Wall
Rooms: 4 (PB) $85-125
Full Breakfast
Credit Cards: A, B
Notes: 2, 3, 4, 5, 10, 12

---

5 Open all year; 6 Pets welcome; 7 Children welcome; 8 Tennis nearby; 9 Swimming nearby;
10 Golf nearby; 11 Skiing nearby; 12 May be booked through travel agent.

KNOXVILLE AREA (TALBOTT)

Arrow Hill

6622 W. Andrew Johnson Hwy., **Talbott** 37877
(423) 585-5777

Arrow Hill, circa 1857 and listed on the National Historic Register, retains the ambience of the antebellum era with its 12-foot ceilings, three-story spiral staircase, original carved woodwork, and widow's walk. Three 1850s-style guest rooms invite a step back in time. Author Helen T. Miller wrote many of her 54 novels in the comfortably furnished library where you may enjoy reading them today. In the morning, a delightful breakfast is served in the elegant tradition of the Old South awaits you.

Hosts: Gary and Donna Davis
Rooms: 3 (1PB; 2SB) $55-65
Full Breakfast
Credit Cards: A, B, C, D
Notes: 2, 3, 4, 5, 7, 8, 9, 10, 11, 12

KODAK

Grandma's House Bed and Breakfast

734 Pollard Road, PO Box 445, 37764
(423) 933-3512; (800) 676-3512;
FAX (423) 933-0748

Located in the center of all the East Tennessee attractions. Colonial style home is on a quite country land at the base of the Great Smoky Mountains. Your hosts are both native East Tennesseans and Southern hospitality just comes naturally to them. A full country breakfast is served, and snacks and soft drinks are always available. Death by

Design Murder Mystery Entertainment weekends are available in the winter months.

Hosts: Charlie and Hilda Hickman
Rooms: 3 (PB) $75-85
Full Breakfast
Credit Cards: A, B
Notes: 2, 5, 10, 11, 12

LIMESTONE

Snapp Inn Bed and Breakfast

1990 Davy Crockett Park Road, 37681
(423) 257-2482

Gracious c. 1815 Federal style home, furnished with antiques. Come to the country for a relaxing weekend getaway. Enjoy the peaceful mountain view or play a game of pool. Located close to Davy Crockett Birthplace State Park. A 15-minute drive to historic Jonesborough or Greenville.

Hosts: Dan and Ruth Dorgan
Rooms: 2 (PB) $65
Full Breakfast
Credit Cards: none
Notes: 2, 5, 6, 7 (one only), 8, 9, 10, 12

LOUDON

Mason Place B&B

600 Commerce Street, 37774
(423) 458-3921

Nestled in a quaint Civil War town along the Tennessee River is a lovely, impeccably restored, 1865 plantation home that offers quality lodging and an opportunity to truly wander back to yester-year without sacrificing the con-

---

NOTES: Credit cards accepted: A Master Card; B Visa; C American Express; D Discover; E Diners Club; F Other; 2 Personal checks accepted; 3 Lunch available; 4 Dinner available;

veniences of today. A grand entrance hall, ten working fireplaces, Grecian swimming pool, gazebo and wisteria-covered arbor are but a few of the amenities available for your enjoyment. Listed on the National Registry of Historic Places, the Mason Place is situated on three acres of lawns and gardens where Civil War bullets and artifacts are still being found. Five delightful antique filled rooms, each complete with a cozy gas-log fireplace, authentic feather bed, and en-suite bathroom. Bountiful breakfast included.

Hosts: Bob and Donna Siewert
Rooms: 5 (PB) $96-120
Full Candlelight Breakfast
Credit Cards: A, B
Notes: 2, 3 (picnic baskets), 5, 8, 9 (on grounds), 10, 11, 12

LYNCHBURG

Cedar Lane Bed and Breakfast

Route 3 Box 155E, 37352
(615) 759-6891; FAX (615) 759-6891

Located on the outskirts of historic Lynchburg (home of Jack Daniel's Distillery). This newly built farmhouse of-

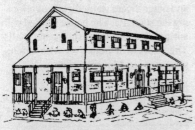

Cedar Lane Bed and Breakfast

fers you comfort and relaxation. You can spend your time antiquing in nearby shops or reading a book in the sunroom. The rooms are beautifully decorated in rose, blue, peach, and green with queen and twin beds. Phones and TVs are available upon request.

Hosts: Elaine and Chuck Quinn
Rooms: 4 (PB) $65-75
Continental Plus Breakfast
Credit Cards: A, B, C
Notes: 2, 4 (by reservation), 5, 7 (over 10), 9, 10

MCMINNVILLE

Historic Falcon Manor Bed and Breakfast

2645 Faulkner Springs Road, 37110
(615) 668-4444; FAX (615) 815-4444
Email: falconmanor@blomand.net
Web site: http://www.blomand.net/~falconmaonor

Relive the peaceful romance of the 1890's in one of the South's finest Victorian mansions. Rock on "gingerbread" verandas, shaded by giant trees. Indulge in the luxury of museum-quality antiques. Enjoy stories about the 10,000 square-foot mansion's history and the innkeepers' adventures restoring it. Ideal base for Tennessee vacation: half-way between Nashville and Chattanooga with easy access from I-24 and I-40. McMinnville is the world's "nursery capital." Fall Creek Falls Park and Cumberland Caverns nearby.

Hosts: George and Charlien McGlothin
Rooms: 6 (2PB; 4SB) $75-105 + tax (8%)
Full Breakfast
Credit Cards: A, B
Notes: 2, 5, 7 (over 11), 8, 9, 10, 12

5 Open all year; 6 Pets welcome; 7 Children welcome; 8 Tennis nearby; 9 Swimming nearby; 10 Golf nearby; 11 Skiing nearby; 12 May be booked through travel agent.

MEMPHIS AREA (CORDOVA)

The Bridgewater House Bed and Breakfast

7015 Raleigh La Grange Road, 38018
(901) 384-0080 (voice and FAX)

A Greek Revival home converted from a school house that is over 100 years old. A lovely, elegant dwelling that is filled with remembrances of travels, antiques, family heirlooms, and Oriental rugs. The Bridgewater House has original hardwood floors cut from trees on the property, enormous rooms, high ceilings, leaded-glass windows, and deep hand-marbelized moldings. There are two very spacious bedrooms with private baths. A certified chef and a food and beverage director serve a full gourmet breakfast and pamper guests with refreshments upon arriving. One mile from the largest city park in the US which offers sailing, walking and biking trails, horseback riding, fishing, canoeing, and more.

Hosts: Steve and Katherine Mistilis
Rooms: 2 (PB) $75-100
Full Breakfast
Credit Cards: A, B, D
Notes: 2, 5

MONTEAGLE

Adams Edgeworth Inn

Monteagle Sunday School Assembly, 37356
(615) 924-4000; FAX (615) 924-3236

Circa 1896, Adams Edgeworth Inn celebrates 100 years of fine lodging and still is the region's leader in elegance and quality. Recently refurbished in English Manor decor, the Inn is a showcase for fine antiques, important original paintings and sculptures, and a prize-winning rose garden. Stroll through the 96-acre Victorian village which surrounds the Inn, or drive six miles to the Gothic campus of Sewanee, University of the South. Cultural activities are year round. 150 miles of hiking trails, scenic vistas, and waterfalls. Tennis, swimming, golf, and riding nearby. Five-course, fine dining by candlelight every night. "One of the best inns I've ever visited anywhere . . ." (Sara Pitzer, recommended by "Country Inns" in *Country Inns Magazine).*

Hosts: Wendy and Dave Adams
Rooms: 14 (PB) $65-150
Continental Breakfast
Credit Cards: A, B, C
Notes: 2, 4, 5, 7, 8, 9, 10, 12

MURFREESBORO

Clardy's Guest House

435 East Main Street, 37130
(615) 893-6030

This large Victorian home was built in 1898 and is located in Murfreesboro's historic district. You will marvel at the ornate woodwork, beautiful fireplaces, and magnificent stained glass overlooking the staircase. The house is filled with antiques, as are local shops and malls. The hosts will help you with dining, shopping, and touring plans.

Hosts: Robert and Barbara Deaton
Rooms: 3 (2PB; 1SB) $38-48 + tax
Continental Breakfast
Credit Cards: none
Notes: 2, 5, 8, 9, 10

NOTES: Credit cards accepted: A Master Card; B Visa; C American Express; D Discover; E Diners Club; F Other; 2 Personal checks accepted; 3 Lunch available; 4 Dinner available;

Simply Southern Bed and Breakfast

Simply Southern Bed and Breakfast

211 North Tennessee Boulevard, 37130
(615) 896-4988
Web site: http://www.bbonline.com/tn/
simplysouthern/

Southern hospitality in the very heart of Tennessee in historic Murfreesboro, site of the famous Civil War Battle of Stones River. Area is rich in history, cultural, and sporting events with many antique shops. This is Walking Horse country and home of Middle Tennessee State University. The house is large, old, nice, and comfortably furnished with private baths and six fireplaces. Basement recreation room with pool table, karaoke, and player piano. Guest sitting area and courtyard. No smoking. Nashville just 15 miles!

Hosts: Carl and Georgia Buckner
Rooms: 3 + a suite (PB) $65-85
Full Breakfast
Credit Cards: A, B, D
Notes: 2, 5, 8, 9, 10, 12

NATCHEZTRACE—SEE PAGE 445 OR NATCHEZTRACE, MISSISSIPPI

NASHVILLE

Bed and Breakfast About Tennessee

PO Box 110227, 37222
(615) 331-5244; (800) 428-2421;
FAX (615) 833-7701
Email: fodom71282@aol.com

From the Great Smoky Mountains to the Mississippi, here is a diversity of attractions that includes fabulous scenery, Tennessee's Grand Ole Opry and Opryland, universities, Civil War sites, horse farms, and much more. With Bed and Breakfast in Tennessee, you make your visit a special occasion. Bed and Breakfast provides an intimate alternative to hotels and motels. You will stay in a private home or inn with a host who will share firsthand knowledge of the area with you. This home-style atmosphere includes the offer of a freshly prepared continental breakfast each morning. Send your guest reservation in today so that we may place you in accommodations which are best suited to your needs. Confirmation and directions will be sent to you immediately.

Owner: Fredda Odom
Rooms: 100 (90PB; 10SB) $55-150
Continental Plus Breakfast
Credit Cards: A, B, C, D, E
Notes: 2, 5, 7 (at some), 8 and 9 (at some), 12

PIGEON FORGE

Day Dreams Country Inn

2720 Colonial Drive, 37863
(423) 428-0370; (800) 377-1469

Delight in the true country charm of this

---

5 Open all year; 6 Pets welcome; 7 Children welcome; 8 Tennis nearby; 9 Swimming nearby; 10 Golf nearby; 11 Skiing nearby; 12 May be booked through travel agent.

antique-filled, secluded two-story log home with its six uniquely decorated guest rooms. Enjoy an evening by our cozy fireplace, relax on the front porch to the soothing sound of Mill Creek, or take a stroll around our three wooded acres. Treat your tastebuds to our bountiful country breakfast each morning. Within walking distance of the parkway. Perfect for family reunions and retreats. From Parkway, take 321 S., go one block, turn left on Florence Drive, go three blocks, and turn right on Colonial Drive.

Hosts: Bob and Joyce Guerrera
Rooms: 6 (PB) $79-99
Full Breakfast
Credit Cards: A, B, D
Notes: 2, 3, 4, 5, 7, 8, 9, 10, 11, 12

Day Dreams Country Inn

Hilton's Bluff B&B Inn
2654 Valley Heights Drive, 37863
(423) 428-9765; (800) 441-4188

Truly elegant country living. Secluded hilltop setting only ½ mile from heart of Pigeon Forge. Minutes from outlet shopping, Dollywood, and Smoky Mountain National Park. The honeymoon, executive, and deluxe rooms, all have private baths; five with two-person jacuzzis, king beds, and waterbeds. Tastefully decorated in romantic mingling of the old and new. Private balconies, covered decks with rockers and checkerboard tables. Den with mountain-stone fireplace; game room/conference room. Southern gourmet breakfast. Group rates for corporate seminars and church groups.

Hosts: Jack and Norma Hilton
Rooms: 10 (PB) $79-129
Full Breakfast
Credit Cards: A, B, C
Notes: 4 (for groups), 5, 7, 8, 9, 10, 11, 12

Little Greenbrier Lodge
3685 Lyon Springs Road., 37862
(615) 429-2500; (800) 277-8100;
FAX (615) 429-4093

Little Greenbrier Lodge Bed and Breakfast is uniquely located on the side of a mountain at the back entrance to the Great Smoky Mountains National Park. The lodge is 150 yards from a hiking trailhead that can connect you to most of the hiking trails in the park. Each of the eleven tastefully decorated Victorian rooms have full access to relaxing decks overlooking tranquil Wears Valley. You're guaranteed to remember the aroma of the hot pecan rolls as you prepare to head for the dining room each morning where a spectacular breakfast awaits!!

Hosts: Barbara and David Matthews
Rooms: 11 (7PB; 4SB) $65-95
Full Breakfast
Credit Cards: A, B, D
Notes: 5, 10, 12

NOTES: Credit cards accepted: A Master Card; B Visa; C American Express; D Discover; E Diners Club; F Other; 2 Personal checks accepted; 3 Lunch available; 4 Dinner available;

Fall Creek Falls B&B Inn

PIKEVILLE

Fall Creek Falls B&B Inn

Route 3, Box 298B, 37367
(423) 881-5494; FAX (423) 881-5040

Elegant mountain inn featured in August '94, *Tennessee* magazine. Eight air-conditioned guest rooms all with private baths. Some heart-shaped whirlpools, and fireplace. Victorian or country decor. One mile from Fall Creek Falls State Resort Park. Beautiful mountains, waterfalls, golfing, boating, fishing, tennis, and hiking. AAA rated, no smoking, full breakfast. Romantic, scenic, and quiet.

Hosts: Doug and Rita Pruett
Rooms: 8 (PB) $75-130
Full Breakfast
Credit Cards: A, B, C
Notes: 2, 3, 4, 5, 8, 9, 10, 12

SEVIERVILLE

Blue Mountain Mist Country Inn and Cottages

1811 Pullen Road, 37862
(423) 428-2335; (800) 497-2335;
FAX (423) 453-1720

Experience the silent beauty of mountain scenery while rocking on the big wraparound porch of this Victorian-style farmhouse. Common rooms filled with antiques lead to twelve individually decorated guest rooms. Enjoy many special touches such as old-fashioned clawfoot tubs, high antique headboards, quilts, and jacuzzi. Nestled in the woods behind the Inn are five country cottages designed for romantic getaways. The Great Smoky Mountains National Park and Gatlinbug are only twenty minutes away.

Hosts: Norman and Sarah Ball
Rooms: 12 + 5 cottages (PB) $89-135
Full Breakfast
Credit Cards: A, B
Notes: 2, 5, 7, 8, 9, 10, 11, 12

Calico Inn

757 Ranch Way, 37862
(423) 428-3833; (800) 235-1054

The Calico Inn located in the Smoky Mountains near Gatlinburg and Dollywood. It is an authentic Log Inn with touches of elegance. Decorated with antiques, collectibles, and country charm. Spectacular mountain view and surrounded with 25 acres of peace and tranquility. Minutes away from fine dining,

---

5 Open all year; 6 Pets welcome; 7 Children welcome; 8 Tennis nearby; 9 Swimming nearby; 10 Golf nearby; 11 Skiing nearby; 12 May be booked through travel agent.

Calico Inn

live entertainment shows, shopping, hiking, fishing, golfing, horseback riding, and all other attractions the area has to offer, yet completely secluded.

Hosts: Lill and Jim Katzbeck
Rooms: 3 (PB) $85-95
Full Breakfast
Credit Cards: A, B
Notes: 2, 5, 7, 8, 9, 10, 11, 12

Persephone's Retreat

2279 Hodges Ferry Road, 37876
(423) 428-3904; FAX (423) 453-7089

A peaceful rural estate nestled in a grove of huge shade trees. Convenient to Gatlinburg, Pigeon Forge, or Knoxville, but ideal for rest and relaxation from busy tourist activities. An elegant two-story home offers three extremely comfortable bedrooms with private baths and large porches overlooking pastures and a beautiful river valley. Enjoy spacious grounds, yard games, farm animals, miniature horses, and hiking. Children welcome.

Hosts: Bob Gonia and Victoria Nicholson
Rooms: 3 (PB) $75-95
Continental or Full Breakfast
Credit Cards: A, B, C
Notes: 2, 7, 10, 12

Von-Bryan Inn

2402 Hatcher Mountain Road, 37862
(423) 453-9832; (800) 633-1459;
FAX (423) 428-8634

A mountaintop log inn with an unsurpassed panoramic view of the Great Smoky Mountains. Greet the sunrise with singing birds and the aroma of breakfast. Swim, hike, rock, rest, read, and relax the day away, then watch the sunset just before the whippoorwills begin their nightly calls. Swimming pool, hot tub, steam shower, whirlpool tubs, library, complimentary dessert, refreshments, and breakfast. Three-bedroom, log chalet is great for families.

Hosts: The Vaughn Family (D.J, JoAnn, David, and Patrick)
Rooms: 6 + 3 bedroom chalet (PB) $90-135, chalet $180
Full Breakfast
Credit Cards: A, B, C, D
Notes: 2, 5, 7, 9 (on-site), 10, 11, 12 (10% com.)

Von-Bryan Inn

WALLAND

Misty Morning Bed and Breakfast

5515 Old Walland Highway, 37886
(423) 681-6373 (voice and FAX)

A three-story log home situated on eight beautiful acres nestled in the foothills of the Smoky mountains. The B&B offers a sense of family and Southern hospitality with full amenities. A restful mountain getaway convenient to Pigeon Forge, Knoxville, Gatlinburg, Cade's Cove, and Knoxville Airport.

Hosts: Darnell and Herman Davis
Rooms: 2 (PB) $69-79
Full Breakfast
Credit Cards: A, B
Notes: 9 (on-site), 10, 11

WAVERLY

Nolan House Inn

385 Highway 13 North, 37185
(615) 296-9063; (615) 296-2511

A Victorian home built in1870 by an Irish immigrant and refurbished into a B&B in 1985. There are three large, antique-filled rooms with private baths. In the spacious Great Room, guests enjoy a Continental Plus breakfast, that also accommodates teas, receptions, and more. The Inn is seven miles from Loretta Lynn's Dude Ranch and is listed on the National Historic Register.

Hosts: Linda and Patrick O'Lee
Rooms: 3 (PB) $60-75
Continental Breakfast
Credit Cards: none
Notes: 2, 6, 7, 8, 9, 10, 12

---

5 Open all year; 6 Pets welcome; 7 Children welcome; 8 Tennis nearby; 9 Swimming nearby; 10 Golf nearby; 11 Skiing nearby; 12 May be booked through travel agent.

TEXAS

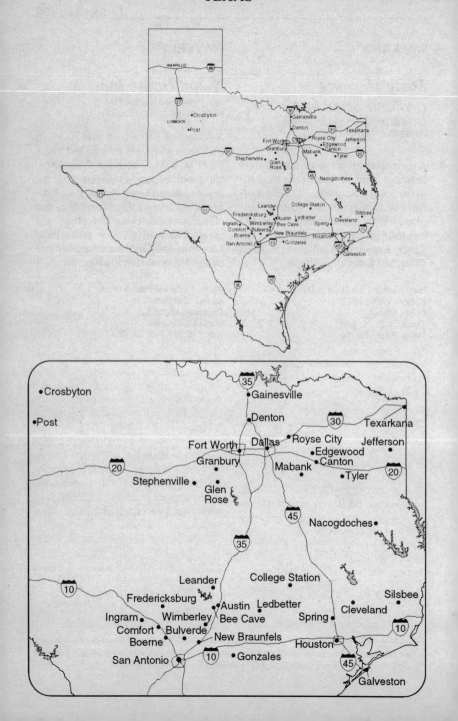

Texas

Reservation Service Bed and Breakfast Texas Style, Inc.

4224 W. Red Bird Lane, **Dallas** 75237
(214) 298-8586; (800) 899-4538;
FAX (214) 298-7118

Bed and Breakfast Texas Style, Inc. is a reservation service established in 1982. We offer you a wide variety of accommodations in private homes, cottages, and small inns. We carefully inspect and approve lodgings to insure comfort and convenience. If you prefer more privacy, you may choose a log cabin on a ranch, cottage on a farm, or a guest house in the woods. Many of our B&B's are historical mansions with Victorian decor. Let us know your desire, we will try to find just the right place for your special needs. For more information, call or write us. Approx. 340 room.; $ 59-150. Major credit cards welcomed. Coordinator, Ruth Wilson.

AUSTIN

Peaceful Hill Bed and Breakfast

6401 River Place Boulevard, 78730-1102
(512) 338-1817

Deer watch you come . . . to country inn on ranch land in beautiful rolling hills. 15 minutes to Austin; five minutes to Lake Travis and The Oasis. Bird watchers paradise; cows, baby calves in field; horses meet you at gate to be fed carrots. On porch, enjoy rocking chairs, porch swing, breakfast at big round table, soaking in countryside and view of city skyline. Nap in hammock built for two in treed yard. Warm, friendly, comfortable home—all yours to enjoy. Grand stone fireplace. Sumptuous home-cooked breakfast. Peaceful is its name and peaceful is the game. Deer watch you go . . .

Hostess: Mrs. Peninnah Thurmond
Rooms: 2 (PB) $60-65 + 6% tax
Full Home-cooked Breakfast
Credit Cards: A, B, C
Notes: 2, 5, 7, 8, 9, 10, 11, 12 (no commissions)

NOTES: Credit cards accepted: A Master Card; B Visa; C American Express; D Discover; E Diners Club; F Other; 2 Personal checks accepted; 3 Lunch available; 4 Dinner available; 5 Open all year; 6 Pets welcome; 7 Children welcome; 8 Tennis nearby; 9 Swimming nearby; 10 Golf nearby; 11 Skiing nearby; 12 May be booked through travel agent.

BEE CAVE

Casa de Angeles

5115 Twin Acres Drive, 78736
(512) 263-REST (7378)

A cozy, convenient, country B&B located 30 minutes from the Austin airport in the rolling Hill Country near Lake Travis. The home was built in the mid 1900s and is turn-of-the-century Texas style. It features a tin roof, wide porches with rocking chairs, and outdoor hot tub. Both guest rooms are upstairs and have whirlpool tubs. We share the home with a loving cat. Come, enjoy our renewing quiet escape.

Hosts: Marilynn and Bill Milligan
Rooms: 2 (PB) $90-105
Full Gourmet Breakfast
Credit Cards: A, B
Notes: 2, 5, 8, 9, 10

BOERNE

Ye Kendall Inn

128 W. Blanco, 78006
(210) 249-2138 (voice and FAX); (800) 364-2138

1859 State and National Historic Land-mark, fully restored and decorated with period antiques. A 200-foot front porch and balcony with railing and columns spans the entire front of the building, complete with rocking chairs. Two restaurants, ladies dress shop, gift and antique shops, tranquil courtyard, ample parking all in the heart of town on the square. Walking distance to Main Street shops and other historic sites; short drive to San Antonio and area attractions.

Host: Shane Schleyer
Rooms: 13 (PB) $80-125
Continental Plus Breakfast
Credit Cards: A, B, C
Notes: 2, 3, 4, 5, 7, 10, 12

Ye Kendall Inn

BULVERDE

Das Holz Haus

1450 Bulverde Road, 78163
(210) 438-2463

Real log home located on seven acres with beautiful oak trees in the hills of western Comal County. Area attractions and historical places are 15, 30, or 45 minutes away, including Natural Bridge Caverns, Sea World, and Fiesta Texas. Enjoy the sounds of country living. Relax in the large living room with 12-foot ceiling and antiques from Opa and Oma's grandparents.

Owner: The Master
Hosts: Lloyd (Opa) and Elva Nell (Oma) Lenz
Rooms: 2 (SB) $55
Continental Breakfast
Credit Cards: none
Notes: 2, 5, 7, 8

NOTES: Credit cards accepted: A Master Card; B Visa; C American Express; D Discover; E Diners Club; F Other; 2 Personal checks accepted; 3 Lunch available; 4 Dinner available;

CANTON AREA

Heavenly Acres Bed and Breakfast

Mail: Route 3 Box 470, **Mabank** 75147
(903) 887-3016; (800) 283-0341;
FAX (903) 887-6108

This wonderful, 100-acre East Texas hideaway, apporpriately named, has a variety of exceptional accommodations overlooking two private and fully stocked fishing lakes. Unique alternative to traditional style B&B with fully equipped and private guest cabins, each with distinctive decor. The cabins provide all the comforts of home with fully equipped kitchen for preparing your own breakfast from food supplied. Enjoy fishing (boats available), paddleboating, and the "Barnyard Petting Zoo" with thoroughly spoiled potbellied pigs, goats, and chickens. This is the perfect place for a country getaway or retreat, filled with peace and serenity.

Hostess: Vickie J. Ragle
Cabins: 6 (PB) $95 ($25-50 per person group rate)
Choice of Full or Continental Breakfast
Credit Cards: A, B, C, D
Notes: 2, 3 + 4 (groups only), 5, 6, 7, 8, 9, 10, 12 (10% com.)

Texas Star Bed and Breakfast

Mail: 1 Box 187-1, **Edgewood** 75117
(903) 896-4277

East Texas countryside, dotted heavily with large oak and cedar trees, hosts our guest house. Four private bedrooms with private baths, private patios, and two additional rooms with shared bath in the main house. Each room reflects a different phase of Texas history and/or culture. Enjoy an exhilerating game of volleyball, horseshoes, or croquet or choose to relax on the shaded porch. Homemade bread and jams are featured in our family-style country breakfast. Within four miles of world-famous Trade Days (flea market) of Canton.

Hosts: David and Marie Stoltzfus
Rooms: 6 (4PB; 2SB) $65-85
Choice of Full or Continental Breakfast
Credit Cards: A, B, C
Notes: 2 (for deposit), 4 (on special request), 5, 7, 8, 10, 12

CLEVELAND

Hilltop Herb Farm at Chain-O-Lakes

One Victorian Place, 77327
(713) 592-58-59; FAX (713) 592-6288

Chain-O-Lakes Resort, nature's heart of the Big Thicket. Spend cozy winters by a crackling fireplace in your own log cabin. Enjoy the colorful palette of springtime flowers and have a splashing good time swimming in pure artesian water. Breakfast is expertly prepared by Hilltop Herb Farm, and a seasonal horse drawn carriage can take you to the restaurant.

Hosts: Jimmy and Beverly Smith (owners)
Rooms: 48 (PB) $120-150
Full Breakfast
Credit Cards: A, B, C, D, E
Notes: 2, 3 and 4 (in season), 5, 7, 9, 10

---

5 Open all year; 6 Pets welcome; 7 Children welcome; 8 Tennis nearby; 9 Swimming nearby; 10 Golf nearby; 11 Skiing nearby; 12 May be booked through travel agent.

COLLEGE STATION

The Flippen Place

1199 Haywood Drive, 77845
(409) 693-7660, FAX (409) 693-7458

A unique B&B in the country which was fashioned from a 150 year old Amish barn that once stood in Ohio. Our goal was create a warm and inviting place where you could really relax. All rooms include private baths, an enjoyable breakfast, and beautiful decor. Guests have acces to the Great Room and Loft. Roam the forty, heavily wooded acres, complete with hiking trails and two fishing ponds.

Hosts: Flip and Susan Flippen
Rooms: 3 (PB) $100-135
Full Breakfast
Credit Cards: A, B, C
Notes: 2, 5, 8, 9, 10, 12

COMFORT

The Meyer Bed and Breakfast

845 High Street, PO Box 1117, 78013
(210) 995-2304 (voice and FAX); (800) 364-2138

A complex of six different buildings, each with its own history, all nestled on a rise overlooking a grassy knoll on the banks of the Cypress Creek — the original Stage Coach Stop, The Maternity House, The White House Hotel, The Meyer Residence, The 1920 Stucco, and The Honeymoon Cottage. Stroll along the creek or sit and enjoy the screened-in summer kitchen conversation area. A secluded hideaway one block from Comfort's historic downtown district.

Rooms: 9 (PB) $69-85
Continental Plus Breakfast
Credit Cards: A, B, C
Notes: 2, 5, 7, 9, 12

The Meyer Bed and Breakfast

CROSBYTON

Smith House

306 West Aspen, 79322
(806) 675-2178; FAX (806) 675-2619

The Inn was built in 1921 by J. Frank Smith, a cowboy from the nearby Two Buckle Ranch. The original oak furniture and iron beds highlight the early West Texas charm. The Inn has a large dining room, a separate meeting room, and a parlor for entertaining. Guests can enjoy a rocking chair on the large front porch. Available for groups, retreats, or dinners.

Hosts: Terry and Sandy Cash
Rooms: 12 (8PB; 4SB) $55-110
Full Breakfast
Credit Cards: A, B
Notes: 2, 5, 7, 8, 9, 12

NOTES: Credit cards accepted: A Master Card; B Visa; C American Express; D Discover; E Diners Club; F Other; 2 Personal checks accepted; 3 Lunch available; 4 Dinner available;

DALLAS—SEE PAGE 461

DENTON

The Redbud Inn

815 N. Locust Street, 76201
(817) 565-6414; (888) 565-6414;
FAX (817) 565-6515

The Redbud Inn has grown into a B&B cluster group which includes The Magnolia Inn and Ginseppe's Italian Restaurant. All are side by side. We have two large, luxury suites which include dinner on the balcony from Ginseppe's. We recently added a hot tub. Inn available for weddings and family reunions.

Hosts: John and Donna Morris
Rooms: 5 + 2 suites (PB) $49-95
Full Breakfast
Credit Cards: A, B, C, D
Notes: 2, 3, 4, 5, 7, 9, 10, 12

The Redbud Inn

FORT WORTH

The Texas White House

1417 Eighth Avenue, 76104
(817) 923-3597; (800) 279-6491;
FAX (817) 923-0410

This historically-designated, award-winning, country-style home has been restored to its original grandeur. It is centrally located near downtown, the medical center, the Forth Worth Zoo, cultural district, Botanic Gardens, and TCU. The three guest rooms are furnished with luxurious queen-sized beds and nice antiques, relaxing sitting areas, and private baths with clawfooted tubs for showers or soaking in bubble baths. Guests are afforded complete privacy; however, if desired, they may enjoy the parlor, living room with fireplace, and large wraparound porch. Breakfast will be a gourmet treat with fresh fruit or baked fruit in compote (seasonal), baked egg casseroles, and homemade breads and muffins, juices, coffee, and tea.

Hosts: Jamie and Grover McMains
Rooms: 3 (PB) $85-105
Full Breakfast
Credit Cards: A, B, C, D
Notes: 2, 5, 10, 12

FREDERICKSBURG

Hill Country Guesthouse and Gardens

407 West Austin Street, 78624
(210) 997-5612 (reservations service)

This 1921 Bungalow style family home, in Fredericksburg's national historic district, was refurbished by one of the eleven children and her husband, maintaining the charm of yesterday while adding the comforts of today. Original furnishings and family heirlooms convey the spirit of German traditions. Country gardens, limestone walkways, old-fashioned swept yard, and the ten-

---

5 Open all year; 6 Pets welcome; 7 Children welcome; 8 Tennis nearby; 9 Swimming nearby; 10 Golf nearby; 11 Skiing nearby; 12 May be booked through travel agent.

Hill Country Guesthouse and Gardens

foot picnic table under the old pecan tree create perfect ambience for relaxation. Neighborhood Sunday morning church bells welcome all visitors.

Hosts: Peter and Corinne Danysh
Rooms: 2 suites (PB) $80-90
Continental Plus Breakfast
Credit Cards: A, B, C, D, E (through reservation service)
Notes: 2, 5, 8, 9, 10, 12

Longhill Home

Mail: 1919 Lakeville Drive, **Kingwood** 77339
(713) 358-3360; reservations (210) 997-5612;
FAX (210) 997-8282

Located six miles east of Fredericksburg on a hill overlooking the Perdenales Valley. Full kitchen stocked with coffee, tea, hot chocolate, and juices. King-size bed upstairs; trundle bed downstairs (house sleeps four). Bath has tub/shower. House is of country decor and located on 30 acres. You are free to roam the area and share it with the cattle that graze here. Central heat/air plus ceiling fans. No firearms or smoking.

Hosts: Danny and Mary Beth Richarson
Rooms: whole house sleeps 4 (PB) $80-110
Breakfast not provided
Credit Cards: A, B, D
Notes: 2, 5, 7, 12

Magnolia House

101 E. Hackberry Street, 78624
(210) 997-0306 (voice and FAX); (800) 880-4374

Circa 1923; restored 1991. Enjoy Southern hospitality in a grand and gracious manner. Outside, lovely magnolias and a bubbling fish pond and waterfall set a soothing mood. Inside, a beautiful living room and a formal dining room provide areas for guests to mingle. Four romantic rooms and two suites have been thoughtfully planned. A Southern-style breakfast completes a memorable experience.

Hosts: Joyce and Patrick Kennard
Rooms: 4 + 2 suites (4PB; 2SB) $80-110
Full Breakfast
Credit Cards: A, B
Notes: 2, 5, 8, 9, 10

Schildknecht-Weidenfeller House

Gastehaus Schmidt Reservations Service: 231 West Main, 78624
(210) 997-5612; FAX (210) 997-8282

Relive history in the Schildknecht-Weidenfeller House located in the heart

Schildknecht-Weidenfeller House

NOTES: Credit cards accepted: A Master Card; B Visa; C American Express; D Discover; E Diners Club; F Other; 2 Personal checks accepted; 3 Lunch available; 4 Dinner available;

of Fredericksburg's historic district. Decorated with antiques and handmade quilts, this guest house accommodates up to ten people. A German-style breakfast is left for you to enjoy at your leisure around the antique farm table in the kitchen. This 1880s German limestone house has been featured on tours of historic homes and in *Country Decorating Ideas*. Member of Historic Accommodations of Texas.

Hosts: Ellis and Carter Schildknecht
Rooms: entire house (8 rooms + 2 baths) $125 and up according to party size
Expanded Continental (German-style) Breakfast
Credit Cards: A, B, D
Notes: 2, 5, 7 (12 and over only), 8, 9, 10, 12

Schmidt Barn Bed and Breakfast

Route 2, Box 112A3, 78624
Reservation service: 231 W. Main, 78624
(210) 997-5612; FAX (210) 997-8282

The Schmidt Barn is located one and one-half miles outside historic Fredericksbug. This 1860's limestone structure has been turned into a charming guesthouse with loft bedroom, living room, bath, and kitchen. The hosts live next door. German-style breakfast is left in the guest house for you. The house has been featured in *Country Living* and *Travel and Leisure* and is decorated with antiques.

Hosts: Dr. Charles and Loretta Schmidt
Guest House: 1 (PB) $79-109
Continental Plus Breakfast
Credit Cards: A, B, D
Notes: 2, 5, 6, 7, 8, 9, 10, 12

Way of the Wolf

HC 12 Box 92H, 78624
(210) 997-0711; (888) WAY-WOLF

This B&B/retreat, on 61 acres in the hill country, offers swimming pool, space for picnics and hikes, wildlife, and scenic views. The four bedrooms and common living area with fireplace are furnished with antiques. A reconstructed Civil War era cabin is also available. This destination B&B is peaceful and secluded while only 15 minutes from shopping, golf, and churches in either Kerrville or Fredericksburg. Assistance in preparing for personal or group retreats is available.

Hosts: Ron and Karen Poidevin
Rooms: 4 (2PB; 2SB) $75-100
Full Breakfast
Credit Cards: none
Notes: 2, 5, 9 (on-site), 10, 12

Yesteryear Gast House

Yesteryear Gast House

405 E. Morse Street, 78624
(210) 997-5612 (reservation service);
FAX (210) 997-8282

The Yesteryear Gast Haus, built in 1912, is in historic Fredericksburg near museums, shops, and restaurants. This

---

5 Open all year; 6 Pets welcome; 7 Children welcome; 8 Tennis nearby; 9 Swimming nearby; 10 Golf nearby; 11 Skiing nearby; 12 May be booked through travel agent.

large house has been restored throughout and is furnished with beautiful antiques, heirlooms, and decorations from the same time period. Relax on the front porch surrounded by honeycomb rock landscaping, or stretch in the back yard and marvel at the old Wisteria that serves as a shaded arbor. Your stay will be filled with nostalgia and tranquility.

Hosts: George and Janice Stehling
Rooms: 2 (1½SB) $95
Coffe Bar Breakfast
Credit Cards: A, B, D
Notes: 2, 5, 8, 9, 10, 12

GAINESVILLE

Alexander Bed and Breakfast Acres (ABBA)

Route 7, Box 788, 76240
(903) 564-7440; (800) 887-8794

Charming three-story Queen Anne home and guest cottage nestled peacefully in the woods and meadows of 65 acres just south of Whitesboro, Texas in the Lake Texoma area. Main house offers parlor and dining room plus third floor sitting area with TV, and wraparound porch for relaxing; five guest bedrooms with private baths and full breakfast. The two-story cottage has three bedrooms which share one bath, there are full kitchen facilities for preparing own breakfast, and it is perfect for families with children.

Hosts: Jimmy and Pamela Alexander
Rooms: Main house-5 + cottage-3 (5PB; 3SB)
$59-125
Full Breakfast for main house
Credit Cards: A, B
Notes: 2, 4, 5, 7 (at cottage), 9, 10, 11 (water), 12

GALVESTON

Carousel Inn

712 - 10th Street, 77550
(409) 762-2166

This 1886 Victorian home—complete with hand-carved carousel horse, player piano, and hand-crank phonograh—is located 4.5 blocks from the beach and has a comfortable, relaxed atmosphere. Each room has a private bath; two rooms have queen-size beds, one has a king-size bed, and the other has a double. Spencer's Carriage House has a sitting room, microwave, and refrigerator. Kathleen's room has a private front porch. The highlights of each breakfast are Jim's scrumptious baked pastries and cinnamon buns. Anniversary discount available.

Hosts: Jim and Kathy Hughes
Rooms: 4 (PB) $80-95
Continental Plus Breakfast
Credit Cards: A, B, C, D
Notes: 2, 5, 9 (ocean)

Coppersmith Inn Bed and Breakfast

1914 Avenue M, 77550
(409) 763-7004; (800) 515-7444

Queen Anne style mansion built in 1887 and designed by a famous architect. The Inn boasts gingerbread trim, double verandah, turret tower, spectacular winding staircase of teak, walnut and curly pine highlighted by stained glass and ornate newel post, large windows with original glass, exquisite heirloom antiques, Victorian decorations with ro-

---

NOTES: Credit cards accepted: A Master Card; B Visa; C American Express; D Discover; E Diners Club; F Other; 2 Personal checks accepted; 3 Lunch available; 4 Dinner available;

mantic themes and interesting faux painting techniques used during restoration, fireplaces, clawfoot porcelain tub, antique tin tub used in Kenny Rogers movie with five water spouts, lovely landscaped gardens, large wooden deck and brick sidewalks, and a generous country breakfast.

Hostess: Lisa Hering
Rooms: 4 (1PB; 3SB) $90-135
Full and/or Continental Breakfast
Credit Cards: A, B, C, D
Notes: 2, 5, 7 (over 5), 9, 12

Coppersmith Inn

Madame Dyer's Bed and Breakfast

1720 Postoffice Street, 77550
(409) 765-5692

From the moment you enter this carefully restored, turn-of-the-century home, you will be entranced by period details such as wraparound porches, high airy ceilings, wooden floors, and lace curtains. Each room is furnished with delightful antiques that bring back memories of days gone by. Come and

enjoy a night or weekend in this 1889 home located in a quiet, historical, residential neighborhood offering its guests a feeling of elegance from the past and still the luxury, comfort, and pleasures of today. Featured on Galveston's Historic Homes Tour.

Hostess: Linda and Larry Bonnin
Rooms: 3 (PB) $95-125
Full Breakfast
Credit Cards: A, B
Notes: 2, 4, 5, 9, 10, 12

GLEN ROSE

Bussey's Something Special B&B

202 Hereford Street (PO Box 1425), 76043
(817) 897-4843

Relax in a private two-story guest cottage, downtown Glen Rose. King and full beds upstairs with livingroom, kitchen, and bath downstairs. Complimentary continental breakfast provided; hosts not on premises. Enjoy the sights and adventures of the River Highlands. Sit on the porch swing, take a leisurely walk to the square for shopping and lunch, visit a nearby historic building or museum, walk to the Paluxy River, or explore the countryside to experience the excitement of the very "Heart" of Texas.

Hosts: Susan and Morris Bussey
Rooms: one guest cottage (PB) $80-125
Continental Plus Breakfast
Credit Cards: none
Notes: 2, 5, 7, 8, 9, 10, 12

---

5 Open all year; 6 Pets welcome; 7 Children welcome; 8 Tennis nearby; 9 Swimming nearby; 10 Golf nearby; 11 Skiing nearby; 12 May be booked through travel agent.

GONZALES

St. James Inn

723 St. James, 78629
(210) 672-7066

A former cattle baron's mansion, the Inn
is a welcome respite from the busy life.
Furnished with antiques, colorful collections, and warm hospitality. The rural area offers hiking, biking, antiquing,
and roaming. Enjoy cold lemonade on
the front porch or spiced tea in front of
a fire.

Hosts: Ann and J.R. Covert
Rooms: 5 (4PB; 1SB) $65-150
Full Breakfast
Credit Cards: A, B, C
Notes: 2, 3, 4, 5, 7, 9, 10, 11, 12

Dabney House

GRANDBURY

Dabney House
Bed and Breakfast

106 South Jones, 76048
(817) 579-1260; (800) 566-1260;
FAX (817) 579-0426

Craftsman-style one-story home built in
1907 by a local banker and furnished
with antiques, hardwood floors, and
original woodwork. Long-term business
rates available per request; romance dinner by reservation only. We offer custom, special occasion baskets in room
upon arrival, by advance order only.
Book whole house for family occasions,
staff retreats, or Bible retreats at discount rates. Hot tub is now available for
all registered guests.

Hosts: John and Gwen Hurley
Rooms: 4 (PB) $60-105
Full Breakfast
Credit Cards: A, B, C
Notes: 2, 5, 8, 9, 10, 12

HOUSTON

Sara's
Bed and Breakfast Inn

941 Heights Boulevard, 77008
(713) 868-1130; (800) 593-1130;
FAX (713) 868-1160

This Queen Anne Victorian with its turret and widow's walk is located in
Houston Heights, a neighborhood of
historic homes, many of which are on
the National Historic Register. Each
bedroom is uniquely furnished, having
either single, double, queen, or king
beds. The Balcony Suite consists of two
bedrooms, two baths, kitchen/living
area, and balcony. Breakfast is served
in the beautiful garden room in the Inn.
The sights and sounds of downtown
Houston are five miles away.

Hosts: Donna and Tillman Arledge
Rooms: 14 (12PB; 2SB) $55-150
Continental Plus Breakfast
Credit Cards: A, B, C, D, E, F
Notes: 2, 5, 7, 8, 9, 10, 12

NOTES: Credit cards accepted: A Master Card; B Visa; C American Express; D Discover;
E Diners Club; F Other; 2 Personal checks accepted; 3 Lunch available; 4 Dinner available;

INGRAM

Lazy Hius Guest Ranch

PO Box G, 78025
(210) 367-5600; (800) 880-0632;
FAX (210) 367-5667

Since the spring of 1959, the Steinruck
family has been welcoming folks from
around the world to Lazy Hius, a 750-
acre spread in the heart of the beautiful
Texas Hill Country. At Lazy Hius we
have earned the reputation of the "family ranch for folks of all ages," so bring
your jeans and boots for a high-riding
Hill Country adventure!

Hosts: Bob and Carol Steinruck
Rooms: 25 (PB) $75-95
Full Breakfast
Credit Cards: A, B, C, D
Notes: 2, 3, 4, 5, 7, 8, 9, 10, 12

JEFFERSON

McKay House
Bed and Breakfast Inn

306 East Delta, 75657
(903) 665-7322; (800) 468-2627 (9-5 only);
FAX (903) 665-8551

Jefferson is a town where one can relax, rather than get tired. The McKay
House, an 1851 Greek Revival cottage,
features a pillared front porch and many
fireplaces and offers genuine hospitality in a Christian atmosphere. Heart-of-
pine floors, 14-foot ceilings, and
documented wallpapers complement
antique furnishings. Guests enjoy a full
"gentle-man's" breakfast. Victorian

McKay House

nightshirts and gowns await pampered
guests in each bed chamber.

Hosts: Alma Anne and Joseph Parker
Rooms: 4 + 3 suites (PB) $75-145 (corporate rates
available)
Full Sit-down Breakfast
Credit Cards: A, B
Notes: 2, 5, 10, 12

LEANDER

Trails End
Bed and Breakfast

12223 Trails End Road #7, 78641
(512) 267-2901; (800) 850-2901

Our B&B is close to Lake Travis and
Austin, Texas. We offer large, comfortable rooms with plenty of outdoor
porches, decks, a swimming pool, bicycles, a gazebo, hiking areas, and a full
breakfast. Each house has a fireplace in
the living areas. Enjoy a cup of hot tea
on the porch swing. Monogramed terry
cloth robes for your use.

Hosts: JoAnn and Tom Patty
Rooms: 4 (2PB; 2SB) $65-95
Full Breakfast
Credit Cards: A, B, C
Notes: 2, 4, 5, 7, 9, 12 (10%)

---

5 Open all year; 6 Pets welcome; 7 Children welcome; 8 Tennis nearby; 9 Swimming nearby;
10 Golf nearby; 11 Skiing nearby; 12 May be booked through travel agent.

LEDBETTER

Ledbetter Bed and Breakfast

PO Box 212, 78946
(409) 249-3066; (800) 240-3066;
FAX (409) 249-3330

Ledbetter B&B, established in 1988, is a collection of multigeneration, family, 1800-1900's homes within walking distance of the remaining 1870s downtown businesses. Full country breakfast buffet can serve up to 70 guests daily. Hayrides, walks, fishing, horse and buggy rides, games, Christmas lights, chuck wagon or romantic dinners, indoor heated swimming pool, VCR, TV, and phone on advance request. Each unit accommodates approximately four people. Only non-alcoholic beverages are allowed outside private quarters. Only outdoor smoking is allowed.

Hosts: Chris and Jay Jervis
Rooms: 16-22 depending on grouping (17PB; 8SB) $70-150
Full Country Buffet Breakfast
Credit Cards: A, B, C (no deposit refunded)
Notes: 2, 3, 4, 5, 7, 8, 9, 10, 11 (water), 12

NACOGDOCHES

Pine Creek Lodge B&B Country Inn

Route 3 Box 1238, 75964
(409) 560-6282; (888) 714-1414

On a beautiful tree covered hill overlooking a springfed creek sits Pine Creek Lodge. Built on a 140-acre property with lots of lawns, rose gardens, and a multitude of flowers, deep in the East Texas woods yet only ten miles from historic Nacogdoches. Our rustic lodge features king-size beds in tastefully decorated rooms with phone, TV/VCR, lots of decks, swimming pool, spa, fishing, biking, and much more. We have become the destination for many city dwellers.

Hosts: The Pitts Family
Rooms: 7 (PB) $55-75
Full Breakfast
Credit Cards: A, B, C
Notes: 2, 3, 4, 5, 7, 9, 10

NEW BRAUNFELS

The Rose Garden

195 S. Academy, 78130
(210) 629-3296; (800) 569-3296

Come to our Rose Garden with designer bedrooms, fluffy towels, scented soaps, and potpourri-filled rooms. Our half-century old home is only one block from downtown. Enjoy a movie, browse our antique shops, or stroll along the Comal Springs—all within walking distance. We offer two guest rooms. The Royal Rose Room has a four poster rice, queen bed with a crystal chandelier and country French decor. The Country Rose Room has a Victorian-style, iron-and-brass queen bed with pine walls also done in country French. A full gourmet breakfast is served in the formal dining room.

Hostess: Dawn Mann
Rooms: 2 (PB) $65-95
Full Breakfast
Credit Cards: A, B
Notes: 2, 5, 8, 9, 10

NOTES: Credit cards accepted: A Master Card; B Visa; C American Express; D Discover; E Diners Club; F Other; 2 Personal checks accepted; 3 Lunch available; 4 Dinner available;

POST

Hotel Garza B&B

302 East Main Street, 79356
(806) 495-3962

This restored 1915 hotel projects friendliness and history of this "Main Street City" where cereal magnate C.W. Post settled in 1907 to create his "Utopia." Guests can enjoy live theatre, colorful shops, museums, and the monthly event of Old Mill Trade Days. The guest rooms boast original furniture. From the comfy library you can look down on a quaint lobby and the dining area where a hearty breakfast is served. Suites are available.

Hosts: Janice and Jim Plummer
Rooms: 12 (8PB; 4SB) $35-95
Full Breakfast (Sat.-Sun.)
Continental (Mon.-Fri.)
Credit Cards: A, B, C
Notes: 2, 3, 4, 5, 7, 8, 9, 10, 12

Hotel Garza

ROYSE CITY

Country Lane B&B

Route 2, Box 94B, 75189
(214) 636-2600; (800) 240-8757;
FAX (214) 635-2300

Just 28 miles east of Dallas, this country getaway has a private pond which is a favorite stopover of egrets and herons. Four guest rooms with private baths are themed to movie characters—Mae West, Roy Rogers, Natalie Wood, and Film Noir Mysteries. Hundreds of vintage and new movies are among the collectibles for your enjoyment.

Hosts: James and Annie Cornelius
Rooms: 4 (PB) $50-85
Full Breakfast
Credit Cards: A, B, C
Notes: 2, 4, 5, 7, 10, 11 (water), 12 (10%)

SAN ANTONIO

Beckmann Inn and Carriage House

222 E. Guenther Street, 78204
(210) 229-1449; (800) 945-1449;
FAX (210) 229-1061

A wonderful Victorian house (1886) located in the King William historic district, across the street from the start of the Riverwalk. Beautifully landscaped, it will take you on a leisurely stroll to the Alamo, downtown shops, and restaurants. You can also take the trolley which stops at the corner and within minutes you're there in style. The beautiful wraparound porch welcomes you to the main house and warm, gracious, Victorian hospitality. The large guest rooms feature antique, ornately carved, Victorian, queen-size beds; private baths; and ceiling fans. Gourmet breakfast, with breakfast dessert, is served in the dining room with china, crystal, and silver. Warm and

---

5 Open all year; 6 Pets welcome; 7 Children welcome; 8 Tennis nearby; 9 Swimming nearby;
10 Golf nearby; 11 Skiing nearby; 12 May be booked through travel agent.

gracious hospitality at its best. AAA, IIA, and Mobil rated.

Hosts: Betty Jo and Don Schwartz
Rooms: 5 (PB) $80-130
Full Breakfast
Credit Cards: A, B, C, D, E
Notes: 2, 5, 7 (over 12), 10, 12

Brackenridge House

230 Madison Street, 78204
(210) 271-3442 (voice and FAX); (800) 221-1412

A Greek Revival home (1903) set in the King William historic district with four two-story white Corinthian columns and first and second floor verdas. The original pine floor, double-hung windows, and high ceilings are enhanced by antique furnishings, many of them family heirlooms. All guest rooms have private baths and entrances, phones, and mini-refrigerators. A bridal suite decorated in all white is available. Breakfast is served in the guest dining room on the second floor. Located only six blocks from downtown, two blocks from the Riverwalk, and one block from the ten cent trolley and the San Antonio Mission Trail. Convenient walking to four delightful restaurants.

Hosts: Bennie and Sue Blansett
Rooms: 5 (PB) $80-115
Full Breakfast
Credit Cards: A, B, C, D, E
Notes: 2, 5, 12

Brookhaven Manor

128 W. Mistletoe, 78212
(210) 733-3939; (800) 851-3666;
FAX (210) 733-3884

Recapture the charm and grace of a by-gone era in an elegant three-story home built in 1914. Each room is distinctly decorated, from the Murphy Room with a queen-size mahogony Murphy bed to the Country French Honeymoon Suite with private dressing room and marble bath with clawfoot tub. Located in a elite, historic district, Brookhaven Manor is five minutes from downtown. Great area for walkers and joggers!

Hosts: Ralph Stutzman
Manager: Nancy Forbes
Rooms: 5 (PB) $75-125
Full Breakfast (Continental for early birds)
Credit Cards: A, B
Notes: 2, 5, 6, 7, 8, 9, 10, 12

Brookhaven Manor

The Riverwalk Inn

329 Old Guilbeau, 78204
(210) 212-8300; (800) 254-4440;
FAX (210) 229-9422

The Riverwalk Inn is comprised of five two-story homes, circa 1840, which have been restored on the downtown San Antonio Riverwalk. Decorated in period antiques which create an ambience of "country elegance." Rock on our 80-foot porch lined with rocking chairs. Enjoy Aunt Martha's evening desserts

---

NOTES: Credit cards accepted: A Master Card; B Visa; C American Express; D Discover; E Diners Club; F Other; 2 Personal checks accepted; 3 Lunch available; 4 Dinner available;

and local story tellers that join us for our expanded continental breakfast. Amenities include fireplaces, refrigerators, private baths, phones, balconies, TV, and conference room. A Texas tradition with a Tennessee flavor awaits you. Call for brochure.

Hosts: Johnny Halpenny and Tammy Hill
Rooms: 11 (PB) $89-145
Expanded Continental Breakfast
Credit Cards: A, B, C, D
Notes: 2, 5, 12

The Victorian Lady Inn

421 Howard Street, 78212
(210) 224-2524 (voice and FAX);
(800) 879-7116

Rediscover the genteel ambiance of 100 years ago in this 1898 historic mansion. Guestrooms are some of the largest in San Antonio and feature period antiques. Your pampered retreat includes a private bath, fireplace, verandah, TV, and phone. Fabulous full breakfasts served daily in the grand dining room. Bicycles and book exchange on premises. Just blocks away are the

The Victorian Lady Inn

Riverwalk, Alamo, and Convention Center. Swimming, golf, horseback riding, and antiquing are all very closeby. AAA rating three diamonds.

Hosts: Joe and Kate Bowski
Rooms: 7 (PB) $79-165
Full Breakfast
Credit Cards: A, B, C, D
Notes: 2, 5, 8, 9, 10, 12

SILSBEE

Sherwood Train Depot Bed and Breakfast

134 Sherwood Trail, PO Box 2281, 77656
(409) 385-0188

A beautiful wooded setting of a two-story cypress home in the midst of beech and oak trees. Within the home is a unique design of knottie cypress wood. Fireplaced living room which at the ceiling begins a "G" scale "LGB" train system that runs on a cypress ceiling-hung rail system that is 430 feet long and runs throughout the downstairs and even spiraling to the upstairs. You have to see this unusual track layout to believe it. The suite features a king bed, private bath, cable TV/VCR, phone, and even has a two-person hot tub. Guests can also enjoy exercise equipment, walking trails, bird watching, and much more.

Host: Jerry Allen
Rooms: 1 (PB) $60-75
Continental and Full Breakfast
Credit Cards: none
Notes: 2, 3, 4, 5, 7, 9, 10

---

5 Open all year; 6 Pets welcome; 7 Children welcome; 8 Tennis nearby; 9 Swimming nearby; 10 Golf nearby; 11 Skiing nearby; 12 May be booked through travel agent.

SPRING

McLachlan Farm Bed and Breakfast

PO Box 538, 77383
(713) 350-2400; (800) 382-3988

The McLachlan family homestead, built in 1911, was restored and enlarged in 1989 by the great-granddaughter, and her husband, of the original McLachlan family who settled the land in 1862. Set back among 35 acres of towering sycamore and pecan trees, neatly mowed grounds, and winding forest trails. It is a quiet oasis that returns guests to a time when life was simpler. Visitors may swing on the porches, walk in the woods, or visit Old Town Spring (one mile south) where there are more than 100 shops to enjoy.

Hosts: Jim and Joycelyn Clairmonte
Rooms: 3-4 (3PB or 2SB) $75-85
Full Country Breakfast
Credit Cards: A, B, C, D
Notes: 2, 5, 10, 12

STEPHENVILLE

The Oxford House

563 N. Graham, 76401
(817) 965-6885 (voice and FAX); (800) 711-7283

The Oxford House is a completely restored, two-story Victorian home constructed in 1898. It's spacious porches surround the magnificent structure which houses antique furnishings, including a pump organ, a sleigh bed, and a fainting couch. Four bedrooms with privacy bathes, a reading room, and a beautiful garden gazebo—just the right setting for the perfect wedding or reception—are all part of this wonderful escape. Enjoy a home cooked country breakfast and a candlelight dinner, and relax and enjoy a memorably romantic weekend at The Oxford House.

Hosts: Bill and Paula Oxford
Rooms: 4 (PB) $65-85
Full Breakfast
Credit Cards: A, B
Notes: 2, 4 (by reservation), 5, 7, 9, 10, 12

Mansion on Main

TEXARKANA

Mansion on Main Bed and Breakfast Inn

802 Main Street, 75501
(903) 792-1835

"Twice as Nice," the motto of Texarkana, USA (Texas and Arkansas), is standard practice at Mansion on Main. The 1895 Neoclassic Colonial mansion, surrounded by 14 tall columns, was recently restored by the owners of McKay House, the popular bed and breakfast in nearby Jerrson. Six bed chambers vary from the Governor's Suite to the

---

NOTES: Credit cards accepted: A Master Card; B Visa; C American Express; D Discover; E Diners Club; F Other; 2 Personal checks accepted; 3 Lunch available; 4 Dinner available;

Butler's Garret. Guests enjoy Southern hospitality, period furnishings, fireplaces, and a gentleman's breakfast. Thirty miles away is the town of Hope, birthplace of President Clinton.

Host: Javeta Hawthorne
Rooms: 4 + 2 suites (PB) $60-99 (corporate rates available)
Full Sit-Down Breakfast
Credit Cards: A, B, C
Notes: 2, 5, 10, 12

Rosevine Inn

TYLER

Rosevine Inn, Bed and Breakfast
415 South Vine, 75702
(903) 592-2221; FAX (903) 593-9500

A quaint two-story with a white picket fence, located in the Brick Street District. The Inn offers many amenities including a covered hot tub outdoors, courtyard complete with a fountain and a fireplace, and lodge-style gameroom. Each of the four bedrooms and two suites are nicely decorated with antiques, wallpapers, and private baths. A full, formal breakfast serves more than you can eat. Your hosts will happily direct you to local restaurants, antique shops, museums, lakes, zoo, and more. The Inn accommodate business travelers and groups.

Hosts: Bert and Rebecca Powell
Rooms: 6 (PB) $85-150
Full Breakfast
Credit Cards: A, B, C, D, E
Notes: 2, 3 (picnic with 12 hour notice), 5, 7, 8, 9, 10, 12

WIMBERLY

Southwind Bed and Breakfast
2701 FM 3237, 78676
(512) 847-5277; (800) 508-5277

Southwind, a prayerful place, sets on 25 secluded acres of hills and trees. Two long porches are provided with rocking chairs to enjoy the fresh air, wildlife, and sunsets. Star gazing is especially grand from the hot tub. A guest living room with fireplace and kitchen and dining room privileges complement the three spacious, private guest rooms. A full, tasty breakfast with coffee or tea served on the porch is a wonderful way to start the day at Southwind. There are two secluded cabins, each with king bed, fireplace, whirlpool tub, kitchen, and porch with swing.

Hostess: Carrie Watson
Rooms: 3 (PB) $70-80
Full Breakfast
Credit Cards: A, B, D
Notes: 2, 5, 6 + 7 (in cabins only), 8, 9, 10, 12

---

5 Open all year; 6 Pets welcome; 7 Children welcome; 8 Tennis nearby; 9 Swimming nearby; 10 Golf nearby; 11 Skiing nearby; 12 May be booked through travel agent.

UTAH

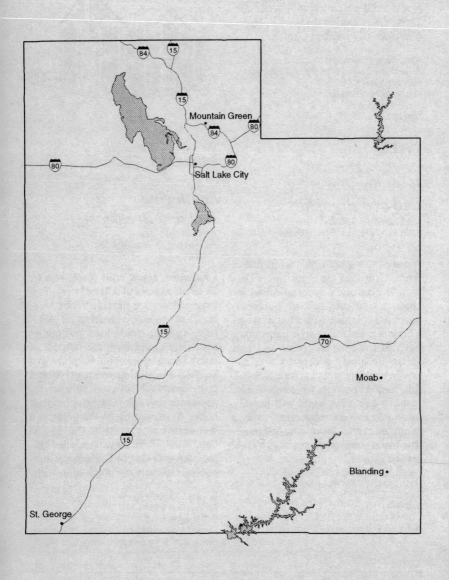

Utah

Mi Casa Su Casa Bed and Breakfast Reservation Service

PO Box 950, **Tempe**, AZ 85280-0950
(602) 990-0682; (800) 456-0682 (reservations);
FAX (602) 990-3390

Over 160 inspected and approved homestays, guest cottages, ranches, and inns in Arizona, Utah, New Mexico, and Nevada. In **Arizona**, listings include Ajo, Apache Junction, Bisbee, Cave Creek, Clarkdale, Dragoon, Flagstaff, Mesa, Page, Patagonia, Payson, Pinetop, Phoenix, Prescott, Scottsdale, Sedona, Sierra Vista, Tempe, Tucson, Tombstone, Yuma, and other cities. In **New Mexico**, we have included Albuquerque, Algodones, Chimayo, Los Cruces, Silver City, Sante Fe, and Taos. In **Utah**, listings include Moab, Monroe, Salt Lake City, Springdale, St. George, and Tropic. In **Nevada**, we list Las Vegas. Rooms with private and shared baths range from $40-175. Credit cards welcomed. Full or continental breakfast. A book with individual descriptions, rates, and pictures is available for $9.50. Ruth Young, coordinator.

BLANDING

Grayson Country Inn Bed and Breakfast

118 East 300 South (86-6), 84511
(801) 678-2388; (800) 365-0868

Grayson Country Inn was first built in 1908 as the home of the William W. Nix family. Located one block east of Main Street at 300 South, the Inn offers country hospitality while adding the modern conveniences of a private bath and television in each of the seven guest rooms. The cozy dining and living rooms are favorite gathering spots for browsing, reading, and enjoying a coun-

---

NOTES: Credit cards accepted: A Master Card; B Visa; C American Express; D Discover; E Diners Club; F Other; 2 Personal checks accepted; 3 Lunch available; 4 Dinner available; 5 Open all year; 6 Pets welcome; 7 Children welcome; 8 Tennis nearby; 9 Swimming nearby; 10 Golf nearby; 11 Skiing nearby; 12 May be booked through travel agent.

try breakfast while you stay for a night, a week's vacation, or a special family event. A great retreat for couples, singles, and family! We specialize in home atmosphere and home cooking. We welcome children and family pets can stay (if requested).

Hosts: Dennis and Lurlene Gutke
Rooms: 11 (PB) $42 (Nov.-March)—$52 (April-Oct.)
Full Breakfast
Credit Cards: A, B, C
Notes: 5, 6 ,7, 12

Home Away From Home
(Arches National Park)

MOAB

Home Away From Home

122 Hillside Drive, 84532
(801) 259-6276

This B&B is minutes from Arches National Park, Colorado Connection, Canyonlands Air Field Airport, and Colorado River rafting, jet skiing, and kayaking. It is walking distance from market and shops, mountain hiking, hiking, horseback riding, water slides, and golf. Some may enjoy dome tent and tepee camping at the enclosed mini park back yard of the B&B. Colorado Connection for deer or elk hunting—bow or rifle. Three hours from Telluride, CO. Ski chair lift winter and summer. TBN dish viewing.

Host: E. M. Smith
Rooms: 4 (1PB; 3SB) advance reservations
Continental Breakfast
Credit Cards: none
Notes: 2, 5, 7, 9, 10, 11, 12

Kane Springs Ranchstead

1705 South Kane Springs Road, PO Box 940, 84532
(801) 259-2821

Just minutes away from Arches National Park; Canyonlands Air Field; Colorado River rafting, jet skiing, and kayaking; hiking; horseback riding; water slides; swimming; and bicycling. Singes: primitive tent camping in canyon, along the rim of the Colorado River —an easy four miles from Moab. Also, accommodations for self-contained RVs among trees along the river near Native American picroglphs with ancient ladder used by inhabitants. Reserve you reservation in advance in order to experience this beautiful Red Rock Canyon—a bed outdoors.

Hosts: Charles and Lucy Nelson
Camping sights: 20 (5SB) RVs and Tents $8-12
No Breakfast
Credit Cards: none
Notes: 2, 5, 7, 9, 10, 11

NOTES: Credit cards accepted: A Master Card; B Visa; C American Express; D Discover; E Diners Club; F Other; 2 Personal checks accepted; 3 Lunch available; 4 Dinner available;

MOUNTAIN GREEN

Hubbard House B&B
5648 W. Old Highway Road, 84050
(801) 876-2005; (800) 815-2220;
FAX (801) 876-2020

Hubbard House, built in the 1920's, has the warmth and charm of days gone by with hardwood floors and stained glass windows. It has an awesome view of God's majestic mountains. Three ski resorts within the area, also fishing, boating, golfing, hiking, and hunting. Piano in dining room. Come and enjoy homemade goodies, laughter, and good old hospitality at Hubbard House. One mile east from Exit 92 off I-84.

Hosts: Donald and Gloria Hubbard
Rooms: 3 (1PB; 2SB) $55-75
Full Country Breakfast
Credit Cards: A, B
Notes: 5, 4, 5, 7, 8, 9, 10, 11

ST. GEORGE

Seven Wives Inn
217 North 100 West, 84770
(801) 628-3737; (800) 600-3737

The Inn consists of two adjacent pioneer adobe homes with massive hand-grained moldings framing windows and doors. Bedrooms are furnished with period antiques and handmade quilts. Some rooms have fireplaces; two have a whirlpool tub. Swimming pool on premises.

Hosts: Donna and Jay Curtis
Rooms: 12 (PB) $55-85; suites $125
Full Breakfast
Credit Cards: A, B, C, D, E
Notes: 2, 5, 7, 8, 9, 10, 12

SALT LAKE CITY

Anton Boxrud Bed and Breakfast
57 South 600 East, 84102
(801) 363-8035; (800) 524-5511;
FAX (801) 596-1316
Email: antonb@kdcol.com

When you are looking for a warm home base from which to explore both Salt Lake City and the Wasatch Ski Resorts, come and stay in casual elegance. Return to a time of polished woods, leaded glass windows, and hand woven lace all wrapped inside a three-story Victorian home built in 1901. A full, hearty homemade breakfast features Gladys' cinnamon buns and is served on real Bavarian China. Chose "Best Place to Stay" by numerous B&B selected guides. AAA three stars.

Hostess: Jane E. Johnson
Rooms: 7 (5PB; 2SB) $65-129
Full Homemade Breakfast
Credit Cards: A, B, C, D
Notes: 2, 5, 8, 9, 10, 11, 12

Anton Boxrud Bed and Breakfast

5 Open all year; 6 Pets welcome; 7 Children welcome; 8 Tennis nearby; 9 Swimming nearby; 10 Golf nearby; 11 Skiing nearby; 12 May be booked through travel agent.

Armstrong Mansion Bed and Breakfast

667 East 100 South, 84102
(801) 531-1333; (800) 708-1333;
FAX (801) 531-0282

The Armstrong Mansion was built in 1893 in fulfillment of a wedding-day promise by Frank Armstrong, then Mayor of Salt Lake City. This Queen Anne Style mansion, alive with the oak staircase in the entry, will take your breath away. The beautiful stenciling in the rooms and the carpeting in the parlor and dining room are reproductions of the original, thanks to photographs which have been made available by the Armstrong descendants. Besides the ornate woodwork and the beautiful stained glass windows, there are fourteen splendidly restored rooms. You are within walking distance of downtown businesses, shopping, entertainment, and historical/cultural attractions. Only a 30-45 minute drive will take you from the Mansion to ten world class ski resorts with the "greatest snow on earth," snowmobiling, and water sports.

Hosts: Juell Delight/Marlene Bennett
Rooms: 14 (PB) $89-189
Full Gourmet Breakfast
Credit Cards: A, B, C, D
Notes: 2, 5, 10, 11, 12

Saltair Bed and Breakfast

164 South 900 East, 84102
(801) 533-8184; (800) 733-8184;
FAX (801) 595-0332

Feel right at home in centrally located Saltair B&B. Antiques and charm complement queen-size brass beds, Amish quilts, and period lamps. Amenities include full breakfast, evening snacks, A/C, hot tub, and goose down comforters. For extended stays, choose Alpine Cottages built around 1870 next door to the B&B. Cottages sleep four and include fireplace, cable TV, full kitchen, sitting room, and private entrance. Near Temple Square, University of Utah, skiing, and canyons.

Hosts: Jan Bartlett and Nancy Saxton
Rooms: 5 (2PB; 3SB) $55-105
Full and Continental Breakfast
Credit Cards: A, B, C
Notes: 2, 5, 8, 9, 10, 11, 12

NOTES: Credit cards accepted: A Master Card; B Visa; C American Express; D Discover; E Diners Club; F Other; 2 Personal checks accepted; 3 Lunch available; 4 Dinner available;

Vermont

American Country Collection of B&B

1353 Union Street, **Schenectady**, NY 12308
(518) 370-4948

This reservation service provides reservations for eastern **New York**, western **Massachusetts**, and all of **Vermont**. Just one call does it all. Relax and unwind at any of our over 100 immaculate, personally inspected bed and breakfasts and country inns. Many include fireplace, jacuzzi, and/or Modified American Plan. We have budget-minded to luxurious accommodations in urban, suburban, and rural locations. $50-200. Gift certificates available and major credit cards accepted. Carol Matos, coordinator.

ALBURG

Thomas Mott Homestead Bed and Breakfast

Rt. 2, Box 149-B, (Blue Rock Road on Lake Champlain) 05440-9620
(802) 796-3736 (voice and FAX);
(800) 348-0843 (USA + Canada)
Web site: http://cimarron.net

Formerly an importer and distributor of fine wines, your host also enjoys gourmet cooking. His completely restored farmhouse has a guest living room with TV and fireplace overlooking the lake, game room with bumper pool and darts, and quilt decor. Full view of Mt. Mansfield and Jay Peak. One hour to Montreal/Burlington; one and one-half hours to Lake Placid and Stowe. Lake activities in winter and summer. Amenities include Ben and Jerry's ice cream, lawn games, and horseshoes. Internet accessible; boat dock. Gift Certificates also available.

Host: Patrick J. Schallert, Sr., M.S., B.A.
Rooms: 5 (PB) $65-85
Full Breakfast
Credit Cards: A, B, C, D
Notes: 2, 5, 7 (over 6), 8, 9, 10, 11, 12

ARLINGTON

The Arlington Inn

Historic Route 7A, PO Box 369, 05250
(802) 375-6532; (800) 443-9442

A stately Greek Revival mansion set on lush, landscaped lawns. Elegantly appointed rooms filled with antiques and amenities. All rooms have private baths and air-conditioning and include break-

VERMONT

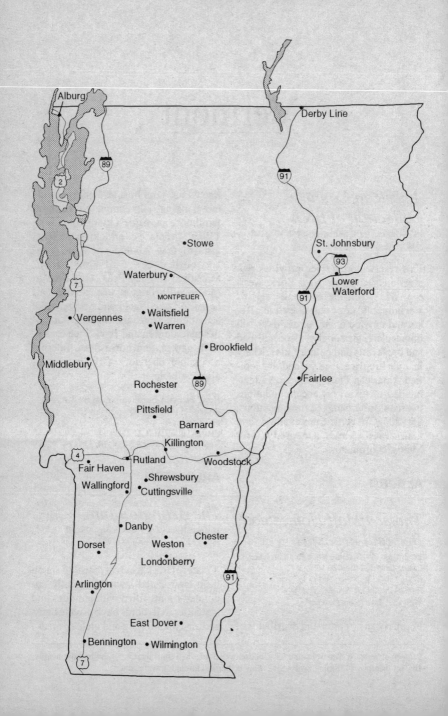

The Arlington Inn

fast. Located between Bennington and Manchester. Antique shops, boutiques, museums, skiing, hiking, biking, canoeing, fly fishing, golf, and many other outdoor activities are nearby. Tennis on our private court. Outstanding cuisine is served by romantic candlelight in our fireplaced, award-winning dining room with superb service. A non-smoking inn. AAA—3 diamonds. Mobile—3 stars.

Hosts: Mark and Deborah Gagnon
Rooms: 19 (PB) $70-185
Full Breakfast
Credit Cards: A, B, C, D, E
Notes: 2 (deposits only), 4, 5, 7, 8 (on-site), 9, 10, 11, 12

Hill Farm Inn

R.R. 2, Box 2015, 05250
(802) 375-2269; (800) 882-2545;
FAX (802) 375-9918

Hill Farm Inn is one of Vermont's original farmsteads granted from King George III in 1775. It has been an inn since 1905 and still retains the character of an old farm vacation inn on 50 beautiful acres between the Taconic and Green Mountains with a mile of frontage on the Battenkill River. We special-

ize in warm country hsopitality. Outside, relax and enjoy the magnificent views from our porches. Inside, savor the aromas of homemade bread fresh from the oven, soup simmering on the stove, and apple crisp baking. Hiking, biking, canoeing, fishing, skiing, and shopping are all nearby. Friendly conversation found everwhere.

Hosts: George and Joanne Hardy
rooms: 13 (8PB; 5SB) $65-120
Full Hot Country Breakfast
Credit Cards: A, B, C, D
Notes: 2, 4, 5, 6 (limited), 7, 8, 9, 10, 11, 12

Hill Farm Inn

Shenandoah Farm

Battenkill Road, 05250
(802) 375-6372

Experience New England in this lovingly restored 1820 Colonial overlooking the Battenkill River. Wonderful "Americana" year-round. Full "farm-fresh" breakfast is served daily and is included.

Host: Woody Masterson
Rooms: 5 (1PB; 4SB) $60-75
Full Breakfast
Credit Cards: A, B
Notes: 2, 5, 8, 10, 11, 12

NOTES: Credit cards accepted: A Master Card; B Visa; C American Express; D Discover; E Diners Club; F Other; 2 Personal checks accepted; 3 Lunch available; 4 Dinner available; 5 Open all year; 6 Pets welcome; 7 Children welcome; 8 Tennis nearby; 9 Swimming nearby; 10 Golf nearby; 11 Skiing nearby; 12 May be booked through travel agent.

BENNINGTON

Bennington Hus

208 Washington Avenue, 05201
(802) 447-7972

Your are welcome at a 1953 custom built house located near downtown the Bennington shops in a quiet neighborhood. Guests have access to livingroom with fireplace and TV and the dining room.

Hostess: AnnaLisa Sparta
Rooms: 4 (2PB; 2SB) $50
Full Breakfast
Credit Cards: none
Notes: 2, 5, 7, 8, 9, 10, 11

BROOKFIELD

Green Trails Inn

By the Floating Bridge, 05036
(802) 276-3412; (800) 243-3412

Green Trails Inn . . . Relax and be pampered . . . enjoy comfortable elegance and true Vermont hospitality on our seventeen-acre country estate in the heart of historic Brookfield. Outdoor lover's paradise — biking, hiking, fishing, swimming, canoeing, ice skating, and cross-country skiing (over 30km) from our front door. Scrumptious meals, spacious lounging areas, and comfy beds to fall into at night. Fabulous antique clock collection!

Hosts: Sue and Mark Erwin
Rooms: 14 (8PB; 6SB) $75-125
Full Breakfast
Credit Cards: A, B
Notes: 2, 4, 5, 7 (10 and over), 9, 10, 11, 12

CHESTER

Henry Farm Inn

PO Box 646, 05143
(802) 875-2674; (800) 723-8213;
FAX (802) 875-2675

The Henry Farm Inn supplies the beauty of Vermont with old-time simplicity. Nestled on 50 acres of rolling hills and meadows, assuring peace and quiet. Spacious rooms, private baths, country sitting areas, and a sunny dining room all guarantee a feeling of home. Come and visit for a day or more!

Hosts: The Bowmans
Rooms: 7 (PB) $50-90
Full Breakfast
Credit Cards: A, B, C
Notes: 2, 5, 7, 8, 9, 10, 11, 12

The Hugging Bear Inn and Shoppe

Main Street, 05143
(802) 875-2412 or 2339; (800) 325-0519;
FAX (802) 875-3823

Teddy bears peek out the windows and are tucked in all the corners of this beautiful Victorian house built in 1850. If you love teddy bears, you'll love the Hugging Bear. There are six guest rooms with private shower baths and a teddy bear in every bed. Full breakfast and afternoon snack are served.

Hosts: Georgette, Diane, and Paul Thomas
Rooms: 6 (PB) $55-90
Full Breakfast
Credit Cards: A, B, C, D
Notes: 2, 5, 6 (limited), 7, 8, 9, 10, 11

NOTES: Credit cards accepted: A Master Card; B Visa; C American Express; D Discover; E Diners Club; F Other; 2 Personal checks accepted; 3 Lunch available; 4 Dinner available;

CUTTINGSVILLE

Buckmaster Inn
Lincoln Hill Road, **Shrewsbury** 05738
(802) 492-3485

The Buckmaster Inn (1801) was an early stagecoach stop in Shrewsbury. Standing on a knoll overlooking a picturesque barn scene and rolling hills, the Inn is situated in the Green Mountains. A center hall, grand staircase, and wide-pine floors grace the home which is decorated with family antiques and crewel handiwork done by your hostess. Extremely large, airy rooms; wood-burning stove; four fireplaces; and two large porches.

Hosts: Sam and Grace Husselman
Rooms: 4 (2PB; 2SB) $55-65 + tax
Full Breakfast
Credit Cards: none (Travelers' Checks accepted)
Notes: 5, 7, 8, 9, 10, 11

DANBY

The Quail's Nest
PO Box 221, Main Street, 05739
(802) 293-5099; FAX (802) 293-6300

Nestled in a quiet mountain village, our inn offers guests friendly conversation around the fireplace, rooms filled with cozy quilts and antiques, and a hearty, home-cooked breakfast in the morning. Hiking, skiing, swimming, and outlet shopping are all very close by as well as our local craft and antique shops. Our guests are all treated as part of the family, which is what makes a real difference.

Hosts: Gregory and Nancy Diaz
Rooms: 6 (4PB; 2SB) $60-89
Full Breakfast
Credit Cards: A, B, C
Notes: 2, 5, 7 (over 8), 8, 9, 10, 11, 12

Silas Griffith Inn
R.R. 1, Box 66F, 05739
(802) 293-5567; (800) 545-1509

Built by Vermont's first millionaire, this Victorian inn was built in 1891 in the heart of the Green Mountains, with a spectacular mountain view. It features 17 delightful, antique-furnished rooms and a fireplace in the living and dining room. Hiking, skiing, and antiquing nearby. Come and enjoy our elegant meals and New England hospitality.

Hosts: Paul and Lois Dansereau
Rooms: 17 (14PB; 3SB) $72-90
Full Breakfast
Credit Cards: A, B
Notes: 2, 4, 5, 7, 9, 10, 11, 12

Silas Griffith Inn

---

5 Open all year; 6 Pets welcome; 7 Children welcome; 8 Tennis nearby; 9 Swimming nearby; 10 Golf nearby; 11 Skiing nearby; 12 May be booked through travel agent.

DERBY LINE

Derby Village Inn

46 Main Street, 05830
(802) 873-3604

Enjoy this charming, old, Victorian mansion situated in the quiet village of Derby Line, within walking distance of the Canadian border and the world's only international library and opera house. The nearby countryside offers year-round recreation: downhill and cross-country skiing, water sports, cycling, fishing, hiking, golf, snowmobiling, sleigh rides, antiquing, and most of all peace and tranquillity. We are a non-smoking facility.

Hosts: Tom and Phyllis Moreau
Rooms: 5 (PB) $55-65
Full Breakfast
Credit Cards: A, B, D
Notes: 2, 5, 7, 8, 9, 10, 11

DORSET

Marble West Inn

Dorset West Road, PO Box 847, 05251-0847
(802) 867-4155; (800) 453-7629

Off the busy main road with stunning mountain views, our informal yet elegant country inn will provide peace and serenity for you. Two trout ponds, with a brook running through them, add to the landscape of herb and flower gardens. Inside our 1840 Greek Revival Inn, you are greeted by delicately stenciled hallways, polished dark floors embellished with Oriental rugs, antiques, fireplaces, a grand piano, library, and comfortable sitting areas.

Hosts: June and Wayne Erla
Rooms: 8 (PB) $90-145
Full Breakfast
Credit Cards: A, B, C
Notes: 2, 5, 8, 9, 10, 11, 12

EAST DOVER

Cooper Hill Inn

PO Box 146, 05341
(802) 348-6333; (800) 783-3229

Set high on a hill in Southern Vermont's Green Mountains Cooper Hill Inn commands a view to the east proclaimed by the *Boston Globe* as "one of the most spectacular mountain panoramas in all New England." A small portion of the Inn was a farmhouse built in 1797. The Inn has ten rooms, all with private bath. The atmosphere is always homey and informal. Country breakfast included in rate. Families welcome.

Hosts: Pat and Marilyn Hunt
Rooms: 10 (PB) $68-110
Full Breakfast
Credit Cards: A, B, D
Notes: 2, 4, 5, 7, 8, 9, 10, 11, 12

Cooper Hill Inn

NOTES: Credit cards accepted: A Master Card; B Visa; C American Express; D Discover; E Diners Club; F Other; 2 Personal checks accepted; 3 Lunch available; 4 Dinner available;

FAIR HAVEN

Maplewood Inn

Route 22A South, 05743
(802) 265-8039; (800) 253-7729;
FAX (802) 265-8210

Rediscover romance in this exquisite, Historic Register Greek Revival. Elegant rooms and suites boast antiques, fireplaces, A/C, color cable TVs, radios, optional phone, and turn-down service. Keeping Room with fireplace, Gathering Room with library, Parlor with games and complimentary cordials. Hot beverages and snacks anytime. Bikes available; pet boarding arranged. Near lakes, skiing, dining, and attractions. Awarded 3 Diamonds by AAA, 3 Stars by Mobil, and 3 Crowns by AB&BA. Recommended by over 25 guidebooks. A true four-season experience!

Hosts: Doug and Cindy Baird
Rooms: 5 (PB) $75-115
Continental Plus Breakfast
Credit Cards: A, B, C, D, E, F
Notes: 2, 5, 7 (over 5), 8, 9, 10, 11, 12

FAIRLEE

Silver Maple Lodge and Cottages

R.R. 1, Box 8, 05045
(802) 333-4326; (800) 666-1946

A historic bed and breakfast country inn is located in a four-season recreational area. Enjoy canoeing, fishing, golf, tennis, and skiing within a few miles of the lodge. Visit nearby flea markets and country auctions. Choose a newly renovated room in our antique farmhouse or a handsome, pine-paneled cottage room. Three cottages with working fireplaces. Many fine restaurants are nearby. Darmouth College is 17 miles away. Also offered are hot air balloon packages, inn-to-inn bicycling, canoeing, and walking tours. Brochures available.

Hosts: Scott and Sharon Wright
Rooms: 16 (14PB; 2SB) $52-76
Continental Breakfast
Credit Cards: A, B, C, D
Notes: 2, 5, 6 (in cottages), 7, 8, 9, 10, 11, 12

The Peak Chalet

KILLINGTON

The Peak Chalet

PO Box 511, South View Path, 05751
(802) 422-4278

The Peak Chalet is a four room B&B located within the beautiful Green Mountains. The exterior is authentically European alpine. The interior is furnished with a fine country inn flavor and reflects high quality with attention to detail. We offer panoramic mountain views with a cozy stone fireplace to unwind by. All rooms have queen-size beds and private baths. Centrally lo-

---

5 Open all year; 6 Pets welcome; 7 Children welcome; 8 Tennis nearby; 9 Swimming nearby; 10 Golf nearby; 11 Skiing nearby; 12 May be booked through travel agent.

cated within Killington Ski Resort, this is a truly relaxing experience.

Hosts: Gregory and Diane Becker
Rooms: 4 (PB) $50-110
Continental Breakfast
Credit Cards: A, B, C, E
Notes: 2, 5, 7 (over 12), 8, 9, 10, 11, 12

LONDONBERRY

Blue Gentian Lodge (Koinonia of Vermont)

R.R. 1 Box 29, 05148
(802) 824-5908; (800) 456-2405;
FAX (802) 824-3531

A special place to stay, nestled at the foot of Magic Mountain — all rooms have private baths, cable color TV, and include a full breakfast in the dining room. Seasonal activities on the grounds, a swimming pool, and walking trails. Recreation Room offers ping pong, bumper pool, board games, and library. There is golf, tennis, fishing, outlet shopping, antiquing, horseback riding, and skiing (downhill and cross-country) nearby.

Hosts: The Alberti Family
Rooms: 13 (PB) $50-80
Full Breakfast
Credit Cards: none
Notes: 2, 4, 5, 7, 8, 9, 10, 11

LOWER WATERFORD

Rabbit Hill Inn

Box 55, Route 18, 05848
(802) 748-5168; (800) 76-BUNNY;
FAX (802) 748-8342

Full of whimsical and charming surprises, this Federal-period inn, estab-

lished in 1795, has been lavished with love and attention. Many guest rooms have fireplaces and canopied beds. Chamber music, candlelit gourmet dining, and turn-down service make this an enchanting and romantic hideaway in a tiny, restore village overlooking the mountains. Award-winning, nationally acclaimed inn—4 Star by Mobil and 4 Diamonds by AAA. Our service is inspired by Philippians 2:7.

Hosts: John and Maureen Magee
Rooms: 21 (PB) $139-219
Full Breakfast
Credit Cards: A, B, C
Closed first two weeks of Nov. and all of April
Notes: 2, 3 (picnic), 4, 8, 9 (on-site), 10, 11 (on-site), 12

The Middlebury Inn

MIDDLEBURY

The Middlebury Inn

14 Courthouse Square, 05753
(802) 388-4961; (800) 842-4666;
FAX (802) 388-4563

This 1827, historic, 75-room landmark overlooks the village green in a picturesque New England college town. Discover Middlebury, Vermont — the splendor of its historic district — Vermont State Craft Center, Middlebury

NOTES: Credit cards accepted: A Master Card; B Visa; C American Express; D Discover; E Diners Club; F Other; 2 Personal checks accepted; 3 Lunch available; 4 Dinner available;

College, boutique shopping, and four season recreation. Elegantly restored rooms, private bath, telephone, color TV, and air-conditioning (in season). The Inn offers breakfast, lunch, dinner, seasonal porch dining, afternoon tea, and Sunday brunch. Recommended by AAA and a member of Historic Hotels of America.

Hosts: Jane and Frank Emanuel, Innkeepers
Rooms: 75 (PB) $86-200 per room, per night (double occupancy)
Full and Continental Breakfast (not included in rate but can be added)
Credit Cards: A, B, C, E
Notes: 3, 4, 5, 6 (limited), 7, 8, 9, 10, 11, 12

PITTSFIELD

Swiss Farm Lodge

PO Box 630, Route 100, 05762
(802) 746-8341; (800) 245-5126

Working Hereford beef farm. Enjoy the casual, family-type atmosphere in our living room with fireplace and TV or in the game room. Home-cooked meals and baking served family style. Our own maple syrup, jams, and jellies. Walk-in cooler available for guests' use. Cross-country trails on site. B&B available all year. M.A.P provided November to April only. Mountain bike trails close by. Owned and operated by the same family for 50 years. Lower rates for children in same room as parents.

Hosts: Mark and Sandy Begin
Rooms: 17 (14PB; 3SB) $50-60
Full Breakfast
Credit Cards: A, B, D
Notes: 2, 4, 5, 7, 8, 9, 10, 11, 12

ROCHESTER

Liberty Hill Farm

R.R. 1 Box 158, Liberty Hill Road, 05767
(802) 767-3926

Come enjoy exploring our award-winning dairy farm in the Green Mountains. Families are welcome to share in the barn chores. Excellent home-cooked meals are served family style in our 1825 farmhouse. Hiking, fishing, swimming, skiing, horseback riding, and golf available. Refresh and restore your spirit and become a member of our "*family.*"

Hosts: Bob and Beth Kennett
Rooms: 7 (SB) $100-120
Full Breakfast and Dinner
Credit Cards: none
Notes: 2, 4, 5, 7, 8, 9, 10, 11, 12

Liberty Hill Farm

RUTLAND

The Inn at Rutland

70 N. Main Street, 05701
(802) 773-0575; (800) 808-0575;
FAX (802) 775-3506

Beautifully restored 1890's Victorian mansion with ten large, comfortable

5 Open all year; 6 Pets welcome; 7 Children welcome; 8 Tennis nearby; 9 Swimming nearby; 10 Golf nearby; 11 Skiing nearby; 12 May be booked through travel agent.

The Inn at Rutland

rooms all with private baths, remote color cable TV, and phones. Some rooms have A/C. Gourmet breakfast included. Large front porch with beautiful views of mountains and valleys. Close to all central Vermont attractions. Common rooms with fireplaces, TV/VCR, and games. Carriage house for ski and bike storage. Ten minutes to Pico and Killington ski areas. Call our toll-free number.

Hosts: Bob and Tanya Liberman
Rooms: 10 (PB) $69-179
Full Breakfast
Credit Cards: A, B, D, E
Notes: 2, 5, 7 (over 8), 8, 9, 10, 11, 12

ST. JOHNSBURY

Sleepy Hollow Bed and Breakfast

RFD 2, Box 83, 05819
(802) 748-5185; (800) 213-8180

Mid-1800s, renovated farmhouse on ten acres. End-of-the-road privacy. Spacious deck overlooking our pond and sheep pasture. Enjoy a nature walk to the brook, or watch the deer grazing at dusk. Cozy up to the fireplace on a cool

evening in our formal parlor brimming with antiques, old photographs, and books. Have a restful night in one of our cozy, newly decorated bedrooms with private and shared baths. Full country breakfast included.

Hosts: Fred and Donna Keenan
Rooms: 3-4 (2PB; 2SB) $55-70
Full Breakfast
Credit Cards: A, B
Notes: 2, 5, 7, 8, 9, 10, 11, 12

Sleepy Hollow Bed and Breakfast

STOWE

Brass Lantern Inn

717 Maple Street, 05672
(802) 253-2229; (800) 729-2980;
FAX (802) 253-7425
Email: brasslatrn@aol.com

Award-winning traditional bed and breakfast inn, in the heart of Stowe, overlooking Mt. Mansfield, Vermont's most prominent mountain. The Inn features period antiques, hand made quilts local artisian wares and A/C. Most rooms have view, some have fireplaces and some have whirlpools. A hint of romance abounds in each room, an intimate Inn for romantics. Special packages include; honeymoon/anniversary, romance, skiing, golf, historic, and more. Non-smoking.

Host. Andy Aldrich
Rooms: 9 (PB) $80-185
Full Breakfast
Credit Cards: A, B, C
Notes: 2, 5, 8, 9, 10, 11, 12

The Siebeness Inn

3681 Mountain Road, 05672
(802) 253-8942; (800) 426-9001;
FAX (802) 253-9232

A warm welcome awaits you at our charming country inn nestled in the foothills of Mt. Mansfield. Romantic rooms have country antiques, private baths, and air-conditioning. Awake to the aroma of freshly baked muffins, which accompany your hearty New England breakfast. Relax in our outdoor hot tub in winter or our pool with mountain views in summer. Fireplace in lounge. Bike, walk, or cross-country ski from the Inn on a recreation path. Honeymoon, golf, and ski packages.

Hosts: Sue and Nils Andersen
Rooms: 11 (PB) $65-140
Full Breakfast
Credit Cards: A, B, C, D
Notes: 2, 4 (winter), 5, 7, 8, 9, 10, 11, 12

Ski Inn

Route 108, 05672
(802) 253-4050

In appearance the Ski Inn is a traditionally old New England inn, but comfortably modern. Built and operated by the Heyer family, original owners. Rooms are large and colorful with both a double and single bed. Located back from the traveled road, it is a quiet place to relax and enjoy. In winter, a skier's delight,

the Inn is close to Mt. Mansfield's downhill trails, with miles of cross-country trails at our back door.

Hostess: Mrs. Larry Heyer
Rooms: 10 (5PB; 5SB) $45-55
Continental Breakfast
Credit Cards: C
Notes: 2, 4 (winter), 5, 6 (advance notice), 7, 8, 9, 10, 11

The Trillium

PO Box 522, 05672
(802) 253-9577

Stowe, Vermont! Magnificent four-story, white Southern Colonial with walls of glass looking into the face of Mt. Mansfield, Vermont's highest peak. Serene, deer-inhabited woodlands. Four bedrooms, four baths, jacuzzi, master whirlpool, fireplace, and decks everywhere. Stunning interior. Cascading book. Incredible views. Extraordinary fall foliage, antiquing, golf, tennis, hiking, biking, splendorous lakes, horse and buggy rides, four-star restaurants, and shopping.

Hosts: Janis and Parker Diamond
Rooms: 4 (PB) $85-135 (foliage rates)
Continental Breakfast
Credit Cards: A, B
Notes: 5, 6 (some), 7, 8, 9, 10, 11, 12

The Trillium

---

5 Open all year; 6 Pets welcome; 7 Children welcome; 8 Tennis nearby; 9 Swimming nearby; 10 Golf nearby; 11 Skiing nearby; 12 May be booked through travel agent.

VERGENNES

Strong House Inn

82 West Main Street, 05491
(802) 877-3337; FAX (802) 877-2599

Experience elegant lodging in a grand 1834 Federal home listed on the National Register of Historic Places. Located in the heart of the Champlain Valley, the area provides superb cycling, hiking, antique shopping, and nearby Shelburne Museum. The fully air-conditioned inn situated on six acres with walking trails and gardens, offers eight rooms, two suites, three working fireplaces, and a full country breakfast.

Hosts: Mary and Hugh Bargiel
Rooms: 8 (PB) $75-165
Full Breakfast
Credit Cards: A, B, C
Notes: 2, 4, 5, 9, 10, 11, 12

WAITSFIELD

1824 House Inn

Route 100, Box 159, 05673
(802) 496-7555; (800) 426-3986;
FAX (802) 496-7559

Enjoy relaxed elegance in one of seven beautiful guest rooms at this quintessential farmhouse on 23 acres. The Inn features antiques, original art, fireplaces, and classical music. Breakfast by the fire includes such whimsical gourmet delights as soufflés, crepes, blueberry buttermilk pancakes, and freshly squeezed orange juice. Cross-country skiing and private river swimming are nearby. Featured in *Glamour* and *Vermont Life*. National Historic Registered. AAA three-diamond and Mobile three-star rated.

Hosts: Susan and Lawrence McKay
Rooms: 7 (PB) $90-135
Full Breakfast
Credit Cards: A, B, C, D
Notes: 2, 5, 8, 9, 10, 11, 12

Mad River Inn

PO Box 75, 05673
(802) 496-7900; (800) 832-8278;
FAX (802) 496-5390

Romantic 1860s country Victorian inn along Mad River. Elegant but comfortable. Picturesque mountain views, flower-filled porches, gardens, and gazebo. Ten guest rooms, feather beds, private baths, jacuzzi, BYOB lounge, and billards. Gourmet breakfast and afternoon tea. Recreation path and swimming along the river. Horseback riding, golf, tennis, Sugarbush and Mad River Glen Ski Resorts, Ben & Jerry's, and Cold Hollow cider mill nearby. Weddings and groups welcome.

Host: Luc Maranda
Rooms: 10 (PB) $69-125
Full Gourmet Breakfast and afternoon tea
Credit Cards: A, B, C
Notes: 2, 5, 7, 8, 9, 10, 11, 12

Mad River Inn

NOTES: Credit cards accepted: A Master Card; B Visa; C American Express; D Discover; E Diners Club; F Other; 2 Personal checks accepted; 3 Lunch available; 4 Dinner available;

Mountain View Inn

RD 1, Box 69, 05673
(802) 496-2426

The Mountain View Inn is an old farmhouse, circa 1826, that was made into a lodge in 1948 to accommodate skiers at nearby Mad River Glen. Today it is a country inn with seven rooms. Meals are served family style around the antique harvest table where good fellowship prevails. Sip mulled cider around a crackling fire in our living room when the weather turns chilly.

Hosts: Fred and Susan Spencer
Rooms: 7 (PB) $35-65 per person
Full Breakfast
Credit Cards: none
Notes: 2, 5, 7, 8, 9, 10, 11, 12

I. B. Munson House B&B Inn

WALLINGFORD

I. B. Munson House B&B Inn

7 S. Main Street, PO Box 427, 05773
(802) 446-2860; FAX (802) 446-3336

The I. B. Munson House is an 1856 Italianate Victorian that was totally and lovingly restored in 1992. High ceilings, beautiful chandaliers, and five opera-

tional, wood-burning fireplaces. Guest rooms and common rooms finely decorated and furnished with comfortable period antiques and fine art. Grounds and gardens expertly maintianed. Off-street parking. Located in a quaint, historic village. Boyhood home of Paul Harris, founder of Rotary International.

Hosts: Phillip and Karen Pimental
Rooms: 7 (PB) $85-145
Full Gourmet Breakfast
Credit Cards: A, B, C, D
Notes: 2, 5, 7 (12 and over), 8, 9, 10, 11, 12

WARREN

Beaver Pond Farm Inn

Golf Course Road, R.D. Box 306, 05674
(802) 583-2861; FAX (802) 583-2860

Beaver Pond Farm Inn, a small gracious country inn near the Sugarbush ski area, is located 100 yards from the first tee of the Sugarbush Golf Course, transformed into 25 kilometers of cross-country ski trails in the winter. *Bed and Breakfast in New England* calls it "The best of the best." Rooms have down comforters and beautiful views. Hearty breakfasts are served, and snacks are enjoyed by the fireplace. Continental dinners are offered three times a week during the winter. Hiking, biking, soaring, and fishing nearby. Bob will take guests out for fly fishing instruction. Ski and golf packages are available.

Hosts: Bob and Betty Hansen
Rooms: 6 (4PB; 2SB) $72-96
Full Breakfast
Credit Cards: A, B, C
Notes: 2, 4 (3 times a week), 7 (over 6), 8, 9, 10, 11, 12

---

5 Open all year; 6 Pets welcome; 7 Children welcome; 8 Tennis nearby; 9 Swimming nearby; 10 Golf nearby; 11 Skiing nearby; 12 May be booked through travel agent.

WATERBURY

Grünberg Haus Bed and Breakfast and Cabins

R.R. 2, Box 1595 CB, Route 100 S., 05676-9621
(802) 244-7726; (800) 800-7760
Email: grunhaus@aol.com

Handbuilt Austrian inn offering romantic guestrooms (each with balcony, antiques, comforters, and quilts), secluded cabins (each with fireplace and mountain-view deck) and a carriage house suite (with skywindow, kitchen, sitting area, and two balconies). Central location is close to Stowe, Burlington, Sugarbush, and Montpelier. All accommodations include full, musical breakfast. Enjoy our jacuzzi, sauna, BYOB pub, fireplaces, tennis court, and groomed cross-country ski trails. Help Mark feed the chickens.

Hosts: Chris Sellers and Mark Frohman
Rooms: 15 (10PB; 5SB) $55-140
Full Musical Breakfast
Credit Cards: A, B, C, D
Notes: 2, 5, 7, 8, 9, 10, 11, 12

Inn at Blush Hill

R.R. 1 Box 1266, 05676
(802) 244-7529; (800) 736-7522;
FAX (802) 244-7314
Email: innatbh@aol.com

Inn at Blush Hill Bed and Breakfast, circa 1790, sits on five acres, high on a hilltop, with unsurpassed views of the mountains. Choose from five individually decorated guest rooms with private baths and featuring Colonial antiques, canopy beds, down comforters, and a fireplace or jacuzzi tub. The large common rooms are spacious and warm, filled with books, antiques, and fireplaces. A full breakfast, featuring many Vermont specialty food products, is served by the garden in summer and fireside in winter. The Inn is located "back to back" to Ben and Jerry's ice cream factory, and the skiing at Stowe and Sugarbush is only minutes away. AAA and Mobil rated.

Hosts: Gary and Pamela Gosselin
Rooms: 5 (PB) $59-130
Full Breakfast
Credit Cards: A, B, C, D
Notes: 2, 5, 7 (over 6), 8, 9, 10, 11, 12

WESTON

The Wilder Homestead Inn

25 Lawrence Hill Road, 05161
(802) 824-8172; (800) 771-8172;
FAX (802) 824-5054

Built in 1827 with Rumford fireplaces and original Moses Eaton stenciling, the Inn has been carefully restored by us and has quiet surroundings and antique furnishings. Walk to village shops, museums, and summer theater. Nearby are Weston Priory, fine restaurants, and skiing. Weston is a village that takes you back in time. Craft Shoppe on premises. No smoking.

Hosts: Peg and Roy Varner
Rooms: 7 (5PB; 2SB) $65-110
Full Breakfast
Credit Cards: A, B (deposit only)
Notes: 2, 7 (over 6), 8, 9, 10, 11, 12 (no fee paid)

NOTES: Credit cards accepted: A Master Card; B Visa; C American Express; D Discover; E Diners Club, F Other; 2 Personal checks accepted; 3 Lunch available; 4 Dinner available;

WILMINGTON

Shearer Hill Farm B&B

PO Box 1453, 05363
(802) 464-3253; (800) 437-3104

Pristine farm setting on country road, large rooms (king, queen, twin), private baths, and delicious Vermont breakfast. Cross-country trails on property. Near downhill skiing, shopping, swimming, fishing, and horseback riding. Only 210 miles from New York, 120 miles from Boston, 90 miles from Hartland, and 70 miles from Albany. Handicap accessible.

Hosts: Bill and Patti Pusey
Rooms: 6 (PB) $80 + tax
Full Vermont Breakfast
Credit Cards: A, B, C, D
Notes: 2 (preferred), 5, 8, 9, 10, 12

Canterbury House

WOODSTOCK

Canterbury House Bed and Breakfast

43 Pleasant Street, 05091
(802) 457-3077; (800) 390-3077

115 year-old Victorian town house is just a stroll to the village green and fine dining. The Inn is beautifully decorated with era antiques and is for the discriminating traveler. The Inn has won awards from *Yankee* magazine and the American B&B Association, and it is recommended as the best value in town by *Glamour* magazine. Each room is decorated to a different theme. 10% discount for three or more days, except Sept. 15 through Oct. 22. No smoking.

Hosts: Celeste and Fred Holden
Rooms: 8 (PB) $85-150
Full Gourmet Breakfast
Credit Cards: A, B, C
Notes: 2, 5, 7 (over 7), 8, 9, 10, 11, 12

The Maple Leaf Inn

PO Box 273, **Barnard** 05031
(802) 234-5342; (800) 51-MAPLE

The Maple Leaf Inn is an elegant Victorian-style inn resplendent with its gables, dormers, wraparound porch, gazebo, gingerbread trim, and soaring chimneys nestled within sixteen acres of maple and birch trees. Most of our guest rooms have king-size beds, wood-burning fireplaces, phone, TV/VCR, and whirlpool tubs. Stenciling, stitchery, and handmade quilts blend with antique and reproduction furnishings to give each guest room a warm and welcoming individuality. The aroma of our gourmet breakfast will entice you to our dining room for breakfast where your candlelit table awaits.

Hosts: Gary and Janet Robison
Rooms: 7 (PB) $100-160
Full Breakfast
Credit Cards: A, B, C, D, E, F (JCB)
Notes: 2, 4, 5, 8, 9, 10, 11, 12

---

5 Open all year; 6 Pets welcome; 7 Children welcome; 8 Tennis nearby; 9 Swimming nearby;
10 Golf nearby; 11 Skiing nearby; 12 May be booked through travel agent.

VIRGINIA

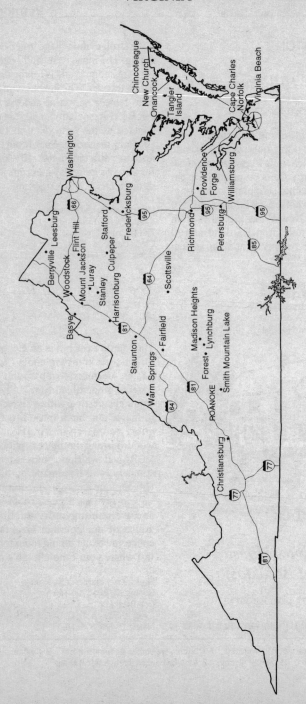

Virginia

ALSO SEE LISTINGS UNDER DISTRICT OF COLUMBIA.

Sky Chalet Mountain Lodge

BASYE

Sky Chalet Mountain Lodge

PO Box 300, Rt. 263, 280 Sky Chalet Lane, 22810
(540) 856-2147; FAX (540) 856-2436

A romantic hideaway in the Shenandoah Valley with unchallenged, spectacular, breathtaking, panoramic mountian and valley views. Rustic lodge open all year. Accommodations are simple, clean, and comfortable. Individual rooms with private baths. Also, the "Treetop" cabin with private baths, living rooms, fireplaces, decks, and rocking chairs. Continental breakfast is delivered to your room or cabin. Restaurant and pub with fireplaces, verandas, and views. Tranquility and nature abound. Hiking, amenities, and attractions nearby. "The Mountain Lovers' Paradise" since 1937.

Hosts: Ken and Mona Sky
Rooms: 10 (PB) $34-79
Continental Breakfast
Credit Cards: A, B, D, E
Notes: 2, 4, 5, 6 (with notice), 7, 8, 9, 10, 11, 12

BERRYVILLE

Blue Ridge B&B Reservation Service

Rocks and Rills Farm, Rt. 2, Box 3895, 22611
(703) 955-1246; (800) 296-1246;
FAX (540) 955-4240

Beautiful antique-filled Colonial Williamsburg reproduction nestled in the foothills of the Blue Ridge Mountains, near the Shenandoah River on eleven acres of fragrant Christmas trees. Perfect getaway; ideal for weekend bikers and hikers. Only 90 minutes from Washington, DC. Also a reservation

---

NOTES: Credit cards accepted: A Master Card; B Visa; C American Express; D Discover; E Diners Club; F Other; 2 Personal checks accepted; 3 Lunch available; 4 Dinner available; 5 Open all year; 6 Pets welcome; 7 Children welcome; 8 Tennis nearby; 9 Swimming nearby; 10 Golf nearby; 11 Skiing nearby; 12 May be booked through travel agent.

service for numerous host homes.

Hostess: Rita Z. Duncan
Rooms: Numerous (most all PB) $50-150
Full Breakfast
Credit Cards: A, B
Notes: 2, 3 and 4 (some, w/reservations), 5, 6, 7, 8, 9, 10, 11, 12

CAPE CHARLES

Sea Gate

9 Tazewell Avenue, 23310
(757) 331-2206

Located in the quiet and sleepy town of Cape Charles, just steps from Chesapeake Bay, on Virginia's undiscovered eastern shore. My home is your home! Day begins with a full breakfast followed by leisure or hiking, birding, bathing, and exploring our historic area. Tea prepares you for the most glorious sunsets on the east coast. Sea Gate is the perfect place to rest, relax and recharge away from the crush of modern America.

Host: Chris Bannon
Rooms: 4 (2PB, 2 shared shower) $75-85 (winter 2 nights $100)
Full Breakfast
Credit Cards: none
Notes: 2, 5, 7 (over 7), 8, 9, 10, 12

Sea Gate

CHINCOTEAGUE

Garden and The Sea Inn and Restaurant

PO Box 275, **New Church** 23415
(804) 824-0672; (800) 824-0672

Casual elegance and warm hospitality await you at this European-style country inn with its romantic, candlelight, fine dining restaurant. Near Chincoteague wildlife refuge and Assateague Island's beautiful beach. Large, luxurious guest rooms, beautifully designed; spacious private baths, some with whirlpools; Victorian detail and stained glass; Oriental rugs; antiques; bay windows; and patios and gardens. Mobil three-star; AAA three diamond. Open April 1- November 26.

Hosts: Tom and Sara Baker
Rooms: 6 (PB) $75-155
Expanded Continental Breakfast
Credit Cards: A, B, C, D
Notes: 2, 3, 4, 6, 7, 8, 9, 10, 12

The Watson House Bed and Breakfast

4240 Main Street, 23336
(804) 336-1564; (800) 336-6787;
FAX (804) 336-5776

The Watson House has been tastefully restored with Victorian charm. Nestled in the heart of Chincoteague, the House is within walking distance of shops and restaurants. Each guest room includes antiques, private bath, and air-conditioning. A full, hearty breakfast and afternoon tea are served in the dining room or on the verandah. Enjoy free use of bicycles to tour the Chincoteague

---

NOTES: Credit cards accepted: A Master Card; B Visa; C American Express; D Discover; E Diners Club; F Other; 2 Personal checks accepted; 3 Lunch available; 4 Dinner available;

The Watson House

National Wildlife Refuge and Beach. AAA—3 diamonds.

Hosts: Tom and Jacque Derrickson, and David and Joanne Snead
Rooms: 6 (PB) $65-115
Full Breakfast plus Afternoon Tea
Credit Cards: A, B
Notes: 2, 7 (over 9), 8, 9, 10

CHRISTIANSBURG

EVERGREEN—The Bell-Capozzi House

201 E. Main Street, 24073
(540) 382-7372; (800) 905-7372;
FAX (540) 382-4376

Victorian Mansion (circa 1890's) on routes I-81, 11, 460, bike Route 76, Wilderness Road, and in the historic district. Amenities include central air-conditioning, fireplaces, swimming pool, art gallery, wisteria covered arbor, gazebo, rockers on wraparound porches, and tea time from 5-6PM. A non-smoking inn.

Hosts: Rocco and Barbara Bell-Capozzi
Rooms: 5 (PB) $75-125
Full, Southern-Style Breakfast
Credit Cards: A, B, C, D, F
Notes: 2, 5, 8, 9, 10, 12

CULPEPER

Fountain Hall

609 S. East Street, 22701
(540) 825-8200; (800) 29-VISIT;
FAX (540) 825-7716

This grad 1859 Colonial Revival structure features tastefully restored and decorated rooms. Some with private porche, whirlpool, or sitting room. Common rooms available for reading, relaxing, TV, and friendly conversation. Complimentary beverages. The grounds are highlighted with flower gardens, stately trees, and mature boxwoods. Enjoy a walk to the quaint historic district; visit antique and gift shops, restaurants, new and used book stores, museum, and more. Conveniently located one mile from Hwy. 29, between Charlottesville; Washington, DC; Richmond; and Blue Ridge Mountains.

Hosts: Steve, Kathi, and Leah-Marie Walker
Rooms: 5 (PB) $85-125
Expanded Continental Breakfast
Credit Cards: A, B, C, D, E, F
Notes: 2, 5, 7, 8, 10, 12

FAIRFIELD

Angels Rest Farm

471 Sunnybrook Road, 24435
(540) 377-6449

Angels Rest Farm is located in the beautiful Shenandoah valley just eight miles north of Lexington, VA. Lexington is home to the Virginia Military Institute and Washington and Lee University as well as a number of historic landmarks and museums. Our home, located on a

---

5 Open all year; 6 Pets welcome; 7 Children welcome; 8 Tennis nearby; 9 Swimming nearby; 10 Golf nearby; 11 Skiing nearby; 12 May be booked through travel agent.

country road, is nestled in a quiet valley surrounded by green pastures with grazing cattle and horses nearby. The pond provides good fishing and a reflected view of the woods as you enjoy the view from either of the porches. A swimming pool is available in summer and hot tub is available year round.

Hosts: John and Carol Nothwang
Rooms: 2 (PB) $55-65
Continental Breakfast
Credit Cards: none
Notes: 2, 5, 9, 11

FOREST

The Summer Kitchen at West Manor

Route 4, Box 538, 24551
(804) 525-0923

Come enjoy a romantic English country cottage located on a beautiful working dairy farm. This private restored summer kitchen, circa 1840, sleeps four with fireplace, loft, sunroom, and jacuzzi. Enjoy a full country breakfast while overlooking 600 acres of rolling cropland, pastures, cattle, and mountains. Afternoon tea and strolls through the gardens complete each day. Come escape to our country haven. Area interests include Thomas Jefferson's Poplar Forest, antique shops, and the Blue Ridge Mountains.

Hosts: Sharon and Greg Lester
Cottage: 1; sleeps four (PB) $115
Full Breakfast
Credit Cards: none
Notes: 2, 5, 7, 10

FREDERICKSBURG

Fredericksburg Colonial Inn

1707 Princess Anne Street, 22401
(540) 371-5666; FAX (540) 371-5697

A restored country inn in the historic district has 32 antique-appointed lodging rooms-private baths, phones, TV, refrigerator, and Civil War motif. Complimentary Continental breakfast, suites, and family rooms available. Wonderful restaurants within walking distance. Beautiful churches nearby! Over 200 antique dealers, 20 major tourist attractions, and battlefields — A Great Getaway! Less than one hour from Washington, D.C. and Richmond, VA. Open year round! AARP welcomed; special group rates upon request! Call for more information. **Mention this ad for a 20% discount!**

Hosts: Mr. Jim Crisp and Mrs. Patsy Nunnally
Rooms: 32 (PB) $45-65
Continental Breakfast
Credit Cards: A, B, C
Notes: 2, 5, 7, 10

La Vista Plantation

4420 Guinea Station Road, 22408
(540) 898-8444; (800) 529-2823;
FAX (540) 898-9414

1838 Classical Revival country home nestled admist ancient tulip poplars, cedars, and hollies, and surrounded by pastures, woods, and fields. The house retains its original charm, with intricate acorn and oak leaf moldings, high ceilings, wide pine floors, and two-story front portico. Guests may choose a spa-

---

NOTES: Credit cards accepted: A Master Card; B Visa; C American Express; D Discover; E Diners Club; F Other; 2 Personal checks accepted; 3 Lunch available; 4 Dinner available;

cious two-bedroom apartment (sleeps six) or a huge formal room with mahogany, rice-carved, king-size, poster bed. Both have A/C, fireplaces, TV, radio, and refrigerator. Brown egg breakfast and stocked pond.

Hosts: Edward and Michele Schiesser
Rooms: 1 + 1 two-bedroom apartment (PB) $95
Full Breakfast
Credit Cards: A, B
Notes: 2, 5, 7, 8, 10, 12

La Vista Plantation

HARRISONBURG

Kingsway Bed and Breakfast

3581 Singers Glen Road, 22801
(540) 867-9696

Enjoy the warm hospitality of your hosts who make your comfort their priority. This private home is in a quiet rural area with a view of the mountains in the beautiful Shenandoah Valley. Hosts' carpentry and homemaking skills, many house plants and outdoor flowers, a large lawn, and the in ground pool help to make your stay restful and refreshing. Just four and one-half miles from downtown; nearby is Skyline Drive, caverns, historic sites, antique shops, and flea markets.

Hosts: Chester and Verna Leaman
Rooms: 2 (PB) $55-60
Full Breakfast
Credit Cards: none
Notes: 2, 5, 7, 9, 10, 12

LEESBURG

Leesburg Colonial Inn

19 South King Street, 22075
(703) 777-5000; (800) 392-1332;
FAX (703) 777-7000

The Leesburg Colonial Inn has well appointed rooms, all in the 18th Century decor, but with all the modern amenities (cable TV, phone, and private bath) a true gourmet breakfast is served as part of the package while staying at the Inn. Some of our rooms have fireplace as well as whirlpool; all rooms have grand period pieces such as rustic farm dresser, fine Persian and Oriental rugs, and queen-size poster bed. The Inn is conveniently located in the center of Historic Leesburg, among many antique shops, where you can find the charm of early Virginia. Our chef can delight the most discriminate palate with his award-winning cuisine. We have conference rooms available; we can cater for two as well as hundred persons. We are surrounded by Virginia's hunt country, yet only 30 minutes from Washington, DC, and 15 minutes from Dulles International Airport.

Host: Mr. Fabian E. Saeidi
Rooms: 10 (PB) $68-150 honeymoon suite
Full Gourmet Breakfast
Credit Cards: A, B, C, D, E, F
Notes: 2, 3, 4, 5, 7, 8, 9, 10, 11, 12

---

5 Open all year; 6 Pets welcome; 7 Children welcome; 8 Tennis nearby; 9 Swimming nearby; 10 Golf nearby; 11 Skiing nearby; 12 May be booked through travel agent.

LURAY

Shenandoah River Roost

4136 US Hwy. 211 W., 22835
(540) 743-3467

Sit on the front porch of the two-story log home and enjoy beautiful views of the mountians and the Shenandoah River. Located three miles west of Luray Caverns and ten miles west of Skyline Drive and Shenandoah National park. Swimming, tubing, canoeing, and golf are all nearby. No smoking. Two bedroom, fully furnished, mobile home, also available and great for two couples or fishermen (two night minimum).

Hosts: Gerry and Ruben McNab
Rooms: 2 (SB) $70 + tax; mobile home $110
Full Breakfast
Credit Cards: none
Notes: 2, 9, 10

LYNCHBURG

Federal Crest Inn Bed and Breakfast

1101 Federal Street, 24504
(804) 845-6155; (800) 818-6155;
FAX (804) 845-1445

A warm and relaxing atmosphere awaits every guest at this elegant 1909 Georgian Revival mansion in the Federal Hill Historic District. Magnificent woodwork and architectural details. Amenties include queen canopy beds, whirlpool tub, bedroom fireplaces, A/C, luxury linens and robes, arrival refreshments, full country breakfast, gift shop, and much more! Convenient to all area colleges, Appomattox, golf, vineyards, antiquing, and museums.

Hosts: Ann and Phil Ripley
Rooms: 4 + 1 suite (PB) $85-115
Full Breakfast
Credit Cards: A, B, C, D
Notes: 2, 3 + 4 (with notice), 5, 8, 9, 10, 11, 12

Federal Crest Inn

MADISON HEIGHTS

Winridge B&B

Route 1, Box 362, Winridge Drive, 24572
(804) 384-7220; FAX (804) 384-1399

Come, enjoy the warm family atmosphere in our grand country home. Stroll through the gardens where birds, butterflies, and flowers abound. Shade trees with swings and hammock. Relax on the large, inviting porches. Scenic mountain views. Hot, hearty breakfasts are served in the family dining room. Greenhouse features perennials, unusual annuals, and container gardening. Close to Blue Ridge Parkway, Lynchburg, Appomattox, and Poplar Forest.

Hosts: LoisAnn and Ed Pfister and Family
Rooms: 3 (1PB; 2SB) $69-85
Full Breakfast
Credit Cards: A, B
Notes: 2, 5, 7, 8, 9, 11, 12

NOTES: Credit cards accepted: A Master Card; B Visa; C American Express; D Discover; E Diners Club; F Other; 2 Personal checks accepted; 3 Lunch available; 4 Dinner available;

MT. JACKSON

Widow Kip's Country Inn
355 Orchard Drive, 22842
(540) 477-2400; (800) 478-8714

A stately 1830 Colonial on seven rural acres in the Shenandoah Valley overlooking the mountains. Friendly rooms filled with family photographs, bric-a-brac, and antiques. Each bedroom has a working fireplace and canopy, sleigh, or Lincoln bed. Two cozy cottages are also available. Pool on the premises. Nearby battlefields and caverns to explore, canoeing, hiking, or downhill skiing. Bicycles, picnics, and grill available.

Hostess: Betty Luse
Rooms: 5 + 2 courtyard cottages (PB) $65-85
Full Breakfast
Credit Cards: A, B
Notes: 2, 5, 6 and 7 (in cottages), 8, 9, 10, 11, 12

NORFOLK

Old Dominion Inn
4111 Hampton Boulevard, 23508
(757) 440-5100; (800) 653-9030;
FAX (757) 423-5238

Our sixty-room inn opened in 1989 and takes its name from the commonwealth of Virginia, "The Old Dominion." Located in the heart of Norfolk's west side, just one block south of the Old Dominion University Campus and only a short drive, up or down Hampton Boulevard, from many of the area's busiest facilities. Each Old Dominion Inn room gives you a remote-controled, color TV with cable service, ceiling fan, and individually controlled heat and air-conditioning. The James W. Sherrill family invites you to share in the warm hospitality of the Old Dominion Inn. As a family owned business, it is our desire that you will feel right at home when you stay with us. We treat our guests like part of "our family." Be our guest for a complimentary, light breakfast each morning of your stay.

Hosts: The Sherrill Family
Rooms: 60 (PB) $61-128
Expanded Continental Breakfast
Credit Cards: A, B, C, D, E
Notes: 5, 7, 12

ONANCOCK

The Spinning Wheel Bed and Breakfast
31 North Street, 23417
(804) 787-7311

This 1890's Folk Victorian home in the historic waterfront town of Onancock, on Virginia's Eastern Shore, has antiques and spinning wheels throughout. All guest rooms have queen beds, private baths, and air-conditioning. Guests can visit Kerr Place (1799 museum), cruise to Tangier Island from Onancock Wharf, and walk to restaurants. Bicycles, tennis, and golf are available. Chincoteague/Assateaque Island beach close by. A calm Eastern Shore getaway from D.C., Maryland, Virginia, Dela-

---

5 Open all year; 6 Pets welcome; 7 Children welcome; 8 Tennis nearby; 9 Swimming nearby; 10 Golf nearby; 11 Skiing nearby; 12 May be booked through travel agent.

ware, and New Jersey on the Chesapeake Bay, five miles from the Atlantic.

Hosts: David and Karen Tweedie
Rooms: 5 (PB) $75-95
Full Breakfast
Credit Cards: A, B
Notes: 2, 8, 9, 10, 12

PETERSBURG

The Owl and The Pussycat

405 High Street, 23803
(804) 733-0505; (888) 733-0505;
FAX (804) 862-0694
Email: owlcat@ctg.net
Web site: http://www.ctg.net/owlcat.htm

Enjoy a stay at a beautiful Queen Anne Victorian mansion near Old Towne. We have lovely, large bedrooms and offer a generous buffet breakfast. Only five minutes from Highways 85 and 95, but quiet and surrounded by a garden. We are near numerous Civil War sites and some splendid plantations. A "purrfect" place to stay on your travels!

Hosts: Juliette and John Swenson
Rooms: 5 (3PB; 2SB) $65-85
Full Breakfast
Credit Cards: A, B
Notes: 2, 6 ($20 deposit), 8, 10, 12

The Owl and The Pussycat

Jasmine Plantation Bed and Breakfast Inn

PROVIDENCE FORGE

Jasmine Plantation Bed and Breakfast Inn

4500 N. Courthouse Road, 23140
(804) 966-9836; (800) NEW-KENT

Restored 1750s farmhouse convenient to Williamsburg, Richmond, and the James River Plantations. Genuine hospitality, a historical setting, and rooms decorated in various period antiques await the visitor. Settled prior to 1683, guests are invited to walk the 47 acres and use their imagination as to what events have occurred here during its 300-year history. Located only 2.4 miles from I-64, the inn offers both convenience and seclusion. Fine dining located nearby.

Hosts: Joyce and Howard Vogt
Rooms: 6 (4PB; 2SB) $75-105
Full Breakfast
Credit Cards: A, B, C
Notes: 2, 5, 7 (over 12), 10, 12

NOTES: Credit cards accepted: A Master Card; B Visa; C American Express; D Discover; E Diners Club; F Other; 2 Personal checks accepted; 3 Lunch available; 4 Dinner available;

RICHMOND

The William Catlin House
2304 E. Broad Street, 23223
(804) 780-3746

Richmond's first and oldest bed and breakfast features antique, canopy poster beds and working fireplaces. A delicious, full breakfast is served in the elegant dining room. Built in 1845, this richly appointed home is in the Church Hill historic district and was featured in *Colonial Homes* and *Southern Living* magazines. Directly across from St. John's Church, where Patrick Henry gave his famous "Liberty or Death" speech. Just two minutes from I-95 and Route 64.

Hosts: Robert and Josie Martin
Rooms: 5 (3PB; 2SB) $95 includes all taxes
Full Breakfast
Credit Cards: A, B, D
Notes: 2, 5, 7 (over 12), 8, 10, 12

ROANOKE—SMITH MOUNTAIN LAKE

The Manor at Taylor's Store Bed and Breakfast Country Inn
Route 1, Box 533, **Smith Mountain Lake** 24184
(703) 721-3951; (800) 248-6267;
FAX (703) 721-5243

This historic 120-acre estate with an elegant manor house provides romantic accommodations in guest suites with fireplaces, antiques, canopied beds, and private porches; use of hot tub, billiards, exercise room, and guest kitchen; and many other amenities. A separate, three-bedroom, two-bath cottage is ideal for a family. Enjoy six private, springfed ponds for swimming, canoeing, fishing, and hiking. Full heart-healthy, gourmet breakfast is served in the dining room with panoramic views of the countryside.

Hosts: Lee and Mary Lynn Tucker
Rooms: 10 (8PB; 2SB) $85-185
Full Breakfast
Credit Cards: A, B
Notes: 2, 3, 4, 5, 7, 8, 9, 10, 11, 12

The Manor at Taylor's Store

SCOTTSVILLE

Deerfield Bed and Breakfast
Route 3, Box 573, 24590
(804) 286-6306; (800) 545-1744

Sophisticated, country getaway! Cassic B&B overlooks the peaceful James River Valley. Southern hospitality on 200-plus acres that are very private. Practice the vanishing art of "porch sitting" on our shady verandas. Explore

---

5 Open all year; 6 Pets welcome; 7 Children welcome; 8 Tennis nearby; 9 Swimming nearby; 10 Golf nearby; 11 Skiing nearby; 12 May be booked through travel agent.

the fields and meadows, observe the wildlife, and visit the historic river town of Scottsville. Nearby are Thomas Jefferson's Moniecello, James Monroe's Ash Lawn-Highland, UVA, Walton's Mountain Museum, and Fork Union Military Academy. Guests rarely need lunch after our full breakfast featuring Callie's homemade goodies.

Hosts: John and Callie Bowers
Rooms: 2 (PB) $95-125
Full Breakfast
Credit Cards: A, B, C
Notes: 2, 11

Renaissance Manor

STAFFORD

Renaissance Manor
2247 Courthouse Road, 22554
(540) 720-3785 (voice and FAX); (800) 720-3784

Designed after Mt. Vernon situated on a winding country road backing to woods. Gardens include gazebo, windmill, fountain, handmade brick patio, rose arbor with landscaping designed to flower in all seasons. Six bedrooms offer king canopied, queen sleigh, double, twin, or an antique nun's bed. Four bathrooms. "Gathering Room" offers fire-

place, piano, library, and music. Afternoon tea and in-room sherry is offered. Ten-foot ceilings, hardwood floors, antiques, and collectible furnishings. Local artists' work is displayed and for sale. Battlefields, vineyards, antique shops, outlet malls, museums, restaurants, beaches, and marina nearby. Four miles off I-95 (Exit 140) near Fredericksburg. One hour to Washington, DC, or Richmond.

Hostesses: Deneen Bernard and JoAnn Houser
  (mother and daughter team)
Rooms: 6 (4PB; 2SB) $55-150
Continental Breakfast
Credit Cards: A, B, C
Notes: 2, 5, 9, 10, 12

STANLEY

Jordan Hollow Farm Inn
326 Hawksbill Park Road, 22851
(540) 778-2285; FAX (540) 778-1759

Peace and serenity surround you at this 200 year old Colonial horse farm. Situated on 150 acres at the base of the Blue Ridge Mountains, the farm offers horseback riding and five miles of hiking trails. Near swimming, canoeing, and caves. Can accommodate retreats and groups. Enjoy genuine Southern hospitality in the Shenandoah Valley.

Hosts: Gail Kyle and Betsy Anderson
Rooms: 21 (PB) $110-140
Full Breakfast
Credit Cards: A, B, C, D, F
Notes: 2, 3, 4, 5, 6 (horses only), 7, 8, 9, 10, 11, 12

NOTES: Credit cards accepted: A Master Card; B Visa; C American Express; D Discover; E Diners Club; F Other; 2 Personal checks accepted; 3 Lunch available; 4 Dinner available;

Ashton Country House

STAUNTON

Ashton Country House

1205 Middlebrook Road, 24401
(540) 885-7819; (800) 296-7819

Ashton is a delightful blend of town and country. This 1860 Greek Revival home is located on 24 acres, yet one mile from the center of Staunton. There are five air-conditioned, comfortable, and attractive bedrooms, each with a private bath. Guests start each day with a hearty country breakfast. Afternoon tea is served in the grand living room or on any porch. Ashton Country House is the perfect place to soothe the spirit, share a weekend with friends, celebrate a special anniversary, or escape to the serenity of the countryside.

Hosts: Dorie and Vince Distefano
Rooms: 5 (PB) $90-125
Full Breakfast
Credit Cards: A, B
Notes: 2, 5, 7 (over 10), 8, 9, 10, 11, 12

Frederick House

28 N. New Street, 24401
(800) 334-5575

An historic town house hotel in the European tradition, Frederick House is located downtown in the oldest city in the Shenandoah Valley. It is convenient to shops and restaurants, adjacent to Mary Baldwin College, and two blocks from Woodrow Wilson's birthplace. All rooms include TV, phone, air-conditioning, private bath, and private entrance.

Hosts: Joe and Evy Harman
Rooms: 14 (PB) $65-105
Full Breakfast
Credit Cards: A, B, C, D, E
Notes: 2, 3, 4, 5, 7, 8, 9, 10, 11, 12

Thornrose House at Gypsy Hill

531 Thornrose Avenue, 24401
(540) 885-7026; (800) 861-4338;
FAX (540) 885-6458

Outside, this turn-of-the century Georgian residence has a wraparound verandah, Greek colonnades, and lovely gardens. Inside, a fireplace and grand piano create a formal but comfortable atmosphere. Five attractive bedrooms with private baths are on the second floor. Your hosts offer afternoon tea, refreshments, and conversation. Adjacent to a 300-acre park that is great for walking, with tennis, golf, and ponds. Other nearby attractions include the Blue Ridge National Park, natural chimneys, Skyline Drive, Woodrow Wilson's birthplace, and the Museum of American Frontier Culture.

Hosts: Otis and Suzanne Huston
Rooms: 5 (PB) $60-80
Full Breakfast
Credit Cards: none
Notes: 2, 5, 7 (over 6), 8, 9, 10

---

5 Open all year; 6 Pets welcome; 7 Children welcome; 8 Tennis nearby; 9 Swimming nearby; 10 Golf nearby; 11 Skiing nearby; 12 May be booked through travel agent.

TANGIER ISLAND

Shirley's Bay View Inn

PO Box 183, 23440
(757) 891-2396

Enjoy a pleasant and restful visit to one
of the last quiet and remote fishing villages on the Chesapeake Bay. Stay at
one of the oldest homes on the island,
filled with the beauty and charm of days
gone by. The beautiful beaches, sunsets,
and customs of Tangier Island will make
your stay a memorable one, and your
hostess will make you feel as part of
the family.

Hostess: Mrs. Shirley Pruitt
Rooms: 6 (3PB; 3SB) $40-70
Full Breakfast
Credit Cards: none
Notes: 2, 5, 7, 9

Sunset Inn

Box 136, 16650 W. Ridge Road, 23440
(804) 891-2535

Enjoy accommodations one-half block
from the beach with a view of the bay.
Deck, air-conditioning, bike riding, and
nice restaurants.

Hosts: Grace and Jim Brown
Rooms: 9 (8PB; 1SB) $50-60
Continental Breakfast
Credit Cards: none
Notes: 2, 5, 7, 9

VIRGINIA BEACH

Barclay Cottage Bed and Breakfast

400 16th Street, 23451
(757) 422-1956

Casual sophistication in a warm historic, inn-like atmosphere. Designed in
turn-of-the-century style, the Barclay
Cottage is two blocks from the beach
in the heart of the Virginia Beach recreational area. The inn is completely
restored with antique furniture to bring
together the feeling of yesterday with
the comfort of today. Formerly the
home of Lillian S. Barclay, the inn has
been a guest home for many years. We
have kept the historic ambiance of the
old inn while modernizing it signifi-
cantly to meet today's needs. We look
forward to welcoming you to the
Barclay Cottage where the theme is
"We go where our dream leads us."

Hosts: Peter and Claire
Rooms: 6 (3PB; 3SB) $65-90
Full Breakfast
Credit Cards: A, B, C
Notes: 8, 9, 10, 12

Barclay Cottage

WARM SPRINGS

Three Hills Inn

PO Box 9, Route 220, 24484
(540) 839-5381; (800) 23-HILLS;
FAX (540) 839-5199

A premier B&B inn in the heart of Bath County, Virginia. Enjoy a casually elegant retreat in a beautifully restored historic manor. Spectacular mountain views, acres of woods and trails—serenity at its best! Elegant suites available, some with kitchens and fireplaces. Four miles from the historic Homestead Resort. Your hosts have missionary backgrounds and speak fluent Spanish. From a romantic getaway to an executive retreat (meeting/conference facility), the Inn is the perfect choice for the discriminating traveler.

Hosts: Doug and Charlene Fike
Rooms: 14 (PB) $59-149
Full Gourmet Breakfast (Afternoon tea weekends)
Credit Cards: A, B, D
Notes: 2, 5, 6, 7, 8, 9, 10, 11, 12

WASHINGTON

Caledonia Farm—1812

47 Dearing Road, **Flint Hill** 22627
(540) 675-3693 (voice and FAX); (800) BNB-1812

Enjoy ultimate hospitality, comfort, scenery, and recreation adjacent to Virginia's Shenandoah National Park. This romantic getaway to history and nature includes outstanding full breakfasts, fireplaces, air-conditioning, hayrides, bicycles, lawn games, VCR, and piano. World's finest dining, caves, Skyline Drive, battlefields, stables,

antiquing, hiking, and climbing are all nearby. Washington, D.C., is 68 miles away; Washington, Virginia, just four miles. A Virginia historic landmark, the farm is listed on the National Register of Historic Places. Unwind in our new spa.

Host: Phil Irwin
Rooms: 2 + 2 suite (2PB; 2SB) $80-140
Full Breakfast
Credit Cards: A, B, D
Notes: 2, 5, 7 (over 12), 8, 9, 10, 11, 12

Applewood Colonial Bed and Breakfast

WILLIAMSBURG

Applewood Colonial Bed and Breakfast

605 Richmond Road, 23185
(800) 899-2753; FAX (757) 229-9405

The owner's unique apple collection is evidenced throughout this restored colonial home. Four elegant guest rooms (one suite with fireplace) are conveniently located four short blocks from Colonial Williamsburg and very close to the College of William and Mary campus. Antiques complement the romantic atmosphere. The dining room has a beautiful built-in corner cupboard and a crystal chandelier above the ped-

---

5 Open all year; 6 Pets welcome; 7 Children welcome; 8 Tennis nearby; 9 Swimming nearby;
10 Golf nearby; 11 Skiing nearby; 12 May be booked through travel agent.

estal table where homemade breakfast is served. Afternoon refreshments. No smoking.

Host: Jan Brown
Rooms: 4 (PB) $75-120
Full Breakfast
Credit Cards: A, B, C, D
Notes: 2, 5, 7, 8, 10, 12

The Cedars Bed and Breakfast

616 Jamestown Road, 23185
(757) 229-3591; (800) 296-3591

Enter this three-story brick Georgian home and the tone will be set for your visit to the 18th Century. An eight-minute walk to historic Williamsburg, across from the College of William and Mary, this elegant inn offers traditional, gracious hospitality and comfort. Candlelit breakfasts are scrumptious and bountiful. Each guest chamber reflects the romance and charm of the Colonial era. Canopy and four-poster beds abound. Fireplaces in parlor and cottage. Offstreet parking. Williamsburg's oldest and largest B&B

Hosts: Carol, Jim, and Brona Malecha
Rooms: 8 + cottage (PB) $95-165
Full Breakfast
Credit Cards: A, B
Notes: 2, 5, 7, 10, 12

Colonial Capital Bed and Breakfast

501 Richmond Road, 23185
(757) 229-0233; (800) 776-0570;
FAX (757) 253-7667

Our Colonial Revival home in the Architectural Preservation District is only three blocks from the historic area. Enjoy our antiques, Oriental rugs, cozy canopied beds, and ensuite baths. Indulge in a full, cooked breakfast before the days activities. Relax afterwards on the porch, patio, or deck sharing tea and wine with friends, new and old. Inroom phone, FAX and IBM PS/1 available. Smoking outdoors only. Free bikes. Gift certificates. Inspected and approved by AAA and BBAV.

Hosts: Barbara and Phil Craig
Rooms: 5 (including one two-room suite) (PB) $76-135
Full Cooked Breakfast
Credit Cards: A, B, C, D
Notes: 2, 5, 7 (8 and over), 8, 9, 10, 12

Colonial Gardens

Colonial Gardens B&B

1109 Jamestown Road, 23185
(757) 220-8087; (800) 886-9715;
FAX (757) 253-1495 (call first)

This beautiful home is conveniently located just four minutes from Colonial Williamsburg and five minutes from Jamestown. Situated on a heavily wooded lot in the heart of the city, it offers the weary traveler a quiet haven of rest and relaxation. English and early 1800s American antiques. Each beautifully decorated bedroom has a private bath. Suites available. Full plantation breakfast. Experience true Southern hospitality and Williamsburg elegance at its best.

Hosts: Scottie and Wilmot Phillips
Rooms: 1 + 2 suites (PB) $95-125
Full Breakfast
Credit Cards: A, B
Notes: 2, 5, 7 (14 and over), 10, 12

Fox and Grape Bed and Breakfast

701 Monumental Avenue, 23185
(757) 229-6914; (800) 292-3699

Lovely two-story Colonial with wraparound porch with rockers and a swing. A perfect place to enjoy your favorite book or plan you day's activities. Rooms are furnished with antiques, counted cross stitch, quilts, and folk art. The sinks are mounted in antique dressers. The front yard has a fox topiary that welcomes guests. December is a special time to enjoy the beautiful greenery and fruit decorations adorning the front of the house.

Hosts: Pat and Bob Orendorff
Rooms: 4 (PB) $84 (Jan.-Mar. first night $90, second night free)
Continental Plus Breakfast
Credit Cards: A, B, D
Notes: 2, 5, 7, 8, 9, 10, 12

Newport House Bed and Breakfast

710 South Henry Street, 23185
(757) 229-1775; FAX (757) 229-6408

A reproduction of an important 1756 home, Newport House has museum-standard period furnishings, including canopy beds. A five-minute walk to the historic area. Full breakfast with Colonial recipes; Colonial dancing in the ballroom every Tuesday evening (beginners welcome). The host is a historian/author(including a book on Christ) and former museum director. The hostess is a gardener, beekeeper, 18-century seamstress, and former nurse. A pet rabit entertains at breakfast. No smoking.

Hosts: John and Cathy Millar
Rooms: 2 (PB) $115-140
Full Breakfast
Credit Cards: none
Notes: 2, 5, 7, 10, 12

Primrose Cottage

706 Richmond Road, 23185
(757) 229-6421; (800) 522-1901;
FAX (757) 259-0717

Primrose Cottage is a nature-lover's delight. In the spring, the front walkway is lined with primroses. In cooler months, the front yard is abloom with banks of pansies. There are two bedrooms upstairs, each with a large, walk-in closet and private bathroom. Desks, chairs, and reading lamps add to the comfort of home. In the morning, the aroma of home cooking usually rouses even the sleepiest traveler. Within walking distance of Williamsburg Historic Area, fine restaurants, and local churches. Complimentary bikes. Off-street parking. Smoke-free atmosphere.

Hostess: Inge Curtis
Rooms: 3 (PB) $85-110
Full Breakfast
Credit Cards: A, B
Notes: 2, 10

5 Open all year; 6 Pets welcome; 7 Children welcome; 8 Tennis nearby; 9 Swimming nearby; 10 Golf nearby; 11 Skiing nearby; 12 May be booked through travel agent.

Spiggle Guest Home

720 College Terrace, 23185
(757) 253-0202

Spend the night with these gracious hosts in their cozy 6,000-square-foot brick home on their beautiful quiet residential street next to the campus of The College of William and Mary and away from the city noise. You'll see all of Williamsburg from this convenient location — just a 10- to 15-minute walk to the restored area of Williamsburg and a ten minute drive to shopping centers, Busch Gardens, and the Pottery Factory. Guest's rooms are comfortably furnished, some with family antiques, and all include wall-to-wall carpeting, central air, inroom refrigerators, coffee and tea maker, phone jacks, TV, and private baths. A great location for seeing all the nearby sights of Jamestown and Yorktown.

Hosts: Phil and Dot Spiggle
Rooms: 4 (3PB; 2SB) $35-50
No Breakfast
Credit Cards: none
Notes: 2, 5

Williamsburg Manor Bed and Breakfast

600 Richmond Road, 23185
(575) 220-8011; (800) 422-8011;
FAX (575) 220-0245

This 1927 Geogian home was built during the reconstruction of historic Colonial Williamsburg. Recently restored to its original elegance and furnished with exquisite pieces including antiques and collectibles. Five well-appointed guest rooms each with private bath, TV, and central air-conditioning. Guests are treated to a lavish fireside breakfast prepared by the executive chef. Home is available for weddings, private parties, dinners, and meetings. Ideal location within walking distance of the historic area. On-site parking. Off season rates available.

Hostess: Laura Sisane
Rooms: 5 (PB) $95-115
Full Breakfast
Credit Cards: A, B
Notes: 2, 4, 5, 8, 9, 10, 12

Williamsburg Sampler Bed and Breakfast

922 Jamestown Road, 23185
(757) 253-0398; (800) 722-1169;
FAX (757) 253-2669

This 18th Century, plantation-style, brick Colonial was proclaimed by Virginia's Governor as the Inn Of The Year, and is a AAA three Diamond and Mobil three Star home, within walking distance to the historic area. Richly furnished bedrooms and suites with king- or queen-size bed, TV, private baths,

Williamsburg Sampler Bed and Breakfast

NOTES: Credit cards accepted: A Master Card; B Visa; C American Express; D Discover; E Diners Club; F Other; 2 Personal checks accepted; 3 Lunch available; 4 Dinner available;

fireplaces, and "Roof Top Garden." A collection of antiques, pewter, and samplers are displayed throughout the house. A "Skip Lunch" breakfast is served. Internationally recognized as a favorite spot for a romantic honeymoon or anniversary.

Hosts: Helen and Ike Sisane
Rooms: 4, includes 2 suites (PB) $95-140
Full Breakfast
Credit Cards: A, B
Notes: 2, 5, 8, 9, 10, 12

Azalea House Bed and Breakfast

WOODSTOCK

Azalea House Bed and Breakfast

551 South Main Street, 22664
(540) 459-3500

A large Victorian house built in 1892 featuring family antiques and stenciled ceilings. It was initially used as a parsonage, serving a church three blocks away for about 70 years. Located in the historic Shenendoah Valley, it is close to Skyline Drive and the mountains. Many Civil War sites are within short driving distance. Nearby activities include antiquing, hiking, and horseback riding.

Hosts: Price and Margaret McDonald
Rooms: 4 (PB) $55-75
Full Breakfast
Credit Cards: A, B, C
Notes: 2, 7 (over 6), 9, 10, 11

---

5 Open all year; 6 Pets welcome; 7 Children welcome; 8 Tennis nearby; 9 Swimming nearby; 10 Golf nearby; 11 Skiing nearby; 12 May be booked through travel agent.

WASHINGTON

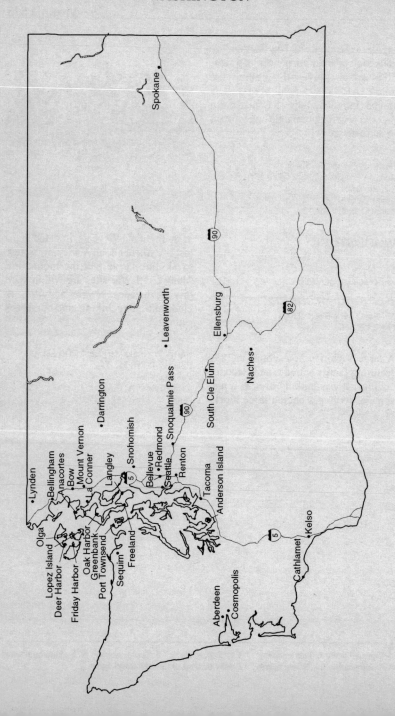

Washington

Bed and Breakfast Service (BABS)

445 W. Lake Samish Drive, **Bellingham** 98226
(360) 733-8642

We are a reservation service referring to hosts associated with us **all over the United States**. Our prices are modest, $40-80, in the European tradition. Call and let us set up your next bed and breakfast stay. Coordinators, George and Delores Herrmann.

Cooney Mansion

ABERDEEN/COSMOPOLIS

Cooney Mansion

1705 Fifth Street, Box 54, **Cosmopolis** 98537
(360) 533-0602

Located two minutes from Aberdeen.

This 1908 National Historic Register home, situated in wooded seclusion, was built by Neil Cooney, owner of one of the largest sawmills of the time. It captures the adventure of the Northwest. Share the lumber baron's history and many of his original "craftsman" style antiques. Enjoy 18 holes of golf (in backyard) or a leisurely walk around Mill Creek Park. Relax in the sauna and jacuzzi, curl up with one of the many books from the library, or watch TV in the ballroom or living room. View us on the Internet at: http//www.techline. com/~cooney/

Hosts: Judi and Jim Lohr
Rooms: 8 (5PB; 3SB) $60-135
Full "Lumber Baron's" Breakfast
Credit Cards: A, B, C, D, E
Notes: 5, 8, 10

ANACORTES

Albatross Bed and Breakfast

5708 Kingsway West, 98221
(360) 293-0677; (800) 622-8864

Our 1927 Cape Cod-style home offers king and queen beds and private baths

---

NOTES: Credit cards accepted: A Master Card; B Visa; C American Express; D Discover; E Diners Club; F Other; 2 Personal checks accepted; 3 Lunch available; 4 Dinner available; 5 Open all year; 6 Pets welcome; 7 Children welcome; 8 Tennis nearby; 9 Swimming nearby; 10 Golf nearby; 11 Skiing nearby; 12 May be booked through travel agent.

in all guest rooms. The quiet, relaxing living room, patio, and deck areas view waterfront, islands, and mountains. You can walk to Washington Park, Skyline marina, fine dining, and inspirational beaches. We also offer sightseeing cruises aboard a 46-sailboat and have two-speed cross bikes available. We are close to the State Ferry Boat terminal for access to the San Juan Islands and Victoria B.C. We are also close to over 25 churches.

Hosts: Ken and Barbie
Rooms: 4 (PB) $75-90
Full Breakfast
Credit Cards: A, B, C
Notes: 2, 5, 7, 8, 9, 10, 12

Blue Rose Bed and Breakfast

1811 Ninth Street, 98221
(360) 293-5175; (888) 293-5175

The main appeal of this memorable old-town B&B is the location. A neighborhood of quiet beaches, histoirc arts and crafts, homes, and passing ships. Ideal for island sunsets. Pleasant surroundings. A grand veranda and rose garden to enjoy a quiet afternoon tea. Floot-to-ceiling closets, open beams, and period built-ins. All on a private floor. Our relaxed atmosphere is readily apparent in everything from our warm hospitality to the wonderful hand-created breakfast and comfortable accommodations.

Host: Creamy Wilkins-Manning
Rooms: 2 (PB) $75-89
Full Breakfast
Credit Cards: A, B
Notes: 8, 10, 11

Sunset Beach Bed and Breakfast

100 Sunset Beach, 98221
(360) 293-5428; (800) 359-3448

On exciting Rosario Straits. Relax and enjoy the view of seven major islands from our decks, stroll on the beach, or walk in the beautiful Washington Park, adjacent to our private gardens. Also enjoy boating, hiking, and fishing. Three bedrooms with private baths, one room with a jacuzzi, and a hot tub is available in a separate building. Private entry and TV. Full breakfast. Five minutes to San Juan Ferries, fine restaurants, and marina and a convenience store nearby. Sunsets are outstanding! No smoking.

Hosts: Joann and Hal Harker
Rooms: 3 (PB) $79-89
Full Breakfast
Credit Cards: A, B
Notes: 2, 5, 7 (over 6), 9, 10, 11, 12

ANDERSON ISLAND

The Inn at Burg's Landing

8808 Villa Beach Road, 98303
(206) 884-9185

Catch the ferry from Steilacoom to stay at this contemporary log homestead built in 1987. It offers spectacular views of Mt. Rainier, Puget Sound, and the Cascade Mountains and is located south of Tacoma off I-5. Choose from three guest rooms, including the master bedroom with queen-size "log" bed with skylight above and private whirlpool bath. The Inn has a private beach. Col-

NOTES: Credit cards accepted: A Master Card; B Visa; C American Express; D Discover; E Diners Club; F Other; 2 Personal checks accepted; 3 Lunch available; 4 Dinner available;

lect seashells and agates, swim on two freshwater lakes nearby, and/or enjoy a game of tennis or golf. Tour the island by bicycle or on foot and watch for sailboats and deer. Hot tub. Full breakfast. Families welcome. No smoking.

Hosts: Ken and Annie Burg
Rooms: 3 (2PB; 1SB) $65-90
Full Breakfast
Credit Cards: A, B
Notes: 2, 5, 7, 8, 9, 10, 11

BELLEVUE

Petersen Bed and Breakfast
10228 SE 8th, 98004
(206) 454-9334

We offer two rooms five minutes from Bellevue Square with wonderful shopping and one-half block from the bus line to Seattle. Rooms have down comforters, and we have a hot tub on the deck. Children are welcome. No smoking.

Hosts: Eunice and Carl Petersen
Rooms: 2 (SB) $50-65
Full Breakfast
Credit Cards: none
Notes: 2, 5, 7

BELLINGHAM

Circle F Bed and Breakfast
2399 Mt. Baker Highway, 98226
(360) 671-9825; (800) 671-9825;
FAX (360) 734-3816

Circle F Bed and Breakfast is a home

away from home for all of our guests. The Victorian-style ranch house was built in 1892 and is located on 330 acres of pasture and woodlands. We are a working farm, and you can enjoy hiking trails and visits with the farm animals. A hearty breakfast is served by a friendly farm family who enjoys the company of all visitors. Children welcome.

Host: Guy J. Foster
Rooms: 4 (1PB; 3SB) $50-65
Full Breakfast
Credit Cards: none
Notes: 2, 5, 7, 11

CATHLAMET

The Gallery B&B at Little Cape Horn
4 Little Cape Horn, 98612
(360) 425-7395; FAX (360) 425-1351

The Gallery is an elegant contemporary home with sweeping views of the majestic Columbia River ship channel. The large deck has a hot tub for relaxing while watching tug boats, seals, eagles, and windsurfers. It is surrounded by tall cedar and fir trees and a tall cliff with waterfalls. A private beach is a few steps

The Gallery B&B at Little Cape Horn

---

away. Breakfast is served with fine china, crystal, and warm Christian hospitality.

Hosts: Carolyn and Eric Feasey
Rooms: 5 (3PB; 2SB with private powder rooms) $80135
Full or Continental Breakfast
Credit Cards: none
Notes: 2, 5, 7, 9, 10

CLE ELUM, SOUTH

The Moore House Bed and Breakfast Country Inn

526 Marie Avenue, PO Box 629, 98943
(509) 674-5939; (800) 2-2-TWAIN (OR and WA only)

Former 1909 Milwaukee Railroad Crew Hotel, now offering 12 bright and airy rooms ranging from economical to exquisite and including two genuine cabooses and a bridal suite with jetted tub. Now on the National Register, the Inn has a museum-like atmosphere with an extensive collection of railroad memorabilia and artifacts. Nestled in the Cascade Mountain foothills, The Moore House is close to cross-country skiing, hiking, biking, rafting, fishing, horse-

back riding, and also fine dining.

Hosts: Eric and Cindy Sherwood
Rooms: 12 (6PB; 6SB) $45-115 + 7.7% tax
Full Breakfast
Credit Cards: A, B, C, D
Notes: 2, 5, 7, 10, 11, 12

DARRINGTON

Sauk River Farm Bed and Breakfast

32629 S.R. 530 NE, 98241
(360) 436-1794 (voice and FAX)

The wild scenic Sauk River runs through this farm nestled in a valley of the North Cascades. All-season recreational opportunities await you. Wildlife abounds year-round. The Native American Loft Room is a collector's delight; The Victoria Room offers pastoral privacy. Hallmarks of the farm are its views of rugged mountains, intimate atmosphere, comfortable accommodations, and solitude for those seeking relaxation. Step back in time and sample Darrington hospitality with its Bluegrass music and crafters. No smoking.

Hosts: Leo and Sharon Mehler
Rooms: 2 (SB) $45-65
Full Breakfast
Credit Cards: none
Notes: 2, 5, 11

ELLENSBURG

Murphy's Country B&B

2830 Thorp Highway South, 98926
(509) 925-7986

Two large guest rooms in a lovely 1915 country home with a sweeping view of

---

NOTES: Credit cards accepted: A Master Card; B Visa; C American Express; D Discover; E Diners Club; F Other; 2 Personal checks accepted; 3 Lunch available; 4 Dinner available;

the valley. Full breakfast. Close to fly fishing and golfing.

Hostess: Doris Callahan-Murphy
Rooms: 2 (SB) $60
Full Breakfast
Credit Cards: A, B, C
Notes: 2, 5, 10

FREELAND

Cliff House and Seacliff Cottage

5440 Windmill Road, 98249
(360) 331-1566

Romantic! Hidden in a lush forest on the very edge of Whidbey Island's west side is a setting so unique. Cliff House, with its secluded nooks, sophisticated yet rugged architecture, fireplace, spa, fully equipped kitchen, video and CD library, and views across the water, is yours alone to enjoy. Explore the island's tiny town, parks, and beaches. Nearby, your hosts also offer Sea Cliff Cottage, a completely private hideaway with fireplace, petite kitchen, window seat, and hammock for two. Down a short path you'll discover a stairway to the beach where you can enjoy hours

Seacliff Cottage

of exploring and may even sight a pod of killer whales.

Hosts: Peggy Moore and Walter O'Toole
Rooms: 1 cottage for 1 couple, $165 +and 1 entire house for 1 or 2 couples, $385 (4PB)
Hearty Continental Breakfast
Credit Cards: none
Notes: 2, 5, 10, 12

States Inn

FRIDAY HARBOR

States Inn

2039 West Valley Road, 98250
(360) 378-6240; FAX (360) 378-6241

Situated in a scenic valley 13 minutes from town, the Inn is located on a 60-acre horse boarding ranch on the west side of San Juan island. We offer nine rooms, each individually decorated with a flavor of a states name. Three diamond rating with AAA. This is a high quality inn in the middle of the Northwest's most scenic vacation area.

Host: Garreth Jeffers
Rooms: 9 (7PB; 2SB, suite) $80-110
Full Breakfast
Credit Cards: A, B
Notes: 2, 5, 12

---

5 Open all year; 6 Pets welcome; 7 Children welcome; 8 Tennis nearby; 9 Swimming nearby; 10 Golf nearby; 11 Skiing nearby; 12 May be booked through travel agent.

Tucker House
Bed and Breakfast
with Cottages

260 B Street, 98250
(360) 378-2783; (800) 965-0123;
FAX (360) 378-6437

Guest House Cottages

A Victorian home (c.1898) with two upstairs bedrooms, queen beds, and shared bath. Three separate cottages with queen beds, private bath, wood-stoves, kitchenettes, TV, outside hot tub, and off-street parking. A full, gourmet breakfast with homemade cinnamon bread. Property abounds in flowers and stately trees and is surrounded by a white picket fence. Two blocks from the ferry landing, and two blocks to the heart of picturesque Friday Harbor. Gift certificates available.

Hosts: Skip and Annette Metzger
Rooms: 2 (SB; upstairs in main Victorian)
Cottages: 3 (PB) $85-135
Full Breakfast
Credit Cards: A, B, C, D
Notes: 2, 5, 6 (under 40 lbs.; $15-25 night each),
7, 8, 9, 10, 12

GREENBANK

Guest House Cottages

3366 S. Highway 525, 98253
(360) 678-3115

Discover privacy, peace, and pampering in each of our seven individually designed cottages in Greenbank, Whidbey Island. Each cottage, four of which are log houses, has a private setting on 25 acres of island greenery. Every cottage features personal jacuzzis, fireplaces, kitchens, and TV/VCRs. Over 400 complimentary movies, an outdoor swimming pool, and hot tub make for a relaxing retreat for two.

Hosts: Don and MaryJane Creger
Rooms: 6 cottages and 1 suite (PB) $110-285
Full Breakfast
Credit Cards: A, B, C, D
Notes: 2, 5, 9, 10, 12

KELSO

Longfellow House B&B

203 Williams-Finney Road, 98626-9513
(360) 423-4545; FAX (360) 414-3130

Longfellow House is the ideal private destination for your special occasion or business trip. A secluded cottage for two in a rural setting, one mile east of I-5. The main floor is yours alone. Enjoy

Longfellow House

NOTES: Credit cards accepted: A Master Card; B Visa; C American Express; D Discover; E Diners Club; F Other; 2 Personal checks accepted; 3 Lunch available; 4 Dinner available;

our 1913 player piano and collection of works by and about Henry Wadsworth Longfellow. Sleep as long as you like. Wake to the smell of gourmet coffee and the breakfast you've selected being prepared. Fine teas are our specialty. Off-street parking, telephone, modem jack, and business services. Visit Mount St. Helens, Pacific Ocean beaches, and Columbia River Gorge.

Hosts: Richard and Sally Longfellow
Rooms: 1 (PB) $89
Full Breakfast
Credit Cards: none
Notes: 2, 5, 8, 9, 10, 11

LACONNER

Benson Farmstead Bed and Breakfast

1009 Avon-Allen Road, **Bow** 98232
(360) 757-0578; (800) 685-7239 or 1930

Located just minutes from the Skagit Valley, tulip fields, the historical town of LaConner, and ferries to the San Juan Islands, the Benson Farmstead is a beautiful restored farmhouse. The Bensons are a friendly couple who serve homemade desserts in the evening and a wonderful breakfast. They have filled their home with charming antiques, old quilts, and curios from their Scandinavian heritage. The extensive yard features an English Garden and a large playground.

Hosts: Jerry and Sharon Benson
Rooms: 4 (2PB; 2SB) $70-80
Full Breakfast
Credit Cards: A, B
Notes: 2, 5 (weekends only Sept.-March), 7, 8, 9, 10, 11

Katy's Inn

503 S. Third, PO Box 869, 98257
(360) 466-3366; (800) 914-7767

Charming 1876 Victorian two blocks up hill from quaint LaConner that has 100 unique shops, galleries, and antique stores. Four lovely guest rooms upstairs (two with private bath) with access to wraparound porch through French doors. Romantic suite with private bath, located by gardens and pond, has a private entrance. Warm hospitality, full breakfast, and hot tub. Great for small retreats (18 max.), weddings, and/or receptions.

Hosts: Bruce and Kathie Hubbard
Rooms: 5 (3PB; 2SB) $69-99
Full Breakfast
Credit Cards: A, B, C, D
Notes: 2, 5, 10, 12

LANGLEY—WHIDBEY ISLAND

The Log Castle B&B

3273 E. Saratoga Road, 98260
(360) 221-5483

A log house on a private, secluded beach features turret bedrooms, wood-burning stoves, porch swings, and panoramic views of the beach and mountains. Rustic elegance — with private baths. Relax before a large stone fireplace or listen to the call of gulls as you watch for bald eagles and sea lions.

Hosts: Congressman Jack and Norma Metcalf, owners, and Karen and Phil, innkeepers
Rooms: 4 (PB) $90-115
Full Breakfast
Credit Cards: A, B, D
Notes: 2, 5, 10

---

5 Open all year; 6 Pets welcome; 7 Children welcome; 8 Tennis nearby; 9 Swimming nearby; 10 Golf nearby; 11 Skiing nearby; 12 May be booked through travel agent.

LEAVENWORTH

All Seasons River Inn

PO Box 788, 8751 Icicle Road, 98826
(509) 548-1425; (800) 254-0555

Riverfront guest rooms, magnificent Cascade views, and warm hospitality are but a few reasons why All Seasons River Inn was selected as one of the "50 most romantic getaways in the Pacific Northwest," and it is also why a stay here will call you back again and again. Built as a bed and breakfast, all guest rooms are very spacious with antique decor, river-view deck, and private bath, some with jacuzzi tub and/or fireplace. Full gourmet breakfast; adults only. No smoking on premises.

Hosts: Kathy and Jeff Falconer
Rooms: 6 (PB) $95-125
Full Breakfast
Credit Cards: A, B
Notes: 2, 5, 8, 9, 10, 11, 12 (with exceptions)

Run of the River

PO Box 285, 98826
(509) 548-7171; (800) 288-6491;
FAX (509) 548-7547

Imagine the quintessential Northwest log bed and breakfast inn. Spacious rooms feature private baths, hand-hewn log beds, and fluffy down comforters. Or, celebrate in a suite with your own heartwarming wood-stove, jetted jacuzzi surrounded by river rock, and a bird's eye loft to laze about with a favorite book. From your room's log porch swing, view the Icicle River, surrounding bird refuge, and the Cascade peaks, appropriately named the Enchantments. To explore the Icicle Valley, get off the beaten path with hiking, biking, and driving guides written just for you by the innkeepers, avid bikers and hikers. Take a spin on complimentary mountain bikes. A hearty breakfast sets the day in motion.

Hosts: Monty and Karen Turner
Rooms: 6 (PB) $95-150
Full Breakfast
Credit Cards: A, B, C, D
Notes: 2, 5, 8, 9, 10, 11, 12

LOPEZ ISLAND

Aleck Bay Inn

Route 1, Box 1920, 98261
(360) 468-3535; FAX (360) 468-3533
Email: abi@pacificrim.net

Aleck Bay Inn provides the luxurious, quiet, and personal care needed for guests celebrating special events, having a romantic getaway, or just wish a relaxing time by the fireplace. Coffee always hot and pastry every present. Repeatedly visited by Congressmen and state dignitaries. The Inn hosts small weddings, business meetings, retreats, and church outings. Guests can walk our beaches, hike through original forests, relax in hot tub, enjoy the game room, and watch the wildlife. Near island churches, golf courses, and tennis courts. Kayak instruction and bike rentals available. Special breakfasts are served in our lovely dining room or in the solarium and begin with fresh fruit,

---

NOTES: Credit cards accepted: A Master Card; B Visa; C American Express; D Discover; E Diners Club; F Other; 2 Personal checks accepted; 3 Lunch available; 4 Dinner available;

followed by a large portion of gourmet selections. Breakfast piano concerts on weekends. Chinese and Spanish spoken.

Hosts: May and David Mendez
Rooms: 4 (PB) $79-149
Full Breakfast
Credit Cards: A, B, C, D, E
Notes: 2, 3, 4, 5, 7, 8, 9, 10, 12

Lopez Farm Cottages

PO Box 610, 98261
(360) 468-3555; (800) 440-3556;
FAX (360) 468-3558

Lopez Farm Cottages offers year-round lodging amidst the peace and quiet of an historic family farm, where lambs frolic in the pasture and deer graze in the 100-year-old orchard. The newly built cottages with private baths, fireplaces, and kitchens are nestled in an old cedar grove. You'll be away from it all yet within minutes of shops and restaurants, parks and beaches, kayak and bicycle rentals, and the ferry landing.

Hosts: John and Ann Warsen
Rooms: 4 separate cottages (PB) $110
Continental Breakfast
Credit Cards: A, B
Notes: 2, 5, 9, 10, 12

MacKaye Harbor Inn

Route 1, Box 1940, 98261
(360) 468-2253; FAX (360) 468-9555

The ideal beachfront getaway. Lopez's only bed and breakfast on a low-bank, sandy beach. Kayak and mountain bike rentals and/or instructions. This 1927

Victorian home has been painstakingly restored. Guests are pampered in comfortable elegance. Eagles, deer, seals, and otters frequent this Cape Cod of the Northwest. Commendations from *Sunset, Pacific Northwest* magazine, the *Los Angeles Times*, and *Northwest Best Places*.

Hosts: Robin and Mike Bergstrom
Rooms: 7 (4PB; 3SB) $69-160
Full Breakfast
Credit Cards: A, B
Notes: 2, 5, 8, 10, 12

LYNDEN

Century House Bed and Breakfast

401 South B.C. Avenue, 98264
(360) 354-2439; (800) 820-3617;
FAX (360) 354-6910

Located on 35 acres at the edge of town, Century House is a 109 year-old Victorian home. You'll find this completely restored home is a quiet retreat with spacious gardens and lawns for your enjoyment. The quaint Dutch village of Lynden is within an easy walk and boasts the best museums in the area and gift shops galore . . . but sorry, the town is closed on Sundays. Take day trips to the Cascade Mountains and Mount Baker, the sea, Seattle, Vancouver, or Victoria, British Columbia.

Hosts: Jan and Ken Stremler
Rooms: 4 (2PB; 2SB) $60-85
Full Breakfast
Credit Cards: A, B
Notes: 2, 5, 7, 8, 9, 10, 11

---

5 Open all year; 6 Pets welcome; 7 Children welcome; 8 Tennis nearby; 9 Swimming nearby; 10 Golf nearby; 11 Skiing nearby; 12 May be booked through travel agent.

MT. VERNON

Dutch Treat

1777 W. Big Lake Boulevard, 98273
(360) 422-5466

Our modest and very Dutch accommodations are in a lovely setting on a lake that lends itself to all water sports, including fishing and swimming. A public boat launch is just down the road. There is a fire pit on the lake's edge where you can roast marshmallows or sip and glass of wine and gaze at the stars. Across the lake is a golf course and a good restaurant. The area is ideal for biking either through the Skagit Valley bulb fields and farmlands or in the foothills of the Cascade Mountains. In winter, there are the birds to watch (eagles, trumpeter swans, and snow geese) or you can ski on Mount Baker or cross-country ski in the foothills. In summer, the typical Dutch breakfast is served on the deck.

Hosts: Ria and Peter Stroosma
Rooms: 2 (PB) $55
Expanded Continental Breakfast
Credit Cards: none
Notes: 2, 3 (picnic), 5, 7, 9, 10, 11

The Parsonage on Pleasant Ridge

1754 Chilberg Road, 98273
(360) 466 1754; (360) 466-1514

Near LaConner, this 1894 restored Victorian farmhouse is on the National Register of Historic Places. Originally, this home was the parsonage for the Bethsaida Swedish Evangelical Lutheran Church. The remains of the 1892 church stand in our garden. Please call for reservations and come visit our adult-oriented, non-smoking environment.

Host: Christopher Barnes
Rooms: 2 (PB) $75
Continental Breakfast
Credit Cards: A, B
Notes: 2, 5, 10

Apple Country Bed and Breakfast

NACHES

Apple Country Bed and Breakfast

4561 Old Naches Highway, 98937
(509) 965-0344; FAX (509) 965-1591

Caring hosts welcome you to this remodeled, 1911 farmhouse is located west of Yokima in the heart of the Naches Valley on a working ranch. Apple Country B&B is the ideal stop for any traveler who is seeking a countryside bed and breakfast. Enjoy a continental breakfast while taking in the sweeping view of the valley from your large bedroom, tastefully decorated with new and antique furniture. Apple Country B&B is just a short drive from many activities offered by its surrounding valleys: fine dining, golfing, antiquing, skiing, fishing, hiking, hunting, and

---

NOTES: Credit cards accepted: A Master Card; B Visa; C American Express; D Discover; E Diners Club; F Other; 2 Personal checks accepted; 3 Lunch available; 4 Dinner available;

wine country tours. *"Truly, A Four Season Country"*.

Hosts: Shirley and Mark Robert
Rooms: 3 (1PB; 2SB) $70-75
Continental Breakfast
Credit Cards: none
Notes: 2, 5, 6, 7, 8, 9, 10, 11, 12

OAK HARBOR

North Island Bed and Breakfast

1589 N. West Beach Road, 98277
(360) 675-7080

North Island Bed and Breakfast is located on 175 feet of private beachfront. Each guest room has a private bath, king-size bed, individual heating, fireplace, and beautiful furnishings. From your deck or patio you'll enjoy a view of the Olympic Mountains and San Juan Islands. A separate entrance and ample parking are provided. All of Whidby Island's wonderful attractions are close by.

Hosts: Jim and MaryVern Loomis
Rooms: 2 (PB) $85-95
Continental Breakfast
Credit Cards: A, B, C, D
Notes: 2, 5, 10

ORCAS ISLAND—DEER HARBOR

Palmer's Chart House

PO Box 51, 98243
(360) 376-4231

The first B&B on Orcas Island (since 1975) with a magnificent water view. The 33-foot, private yacht *Amante* is available for a minimal fee with skipper Don. Low-key, private, personal attention makes this B&B unique and attractive. Well-traveled hosts speak Spanish.

Hosts: Don and Majean Palmer
Rooms: 2 (PB) $60-70 + tax
Full Breakfast
Credit Cards: none
Notes: 2, 5, 7 (over 12), 8, 10, 11, 12

ORCAS ISLAND—OLGA

Buck Bay Farm

Star Route Box 45, 98279
(360) 376-2908

Buck Bay Farm is located on beautiful Orcas in the San Juan Islands of Washington State. Orcas is an idyllic vacation destination with lots of outdoor fun: hiking, bicycling, boating or kayaking, whale watching, golf, fishing, and much more. The B&B is a farmhouse recently rebuilt by the owner. A warm welcome and hearty, home-style breakfast await you.

Hosts: Rick and Janet Bronkey
Rooms: 5 (3PB; 2SB) $75-95
Full Breakfast
Credit Cards: A, B, C, D
Notes: 2, 5, 7 (by arrangement), 8, 9, 10

PORT TOWNSEND

Ann Starrett Mansion 1889 Victorian B&B Inn

744 Clay Street, 98368
(360) 385-3205; (800) 321-0644;
FAX (360) 385-2976

Just as the Taj Mahal was built as a trib-

5 Open all year; 6 Pets welcome; 7 Children welcome; 8 Tennis nearby; 9 Swimming nearby; 10 Golf nearby; 11 Skiing nearby; 12 May be booked through travel agent.

ute to love, so was this mansion. The most photographed Victorian in the Northwest was awarded "The Great American Home Award" by the National Trust. A 60-foot octagonal tower with a free floating staircase leads to a celestial calendar and frescoed maidens dancing in the clouds depicting Ann. "The Crown Jewel of the Pacific Northwest." Step back in time to serenity and beauty.

Hosts: Bob and Edel Sokol
Rooms: 11 (PB) $70-225
Full Breakfast
Credit Cards: A, B, C, D
Notes: 2, 5, 7, 8, 9, 10, 11, 12

The English Inn

The English Inn

718 F Street, 98368
(360) 385-5302; (800) 254-5302;
FAX (360) 385-6562
Internet: www.english-inn.com

The English Inn was built in 1885 in the Italianate style. It is one of the more gracious Victorian mansions in Port Townsend. It has five large, sunny bedrooms with private baths and views of the Olympic Mountains. Beautiful scenery, hiking, antiquing, and only two hours from Seattle. A lovely garden

with hot tub, Internet access in-room, special events, and corporate rates.

Hostess: Nancy Borino
Rooms: 5 (PB) $65-95
Full Breakfast
Credit Cards: A, B, C, D, E
Notes: 2, 5, 8, 9, 10, 12

REDMOND

Lilac Lea Christian Bed and Breakfast

21008 NE 117th Street, 98053
(206) 861-1898; FAX (206) 883-0285

Custom built Dutch Colonial on a country dead end lane and surrounded by large firs and next to 80 acres of wilderness preserve. Secluded and quiet, yet just 17 miles from downtown Seattle. Private cottage with separate entrance, queen bed, private bath, TV, and study area. Near hiking and biking trails. Large deck and wooded picnic area available. You're special to us—our only guest!

Hosts: Chandler Haight and Ruthanne Hayes
        Haight
Rooms: 1 suite (PB) $85 + tax
Self-catered Extended Continental Breakfast
Credit Cards: none
Notes: 2, 5, 8, 9, 10, 11

RENTON

Holly Hedge House

908 Grant Avenue South, 98055
(206) 226-2555 (voice and FAX)

Experience the ultimate in pampering and privacy in this meticulously restored 1900 scenic hilltop retreat. This unique lodging facility reserves the entire house for one couple at a time to indulge in the beauty and affordable luxury. Landscaped grounds; wood deck with hot tub; swimming pool; stocked gourmet kitchen; whirlpool bath tub; CD, video, and reading libraries; fireplace; glassed-in-verandah. Ten minutes from Sea Tac International Airport; twenty minutes from Seattle; five minutes from Lake Washington. A vacation, honeymoon, or corporate travel getaway that will long be remembered! Ask about the "Spirit Package."

Hosts: Lynn and Marian Thrasher
Rooms: 1 (PB) $110 (2 night minimun), $125 (one night upon availability)
Full Breakfast
Credit Cards: A, B
Notes: 2, 5, 8, 9, 10, 11

SEATTLE

Chambered Nautilus Bed and Breakfast Inn

5005 - 22nd Avenue N.E., 98105
(206) 783-5621; FAX (206) 528-0898

A gracious 1915 Georgian Colonial that is nestled on a hill and furnished with a mixture of American and English antiques and fine reproductions. A touch of Mozart, Persian rugs, a grand piano, two fireplaces, four lovely porches, and national award-winning breakfasts help assure your special comfort. Excellent access to Seattle's theaters, restaurants, public transportation, shopping, bike and jogging trails, churches, Husky Stadium, and the University of Washington campus.

Hosts: Joyce Schulte and Steve Poole
Rooms: 6 (4PB; 2SB) $79.50-109.50
Full Breakfast
Credit Cards: A, B, C
Notes: 2, 5, 8, 9, 10, 11, 12

SEQUIM

Greywolf Inn

395 Keeler Road, 98382
(360) 683-5889; (800) 914-WOLF;
FAX (360) 683-1487

Nestled in a crescent of towering evergreens, this Northwest country estate overlooking the Dungeness Valley is the ideal starting point for year-round, light adventure on the Olympic peninsula . . . hiking, fishing, biking, boating, bird-watching, sightseeing, and golf. Enjoy Greywolf's sunny decks, Japanese-style hot tub, and meandering five-acre woodswalk, or curl up by the fire with a good book. Then, retire to one of the Inn's cozy, comfortable theme rooms. It is the perfect ending to an exciting day.

Hosts: Peggy and Bill Melang
Rooms: 5 (PB) $65-115
Full Breakfast
Credit Cards: A, B, C
Notes: 2, 3, 5, 7 (over 12), 8, 9, 10, 11, 12

Margie's Inn on the Bay

120 Forrest Road, 98382
(360) 683-7011 (voice and FAX); (800) 730-7011

Sequim's only waterfront bed and breakfast. A contemporary ranch-style home with 180 feet on the water. Enjoy

---

5 Open all year; 6 Pets welcome; 7 Children welcome; 8 Tennis nearby; 9 Swimming nearby; 10 Golf nearby; 11 Skiing nearby; 12 May be booked through travel agent.

a terrific view of the water from our hot tub. Five well-appointed bedrooms with private baths. A large sitting room with VCR and movies. Two Persian cats and a talking parrot. Close to the marina, fishing, Dungeness National Wildlife Refuge and Spit, Olympic Game Farm, hiking, biking, Hurricane Ridge, gift shops, and much more. Great restaurants in the area. AAA inspected.

Hosts: Margie and Don Vorhies
Rooms: 5 (PB) $69-125
Full Breakfast
Credit Cards: A, B, C, D
Notes: 2, 5, 7 (over 12), 8, 9, 10, 11, 12

Redmond House

SNOHOMISH

Redmond House
Bed and Breakfast

317 Glen Avenue, 98290
(360) 568-2042

Enter a world of comfort, luxury, and simple elegance that makes time stand still. Located in the Victorian era town of Snohomish, Redmond House is within walking distance of the "Antique Capital of the Northwest" with its 400 antique dealers, gift shops, and wonder-ful restaurants. The House is graced by beautiful gardens and a wraparound porch. Comfortably furnished with period antiques. Luxurious bedrooms are filled with quilts, linens, and queen-size featherbeds and are available with clawfoot soaking tubs. Near hiking, boating, golf, skiing, hot air ballooning, parachuting, wineries, and sports events.

Hosts: Ken and Mary Riley
Rooms: 4 (2PB; 2SB) $85-100
Full Breakfast
Credit Cards: A, B
Notes: 2, 5, 7, 8, 9, 10, 11

SNOQUALMIE PASS

Frantzian Mountain Hideaway

PO Box 174 (7 Ober Strasse, Alpental), 98068
(206) 434-6270

Rustic, but charming, private, self-contained, fully furnished apartment in hosts' home. Apartment features small kitchenette, living room with fireplace and loft, private bedroom, and bathroom with shower. Great for families or small groups of 4-6 people. Breakfast provisions provided. Bavarian and Mt. Alpine setting adjacent to four ski areas adn the Pacific Crest Trail. Only 55 minutes east of Seattle and five minutes to skiing, sledding, hiking, mountain biking, and other outdoor recreational activities.

Hosts: Pat and Forrest Frantz
Rooms: 1 apartment sleeps 4-6 (1PB) $55-75
Continental Breakfast (provisions provided)
Credit Cards: none
Notes: 2, 5, 7, 11

NOTES: Credit cards accepted: A Master Card; B Visa; C American Express; D Discover; E Diners Club; F Other; 2 Personal checks accepted; 3 Lunch available; 4 Dinner available;

SPOKANE

Marianna Stoltz House Bed and Breakfast

E 427 Indiana Avenue, 99207
(509) 483-4316; (800) 978-6587;
FAX (509) 483-6773

Our 1908 historic home is situated five minutes from downtown. Furnished with antiques, old quilts, and Oriental rugs. We offer wraparound veranda, sitting room, and parlor which provide relaxation and privacy. Enjoy king, queen, or single beds with private or shared baths, air-conditioning, and TV. A tantalizing, unique, and hearty breakfast is prepared each morning. Close to shopping, opera house, convention center, Centennial Trail, riverfront park, and bus.

Hosts: Jim and Phyllis Maguire
Rooms: 4 (2PB; 2SB) $65-80
Full Breakfast
Credit Cards: A, B, C, D, E
Notes: 2, 5, 8, 9, 10, 11, 12

Oslo's Bed and Breakfast

1821 East 39th Avenue, 99203
(509) 838-3175; (888) 838-3175

An attractive South Hill home on a quiet street. Comfortable bedrooms with private baths, and living room available where you may relax and read or visit in a Norwegian atmosphere. Central air-conditioning. A large terrace overlooking the garden may be enjoyed with a full breakfast served at 9:00 A.M., Scandinavian cuisine if desired. Earlier breakfast may be arranged if planned in advance. A small park is located ½ block away. It has tennis courts, exercise stops, and paths for walking. The network of skywalks downtown may be worth investigating, also the Cheney Cowles Museum and the Bing Crosby Library at Gonzaga University.

Host: Aslaug Stevenson
Rooms: 2 (PB) $55-70
Full Breakfast
Credit Cards: none
Notes: 2, 5, 6, 8, 10, 11, 12

TACOMA/SEATTLE

Commencement Bay Bed and Breakfast

3312 N. Union Avenue, 98407
(206) 752-8175; FAX (206) 759-4025
Email: greatviews@aol.com

An elegant Colonial home in scenic North Tacoma with dramatic bay and mountain views. Located in an historic area near quaint shops, numerous fine restaurants, and waterfront parks. Featured in "Northwest Best Places," the Inn serves fantastic breakfasts and offers large rooms private baths, a relaxing fireside area, a secluded garden hot tub, and full services for business travelers. Gourmet coffees served daily.

Hosts: Bill and Sharon Kaufmann
Rooms: 3 (PB) $75-105
Full Breakfast
Credit Cards: A, B, C, D
Notes: 2, 5, 7 (12 and up), 8, 9, 10, 11, 12

---

5 Open all year; 6 Pets welcome; 7 Children welcome; 8 Tennis nearby; 9 Swimming nearby; 10 Golf nearby; 11 Skiing nearby; 12 May be booked through travel agent.

WEST VIRGINIA

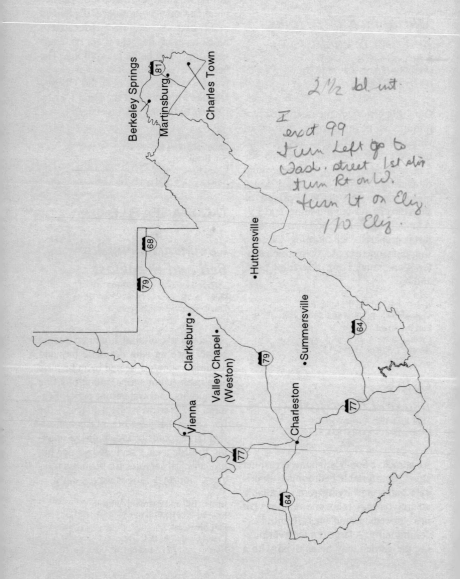

2½ bl. wt.

I
exot 99
turn Left go to
Wash. street 1st str
turn Rt on W.
turn Lt on Eliz.
110 Eliz.

West Virginia

BERKELEY SPRINGS

The Country Inn and Renaissance Spa

207 S. Washington Street, 25411
(304) 258-2210; (800) 822-6630;
FAX (304) 258-5111

Retaining the best of the past. . .less than 100 miles from Balto. Enjoy the warmth and service of a unique and charming country inn. 70 distinctive rooms, creative cuisine, and light specialties. Relax in our full service spa, art gallery, and serene gardens. Many irresistible packages available. Call for reservations.

Hosts: Mr. and Mrs. Jack Barker (innkeepers)
Rooms: 70 (57PB; 13SB) $35-80
Full Breakfast
Credit Cards: A, B, C, D, E
Notes: 2, 3, 4, 5, 7, 8, 9, 10, 11, 12

CHARLESTON

Historic Charleston Bed and Breakfast

114 Elizabeth Street, 25311
(304) 345-8156;
(800) CALLWVA (ask for Historic Charleston);
FAX (304) 342-1572

Historic Charleston Bed and Breakfast

Built in 1905 this American Foursquare home was opened in 1991 as the FIRST bed and breakfast in Charleston. Located in the historic district of the city, one block from the Capitol, Cultural Center and Governor's Mansion. A great place for evening walks along the Kanawha River with a view of Charleston University and many beautiful homes. Many other attractions in the city and nearby to take part in. Three antique-filled, non-smoking guest rooms with private baths and a sitting area await your arrival. A full breakfast is included; stuffed French toast, blueberry pancakes, and Belgian waffles are just a few of the many delicious entrees served. We offer affordable elegance

NOTES: Credit cards accepted: A Master Card; B Visa; C American Express; D Discover; E Diners Club; F Other; 2 Personal checks accepted; 3 Lunch available; 4 Dinner available; 5 Open all year; 6 Pets welcome; 7 Children welcome; 8 Tennis nearby; 9 Swimming nearby; 10 Golf nearby; 11 Skiing nearby; 12 May be booked through travel agent.

that will entice a return visit. While visiting in Charleston, we welcome you in our bed and breakfast.

Hosts: Jean and Bob Lambert
Rooms: 3 (PB) $70-75
Full Breakfast
Credit Cards: A, B, C
Notes: 2, 8, 9, 10

COLONIAL CHARLES TOWN

Washington House Inn

216 South George Street, 25414
(304) 725-7923; (800) 297-6957;
FAX (304) 728-5150
Email: mnuogel@intrepid.net
Web site: http://www.intrepid.net/whib+b

In charming Colonial Charles Town, nestled in the Blue Ridge Mountains where the Shenandoah and Potomac Rivers meet, the Washington House Inn is a wonderful example of late Victorian architecture. Built at the turn of the century, by descendants of President Washington's brothers, the Inn is graced with antique furnishings, carved oak mantles, seven fireplaces, and spacious guest rooms. Just 60 miles from Washington D.C.

Hosts: Mel and Nina Vogel
Rooms: 6 (PB) $70-125
Full Breakfast
Credit Cards: A, B, C, D
Notes: 2, 5, 7 (over 10), 8, 9, 10, 12

CLARKSBURG

Main Street B&B

151 East Main Street, 26301
(304) 623-1440 (voice and FAX); (800) 526-9460

Main Street Bed and Breakfast is lo-

Main Street Bed and Breakfast

cated just five blocks from the heart of Clarksburg. Our 1872 home is one of the oldest in the county and part of a nationally registered historic district of distinguished homes. It was built in the Carpenter-Gothic style and is colorfully decorated in a pleasing multi-colored scheme. The three large guest rooms have queen- or king-sized beds, private baths, and comfortable sitting areas.

Hosts: Bethlyn and David Cluphf
Rooms: 3 (PB) $60-70
Full Breakfast
Credit Cards: A, B, C, D
Notes: 2, 5, 7, 10, 12

HUTTONSVILLE

Hutton House Bed and Breakfast

PO Box 88, Route 250 and 219, 26273
(304) 335-6701

Meticulously restored and decorated, this Queen Anne Victorian on the National Register of Historic Places is conveniently located near Elkins, Cass Railroad, and Snowshoe Ski Resort. It has a wraparound porch and deck for relaxing

NOTES: Credit cards accepted: A Master Card; B Visa; C American Express; D Discover; E Diners Club; F Other; 2 Personal checks accepted; 3 Lunch available; 4 Dinner available;

and enjoying the view, TV, game room, lawn for games, and a friendly kitchen. Breakfast and afternoon refreshments are served at your leisure; other meals are available with prior reservation or good luck! Come see us!

Hosts: Loretta Murray and Dean Ahren
Rooms: 6 (PB) $60-70
Full Breakfast
Credit Cards: A, B
Notes: 2, 5, 7, 8, 10, 11, 12

MARTINSBURG

Boydville, The Inn at Martinsburg

601 South Queen Street, 25401
(304) 263-1448

A stone manor house, set well back from Queen Street. To reach the front door you turn up a drive through ten acres with over-arching maples on both sides of the road. This is an experience in itself, because it feels as if you are being led away from a busy world into an earlier and more peaceful time. Handsomely appointed and furnished with English and American antiques, the Inn dates back to 1812. Guests enjoy leisurely walks on the grounds, in the brick-walled courtyard, and the surrounding gardens. Boydville is ideal for a business retreat or a romantic getaway. On the National Register of Historic Places.

Hosts: LaRue Frye, Bob Boege, Carolyn Snyder, and Pete Bailey
Rooms: 6 (4PB; 2SB) $90-110
Expanded Continental Breakfast
Credit Cards: A, B
Notes: 2, 5 (except Aug.), 7 (over 12), 8, 10, 11, 12

Pulpit and Pallette Inn

316 W. John Street, 25401
(304) 263-7012

An 1870 Italianate Victorian home situated on land purchased in 1839 from Alexander Stephen, brother of Martinsburg founder Adam Stephen. An Oriental ambiance — Tibetan rugs and art treasures from India, Nepal, Thailand, and Hong Kong with a mix of American antiques. Two bedrooms share a bath. Morning coffee/tea, shortbread, and newspaper in bed, afternoon English tea, evening complimentary drinks and hor d'oeuvres, and gourmet breakfasts. Antique mall, 50-store outlet, craft mall one block.

Hosts: Bill and Janet Starr
Rooms: 2 (SB) $75
Full Breakfast and Afternoon Tea
Credit Cards: A, B
Closed January and February
Notes: 2, 10

SUMMERSVILLE

Historic Brock House Bed and Breakfast Inn

1400 Webster Road, 26651
(302) 872-4887 (voice and FAX)

Tucked away among towering maples and oaks, Historic Brock House Bed and Breakfast Inn has hosted travelers for over 100 years. On lazy summer afternoons, guests can enjoy the rockers and wicker furniture on the wide, wraparound porch. On cooler days a cozy fireside is available for quiet moments, a cup of tea, card playing, or visiting

---

5 Open all year; 6 Pets welcome; 7 Children welcome; 8 Tennis nearby; 9 Swimming nearby; 10 Golf nearby; 11 Skiing nearby; 12 May be booked through travel agent.

with new friends. Guests can choose from a full or light breakfast with a variety of homebaked items. Antique shops, Civil War battlefields, canoeing, water skiing, horseback trails, kayaking, rock climbing, and white water rafting abound in this area.

Hosts: Margie and Jim Martin
Rooms: 6 (4PB; 2SB) $70-90
Full Breakfast
Credit Cards: A, B
Notes: 2, 4, 10, 12

Ingeberg Acres

VALLEY CHAPEL (WESTON)

Ingeberg Acres Bed and Breakfast

PO Box 199, 26446
(304) 269-2834 (voice and FAX)

An unique experience can be yours at this scenic 450-acre horse and cattle farm. Ingeberg Acres is located in the heart of West Virginia seven miles from Weston, overlooking its own private valley. Hiking, swimming, hunting, and fishing or just relaxing can be the orders of the day. Observe or participate in numerous farm activities. Craft outlets and antique stores nearby. Come enjoy the gardens, the pool, and the friendly atmosphere. German spoken.

Hosts: Inge and John Mann
Rooms: 3 (SB) $59; cabin $80
Full Breakfast
Credit Cards: none
Notes: 2, 5, 7, 9, 10

VIENNA

Williams House B&B

5406 Grand Central Avenue (Route 14), 26105
(304) 295-7212

Reminiscent of day's spent long ago at Grandma's, the home is filled with old things, antiques, memorabilia from a wonderful family now grown. Clean comfortable, private rooms with baths and TV are named for our grown children. Delectable homemade dishes served every morning. Beautiful porches. Home is four square, three-story. Large common and sitting areas, fireplaces, central air, and wonderful pool. Area attractions include Fenton Art Glass Factory, Blennerhassett Island Historical Park, Middleton Doll Factory, and historical Marietta, Ohio.

Hosts: Bob and Barbara Williams
Rooms: 6 (3PB; 3SB) $52-62
Full Breakfast
Credit Cards: A, B, C
Notes: 2, 8, 9, 10, 12

Williams House

NOTES: Credit cards accepted: A Master Card; B Visa; C American Express; D Discover; E Diners Club; F Other; 2 Personal checks accepted; 3 Lunch available; 4 Dinner available;

Wisconsin

Albany Guest House

ALBANY

Albany Guest House

405 S. Mill Street, 53502
(608) 862-3636

A two-acre park-like setting, with flower gardens galore and a brick walk, is where you'll find the restored 1908 three story block home. With blooming plants everywhere you'll find king- and queen-sized beds, and a wood-burning fireplace in the master bedroom. Be amazed with the complete, antique, four piece, solid birdseye maple bedroom set, a family heirloom. After a full, wholesome breakfast, recover on the porch swing or rocker or stroll the grounds before exploring, biking, tub-

ing, or canoeing the river. A great reunion or retreat site.

Hosts: Bob and Sally Braem
Rooms: 4 (PB) $55-75
Full Breakfast
Credit Cards: A, B
Notes: 2, 5, 7 (disciplined), 10, 11

Oak Hill Manor Bed and Breakfast

401 E. Main Street, 53502
(608) 862-1400; FAX (608) 862-1404

Step back into time in our 1908 manor home. Enjoy rich oak woodwork, gasoliers, and period furnishings. Spacious, sunny corner rooms are air-conditioned and include queen-size beds and cozy reading areas. Choose a room with a fireplace, porch, or canopy bed. Relax in the garden gazebo or lounge on our spacious porch. Sumptuous breakfast served by fireside and candlelight. On the Sugar River Bike Trail. Bicycles available at no charge. No smoking. Come and enjoy!

Hosts: Donna and Colen Rothe
Rooms: 4 (PB) $60-70
Full Breakfast
Credit Cards: A, B
Notes: 2, 5, 7 (12 and older), 8, 10, 11

---

5 Open all year; 6 Pets welcome; 7 Children welcome; 8 Tennis nearby; 9 Swimming nearby;
10 Golf nearby; 11 Skiing nearby; 12 May be booked through travel agent.

WISCONSIN

Sugar River Inn Bed and Breakfast

304 S. Mill Street, 53502
(608) 862-1248

Our turn-of-the century inn, with many original features, has the charm of yesteryear and Christian fellowship. We are located in a quiet village in southern Wisconsin along the Sugar River. We have spacious lawn, canoeing, and fishing in the back yard. We are minutes away from the bike trail. Comfortable, light, airy rooms await you with queen-size beds, fine linens, afternoon refreshments, and wake up coffee. We are near New Glarus, House on the Rock, Little Norway, and the state capital in Madison. Only two hours from Chicago.

Hosts: Jack and Ruth Lindberg
Rooms: 4 (1PB; 3SB) $45-60
Full Breakfast
Credit Cards: A, B
Notes: 2, 5, 7 (by arrangement), 9, 10

ALGOMA

Amberwood Inn

N7136 Hwy. 42, 54201
(414) 487-3471

Luxury Lake Michigan beachfront accommodations. Located on two and one-half private acres with 300 feet of beach. Each suite is large, romantic, and very private. Private baths, whirlpool tubs, hot tub, sauna, and private decks open to the water. Two condos with full kitchens, one or two bedrooms, and whirlpool tubs are the ultimate in luxury and privacy. Awaken to a sunrise over

Amberwood Inn

water; sleep to the sound of the waves. Ten minutes to Door County.

Hosts: Jan and George Davies
Rooms: 7 (PB) $75-95
Full Breakfast
Credit Cards: A, B
Notes: 2, 7, 9, 10

BARABOO

Pinehaven B&B

E13083 Highway 33, 53913
(608) 356-3489

Our home is located in a scenic valley with a small, private lake and Baraboo Bluffs in the background. The guest rooms are distinctly different with wicker furniture and antiques, queen and twin beds. Take a walk in this peaceful country setting. Area activities

Pinehaven Bed and Breakfast

NOTES: Credit cards accepted: A Master Card; B Visa; C American Express; D Discover; E Diners Club; F Other; 2 Personal checks accepted; 3 Lunch available; 4 Dinner available; 5 Open all year; 6 Pets welcome; 7 Children welcome; 8 Tennis nearby; 9 Swimming nearby; 10 Golf nearby; 11 Skiing nearby; 12 May be booked through travel agent.

include Devil's Lake State Park, Circus World Museum, Wisconsin Dells, and ski resorts. Ask about our private guest cottage. No pets and no smoking. Gift certificates available.

Hosts: Lyle and Marge Getschman
Rooms: 4 (PB) $65-75
Full Breakfast
Credit Cards: A, B
Notes: 2, 5, 7 (over 5), 9, 10, 11

The Victorian Rose Bed and Breakfast

423 Third Avenue, 53913
(608) 356-7828

Nostalgic retreat. A place for all seasons. Spend tranquil moments with memories to treasure. Nestled in the heart of historical Baraboo. Centrally located to all area attractions. Enjoy the splendor of the Victorian era by resting on the wraparound front porch or relaxing in two formal parlors with beautiful cherub fireplace and TV/VCR. Romantic guestrooms, candlelight breakfast, and Christian hospitality.

Hosts: Robert and Carolyn Stearns
Rooms: 3 (PB) $70-90
Full Breakfast
Credit Cards: D
Notes: 2, 5, 8, 9, 10, 11, 12

Abendruh Bed and Breakfast Swisstyle

BELLEVILLE

Abendruh Bed and Breakfast Swisstyle

7019 Gehin Drive, 53508
(608) 424-3808

Experience B&B Swisstyle. This highly acclaimed, Wisconsin B&B offers true Swiss charm and hospitality. The serenity of this peaceful retreat is one of many treasures that keeps guests coming back. Spacious guestrooms adorned with beautiful family heirlooms. Sitting room with high cathedral ceiling and cozy fireplace. An Abendruh breakfast is a perfect way to start a new day or end a peaceful stay.

Hostess: Mathilde Jaggi
Rooms: 2 (PB) $60-65 + tax
Full Breakfast
Credit Cards: A, B
Notes: 2, 5, 8, 9, 10, 11, 12

Cameo Rose Bed and Breakfast

1090 Severson Road, 53508
(608) 424-6340

Romantic, Victorian country mansion set amid 120 acres of wooded hills and trails. Enjoy the gazebo porch with wicker swing and furniture, guest livingroom with fireplace, and tower sunroom. Ultimate quiet and relaxation. Memorable breakfast served on antique china and vintage lace. Five charming guest rooms with king or queen beds, private baths, central air, and smokefree; one with whirlpool. Ten miles to Madi-

---

NOTES: Credit cards accepted: A Master Card; B Visa; C American Express; D Discover; E Diners Club; F Other; 2 Personal checks accepted; 3 Lunch available; 4 Dinner available;

son or New Glarus. Antiques combined with comfort. Welcome!

Hosts: Dawn and Gary Bahr
Rooms: 5 (PB) $89-139
Full Breakfast
Credit Cards: A, B
Notes: 2, 5, 8, 9, 10, 11, 12

CHETEK

Trails End Bed and Breakfast

641 Ten Mile Lake Drive, 54728
(715) 924-2641

Peace and tranquillity await you in this modern, spacious, log lodge, situated on our private island. The log home boasts antiques of every sort, with stories behind most every unique feature of the home from an 1887 jail door to a 300 pound, seven-foot wagon wheel and a huge stone fireplace. Each guest's bedroom—the Romantic, Indian, and Western Rooms—are decorated for utmost comfort and relaxation.

Hosts: Richard and Bonnie Flood
Rooms: 3 (2PB; 1SB) $80-95
Full Breakfast
Credit Cards: A, B, C, D
Notes: 2, 9, 10

Trails End Bed and Breakfast

McGilvray's Victorian Bed and Breakfast

CHIPPEWA FALLS

McGilvray's Victorian Bed and Breakfast

312 West Columbia Street, 54729
(715) 720-1600

Built in 1893, this beautifully restored home is furnished with antiques typical of the turn-of-the-century. The style is Neo-classicism and Georgian Revival with a portico featuring two-story columns. The Rose bedroom has a queen-size oak bed and a half bath. The Secret Garden has a full-size bed and shares a bath across the sitting room. The Room With a View has a full-size bed and shares a bath with The Secret Garden. Guests of all three rooms are served a full breakfast in the formal dining room.

Hostess: Melanie J. Berg
Rooms: 3 (1PB; 2SB) $55-65
Full Breakfast
Credit Cards: none
Notes: 2, 5, 7 (over 12), 8, 9, 10, 11

CRANDON

5 Open all year; 6 Pets welcome; 7 Children welcome; 8 Tennis nearby; 9 Swimming nearby; 10 Golf nearby; 11 Skiing nearby; 12 May be booked through travel agent.

Courthouse Square Bed and Breakfast

Courthouse Square Bed and Breakfast

210 E. Polk Street, 54520
(715) 478-2549

Guests frequently comment about the peace and tranquillity of the setting. Enjoy birds and squirrels at the many benches placed throughout the flower and herb gardens or stroll down the hill to the lake through the forget-me-nots and view the wildlife. *The Rhinelander Daily News* wrote, "Traditional hospitality is emphasized at Courthouse Square B&B, and it's evident from the moment you enter this delightful home where tranquillity and peace abounds. You will no doubt smell something delicious baking in Bess's kitchen as gourmet cooking is one of her specialties."

Hosts: Les and Bess Aho
Rooms: 3 (1PB; 2SB) $50-60
Full Gourmet Candlelit Breakfast
Credit Cards: C
Notes: 2, 5, 7 (ask about 12+), 8, 9, 10, 11

DOOR COUNTY SEE—ALGOMA, EPHRAIM, GILLS ROCK, AND STURGEON BAY

EAGLE RIVER

Brennan Manor Bed and Breakfast

1079 Everett Road, 54521
(715) 479-7353

We welcome you to our English Tudor mansion located on the world's largest inland chain of lakes in Eagle River. We offer four large guest rooms, each with private bath, queen bed, hand-sewn quilts, and antiques. All rooms lead to an open balcony overlooking the spacious great room with its arched windows, hand-carved woodwork, and 30-foot stone fireplace. A four-bedroom guest house is also available. We welcome you!

Hosts: Bob and Connie Lawton
Rooms: 4 (PB) $79-99
Full Breakfast
Credit Cards: B, C
Notes: 2, 5, 9, 10, 11 (cross-country)

EAU CLAIRE

The Atrium Bed and Breakfast

5572 Prill Road, 54701
(715) 833-9045

Named for its most unique feature, the heart of this contemporary home is a 20' x 20' garden room where a palmtree and bougainvillea vines stretch toward the glassed ceiling. The home is nestled on 15 wooded acres on Otter Creek that beckons the explorer. Nearby you'll fine bicycling, canoeing, antiquing, and an Amish community. The Atrium offers

NOTES: Credit cards accepted: A Master Card; B Visa; C American Express; D Discover; E Diners Club; F Other; 2 Personal checks accepted; 3 Lunch available; 4 Dinner available;

the best of both worlds; relaxed seclusion, only minutes from numerous restaurants, shopping, and the University of Wisconsin-Eau Claire.

Hosts: Celia and Dick Stoltz
Rooms: 4 (2PB; 2SB) $65-80
Full Breakfast weekends; Continental Breakfast weekdays
Credit Cards: A, B
Notes: 2, 5, 7 (12 and over), 8, 9, 10, 11 (cross-country)

The Atrium Bed and Breakfast

Otter Creek Inn
2536 Highway 12, 54701
(715) 832-2945

Pamper yourself with breakfast in bed amid the antiques of yesteryear in this spacious 6,000 square-foot, three-story inn. Discover amenities of today tucked amidst the country Victorian decor as every guest room contains a double whirlpool, private bath, phone, AC, and cable TV. Explore the creek or snuggle up inside near the fire to watch the wildlife saunter by. All this country charm is located less than one mile from numerous restaurants and shops.

Hosts: Randy and Shelley Hansen
Rooms: 5 (PB) $79-139
Full Breakfast
Credit Cards: A, B, C, D, E
Notes: 2, 5, 8, 9, 10, 11

EPHRAIM

Hillside Hotel of Ephraim
9980 Hwy. 42, PO Box 17, 54211-0017
(414) 854-2417; (800) 423-7023;
FAX (414) 854-4604

Authentic, restored country, Country-Victorian inn featuring full, specialty breakfasts and afternoon teas, feather beds, original antiques, gorgeous harbor view, 100-foot veranda overlooking the harbor, individually decorated guest rooms, clawfoot tubs with showers, and brass fixtures. We have 13 years experience and *love* what we do!!

Hosts: David and Karen McNeil
Rooms: 11 (SB) $84-115
Cottages: 2 (PB) $160-180
Full Breakfast and Afternoon Tea
Credit Cards: A, B, D
Notes: 2, 5, 7, 8, 9, 10, 11

FORT ATKINSON

The Lamp Post Inn
408 S. Main Street, 53538
(414) 563-6561

We welcome you to the charm of our 122-year-old Victorian home filled with beautiful antiques. Five gramophones for your listening pleasure. For the modern, one of our baths features a large jacuzzi. We are located seven blocks from the famous Fireside Playhouse. You come a stranger, but leave here a friend. No smoking.

Hosts: Debbie and Mike Rusch
Rooms: 3 (2PB; 1SB) $60-95
Full Breakfast
Credit Cards: none
Notes: 2, 5, 7, 8, 9, 10, 11

5 Open all year; 6 Pets welcome; 7 Children welcome; 8 Tennis nearby; 9 Swimming nearby; 10 Golf nearby; 11 Skiing nearby; 12 May be booked through travel agent.

GILLS ROCK (DOOR COUNTY)

Harbor House Inn

12666 Hwy. 42, 54210
(414) 854-5196

1904 Victorian bed and breakfast with a new Scandinavian country wing overlooking the quaint fishing harbor, bluffs, and sunsets. The Inn has been restored to its original charm and tastefully done in period furniture. All rooms have Victorian old world charm, private baths, TVs, air-conditioning, and period furnishings. Two cottages are also available, both with full kitchens and one with a fireplace. Enjoy the Inn's fireplace, gazebo, one of the many decks, private beach, Scandinavian sauna cabin, whirlpool, and bike rentals. Walk to the ferry, shopping, and dining. AAA three-diamond rated.

Hosts: David and Else Weborg
Rooms: 12 (PB) $49-89
Cottages: 2 (PB) $99-105
Continental Plus Breakfast
Credit Cards: A, B, C
Open May 1 through October 30
Notes: 2, 6, 7, 9, 10

Harbor House Inn

Jordan House

HARTFORD

Jordan House B&B

81 S. Main Street, 53027
(414) 673-5643

Warm and comfortable Victorian home furnished with period antiques. Forty miles from Milwaukee. Near majestic Holy Hill Shrine, Horizon Wildlife Refuge, and Pike Lake State Park. Walk to the state's largest antique auto museum, antique malls, and downtown shops. Call or write for brochure.

Hosts: Kathy Buchanan and Art Jones
Rooms: 4 (1PB; 3SB) $55-65
Full Breakfast
Credit Cards: A, B
Notes: 2, 5, 7, 8, 9, 10, 11

HAYWARD

Shepherds Inn B&B

Route 3, Box 3306A, 54843
(715) 634-6142

Our bed and breakfast is nestled on the edge of a meadow, surrounded by 54 acres. We are minutes from the Birkie Ski Trail and Camba Bike Trails. We offer ski wax building and bike storage. Our inn is clean, cozy, and friendly.

Hosts: Pam and Steve Miles
Rooms: 3 (SB) $50-60
Continental Breakfast
Credit Cards: none
Notes: 2, 5, 9, 11

HAZEL GREEN

Wisconsin House Stage Coach Inn

2105 E. Main, 53811
(608) 854-2233

Built as a stage coach inn in 1846, the Inn now offers six rooms and two suites for your comfort. Join us for an evening's rest. Dine and be refreshed in the parlor where General Grant spent many evenings with his friend Jefferson Crawford. Most conveniently located for all the attractions of the Tri-State Area. Galena, Illinois, is ten minutes away; Dubuque, Iowa, 15 miles away; and Platteville is 20 miles away.

Hosts: Ken and Pat Disch
Rooms: 8 (6PB; 2SB) $55-110
Full Breakfast
Credit Cards: A, B, D
Notes: 2, 4, 5, 7, 12

IOLA

Taylor House Bed and Breakfast

210 E. Iola Street, PO Box 101, 54945
(715) 445-2204

Turn-of-the-century Victorian home. Four antique-furnished rooms, one with fireplace. Parlor with fireplace. Queen-size beds. No smoking. Air-conditioned. Paved country roads are ideal for biking. Twenty minutes from the Waupaca Chain O'Lakes area. We offer a glimpse of the lifestyle of the 1800s with all the conveniences of the modern age. Call or write for a free brochure.

Hosts: Crystal and Richard Anderson
Rooms: 4 (2PB; 2SB) $46-59.95
Full Breakfast
Credit Cards: none
Notes: 2, 5, 7, 9, 10, 11

LA FARGE

Trillium

E10596 East Salem Ridge Road, 54639
(608) 625-4492

An unusual opportunity to relax and unwind in the peaceful beauty of rural life. The private guest cottage, located on our 85-acre farm, faces woods and fields and is joined on two sides by our organic garden and orchard. Much wildlife to be observed. The cottage is completely furnished with two double beds, a crib, and all modern conveniences and includes a sunny kitchen-dining area, a wood-burning cookstove, stone fireplace, hammock under the trees, and porch. A generous farm cottage breakfast is served to the cottage. Many farm and area activities throughout the year; near an Amish community and good restaurants.

Hostess: Rosanne Boyett
Cottage: 2 bedrooms (2PB) $63-75
Full Breakfast
Credit Cards: none
Notes: 2, 5, 7, 8, 9, 10, 11

---

5 Open all year; 6 Pets welcome; 7 Children welcome; 8 Tennis nearby; 9 Swimming nearby; 10 Golf nearby; 11 Skiing nearby; 12 May be booked through travel agent.

LIVINGSTON

Oak Hill Farm

9850 Highway 80, 53554
(608) 943-6006

A comfortable country home with a warm hospitable atmosphere that is enhanced with fireplaces, porches, and facilities for picnics, bird-watching, and hiking. In the area you will find state parks, museums, and lakes.

Hosts: Elizabeth and Victor Johnson
Suites: 4 (1PB; 3SB) $42
Continental Breakfast
Credit Cards: none
Notes: 2, 6, 7, 8, 9, 10, 11, 12

LODI

Victorian Treasure Bed and Breakfast Inn

115 Prairie Street, 53555
(608) 592-5199; (800) 859-5199;
FAX (608) 592-7147

The Victorian Treasure is a balance between timeless ambiance, thoughtful amenities, and gracious hospitality. Eight unique guest rooms in two historic Queen Anne Victorians with architectural details and classic Victorian flair. Guests of the 1897 Bissell Mansion experience a more traditional B&B stay with a formal front parlor, sitting room with fireplace, and wraparound verandah. All guests enjoy fternoon refreshments and a full gourmet breakfast in the formal dining room. Guests of the

1893 Palmer House escape to luxurious suites with canopied bed, sitting area, fireplace, wet bar, microwave, refrigerator, stereo with CD, and whirlpool bath. The owners, also the innkeepers, are fussy about the details and genuinely interested in exceeding guest's expectations!

Hosts: Todd and Kimberly Seidl
Rooms: 4 (PB) $65-110
Full Breakfast
Credit Cards: A, B
Notes: 2, 5, 8, 9, 10, 11, 12

MADISON

Annie's Bed and Breakfast

2117 Sheridan Drive, 53704
(608) 244-2224; FAX (608) 242-9611

When you want the world to go away, come to Annie's, the quiet inn on Warner Park with the beautiful view. Luxury accommodations at reasonable rates. Close to the lake and park. It is also convenient to downtown and the University of Wisconsin campus. There are unusual amenities in this charming setting, including a romantic gazebo surrounded by butterfly gardens, a shaded terrace, and pond. Two beautiful two-bedroom suites. Double jacuzzi. Full air-conditioning. Winter cross-country skiing, too!

Hosts: Anne and Larry Stuart
Suites: 2 (two-room suites) (PB) $75-119
Full Breakfast
Credit Cards: A, B, C
Notes: 2, 5, 7 (over 12), 8, 9, 10, 11

NOTES: Credit cards accepted: A Master Card; B Visa; C American Express; D Discover; E Diners Club; F Other; 2 Personal checks accepted; 3 Lunch available; 4 Dinner available;

Harrisburg Inn

Mansion Hill Inn

424 N. Pinckney Street, 53703
(608) 255-3999; (800) 798-9070;
FAX (608) 255-2217

Eleven luxurious rooms, each with a sumptuous bath. Whirlpool tubs with stereo headphones, hand-carved marble fireplaces, minibars, and elegant Victorian furnishings help make this restored mansion into Madison's ONLY Four Diamond Inn. Private wine cellar, VCR's, and access to private dining and athletic clubs available upon request. Turndown service and evening refreshments in our parlor. Ideal for honeymoons. Listed on the National Register of Historic Places.

Hostess: Janna Wojtal
Rooms: 11 (PB) $120-130
Continental, Silver Service Breakfast
Credit Cards: A, B, C
Notes: 2, 5, 9, 12

MAIDEN ROCK

Harrisburg Inn

W3334 Highway 35, PO Box 15, 54750
(715) 448-4500

Our slogan, "a view with a room," can't begin to describe the sweeping vista enjoyed from every room. Miles of Mississippi valley spread out with boating, fishing, bird watching, and biking readily available. The Harrisburg Inn nestles on a bluff with the ambience of yesteryear in simple country decor and the beauty of nature pleasing the eye. Hearty food and happy hosts welcome you to Wisconsin's west coast. Explore twelve vintage villages of the Lake Pepin area and "inn-joy."

Hosts: Bern Paddock and Carol Crisp Paddock
Rooms: 4 (PB) $68-98
Full Breakfast Weekends (Continental Breakfast
   Monday - Thursday)
Credit Cards: A, B, D
Notes: 2, 7 (weekdays), 9, 10, 11

MENOMONIE

The Wilson Park Bed and Breakfast

814 Ninth Avenue East, 54751
(715) 235-4552

A comfortabe home built in 1909, furnished with antiques and decorated with warm and hospitality. Full breakfast served with homemade muffins, rolls,

---

5 Open all year; 6 Pets welcome; 7 Children welcome; 8 Tennis nearby; 9 Swimming nearby;
10 Golf nearby; 11 Skiing nearby; 12 May be booked through travel agent.

coffee cakes, and plenty of fresh brewed coffee. No smoking. Walking distance to historic downtown, Wilson Park, museum, and University of Wisconsin-Stout. Also near antique shops, hiking, biking, fishing, water sports, Crystal Cave, and Eau Claire, a half hour.

Hosts: Judith and Robert Reuter
Rooms: 3 (SB) $40-60
Full Breakfast
Credit Cards: none
Notes: 2, 5, 8, 9, 10, 11

MEQUON

Port Zedler Motel

10036 North Port Washington Road, 53705
(414) 241-5850 (voice and FAX)

AAA Approved. Air-conditioned. Convenient to downtown, casino, and excellent restaurants. Twelve minutes north of downtown Milwaukee. Touch-tone, in-room phones. Full private bath/shower. Winter plug-ins. In-room refrigerator and microwave oven on request. Rates include color cable TV (HBO/Showtime). Free, ample parking and ice. No charge for children under 12. Senior/AARP/AAA discounts. German is spoken. I-43 northbound one-half mile northwest of exit 83 (Hwy. W. North). I-43 southbound exit 82A, one block east and one and one-half mile north on Port Washington Road (Hwy. W. North).

Hostess: Sheila
Rooms: 16 (PB) $34-95-59.95
Continental Breakfast
Credit Cards: A, B, C, D
Notes: 5, 6, 7, 8, 9, 10, 11, 12

Victorian Garden Bed and Breakfast

MONROE

Victorian Garden B&B

1720 16th Street, 53566
(608) 328-1720

1890 Victorian home has a wraparound porch and a large flower garden. The light and airy interior welcomes you into a pet and smoke free home. The sitting room with a baby grand piano, a formal parlor, and an informal parlor with TV are for your enjoyment. A three-course breakfast is served in the formal dining room. The new kitchen is always a favorite spot to enjoy the view of the yard from the bay window.

Hosts: Pete and Jane Kessenich
Rooms: 3 (PB) $65-80
Full Breakfast
Credit Cards: A, B, D
Notes: 2, 5, 8, 9, 11 (cross-country), 12

OSCEOLA

Pleasant Lake
Bed and Breakfast

2238 60th Avenue, 54020-4509
(715) 294-2545; (800) 294-2545

Enjoy a romantic getaway on beautiful

Pleasant Lake. While here you may take a leisurely walk in the woods, watch the birds and other wildlife, enjoy the lake in the paddle boat or canoe, sit around the bonfire, and watch the moon and stars reflecting on the lake then relax on your private deck or in one of the whirlpools. Enjoy a full country breakfast which includes homemade whole wheat cinnamon toast, muffins, and homemade jam.

Hosts: Richard and Charlene Berg
Rooms: 4 (PB) $55-110
Full Breakfast
Credit Cards: A, B, D
Notes: 2, 5, 9, 10, 11

Pleasant Lake Bed and Breakfast

PLAIN

Bettinger House Bed and Breakfast

Highway 23, PO Box 243, 53577
(608) 546-2951 (voice and FAX)

Hostess's grandparents' 1904 Victorian farmhouse; Grandma was a midwife and delivered 300 babies in this house. Choose from five spacious bedrooms that blend the old with the new, each

named after note-worthy persons of Plain. Central air-conditioning. Start your day with one of the old-fashioned, full-course breakfasts we are famous for. Near "House on the Rock," Frank Lloyd Wright's original Taliesin, American Players Theatre, White Mound Park, and much more.

Hosts: Jim and Marie Neider
Rooms: 5 (2PB; 3SB) $50-65
Full Breakfast
Credit Cards: A, B
Notes: 2, 5, 7 (inquire first), 8, 9, 10, 11, 12

PORT WASHINGTON

The Inn at Old Twelve Hundred Bed and Breakfast and Guest House

806 W. Grand Avenue, 53074
(414) 268-1200; FAX (414) 284-6885

Beautifully restored and decorated Queen Anne. Alls rooms have fireplaces; some offer oversized whirlpools, private sitting rooms, and/or porches. Guest House rooms offer all the amenities and ultimate privacy, but do not include breakfast. Air-conditioned. Restricted smoking. Croquet, Tandem bicycles, and spacious yard. Minutes to Cedarburg and Harrison Beach State Park.

Hostesses: Stephanie and Ellie Bresette
Rooms: 4 B&B suites and 3 Guest House suites
(PB) $95-145
Continental Breakfast in B&B only
Credit Cards: A, B, C
Notes: 2, 5

---

5 Open all year; 6 Pets welcome; 7 Children welcome; 8 Tennis nearby; 9 Swimming nearby; 10 Golf nearby; 11 Skiing nearby; 12 May be booked through travel agent.

REEDSBURG

Parkview
Bed and Breakfast

211 N. Park Street, 53959
(608) 524-4333
Email: parkview@tcs.itis.com

Our 1895 Queen Anne Victorian home
overlooks City Park in the historic district. Many of the original features of
the home remain, such as hardware,
hardwood floors, intricate woodwork,
leaded and etched windows, plus a suit-
ors window. Wake-up coffee is followed by a full, homemade breakfast.
Central air and ceiling fans add to
guests' comfort. Located one block
from downtown. Close to Wisconsin
Dells, Baraboo, and Spring Green.
Three blocks from 400 Bike Trail.

Hosts: Tom and Donna Hofmann
Rooms: 4 (2PB; 2SB) $60-75
Full Breakfast
Credit Cards: A, B, C
Notes: 2, 5, 7 (inquire), 8, 10, 11, 12

RICHLAND CENTER

Lamb's Inn
Bed and Breakfast

Route 2, Box 144, 53581
(608) 585-4301

Relax on our 180-acre farm, located in
scenic valley surrounded by spectacular hills. Beautifully renovated farmhouse, furnished with country antiques
. . . porch for watching deer and other
wildlife . . . cozy library for rainy days.
Our new cottage has a spiral stair to the
loft and a deck to relax on. Large homemade breakfasts served at the B&B with
homemade breads, egg dishes, and often old-fashioned bread pudding. Our
hope is that your stay will be a memorable and relaxing time for you.

Hosts: Dick and Donna Messerschmidt
Rooms: 2 + 2 suites in cottage (PB) $70-115
Full Breakfast in B&B; Continental Breakfast in
    Cottage
Credit Cards: A, B
Notes: 2, 5, 7 (in cottage), 8, 9, 10, 12

Lamb's Inn

SPARTA

The Franklin Victorian
Bed and Breakfast

220 E. Franklin Street, 54656
(608) 269-3894; (800) 845-8767

This turn-of-the-century home welcomes you to bygone elegance with
small-town quiet and comfort. The four
spacious bedrooms provide a perfect
setting for ultimate relaxation. Full
home-cooked breakfast is served before
starting you day of hiking, biking, skiing, canoeing, antiquing, or exploring
this beautiful area.

Hosts: Lloyd and Jane Larson
Rooms: 4 (2PB; 2SB) $70-92
Full Breakfast
Credit Cards: A, B
Notes: 2, 5, 7 (over 10), 8, 9, 10, 11

NOTES: Credit cards accepted: A Master Card; B Visa; C American Express; D Discover;
E Diners Club; F Other; 2 Personal checks accepted; 3 Lunch available; 4 Dinner available;

Strawberry Lace Inn Bed and Breakfast

603 North Water Street, 54656
(608) 269-7878

Return to an era of romance and elegance. The home is an excellent example of an Italianate Victorian (circa 1875). Rest in your own private retreat with private bath, king or queen bed with mountains of pillows, and distinctive antique decor. Partake in your hosts' four-course breakfast presented on crystal and linen. Relax by visiting, reading, or playing games on the four-season porch. Known as "the biking capital of America," the area offers bike trails, golf, water sports, antiquing, restaurants, winter sports, and much more.

Hosts: Jack and Elsie Ballinger
Rooms: 5 (PB) $79-125
Full Four-course Breakfast
Credit Cards: A, B
Notes: 2, 5, 8, 9, 10, 11

Strawberry Lace Inn

STEVENS POINT

Dreams of Yesteryear Bed and Breakfast

1100 Brawley Street, 54481
(715) 341-4525; FAX (715) 344-3047

Featured in *Victorian Homes Magazine* and listed on the National Register of Historic Places. Your hosts are from Stevens Point and enjoy talking about the restoration of their turn-of-the-century home which has been in the same family for three generations. All rooms are furnished in antiques. Guests enjoy use of parlors, porches, and gardens. Two blocks from the historic downtown, antique and specialty shops, picturesque Green Circle Trails, the university, and more. Dreams of Yesteryear is truly "a Victorian dream come true."

Hosts: Bonnie and Bill Maher
Rooms: 6 (4PB; 2SB) $55-129
Full Breakfast
Credit Cards: A, B, C, D
Notes: 2, 5, 7 (over 12), 8, 9, 10, 11, 12

STURGEON BAY

Hearthside Bed and Breakfast

2136 Taube Road, 54235
(414) 746-2136

Our 1800s farmhouse has a blend of contemporary and antique furnishings. The old barn still stands nearby. Within

---

5 Open all year; 6 Pets welcome; 7 Children welcome; 8 Tennis nearby; 9 Swimming nearby;
10 Golf nearby; 11 Skiing nearby; 12 May be booked through travel agent.

easy driving distance are fantastic state parks, beaches for swimming in summer, or areas for skiing in the winter. Lighthouses, U.S. Coast Guard Station, lake cruises, airport, ship building, and weekend festivals. The rooms are charming; three with queen beds. Our family room has twin beds with an adjoining room that has a double bed. Guests may use TVs, VCRs, living room, and sun room.

The Scofield House

Hosts: Don and Lu Kleussendorf
Rooms: 4 (PB) $35-65
Full Home-cooked Breakfast
Credit Cards: none
Notes: 2, 5, 7, 8, 9, 10, 11

The Scofield House Bed and Breakfast

908 Michigan Street, 54235-1849
(414) 743-7727 (voice and FAX); (888) 463-0204

"Door County's most elegant bed and breakfast." This 1902, multi-colored, three-story Victorian was restored in 1987 by the present hosts. Guests keep coming back for Bill's wonder gourmet breakfasts and Fran's homemade "sweet treats" served fresh daily. The Scofield House has six guest rooms, of which four are suites, all with private bath, color TV/VCR, and a "free" video library. Double whirlpools, fireplaces, and central A/C. Smoke free environment.

Hosts: Bill and Fran Cecil
Rooms: 6 (PB) $89-190
Full Breakfast
Credit Cards: none
Notes: 2, 5, 8, 9, 10, 11

TWO RIVERS

Red Forest Bed and Breakfast

1421 25th Street, 54241
(414) 793-1794

We invite you to step back in time to 1907 and enjoy our gracious three-story shingle style home. Highlighted with stained glass windows, heirloom antiques, and cozy fireplace. Four beautifully appointed guest rooms await your arrival. Stroll along our sugar sand beaches or through downtown antique shops. The Red Forest is located on Wisconsin's East Coast, minutes from Manitowoc, Wisconsin's port city of Lake Michigan Carferry. Also located midway from Chicago and the Door County Pennisula.

Hosts: Alan and Kay Rodewald
Rooms: 4 (2PB; 2SB) $65-85
Full Breakfast
Credit Cards: A, B, C, D
Notes: 2, 5, 7 (older), 8, 9 (beach), 10, 11, 12 (12% comm.)

NOTES: Credit cards accepted: A Master Card; B Visa; C American Express; D Discover; E Diners Club; F Other; 2 Personal checks accepted; 3 Lunch available; 4 Dinner available;

VIROQUA

Viroqua Heritage Inn

220 East Jefferson, 54665
(608) 637-3306

Two elegant 1890s homes furnished with period antiques and located in this quaint small town in the beautiful Hidden Valleys region of southwestern Wisconsin. Historic homes and churches are abundant in this area, known for its wholesome Midwest lifestyle. Full breakfast and personal service. Located just nineteen miles from the Mississippi Rive and eight miles from an Amish farm community with quilt shops, Bentwood furniture shops, Amish rugs, baked goods, and so forth. Six downhill ski areas nearby; minute from the Kickapoo River.

Hosts: Nancy Rhodes
Rooms: 8 (1PB; 7SB) $40-60
Full Breakfast
Credit Cards: A, B, C
Notes: 2, 7, 8, 9, 10, 11

WISCONSIN DELLS

Historic Bennett House

825 Oak Street, 53965
(608) 254-2500

The 1863 home of honored pioneer photographer H. H. Bennett is warm and inviting in its casual elegance and welcoming atmosphere. Traveling with another couple? We have the ideal situations for you. Two lovely bedrooms, one with queen canopy bed and English armoire and the other with queen brass bed with wicker accents. Share a carpeted bedroom-size bath with Italian sinks and Bennett's clawfooted tub. You may, of course, reserved just one room. The library has become part of a two-room suite with private bath. View a favorite movie from our 100-plus collection. Enjoy East Lake bedroom. Savor a delicious gourmet breakfast, and visit Dells attractions; state parks; Bennett, Rockwell, Circus, and Railroad museums; river boat tours; skiing; and the C Vane Foundation.

Hosts: Gail and Rich Obermeyer
Rooms: 3 (1PB; 2SB) $70-90
Full Breakfast
Credit Cards: none
Notes: 2, 5, 8, 9, 10, 11

Terrace Hill Bed and Breakfast

922 River Road, 53965
(608) 253-9363

Serendipity, the unexpected. A quiet niche with private parking in rear and adjoining the parking area is a secluded city park which wraps around our residences down to River Road and overlooks the Wisconsin River. Only one block from downtown Dells. Victorian decor includes little surprises tucked in places throughout the house for your enjoyment and reminiscing pleasure. In this hectic world, let time stand still and enjoy a memorable stay.

Hosts: The Novak Family
Rooms: 5 (PB) $65-110
Full Breakfast
Credit Cards: none
Notes: 2, 5, 7, 8, 9, 10, 11, 12

5 Open all year; 6 Pets welcome; 7 Children welcome; 8 Tennis nearby; 9 Swimming nearby; 10 Golf nearby; 11 Skiing nearby; 12 May be booked through travel agent.

WYOMING

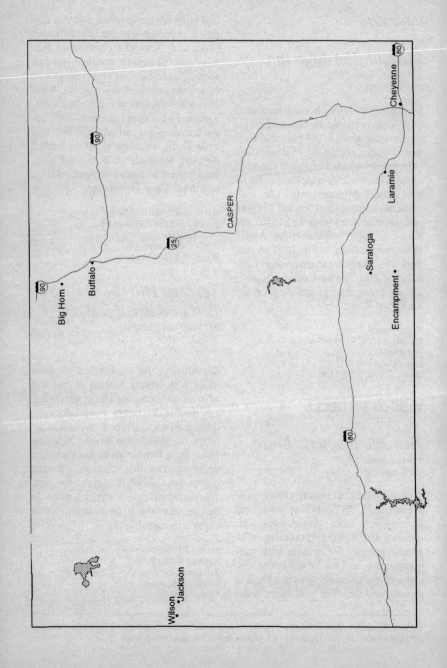

Wyoming

BIG HORN

Spahn's Bighorn Mountain Bed and Breakfast

PO Box 579, 82833
(307) 674-8150

Towering log home and secluded guest cabins on the mountainside in whispering pines. Borders one million acres of public forest with deer and moose. Gracious mountain breakfast served on the deck with binoculars to enjoy the 100-mile view. Owner is former Yellowstone ranger. Ten minutes from I-90 near Sheridan.

Hosts: Ron and Bobbie Spahn
Rooms: 2 + 2 cabins (PB) $65-120
Full Breakfast
Credit Cards: A, B
Notes: 2, 3, 4, 7

BUFFALO

Historic Mansion House Inn

313 North Main Street, 82834
(307) 684-2218

Turn-of-the-century Victorian Home located on historic Main Street and Highway 16, scenic route from the Black Hills of South Dakota to Yellowstone National Park. All rooms are comfortably decorated, each with private bath, TV, and air-conditioning. Continental Breakfast provided. Open year-round.

Hosts: Phil and Diane Mehlhaff
Rooms: 18 (PB) call for rates
Continental Breakfast
Credit Cards: A, B, D
Notes: 5, 7, 8, 9, 10, 11, 12

NOTES: Credit cards accepted: A Master Card; B Visa; C American Express; D Discover; E Diners Club; F Other; 2 Personal checks accepted; 3 Lunch available; 4 Dinner available; 5 Open all year; 6 Pets welcome; 7 Children welcome; 8 Tennis nearby; 9 Swimming nearby; 10 Golf nearby; 11 Skiing nearby; 12 May be booked through travel agent.

CHEYENNE

A. Drummond's Ranch Bed and Breakfast

399 Happy Jack Road, **Laramie** 82007
(307) 634-6042; FAX (307) 634-6042

A quiet, gracious retreat, situated on 120 acres near Medicine Bow National Forest and Curt Gowdy State Park. Between Cheyenne and Laramie at 7,500 feet elevation. Privacy with personalized service. Hiking, mountian biking, cross-country skiing, llama packing, or simply relaxing. Outdoor hot tubs and glorious night skies. Boarding for horses and pets in transit. Dietary restrictions accommodated when possible. No smoking please. Reservations required.

Hostess: Taydie Drummond
Rooms: 4 (2PB; 2SB) $65-150
Full Breakfast
Credit Cards: A, B
Notes: 2, 3, 4, 5, 6, 7, 10, 11, 12

A. Drummond's Ranch

The Storyteller, Pueblo Bed and Breakfast

5201 Ogden Road, 82009
(307) 634-7036; FAX (307) 638-4924

Native American art from over 30 tribes: pottery, beadwork, baskets, and rugs. Contemporary home of country and primitive antiques. Down home hospitality on a quiet street. Convenient to shopping and major restaurants. Breakfast with all the amenities. Fireplaces and family rooms for your enjoyment. Reservations recommended. Special rates during the last ten days of every July.

Hosts: Howard and Peggy Hutchings
Rooms: 3 (1PB; 12SB) $40-55
Full Breakfast
Credit Cards: none
Notes: 2, 5, 7 (by arrangement), 8, 9, 10, 11, 12

ENCAMPMENT

Rustic Mountain Lodge

Star Route, Box 49, 82325
(307) 327-5539 (voice and FAX)

A peaceful mountain view, located on a working ranch with wholesome country atmosphere and lots of Western hospitality. Enjoy daily fishing on a private pond, big game trophy hunts, cookouts, retreats, pack trips, photo safaris, youth programs, cattle drives, trail rides, hiking, rock hunting, numerous ranch activities, mountain biking and four wheeling trails, and survival workshops. Individuals, families, and groups welcome! A terrific atmosphere for workshops. Lodge and cabin rentals available. Reservations only. Private fishing cabins available May through September. Write for a complete brochure!

Hosts: Mayvon and Ron Platt
Rooms: 4 (SB) $55
Full Breakfast
Credit Cards: none
Notes: 2, 3, 4, 5, 6, 7, 8, 9, 10, 11

NOTES: Credit cards accepted: A Master Card; B Visa; C American Express; D Discover; E Diners Club; F Other; 2 Personal checks accepted; 3 Lunch available; 4 Dinner available;

JACKSON

H.C. Richards Bed and Breakfast

PO Box 2606, 83001
(307) 733-6704; FAX (307) 733-0930

One and one-half blocks from the center of town. Homer and Eliza Richards' granddaughter, Jackie will be your hostess. Amenities included in every room: private baths, goosedown comforters, tea service, telephones, and cable TV. Gourmet breakfasts. Take your afternoon tea in the sitting room in front of a glowing fire. Many of the beautiful antiques were Homer and Eliza's and you feel the warmth of their presence and the love that they shared just relaxing amidst their treasured belongings.

Hostess: Jackie Williams
Rooms: 3 (PB) $81.00 - 97.20
Full Breakfast
Credit Cards: A, B
Notes: 2, 5, 6, 7 (over 9), 8, 9, 10, 11, 12

SARATOGA

Far Out West Bed and Breakfast

304 N. Second Street, PO Box 1230, 82331-1230
(307) 326-5869; FAX (307) 326-9864

Historic home with six guest rooms that are comfortably decorated with a country flair and include all private baths. Each room is named for an historical figure famous in the area. We provide a separate area to clean your fish and equipment, store your skis, and wax your skis. Every effort is taken to make your stay relaxing and stress free.

Hosts: Bill and B. J. Farr
Rooms: 6 (PB) $95 + tax
Full Breakfast
Credit Cards: A, B
Notes: 2, 5, 7, 9, 10, 11

WILSON

Teton View Bed and Breakfast

2136 Coyote Loop, PO Box 652, 83014
(307) 733-7954

Rooms have mountain views. The lounge/eating area, where homemade pastries, fresh fruit, and coffee are served, connects to a private upper deck with fantastic mountain and ski resort views. Private, guest entrance. Convenient to Yellowstone and Grand Teton National Parks. Approximately four miles from the ski area.

Hosts: John and Joanna Engelhart
Rooms: 3 (1PB; 2SB) $60-90
Full Breakfast
Credit Cards: A, B
Close April and November
Notes: 2, 4, 7, 8, 9, 10, 11, 12

5 Open all year; 6 Pets welcome; 7 Children welcome; 8 Tennis nearby; 9 Swimming nearby; 10 Golf nearby; 11 Skiing nearby; 12 May be booked through travel agent.

ALBERTA

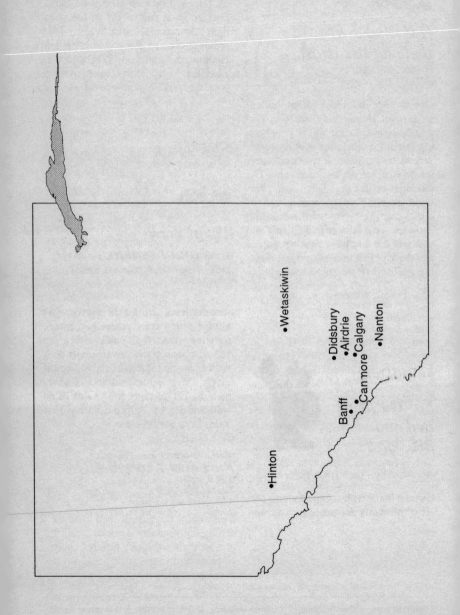

- •Wetaskiwin
- •Didsbury
- •Airdrie
- •Calgary
- •Canmore
- •Nanton
- •Banff
- •Hinton

Alberta

AIRDRIE

Big Springs Bed and Breakfast

RR 1, T4B 2A3
(403) 948-5264; FAX (403) 948-5851
Email: whittake@cadvision.com
Web site: bigsprings@cadvision.com

Overlooking picturesque valley on private 35 pastoral acres. Beautifully landscaped and treed. Spacious 5,000 square foot hillside bungalow. Choose from The Bridal Room, The Manor Room, or The Victorian Room. Relax in the secluded English Garden sitting room. Full gourmet breakfast experience. Fifteen minutes to Calgary city limits, 25 minutes to airport. Great access to Banff, Lake Louise, Kananaskis Country, Calgary Stampede, and Calgary Zoo.

Hosts: Earle and Carol Whittaker
Rooms: 3 (PB) $85-100
Full Gourmet Breakfast
Credit Cards: B
Notes: 5, 7, 9, 10, 11, 12

BANFF

Pension Tannenhof

PO Box 1914, 121 Cave Avenue, T0L 0C0
(403) 762-4636; FAX (403) 762-5660

Quietly located on the foot of Sulphur Mountain, fifteen minutes walking to downtown on the Eave and Basin (birthplace of Banff and Banff National Park). Featuring a large living room with wood-burning fireplace, CCTV, lovely breakfast room, and a homey, yet elegant, atmosphere. Recreational facilities within short walking distance.

Hosts: Herbert and Fannye Riedinger
Rooms: 14 (7PB; 7SB) $70-135 (Canada $)
Full Breakfast
Credit Cards: A, B
Notes: 2, 5, 7, 8, 9, 10, 11

CALGARY

Paradise Acres B&B

Box 20 Site 2 RRH6, T2M 4L5
(403) 248-4748 (voice and FAX)

Come enjoy our friendly and luxurious setting with country quietness and city access. Paradise Acres features choice of breakfasts, queen-size beds, private

---

NOTES: Credit cards accepted: A Master Card; B Visa; C American Express; D Discover;
E Diners Club; F Other; 2 Personal checks accepted; 3 Lunch available; 4 Dinner available;
5 Open all year; 6 Pets welcome; 7 Children welcome; 8 Tennis nearby; 9 Swimming nearby;
10 Golf nearby; 11 Skiing nearby; 12 May be booked through travel agent.

baths, plus guest sitting rooms with TV/VCR. Located close to the TransCanada Highway and Calgary airport with a city and mountain view. Airport pickup available.

Hosts: Brian and Char Bates
Rooms: 3 (PB) $55-70
Both Full and Continental Breakfast
Credit Cards: A, B, C
Notes: 2, 5, 8, 9, 10, 11, 12

Rosedale House B&B

1633 7A Street NW, T2M 3K2
(403) 284-0010 (voice and FAX)

This large executive home offers the charm of a turn-of-the-century home with all the modern conveniences. The guest rooms have ensuite bathrooms, excellent queen beds, writing tables, and phone jacks. The lounge offers a TV, VCR, fireplace, pool table, and beverage station with microwave. The full breakfast is served in a formal dining room with linen and china. Excellent central location.

Hosts: Beth and Dennis Palmquist
Rooms: 3 (PB) $80-110 (Canadian)
Full Breakfast
Credit Cards: A, B, C
Notes: 2, 5, 7, 8, 9, 10, 11

CANMORE

Cougar Creek Inn B&B

PO Box 1162, T0L 0M0
(403) 678-4751; FAX (403) 678-9529

Quiet, rustic, cedar chalet with mountain views in every direction. Grounds border on Cougar Creek and are surrounded by rugged mountain scenery which invites all types of outdoor activity. Hostess has strong love for the mountains and can assist with plans for local hiking, skiing, canoeing, mountain biking, backpacking, etc., as well as scenic drives. The Bed and Breakfast has a private entrance with sitting area, fireplace, games, TV, sauna, and numerous reading materials for guests' use. Breakfasts are hearty and wholesome with many home-baked items.

Hostess: Mrs. Patricia Doucette
Rooms: 4 (2PB; 2SB) $55-60 (Canada $)
Full Breakfast
Credit Cards: none
Open May to September
Notes: 2, 3, 7, 8, 9, 10, 11

DIDSBURY

Grimmon House B&B

1601-15 Avenue, PO Box 1268, T0M 0W0
(403) 335-8353; FAX (403) 335-3640

"Love in any language, color, or creed fluently spoken here." Relax and enjoy the unique benefits of a rural experience just 45 minutes from Calgary. Three rooms charmingly furnished with brass beds, antiques, and quilts. Hearty breakfast overlooking the garden, private entrance, off-street parking, wake-up coffee delivered to your door. On-site antique store for browsing. Welcome lemonade and evening outdoor fire, weather permitting.

Hosts: John and Myrna Grimmon
Rooms: 3 (SB) $55 (includes tax)
Full Breakfast
Credit Cards: none
Notes: 2, 5, 7 (by prior arrangement), 8, 9, 10, 11, 12

NOTES: Credit cards accepted: A Master Card; B Visa; C American Express; D Discover; E Diners Club; F Other; 2 Personal checks accepted; 3 Lunch available; 4 Dinner available;

HINTON

Cozy Quarters Bed 'n Breakfast

289 Collinge Road, T7V 1L3
(403) 865-3996 (voice and FAX)

Cozy Quarters is conveniently located on a quiet residential street in the town of Hinton, just 15 minutes from Jasper Park gates. It's hilltop location offers a glimpse of the Rockies, while just across the street guests have access to the woodland wilderness and Hinton's vast hiking/biking trail system. Clean and cozy accommodations include a choice of two bedrooms with adjacent full bath. Family room with coffe bar, TV, and VCR. Full homemade breakfast. Backyard patio with fire pit.

Hosts: Ed and Debbie Braun
Rooms: 2 (SB) $50-65
Full Breakfast
Credit Cards: none
Notes: 5, 8, 9, 10, 11, 12

NANTON

Timber Ridge Homestead

Box 94, T0L 1R0
Summer: (403) 646-5683; Winter: (403) 646-2480

Timber Ridge Homestead is a rustic establishment in beautiful foothills ranching country about 70 miles SW of Calgary. We have good, quiet horses to help you see the abundant wildflowers, wildlife, and wonderful views of the Rockies. Good plain cooking if you want it. To get here, go to Nanton, 50 miles south of Calgary, drive West on Highway 533 for four miles, turn south, and follow winding road into hills for twelve miles and the gate is on the right.

Hostess: Bridget Jones
Rooms: 3 (SB) $50
Full Breakfast
Credit Cards: none
Notes: 2, 3, 4, 7

WETASKIWIN

Norwood Bed and Breakfast

201 Norwood Court, T9A 3P2
(403) 352-8850 (voice and FAX); (888) 352-7880
Email: norwd201@agt.net

Country charm and old-fashioned hospitality are combined in Norwood Bed and Breakfast, a modern home decorated with antiques and memorabilia. Guests will enjoy extra special amenities that include jacuzzi on outside deck and a baby grand piano, library, and CD system in the sitting room. A full breakfast is served in the formal dining room or on a sunny patio and includes homemade breads and jams. Resident cat. Near Canada's Aviation Hall of Fame, The Alberta Central Railroad Museum, golf, fashionable shops, and a tea house. 45 minutes from Edmonton and 30 minutes from the international airport.

Hosts: Pat and Roland Jensen
Rooms: 3 (1PB; 2SB) $55
Full Breakfast
Credit Cards: A, B, C
Notes: 2, 7 (by prior arrangement), 8, 9, 10

5 Open all year; 6 Pets welcome; 7 Children welcome; 8 Tennis nearby; 9 Swimming nearby; 10 Golf nearby; 11 Skiing nearby; 12 May be booked through travel agent.

BRITISH COLUMBIA

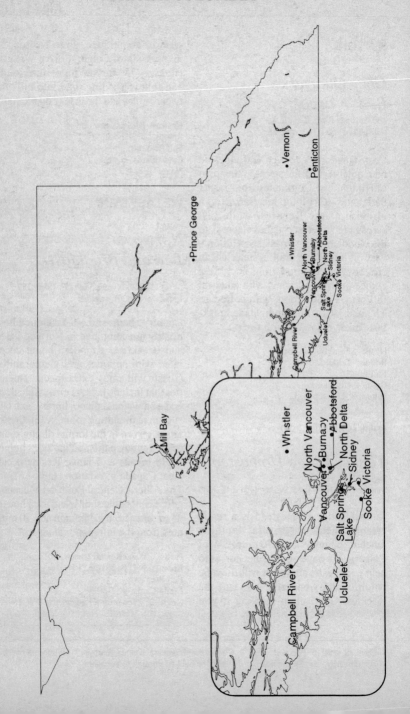

Vernon
Penticton
Prince George
Whistler
North Vancouver
Burnaby
Vancouver
Abbotsford
North Delta
Sidney
Salt Spring Lake
Sooke Victoria
Ucluelet
Campbell River
Mill Bay

North Vancouver
Burnaby
Vancouver
Abbotsford
North Delta
Sidney
Salt Spring Lake
Sooke Victoria
Ucluelet
Campbell River
Whistler

British Columbia

ABBOTSFORD

Everett House
Bed and Breakfast

1990 Everett Road, V2S 7S3
(604) 859-2944; FAX (604) 859-9180

We invite you to join us in our Victorian styled home in Abbotsford. Easily accessible to the freeway and overlooking the Fraser Valley, our home is the perfect retreat removed from the hustle of the city. It is also that "someplace special" for you while you conduct your business in the Fraser Valley. A stay at our home will provide you with a refreshing break from ordinary life.

Hosts: David and Cindy Sahlstrom
Rooms: 3 (PB) $65-95
Full Breakfast (early departure; Continental)
Credit Cards: A, B
Notes: 5, 7, 8, 9 (public pools), 10, 11, 12

CAMPBELL RIVER

Arbour's Guest House

375 S. Murphy Street, V9W 1Y8
(250) 287-9873; FAX (250) 287-2353

Arbour's Guest House Bed and Breakfast, reservations suggested, seasonal, complimentary glass of wine on arrival. Antique decor, with spectacular view of the mountains, ocean, and fishing grounds, from large treed property. TV room, bicycle rentals available, golf courses close by. Boat rental arrangements made and experienced fishing guides available for salt water salmon fishing. No smoking and no pets, please. Adult oriented.

Hosts: Ted and Sharon Arbour
Rooms: 2 (1PB; 1SB) $70-95
Continental Breakfast
Credit Cards: A, B
Open April through October
Notes: 8, 9, 10, 12

MILL BAY/VANCOUVER ISLAND

Pine Lodge Farm
Bed and Breakfast

3191 Mutter Road, V0R 2P0
(604) 743-4083; FAX (604) 743-7134

Our beautiful antique-filled lodge is located 25 miles north of Victoria. It is situated on a 30-acre farm overlooking ocean and islands. Arbutus trees, walk-

---

NOTES: Credit cards accepted: A Master Card; B Visa; C American Express; D Discover; E Diners Club; F Other; 2 Personal checks accepted; 3 Lunch available; 4 Dinner available; 5 Open all year; 6 Pets welcome; 7 Children welcome; 8 Tennis nearby; 9 Swimming nearby; 10 Golf nearby; 11 Skiing nearby; 12 May be booked through travel agent.

ing trails, farm animals, and wild deer add to the idyllic setting. Each room has en suite baths and shower. Full farm breakfast. No smoking.

Hosts: Cliff and Barb Clarke
Rooms: 7 (PB) $75-95
Full Breakfast
Credit Cards: A, B
Notes: 2, 12

NORTH DELTA (VANCOUVER AREA)

"Sunshine Hills Bed and Breakfast"

11200 Bond Boulevard, V4E 1M7
(604) 596-6496; FAX (604) 596-2560

Private entrance. Two cozy bedrooms with TV, shared bathroom, and a beautiful garden. Close to US Border, airport, and ferries (20 minutes). Kitchenette. We are originally Dutch, very European. Breakfast includes fresh fruit, orange juice, and much more. Your host knows the city very well and can be of help to all the guests.

Hosts: Putzi and Wim Honing
Rooms: 2 (SB) $50 (Canada $)
Full Breakfast
Credit Cards: none
Notes: 7, 8, 10

NORTH VANCOUVER

Sue's Victorian Guest House—Circa 1904

152 E. Third Street, V7L 1E6
(604) 985-1523; (800) 776-1811

Located centrally for many tourist at-

tractions, this lovely, restored, 1904, non-smoking home, just four blocks from the harbor, seabus terminal, and Quay market; and even closer are restaurants, ships and public transportation. We have Victorian soaker baths (no showers), and each room is individually keyed, has a fan, TV, video, and phone (for short local calls). Minimum stay of three nights. Cats in residence; shoes off at door. Longer stays encouraged. Parking behind 152 and 158 East Third Street.

Hostesses: Gail Fowler and Sue Chalmers
Rooms: 3 (1PB; 2SB) $75 (Canada $) $65 single
Self-serve kitchen privileges (4 PM - 10 AM)
Credit Cards: B (for deposit only, cash or traveller's cheque upon arrival please)
Notes: 5

PENTICTON

God's Mountian Crest Chalet

RR 2, S 15, Comp. 41, V2A 6J7
(604) 490-4800 (voice and FAX)

Scenic, private, 100-acre mountain park has majestic cliffs and lake views. The Chalet is set in our vineyard above Skaha Lake. Enjoy observing wildlife, relax around the pond and patios, and feel spoiled and pampered like a European spa. Enjoy a fine mix of luxury and class. Downtown Penticton, airport, shopping, restaurants, local wineries, golf courses, and beaches are only ten minutes away. Your host family extends a cordial welcome in English, French,

---

NOTES: Credit cards accepted: A Master Card; B Visa; C American Express; D Discover; E Diners Club; F Other; 2 Personal checks accepted; 3 Lunch available; 4 Dinner available;

or German and is dedicated to making you feel at home.

Hosts: Ghitta and Ulric Lejeune
Rooms: 7 (PB) $95
Full Breakfast
Credit Cards: E
Notes: 2, 4, 5, 6, 7, 8, 9, 10, 11, 12

PRINCE GEORGE

Beaverly Bed and Breakfast

12725 Miles Road, V2N 5C1
(250) 560-5255

Beaverly B&B is located 18 kilometers west of Prince George on ten acres of beautiful British Columbia wilderness. You will feel very welcome and comfortable in our new home. Many trees surround us and it is a birder's paradise. We serve a luxurious full breakfast, and you will enjoy our Dutch touch.

Hosts: Anneke and Adrian VanPeenen
Rooms: 2 (PB) $55 ($45 single)
Full Breakfast
Credit Cards: none
Notes: 5, 9, 10, 11, 12

SALT SPRING ISLAND

Pauper's Perch Bed and Breakfast

225 Armand Way, U8K 2B6
(250) 653-2030; FAX (250) 653-2045
Email: libby@saltspring.com

This new architecturally designed, West Coast contemporary home has private entrances and decks. Perched 1,000 feet above sea level, guest can watch the sun rise over ocean views from the Sunshine Coast to the San Juan Islands, with the majestic Coastal mountains as a backdrop. For romance, at night, across the Straight of Georgia, we see the lights of Vancouver, Whiterock, and Bellingham. Duvets and feather pillows. Four-course breakfasts include free range eggs, homemade jams, West Coast seafoods, or vegetarian alternatives. The hostess is a watercolour artist and instructor, and holds an hotel management diploma. For the discerning guest, immaculate comfort in an adult oriented, smoke free environment.

Hostess: Libby Jutras
Rooms: 3 (PB) $125-165 (Canadian $)
Full Breakfast
Credit Cards: A, B
Notes: 5, 8, 9, 10, 12

Pauper's Perch Bed and Breakfast

SIDNEY (VICTORIA)

Borthwick Country Manor Bed and Breakfast

9750 Ardmore Drive, V8L 5H5
(250) 656-9498; FAX (250) 656-9498

An English Tudor manor house is set on an acre of gorgeous landscaped gar-

---

5 Open all year; 6 Pets welcome; 7 Children welcome; 8 Tennis nearby; 9 Swimming nearby;
10 Golf nearby; 11 Skiing nearby; 12 May be booked through travel agent.

dens in the quite countryside area of Patricia Bay on Vancouver Island. Relax in the outdoor hot tub or walk to the nearby beach. Enjoy a delicious gourmet breakfast on the patio. Large bedrooms, king- and queen-size beds. Minutes from Butchart Gardens, Victoria, airport, BC and Washington State Ferries, golf, fishing, boating, and beaches.

Hostess: Susan Siems
Rooms: 4 (PB) $89-130 (Canadian $)
Full Breakfast
Credit Cards: A, B, C, E
Notes: 5, 10, 12

Peggy's Cove Bed and Breakfast

279 Coal Point Lane, V8L 5P1
(250) 656-5656; FAX (250) 655-3118

Spoil yourself! Come join me in my beautiful home bordered by spectacular ocean views on all sides. Imagine a gourmet breakfast on the sundeck, watching sea lions at play, eagles soaring, and if you are lucky, a family of killer whales may appear. Enjoy fishing at your doorstep, a stroll on the beach, and, in the evening, canoe into the sunset then spend a romantic moment in the **"hot tub under the stars."** Victoria's world famous Butchart Gardens, BC and Anacortes Ferries are only minutes away. Many consider Peggy's Cove a honeymoon paradise.

Hostess: Peggy Waibel
Rooms: 2 (1PB; 2SB) $100 + (US $)
Full Gourmet Breakfast
Credit Cards: none
Notes: 2, 5, 5, 8, 9, 10, 12

SOOKE

Ocean Wilderness Country Inn

109 West Coast Road, RR#2, V0S 1N0
(604) 646-2116; (800) 323-2116;
FAX (604) 646-2371

Nine guest rooms on five forested acres of ocean front with breathtaking views of forests, Strait of Juan de Fuca, and the Olympic Mountians. Large, beautifully decorated rooms with private baths, and canopied beds. A silver service of coffee is delivered to your door as a gentle wake-up call. Country breakfast from local produce is a wonderful treat. Try our seafood dinner on the beach Thursdays and Sundays. The hot tub in a Japanese gazebo is popular with weary vacationers. Book your time for a private soak. Several rooms have private soak tubs for two overlooking the ocean.

Host: Marion Rolston
Rooms: 9 (PB) $85-175 (Canadian $)
Full Breakfast
Credit Cards: B
Notes: 4, 5, 6, 9, 10, 12 (commissionable)

UCLUELET

Bed and Breakfast at Burley's

Box 550, 1078 Helen Road, V0R 3A0
(604) 726-4444

A waterfront home on a small "drive to" island at the harbor mouth. Watch the ducks and birds play, heron and kingfisher work, and eagles soar. In the

---

Harbor, trollers, draggers, and seiners attract the gulls. Loggers work in the distant hills. There is a view from every window, a large living room, fireplace, books, and recreation room with pool table.

Hosts: Ron Burley and Micheline Burley
Rooms: 6 (SB) $45-65
Continental Breakfast
Credit Cards: A, B
Notes: 8, 9, 10

VANCOUVER

AB&C Bed and Breakfast Agency

4390 Frances Street, **Burnaby**, V5C 2R3
(604) 298-8815; (800) 488-1941 (US only);
FAX (604) 298-5917

A professional reservation agency offering modest to luxurious accommodations. Single, twin, queen, and king beds, private and shared baths. Vancouver, Victoria, and throughout BC. 18 years in tourism.

Manager: Norma McCurrach
Homes: 60; $75-160
Full Breakfast
Credit Cards: A, B
Notes: 5, 8, 9, 10, 11, 12

Wrays Lakeview Bed and Breakfast

VERNON

Wrays Lakeview Bed and Breakfast

7368 L and A Road, V1B 3S6
(250) 545-9821; FAX (250) 545-9924

Come and relax in the peace and seclusion of our spotless, but cozy, air-conditioned home in a beautiful country setting. We offer three immaculate guest rooms with ensuite or private baths. A full breakfast is served in our formal dining room or on the deck. Enjoy a comfortable sitting room with library, TV, and piano. Warm hospitality is quaranteed. Adults only; no smoking or pets. Easy access to skiing, golfing, boating, beaches, hiking, dining, and shopping.

Hosts: Irma and Gord Wray
Rooms: 3 (PB) $65
Full Breakfast
Credit Cards: A, B
Notes: 5, 9, 10, 11

VICTORIA

AA-Accommodations West Reservation Service

660 Jones Terrace, V8Z 2L7
(604) 479-1986; FAX (604) 479-9999
Email: dwensley@vanisle.net
Internet: http://www.bactravel.com/gardencity.html

No reservation fee. Over seventy choice locations inspected and approved. Ocean view, farm tranquillity, cozy cottage, city convenience, and historic heritage! Assistance with itineraries

---

5 Open all year; 6 Pets welcome; 7 Children welcome; 8 Tennis nearby; 9 Swimming nearby; 10 Golf nearby; 11 Skiing nearby; 12 May be booked through travel agent.

includes **Victoria, Vancouver Island,** and some adjacent islands. For competent, caring service, call Doreen. 9AM - 9PM Monday through Saturday and 2PM - 9PM on Sundays.

Manager: Doreen Wensley
Credit Cards: A, B, C
Notes: 2, 5, 7, 8, 9, 10, 12

All Seasons Bed and Breakfast Agency Inc.

PO Box 5511 Station B, V8R 6S4
(604) 655-7173; FAX (604) 655-7193

All the best B&B of Victoria, Vancouver Island, and the Gulf Islands. Specializing in waterfront and garden homes and inns. There's an accommodation style for everyone. When you want to get away from it all, trips are much more enjoyable with a bit of advance planning. You know where you'll be welcome at night, so you can travel for the mere fun of it. Listing approximately 40 B&B's. Visa, Master-Card, and personal checks accepted. Kate Catterill, coordinator.

Battery Street Guest House

670 Battery Street., V8V 1E5
(604) 385-4632

Newly renovated guest house built in 1898 with four bright comfortable rooms, two with bathrooms. Centrally located within walking distance to downtown, Beacon Hill Park, and Victoria's scenic Marine Drive, only one block away. A full, hearty breakfast served by a Dutch hostess. No smoking.

Hostess: Pamela Verduyn
Rooms: 4 (2PB; 2SB) $75-95 (Canadian $)
Full Breakfast
Credit Cards: B
Notes: 2, 5

Craigmyle Bed and Breakfast Inn Ltd.

1037 Craigdarroch Road, V8S 2A5
(604) 595-5411; FAX (604) 370-5276

Craigmyle guesthouse is a large, old B&B situated only one kilometer from the city center of Victoria in the prestigious Rockland area. Sitting in the shadow of the Craigdarrock Castle, Craigmyle offers a relaxed and quiet atmosphere in the tradition of English-style bed and breakfast. Craigmyle was built in 1913 and was designed by the famous Victorian architect Samuel McClure. Craigmyle has been owned and operated since 1975 by Jim and Cathy Pace.

Hosts: Jim and Cathy Pace
Rooms: 17 (PB) $80-95 (Canadian $)
Full English Breakfast
Credit Cards: A, B, C
Notes: 5, 7, 8, 9, 10, 12

Gregory's Guest House

5373 Patricia Bay Highway, V8Y 1S9
(604) 658-8404; FAX (604) 658-4604

Early 1900's restored, historic farmstead overlooking Beaver/Elk Lake and park. Ten minutes to downtown Victoria.

NOTES: Credit cards accepted: A Master Card; B Visa; C American Express; D Discover; E Diners Club; F Other; 2 Personal checks accepted; 3 Lunch available; 4 Dinner available;

Convenient to ferries, airport, and Burchart Gardens. Children of all ages enjoy our farm animals and unique hobby farm setting. The Little Garden Farm has four character guest rooms decorated with antiques and down quilts. Private bathrooms are available. Our library welcomes guests with fireplace and lake view. Lake activities include swimming, hiking, canoeing, and windsurfing. A full country breakfast is included.

Hosts: Elizabeth and Paul Gregory
Rooms: 4 (2PB; 2SB) $65-85 ($20 each additional person)
Full Breakfast
Credit Cards: A, B
Notes: 2, 5, 7, 8, 9, 10 , 12

Hibernia Bed and Breakfast

Hibernia Bed and Breakfast

747 Helvetia Crescent, V8Y 1M1
(604) 658- 5519; FAX (604) 658-0588

Lovely, quiet country home. 15 minutes from Victoria, Butchart Gardens, ferries, and airport. Five minutes from good restaurants, sea, and lakes. A registered BC B&B. Owner is Irish-born. Large home with trees, lawns, and vines. Antique furnishings duvets. Guest lounge with grand piano and TV.

Full Irish breakfast on vine-covered terrace. We try to make your stay as comfortable as possible, and are happy to help with sight-seeing and more.

Hosts: Mrs. Aideen Lydon
Rooms: 4 (2PB; 2SB) $65-75 (Canadian $); $55-65 (US $)
Full Irish Breakfast
Credit Cards: A, B
Notes: 5, 7 (over 6), 8, 9, 10, 12

Lavigne's Gourmet Bed and Breakfast

999 Easter Road, V8X 2Z9
(604) 480-0999

Lovely 1940 home located in a charming residential area surrounded by historic Garry Oaks. Guests will enjoy the beautifully decorated guest rooms, coved ceilings, the Samuel McClure stone fireplace, and the private garden. A gourmet breakfast is often served on the sunny deck with hillside views. Fresh fruit and home baking precede such specialties as smoked salmon soufflé. Within walking distance to Swan Lake Nature Sanctuary and Playfair Park.

Hosts: Len and Lynne Lavigne
Rooms: 2 (1PB; 2SB) $55-80 (Canada $)
Full Breakfast
Credit Cards: none
Notes: 2, 5, 7 (over 10), 8, 9, 10, 12

Oak Bay Guest House

1052 Newport Avenue, V8S 5E3
(604) 598-3812; (800) 575-3812;
FAX (604) 598-0369
Email: OakBay@beds-breakfasts.com
Internet: http//beds-breakfasts.com/OakBay

Built from designs by famous architect

---

5 Open all year; 6 Pets welcome; 7 Children welcome; 8 Tennis nearby; 9 Swimming nearby; 10 Golf nearby; 11 Skiing nearby; 12 May be booked through travel agent.

Oak Bay Guest House

Samuel McLure. This classic 1912 inn, established since 1922, has your comfort at heart. Set in beautiful gardens in the prime, peaceful location of Oak Bay, only one block from the water and minutes from downtown. Eleven rooms with private bathrooms and antiques; sitting room with Inglenook fireplace; sunroom with library and TV. Home-cooked breakfast. Golf, shopping, and the city bus at door.

Hosts: Karl and Jackie Morris
Rooms: 11 (PB) $79-165 (Canadian $)
Full Breakfast
Credit Cards: A, B, C
Notes: 5, 8, 9, 10, 12

Top O'Triangle Mountain

3442 Karger Terrace, V9C 3K5
(604) 478-7853; FAX (604) 478-2245

Our home, built of solid cedar construction, boasts a spectacular view of Victoria, the Juan de Fuca Strait, and the Olympia Mountains in Washington. We are a relaxed household with few rules, lots of hospitality, and clean, comfortable rooms. A hearty breakfast is different each morning.

Hosts: Henry and Patricia Hansen
Rooms: 3 (PB) $70-90 (Canadian $)
Full Home-cooked Breakfast
Credit Cards: A, B
Notes: 5, 7, 8, 9, 10, 12

Wellington Bed and Breakfast

66 Wellington Avenue, V8V 4H5
(604) 383-5976 (voice and FAX)

You're in for a treat of the finest Victorian hospitality in this 1912, fully restored, Edwardian B&B. Inge is an interior designer and each room is specially designed with private baths, queen or king bed, walk-in closet, duvets, lace, and some fireplaces. A guest living room offers books and relaxation. Only a half block from ocean and bus. A 20-minute walk will take you to downtown through the park. Only minutes from shops, restaurants, and sites. A full, delicious breakfast is served in the dining room.

Hosts: Inge Ranzinger
Rooms: 3 (3PB) $70-95 (Canada $) or $50-70 (US $)
Full Breakfast
Credit Cards: A
Notes: 2, 5, 7 (over 12), 8, 9, 10, 12

WEST VANCOUVER

Beachside Bed and Breakfast

4208 Evergreen Avenue, V7V 1H1
(604) 922-7773; (800) 563-3311;
FAX (604) 926-8073
Email: beach@uniserve.com

Guests are welcomed to this beautiful waterfront home with a basket of fruit and fresh flowers. Situated on a quiet cul-de-sac in an exclusive area of the city, the house, with Spanish architecture accented by antique stained glass windows, affords a panoramic view of

---

NOTES: Credit cards accepted: A Master Card; B Visa; C American Express; D Discover; E Diners Club; F Other; 2 Personal checks accepted; 3 Lunch available; 4 Dinner available;

Vancouver's busy harbor. There are private baths, a patio leading to the beach, and a large jacuzzi at the seashore, where you can watch seals swim by daily. Near sailing, fishing, hiking, golf, downhill skiing, and antique shopping.

Hosts: Gordon and Joan Gibbs
Rooms: 3 (PB) $125-200
Full Breakfast
Credit Cards: A, B
Notes: 2, 5, 8, 10, 11, 12, 13

WHISTLER

Golden Dreams Bed and Breakfast

6412 Easy Street, V0N 1B6
(604) 932-2667; (800) 668-7055;
FAX (604) 932-7055
Email: golden@whistler.net

Uniquely decorated Victorian, Oriental, and Aztec theme rooms feature sherry decanter and cozy duvets. Relax in the luxurious, private jacuzzi and awake to a nutritious vegetarian breakfast including homemade jams and fresh herbs served in the country kitchen. A short walk to the valley trail to village activities and restaurants.

Hosts: Ann and Terry Spence
Rooms: 3 (1PB; 2SB) $75-105 (Canada $)
Full Breakfast
Credit Cards: A, B
Notes: 2, 5, 7, 8, 9, 10, 11

Golden Dreams Bed and Breakfast

---

5 Open all year; 6 Pets welcome; 7 Children welcome; 8 Tennis nearby; 9 Swimming nearby; 10 Golf nearby; 11 Skiing nearby; 12 May be booked through travel agent.

MANITOBA

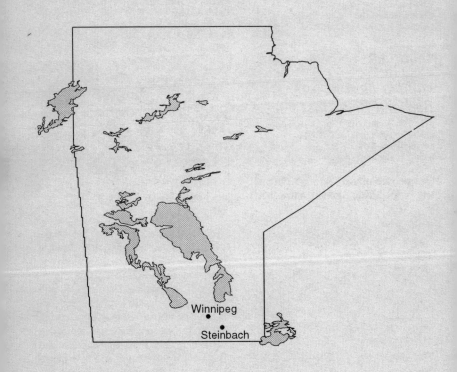

Winnipeg

Steinbach

Manitoba

Forest Glen Tea Room/Bed and Breakfast

STEINBACH

Forest Glen Tea Room/ Bed and Breakfast

Box 2503, R0A 2A0
(204) 326-5053

Forest Glen, on Highway 12 in the south side of town, is a modest home set in a wooded yard—a forested hideaway right in town. Travellers are welcome to picnic at no charge. Drinking water provided when hostess is home. Children are always welcome and people with special needs are invited. (Not readily wheelchair accessible.) Steinbach has the internationally known Mennonite Heritage Village and many other attractions. Forty miles from Winnepeg.

Hostess: Elma Brandt
Rooms: 2 (SB) $30-45
Full Breakfast
Credit Cards: A, B
Notes: 2, 3, 4, 5, 7, 8, 9, 10, 11

WINNIPEG

Bed and Breakfast of Manitoba

434 Roberta Avenue, R2K 0K6
(204) 661-0300

We are an association of bed and breakfast homes in Winnipeg and areas of rural Manitoba. All homes are clean and safe; your hosts are friendly and knowledgeable about local attractions and events. Call or write for a free brochure listing for your assistance in reserving accommodations for your Winnipeg visit. Our goal is to match guest and hosts as closely as possible to enhance your stay. Welcome to Winnipeg!

Coordinator: Ms. P. Carlson
Rooms: 1-4 per home; $40-50 (Canadian $)
Full Breakfast
Credit Cards: none
Notes: 5, 6, 7, 10

NOTES: Credit cards accepted: A Master Card; B Visa; C American Express; D Discover; E Diners Club; F Other; 2 Personal checks accepted; 3 Lunch available; 4 Dinner available; 5 Open all year; 6 Pets welcome; 7 Children welcome; 8 Tennis nearby; 9 Swimming nearby; 10 Golf nearby; 11 Skiing nearby; 12 May be booked through travel agent.

NEW BRUNSWICK

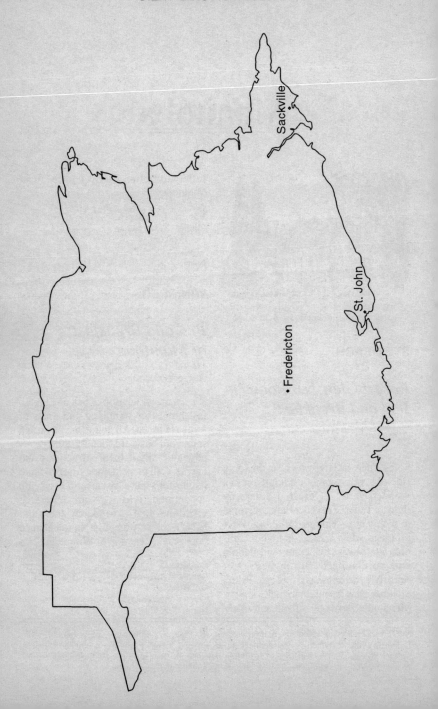

New Brunswick

FREDERICTON

Applelot
Bed and Breakfast

RR 4 (located on Hwy. 105), E3B 4X5
(506) 444-8083

Attractive farmhouse overlooking the St. John River. Three bedrooms with a view in a restful country atmosphere. Full homemade breakfast served on the spacious sunporch. Orchards and woodlands with walking trails, "a bird-watcher's delight." Board games, TV, VCR, books, and piano inside; picnic table, gas BBQ, and lawn swing outside. Area attractions include several golf courses, Mactaquac Park, Kings Landing Historical Village, museums in Fredericton, the Beaverbrook Art Gallery, and the Provincial Archives.

Hostess: Elsie Myshrall
Rooms: 3 (1PB; 2SB) $55-60
Full Breakfast
Credit Cards: none
Open May 1 through Oct. 31
Notes: 2, 9, 10, 12

Carriage House Inn

230 University Avenue, E3B 4H7
Mail: PO Box 1088 Station A, E3B 5C2
(506) 452-9924; (800) 267-6068;
FAX (506) 458-0799

The Carriage House may be Fredericton's Heritage Inn, but is offers modern conveniences: off-street parking, wake-up calls, a library, and FAX service. The location is perfect, just a few paces from Fredericton's Green along the St. John River at the edge of the historic preservation area. Within strolling distance are the Christ Church Cathedral, art galleries, the Legislative Assembly Building, restaurants, and craft shops. Three-star property.

Hosts: Joan, Frank, and Nathan Gorham
Rooms: 10 (5 PB; 5SB) $60-75
Full Breakfast
Credit Cards: A, B, D, E
Notes: 2, 5, 6, 7, 8, 9, 10, 11, 12

Applelot Bed and Breakfast

NOTES: Credit cards accepted: A Master Card; B Visa; C American Express; D Discover; E Diners Club; F Other; 2 Personal checks accepted; 3 Lunch available; 4 Dinner available; 5 Open all year; 6 Pets welcome; 7 Children welcome; 8 Tennis nearby; 9 Swimming nearby; 10 Golf nearby; 11 Skiing nearby; 12 May be booked through travel agent.

Marshlands Inn

SACKVILLE

Marshlands Inn

59 Bridge Street, PO Box 1440, E0A 3C0
(506) 536-0170; (800) 561-1266;
FAX (506) 536-0721

One of Canada's oldest and best known country inns. . .located in a small university town, adjacent to famous Tantramar Marshes, in the geographic centre of Maritime Canada Famous for its fine dining, wonderful gardens and antique furnishings. Come relax, replenish, and retire.

Hosts: Peter and Diane Weedon
Rooms: 20 (17PB; 3SB) $65-95
Full and/or Continental Breakfast
Credit Cards: A, B, C, E
Notes: 3, 4, 5, 7, 8, 9, 10, 11, 12

ST. JOHN

Five Chimneys
Bed and Breakfast

238 Charlotte Street West, E2M 1Y3
(506) 635-1888; FAX (506) 635-8402
Email: ajdg@nbnet.nb.ca

Five Chimneys was built in 1854 in a variation of the Greek Revival style. Our three guest rooms are named in honor of former owners of our home, the Ambrose, Colwell, and Wilson families. My breakfast specialties include muffins, cheesy eggs, and oatmeal/whole wheat pancakes. As well, due to food allergies, I am accustomed to cooking without milk or wheat, etc. We are located midway between Route 1 (exit 109) and the Digby Ferry terminal.

Hostess: Linda Gates
Rooms: 3 (1PB; 2SB) $55-65 (Canadian $)
Full Breakfast
Credit Cards: A, B
Notes: 2, 5, 7, 8, 9

Linden Manor

267 Charlotte Street West, E2M 1Y2
(506) 674-2754

A large Colonial home, circa. 1830. Within walking distance of ferry to Nova Scotia, historic Martello tower (1812), and five churches. A five-minute drive to nature park, downtown, and world famous Reversing Falls. After a restful sleep in our king- and queen-size beds, enjoy breakfast in the dining room or cozy kitchen. Fresh baked muffins with fruit, coffee, or tea await you while french toast, eggs of any style, or cereal are being prepared.

Hosts: Linda and Gregg Molloy
Rooms: 3 (PB) $69-74 (Canadian $)
Full Breakfast
Credit Cards: A, B
Notes: 2, 5, 8, 9

Linden Manor

NOTES: Credit cards accepted: A Master Card; B Visa; C American Express; D Discover;
E Diners Club; F Other; 2 Personal checks accepted; 3 Lunch available; 4 Dinner available;

Nova Scotia

AMHERST

Victoria Garden

196 Victoria Sreet East, B4H 1Y9
(902) 667-2278

Situated on the famous Sunrise Trail
in downtown Amherst is an elegant,
circa 1903, Victorian home on a tree-
lined street in the midst of heritage
properties. Each room is tastefully
decorated and has antique furniture. For
the guests enjoyment, we also have fireplace, piano, organ, TV/VCR, and barbecue. Full breakfast; the house
specialty is Nova Scotia blueberry pancakes with Nova Scotia maple syrup.
Pleased to cater to special diets with
prior notice. Tea and sweets served in
the evening. Smoking is limited to the
out of doors. Rated 3½ stars by the
Tourism Industry of Nova Scotia
Canada Select.

Hosts: Carl and Beatrice Brander
Rooms: 3 (1PB; 2SB) $50-60
Full Breakfast
Credit Cards: A, B
Notes: 8, 9, 10, 11, 12

Gray Gables Bed and Breakfast

CHESTER

Gray Gables Bed and Breakfast

RR #1, B0J 1J0
(902) 275-3983

Beautiful view of Mahone Bay and
Graves Island Park. Modern, new Cape
Cod, elegantly decorated. Three rooms,
two queen and one twin/king, all with
four-piece bath ensuite, sitting areas,
and ocean view. Relax in the main floor
gathering room with fireplace, in front
of the CBTV and VCR in upstairs sit-

---

5 Open all year; 6 Pets welcome; 7 Children welcome; 8 Tennis nearby; 9 Swimming nearby;
10 Golf nearby; 11 Skiing nearby; 12 May be booked through travel agent.

NOVA SCOTIA

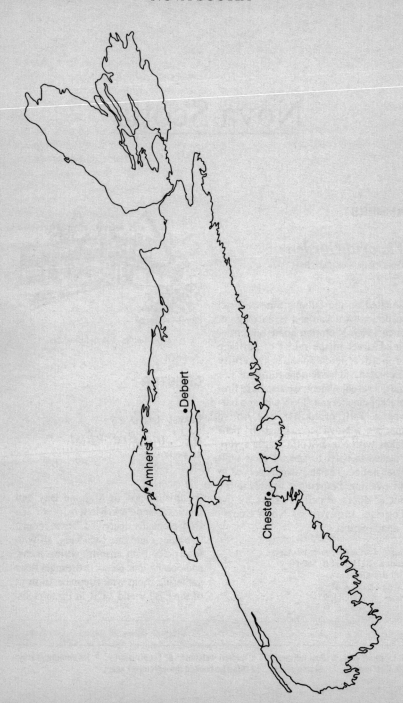

- Debert
- Amherst
- Chester

ting area, or on the large verandah. Full, delicious breakfast served 7-9AM. Laundry facilities. Nearby attractions include 18-hole golf course, Peggy's Cove, Lunenburg, Mahone Bay, and Halifax.

Hosts: David and Jeannette Tomsett
Rooms: 3 (PB) $75-85 + tax
Full Breakfast
Credit Cards: A, B
Notes: 9, 10, 11

DEBERT

Shady Maple
Bed 'n Breakfast
R.R. 1, Masstown, B0M 1G0
(902) 662-3565; (800) 493-5844;
FAX (902) 662-3565

Welcome to our fully operating farm; Exit 12 off Highway 104. Travel 1½ miles into Masstown or, Exit 14A off Hwy. 102, six miles to Masstown. Walk through fields and wooded trails, view the milking, pet the animals, or have a swim in our outdoor, heated pool and an outdoor year-round spa. In the evening, come and sit by the fireplace in our country home. Close proximity to the Tidal Bore, Truro, Ski Wentworth, and only 45 minutes from Halifax Airport. We offer homemade jams, jellies, and maple syrup. Farm fresh eggs and an in-house gift shop. Cribs and cots available. Honeymoon package available. Open all year.

Hosts: James and Ellen Eisses
Rooms: 3 (1 suite PB; 2SB) $40-75
Full Breakfast and Evening Snack
Credit Cards: B
Notes: 5, 6, 7, 9, 10, 11, 12

ONTARIO

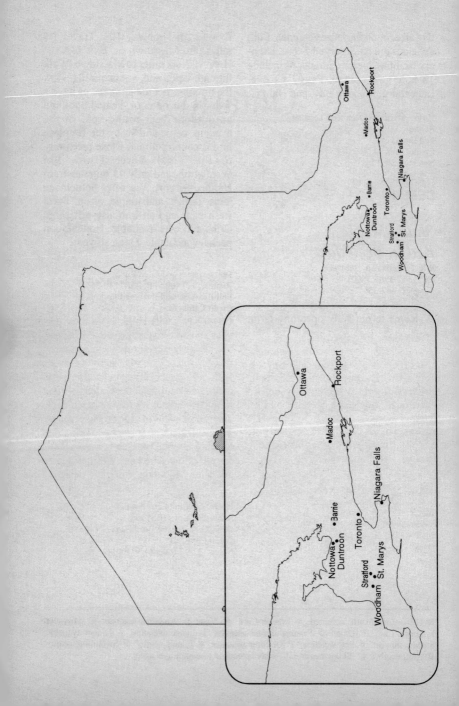

Ontario

BARRIE

Cozy Corner
Bed and Breakfast
2 Morton Crescent, L4N 7T3
(705) 739-0157

Escape to peace and tranquillity in this comfortable home, nestled amidst sparkling lakes and forests. 36 miles north of Toronto. Charita, a former school teacher, spent four years as governess to Julio Iglesias's children. Her English born husband completed three years of culinary training in Germany before moving to the Savoy Hotel, London. Sample Harry's expertise at breakfast and other meals. Sandy beaches and golf on our doorstep. Air-conditioned. Jacuzzi. Brochure available.

Hosts: Charita and Harry Kirby
Suite: 1 (4 piece bath and jacuzzi)
Rooms: 2 (1SB) $55-85
Full Breakfast
Credit Cards: B
Notes: 2, 4, 5, 8, 9, 10, 11, 12

DUNTROON

Conrad Heritage Place
Box 103, L0M 1H0
(705) 444-5073; (705) 444-6825 (voice and FAX)

Conrad Heritage Place, in country setting, exudes the fascination and history of the original home dating to 1856. Guest suites feature extraordinary privacy, ensuite baths, private entrances, televisions, refrigerators, and microwaves. A spacious guest living room with a fireplace offers relaxation. All areas are beautifully decorated in stunning coordinates. A flower-laden deck and pool invite outdoor enjoyment. Your refrigerator is stocked with a deluxe continental breakfast "in a basket" for a flexible schedule. Wasaga Beach and Blue Mountain skiing are nearby.

Hosts: Sara and Larry Swalm
Rooms: 3 suties (PB) $65
Deluxe Continental Breakfast
Credit Cards: B
Notes: 2, 5, 7 (over 6), 9, 10, 11

NOTES: Credit cards accepted: A Master Card; B Visa; C American Express; D Discover; E Diners Club; F Other; 2 Personal checks accepted; 3 Lunch available; 4 Dinner available; 5 Open all year; 6 Pets welcome; 7 Children welcome; 8 Tennis nearby; 9 Swimming nearby; 10 Golf nearby; 11 Skiing nearby; 12 May be booked through travel agent.

Camelot Country Inn

MADOC

Camelot Country Inn

RR 5, K0K 2K0
(613) 473-0441

Relax in the quiet, country setting of our 1853 brick and stone home. It is surrounded by plantings of red and white pine on 25 acres of land in the heart of Hastings County. Original woodwork and oak floors have been lovingly preserved. There are three guest rooms available with two doubles and one twin. The full breakfast may be chosen by guests from the country breakfast or one of two gourmet breakfasts.

Hostess: Marian Foster
Rooms: 3 (SB) $45
Full Breakfast
Credit Cards: none
Notes: 5, 7, 8, 10

NIAGARA FALLS

Bed of Roses B&B

4877 River Road, L2E 3G5
(905) 356-0529 (voice and FAX)

Christian hosts welcome you. We have two efficiency units with bedroom, living room with pull out sofa bed, furnished kitchenette, dining area, bath and a private entrance. A full breakfast is served "room service style." We are located on the famous River Road near Niagara Falls, bridges to U.S.A, bike and hiking trails, golf course, and all major attractions. Free pick up from bus and train station. Come and enjoy your stay in Niagara Falls, Ontario.

Hosts: Norma and Don Lambertson
Rooms: 2 Efficiency Apts. (PB) $75-95
Full Breakfast
Credit Cards: B
Notes: 5, 7, 10

Gretna Green B&B

5077 River Road, L2E 3G7
(905) 357-2081

A warm welcome awaits you in this Scots-Canadian home overlooking the Niagara River Gorge. All rooms are air-conditioned and have their own TV. Included in the rate is a full breakfast with homemade scones and muffins. We also pick up at the train or bus stations. Many people have called this a "home away from home."

Hosts: Stan and Marg Gardiner
Rooms: 4 (PB) $45-70
Full Breakfast
Credit Cards: none
Notes: 5, 7, 8, 10

NOTTAWA (NEAR COLLINGWOOD)

Pretty River Valley "Country" Inn

RR #1, L0M 1P0
(705) 445-7598 (voice and FAX)

Cozy, quiet, country inn in the scenic

NOTES: Credit cards accepted: A Master Card; B Visa; C American Express; D Discover; E Diners Club; F Other; 2 Personal checks accepted; 3 Lunch available; 4 Dinner available;

Blue Mountains overlooking Pretty River Valley Wilderness Park. Distinctive pine furnished studios and suites with **fireplaces and in-room whirlpools for two**. Spa and air-conditioning. Close to Collingwood, beaches, golfing, fishing, hiking (Bruce Trail), bicycle paths, antique shops, and restaurants. Complimentary tea served upon arrival. No smoking.

Hosts: Steve and Diane Szelestowski
Rooms: 8 (6 studios + 2 suites) (PB) $69-110
  (Canada $)
Full Breakfast
Credit Cards: A, B
Notes: 5, 7 (well-behaved), 8, 9, 10, 11, 12

Auberg McGEE'S Inn

OTTAWA

Auberg McGEE'S Inn

185 Daly Avenue, K1N 6E8
(613) 237-6089; (800) 2 MCGEES;
FAX (613) 237-6021

A 14-room, smoke-free, historic Victorian inn celebrating twelve-plus years of award-winning hospitality! Centrally located downtown on a quiet avenue within walking distance of excellent restaurants, museums, Parliament, Rideau Canal, and University of Ottawa. Rooms with cable TV, phone, and jacuzzi ensuites. Kitchenette facilities for longer stays. Recommended by AAA. Full breakfast served in Art Deco dining room. All denominations welcome.

Hostesses: Anne Schutte and Mary Unger
Rooms: 14 (10PB; 4SB) $58-150 (Canada $)
Full Breakfast
Credit Cards: A, B
Notes: 5, 7, 8, 9, 10, 11

Australis Guest House

35 Marlborough Avenue, K1N 8E6
(613) 235-8461 (voice and FAX)

We are the oldest, established, and still operating bed and breakfast in the Ottawa area. Located on a quiet, tree-lined street one block from the Redeau River with ducks and swans, and Strathcona Park. We are a 20-minute walk from the Parliament buildings. This period house boasts leaded-glass windows, fireplaces, oak floors, and unique eight-foot high stained-glass windows overlooking the hall. Hearty, home-cooked breakfasts with home-baked breads and pastries. Past winner of the Ottawa Hospitality Award, recommended by *Newsweek*, featured in the *Ottawa Sun* newspaper for our Australian bread, and gold award recipient for Star of City for Ottawa Tourism 1996.

Hosts: Carol and Brian Waters
Rooms: 3 (1PB; 2SB) $58-75 (Canadian $)
Full Breakfast
Credit Cards: none
Notes: 5, 7, 8

---

5 Open all year; 6 Pets welcome; 7 Children welcome; 8 Tennis nearby; 9 Swimming nearby; 10 Golf nearby; 11 Skiing nearby; 12 May be booked through travel agent.

ROCKPORT

Houseboat Amaryllis Bed and Breakfast

Box C-10, K0E 1V0
(613) 659-3513

The 100-foot, double deck houseboat *Amaryllis* is located on its own island in the middle of the 1,000 Islands region. Originally built in 1921 as a private summer residence on the St. Lawerence River, it has a unique atmosphere of comfort and relaxation. A large verandah deck, living room with fireplace, and dining room all overlook the water and forested shores. The four guest rooms also look out onto the river and each has its own private bathroom. The Island is 4.5 acres with paths winding through many species of trees and wildflowers. Stroll, swim, fish, or relax in tranquil surroundings. Full breakfast and boat transportation from the village of Rockport included. Available for groups. One and a half hours from Ottawa, three hours from Montreal.

Hosts: Karin and Pieter Bergen
Rooms: 4 (PB) $65 95 (US $)
Full Breakfast
Credit Cards: none
Notes: 2, 7, 8, 9, 10

Houseboat Amaryllis Bed and Breakfast

Eagleview Manor

ST. MARYS

Eagleview Manor Bed and Breakfast

Box 3183, 178 Widder Street East, N0M 2P0
(519) 284-1811

"St. Marys is a town time forgot." Beautiful Victorian home overlooking a quaint, peaceful town. Minutes from London and Stratford. Sweeping staircase, stained-glass windows, jacuzzi, quilts, antiques, fireplaces, in-ground pool, and four spacious guest rooms. Nanny's Tea Room available for afternoon or Victorian teas. Reservations necessary. Open year-round. Theme weekends and retreats. Amtrack stops here. Future home of Canadian Baseball Hall of Fame.

Hosts: Bob and Pat Young
Rooms: 4 (SB) $50-70 (Canadian $)
Full Menu Breakfast
Credit Cards: none
Notes: 2, 5, 7, 8, 9, 10, 11, 12

NOTES: Credit cards accepted: A Master Card; B Visa; C American Express; D Discover; E Diners Club; F Other; 2 Personal checks accepted; 3 Lunch available; 4 Dinner available;

STRATFORD

Burnside Guest Home

139 William Street, N5A 4X9
(519) 271-7076 (voice and FAX)

Burnside is a turn-of-the century Queen Anne Revival home on the north shore of Lake Victoria, the site of the first Stratford logging mill. The home features many family heirlooms and antiques and is central air-conditioned. Our rooms have been redecorated with light and cheery colors. Relax in the gardens overlooking the Avon River on hand-crafted furniture amid the rose, herb, herbaceous, and annual flower gardens. A full home-cooked, nutritional breakfast is provided. Within walking distance of Shakespearean theaters. Close to Protestant and Roman Catholic churches of Stratford. Stratford is the home of a world renowned Shakespearean festival from early-May to mid-November.

Host: Lester J. Wilker
Rooms: 4 (SB) $50-70
Full Five-course Breakfast
Credit Cards: A
Notes: 2, 5, 7, 8, 9, 10, 11

TORONTO

Toronto Bed and Breakfast, Inc.

Box 269, 253 College Street, M5T 1R5
(416) 588-8800 or (416) 690-1407;
FAX (416) 690-5089

One call to us and we will arrange your stay at one of our friendly B&B homes. All are centrally located near safe, clean public transportation. You will stay with real Torontoians who love their city and their neighborhoods. This very personal registry has been providing accommodations for 18 years. Referrals for **Toronto, Ottawa and Niagara Falls!** Free brochure on request.

Coordinator: Marcie Getgood
Rooms: 47 (18PB; 29SB) $56-85 (Canadian)
Both Full and Continental Breakfasts
Credit Cards: A, B, C, F

WOODHAM (NEAR EXETER)

Country Haven Bed and Breakfast

RR 1, N0K 2A0
(519) 229-6416

Relax in the peaceful atmosphere of our mixed farming operation, centrally located between attractions at Grand Bend, Stratford, and London. Enjoy the beauty of nature while exploring the grounds or trails in the woods. One spacious bedroom includes two double beds and ensuite bath. Excellent for families! Two other attractive, cozy bedrooms avaiable. Awaken to a nourishing home-cooked breakfast served in the warmth of our family dining room. Central air-conditioning.

Hosts: Earl and Marilyn Miller
Rooms: 3 (1PB; 2SB) $50 (Canadian $)
Full Breakfast
Credit Cards: none
Notes: 2. 5. 7, 10

---

5 Open all year; 6 Pets welcome; 7 Children welcome; 8 Tennis nearby; 9 Swimming nearby;
10 Golf nearby; 11 Skiing nearby; 12 May be booked through travel agent.

PRINCE EDWARD ISLAND

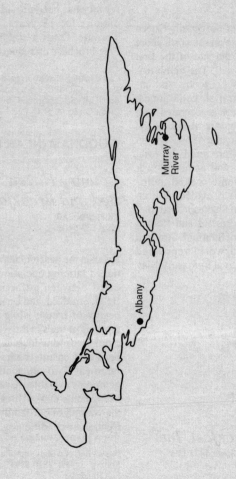

Prince Edward Island

ALBANY

The Captain's Lodge

Seven Mile Bay, RR #2, C0B 1A0
(902) 855-3106; (800) 261-3518

A quiet, secluded bed and breakfast surrounded by flower gardens and fields of clover, grain, and potato blossoms. A short walk to a warm water beach with red sand, and convenient to Borden ferry. Three guest rooms include private baths, ceiling fans, fresh flowers, slippers, duvets, bathrobes, and a gourmet breakfast. Enjoy the sunporch, TV room, living room, and veranda. No smoking. Resident cat and dog.

Hosts: Jim and Sue Rogers
Rooms: 3 (PB) $60-75
Full Breakfast
Credit Cards: A, B
Notes: 2, 9, 10

MURRAY RIVER

Bayberry Cliff Inn

RR 4, Little Sands, C0A 1W0
(902) 962-3395 (voice and FAX)

Located on the edge of a 40-foot cliff are two uniquely decorated post-and-beam barns, antiques, and marine art. Seven rooms have double beds, three with extra sleeping lofts. One room has two single beds. Two rooms, including the honeymoon suite, have private bath. Seals, occasional whale sightings, restaurants, swimming, inner-tubing, and crafts shops are all nearby.

Hosts: Don and Nancy Perkins
Rooms: 8 (2PB; 6SB) $65-125
Full Breakfast
Credit Cards: A, B
Notes: 2 ($50 limit), 7, 9, 10, 12

Mary Catherine Bed and Breakfast and Cottage

Highway 4, C0A 1W0
(902) 962-3437; (800) 227-6406

Beautiful rural, quiet setting with flower and vegetable gardens. Relaxing sitting areas scattered around the property. Walk to seal cruises, craft shops, and restaurants. Tastefully decorated throughout the B&B with antiques and matching bed ensembles. Full breakfast is served on request in the guest home. Laundry service available.

Hostess: Catherine M. Foley
Rooms:
Full Breakfast
Credit Cards: B
Notes: 2, 5, 9, 10

NOTES: Credit cards accepted: A Master Card; B Visa; C American Express; D Discover; E Diners Club; F Other; 2 Personal checks accepted; 3 Lunch available; 4 Dinner available; 5 Open all year; 6 Pets welcome; 7 Children welcome; 8 Tennis nearby; 9 Swimming nearby; 10 Golf nearby; 11 Skiing nearby; 12 May be booked through travel agent.

QUEBEC

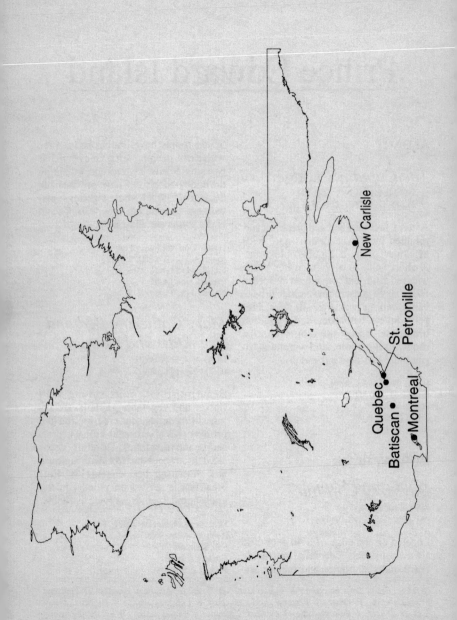

New Carlisle

St.
Petronille

Quebec ●
Batiscan ●
Montreal ●

Quebec

BATISCAN

Au Bois Dormant

1521 Rue Principale, G0X 1R0
(418) 362-3182

Au Bois Dormant is a tranquil country home located on the Batiscan River near St. Lawrence Seaway. Guest may enjoy our art gallery and antiques, or a drive along the ancestral "Chemin du Roi," which runs through the picturesque countryside along the waterway from Montreal to Quebec City. Romance and the flavor of yesteryear await you. No smoking indoors.

Hosts: Pierre and Ginette Lajoie
Rooms: 3 (SB) $45 (US $)
Full Breakfast
Credit Cards: B
Notes: 5, 7, 8, 9, 10, 11

MONTREAL

Armor and Manoir Sherbrooke

157 Sherbrooke Est., H2X 1C7
(514) 845-0915; (800) 203-5485;
FAX (514) 284-1126

The Armor and Manoir Sherbrooke are

two small hotels with European character and offering a family atmosphere. Convenient to Métro, Saint Denis, and Prince Arthur streets. Within walking distance of Old Montréal, the Palais of Congress, and numerous shopping centers. Three guest rooms offer jaccuzi.

Hosts: Annick Le Gall Morvan
Rooms: 22 (14 PB; 8 SB) $42-99
Continental Breakfast
Credit Cards: A, B
Notes: 5, 7, 12

Auberge de la Fontaine

Auberge de la Fontaine

1301 Rachel Street East, H2J 2K1
(514) 597-0166; (800) 597-0597;
FAX (514) 597-0496

The Auberge de la Fontaine is a nice

NOTES: Credit cards accepted: A Master Card; B Visa; C American Express; D Discover; E Diners Club; F Other; 2 Personal checks accepted; 3 Lunch available; 4 Dinner available; 5 Open all year; 6 Pets welcome; 7 Children welcome; 8 Tennis nearby; 9 Swimming nearby; 10 Golf nearby; 11 Skiing nearby; 12 May be booked through travel agent.

stone house, newly renovated, where the 21 rooms, in a warm and modern decor, are of unique style in Montréal. Located in front of a magnificent park. Comfortable, friendly atmosphere and attentive, personal service are greatly appreciated by our corporate and leisure travelers. Each room is tastefully decorated. The suites with whirlpool baths, as well as the luxurious rooms, have brick walls and exclusive fabrics. It will settle you in an elegant and quiet environment. Duvet and decorative pillows will ensure you a cozy comfort. Breakfast is a given at the Auberg. A delicious variety of breakfast foods are set out each morning and you have access to the kitchen for snacks. There are no parking fees. We want our guests to feel comfortable and be entirely satisfied with their stay.

Hostesses: Céline Boudreau and Jean Lamothe
Rooms: 21 (PB) $99-175 (Canada $)
Generous Continental Buffet Breakfast
Credit Cards: A, B, C, E, F
Notes: 5, 7, 8, 9, 12

NEW CARLISLE WEST

Bay View Farm

377 Main Hwy., Route 132, Box 21, G0C 1Z0
(418) 752-2725 or (418) 752-6718

On the coastline of Quebec's picturesque Gaspé Peninsula, guests are welcomed into our comfortable home located on Route 132 Main Highway. Enjoy fresh sea air from our wraparound veranda, walk or swim at the beach. Visit natural and historic sites. Country breakfast; fresh farm, garden and or-

Bay View Farm

chard produce; home baking; and genuine Gaspesian hospitality. Light dinners by reservation. Craft, quilting, and folk music workshops. August Folk Festival. Also, a small cottage for $350 per week. English and French spoken.

Hostess: Helen Sawyer
Rooms: 5 (1PB; 4SB) $35
Full Breakfast
Credit Cards: none
Notes: 3, 4, 5, 7, 8, 9, 10, 11

Bay View Manor/Manoir Bay View

395, Route 132, Bonaventure East, PO Box 21, G0C 1Z0
(418) 752-2725 or (418) 752-6718

Comfortable, two-story, wood frame, home on the beautiful Gaspe Peninsula across the highway from the beach and beside an 18-hole golf course. The building was once a country store and rural post office. Stroll our quiet, natural beach; see nesting seabirds along the rocky cliffs; watch fishermen tend their nets and lobster traps; enjoy beautiful sunrises and sunsets; view the lighthouse beacon on the nearby point; and fall asleep to the sound of waves on the shore. Visit museums, archaeological caves, fossil site, bird sanctuary, or

NOTES: Credit cards accepted: A Master Card; B Visa; C American Express; D Discover; E Diners Club; F Other; 2 Personal checks accepted; 3 Lunch available; 4 Dinner available;

Bay View Manor

Bristish Heritage Village. Hike, fish, canoe, horseback ride, or birdwatch.

Hostess: Helen Sawyer
Rooms: 5 + cottage (1PB; 4SB) $35
Full Breakfast
Credit Cards: none
Notes: 5, 7, 8, 9, 10, 11

QUEBEC

Hotol Manoir des Remparts

3½-rue des Remparts, G1R 3R4
(418) 692-2056; FAX (418) 692-1125

Located minutes from the train/bus terminal and the famed Chateau Frontenac, with some rooms overlooking the majestic St. Lawrence River, the Manoir des Remparts boasts having one of the most coveted locations available in the old city of Quebec. Newly renovated, it is able to offer its guests a vast choice of rooms, ranging from a budget room with shared washrooms to an all inclusive room with private terrace.

Hostess: Sitheary Ngor
Rooms: 36 (22PB; 14SB) $35-75
Continental Breakfast
Credit Cards: A, B, C
Notes: 5, 7, 11, 12

ST. PÉTRONILLE

Auberge La Goéliche

22 Chemin Du Quai, G0A 4C0
(418) 828-2248; FAX (418) 828-2745

Overhanging the St. Lawrence River, this castle-like inn offers a breathtaking view of Quebec City, a 15-minute drive away. It is also close to famous Mt. St. Anne Ski Center. Its 24 rooms are warmly decorated in Victorian style. Outdoor swimming pool.

Host: Andrée Marchand
Rooms: 18 (PB) $55
Continental Breakfast
Credit Cards: A, B, C, F
Notes: 3, 4, 5, 7, 8, 9, 10, 11, 12

La Vielle École

25 Ch du Bout ele l'Île, G0A 4C0
(418) 828-2737

Located near the bridge to the island in a charming house dating back to 1844 with a view of the St. Lawerence River and Quebec City. This completely renovated home offers two bedrooms for two to six people. Come to enjoy a hearty breakfast in a warm and unassuming atmosphere.

Hostess: Sissi Leeb
Rooms: 2 (SB) $50-55
Full Breakfast
Credit Cards: none
Notes: 7, 8, 9, 10

---

5 Open all year; 6 Pets welcome; 7 Children welcome; 8 Tennis nearby; 9 Swimming nearby; 10 Golf nearby; 11 Skiing nearby; 12 May be booked through travel agent.

SASKATCHEWAN

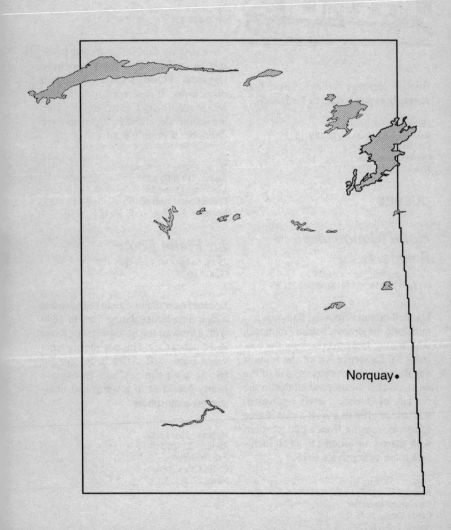

Norquay•

Saskatchewan

NORQUAY

Vintage Country Vacations

Box 537, S0A 2V0
(306) 594-2629 (voice and FAX)

Private. . .quiet. . .romantic. . .secure all-season escape. A family resort offering designer holidays and retreats for individuals, couples, families, or business groups. Located on a well-preserved pioneer homestead, much care has been taken to maintain the vast collection of vintage clothing, furniture, and dinnerware. A private Victorian cottage if fully furnished in antiques and sleeps up to nine. Our modern home features twin suites with shared bath. Our authentic pioneer cabin will take you back in time with its rustic accommodations for four and outside toilet. Breakfast is served in a variety of styles and settings, from hearty country style to elegant gourmet. Lunch and dinner are also offered making your stay completely carefree. All food is fresh and homemade. We provide complete holiday planning, and we rent snowmobiles and the necessary clothing for the sport.

Hosts: Doug and Donna Bernard
Rooms in house: 2 (SB); Cottage: 3 bedrooms (SB); Rustic Cabin: sleeps 4 (SB, outside) $55-75 (Canada $)
Full Breakfast
Credit Cards: A, B
Notes: 2, 3, 4, 5, 6, 7, 9, 10, 11

NOTES: Credit cards accepted: A Master Card; B Visa; C American Express; D Discover; E Diners Club; F Other; 2 Personal checks accepted; 3 Lunch available; 4 Dinner available; 5 Open all year; 6 Pets welcome; 7 Children welcome; 8 Tennis nearby; 9 Swimming nearby; 10 Golf nearby; 11 Skiing nearby; 12 May be booked through travel agent.

JAMAICA

MONTEGO BAY

Glencoe ●

KINGSTON

Jamaica

CLAREDON

Glencoe
Bed and Breakfast
Spalding PO
(809) 964-2286 or (809) 987-8025

Glencoe Bed and Breakfast was built in 1891 by the Nash family 3,00 feet above sea level. As you enter this small, chaming estate, you will begin to feel the warmth and tranquility that awaits. Once settled into your room, you may want to take a stroll around the 7.5-acre working farm and enjoy the wonders of nature. For the avid golfer, you may want to tee-off at a nearby golf course. Curl up in the library with a good book. Wake to birds singing, chickens cackling and pristine mountain air. Enjoy a full breakfast made with organic fresh fruit, milk, eggs, and home-grown Jamaican coffee. Whichever way you choose to spend your time, Glencoe will be an experience you will wish to rediscover time after time.

Hostess: Lucy A. Nash
Rooms: 5 (PB) $40-60
Full Breakfast
Credit Cards: none
Notes: 4, 5, 7, 10

NOTES: Credit cards accepted: A Master Card; B Visa; C American Express; D Discover; E Diners Club; F Other; 2 Personal checks accepted; 3 Lunch available; 4 Dinner available; 5 Open all year; 6 Pets welcome; 7 Children welcome; 8 Tennis nearby; 9 Swimming nearby; 10 Golf nearby; 11 Skiing nearby; 12 May be booked through travel agent.

PUERTO RICO

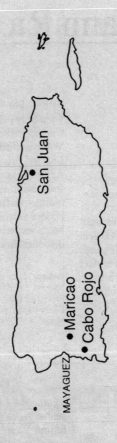

Puerto Rico

CABO ROJO

Parador Perichi's

HC 01 Box 16310, 00623
(787) 851-3131; (800) 443-0266;
FAX (787) 851-0560

Excellece has distinguished Perichi's in its 12 years of hospitality and service. Guest rooms are air-conditioned with private baths and balconies, TVs, and phones. Perichi's award-winning restaurant features gourmet delights that are not to be missed. Well-stocked and cozy lounge; comfortable banquet room for 300; live music by the pool on weekends. Visit golden sand beaches, century-old lighthouse, Mayaguez Zoo, Caribbean wildlife refuge, and more.

Hosts: Julio Cl Perichi
Rooms: 48 (PB) $65-75
Both Full and Continental Breakfasts
Credit Cards: A, B, C, D, E
Notes: 3, 4, 5, 7, 8, 9, 10, 12

MARICAO

Parador La Hacienda Juanita

PO Box 777, Road 105, KM 23-5, 00606
(787) 838-2550; FAX (787) 2551

C. 1830. This hacienda-style building once served as the main lodge for a coffee plantation. Twenty-four acres, 1,600 feet above sea level in the cool tropical mountains of the Puerto Rican rain forest. Bird watchers' paradise.

Hosts: Luis J. Rivera Lugo
Rooms: 21 (PB) $72
Continental Breakfast
Credit Cards: A, B, C
Notes: 2, 3, 4, 5, 7, 8, 9, 12

SAN JUAN

El Canario Inn

1317 Ashford Avenue Condado, 00907
(787) 722-3861; (800) 533-2649;
FAX (787) 722-0391

San Juan's most historic and unique B&B inn. All 25 guest rooms are air-conditioned with private baths, cable TV, and telephone, and come with complimentary continental breakfast. Our tropical patios and sundeck provide a friendly and informal atmosphere. Centrally located near beach, casinos, restaurants, boutiques, and public transportation.

Hosts: Jude and Keith Olson
Rooms: 25 (PB) $65 -95
Continental Breakfast
Credit Cards: A, B, C, D, E
Notes: 5, 7, 8, 9, 12

NOTES: Credit cards accepted: A Master Card; B Visa; C American Express; D Discover; E Diners Club; F Other; 2 Personal checks accepted; 3 Lunch available; 4 Dinner available; 5 Open all year; 6 Pets welcome; 7 Children welcome; 8 Tennis nearby; 9 Swimming nearby; 10 Golf nearby; 11 Skiing nearby; 12 May be booked through travel agent.

VIRGIN ISLANDS

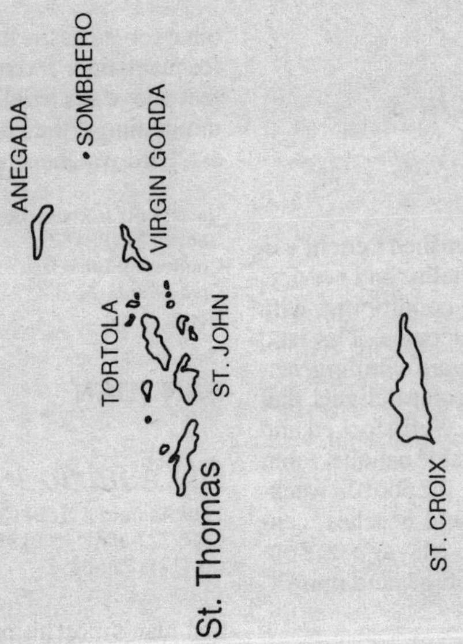

ANEGADA

• SOMBRERO

VIRGIN GORDA

TORTOLA

ST. JOHN

St. Thomas

ST. CROIX

Virgin Islands

ST. THOMAS

Danish Chalet Inn

PO Box 4319, 00803
(809) 774-5764; (800) 635-1531;
FAX (809) 777-4886

Ten minutes from the Cyril King Airport, overlooking Charlotte Amalie Harbor with cool mountian and bay breezed. Five-minute walk to town with duty-free shopping, restaurants, and waterfront activities. Complimentary, continental breakfast; sundeck; in-room phones; air-conditioning or ceiling fans. Can arrange day sails, sight-seeing trips, car rental, etc. Special honeymoon packages available. We have been in the hospitality profession for nearly fifty years and welcome your visit.

Hostess: Frank and Mary Davis
Rooms: 10 (6PB; 4SB) $60-95
Continental Breakfast
Credit Cards: A, B
Notes: 5, 6, 7, 8, 9, 10, 12

NOTES: Credit cards accepted: A Master Card; B Visa; C American Express; D Discover; E Diners Club; F Other; 2 Personal checks accepted; 3 Lunch available; 4 Dinner available; 5 Open all year; 6 Pets welcome; 7 Children welcome; 8 Tennis nearby; 9 Swimming nearby; 10 Golf nearby; 11 Skiing nearby; 12 May be booked through travel agent.

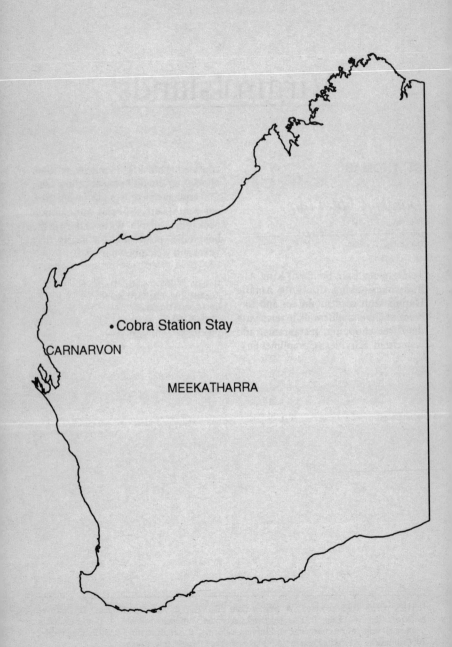

AUSTRALIA (WESTERN)

• Cobra Station Stay

CARNARVON

MEEKATHARRA

Australia

WEST AUSTRALIA (MOUNT AUGUSTUS NATIONAL PARK)

Cobra Station Stay

P. M. B. 28 Cobra Station, via Carnarvon, W. Australia 6701
(099) 430 565; FAX (099) 430 992

Originally established in 1896 as the Historical Bangemall Wayside Inn for the miners in the nearby El-Dorado Gold Mine. Situated about 400 kilimeters from Carnarvon, Meekatharra, and Murchion Shire. We welcome visitors yearround, but we consider our best climate to be from July to October (our winter). Units in the motel are fully air-conditioned with private baths. Station rooms are not air-conditioned but fans are provided. A R.F.D.S. standard airstrip is available. Camping facilities available. The Cobra is being stocked as a working sheep station. Visit the adjoining Mount Augustus National Park (Aborigial name is *Burringurrah* meaning "sleeping man.") boasting the largest rock in the world rich in Aborigial art, or Edithana Pool filled with birds and native fauna. Stroll the original Cobra Homestead and pioneer graves. The water holes provide a cooling swim. A true Australian adventure! We promise, no cobras under the beds.

Hosts: Dennis and Alexa Lang and, daughter, Elizabeth
Rooms: 19 (6PB; 7SB) $50-65
Breakfast
Credit Cards: A, B, F (EFTPOS)
Notes: 2, 3, 4, 5 (closed Saturdays all day), 6 (restrained), 7, 9, 12

NOTES: Credit cards accepted: A Master Card; B Visa; C American Express; D Discover; E Diners Club; F Other; 2 Personal checks accepted; 3 Lunch available; 4 Dinner available; 5 Open all year; 6 Pets welcome; 7 Children welcome; 8 Tennis nearby; 9 Swimming nearby; 10 Golf nearby; 11 Skiing nearby; 12 May be booked through travel agent.

ENGLAND

England

NANTWICH, CHESHIRE

The Brambles
2A Heathside, CW5 5PW
(0) 1270-624664

Extremely comfortable accommodations in home of retired pastor and wife. En-suite rooms with TV and tea/coffee making facilities. Full English breakfast is offered. Nantwich is an historic, small town in an excellent situation for visiting North Whales, the Peak District, the potteries, and the surrounding beautiful English countryside. Manchester Airport is approx. 40 minutes drive. Brambles offers you an ideal vacation spot with helpful, friendly hosts. No smoking in house please. Spanish spoken. Make this your home while visiting or working in South Cheshire!

Hosts: Mr. and Mrs. L. A. Jones
Rooms: 3 (2PB; 1SB) £16.50-18.50 per person
Both Full and Continental Breakfast Offered.
Credit Cards: none
Notes: 2, 4, 5, 6, 7, 8, 9

NOTES: Credit cards accepted: A Master Card; B Visa; C American Express; D Discover; E Diners Club; F Other; 2 Personal checks accepted; 3 Lunch available; 4 Dinner available; 5 Open all year; 6 Pets welcome; 7 Children welcome; 8 Tennis nearby; 9 Swimming nearby; 10 Golf nearby; 11 Skiing nearby; 12 May be booked through travel agent.

The Christian Bed and Breakfast Directory

P.O. Box 719
Uhrichsville, OH 44683

INN EVALUATION FORM

Please copy and complete this form for each stay and mail to the address above. Since 1990 we have maintained files that include thousands of evaluations from inngoers. We value your comments. These help us to keep abreast of the hundreds of new inns that open each year and to follow the changes in established inns.

Name of inn: _____

City and State: _____

Date of stay: _____

Length of stay: _____

Please use the following rating scales for the next items.
A: Outstanding. B: Good. C: Average. D: Fair. F: Poor.

Attitude of innkeepers: _____   Attitude of helpers: _____

Food Service: _____   Handling of Reservations: _____

Cleanliness: _____   Privacy: _____

Beds: _____   Bathrooms: _____

Parking: _____   Worth of price: _____

Comments on the above: _____
_____
_____
_____
_____

What did you especially like? _____
_____
_____
_____

Suggestions for improvements: _____
_____
_____
_____

RECOMMENDATION FORM

As *The Christian Bed and Breakfast Directory* gains approval from the traveling public, more and more bed and breakfast establishments are asking to be included on our mailing list. If you know of another bed and breakfast who may not be on our list, give them a great outreach and advertising opportunity by providing us with the following information:

1) B&B Name _____

Host's Name _____

Address _____

City _____ State _____ Zip Code _____

Telephone _____ FAX _____

2) B&B Name _____

Host's Name _____

Address _____

City _____ State _____ Zip Code _____

Telephone _____ FAX _____

3) B&B Name _____

Host's Name _____

Address _____

City _____ State _____ Zip Code _____

Telephone _____ FAX _____

Please return this form to: *The Christian Bed and Breakfast Directory*
PO Box 719, Uhrichsville, OH 44683
(614) 922-6045; FAX (614) 922-5948